Biology for CSEC® Examinations

Fourth edition

Louis Chinnery
Joyce Glasgow
Mary Jones
Geoff Jones

CORAL REEF BIOLOGY
Eugenie Williams

CAMBRIDGE
UNIVERSITY PRESS

CAMBRIDGE
UNIVERSITY PRESS

University Printing House, Cambridge CB2 8BS, United Kingdom

One Liberty Plaza, 20th Floor, New York, NY 10006, USA

477 Williamstown Road, Port Melbourne, VIC 3207, Australia

314–321, 3rd Floor, Plot 3, Splendor Forum, Jasola District Centre, New Delhi – 110025, India

79 Anson Road, #06–04/06, Singapore 079906

Cambridge University Press is part of the University of Cambridge.

It furthers the University's mission by disseminating knowledge in the pursuit of education, learning and research at the highest international levels of excellence.

www.cambridge.org
Information on this title: www.cambridge.org/9780521701143

First published 1987
Second edition 1992
Third edition 2001
Fourth edition 2009

20 19 18 17 16 15 14 13 12 11 10 9 8

Printed in Great Britain by CPI Group (UK) Ltd, Croydon CR0 4YY

A catalogue record for this publication is available from the British Library

ISBN 978-0-521-70114-3 Paperback

ACKNOWLEDGEMENTS
Cover image: © Plush Studios/D. Sanner/Plush Studios/Corbis
Adviser: Anna-May Edwards-Henry
Typesetter: Geoff Jones

Contents

Introduction

This book is for students preparing for the Caribbean Secondary Education Certificate (CSEC) in Biology.

The eighteen chapters cover all of the content of the CSEC syllabus. In this new edition, the content has been partly reorganised so that it is now arranged in the same sequence as the syllabus itself. The content has also been revised and updated. Each chapter is lavishly illustrated with diagrams drawn by a biologist and numerous photographs. Short questions at intervals in the text will help students to check that they have absorbed and understood the information that precedes the questions. There are also questions at the end of each chapter, which test a wide range of the facts and concepts covered in the chapter.

Investigations throughout the book provide opportunities for students to carry out practical activities that will help them to understand and apply the biological principles they have read about. At the beginning of each Investigation, there is a list of the SBA (school-based assessment) skills that the Investigation addresses. The Investigations are ideal for helping students to develop these skills, and also for the assessment of the SBA skills. Details of the apparatus and materials required for the Investigations are listed in Appendix 1. Appendix 2 explains the requirements for the assessment of SBA skills, and Appendix 3 lists the skills that are relevant to each Investigation. Many new Investigations have been introduced in this new edition, including several which ask students to design and carry out their own experiments.

Biology has a very large number of specialist terms, and it is important that students become familiar with these terms and learn to use them appropriately. In general, each term is carefully explained or defined when it first appears. The term is shown in **brown**, and its definition (or the definition of a closely related term) is included in the extensive glossary.

The authors

Joyce Glasgow is a well-known teacher and educator. She was formerly Senior Lecturer in Science Education at the University of West Indies, Mona, Jamaica and was chief examiner for CXC Biology. She is now a consultant in environmental and science education.

Louis Chinnery is Senior Lecturer and Head of the Department of Biological and Chemical Sciences, the University of the West Indies, Barbados.

Mary Jones has written many successful textbooks for CSEC, GCSE, O Level and A Level Biology and is a senior examiner for IGCSE and A level Biology. She runs training courses for teachers all over the world.

Geoff Jones was formerly a teacher of biology in schools and colleges. He is the designer and illustrator of many textbooks in biology and other sciences, and produces multimedia materials.

Eugenie Williams (coral reef biology material in Chapters 17 and 18) teaches in the Science Department at Parkinson Memorial School, Barbados.

Acknowledgements

The author and publishers are grateful for the permissions granted to use photographs. While every effort has been made, it has not always been possible to identify the sources of all the images used, or to trace all copyright holders. If any omissions are brought to our notice we will be happy to include the appropriate acknowledgements on reprinting.

Cover © Plush Studios/D. Sanner/Plush Studios/Corbis; pp. 5, 14*l*, 14*br*, 156*t*, 156*b*, 158, 170*t*, 170*b*, 178, 244, 250, 270*t*, 325*tr*, 325*cr*, 336*l*, 338, 339, 358, 360*l*, 360*tr*, 370*l* Wendy Lee; p. 7*t* © Rough Guides/Alamy; p. 7*b* © Glow Images/Alamy; pp. 8*tl*, 330*b* © blickwinkel/Alamy; pp. 8*tr*, 343*tr* © Charles Stirling (Diving)/Alamy; p. 8*bl* © Redmond Durrell/Alamy; p. 8*br* © Zach Holmes/Alamy; pp. 14*tr*, 341, 343*bc* © Masa Ushioda/Alamy; pp. 16, 57*r*, 130, Andrew Syred/SPL; pp. 17, 203 © Donald Enright/Alamy; pp. 19, 157*tl*, 157*bl*, 157*br*, 324*l*, 324*r*, 325*br*, 367 Geoff Jones; pp. 23, 24*t* Eleanor Jones; pp. 24*b*, 57*l*, 82, 107*t*, 107*b*, 117, 133, 359*b* Biophoto Associates/SPL; p. 42 © Visual&Written SL/Alamy; pp. 62, 221*r* Nigel Cattlin/Alamy; p. 77 WK Fletcher/SPL; pp. 79, 124, 126, 242, 246*t*, 255*t*, 302, 305, 335 © Phototake Inc./Alamy; p. 87 © Adams Picture Library t/a apl/Alamy; p. 96 © Maximilian Weinzierl/Alamy; p. 104 © Rick Rickman/Newsport/Corbis; p. 119*l* Janine Wiedel Photolibrary; p. 119*r* Prof. P. Motta/SPL; p. 131 J.C. Revy/SPL; p. 142 Hywit Dimyadi/Shutterstock; p. 157*tr* © Andy Sutton/Alamy; p. 164*l* J. Gross, Biozentrum/SPL; p. 164*tr* Medimage/SPL; p. 164*br* Astrid & Hanns-Frieder Michler/SPL; pp. 169, 306 NIBSC/SPL; p. 171 © Florida Images/Alamy; p. 181 © Visual Ideas/Nora Pelaez/Blend Images/Corbis; p. 199 Dr M.A. Ansary/SPL; p. 221*l* © geogphotos/Alamy; p. 235 Steve Gschmeissner/SPL; p. 243 Gary Watson/SPL; p. 246*b* Susumu Nishinaga/SPL; p. 247*t* © Pictox/Alamy; p. 247*b* © tbkmedia.de/Alamy; pp. 256*tl*, 256*bl* Dept. of Clinical Cytogenetics, Addenbrookes Hospital/SPL; p. 256*r* Joyce Glasgow; p. 264 Kevin Beebe, Custom Medical Stock Photo/SPL; p. 265*l* Bruno Morandi/Getty Images; p. 265*r* Biology Media/SPL; pp. 270*c*, 368 © imagebroker/Alamy; pp. 207*b*, 282 the Jamaica Livestock Association Ltd; p. 255*b* Cheryl Power/SPL; p. 272*t* © Mary Evans Picture Library/Alamy; p. 272*b* Pat & Tom Leeson/SPL; pp. 274*t*, 274*b* Stephen Dalton/NHPA; p. 276 Agence Nature/NHPA; p. 291 © Enigma/Alamy; p. 292*t* © Phil Grain/Alamy; p. 292*b* © Custom Medical Stock Photo/Alamy; p. 293*l* Zephyr/SPL; pp. 293*c*, 293*r* Tropical Metabolism Research Institute, University of the West Indies; p. 295 Pascal Goetgheluck/SPL; p. 296*l* © Darrin Jenkins/Alamy; p. 296*tr* Franklyn Williams/© 2009 Keen i Media Ltd; p. 296*br* St Bartholomew's Hospital/SPL; p. 297 Vaughan Fleming/SPL; p. 298 © Interfoto Pressebildagentur/Alamy; p. 312*tl* © Steve Hamblin/Alamy; pp. 312*tr*, 312*cr* Wayne Nishijima and Scot Nelson, College of Tropical Agriculture and Human Resources, University of Hawaii and Manoa; p. 312*cl* Cn Boon/Alamy; pp. 312*bl*, 312*br* Coconut Industry Board; p. 325*tl* Rolf Richardson/Alamy; p. 325*cl* © Helene Rogers/Alamy; p. 325*bl* © Trip/Alamy; p. 330*t* © Bob Ferry/Alamy; p. 331*t* Agripicture Images/Alamy; p. 331*b* David C Clegg/SPL; p. 333 © Claudia Adams/Alamy; p. 334*t* © Andre Seale/Alamy; p. 334*b* © Malcolm Schuyl/Alamy; p. 336*r* © Kumar Sriskandan/Alamy; pp. 340, 346*r* © Brandon Cole Marine Photography/Alamy; p. 342 © Robert Fried/Alamy; p. 343*tl* © David W. Hamilton/Alamy; p. 343*bl* © Images&Stories/Alamy; p. 343*br* © James Gritz/Alamy; pp. 344*t*, 344*b* © Waterframe/Alamy; p. 345 © David Taylor Photography/Alamy; p. 346*l* © Chris Howes/Wild Places Photography/Alamy; p. 349 © Paul Thompson Images/Alamy; p. 355 © Sylvia Cordaiy Photo Library Ltd/Alamy; p. 357 Armand-Photo-Travel/Alamy; p. 359*t* NASA/SPL; p. 360*br* Charles Glasgow; p. 361 International Centre for Environmental and Nuclear Sciences, UWI; p. 365 © Justin Kase zfivez/Alamy; p. 366*t* © Jane Gould/Alamy; p. 366*c* © F.Bttex – Mysterra.org/Alamy; p. 366*b* © Guillen Photography/UW/Bonaire/Alamy; p. 370*r* © Roberd Harding Picture Library/Alamy; p. 372*t* David Nunuk/SPL; p. 372*b* © Alan Myers/Alamy

Acknowledgements

The author and publishers are grateful for the permissions granted to use photographs. While every effort has been made, it has not always been possible to identify the sources of all the images used, or [illegible] all copyright holders. If any omissions are brought to our notice we will be happy to include the appropriate acknowledgements on reprinting.

[illegible]

1 Life

In this chapter, you will find out:

- what makes living things (organisms) different from non-living things
- some of the ways in which organisms interact with their environment
- why organisms are given Latin names
- the special features of some of the main groups of organisms
- how to use a key to identify an unknown organism
- about food chains, food webs and trophic levels
- some examples of symbiosis, including parasitism, commensalism and mutualism
- how carbon and nitrogen are cycled between organisms and their environment.

Living things

1.1 Biology is the study of life.

Biology is the study of living things, which are called **organisms**. Biology deals with how organisms function, how they react to each other and how the environment affects their lives. There are many different kinds of organisms, ranging from microscopic bacteria to large plants and complex animals.

1.2 All living things have certain characteristics.

Living organisms have several features or characteristics which make them different from objects that are not alive.

1 They **reproduce**.
2 They **feed**.
3 They **respire** – that is, they release energy from their food, often by combining it with oxygen.
4 They **grow**.
5 They **excrete** – that is, they get rid of substances which they do not want. These have been made by some of the chemical reactions going on inside them.
6 They **move**.
7 They are **sensitive** – that is, they can sense and respond to changes in their surroundings.
8 They are made of **cells**.

1.3 Organisms interact with their environment.

One very important way of studying living things is to study them where they live. Animals and plants do not live in complete isolation. They are affected by their surroundings, called their **environment**. Their environment is also affected by them. The study of the interaction between living organisms and their environment is a branch of biology called **ecology**.

1.4 Special terms are used in ecology.

Many special scientific words are used in ecology and other branches of biology and you need to be familiar with them. Throughout this book these words are printed in brown type.

In ecology, the place where an organism lives is called its **habitat**. The habitat of a fish might be a pond. There will probably be many fish in the pond, forming a **population** of fish. A population is a group of organisms of the same species, living in the same place at the same time and able to breed with one another.

But fish will not be the only organisms living in the pond. There will be many other kinds of animals and plants which together make up the pond **community**. A community is all the organisms, of all the different species, living in the same habitat. The living organisms in the pond, the water in it, the stones and the mud at the bottom, make up an **ecosystem**. An ecosystem consists of a community and its environment. Within an ecosystem, the living and non-living things are constantly interacting with one another.

Within the ecosystem, each living organism has its own life to live and role to play. The way in which an organism lives its life – the way it fits into the ecosystem – is called its **niche**. Fish, for example, eat algae or small animals in the pond, disturb pebbles and mud at the bottom of shallow areas in the pond, excrete ammonium salts into the water, breathe in oxygen from the water, and breathe out carbon dioxide. All these activities, and many others, help to describe the role, or niche, of fish in the ecosystem.

Figure 1.1 shows an example of a pond ecosystem.

Questions

1.1 List the characteristics of living things.

1.2 What is ecology?

1.3 What is a population?

1.4 Give two examples of an ecosystem, other than a pond.

1.5 How does a niche differ from a habitat?

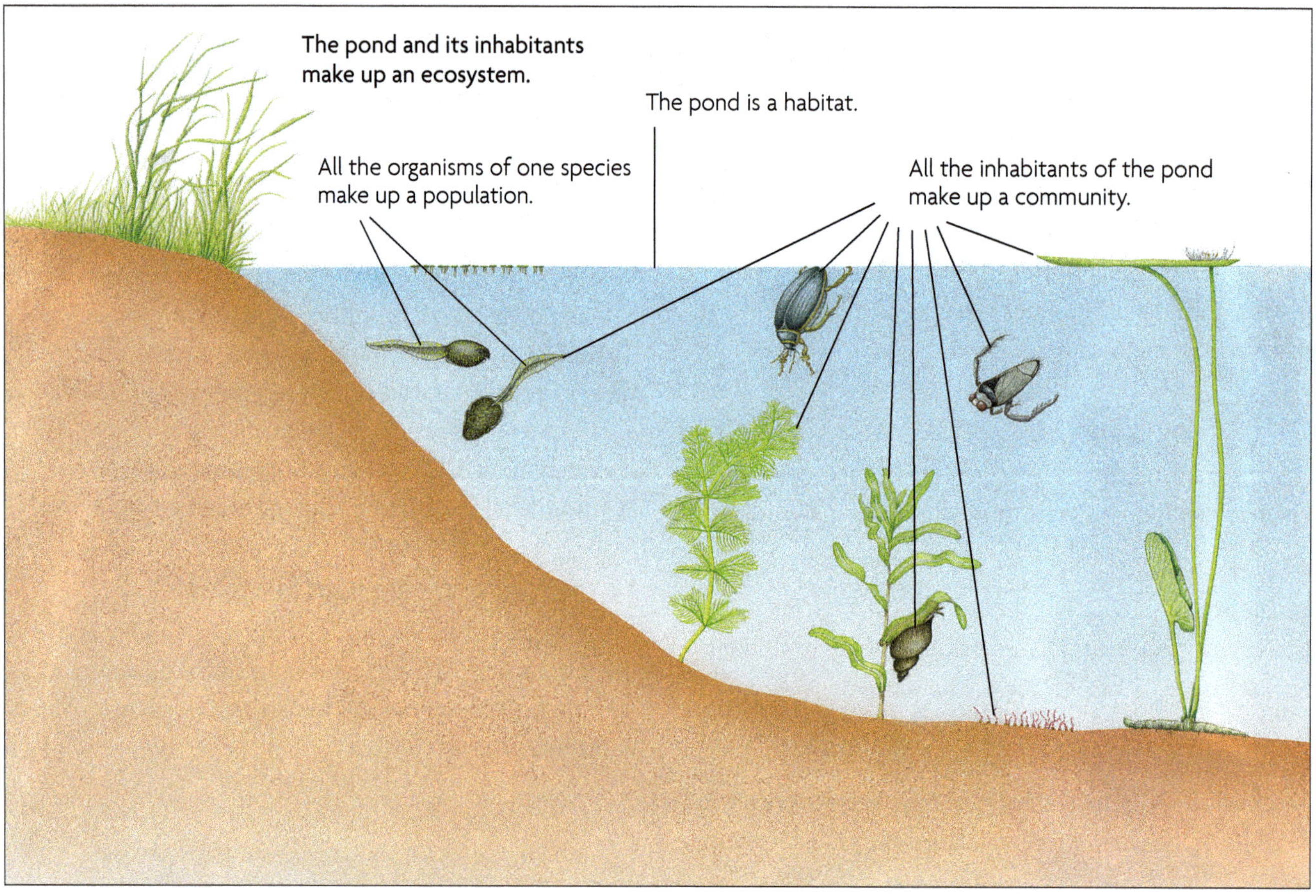

The pond and its inhabitants make up an ecosystem.
The pond is a habitat.
All the organisms of one species make up a population.
All the inhabitants of the pond make up a community.

Figure 1.1 A pond and its inhabitants – an example of an ecosystem.

Studying ecosystems

1.5 Different types of organisms have different names.

When you are studying an ecosystem, you will want to try to identify all of the different kinds of organisms that you find there. Each type of organism has its own name. Groups of similar organisms which are able to interbreed make up a **species**. Each species has its own scientific name which consists of two Latin words called the **generic name** and the **specific name**. Closely related species share the same generic name but have different specific names.

The scientific name for an organism is used by all scientists throughout the world. The scientific name for humans is *Homo sapiens*, that for English potatoes is *Solanum tuberosum* and that for egg plants is *Solanum melongena*. *Homo sapiens* means humans in all languages, whereas the common name for a man varies. In French it is 'homme', in Spanish 'hombre' and in St Lucian Creole 'mun'. Many other languages are written in a different kind of writing; these languages include the Asian languages spoken by more than one third of the world's population. The scientific name for humans in all these countries is the same two Latin words, *Homo sapiens*.

Much confusion is caused by the use of different common names for the same organism or the use of a single common name for more than one species. For example, Jamaicans use the name 'ackee' for the sweet fruit of *Blighia sapida* which is used as a vegetable, whereas Barbadians use the word 'ackee' for the sweet fruit of *Melicoccus bijugatus* (Figure **1.2**). In other parts of the Caribbean *Melicoccus bijugatus* is known as 'chenette', 'chenip', 'genip', 'kinip', 'mapo', 'quenette' and 'skinip'. The consistent use of scientific names by biologists prevents any confusion. This does not mean that you have to know the scientific names of all the organisms you encounter. But you must be sure that the common names you use mean the same thing to all the people likely to read your work.

Figure 1.2 Although their common names are the same, these two plants have completely different scientific names. **a** Jamaican ackee, *Blighia sapida*. **b** Barbadian ackee, *Melicoccus bijugatus*.

1.6 Organisms are classified into groups.

Different types of organisms can be identified – that is, given names – from their characteristics. You identify your classmates by subconsciously noticing their characteristics, such as height, weight, complexion, eye colour, hair style, and so on.

Biologists group organisms according to characteristics that they share. Figure **1.3** shows the main groups into which all organisms are placed. These are the five **kingdoms**. Within each kingdom, organisms are grouped into **phyla** (singular: phylum) and then **classes**. Figures **1.4** to **1.8** (pages **4–6**) show some of the groups of animals that you may meet when you are studying an ecosystem.

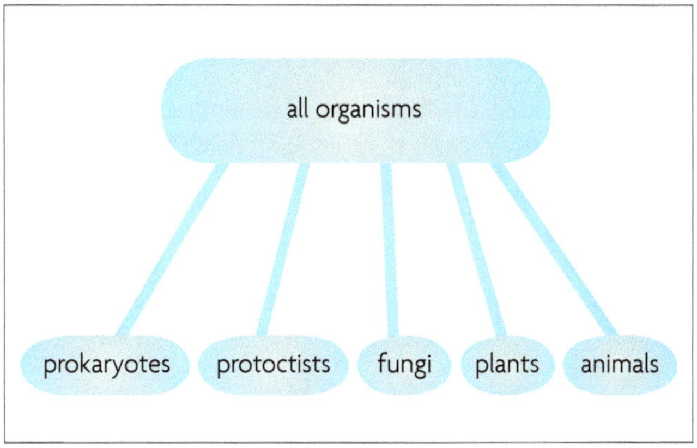

Figure 1.3 The main groups into which all organisms are placed.

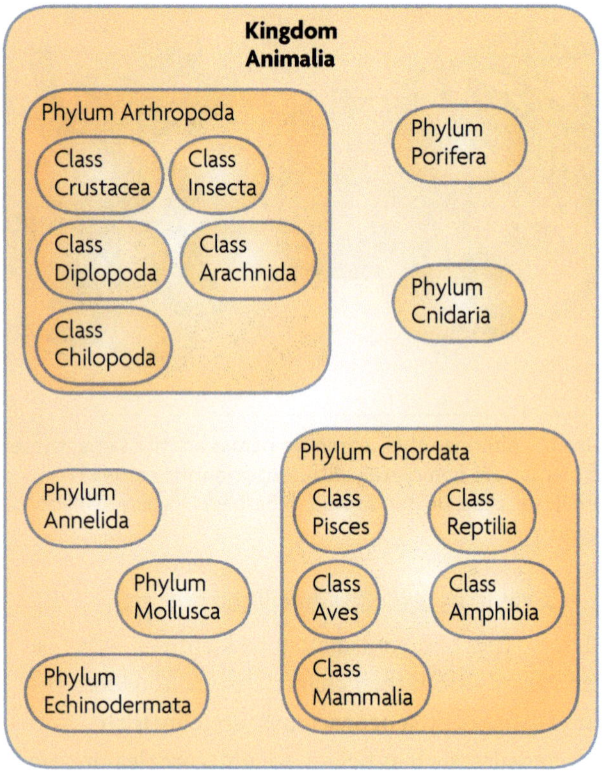

Figure 1.4 Classification of the animal kingdom.

Phylum Cnidaria
These are the corals, jellyfish and sea anemones. They all live in water, because their soft bodies would dry out very quickly on land. They have a ring of tentacles surrounding a mouth. The mouth is the only opening in their digestive system – they have no anus.

Characteristics:
- body wall made of only two layers of cells
- ring of tentacles, with a mouth in the centre
- only one opening to gut.

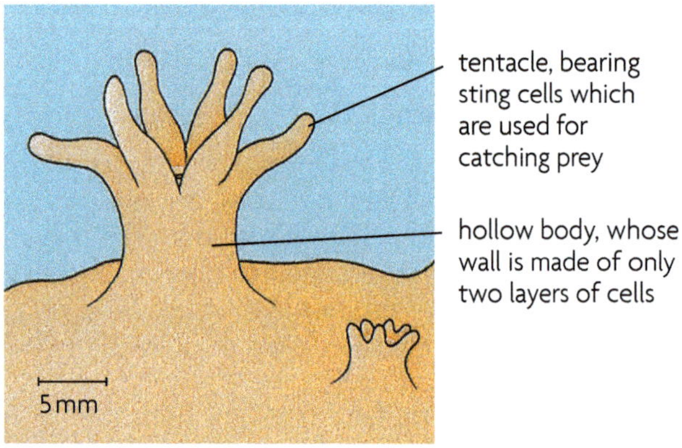

coral polyps – they are joined to make a large colonial organism

Figure 1.5 Classification of the cnidarians.

Phylum Echinodermata
These are starfish, sea urchins and sand dollars. They are found in the sea.

Characteristics:
- five-part radial symmetry
- body wall contains calcareous particles
- many have a 'shell' with projecting spines.

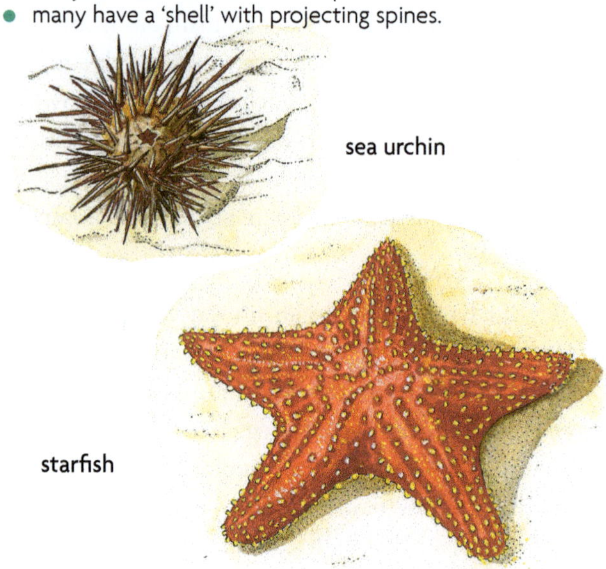

Figure 1.6 Classification of the echinoderms.

Phylum Arthropoda
Arthropods are animals with jointed legs, but no backbone. They are a very successful group, because they have a waterproof exoskeleton that has allowed them to live on dry land. There are more kinds of arthropod in the world than all the other kinds of animals put together.

Characteristics:
- several pairs of jointed legs
- exoskeleton.

Class Crustacea
These are the crabs, lobsters and woodlice. They breathe through gills, so most of them live in wet places and many are aquatic.

Characteristics:
- arthropods with more than four pairs of jointed legs
- not millipedes or centipedes
- breathe through gills.

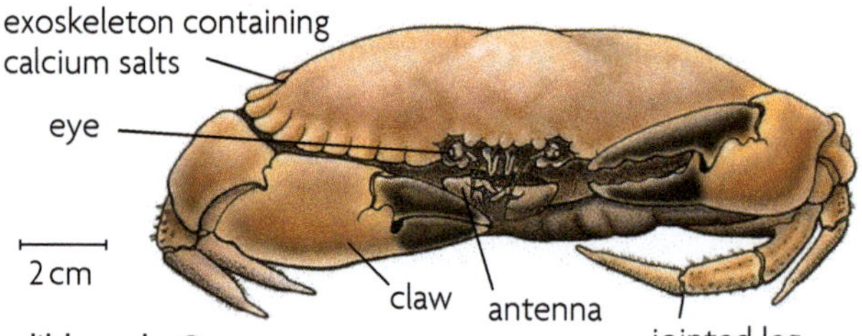

edible crab, *Cancer pagurus*

Figure 1.7 Classification of the arthropods (*continues on page 5*).

(... *continued*)

Class Arachnida
These are the spiders, ticks and scorpions. They are land-dwelling organisms.

Characteristics:
- arthropods with four pairs of jointed legs
- breathe through gills called book lungs.

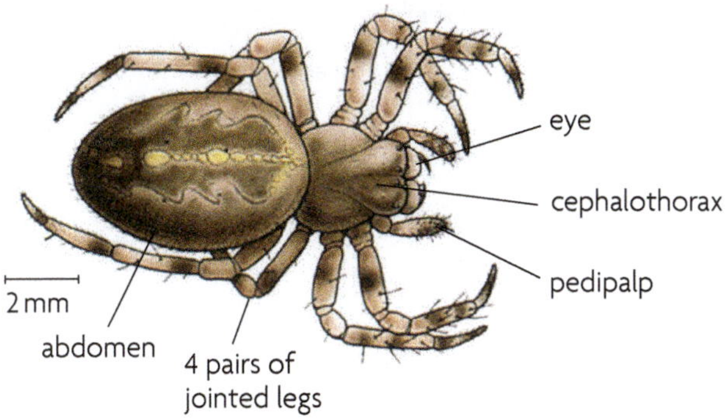

spider, *Araneus diadematus*

Class Insecta
Insects are a very successful group of animals. Their success is mostly due to their exoskeleton and tracheae which are very good at stopping water from evaporating from the insects' bodies, so they can live in very dry places. They are mainly terrestrial.

Characteristics:
- arthropods with three pairs of jointed legs
- two pairs of wings (one or both may be vestigial)
- breathe through tracheae.

locust

moth

Class Diplopoda
These are the millipedes.

Characteristics:
- body consists of many segments
- each segment has two pairs of legs.

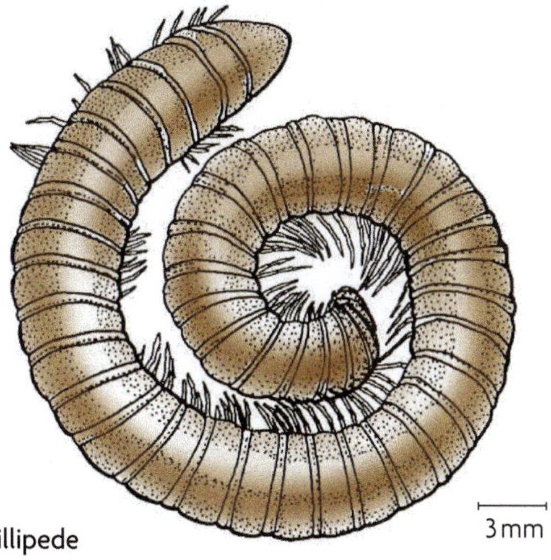

millipede

Class Chilopoda
These are the centipedes.

Characteristics:
- body consists of many segments
- each segment has one pair of legs
- front segment has a large pair of poison claws.

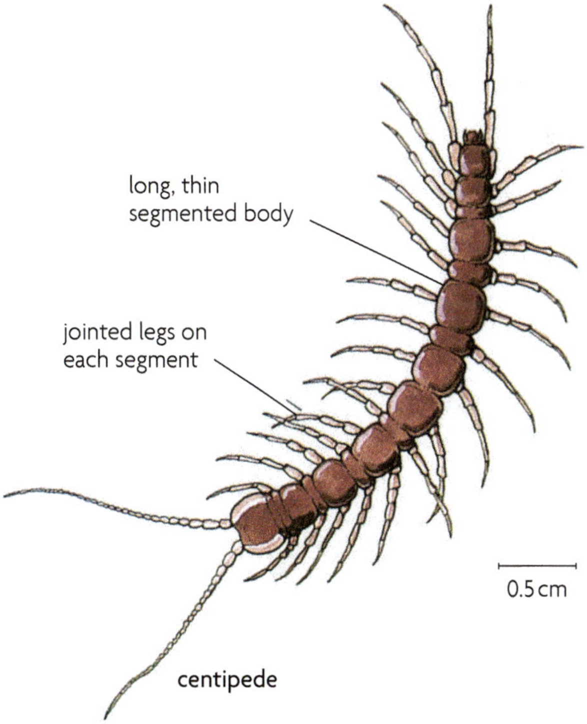

centipede

Figure 1.7 Classification of the arthropods.

Phylum Chordata

These are animals with a supporting rod running along the length of the body. The most familiar ones have a backbone, and are called vertebrates.

Class Pisces

The fish all live in water, except for one or two like the mudskipper, which can spend short periods of time breathing air.

Characteristics:

- vertebrates with scaly skin
- have gills
- have fins.

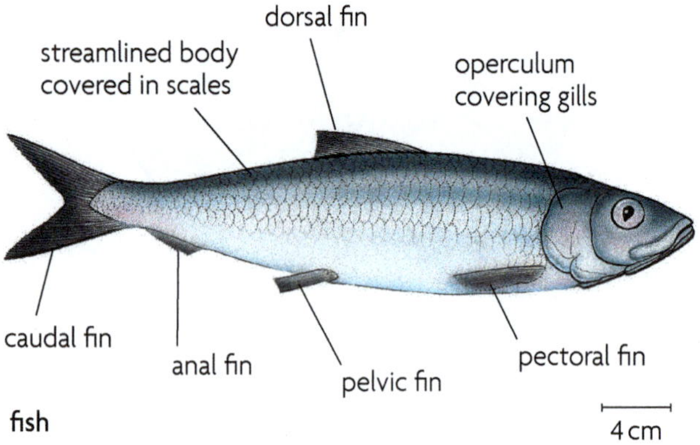

fish

Class Amphibia

Although most adult amphibians live on land, they always go back to the water to breed. Frogs and toads are amphibians.

Characteristics:

- vertebrates with moist, scale-less skin
- eggs laid in water, larva (tadpole) lives in water
- adult often lives on land
- larva has gills, adult has lungs.

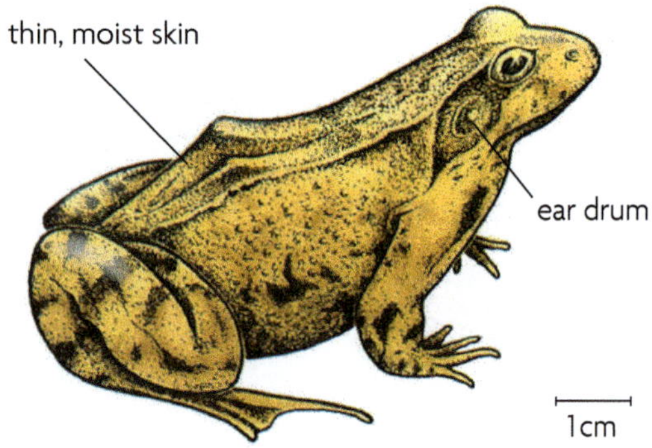

frog

Class Reptilia

These are the crocodiles, lizards, snakes, turtles and tortoises. Reptiles do not need to go back to the water to breed because their eggs have a waterproof shell which stops them from drying out.

Characteristics:

- vertebrates with scaly skin
- lay eggs with rubbery shells.

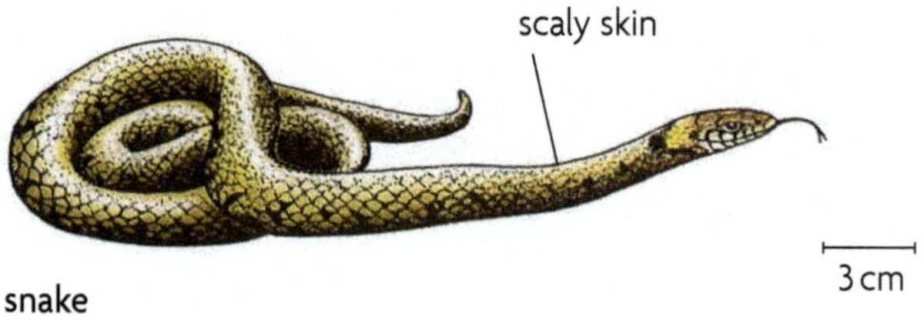

snake

Class Aves

The birds, like reptiles, lay eggs with waterproof shells.

Characteristics:

- vertebrates with feathers
- forelimbs have become wings
- lay eggs with hard shells
- homeothermic
- have a beak.

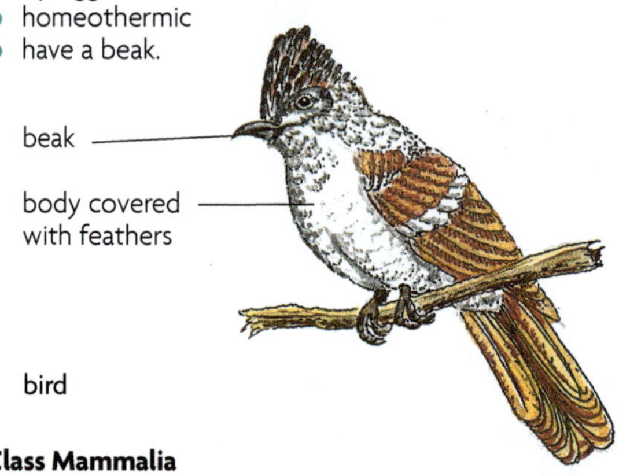

bird

Class Mammalia

This is the group that humans belong to.

Characteristics:

- vertebrates with hair
- have a placenta
- young feed on milk from mammary glands
- homeothermic
- have a diaphragm
- heart has four chambers
- have different types of teeth (incisors, canines premolars and molars)
- cerebral hemispheres are very well developed.

ocelot

Figure 1.8 Classification of the vertebrates.

Table **1.1** shows that the number of legs an organism has helps you to identify its type.

Table 1.1 Number of legs on different types of organisms

Number of legs	Types of animal
0	molluscs, echinoderms
2	birds
4	mammals, reptiles, amphibians
6	insects
8	spiders
2 per body segment	centipedes
4 per body segment	millipedes

In the Caribbean, the phrase 'tail up goat, tail down sheep' is often quoted. This is one characteristic which can be used to distinguish hair sheep – for example, Barbados black-belly – from goats (Figure **1.9**).

Figure 1.9 We can tell sheep and goats apart by whether their tail stands up or hangs down. **a** Goat. **b** Barbados black-belly sheep.

1.7 Keys are used for identification.

You may be able to identify some organisms, particularly larger ones, quite quickly from pictures in books. But there will almost certainly be many that you cannot find pictures of, or where you are not sure if the picture really is of your plant or animal.

When this happens you will need to use a **key**. A key leads you through to the name of your organism by giving you two descriptions at a time, and asking you to choose between them. Each choice you make then leads you on to another pair of descriptions, until you end up with the name of your organism.

An example of a key like this is shown in Figure **1.10**. It is called a **dichotomous key** because you choose between two descriptions each time ('di' means two).

1	Animals of only one cell, normally living in water	Protoctista
	Animals of more than one cell	2
2	Animals without legs	3
	Animals with legs	9
3	Animals with scales	4
	Animals without scales	5
4	Animals with fins, living in water	Fish
	Animals without fins, normally living on land	Reptiles
5	Sessile animals with no mouth or digestive system	Sponges
	Animals with a mouth	6
6	Animals with bodies made up of ring-like segments	Annelids
	No ring-like segments	7
7	Animals with an obvious central body cavity and tentacles	Cnidarians
	Animals without tentacles or with a muscular foot	8
8	Animals with five-fold radial symmetry	Echinoderms
	Animals without five-fold radial symmetry	Molluscs
9	Animals with two legs and feathers	Birds
	Animals with more than two legs	10
10	Animals with four legs	11
	Animals with more than two pairs of legs	13
11	Animals with hair or fur	Mammals
	Animals without hair or fur	12
12	Animals with scales	Reptiles
	Animals without scales	Amphibians
13	Animals with three pairs of legs	Insects
	Animals with more than six legs	14
14	Animals with eight legs	Arachnids
	Animals with more than four pairs of legs	15
15	Animals often with a pair of claws	Crustaceans
	Animals with 15 or more pairs of legs	16
16	Animals with one pair of legs per body segment	Centipedes
	Animals with two pairs of legs per segment	Millipedes

Figure 1.10 A dichotomous key to help to identify an unknown animal.

Questions

1.6 Use the key in Figure **1.10** (page **7**) to identify each of the animals in **a** to **d**. Each time, make a list of the numbers that you worked through to get to your identification – for example, 1, 2, 9 and so on.

1.7 Construct a dichotomous key to help someone to identify four of the people in your class. Take care to use features that a stranger could easily distinguish. For example, choosing between 'tall' and 'short' is not a good idea, because what one person thinks is tall another might think is short. Keep the key as short and simple as possible.

1.8 Care should be taken when observing and collecting organisms.

When you carry out an investigation of an ecosystem you may need to move rocks or stones to see if there are any organisms underneath. But you must always replace them exactly as you found them. The reason for doing this is that the sheltered conditions under the rock provide a protected home for the animals found there. If these conditions are destroyed the animals may die.

You should only collect organisms which you or your teacher cannot identify in the field, or as a single representative of a commonly occurring species which you may want to draw. *Rare animals and plants should not be collected.* When collecting plants, you should only take pieces large enough to show all their characteristics (leaves, flowers and fruits). *Remember all living things have a right to life.*

Another reason for taking care in handling plants and animals is your own safety. Many plants have spines or bristles on them and others produce toxic juices. Animals may bite or sting and some can be extremely dangerous – for example, some snakes, centipedes and spiders.

Questions

1.8 What is a species?

1.9 What is a dichotomous key?

1.10 Why should you take care when collecting organisms?

Food and energy in an ecosystem

1.9 The green plants are food producers.

By the process of photosynthesis (described in Chapter **4**) green plants are able to capture some of the energy in sunlight. Plants use this energy to make organic substances. Later, some of the energy from these organic substances can be released by the process of respiration (described in Chapter **6**).

All organisms need energy to stay alive, and this is where all of their energy comes from. Animals get theirs from the plants that they eat, or from eating other animals that have eaten plants. Plants are the only source of energy for all living organisms. Thus, plants are the **primary producers** of food in any ecosystem.

1.10 There are many different types of feeding relationships.

Animals that feed on plants are called **herbivores**. Sheep, cattle, slugs and the caterpillars of the white cabbage butterfly are all examples of herbivores.

Animals that eat other animals are called **carnivores**. Some carnivores kill the animals that they eat, and they are called **predators**. Other carnivores, such as hyenas, eat animals that are already dead (perhaps killed by a predator). Sharks, lizards and spiders are all carnivores.

Animals whose diet consists of both animals and plants are called **omnivores**. Humans are omnivores.

Humming-birds visit flowers to obtain nectar and therefore are herbivores. As a result of their visits they carry pollen from one plant to another and are said to be **pollinators** of the plants involved. Humming-birds also capture small insects to feed their young so they are also carnivores.

Parasites live on or inside another species, the **host**, on which they feed. For example, the tapeworm is a parasite of humans. Parasites do not usually kill their host. However, insect parasitoids are predators that live for part of their life inside their insect host. The host is eventually killed. *Apanteles plutellae*, a very small wasp, is a parasitoid which kills the diamond-back moth, *Plutella xylostella*. The diamond-back moth is a serious pest of cabbages and related crops. Researchers in Barbados and other countries are investigating the use of *Apanteles* to control the moth.

1.11 Food chains and food webs show feeding relationships.

The sequence by which energy, in the form of food, passes from plant to animal and then to other animals, is called a **food chain**. Figure **1.11** shows an example of a simple food chain.

In nature, organisms often have more than one food source. As a result, a diagram called a food web better represents their feeding relationships. A simple food web is shown in Figure **1.12**. Figure. **1.13** shows an aquatic (in water) food web, and Figure **1.14** (overleaf) shows a terrestrial (on land) food web.

As you can see, in any community, the feeding relationships between all the organisms present are extremely complex. You can find an example of a food web on a coral reef on page **345**.

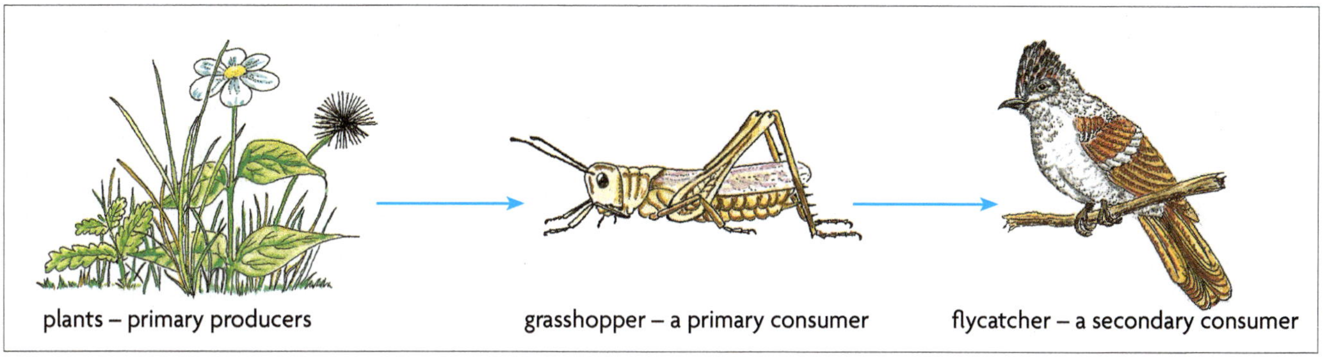

Figure 1.11 A food chain.

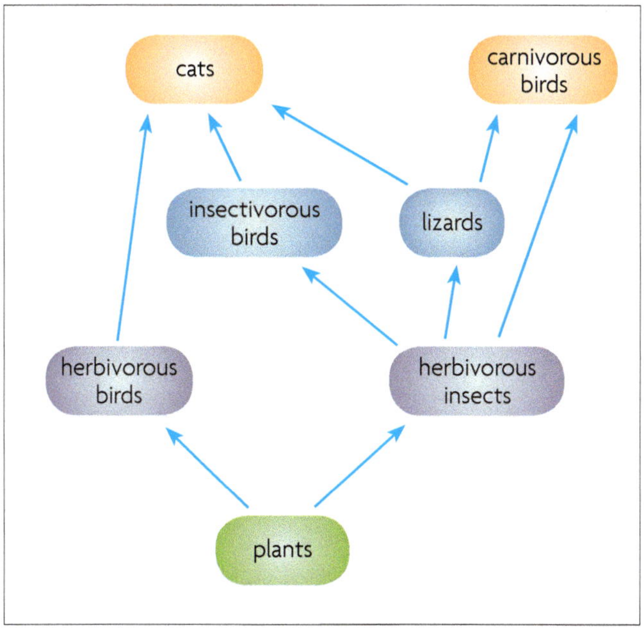

Figure 1.12 A food web.

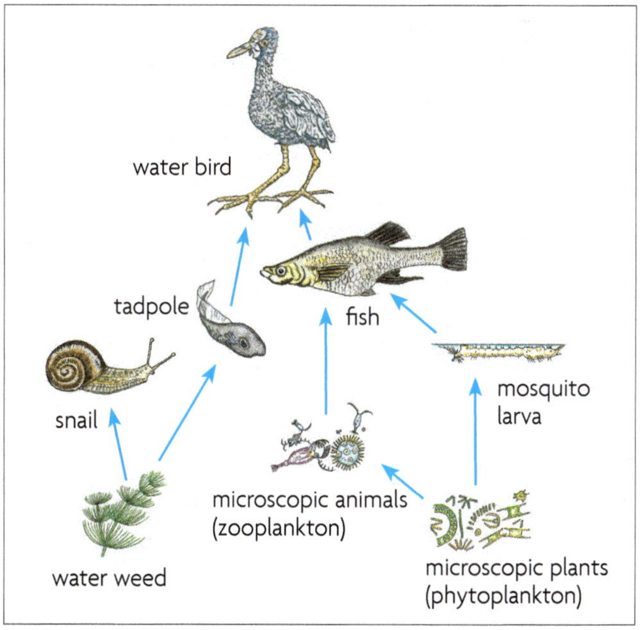

Figure 1.13 An aquatic food web.

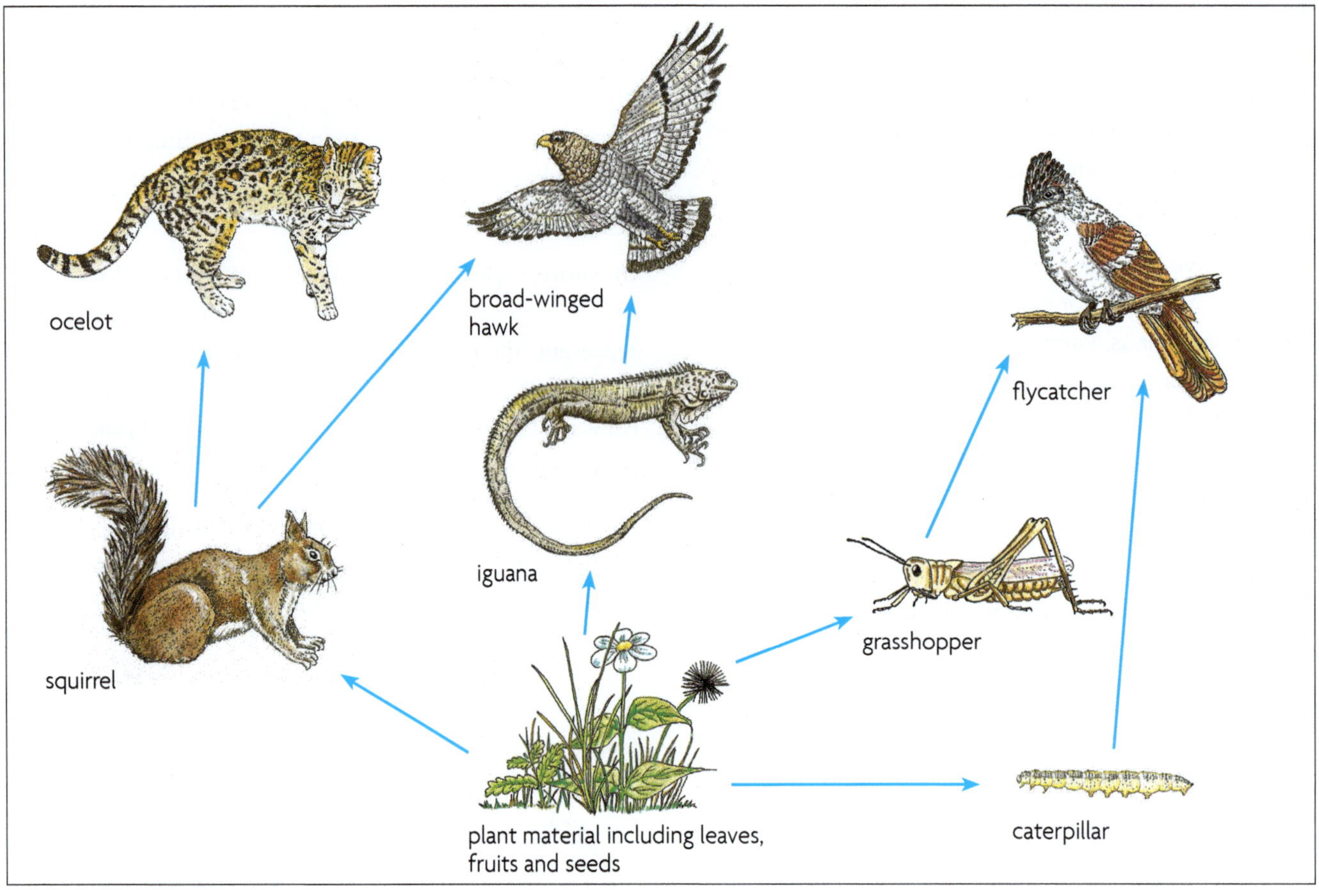

Figure 1.14 A terrestrial food web.

> **Question**
>
> **1.11** This paragraph describes a food web in a mangrove ecosystem. Use the information to draw a food web.
>
> Leaves from mangrove trees are eaten by molluscs, crabs and prawns. Fish eat small prawns. Herons eat molluscs, crabs, prawns and fish. Pelicans eat fish.

1.12 Organisms feed at different trophic levels.

Trophic level is a useful term. It indicates the number of stages in a food chain between the feeder and the Sun.

Plants are at the **first trophic level**. They are **primary producers** – they make the food that supports the rest of the food chain. Primary producers are always at the first trophic level.

Herbivores are at the **second trophic level**. They feed on plants directly and so are **primary consumers**. Carnivores, which feed on herbivores, are at the **third trophic level** and are **secondary consumers**. Top carnivores may feed on the secondary consumers.

If all the organisms in the ecosystem are counted and classified as primary producers, herbivores and carnivores, we can construct a diagram like Figure **1.15**. This is called a **pyramid of numbers**.

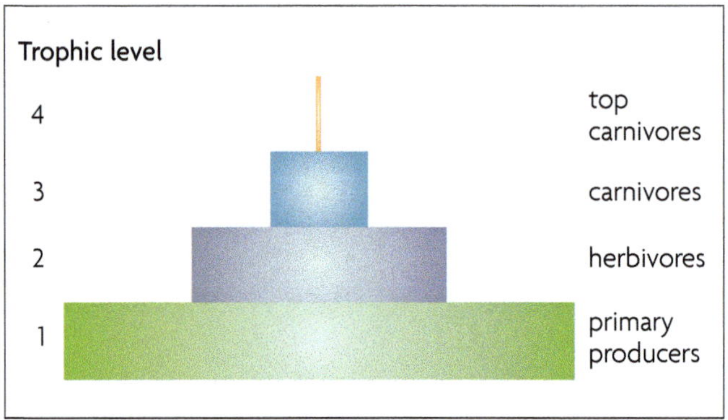

Figure 1.15 A pyramid of numbers for a typical ecosystem.

However, pyramids of numbers are not always this shape. For example, in a tropical rainforest there are relatively few plants, many of which are large trees. The herbivores are mainly small insects that feed on leaves and other parts of the trees. A pyramid of numbers for a tropical rainforest may look like Figure **1.16**.

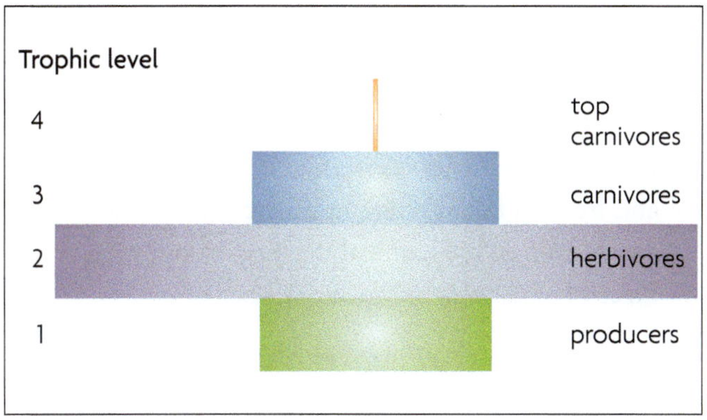

Figure 1.16 A pyramid of numbers in a tropical rainforest.

If, instead of the number of organisms, we use the mass of all the organisms at each trophic level we should get a pyramid shaped approximately like that in Figure **1.15** for any ecosystem. This pyramid is called a **pyramid of biomass**. Biomass is an abbreviation for biological mass. It is measured in grams or kilograms. Figure **1.17** shows a pyramid of biomass for a tropical rainforest.

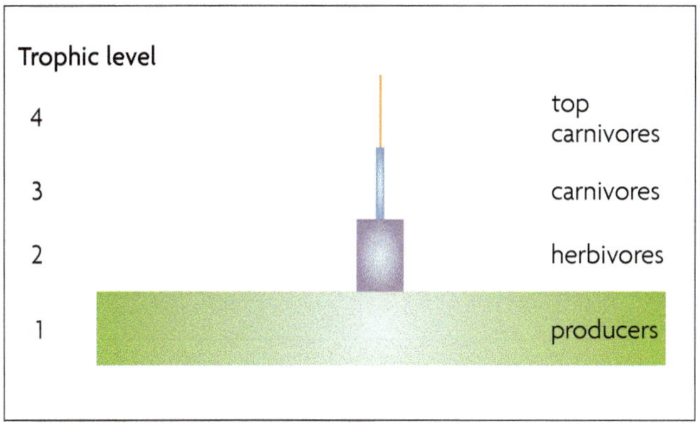

Figure 1.17 A pyramid of biomass in a tropical rainforest.

FACT!

The larvae of the polyphemus moth (*Antheraea polyphemus*) can eat 86 000 times their own birth weight in food in the first 48 hours of their life.

1.13 Understanding energy flow helps agriculture.

Understanding how energy is passed along a food chain can be useful in agriculture. We can eat a wide variety of foods, and can feed at several different trophic levels. Which is the most efficient sort of food for a farmer to grow, and for us to eat?

The nearer to the beginning of the food chain we feed, the more energy is available for use. This is why our staple foods – wheat, rice, potatoes – are plants.

When we eat meat, eggs or cheese or drink milk, we are feeding further along the food chain. Less energy is available for us from the original energy provided by the Sun. It would be more efficient in principle to eat the grass in a field, rather than to let cattle eat it, and then eat them.

In fact, however, although there is far more energy in the grass than in the cattle, it is not available to us. We simply cannot digest the grass, and so we cannot release the energy from it. The cattle can; they turn the energy in cellulose into energy in protein and fat, which we can digest.

However, there are many plant products that we can eat. Soya beans, for example, yield a large amount of protein, much more efficiently and cheaply than cattle or other animals. A change towards vegetarianism would enable more food to be produced on the Earth, if the right crops were chosen.

Questions

1.12 Why are green plants called primary producers?

1.13 Name three herbivores and three carnivores.

1.14 List three food chains from Figure 1.14.

1.15 What does a pyramid of numbers show?

1.16 At which trophic level are you feeding, when you eat

- **a** fish
- **b** bread
- **c** eggs
- **d** a mango
- **e** sugar
- **f** a meal containing all of these?

Investigation 1.1
Studying an ecosystem

SBA skills

Observation/Recording/Reporting *Drawing*
Analysis/Interpretation

Among the first things a biologist needs to know about an organism is where it lives and how it relates to other organisms in the ecosystem. In this investigation, you will find out which organisms live in a particular ecosystem and the relationships between them. Your teacher will choose the ecosystem to be studied.

Remember that you must disturb the ecosystem as little as possible. Do not take plants or animals away from the ecosystem unless your teacher tells you that you can do this. If you have a digital camera, take photographs of the organisms rather than collecting them.

1 Search the area thoroughly and try to identify all the types of plants in the area. If you cannot identify a plant, and there appears to be a lot of it, then collect samples of leaves and flowers to take back to your laboratory, where you can spend longer trying to find out what it is. Better still, take photographs of the plant so that you do not need to take samples from it.

2 Try to identify any small animals you see. Record where you found them, e.g. 'on the underside of the leaves of ...', 'on the ground near ...'. If possible, name the plant on or near which you found each kind of animal. Where possible, take photographs of each kind of animal.

3 Collect decaying leaves from underneath bushes and trees and place them in plastic bags. Using a pencil, write the name of the bush or tree on a piece of paper and put this in the bag.

4 Examine the soil surface and wherever it appears to be disturbed, try to find the organisms responsible.

5 Make notes about the large animals in the area, e.g. the types of birds present and what they are feeding on.

6 In the laboratory, examine your collections and, with your teacher's assistance, complete the identifications of all the organisms found.

7 Make a table like the one below to summarise all the class results.

place where animal found	types of animal			
	ants	caterpillars	beetles	
on mahogany tree	red on bark, black on ground	none	none	
on grass	many types	green	none	
on *Crotalaria* plants	none	yellow and black	none	
on ground				

8 Draw any animals you brought back to the laboratory.

9 Construct a food web for this ecosystem.

Investigation 1.2
Do animals prefer particular types of plants to eat?

SBA skills
Observation/Recording/Reporting
Analysis/Interpretation

It is important for a biologist to know the types of food that different animal species eat. For those animals that eat plants, one way to obtain this information is to give the animals different types of food and see which they prefer.

1 Collect 12 slugs or other small herbivores of the same species.

2 Collect leaves from four different kinds of plant growing in the same area.

3 Identify the plants and call them A, B, C and D.

4 Place pairs of undamaged leaves into six jars as follows:

A and B	B and C	A and C
B and D	A and D	C and D

Make sure that you label the jars.

5 To each jar add two of your animals and put the lid on.

6 On the next day, remove the animals and examine the leaves.

7 Draw up a suitable results table. For each leaf record the amount eaten as follows:

No damage	0
Leaf nibbled	1
Less than half eaten	2
More than half eaten	3
Leaf completely eaten	4

8 For each type of leaf, add the scores. Construct a histogram or pie chart to show the results.

Questions

1 Which kind of plant did your animals prefer?

2 Can you suggest why your animals preferred this kind of plant?

3 Why must undamaged leaves be used in the experiment?

4 Why were the leaves used in pairs rather than one at a time?

5 Do you think that it would have been better to give the animals all the leaves at one time?

Symbiosis

1.14 Symbiosis means living together.

When two different species live together intimately their relationship is called **symbiosis**. There are three types of symbiosis.

- **Parasitism** This is where one partner, usually the smaller, benefits from the association and the other suffers. The one that benefits is called the parasite, and the one that is harmed is called the host.
- **Commensalism** **Commensalism** is where one partner benefits and the other partner usually does not gain from the relationship, but does not suffer.
- **Mutualism** **Mutualism** is where both organisms gain from the association. In extreme cases, neither can live without the other.

These three types only represent points on a continuous line of degrees of harm and benefit and degree of intimacy. Therefore it is often difficult to distinguish the type of relationship existing between a pair of symbiotic species.

You may sometimes come across the word symbiosis used to mean the same as mutualism. This is an older meaning of the word and most scientists now use symbiosis to mean parasitism, commensalism and mutualism.

1.15 Parasitism is one extreme form of symbiosis.

The **tapeworm**, which affects humans and cattle, is a parasite (Figure **17.28**, page **335**). The tapeworm gains nourishment and shelter from its host and gives nothing in return. Humans with tapeworms have to eat more than usual or they will lose weight and could die.

Plasmodium, a unicellular animal, is a parasite which causes malaria in humans (Figure **16.28**, page **309**).

Many plant diseases are caused by parasitic fungi (Figure **1.18**). Sugar cane smut is the result of the plant becoming parasitised by the fungus *Ustilago scitaminea*.

Figure 1.18 Sugar cane plant suffering from fungal disease.

FACT!

Sugar cane smut disease was first found in the Caribbean in 1974 and is thought to have been carried on high-altitude winds from West Africa.

1.16 Commensalism is another type of symbiosis.

One of the best-known examples of commensalism involves two species of fish – remora and shark (Figure **1.19**). The remora is a small fish which has a suction cap on the top of its head. It uses this to attach itself to the body of a shark. It is carried around by the shark and eats leftover scraps when the shark feeds. Although the remora may remove parasitic crustaceans from the shark's skin, the shark can live in the absence of its passenger. The remora benefits greatly from this association.

Figure 1.19 Remora fish stay close to sharks so that they can steal some of their food.

Often one sees a plant growing on another one (Figure **1.20**). If the roots of this plant do not enter the soil, the plant is called an **epiphyte**. The epiphyte may be a lichen, a moss, a fern or a flowering plant, commonly an orchid or bromeliad (pineapple family). Although the epiphytic plant does not obtain food from the host plant, it benefits in a number of ways. It is able to live above the ground,

Figure 1.20 An epiphytic orchid (a species of *Broughtonia*) is growing on the trunk of a tree.

closer to the light. This is important in a shady forest. It might also escape some herbivores which could graze it if the epiphyte were growing on the ground. This is an example of commensalism because the tree does not suffer, unless the weight of the epiphytes becomes excessive.

In the Caribbean, cattle egrets are often seen riding on the backs of cattle and sheep. From their perch they are able to see animals disturbed by their companion. Cattle egrets are carnivores that eat insects, lizards, centipedes and mice. They may also eat ticks and fleas from their host's body. Cattle egrets and cattle can both live without each other. This is a common feature of many commensal relationships.

Plants provide microhabitats for small animals where they can gain shelter from their enemies and adverse weather conditions. For example, the bases of palm leaves often shelter wood lice and ants. These are also examples of commensalism.

1.17 Mutualism is symbiosis for mutual benefit.

When both partners of a symbiotic relationship are unable to live without each other, the relationship is said to be an **obligate** one. That is, the two species are obliged to live together. Many mutualisms are obligate.

Termites feed on wood but, like most organisms, cannot digest wood's main constituent, cellulose. Small unicellular organisms, *Trichonympha,* are found in the intestines of termites. The *Trichonympha* are able to break down the cellulose into sugars (section **3.5**). The termite is able to digest many of these sugars and thus is able to live on a diet of wood. The *Trichonympha* obtain food and protection by living in their hosts' intestines and do not live anywhere else.

A very important mutualistic relationship exists between corals and the tiny unicellular zooxanthellae which live in their tissues. This is described on page **342**.

There are many other examples of mutualistic relationships. Two of these mutualisms are important in agriculture.

Rhizobium is a bacterium which is able to use nitrogen gas from the air spaces in the soil, and combine it with other substances to make ammonium ions and other compounds. It is a **nitrogen-fixing** bacterium. Flowering plants require nitrogen compounds but cannot use nitrogen gas to make them. However, they can use ammonium ions. The legumes are a group of plants which exploit these bacteria. The bacteria live in swellings, called nodules, on the roots of these plants. The plants benefit because they can use the ammonium produced by the bacteria to make proteins. The bacteria benefit because they obtain sugars from the plant. Pea and bean plants are legumes and due to the presence of their mutualistic bacteria they do not normally need to be fertilised with nitrogenous fertilisers.

When the roots of most plants are examined they are found to have fungi growing in and on them. Some of these fungi are disease organisms (pathogens), including those that cause root rot. But many of the fungi do not cause disease, and are beneficial to the host plant. These form mutualisms called **mycorrhizae** ('myco' means fungus, 'rhizae' means roots). Plants with these root partners are better at taking up phosphates from the soil, are more tolerant of drought conditions and are less likely to suffer from root diseases. The fungi obtain sugars and other organic substances from their hosts.

1.18 The type of symbiosis between species may change in different ecosystems.

Although in the Caribbean the relationship between cattle egrets and cattle is commensalism, in Africa it is mutualism. On that continent there are many large predators of cattle and other hoofed animals. From their perch on their partner's back the egrets are able to see approaching predators. The alarm 'cries' of the egrets warn the cattle of their approach. Thus the benefit is mutual.

Question

1.17 Decide whether each of these relationships is parasitism, mutualism or commensalism.

- **a** Fleas live on the skin of dogs, feeding on their blood.
- **b** Clown fish live amongst the tentacles of sea anemones, feeding on scraps of waste food.
- **c** Dodder is a plant with no leaves, which climbs up over other plants and takes nutrients from their stems.

Nutrient cycles

Nothing is wasted in an ecosystem. Food that goes uneaten by one organism will be used by another.

Our bodies contain molecules of many different substances, especially carbohydrates, proteins and fats. You can read more about these in Chapter **3**. These substances contain four **elements** – carbon, hydrogen, oxygen and nitrogen. Atoms of these elements are passed around the ecosystem, from one organism to another, as well as into the air or the soil. Most of the atoms in your body were once part of something else's body.

1.19 Decomposers release minerals from dead organisms.

One very important group of organisms that it is easy to overlook when you are studying an ecosystem, is the **decomposers**. They feed on waste material from animals and plants, and on their dead bodies (Figure **1.21**). Many fungi and bacteria are decomposers. You can read more about how fungi feed on page **85**.

Decomposers are extremely important, because they help to release substances from dead organisms, so that they can be used again by living ones. Two of these substances are carbon and nitrogen.

Figure 1.21 These fungi are growing on cattle dung. They break the dung down and feed on the nutrients released from it.

1.20 Carbon is recycled.

Carbon is a very important component of living things, because it is an essential part of carbohydrates, fats and proteins.

Figure **1.22** shows how carbon circulates through an ecosystem. The air contains about 0.04% carbon dioxide. When plants photosynthesise, carbon atoms from carbon dioxide become part of glucose or starch molecules in the plant (section **4.4**).

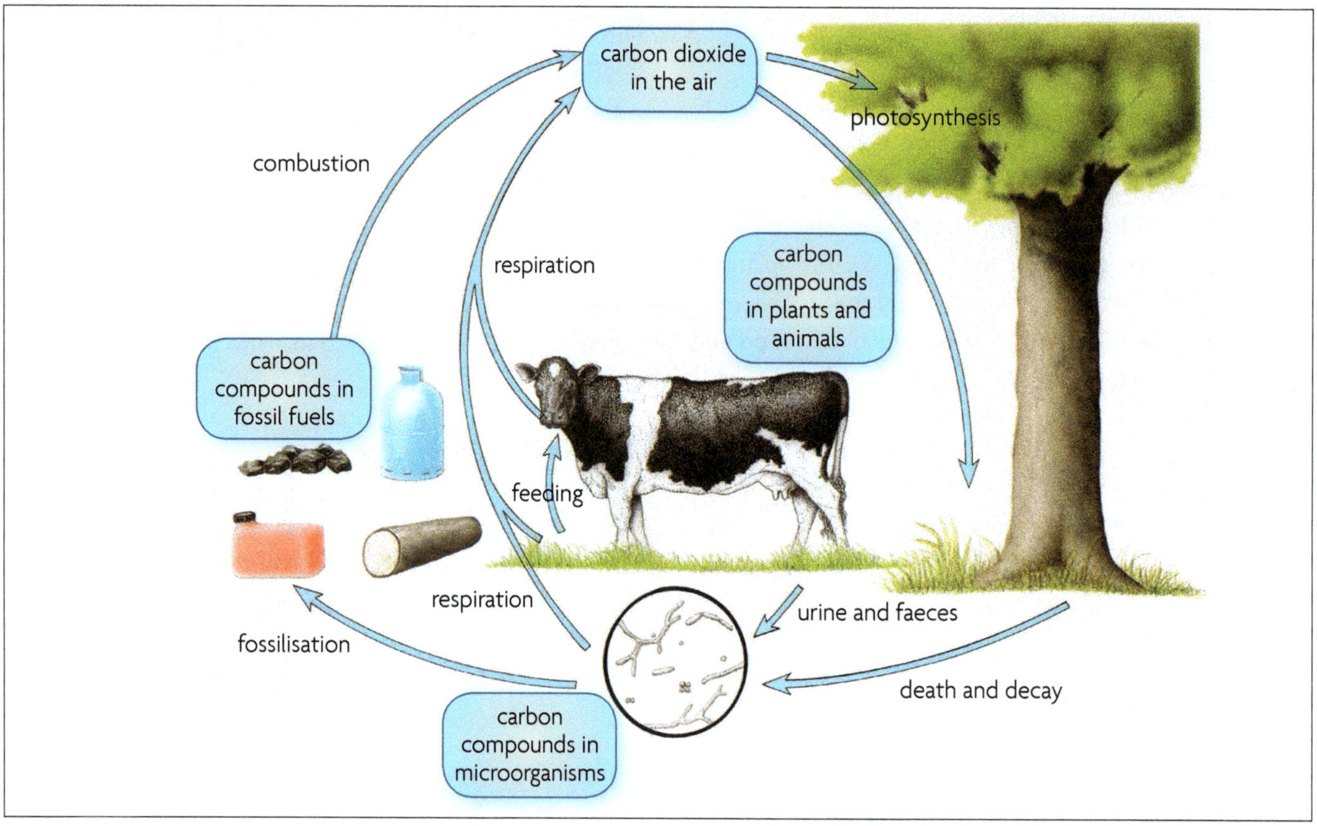

Figure 1.22 The carbon cycle.

Some of the glucose is later broken down by the plant in respiration. The carbon in the glucose becomes part of a carbon dioxide molecule again, and is released back into the air.

Some of the carbon in the plant will be eaten by animals. The animals respire, releasing some of it back into the air as carbon dioxide.

When the plant or animal dies, or when it produces waste materials, decomposers will feed on them. The carbon becomes part of the decomposers' bodies. When the decomposers respire, they release carbon dioxide into the air again.

Millions of years ago, the Earth was wetter and warmer than it is today. Much of the land was covered by swamps. The plants that grew in these swamps fell into the marshy ground when they died. There was not much oxygen in the wet ground, so decomposers could not rot them away completely. Instead, the plants became compressed into the rocks, forming coal. Oil and natural gas were formed in a similar way. These are **fossil fuels**. When we burn them, the carbon in them is oxidised to carbon dioxide, and released into the atmosphere.

Questions

1.18 What does a decomposer do? What kinds of organisms can be decomposers?

1.19 Why are decomposers important?

1.20 Why do living organisms need carbon?

1.21 How do carbon atoms become part of a plant?

1.22 What happens to some of these carbon atoms when a plant respires?

1.23 How do decomposers help in the carbon cycle?

1.24 Oxygen is used in respiration and combustion. It is produced by photosynthesis. Draw a simple diagram to show how plants, animals, decomposers and fossil fuels are involved in an 'oxygen cycle'.

1.21 Few organisms can use nitrogen gas.

Living things need nitrogen to make proteins. There is plenty of nitrogen around. The air is about 79% nitrogen gas. Molecules of nitrogen gas, N_2, are made of two nitrogen atoms joined together (Figure **1.23**). These molecules are very inert, which means that they will not readily react with other substances.

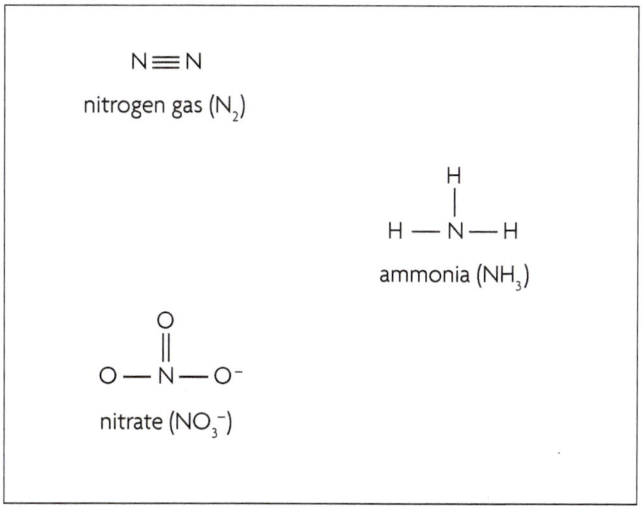

Figure 1.23 Nitrogen gas is very unreactive and cannot be used by most living organisms. It must be combined with hydrogen (to make ammonia) or oxygen (to make nitrate ions) before plants can make use of it.

So, although the air is full of nitrogen, it is in such an unreactive form that plants and animals cannot use it at all. It must first be changed into a more reactive form, such as ammonia (NH_3) or nitrates (NO_3^-).

FACT!

The cattle egret, *Bubulcus ibis*, was first sighted in the New World in 1877. Since then it has spread from Suriname to eastern and central North America, Central America and throughout northern South America and the Caribbean.

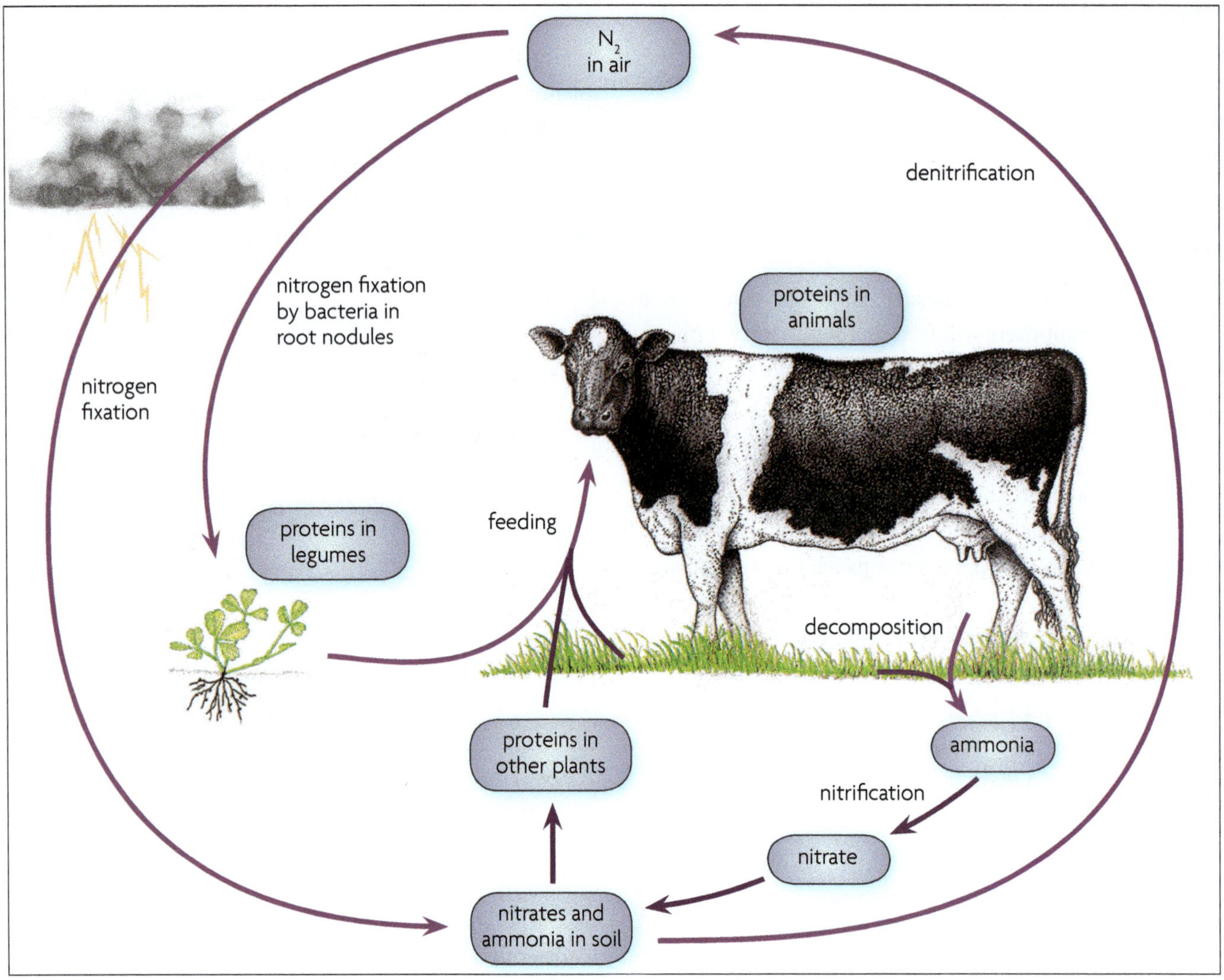

Figure 1.24 The nitrogen cycle.

Changing nitrogen gas into a more reactive form is called **nitrogen fixation** (Figure **1.24**). There are several ways that it can happen.

- **Lightning** Lightning causes some of the nitrogen gas in the air to combine with oxygen, forming nitrogen oxides. These dissolve in rain, and are washed into the soil, where they form nitrates.
- **Artificial fertilizers** Nitrogen and hydrogen can be made to react in an industrial chemical process, forming ammonia. The ammonia is used to make ammonium compounds and nitrates, which are sold as fertilizers.
- **Nitrogen-fixing bacteria** These bacteria live in the soil, or – as we have seen – in root nodules (small swellings) on plants like peas and beans. They use nitrogen gas from the air spaces in the soil, and combine it with other substances to make ammonia.

1.22 Fixed nitrogen moves around in a cycle.

Once the nitrogen has been fixed, it can be absorbed by the roots of plants, and used to make proteins. Animals eat the plants, so animals get their nitrogen in the form of proteins.

When an animal or plant dies, bacteria and fungi decompose the bodies. The proteins, containing nitrogen, are broken down to ammonia and this is released.

Another group of bacteria, called **nitrifying bacteria**, turn the ammonia into nitrates, which plants can use again.

Nitrogen is also returned to the soil when animals excrete nitrogenous waste material. It may be in the form of ammonia or urea. Again, nitrifying bacteria will convert it to nitrates.

1.23 Denitrifying bacteria make nitrogen gas.

A third group of bacteria completes the nitrogen cycle. They are called **denitrifying bacteria**, because they undo work done by nitrifying bacteria. They turn nitrates and ammonia in the soil into nitrogen gas, which goes into the atmosphere.

1.24 Carnivorous plants get nitrogen from insects.

Nitrogen-fixing bacteria can only use nitrogen gas if there is plenty of air in the soil where they live. They need to get nitrogen as a gas from the air spaces in the soil.

If the soil is waterlogged, nitrogen-fixing bacteria cannot live there, but denitrifying ones can. So boggy soil is usually very short of nitrates. Plants living in these places either have to manage with very little nitrogen, or get it from somewhere else. Some of them have become carnivorous. Plants like the pitcher plant (Figure **1.25**) or the sundews supplement their diet with insects. They digest them with enzymes, and get extra nitrogen from the proteins in the insects' bodies.

Figure 1.25 An insectivorous pitcher plant.

1.25 The water cycle.

A continuous supply of water is essential for life. In nature, a constant recycling process maintains this supply (Figure **1.26**). Water vapour, a gas, is released into the air when water **evaporates** from oceans, lakes, streams and rivers. When plants transpire (section **7.39**), and living organisms respire, water vapour is also passed out into the air. The vapour rises and cools until it **condenses** to form water droplets. These form clouds. Eventually the water droplets fall back to the earth as rain, snow or hail. This is called **precipitation**. Then the cycle begins again.

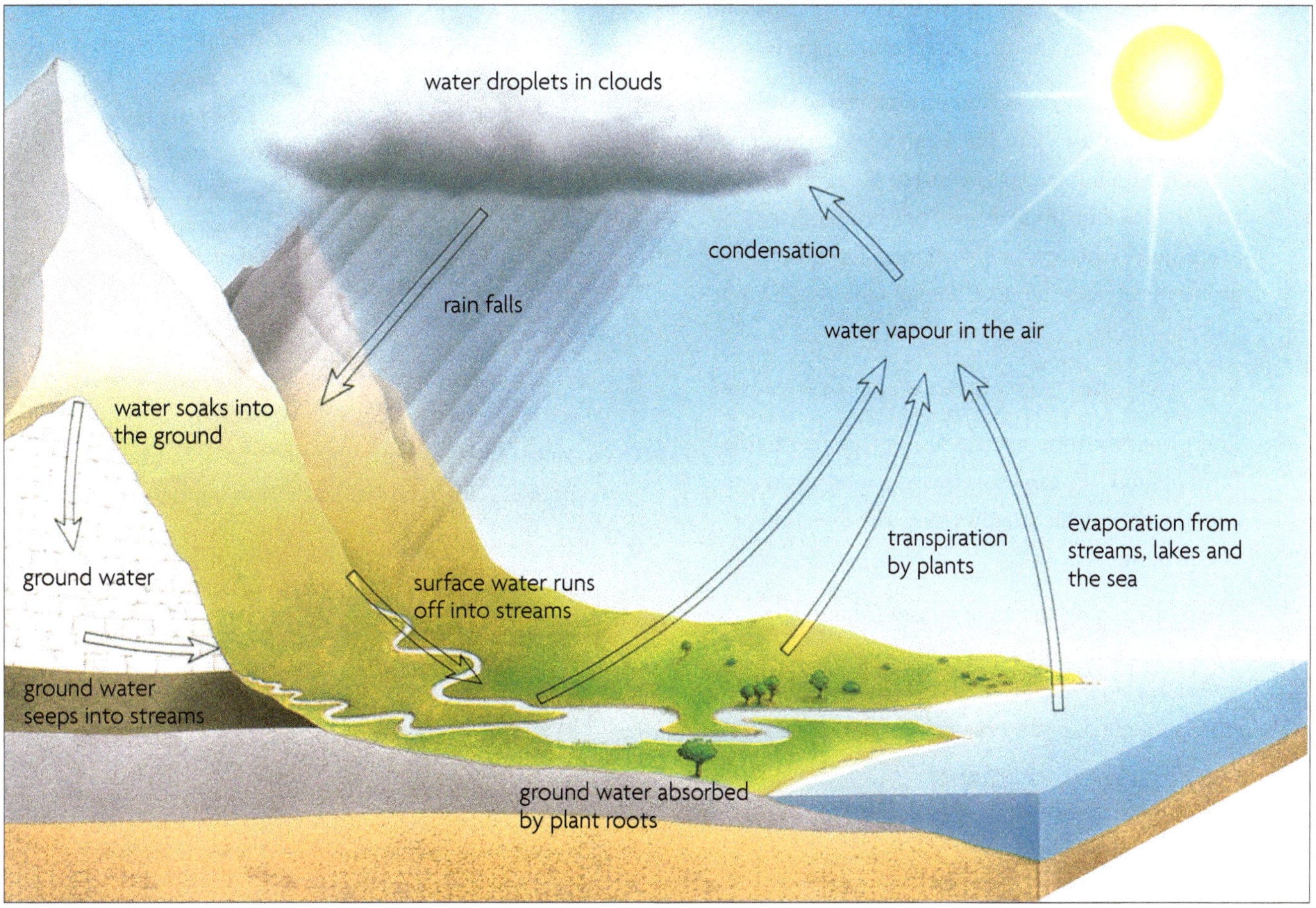

Figure 1.26 The water cycle.

Questions

1.25 Why do living organisms need nitrogen?

1.26 Why can plants and animals not use the nitrogen in the air?

1.27 What is nitrogen fixation?

1.28 How do animals obtain nitrogen?

1.29 What do nitrifying bacteria do?

1.30 Which type of bacteria return nitrogen to the air?

Key ideas

- Living organisms reproduce, feed, respire, grow, excrete, move, are sensitive and are made of cells.
- All the living organisms in an area and their environment are called an ecosystem.
- A habitat is a place where an organism lives. All the organisms of one species in a habitat are called a population. All the populations of different species make up the community. Each species of organism has a particular role to play in the ecosystem, called its niche.
- Each species of organism is given a unique two-word Latin name, made up of its genus and its species.
- Biologists classify organisms into groups according to features that they share. For example, all invertebrate animals with jointed legs belong to the arthropod phylum. We can group arthropods into insects, arachnids, crustacea, millipedes and centipedes. We group vertebrates into fish, amphibians, reptiles, birds and mammals.
- Keys can be used to identify an unknown organism.
- Energy passes from one organism to another in the form of food. We can show this as a food chain or a food web, in which arrows show the direction of energy flow.
- The position at which an organism feeds in a food chain is its trophic level. Plants are primary producers (first trophic level) because they use energy from sunlight to make organic substances such as carbohydrates, which contain energy that can be passed on to other organisms. All other organisms are consumers.
- Energy is lost as it passes along a food chain. There are therefore fewer organisms at the end of a food chain than near the beginning. Pyramids of numbers and biomass show this.
- Sometimes two different species live closely with one another. This is called symbiosis. If one benefits and the other is harmed, the relationship is parasitism. If one benefits and the other is not very much affected, it is commensalism. If both benefit, it is mutualism.
- Decomposers break down dead bodies and waste material. Many are fungi or bacteria. They release substances which can then be reused by other organisms.
- Plants take carbon dioxide from the air during photosynthesis. The carbon becomes part of carbohydrate and other molecules in the plant. Animals get carbon when they eat plants or other animals. Decomposers get carbon when they feed on dead plants or animals, or their wastes.
- Respiration in every living organism returns carbon dioxide to the air.
- Plants and animals cannot use nitrogen gas because it is too unreactive. It must be fixed – changed into a compound – by lightning, bacteria or industrial processes. This produces nitrates and ammonia.
- Plants can use nitrates or ammonia to make proteins. Animals eat plants or other animals to get their nitrogen, in the form of proteins. Decomposers break down their dead bodies or wastes.
- Nitrifying bacteria change ammonia into nitrates. Denitrifying bacteria change nitrates into nitrogen gas, which is released into the air.
- Plants play an important role in the water cycle, because they take up water from the soil and allow it to evaporate into the air, in transpiration.

End-of-chapter questions

1 Explain why a crystal growing in a super-saturated solution of a salt is not considered to be alive.

2 For each of the following, state the habitat in which you would expect to find it and describe its niche.
   a cockroach
   b centipede
   c cow
   d cattle egret
   e crested humming-bird

3 Examine the table below and construct a food web.

Organism	Food source
Pinsonus	seeds of *Anathema* and *Bumus*
Sauterella	leaves of *Bumus*
Feuillus	leaves of *Cynaria* and *Daedaelus*
Fructueux	fruits of *Daedaelus*
Chassum	*Feuillus, Fructueux* and *Sauterella*
Unguis	*Chassum* and *Pinsonus*
Kermesinus	*Fructueux*
Summus	*Chassum* and *Kermesinus*

Which of the organisms in your food web are:
   a primary producers
   b herbivores
   c carnivores
   d top carnivores?

4 Scale insects are sedentary organisms which spend most of their lives sucking juices from plants to which they are fixed by their mouths. The insects excrete a sugary substance called 'honeydew' which black ants love to eat. Scale insects in colonies which have ants associated with them are less often parasitised or eaten by predators. The parasitoids are small wasps, and ladybird beetles are common predators.
   a What type of relationship exists between the ants and the scale insects?
   b At which trophic levels are each of these organisms feeding?

5 Describe the differences between parasitism, commensalism and mutualism. What other types of relationships exist between pairs of species?

6 a Why is nitrogen important to living organisms?
   b In what form do each of the following obtain their nitrogen?
      i green plant
      ii nitrogen-fixing bacteria
      iii a mammal.
   c In the sea, the main nitrogen-fixing organisms are blue-green algae, which float near the top of the water in the plankton. Construct a diagram or chart similar to Figure 1.24, showing how nitrogen is circulated among marine organisms.

7 A fish tank was filled with water, and some bacteria were added. Some phytoplankton (microscopic plants) were then introduced. The tank was put into a dark place, and left for eight months. At intervals, the water was tested to find out what it contained. The results are shown in the graph in Figure 1.27.

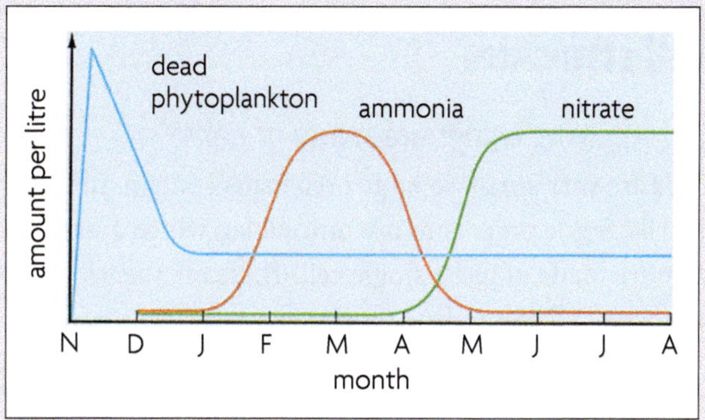

Figure 1.27

   a Why did the phytoplankton die so quickly?
   b The phytoplankton contain nitrogen in their cells. In what form is most of this nitrogen?
   c Why does the quantity of dead phytoplankton decrease during the first two months of the experiment?
   d After one month, ammonia begins to appear in the water. Where has this ammonia come from?
   e What kind of bacteria are responsible for its production?
   f When does nitrate begin to appear in the water?
   g What kind of bacteria are responsible for its production?

2 Cells

In this chapter, you will find out:

- about plant and animal cells, including their similarities and differences
- about the functions of each of the different parts of a cell
- how to look at cells using a microscope
- how to make good drawings of biological specimens
- about how cells are organised into tissues, organs, organ systems and organisms
- how substances move into and out of cells by diffusion and osmosis.

Cell structure

2.1 All living things are made of cells.

Cells are very small, so large organisms contain millions of cells. Some organisms are unicellular, which means that they are made of just a single cell. These are the bacteria, protozoa and some algae.

2.2 Microscopes are used to study cells.

To see cells clearly, you need to use a microscope (Figure **2.1**). The kind of microscope used in a school laboratory is called a **light microscope** because it shines light through the piece of animal or plant you are looking at. It uses glass lenses to magnify and focus the image. A very good light microscope can magnify about 1500 times, so that all the structures in Figures **2.2** and **2.3** can be seen.

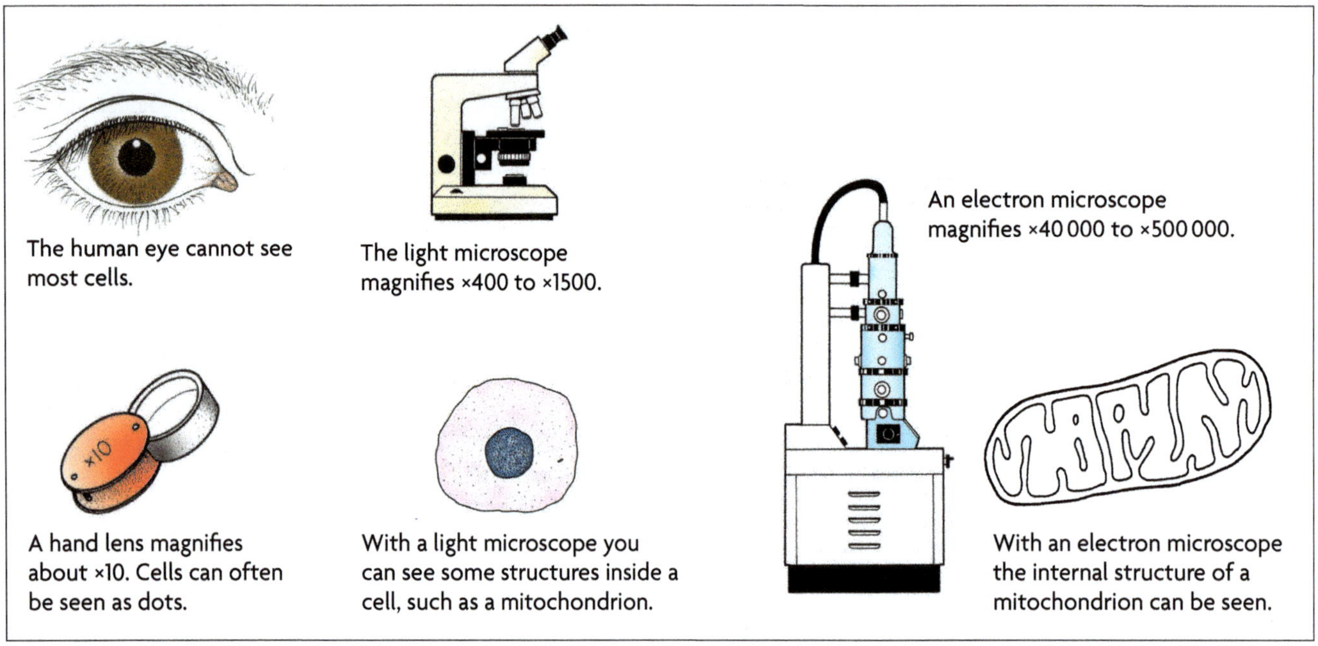

The human eye cannot see most cells.
The light microscope magnifies ×400 to ×1500.
An electron microscope magnifies ×40 000 to ×500 000.
×10
A hand lens magnifies about ×10. Cells can often be seen as dots.
With a light microscope you can see some structures inside a cell, such as a mitochondrion.
With an electron microscope the internal structure of a mitochondrion can be seen.

Figure 2.1 Equipment used for looking at biological material.

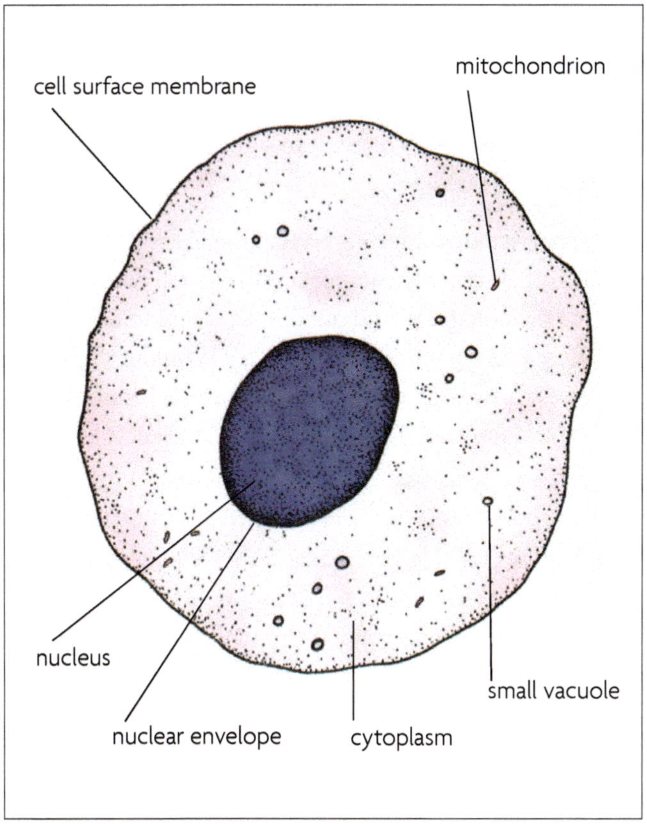

Figure 2.2 A typical animal cell as seen with a light microscope.

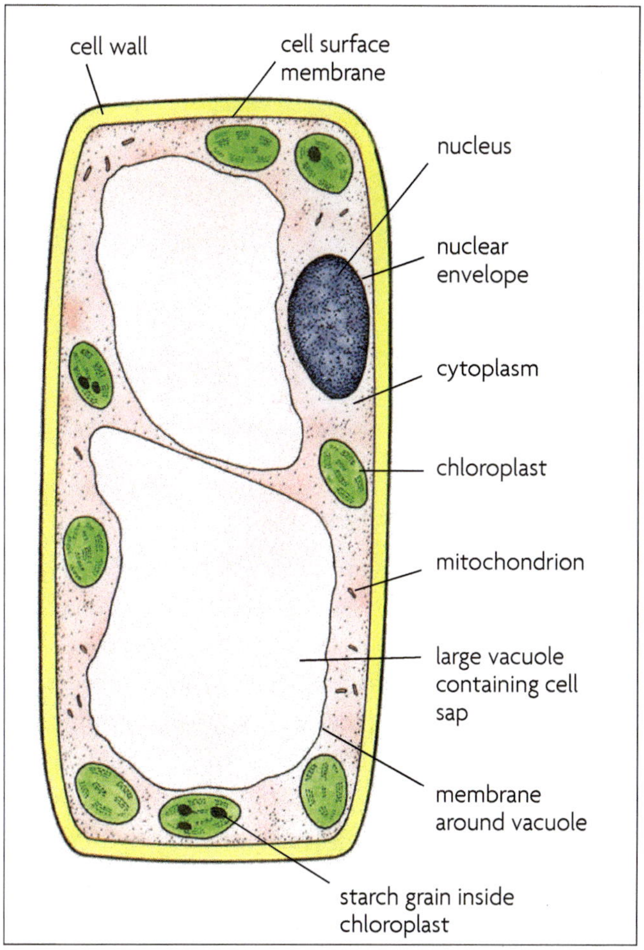

Figure 2.3 A typical plant cell as seen with a light microscope.

Photomicrographs of plant and animal cells are shown in Figure 2.4 and Figure 2.5 (page 24).

To see even smaller things inside a cell, an electron microscope is used. This uses a beam of electrons instead of light, and can magnify up to 500 000 times. This means that a lot more detail can be seen inside a cell. We can see many structures more clearly, and also some structures that could not be seen at all with a light microscope.

Questions

2.1 How many times can a good light microscope magnify?

2.2 If an object was 1 mm across, how big would it look if it was magnified 10 times?

FACT!

The largest cells in the human body are nerve cells (neurones) which can be as much as one metre long. The smallest cells in the human body are sperm cells, which are about 60 micrometres long. A micrometre is one thousandth of a millimetre.

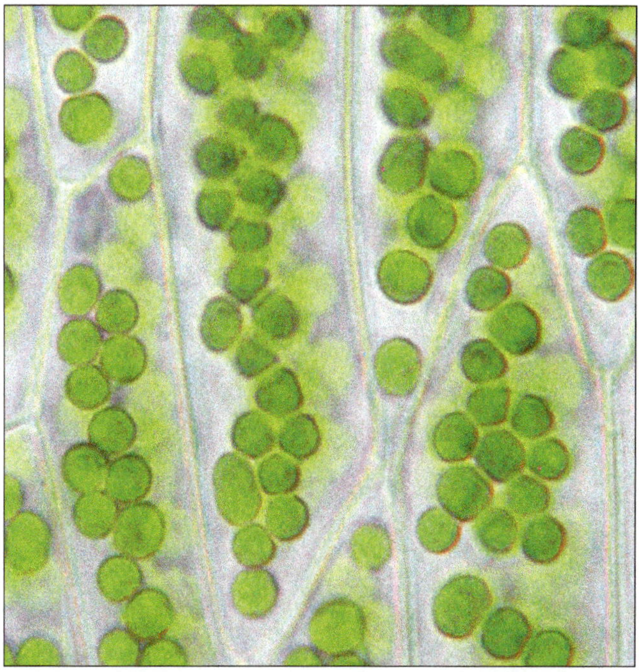

Figure 2.4 Many plant cells contain green structures, called chloroplasts. Even if it does not have any chloroplasts, you can still identify a plant cell because it has a cell wall around it.

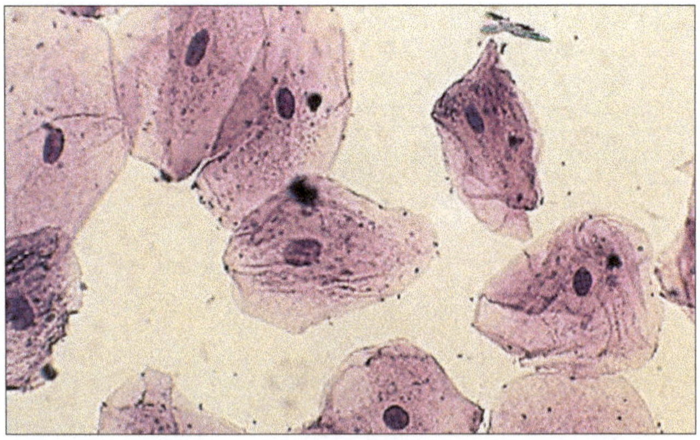

Figure 2.5 Cells from the trachea (wind pipe) of a mammal, seen through a light microscope.

2.3 All cells have a cell membrane.

Whatever sort of animal or plant they come from, all cells have a **cell membrane** around the outside. Inside the cell membrane is a jelly-like substance called cytoplasm, in which are found many small structures called **organelles**. The most obvious of these organelles is usually the **nucleus**. The whole content of the cell is called **protoplasm**.

2.4 Plant cells have a cell wall.

All plant cells are surrounded by a cell wall made mainly of **cellulose**. Paper, which is made from cell walls, is also made of cellulose. Animal cells never have cell walls made of cellulose. Cellulose belongs to a group of substances called polysaccharides, which are described in section **3.5**. Cellulose forms fibres which criss-cross over one another to form a very strong covering to the cell (Figure **2.6**). This helps to protect and support the cell. If the cell absorbs a lot of water and swells, the cell wall stops it bursting.

Because of the spaces between fibres, even very large molecules are able to go through the cellulose cell wall. It is therefore said to be **fully permeable**.

Figure 2.6 Cellulose fibres from a plant cell wall. This picture was taken using an electron microscope (magnification ×50 000).

2.5 Cell membranes are partially permeable.

All cells have a membrane surrounding the cell. It is called the cell surface membrane or **plasma membrane**. In a plant cell, it is very difficult to see, because it is right against the cell wall.

The cell surface membrane is a very thin layer of protein and fat. It is very important to the cell because it controls what goes in and out of it. It is said to be **partially permeable**, which means that it will let some substances through but not others. Another term for this is **selectively permeable**.

2.6 Cytoplasm is a complex solution.

Cytoplasm is a clear jelly. It is nearly all water; about 70% is water in many cells. It contains many substances dissolved in it, especially proteins. Many different **metabolic reactions** (the chemical reactions of life) take place in the cytoplasm.

2.7 Most cells contain vacuoles.

A vacuole is a space in a cell, surrounded by a membrane, and containing a solution. Plant cells have very large vacuoles, which contain a solution of sugars and other substances called **cell sap**. Animal cells have much smaller vacuoles, which may contain food or water.

2.8 Chloroplasts trap the energy of sunlight.

Chloroplasts are never found in animal cells, but most of the cells in the green parts of plants have them. They contain the green colouring or pigment called **chlorophyll**. Chlorophyll absorbs sunlight, and the energy of sunlight is then used for making food for the plant by **photosynthesis** (Chapter **4**).

Chloroplasts often contain starch grains, which have been made by photosynthesis. Animal cells never contain starch grains.

2.9 Mitochondria release energy from food.

Almost every cell has mitochondria, because it is here that the cell releases energy from food. The energy is needed to help it move and grow. Mitochondria are sometimes called the 'powerhouses' of the cell. The energy is released by combining food with oxygen, in a process called **respiration**. The more active a cell, the more mitochondria it has.

2.10 The nucleus stores inherited information.

The nucleus is where the genetic information is stored which helps the cell to make the right sorts of proteins. The information is kept on the **chromosomes**, which are inherited from the organism's parents. The chromosomes are made of **DNA**.

Chromosomes are very long, but so thin that they cannot easily be seen even using the electron microscope. However, when the cell is dividing, they become short and thick, and can be seen with a good light microscope.

Table 2.1 A comparison between animal and plant cells

Similarities

1 Both have a cell surface membrane surrounding the cells.
2 Both have cytoplasm.
3 Both contain a nucleus.
4 Both contain mitochondria.

Differences

	Plant cells	Animal cells
1	have a cellulose cell wall outside the cell membrane	have no cell wall
2	often have chloroplasts containing chlorophyll	have no chloroplasts
3	often have large vacuoles containing cell sap	have only small vacuoles
4	often have starch grains	never have starch grains: sometimes have glycogen granules
5	often regular in shape	often irregular in shape

Animal and plant cells obtain their food in different ways. Plants make their own food, so their cells contain chloroplasts. Starch granules store some of the food they make. Animals often have to move to find their food. This is made easier if their cells do not have a rigid wall.

Investigation 2.1
Looking at animal cells

SBA skills
Observation/Recording/Reporting *Drawing*

Some simple animal cells line the mouth and trachea (or windpipe). If you colour or stain the cells, they are quite easy to see using a light microscope (see diagram below and Figure 2.5).

1 Using a section lifter, gently rub off a little of the lining from the inside of the trachea provided.

2 Put your cells onto the middle of a clean microscope slide, and gently spread them out. You will probably not be able to see anything at all at this stage.

3 Put on a few drops of methylene blue.

4 Gently lower a coverslip over the stained cells, trying not to trap any air bubbles.

5 Use filter paper or blotting paper to clean up the slide, and then look at it under the low power of a microscope.

6 Make a labelled drawing of a few cells.

Questions

1 Which part of the cell stained the darkest blue?
2 Is the cell membrane permeable or impermeable to methylene blue? Explain your answer.

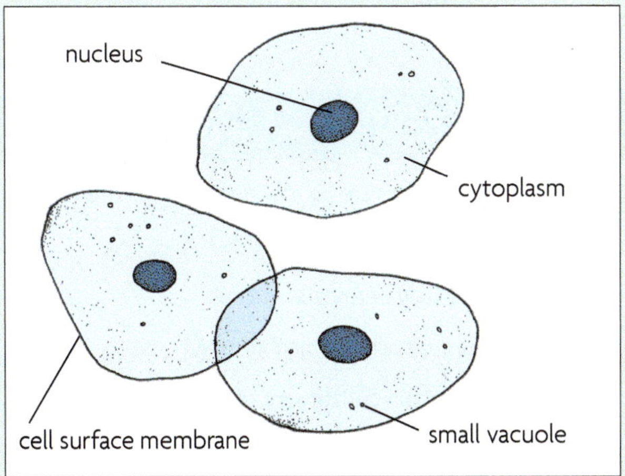

Investigation 2.2
Looking at plant cells

SBA skills

Observation/Recording/Reporting *Drawing*

To be able to see cells clearly under a microscope, you need a very thin layer. It is best if it is only one cell thick (see diagram below). An easy place to find such a layer is inside an onion bulb.

1 Cut a small piece from an onion bulb, and use forceps to peel a small piece of thin skin, called epidermis, from the inside of it. Do not let it get dry.

2 Put a drop or two of water onto the centre of a clean microscope slide. Put the piece of epidermis into it, and spread it flat.

3 Gently lower a coverslip onto it.

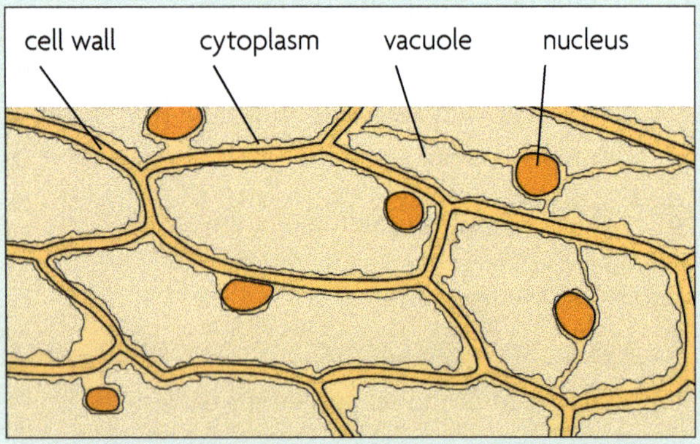

A drawing of onion epidermis cells seen through a light microscope after staining with iodine.

4 Use filter paper or blotting paper to clean up the slide, and then look at it under the low power of a microscope.

5 Make a labelled drawing of a few cells.

6 Using a pipette, take up a small amount of iodine solution. Very carefully place some iodine solution next to the edge of the coverslip. The iodine solution will seep under the edge of the coverslip. To help it do this, you can place a small piece of filter paper next to the opposite side of the coverslip, which will soak up some of the liquid and draw it through.

7 Look at the slide under the low power of the microscope. Note any differences between what you can see now and what it looked like before adding the iodine solution.

Questions

1 Name two structures which you can see in these cells, but which you could not see in the tracheal cells (Investigation **2.1**).

2 Most plant cells have chloroplasts, but these onion cells do not. Suggest a reason for this.

3 Iodine solution turns blue-black in the presence of starch. Did any of the onion cells contain starch?

Questions

2.3 What sort of cells are surrounded by a cell membrane?

2.4 What are plant cell walls made of?

2.5 What does fully permeable mean?

2.6 What does partially permeable mean?

2.7 What is the main constituent of cytoplasm?

2.8 What is a vacuole?

2.9 What is cell sap?

2.10 Chloroplasts contain chlorophyll. What does chlorophyll do?

2.11 What happens inside mitochondria?

2.12 What is stored in the nucleus?

2.13 Why can chromosomes be seen only when a cell is dividing?

Cells and organisms

2.11 Structures within a cell are called organelles.

A nucleus, mitochondria and chloroplasts are **organelles**. Organelles are structures in the cell with special functions. You will find out more about their functions later in this book. Organelles are discrete and the nucleus, mitochondria and chloroplasts are surrounded by their own membranes.

2.12 There is division of labour between cells.

A large organism such as yourself may contain many millions of cells, but not all the cells are alike. Almost all of them can carry out the activities which are characteristic of living things, but many of them specialise in doing some of these better than other cells do. Muscle cells, for example, are specially adapted for movement. Most cells in the leaf of a plant are specially adapted for making food by photosynthesis.

2.13 Similar cells are grouped to form tissues.

Often, cells which specialise in the same activity are found together. A group of cells like this is called a **tissue**. An example of a tissue is a layer of cells lining your stomach. These cells make enzymes to help to digest your food (Figure 2.7).

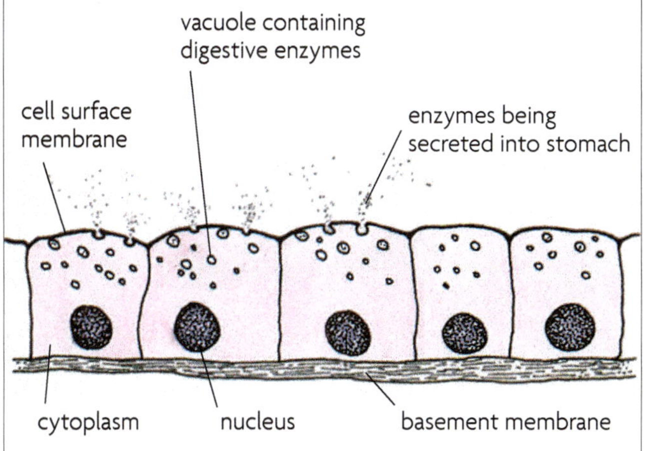

Figure 2.7 Cells lining the stomach – an example of a tissue.

The stomach also contains other tissues. For example, there is a layer of muscle in the stomach wall, made of cells which can move. This muscle tissue makes the wall of the stomach move in and out, churning the food and mixing it up with the enzymes.

Plants also have tissues. You may already have looked at some epidermis tissue from an onion bulb. Inside a leaf, a layer of cells makes up the palisade tissue, in which the cells are specialised to carry out photosynthesis.

2.14 An organ contains tissues working together.

All tissues in the stomach work together, although they have their own job to do. A group of tissues like this makes up an **organ**. The stomach is an organ. Other organs include the heart, the kidneys and the lungs.

In a plant, an onion bulb is an organ. A leaf is another example of a plant organ.

2.15 An organ system contains organs working together.

The stomach is only one of the organs which help in the digestion of food. The mouth, the intestines and the stomach are all part of the digestive system. The heart is part of the circulatory system, while each kidney is part of the excretory system.

The way in which organisms are built up can be summarised like this:

> **Organelles** make up **cells** which make up **tissues** which make up **organs** which make up **organ systems** which make up **organisms**.

Movement into and out of cells

2.16 Diffusion results from random movement.

Atoms, molecules and ions are always moving. The higher the temperature, the faster they move. In a solid substance the molecules cannot move very far, because they are held together by attractive forces between them. In a liquid they can move more freely, knocking into one another and rebounding. In a gas they are freer still, with no attractive forces between molecules. Molecules and ions can also move freely when they are in solution.

When they can move freely, molecules tend to spread themselves out as evenly as they can. This happens with gases, solutions, and mixtures of liquids. Imagine, for example, a rotten egg in one corner of a room, giving off hydrogen sulfide gas. To begin with, there will be a very high concentration of the gas near the egg, but none in the rest of the room. However, before long the hydrogen sulfide molecules have spread throughout the air in the room. Soon, you will not be able to tell where the smell first came from – the whole room will smell of hydrogen sulfide.

Investigation 2.3
Demonstrating diffusion in a solution

SBA skills

Observation/Recording/Reporting

Analysis/Interpretation

1 Fill a gas jar with water. Leave it for several hours to let the water become very still.

2 Carefully place a small crystal of potassium permanganate into the water.

3 Make a labelled drawing of the gas jar to show how the colour is distributed at the start of your experiment.

4 Leave the gas jar completely undisturbed for several days.

5 Make a second drawing to show how the colour is distributed.

You can try this with other coloured salts as well, such as copper sulfate or potassium dichromate.

Questions

1 Why was it important to leave the water to become completely still before the crystal was put in?

2 Why had the colour spread through the water at the end of your experiment?

3 Suggest three things that you could have done to make the colour spread more quickly.

The hydrogen sulfide molecules have spread out, or diffused, through the air. **Diffusion** is the movement of particles from a place where they are in a high concentration to a place where they are in a lower concentration, as a result of their random movements. Diffusion evens out the molecules.

2.17 Diffusion is important to living organisms.

Living organisms obtain many of their requirements by diffusion. They also get rid of many of their waste products in this way. For example, plants need carbon dioxide for photosynthesis. This diffuses from the air into the leaves, through the stomata. It does this because there is a lower concentration of carbon dioxide inside the leaf, as the cells are using it up. Outside the leaf in the air, there is a higher concentration. Carbon dioxide molecules therefore diffuse into the leaf, down this concentration gradient.

Oxygen, which is a waste product of photosynthesis, diffuses out in the same way. There is a higher concentration of oxygen inside the leaf, because it is being made there. Oxygen therefore diffuses out through the stomata into the air.

Diffusion is also important in gas exchange for respiration in animals and plants (Figure **2.8**). Some of the products of digestion are absorbed from the ileum of mammals by diffusion (section **5.21**).

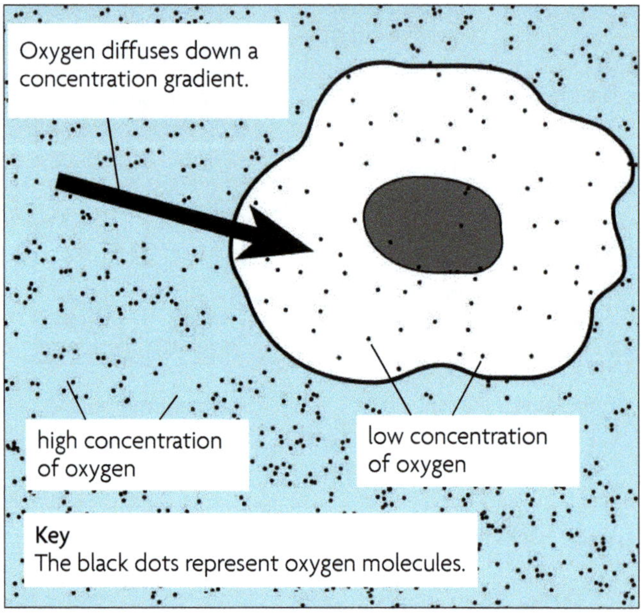

Figure 2.8 Diffusion of oxygen into a cell.

Investigation 2.4

Diffusion of substances through a membrane

SBA skills

Observation/Recording/Reporting
Manipulation/Measurement
Analysis/Interpretation

You are going to investigate diffusion of two different substances dissolved in water. When a substance is dissolved, its particles are free to move around.

In this investigation, you will use starch solution and iodine solution. The solutions will be separated by a membrane made out of Visking tubing. Visking tubing has microscopic holes in it. The holes are big enough to let water molecules and iodine molecules through, but not starch molecules, which are bigger than the holes.

1. Collect a piece of Visking tubing. Moisten it and rub it until it opens.
2. Tie a knot in one end of the tubing.
3. Using a pipette, carefully fill the tubing with some starch solution.
4. Tie the top of the tubing very tightly, using thread.
5. Rinse the tubing in water, just in case you got any starch on the outside of it.
6. Put some iodine solution into a beaker.
7. Gently put the Visking tubing into the iodine solution, so that it is completely covered.
8. Leave the apparatus for about 10 minutes.

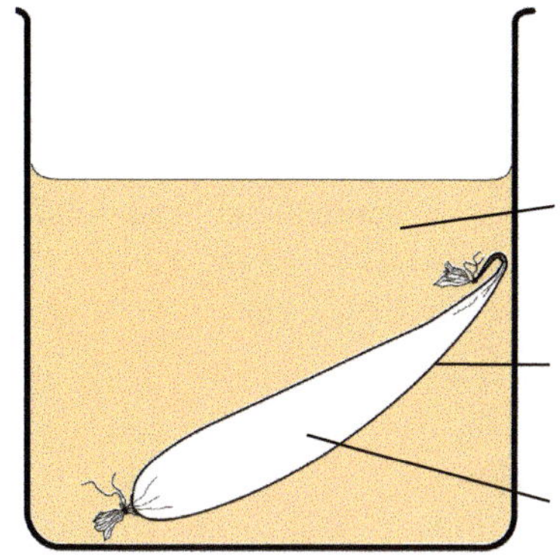

Questions

1. What colour were the liquids inside and outside the tubing at the start of the experiment?
2. What colour were the liquids inside and outside the tubing at the end of the investigation?
3. When starch and iodine mix, a blue-black colour is produced. Where did the starch and iodine mix in your experiment?
4. Did either the starch particles or the iodine particles diffuse through the Visking tubing? How can you tell?
5. Copy and complete these sentences.

   At the start of the experiment, there were starch molecules inside the tubing but none outside the tubing. Starch particles are too .... to go through Visking tubing.

   At the start of the experiment, there were iodine molecules .... the tubing but none .... the tubing. The iodine molecules diffused into the tubing, down their .... gradient.

   When the starch and iodine molecules mixed, a .... colour was produced.

2.18 In osmosis, water diffuses through a partially permeable membrane.

Figure **2.9** illustrates a concentrated sugar solution, separated from a dilute sugar solution by a membrane. The membrane has holes or pores in it which are very small. An example of a membrane like this is Visking tubing.

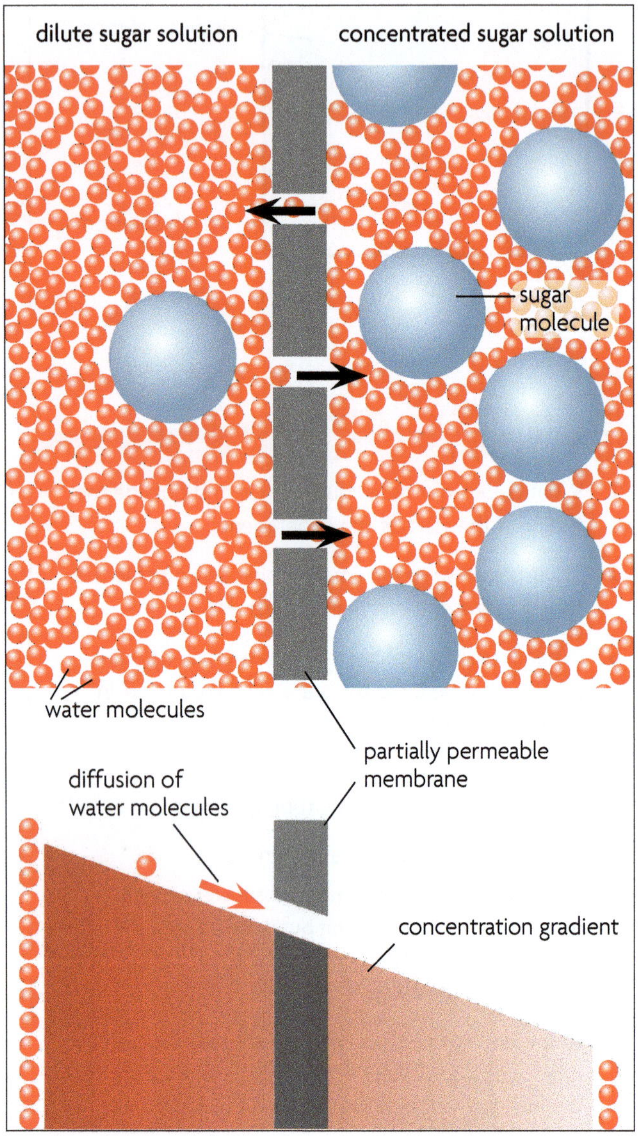

Figure 2.9 Osmosis.

Water molecules are very small. Each one is made of two hydrogen atoms and one oxygen atom. Sugar molecules are many times larger than this. In Visking tubing, the holes are big enough to let the water molecules through, but not the sugar molecules. It is called a **partially permeable membrane** (sometimes known as a **selectively permeable membrane**) because it will let some molecules through but not others.

There is a higher concentration of sugar molecules on the right-hand side of the membrane in Figure **2.9**, and a lower concentration on the left-hand side. If the membrane was not there, the sugar molecules would diffuse from the concentrated solution into the dilute one until they were evenly spread out. However, they cannot do this because the pores in the membrane are too small for them to get through.

There is also a concentration gradient for the water molecules. On the left-hand side of the membrane, there is a high concentration of water molecules. On the right-hand side, the concentration of water molecules is lower because a lot of space is taken up by sugar molecules. The water molecules therefore diffuse from the left-hand side into the right-hand side. They can do this because the pores in the membrane are large enough for them to get through.

What is the result of this? Water has diffused from the dilute solution, through the partially permeable membrane, into the concentrated solution. The concentrated solution becomes more dilute, because of the extra water molecules coming into it.

This process is called **osmosis**. Osmosis is the diffusion of water molecules from a place where they are in a higher concentration (such as a dilute sugar solution), to a place where the water molecules are in a lower concentration (such as a concentrated sugar solution) through a partially permeable membrane.

Investigation 2.5
Measuring the rate of osmosis

SBA skills

Observation/Recording/Reporting *Planning/Design*
Manipulation/Measurement
Analysis/Interpretation

1 Collect a piece of Visking tubing. Moisten it and rub it between your fingers to open it. Tie one end tightly.

2 Use a dropper pipette to put some concentrated sugar solution into the tubing.

3 Place a long glass tube into the tubing, as shown in the diagram. Tie it very, very tightly, using thread.

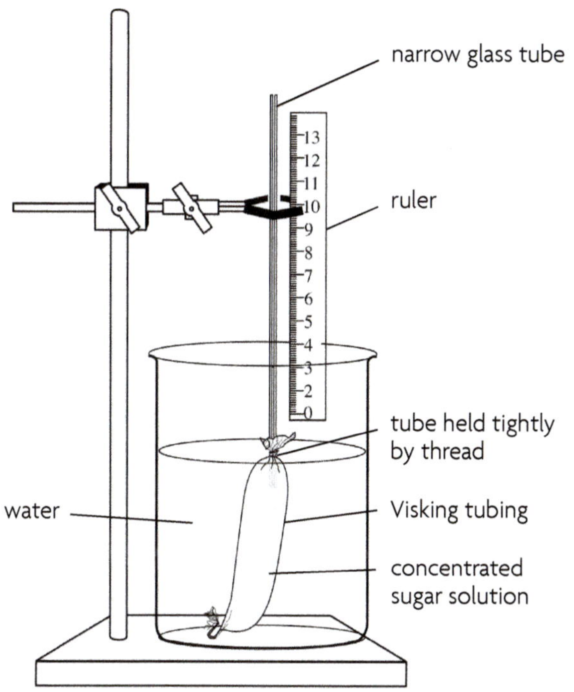

4 Place the tubing inside a beaker of water, as shown in the diagram.

5 Mark the level of liquid inside the glass tube.

6 Make a copy of this results chart. Every 2 minutes, record the level of the liquid in the glass tube.

time in minutes	0	2	4	6	8	10	12	14	16
height of liquid in mm									

7 Collect a sheet of graph paper. Draw a line graph of your results. Put *time in minutes* on the *x*-axis, and *height in mm* on the *y*-axis.

Questions

1 Describe what happened to the liquid level inside the glass tube.

2 Explain why this happened.

3 Use your graph to work out the mean (average) rate at which the liquid moved up the tube, in mm per second. (Ask your teacher for help if you are not sure how to do this.)

4 Predict what would have happened to the rate of osmosis in this experiment if you had used a kind of Visking tubing with ridges and grooves in it, giving it a larger surface area. Explain your answer.

5 When temperature rises, particles move more quickly. Describe how you could use this apparatus to carry out an experiment to investigate the effect of temperature on the rate of osmosis. Think about these things:

- What will you vary in your experiment?
- What will you keep the same?
- What will you measure, when will you measure it and how will you measure it?
- How will you record and display your results?

Predict the results that you would expect.

2.19 Cell membranes are partially permeable.

Cell membranes behave very like Visking tubing. They will let some substances pass through them, but not others. They are partially permeable membranes.

There is always cytoplasm on one side of any cell membrane. Cytoplasm is a solution of proteins and other substances in water. There is usually a solution on the other side of the membrane, too. Inside large animals, cells are surrounded by tissue fluid (section **7.23**). In the soil, the roots of plants are often surrounded by a film of water. Single-celled organisms such as *Amoeba* are also surrounded by water.

So, cell membranes often separate two different solutions – the cytoplasm, and the solution around the cell. If the solutions are of different concentrations, then osmosis will occur.

2.20 Osmosis and animal cells.

Figure **2.10** illustrates an animal cell in pure water. The cytoplasm inside the cell is a fairly concentrated solution. The proteins and many other substances dissolved in it are too large to get through the cell membrane. Water molecules, though, can get through.

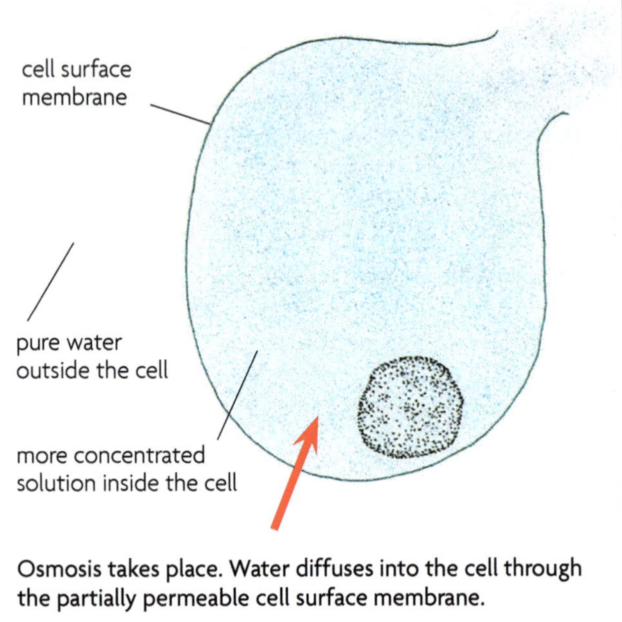
cell surface membrane
pure water outside the cell
more concentrated solution inside the cell
Osmosis takes place. Water diffuses into the cell through the partially permeable cell surface membrane.

Figure 2.10 Animal cells burst in pure water.

If you compare this situation with Figure **2.9** (page **30**), you will see that they are similar. The dilute solution in Figure **2.9** and the pure water in Figure **2.10** are each separated from a concentrated solution by a partially permeable membrane. In Figure **2.10**, the concentrated solution is the cytoplasm and the partially permeable membrane is the cell membrane. Therefore osmosis will occur.

Water molecules will diffuse from the dilute solution into the concentrated solution. What happens to the cell? As more and more water enters the cell, it swells. The cell membrane has to stretch as the cell gets bigger, until eventually the strain is too much, and the cell bursts.

Figure **2.11** illustrates an animal cell in a concentrated solution. If this solution is more concentrated than the cytoplasm, then the water molecules will diffuse out of the cell. Look at Figure **2.9** (page **30**) to see why.

As the water molecules go out through the cell membrane, the cytoplasm shrinks. The cell shrivels up.

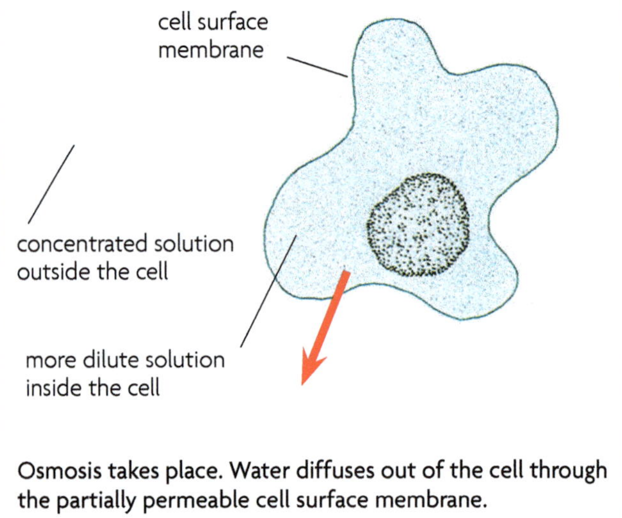
cell surface membrane
concentrated solution outside the cell
more dilute solution inside the cell
Osmosis takes place. Water diffuses out of the cell through the partially permeable cell surface membrane.

Figure 2.11 Animal cells shrink in a concentrated solution.

2.21 Osmosis and plant cells.

Plant cells do not burst in pure water. Figure **2.12** illustrates a plant cell in pure water. Plant cells are surrounded by a cell wall. This is fully permeable, which means that it will let any molecules go through it.

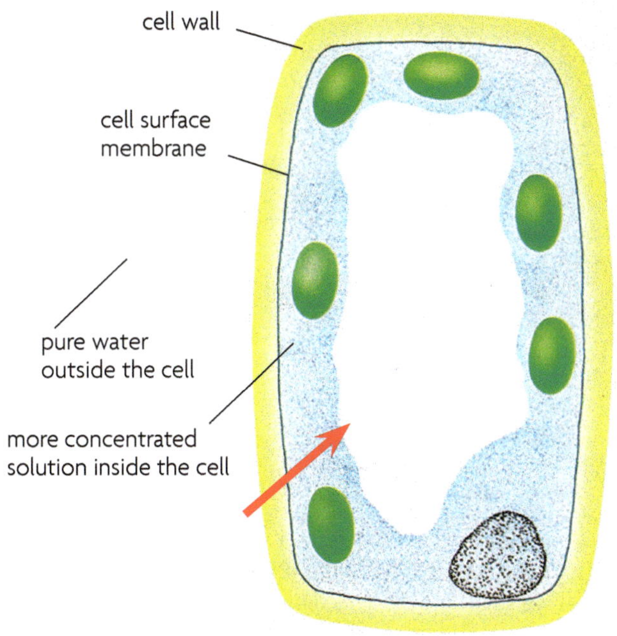

Osmosis takes place. Water diffuses into the cytoplasm and vacuole through the partially permeable cell surface membrane. The cell swells and becomes turgid.

Figure 2.12 Plant cells become turgid in pure water.

Although it is not easy to see, a plant cell also has a cell surface membrane just like an animal cell. The cell membrane is partially permeable. A plant cell in pure water will take in water by osmosis through its partially permeable cell membrane in the same way as an animal cell. As the water goes in, the cytoplasm and vacuole will swell.

However, the plant cell has a very strong cell wall around it. The cell wall is much stronger than the cell membrane and it stops the plant cell from bursting. The cytoplasm presses out against the cell wall, but the wall resists and presses back on the contents.

A plant cell in this state is rather like a blown-up tyre – tight and firm. It is said to be **turgid**. The turgidity of its cells helps a plant that has no wood in it to stay upright, and keeps the leaves firm. Plant cells are usually turgid.

Figure **2.13** illustrates a plant cell in a concentrated solution. Like the animal cell in Figure **2.11**, it will lose water by osmosis. The cytoplasm shrinks, and stops pushing outwards on the cell wall. Like a tyre when some of the air has leaked out, the cell becomes floppy. It is said to be **flaccid**. If the cells in a plant become flaccid, the plant loses its firmness and begins to **wilt**.

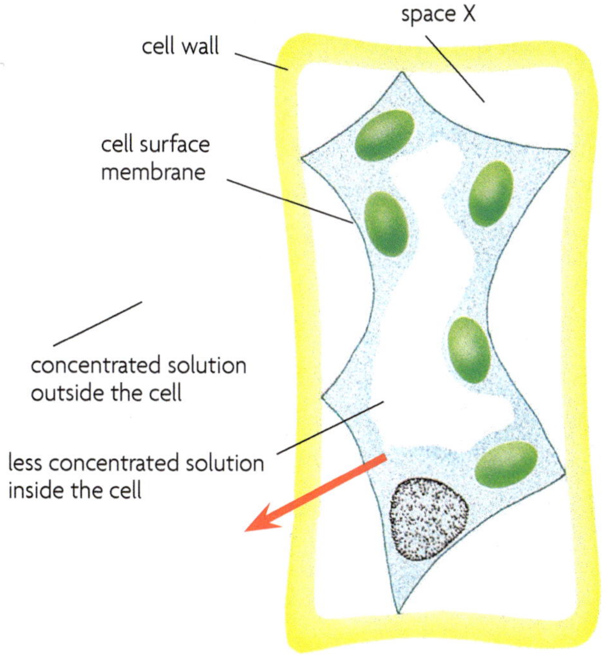

Osmosis takes place. Water diffuses out of the cytoplasm and vacuole through the partially permeable cell surface membrane. First, the cell shrinks slightly and becomes flaccid. Then the cell membrane pulls away from the cell wall, and the cell is plasmolysed.

Figure 2.13 Plant cells become flaccid and may plasmolyse in a concentrated solution.

If the solution is very concentrated, then a lot of water will diffuse out of the cell. The cytoplasm and vacuole go on shrinking. The cell wall, though, is too stiff to be able to shrink much. As the cytoplasm shrinks further and further into the centre of the cell, the cell wall gets left behind. The cell membrane, surrounding the cytoplasm, tears away from the cell wall (Figure **2.13**).

A cell like this is said to be **plasmolysed**. This does not normally happen because plant cells are not usually surrounded by very strong solutions. However, you can make cells become plasmolysed if you do Investigation **2.6**. Plasmolysis usually kills a plant cell because the cell membrane is damaged as it tears away from the cell wall.

Investigation 2.6

Experiment to investigate the effect of different solutions on plant cells

SBA skills

Observation/Recording/Reporting *Drawing*
Manipulation/Measurement
Analysis/Interpretation

1 Set up a microscope.

2 Take three clean microscope slides. Label them A, B and C.

3 Put a drop of distilled water onto the centre of slide A.

4 Put a drop of medium concentration sugar solution onto slide B.

5 Put a drop of concentrated sugar solution onto slide C.

6 Peel off a very thin layer of coloured epidermis from a *Rhoeo* ('Moses in the cradle' or 'Lady in a boat') leaf. To get good results, it should be as thin as possible (only one cell thick).

7 Cut three squares of this epidermis, each with sides about 5 mm long.

8 Put one square into the drop of solution on each of your three slides.

9 Carefully cover each one with a coverslip. Clean excess liquid from your slides with filter paper.

10 Look at each of your slides under the microscope. Make a labelled drawing of a few cells from each one.

Questions

1 Which part of the cell is coloured?

2 What has happened to the cells in pure water? Explain your answer.

3 What has happened to the cells in medium concentration sugar solution? Explain your answer.

4 What has happened to the cells in concentrated sugar solution? Explain your answer.

Questions

2.14 What happens to an animal cell in pure water?

2.15 Explain why this does not happen to a plant cell in pure water.

2.16 Which part of a plant cell is

a fully permeable

b partially permeable?

2.17 What is meant by a turgid cell?

2.18 What is plasmolysis?

2.19 How can plasmolysis be brought about?

2.20 In Figure 2.13, what fills space X? Explain your answer.

Investigation 2.7
Osmosis and potato strips

SBA skills

Observation/Recording/Reporting *Planning/Design*
Manipulation/Measurement
Analysis/Interpretation

1 Peel a potato or other plant tuber or root. Very carefully cut five strips from it, each exactly 40 mm long, 10 mm wide and 10 mm deep.

2 Make a copy of the results table below.

container	A	B	C	D	E
concentration of solution					
initial length of strip in mm					
final length of strip in mm					
change in length of strip in mm					

3 Take five containers and label them A, B, C, D and E. Pour a different solution into each one, as provided by your teacher. Write down the concentration of the solution in the results table.

4 Place one potato strip into each container, so that they are completely covered by the liquid. Leave them for at least half an hour.

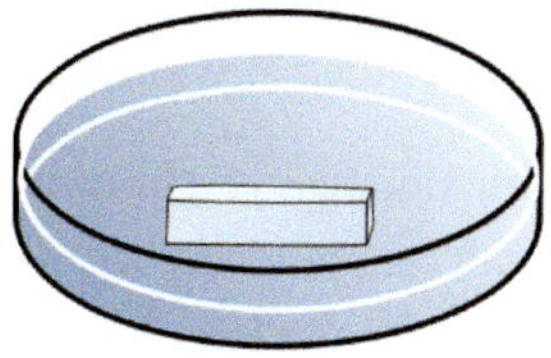

5 Remove the strip from container A and measure it. Write the results in the table.

6 Repeat for all the other strips.

7 Now calculate the change in length of each strip. If it got smaller, show this with a minus sign.

Questions

1 Which strips, if any, got shorter?

2 Complete these sentences, to explain why these strips got shorter.

Potato strips are made of plant cells. Each cell is surrounded by a partially permeable cell .... When the strip is in a solution that is more concentrated than the cytoplasm in the cells, water moves .... the potato cells by osmosis. This makes the cells get .... , so the whole strip becomes smaller.

3 Which strips, if any, got longer?

4 Write some sentences, like the ones in Question 2, to explain why these strips got longer.

5 Describe how you could use this technique to find out the concentration of the cell contents in a potato strip.

Key ideas

- Cells are the smallest units of living things. They are too small to be seen with the naked eye, so we need to use microscopes to see their structures.
- Cells have a cell membrane, cytoplasm, a nucleus and mitochondria. Plant cells also have a cell wall, and often have chloroplasts and a large vacuole containing cell sap.
- The cell membrane is partially (selectively) permeable, and it controls what enters and leaves the cell.
- The cytoplasm is a jelly-like solution of many different substances in water. It is the site of many different metabolic reactions.
- The nucleus contains the chromosomes, which are made of DNA. This is the genetic information and it controls the activities of the cell.
- Mitochondria are the power-houses of the cell, where energy is released from glucose during aerobic respiration.
- The cell wall of a plant cell is made of criss-crossing fibres of cellulose. It is fully permeable. It helps to support the cell, and prevents the cell bursting if it absorbs a lot of water.
- The vacuole of a plant cell contains cell sap, which is a solution of sugars and other substances in water.
- Chloroplasts contain the green pigment chlorophyll, which absorbs sunlight for photosynthesis. There may be starch grains inside the chloroplasts, which are the form in which plants store the food that they make in photosynthesis.
- A tissue is a group of similar cells which work together to carry out a particular function. Tissues are grouped into organs, and organs are grouped into organ systems.
- Particles in gases, liquids and solutions are in constant random motion. As a result of this, there is a net movement from where they are in a high concentration to where they are in a low concentration. This is diffusion.
- Diffusion is important to cells. For example, oxygen enters a respiring cell by diffusion, and carbon dioxide diffuses out of it.
- Water molecules are small and can diffuse through a partially permeable (selectively permeable) membrane. Larger molecules dissolved in the water cannot do this. The diffusion of water through a partially permeable membrane is called osmosis.
- Osmosis is important to cells. In a dilute solution, water passes into a cell through its partially permeable membrane. The cells gets bigger. Animal cells may burst, but plant cells do not because of their strong cell wall.
- In a concentrated solution, water passes out of a cell by osmosis through its partially permeable membrane. The cell shrinks. Plant cells may become plasmolysed – that is, the cell membrane pulls away from the cell wall.

End-of-chapter questions

1 Arrange these structures in order of size, beginning with the smallest:
stomach, mitochondrion, starch grain, tracheal cell, nucleus, ribosome.

2 For each of the following, state whether it is an organelle, a cell, a tissue, an organ, an organ system, or an organism.
   a heart
   b chloroplast
   c nucleus
   d trachea
   e onion epidermis
   f onion bulb
   g onion plant
   h mitochondrion
   i human being
   j lung

3 State which part of a plant cell:
   a makes food by photosynthesis
   b releases energy from food
   c controls what goes in and out of the cell
   d stores information about making proteins
   e contains cell sap
   f protects the outside of the cell.

4 Which of **a–d** below is an example of:
(i) diffusion, (ii) osmosis, or (iii) neither?
Explain your answer in each case.
   a Water moves from a dilute solution in the soil into the cells in a plant's roots.
   b Saliva flows out of the salivary glands into your mouth.
   c A spot of blue ink dropped into a glass of still water quickly colours all the water blue.
   d Carbon dioxide goes into a plant's leaves when it is photosynthesising.

5 Pumpkin growers can make their prize specimens even larger by injecting a concentrated sugar solution into the growing pumpkin. The increase in size can be dramatic. Can you explain why? You may be able to think of more than one reason.

3 The chemicals of life

In this chapter, you will find out:

- why water is so important to living organisms
- what carbohydrates, lipids and proteins are made of, and their properties
- the roles of carbohydrates, lipids and proteins in living organisms
- how to test for the presence of carbohydrates, lipids and proteins
- some good sources of foods containing carbohydrates, lipids and proteins
- what enzymes are and what they do
- how to investigate the effect of various factors on the activity of enzymes.

The bodies of all living things are made of many different kinds of chemicals. Most of our bodies are made up of water. We also contain carbohydrates, proteins and fats. These substances are what our cells are made of. Each of them is vital for life.

In this chapter, we will look at each of these kinds of substances in turn. As you work through your biology course, you will keep meeting them over and over again.

It will help if you have a basic understanding of the meanings of the terms atom, element and molecule. If you are not sure about these, ask your biology or chemistry teacher to explain them to you.

3.1 Water dissolves substances in cells.

In most organisms, almost 80% of the body is made up of water. We have seen that cytoplasm is a solution of many different substances in water. The spaces between our cells are also filled with a watery liquid.

Inside every living organism, chemical reactions are going on all the time. These reactions are called **metabolism**. Metabolic reactions can only take place if the chemicals which are reacting are dissolved in water. This is one reason why water is so important to living organisms. If their cells dry out, the reactions stop, and the organism dies.

Water is also needed for other reasons. For example, plasma, the liquid part of blood, must contain a lot of water, so that substances like glucose can dissolve in it. These dissolved substances are transported around the body.

We also need water to help us to get rid of waste products. As you will see in Chapter **8**, the kidneys remove the waste product urea from the body. The urea is removed dissolved in water, forming urine.

Water also helps us to keep cool. When we are too hot, the sweat glands in the skin release sweat, which is mostly water. The water in the sweat evaporates, and this cools us down.

Carbohydrates

3.2 Starch and sugars are carbohydrates.

Carbohydrates include starches and sugars. Their molecules contain three kinds of atom – carbon (C), hydrogen (H), and oxygen (O). A carbohydrate molecule has about twice as many hydrogen atoms as carbon or oxygen atoms.

3.3 Glucose is a simple sugar.

The simplest kinds of carbohydrates are the **simple sugars** or **monosaccharides**. **Glucose** is a simple sugar. A glucose molecule is made of six carbon atoms joined in a ring, with the hydrogen and oxygen atoms pointing out from and into the ring (Figure **3.1**).

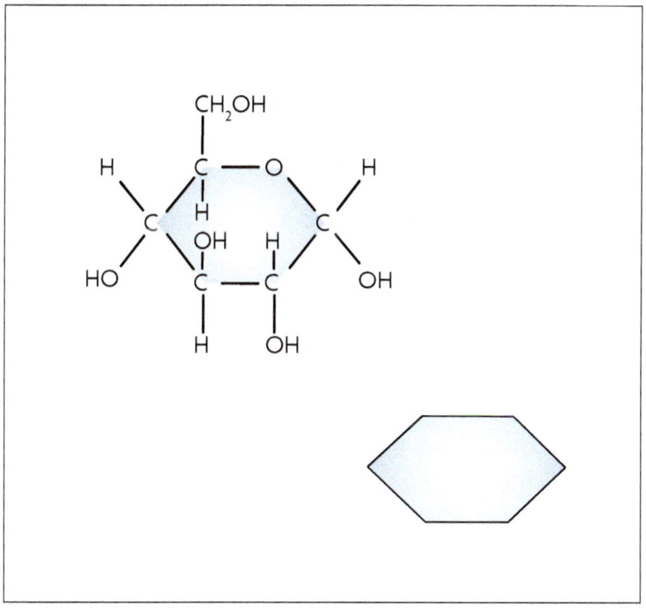

Figure 3.1 The structure of a glucose molecule. You do not need to remember this, but you should remember that glucose is made of carbon, hydrogen and oxygen atoms.

The molecule contains six carbon atoms, twelve hydrogen atoms, and six oxygen atoms. To show this, its molecular formula can be written $C_6H_{12}O_6$. This formula stands for one molecule of a simple sugar, and tells you which atoms it contains, and how many of each kind.

Although they contain many atoms, simple sugar molecules are very small (Figure **3.2a**). They are soluble in water, and they taste sweet.

3.4 Sucrose is a complex sugar.

If two simple sugar molecules join together, a larger molecule called a **complex sugar** or **disaccharide** is made (Figure **3.2b**). Two examples of complex sugars are **sucrose** (the sugar you use on the table) and **maltose** (malt sugar). Like simple sugars, they are soluble in water and they taste sweet.

3.5 Starch is a polysaccharide.

If many simple sugars join together, a very large molecule called a **polysaccharide** is made. Some polysaccharide molecules contain thousands of sugar molecules joined together in a long chain. The **cellulose** of plant cell walls is a polysaccharide and so is **starch**, which is often found inside plant cells (Figure **3.2c**).

Most polysaccharides are insoluble, and they do not taste sweet.

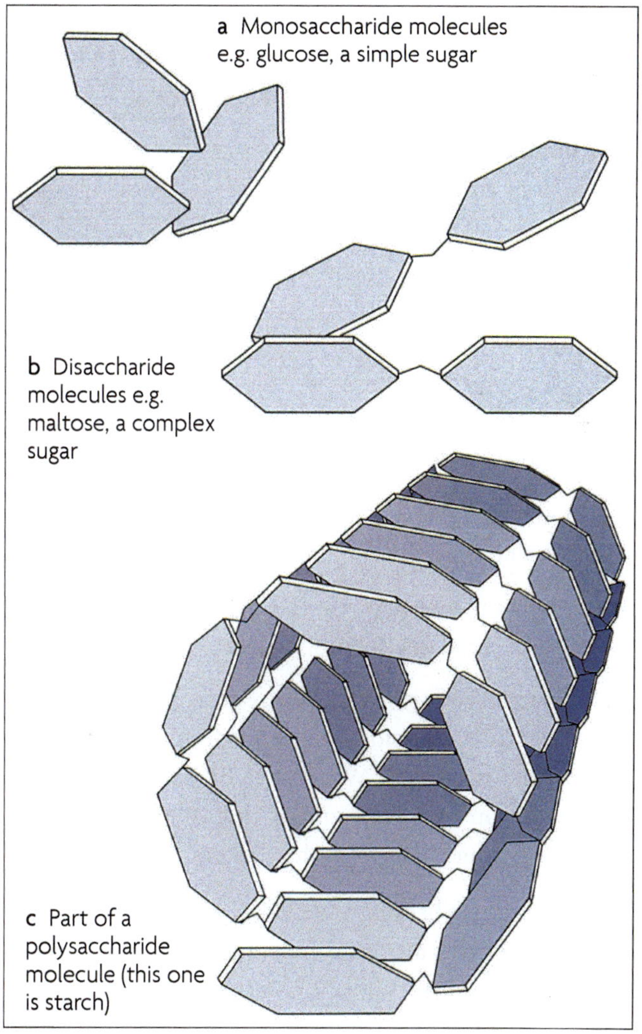

Figure 3.2 Carbohydrate molecules.

3.6 Living organisms get energy from carbohydrates.

Carbohydrates are needed for energy. One gram of carbohydrate releases 17 kJ (kilojoules) of energy. The energy is released by respiration (Chapter **6**).

The carbohydrate that is normally used in respiration is glucose. This is also the form in which carbohydrate is transported around an animal's body. Human blood plasma contains dissolved glucose, being transported to all the cells. The cells then use the glucose to release the energy that they need to carry out the processes of life.

Plants also use glucose in respiration, to provide them with energy. However, they do not transport glucose around their bodies. Instead, they transport sucrose. The cells change the sucrose to glucose when they need to use it.

Plants store carbohydrates as starch. It is quick and easy to change glucose into starch, or starch into glucose.

Investigation 3.1
Testing foods for sugars

SBA skills
Observation/Recording/Reporting

All simple sugars are reducing sugars. This means that they will react with a blue liquid called Benedict's solution. We can use this reaction to find out if a food or other substance contains a reducing sugar.

To test for reducing sugars

1 Draw a results chart.

Food	Colour with Benedict's solution	Simple sugar present

2 Cut or grind a little of the food into very small pieces. Put these into a test tube. Add some water, and shake it up to try to dissolve it.

3 Add some Benedict's solution. Benedict's solution is blue, because it contains copper salts.

4 Heat the tube strongly. If there is reducing sugar in the food, the solution will turn orange-red.

5 Record your result in your results chart. If the Benedict's solution does not change colour, do not write 'no change'. Write down the actual colour that you see – for example, blue. Then write down your conclusion from the result of the test.

This test works because the reducing sugar reduces the blue copper salts to a red compound. All simple sugars are reducing sugars, and also some complex sugars. For example, the complex sugar maltose is reducing sugar.

To test for non-reducing sugars

Some complex sugars, such as sucrose, are not reducing sugars, so they will not turn Benedict's solution orange–red. To test for them, you first have to break them down to simple sugars. Then you must do the Benedict's test.

1 Draw a results chart.

2 Make a solution of the food to be tested.

3 Put a little of the solution into a test tube, and do the simple sugar test, to check that there is no reducing sugar in the food.

4 Boil a fresh tube of food solution with hydrochloric acid. This breaks apart each complex sugar molecule into two simple sugar molecules.

5 Add sodium hydrogencarbonate solution until the contents stop fizzing. This neutralises any left-over hydrochloric acid in the tube.

6 Now add Benedict's solution and heat. A red colour shows that there is now reducing sugar in the food, which was produced from non-reducing sugar.

Questions

1 Why should you cut food into small pieces and try to dissolve it before you do a test for sugar?

2 If you test a food, and find that it contains a reducing sugar, there is no point in doing the non-reducing sugar test. Why not?

Some plants store large quantities of starch in their seeds or tubers, and we use these as food.

Animals do not store starch. Instead, they store carbohydrates in the form of a polysaccharide called **glycogen**. However, only small quantities of glycogen can be stored. It is mostly stored in the cells in the liver and the muscles.

3.7 Carbohydrates come mostly from plant-based foods.

Plants make their own carbohydrates, by photosynthesis. Animals and fungi get their carbohydrates from the food that they eat.

Figure 3.3 shows some foods that contain carbohydrates. Almost all of the carbohydrate that we get in our diet comes from foods derived from plants. This is because animals store only a very little carbohydrate in their bodies. So meat and fish contain hardly any carbohydrate at all.

Carbohydrates are needed for energy.

Figure 3.3 Carbohydrate foods.

Investigation 3.2
Testing foods for starch

SBA skills

Observation/Recording/Reporting

There is no need to dissolve the food for this test.

1 Draw a results chart.

2 Put a small piece of the food onto a white tile.

3 Add a drop or two of iodine solution. Iodine solution is brown, but it turns blue–black if there is starch in the food. Record each of your results and conclusions.

Question

How could you test a solution to see if it contained iodine?

Questions

3.1 What is metabolism?

3.2 Why do organisms die if they do not have enough water?

3.3 Which three elements are contained in all carbohydrates?

3.4 The molecular formula for glucose is $C_6H_{12}O_6$. What does this tell you about a glucose molecule?

3.5 To which group of carbohydrates does each of these substances belong: **(a)** glucose, **(b)** starch, **(c)** sucrose?

3.6 In what form:

- **a** do most organisms use carbohydrates in respiration?
- **b** do animals transport carbohydrates in their blood?
- **c** do animals store carbohydrates in their cells?
- **d** do plants transport carbohydrates round their bodies?
- **e** do plants store carbohydrates in their cells?

Lipids

3.8 Lipids are made of glycerol and fatty acids.

Lipids are fats and oils. Like carbohydrates, they contain only three kinds of atom – carbon, hydrogen and oxygen. A lipid molecule is made of four molecules joined together. One of these is **glycerol**. Attached to the glycerol are three long molecules called **fatty acids** (Figure **3.4**).

Lipids are insoluble in water.

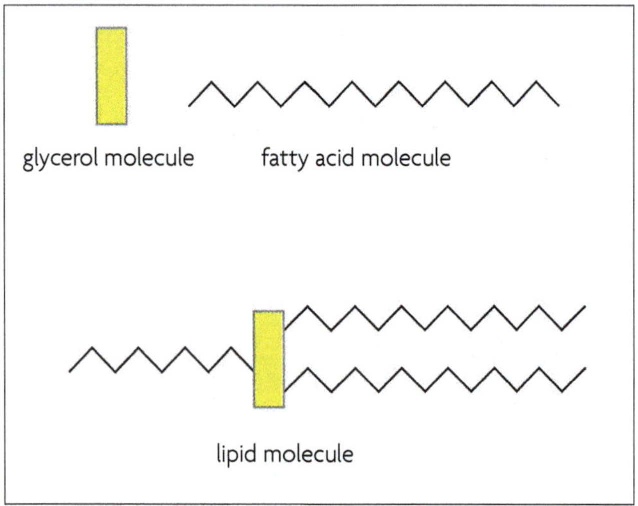

Figure 3.4 A lipid molecule.

3.9 Lipids are good storage products.

Like carbohydrates, fats and oils can be used in a cell to release energy. A gram of fat gives about 39 kJ of energy. This is more than twice as much energy as that released by a gram of carbohydrate. However, most cells use carbohydrates first when they need energy, and only use fats when all the available carbohydrates have been used.

The extra energy which lipids contain makes them very useful for storing energy. In mammals, some cells, particularly ones underneath the skin, become filled with large drops of fats or oils. These stores can be used to release energy when needed. This layer of cells is called **adipose tissue**. Adipose tissue also helps to keep heat inside the body – that is, it insulates the body. Animals such as seals and some whales, which live in very cold places, often have especially thick layers of adipose tissue, called blubber (Figure **3.5**). Many plants store oils in their seeds – for example, castor oil, coconut and peanut. The oils provide a good store of energy for germination.

Figure 3.5 Animals that live in very cold places, such as this bowhead whale, may have thick layers of blubber under their skin to keep in body heat.

3.10 Lipids are found in foods from plants and from animals.

We have seen that plants make carbohydrates by photosynthesis. They use some of these carbohydrates to make lipids. We get lipids from eating plants or animals.

Figure **3.6** shows some foods that contain lipids.

Lipids are needed for energy and for keeping warm.

Figure 3.6 Foods containing lipids.

Questions

3.7 Which three elements are found in all fats and oils?

3.8 State two uses of lipids to living organisms.

3.9 We get cooking oil mostly from the seeds of plants. Why do plant seeds contain oil?

Investigation 3.3
Testing foods for lipids

SBA skills
Observation/Recording/Reporting

There are two different tests that you can do for lipids. One is the emulsion test, and the other is the grease-spot test.

The emulsion test
Lipids will not dissolve in water, but they will dissolve in alcohol. If a solution of lipid (fat or oil) in alcohol is added to water, the lipid forms tiny globules which float in the water. This is called an **emulsion**. The globules of lipid make the water look milky.

1 Draw a results chart.

2 Chop or grind a small amount of food, and put some into a very clean, dry test tube. Add some absolute (pure) alcohol (ethanol). Shake it thoroughly.

3 Put some distilled water in another tube.

4 Pour some of the liquid part, but not any solid, from the first tube into the water. A milky appearance shows that there is lipid in the food.

The grease-spot test

1 Draw a results chart.

2 Rub some of the food onto some filter paper.

3 A translucent mark suggests that there is fat in the food. To check that it is a greasy mark, and not a wet one, dry the paper gently. If the mark goes, it was made by water. If it stays, it was made by fat.

Questions

1 What is an emulsion?

2 Sometimes, a food gives a positive result with the emulsion test, but not with the grease-spot test. Can you suggest why?

Proteins

3.11 Proteins are long chains of amino acids.

Protein molecules contain some kinds of atoms which carbohydrates and lipids do not. As well as carbon, hydrogen and oxygen, they also contain nitrogen (N) and small amounts of sulfur (S) (Figure 3.7).

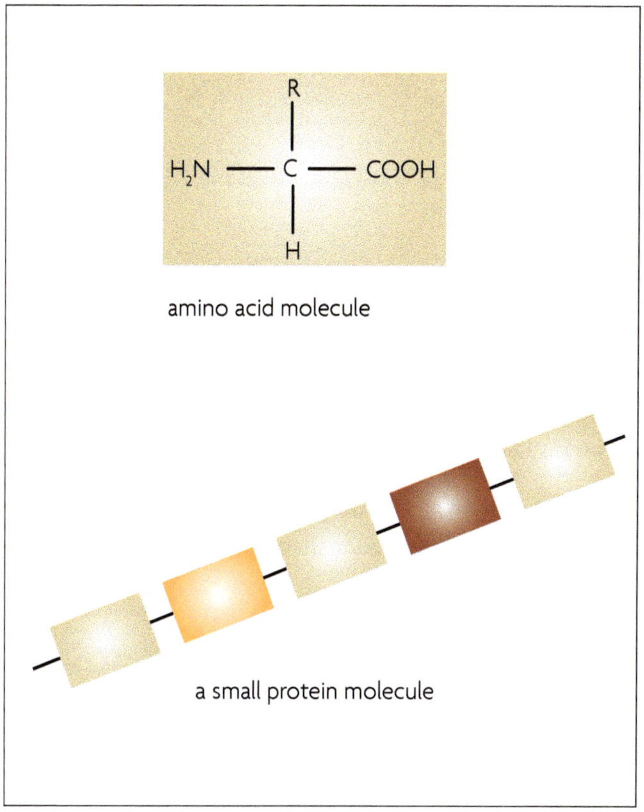

Figure 3.7 Structure of a protein molecule.

Like polysaccharides, protein molecules are made of long chains of smaller molecules joined end to end. These smaller molecules are called **amino acids**. There are about 20 different kinds of amino acid. Any of these 20 can be joined together in any order to make a protein molecule (Figure 3.7). Each protein is made of molecules with amino acids in a precise order. Even a small difference in the order of amino acids makes a different protein, so there are millions of different proteins which could be made.

Some proteins are soluble in water; an example is haemoglobin, the red pigment in blood. Others are insoluble in water; for example, keratin. Hair and fingernails are made of keratin.

3.12 Proteins are used for growth and repair.

Unlike carbohydrates, proteins are not normally used to provide energy. Many of the proteins in the food you eat are used for making new cells. New cells are needed for growing, and for repairing damaged parts of the body. In particular, cell membranes and cytoplasm contain a lot of protein.

Proteins are also needed to make antibodies. These fight bacteria and viruses inside the body. Enzymes are also proteins.

3.13 Plant foods and animal foods are good sources of protein.

Plants use some of their carbohydrates to make proteins. To do this, they need ammonium ions or nitrate ions. These ions contain nitrogen, which the plant has to combine with the carbohydrates to make amino acids. The amino acids are then linked into a long chain to make a protein.

We get proteins when we eat plants or animals. Figure **3.8** shows some foods that are especially good sources of protein.

Proteins are needed for growth, repair and fighting disease.

Figure 3.8 Foods containing protein.

Investigation 3.4
Testing foods for protein

SBA skills
Observation/Recording/Reporting

The biuret test

The biuret test uses potassium hydroxide solution and copper sulfate solution. You can also use a ready-mixed reagent called biuret reagent, which contains these two substances already mixed together.

1 Draw a results chart.

2 Put the food into a test tube, and add a little water.

3 Add some potassium hydroxide solution.

4 Add two drops of copper sulfate solution.

5 Shake the tube gently. If a purple colour appears, then protein is present.

Questions

3.10 Name two elements found in proteins that are not found in carbohydrates.

3.11 How many different amino acids are there?

3.12 In what way are protein molecules similar to polysaccharides?

3.13 Give two examples of proteins.

3.14 State three functions of proteins in living organisms.

Table 3.1 Carbohydrates, lipids and proteins

	Carbohydrates	Lipids	Proteins
Elements they contain	C, H, O	C, H, O	C, H, O, N
Smaller molecules of which they are made	simple sugars (monosaccharides)	fatty acids and glycerol	amino acids
Solubility in water	sugars are soluble	insoluble	some are soluble and some are insoluble
Why organisms need them	easily available energy (17 kJ/g)	storage of energy (39 kJ/g); insulation; making cell membranes	making cells, antibodies, enzymes, haemoglobin and many other substances; also used for energy
Some foods that contain them	bread, cakes, potatoes, rice, yams, eddoes	butter, lard, margarine, oil, fatty meat, milk, peanuts	meat, fish, eggs, milk, cheese, peas, beans, tofu

Table **3.1** compares carbohydrates, lipids and proteins.

Enzymes – special proteins

3.14 Enzymes can speed up reactions.

If you made a solution of starch in water, and kept it at the temperature of your body, it would be a very long time before any of the starch molecules changed into glucose molecules. Yet this reaction happens quite quickly inside your alimentary canal.

Many chemical reactions can be speeded up by substances called **catalysts**. A catalyst alters the rate of a chemical reaction, without changing itself.

Almost all the chemical reactions which go on inside the body are controlled by catalysts. The catalysts which are found in living organisms are special proteins called **enzymes**.

3.15 Enzymes help with hydrolysis and condensation.

For example, in several parts of the alimentary canal, digestive juices are secreted. These digestive juices contain enzymes which speed up the breakdown of large molecules to small ones (Figure **3.9**). They are called **digestive enzymes**. This breakdown is called **hydrolysis** because water is also involved ('lysis' means splitting, and 'hydro' means water). Similarly, the food stored in seeds is broken down to small molecules to provide the energy for germination.

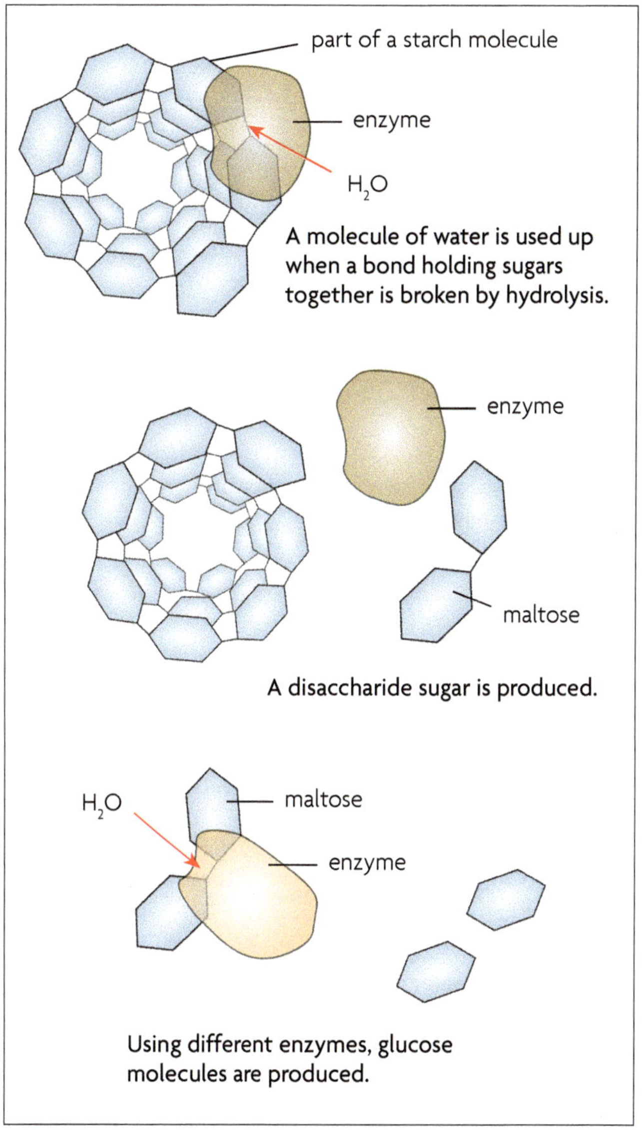
part of a starch molecule
enzyme
H_2O
A molecule of water is used up when a bond holding sugars together is broken by hydrolysis.
enzyme
maltose
A disaccharide sugar is produced.
H_2O
maltose
enzyme
Using different enzymes, glucose molecules are produced.

Figure 3.9 Hydrolysis of starch. Digestive enzymes break down large molecules into small ones.

But digestive enzymes are only one of many different kinds of enzymes. Some enzymes, for example, build up molecules rather than breaking them down. They can link together small molecules to make long chains (Figure 3.10). This is called a **condensation reaction**.

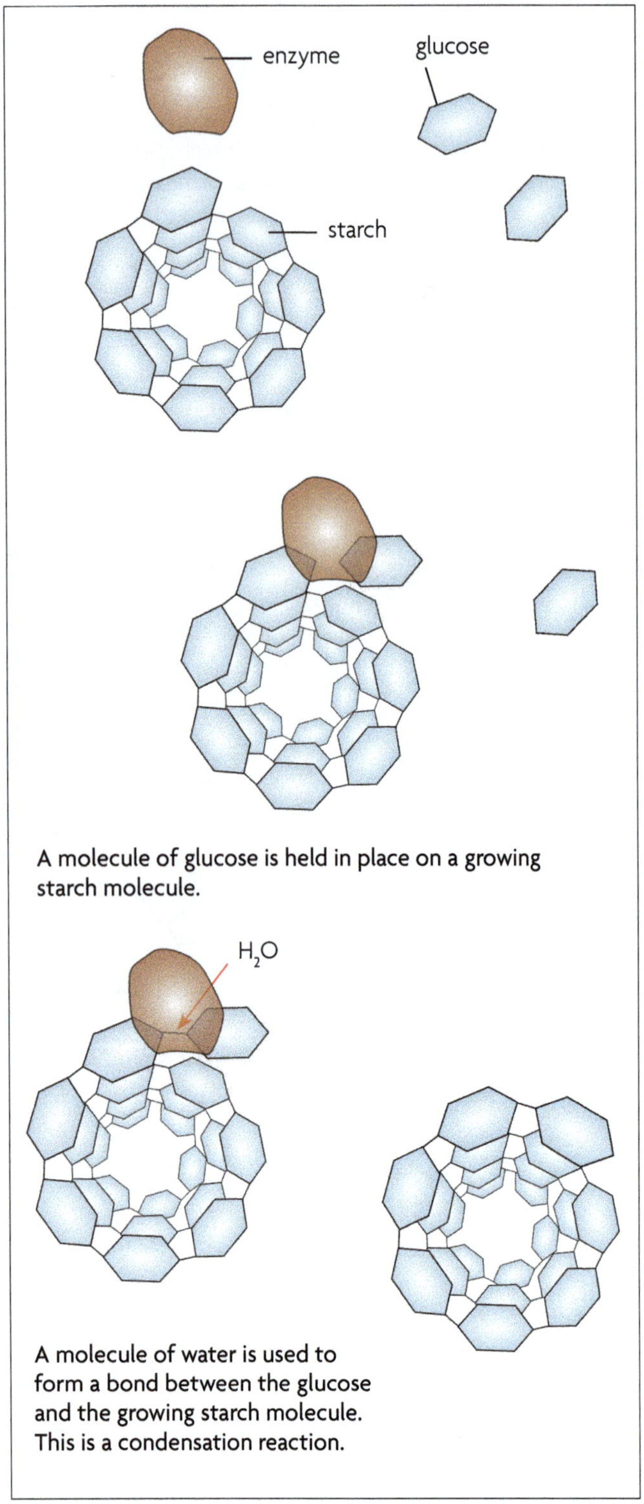

enzyme
glucose
starch
A molecule of glucose is held in place on a growing starch molecule.
H_2O
A molecule of water is used to form a bond between the glucose and the growing starch molecule. This is a condensation reaction.

Figure 3.10 Condensation of glucose molecules to form starch. This happens inside plant cells.

Questions

3.15 Using Figures 3.7 and 3.9 as guides, draw and label a diagram showing the hydrolysis of a protein molecule.

3.16 Using Figures 3.7 and 3.10 as guides, draw and label a diagram showing how amino acids are linked together by condensation reactions to make proteins.

3.16 Enzymes are given special names.

Enzymes are named according to the reaction that they catalyse. For example, enzymes which catalyse the breakdown of carbohydrates are called **carbohydrases**. If they break down proteins, they are **proteases**. If they break down fats (lipids) they are **lipases**.

Sometimes, they are given more specific names than this. For example, a carbohydrase that breaks down starch is called **amylase**. One that breaks down maltose is called **maltase**. One that breaks down sucrose is called **sucrase**.

3.17 Enzymes change substrates to products.

A chemical reaction always involves one substance changing into another. The substance which is present at the beginning of the reaction is called the **substrate**. The substance which is made by the reaction is called the **product**.

For example, in saliva there is an enzyme called amylase. It catalyses the breakdown of starch to the complex sugar maltose.

$$\text{starch} \xrightarrow{\text{amylase}} \text{maltose}$$

In this reaction, starch is the substrate, and maltose is the product.

Figure 3.11 shows how amylase does this. An amylase molecule has a dent in it called its **active site**. This is exactly the right size and shape for part of a starch molecule to fit in. When the starch molecule is in the active site, the enzyme breaks it apart.

All enzymes have active sites. Each enzyme has an active site that exactly fits its substrate. This means that each enzyme can only act on a particular kind of substrate. Amylase, for example, cannot break down protein molecules, because they do not fit into its active site.

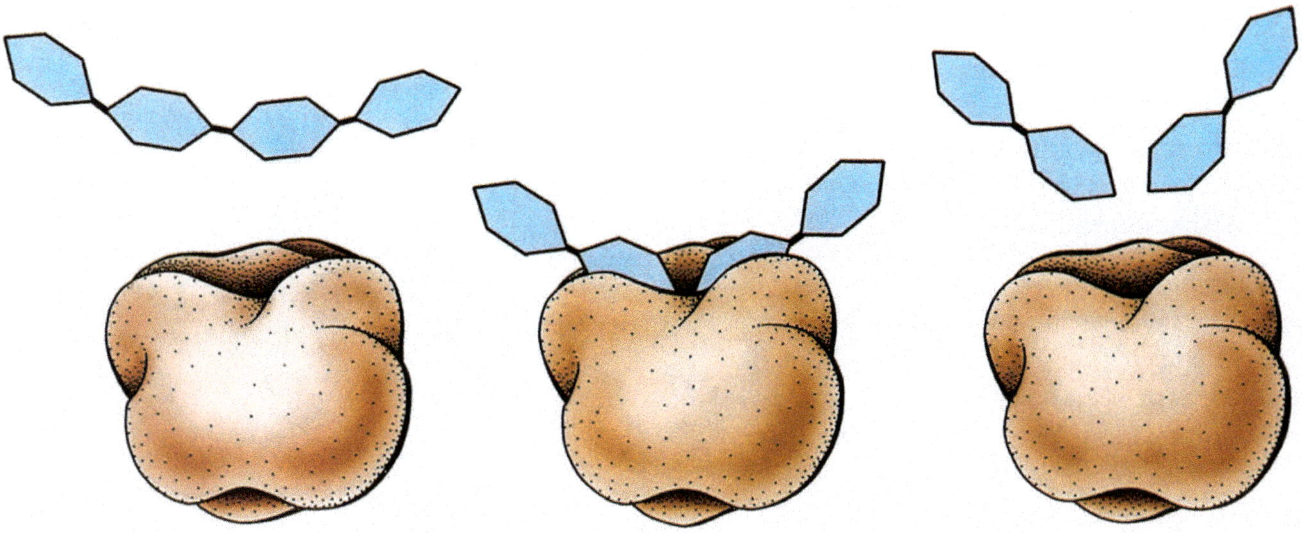

Each enzyme has an active site into which its substrate molecule fits exactly. This enzyme is amylase, and its active site is just the right size and shape for a starch molecule.

The substrate molecule (starch in this case) slots into the active site.

The starch is split into maltose molecules. The enzyme is unaltered, and ready to accept another part of the starch molecule.

Figure 3.11 How an enzyme works.

3.18 All enzymes have certain properties.

1 **All enzymes are proteins** This may seem rather odd, because some enzymes actually digest proteins.

2 **Enzymes are made inactive by high temperature** This is because they are protein molecules, which are damaged by heat.

3 **Enzymes work best at a particular temperature** Enzymes which are found in the human body usually work best at about 37 °C.

4 **Enzymes work best at a particular pH** pH is a measure of how acid or alkaline a solution is. Some enzymes work best in acid conditions (low pH). Others work best in alkaline conditions (high pH).

5 **Enzymes are catalysts** They are not changed in the chemical reactions which they control. They can be used over and over again, so a small amount of enzyme can change a lot of substrate into a lot of product.

6 **Enzymes are specific** This means that each kind of enzyme will only catalyse one kind of chemical reaction.

3.19 High temperature denatures enzymes.

Most chemical reactions happen faster at higher temperatures. This is because the molecules are moving around faster, so they bump into each other more frequently. This means that at higher temperatures an enzyme is likely to bump into its substrate more often than at lower temperatures. They will also hit each other with more energy, so the reaction is more likely to take place (Figure 3.12).

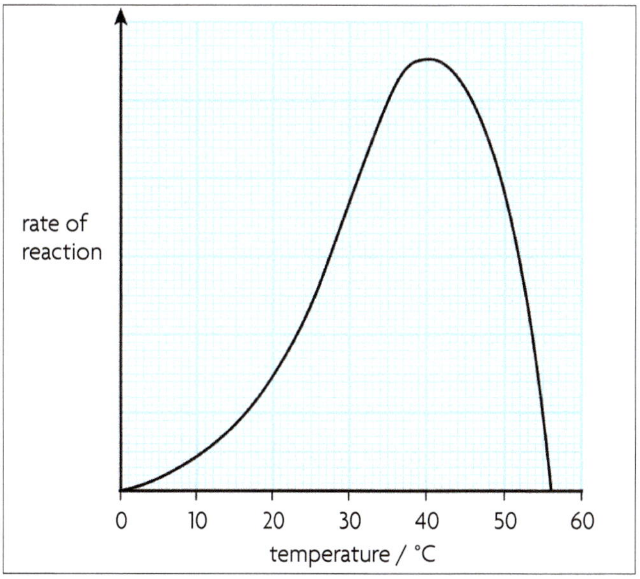

Figure 3.12 How temperature affects enzyme activity.

However, enzymes are damaged by high temperatures. For most human enzymes, this begins to happen from about 40 °C upwards. As the temperature increases beyond this, the enzyme molecules start to lose their shapes. The active site no longer fits perfectly with the substrate. The enzyme is said to be **denatured**. It can no longer catalyse the reaction.

The temperature at which an enzyme works fastest is called its **optimum** temperature. Different enzymes have different optimum temperatures. For example, enzymes from the human digestive system generally have an optimum of around 37 °C. Enzymes from plants often have optimums around 28 °C to 30 °C. Enzymes from bacteria that live in hot springs may have optimums as high as 75 °C.

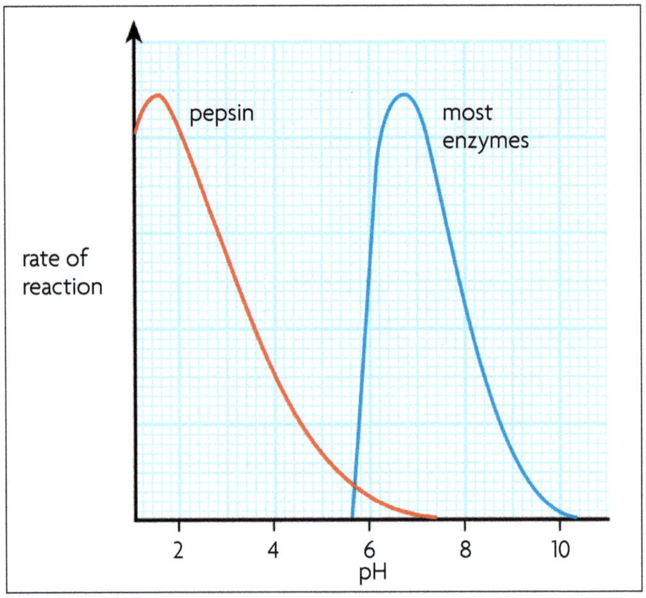

Figure 3.13 How pH affects enzyme activity.

3.20 pH affects enzymes.

The pH of a solution affects the shape of an enzyme. Most enzymes are their correct shape at a pH of about 7 – that is, neutral. If the pH becomes very acidic or very alkaline, then they lose their shape. This means that the active site no longer fits the substrate, so the enzyme can no longer catalyse its reaction (Figure **3.13**).

Some enzymes have an optimum pH that is not neutral. For example, there is a protease enzyme in the human stomach that has an optimum pH of about 2. This is because we have hydrochloric acid in the stomach. Pepsin must be able to work well in these very acidic conditions.

Questions

3.17 What is a catalyst?

3.18 What are the catalysts inside a living organism called?

3.19 Which kinds of reaction inside a living organism are controlled by enzymes?

3.20 What is meant by a carbohydrase?

3.21 Give one example of a carbohydrase.

3.22 Name the substrate and product of a reaction involving a carbohydrase.

3.23 Why are enzymes damaged by high temperatures?

3.24 What is meant by an optimum temperature?

Investigation 3.5
Investigating the effect of pH on the activity of catalase

SBA skills

Observation/Recording/Reporting

Manipulation/Measurement

Analysis/Interpretation

Catalase is a common enzyme which is the catalyst in the breakdown of hydrogen peroxide, H_2O_2. Catalase is found in almost every kind of living cell. Hydrogen peroxide is a toxic substance formed in cells. The reaction is as follows:

$$2H_2O_2 \longrightarrow 2H_2O + O_2$$

The rate of the reaction can be determined from the rate of oxygen production. One indirect but simple way to measure rate of oxygen production is to soak up a catalase solution onto a little square of filter paper and then drop it into a solution of H_2O_2.

(*continues on page* **49**)

(*... continued*)

The paper sinks at first, but as the reaction proceeds, bubbles of oxygen collect on its surface and it floats up. The time between placing the paper in the beaker and it floating to the surface is a measure of the rate of the reaction.

In this investigation, you will test this hypothesis:

Catalase works best at a pH of 7 (neutral).

1 Label five 50 cm^3 beakers pH 5.6, 6.2, 6.8, 7.4, 8.0.

2 Measure 5 cm^3 of 3% hydrogen peroxide into each beaker.

3 Add 10 cm^3 of the correct buffer solution to each beaker. (A buffer solution keeps the pH constant at a particular value.)

4 Cut out 20 squares of filter paper exactly 5 mm × 5 mm. Alternatively, use a hole punch to cut out circles of filter paper all exactly the same size. Avoid handling the paper with your fingers, as you may get grease onto it. Use forceps (tweezers) instead.

5 Prepare a leaf extract by grinding the leaves in a pestle and mortar. Add 25 cm^3 of water and stir well.

6 Allow the remains of the leaves to settle and then pour the fluid into a beaker. This fluid contains catalase.

7 Prepare a results table like the one below.

Time taken for paper to float in seconds	pH of buffer solution				
	5.6	6.2	6.8	7.4	8.0
tests 1					
2					
3					
mean					
boiled extract					

8 Pick up a filter paper square with the forceps and dip it into the leaf extract.

9 Make sure you are ready to start timing. Then drop the filter paper square into the mixture of H_2O_2 and pH 5.6 buffer solution. (Do not let it fall near the side of the beaker.) As you drop the square into the beaker, start a stopwatch. Stop the watch when the paper floats horizontally at the surface.

10 Record the time in your table and repeat steps 8 and 9 twice more.

11 Follow steps 8–10 for each of the other pHs.

12 Pour some of the remaining leaf extract into a test tube and boil for 2 minutes. Cool under a tap.

13 Repeat steps 8–10, using the boiled extract.

14 Calculate the mean (average) time taken at each pH and enter it into your table.

15 Draw a graph to show time taken for flotation plotted against pH.

Questions

1 Does the enzyme have an optimum pH? If it does, what do your results suggest it to be?

2 Do your results support the hypothesis you were testing, or do they disprove it? Explain your answer.

3 What is the effect of boiling the extract?

4 Why do the filter paper squares have to be exactly the same size?

5 What concentration of hydrogen peroxide did you use with the extract?

6 In most experiments in Biology, we can never be quite sure that we would get exactly the same results if we did it again! There are always some limitations on the reliability of the data that we collect. Can you think of any reasons why the results you got in your experiment might not be absolutely reliable? For example:

- Might there have been any variables that were not controlled and that might have affected the results?
- Were you able to measure the volumes and times as accurately as you would have liked?

Investigation 3.6
Investigating the effect of temperature on the activity of catalase

SBA skills

Observation/Recording/Reporting
Planning/Design
Manipulation/Measurement
Analysis/Interpretation

You are going to plan this investigation yourself. You can use ideas from Investigation **3.5** to help you.

You can vary temperature by using a water bath. Your teacher may be able to provide electrically controlled water baths. If not, you can make one by placing a beaker of water on a tripod and gauze over a Bunsen burner. You can make cold temperatures by using ice. Your teacher will show you how to do this.

You need to think about each of the following points carefully. Once you have an idea about how you will do your experiment, write it down as a list of points. Then think through it again, and make improvements to your plan. Once you are fairly happy with it, show your teacher. You must not try to do your experiment until your teacher says that you may begin.

- What is the hypothesis you are going to test? (Hint: use similar wording to the hypothesis in Investigation **3.5**. Also look at section **3.18**, point 3.)
- What apparatus and other materials will you need for your experiment?
- What will you vary in your experiment? How will you vary it?
- What will you keep the same in all the tubes or beakers in your experiment? How will you do this?
- What will you measure in your experiment? How will you measure it? When will you measure it? Will you do repeat measurements and calculate a mean?
- How will you record your results? (You can sketch out a results chart, ready to fill in.)
- How will you display your results? (You can sketch the axes of the graph you plan to draw.)
- What will your results be if your hypothesis is correct? (You can sketch the shape of the graph you think you will get.)

Once you have approval from your teacher, you should do your experiment. Most scientific researchers find that they want to make changes to their experiment once they actually begin doing it. This is a good thing to do. Make careful notes about all the changes that you make.

Finally, write up your experiment in the usual way, including:

- a heading, and the hypothesis that you tested
- a diagram of the apparatus that you used, and a full description of your method
- a neat and carefully headed table of results, including means if you decided to do repeats
- a neat and carefully headed line graph of your results
- a conclusion, in which you say whether or not your results support your hypothesis
- a discussion, in which you use what you know about enzymes to try to explain the pattern in your results
- an evaluation, in which you explain the main limitations that you feel might have affected the reliability of your data.

Investigation 3.7
The effect of temperature on the action of amylase

SBA skills

Observation/Recording/Reporting
Manipulation/Measurement
Analysis/Interpretation

Saliva is the digestive fluid in your mouth. It contains the enzyme amylase. Before doing this investigation, review the food tests in Investigations **3.1** and **3.2**.

1 Set up water baths at 0, 20, 40, 60, and 80 °C.

2 Label five test tubes, 0, 20, 40, 60 and 80.

3 Measure 2 cm^3 of 1% starch suspension into each test tube. Then measure 2 cm^3 of amylase solution into each of five further test tubes. Put the test tubes into the appropriate water baths, as shown in the diagram below. Leave them for at least 5 minutes so that the contents come to the same temperature as the water bath.

4 Prepare a results table like the one below.

	Temperature in °C				
Time in minutes	0	20	40	60	80
starch test 0					
5					
10					
15					
20					
test for sugars					

5 Add the amylase solution to each of the starch tubes in the water baths. Stir each with a separate glass rod (see diagram below).

6 Check the temperature in each water bath regularly and adjust if necessary.

7 At five-minute intervals, including the start, remove a drop of mixture from each test tube and test for starch with iodine solution. Record the result of each test in your table.

8 After 20 minutes, test the remaining solutions in the test tubes for reducing sugars by adding equal volumes of Benedict's solution and heating.

9 Record any colour changes in your table.

Questions

1 Write down a hypothesis that your experiment could have been testing.

2 Does the temperature have any effect on the reactions in the test tubes?

3 How can you explain the results in your table?

4 How do your results relate to the normal range of body temperature in humans?

5 State two reasons for using a solution of amylase rather than fresh saliva.

6 Suggest the main limitations of the method of this experiment, and how these may have affected the reliability of your results.

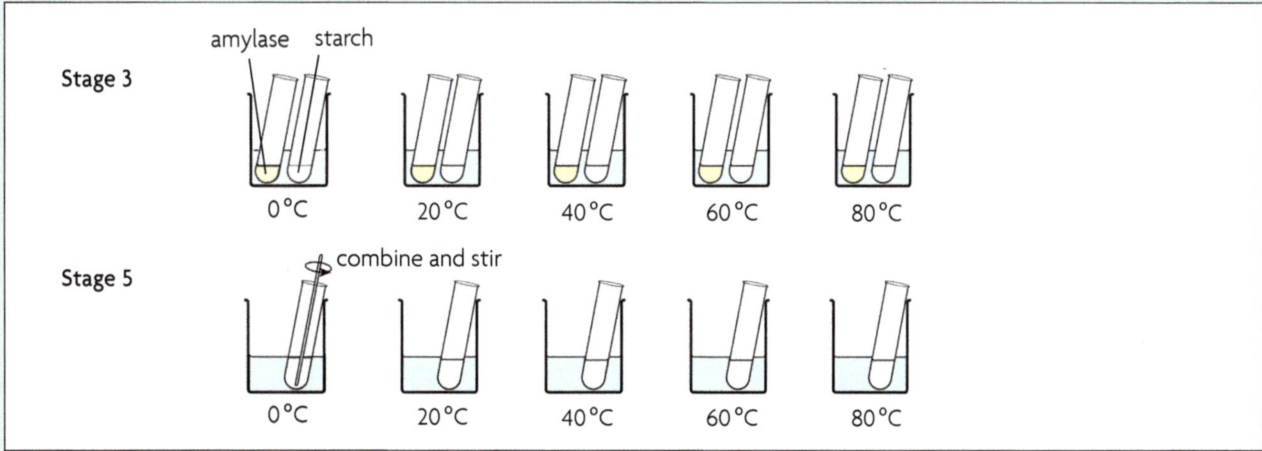

Investigation 3.8
The effect of substrate concentration on the rate of activity of catalase

SBA skills

Observation/Recording/Reporting
Manipulation/Measurement
Analysis/Interpretation

Remember that the chemical acted on by an enzyme is known as its substrate. In Investigations 3.5 and 3.7 the concentration of the substrate was kept constant. In this experiment, you will vary the concentration of the substrate – hydrogen peroxide – and keep all other variables constant.

The catalase in this experiment comes from the potato tissue. Instead of using floating filter paper as a way of measuring the rate at which oxygen is given off, you will count the rate at which bubbles of oxygen are given off from the mixture in the test tube.

1 Set up the apparatus shown in the diagram.

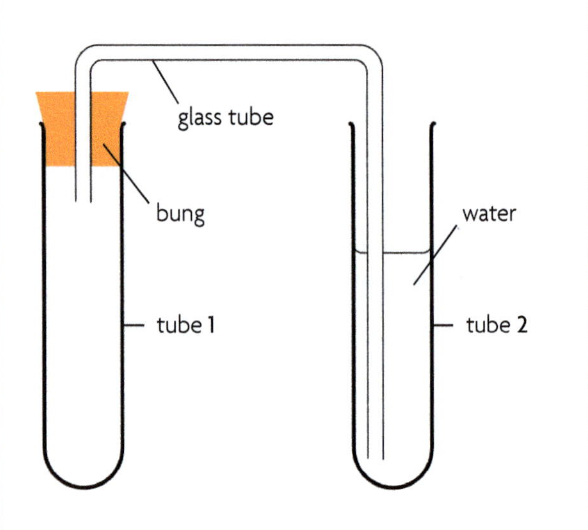

2 Using a large cork borer, cut cylinders from an Irish potato. Immerse the cylinders in a beaker of distilled water.

3 Add 10 cm^3 of 0.5 mol / dm^3 hydrogen peroxide (H_2O_2) solution to tube **1**.

4 Add water to tube **2** so that the end of the glass tube is well below the water surface (as shown).

5 Cut ten thin (1–2 mm thick) complete slices (discs) from a potato cylinder. Place all the slices in tube **1**. Replace the bung tightly and gently shake the tube to separate the slices.

6 Wait 45 seconds and then count the number of bubbles produced in 1 minute.

7 Prepare a results table as shown below, and enter the first number.

		Concentration of H_2O_2 in mol / dm^3			
		0.5	1.0	1.5	2.0
Relative rates of reaction in bubbles per minute	Ist count				
	2nd count				
	3rd count				
	Mean				

8 Discard the contents of tube **1**, wash the tube and repeat steps 5 and 6 twice. Record in your table the numbers of bubbles produced.

9 Repeat the experiment using 1.0, 1.5 and 2.0 mol / dm^3 H_2O_2. Record the numbers in your table and calculate means for each concentration.

10 Draw a graph to show the mean number of bubbles produced against substrate (H_2O_2) concentration.

Questions

1 Suggest a hypothesis that was being tested in this investigation.

2 From your results, what were the effects of the concentration of the substrate on the rate of this reaction?

3 How do you explain your results?

4 Why was tube 1 shaken to separate the slices?

5 Why were the slices changed after taking only one count, instead of taking three counts with each set of slices?

6 Suggest the main limitations of the method of this experiment, and how these may have affected the reliability of your results.

Key ideas

- Water is needed in the body as a solvent, for transport, for the removal of waste products and for keeping cool.
- Carbohydrates include sugars, starch, glycogen and cellulose. They are made of carbon, hydrogen and oxygen.
- The simplest carbohydrates are called simple sugars or monosaccharides. They include glucose and fructose. Two molecules of simple sugars can join together by a condensation reaction to form a complex sugar or disaccharide. These include sucrose and maltose. All sugars are soluble in water and taste sweet.
- Many simple sugar molecules can link together to form a very long chain. These make up polysaccharides. Examples include cellulose, starch and glycogen. They do not taste sweet and are not soluble in water.
- Glucose is the main fuel for most cells. Energy is released from it in respiration. Energy can be stored in the form of starch (in plants) or glycogen (in animals). Cellulose forms plant cell walls.
- The Benedict's test is used to test for reducing sugars. Non-reducing sugars must first be hydrolysed with hydochloric acid before they give a positive result with the Benedict's test. Iodine solution is used to test for starch.
- Lipids include fats and oils. They are made of carbon, hydrogen and oxygen. Some types of lipid molecule are made up of one molecule of glycerol joined to three fatty acids. Lipids are insoluble in water.
- Lipids are used as an energy source. They are especially useful for energy storage, because they contain more than twice as much energy per gram as carbohydrates.
- The grease-spot test and the emulsion test are used to test for lipids.
- Proteins contain carbon, hydrogen, oxygen, nitrogen and sometimes sulfur. They are made of many amino acids linked in a long chain. Some are soluble in water and some are insoluble.
- Proteins are needed for the growth and repair of the body. They are also needed to produce enzymes, antibodies, haemoglobin and many other vital chemicals in the body. They can also be used as a source of energy.
- The biuret test is used to test for proteins.
- Enzymes are biological catalysts. They are proteins. Each one is able to catalyse one particular kind of reaction, because their active site must precisely fit a particular substrate. Each enzyme has a particular temperature at which it works fastest, known as its optimum temperature. It also has an optimum pH.

End-of-chapter questions

1 For each of these carbohydrates, state: (i) whether it is a monosaccharide, disaccharide or polysaccharide; (ii) whether it is found in plants only, animals only or in both plants and animals; (iii) one function.

a glucose b starch c cellulose d glycogen

2 Name:

a an element found in proteins but not in carbohydrates or lipids

b the small molecules that are linked together to form a protein molecule

c the reagent used for testing for reducing sugars

d the substance which the emulsion test detects

e the form in which carbohydrate is transported in a plant

f the term that describes all the chemical reactions taking place in an organism.

3 A protease enzyme is found in the small intestine. It catalyses the hydrolysis of long chains of amino acids into individual amino acid molecules.

a Explain the meaning of each of these terms: (i) *enzyme;* (ii) *catalyse;* (iii) *hydrolysis.*

b Suggest the optimum temperature for the activity of this protease enzyme.

c Explain why the rate of an enzyme-controlled reaction is relatively slow at low temperatures.

d Explain why the rate of the reaction slows down above the enzyme's optimum temperature.

4 How green plants feed

In this chapter, you will find out:

- the difference between autotrophic and heterotrophic nutrition
- how plants make carbohydrates by photosynthesis
- about the structure of leaves
- the ways in which leaves are adapted for photosynthesis
- how plants use the glucose they produce in photosynthesis
- how to carry out investigations into photosynthesis
- about the factors that affect the rate of photosynthesis
- about the importance of photosynthesis for all living things

Types of nutrition

4.1 All organisms feed.

All living organisms need to take many different substances into their bodies. Some of these may be used to make new parts, or repair old parts. Others may be used to release energy. Taking in useful substances is called feeding, or **nutrition**.

4.2 Animals take complex substances from plants.

Animals and fungi cannot make their own food. They feed on **organic** substances that have originally been made by plants. This is called **heterotrophic nutrition**. 'Hetero' means other and 'trophic' means feeding, so 'heterotrophic' means that an animal feeds on substances made by other organisms. Some animals eat other animals, but all the substances passing from one animal to another were first made by plants. Heterotrophic nutrition is described in Chapter **5**.

4.3 Green plants can make complex substances from simple chemicals.

Green plants make their own food. They use simple **inorganic** substances – carbon dioxide, water and minerals, from the air and soil. Plants build these substances into complex materials, making all the carbohydrates, lipids, proteins and vitamins that they need. Substances made by living things are termed **organic**. Green plants are termed **autotrophic**, since they feed themselves ('auto' means self).

Photosynthesis

4.4 Photosynthesis is a chemical process.

Green plants first make the carbohydrate glucose (section **3.3**) from carbon dioxide and water. At the same time oxygen is produced.

carbon dioxide + water ⟶ glucose + oxygen

But the carbon dioxide and water have to be given energy before they will combine. Green plants use the energy of sunlight for this. The reaction is therefore called **photosynthesis** ('photo' means light, and 'synthesis' means manufacture).

Sunlight energy first has to be trapped before the plant can use it in photosynthesis. The green pigment (colouring matter) **chlorophyll** does this. Chlorophyll is kept inside the **chloroplasts** of plant cells. The chlorophyll is arranged on a series of membranes inside the chloroplasts (Figure **4.9**, page **59**). Spread out like this, chlorophyll is well exposed to the light. Therefore it can trap the maximum amount of energy possible. This energy when released, makes possible the combination of carbon dioxide and water. Enzymes inside the chloroplasts help the process.

The full equation for photosynthesis is written like this:

$$\text{carbon dioxide + water} \xrightarrow[\text{chlorophyll}]{\text{sunlight}} \text{glucose + oxygen}$$

To show the number of molecules involved in the reaction, a balanced equation needs to be written. Carbon dioxide contains two atoms of oxygen, and one of carbon, so its molecular formula is CO_2. Water has the formula H_2O. Glucose has the formula $C_6H_{12}O_6$. Oxygen molecules contain two atoms of oxygen, and so they are written O_2.

The balanced equation for photosynthesis is this:

$$6CO_2 + 6H_2O \xrightarrow[\text{chlorophyll}]{\text{sunlight}} C_6H_{12}O_6 + 6O_2$$

4.5 Photosynthesis happens in two stages.

There are two main steps in photosynthesis.

First, the energy in sunlight is used to split water molecules into hydrogen and oxygen. The oxygen is given off as a waste product. This is where the oxygen in our atmosphere comes from.

Next, the hydrogen combines with carbon dioxide, making carbohydrates. This is a **reduction** reaction.

Both of these stages happen inside the chloroplast. Figure **4.1** summarises what happens in each stage.

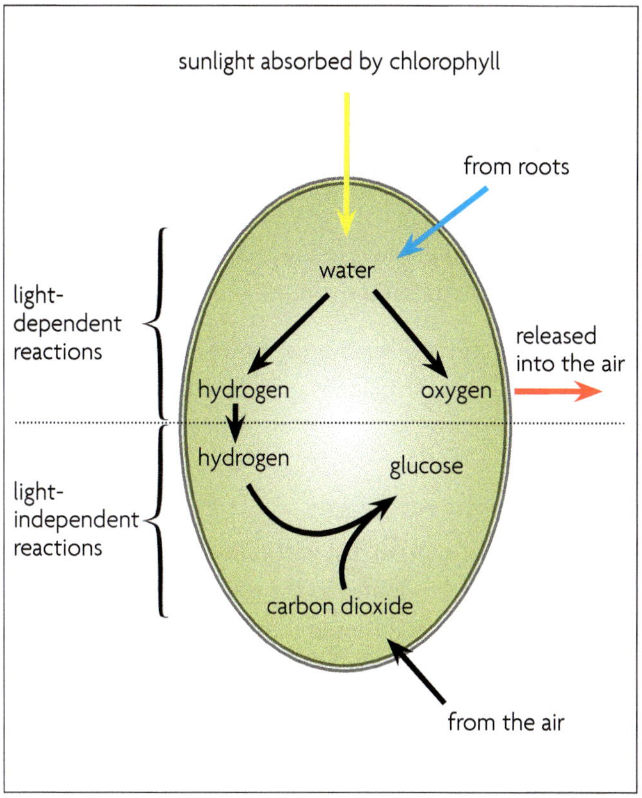

Figure 4.1 The reactions of photosynthesis.

Questions

4.1 Give one example of an organic substance.

4.2 Explain the difference between autotrophic and heterotrophic nutrition.

4.3 Name two groups of organisms that have heterotrophic nutrition.

4.4 Which inorganic substances does a plant use to make food?

4.5 What is chlorophyll, and how does it help the plant?

4.6 What does a balanced equation show?

4.7 For which step in photosynthesis is light required?

4.8 A student wrote, 'In photosynthesis, carbon dioxide is changed into oxygen.' Why is this wrong?

Leaves

4.6 Plant leaves are food factories.

Photosynthesis happens inside chloroplasts. This is where the enzymes and chlorophyll are that catalyse and supply energy to the reaction. In a typical plant, most chloroplasts are in the cells in the leaves. A leaf is a factory for making carbohydrates.

Leaves are therefore specially adapted to allow photosynthesis to take place as quickly and efficiently as possible.

4.7 The structure of leaves.

A leaf consists of a broad, flat part called the **lamina** (Figure **4.2**), which is joined to the rest of the plant by a leaf stalk or **petiole**. Running through the petiole are **vascular bundles** (section **7.33**), which then form the **veins** in the leaf. These contain tubes which carry substances to and from the leaf.

Although a leaf looks thin, it is in fact made up of several layers of cells. You can see these if you look at a transverse section (TS) of a leaf under a microscope (Figures **4.3** and **4.4**).

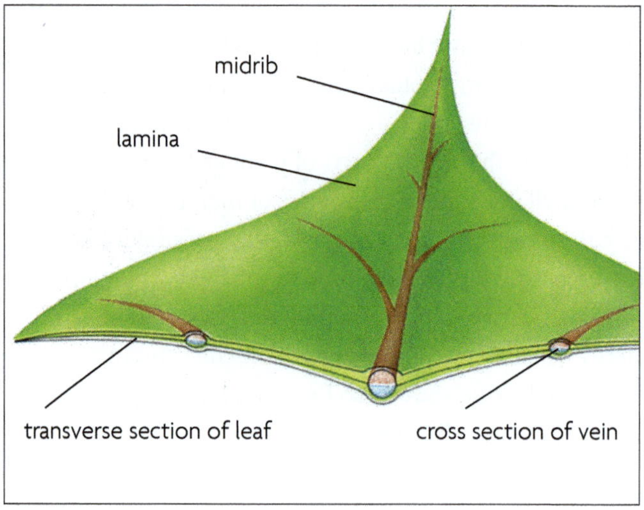

Figure 4.2 The structure of a leaf

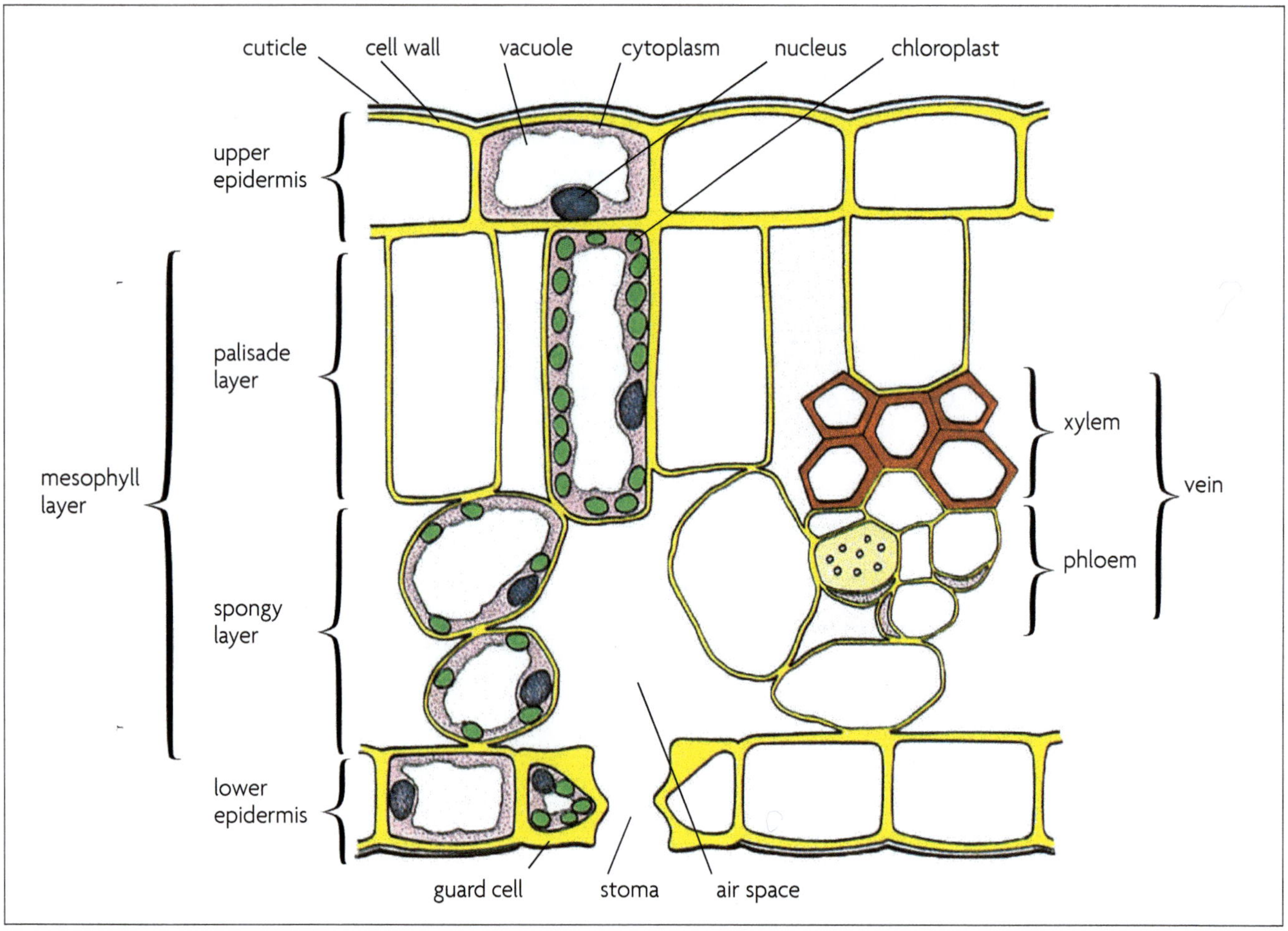

Figure 4.3 Transverse section through a small part of a leaf.

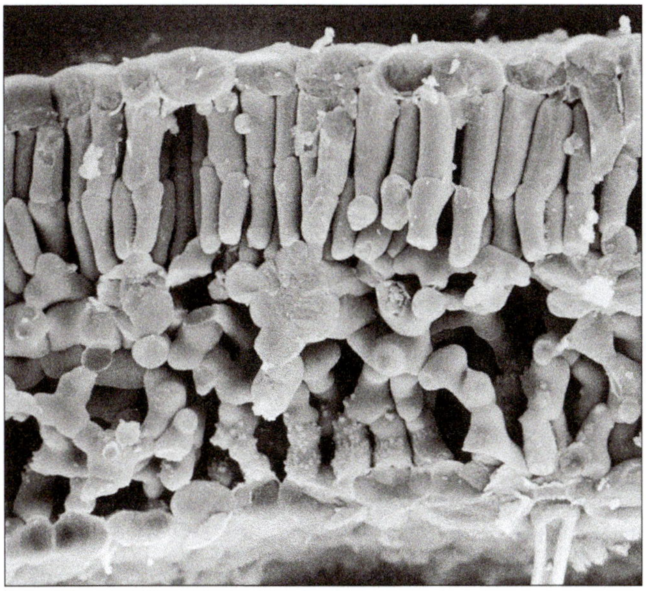

Figure 4.4 A photograph taken with a scanning electron microscope, showing the cells inside a leaf. Notice the many air spaces between the cells.

The top and bottom of the leaf are covered with a layer of closely fitting cells called the **epidermis** (Figure **4.5**). These cells do not contain chloroplasts. Their function is to protect the inner layers of cells in the leaf. The cells of the upper epidermis often secrete a waxy substance, that lies on top of them. It is called the **cuticle**, and it helps to stop water evaporating from the leaf. There is sometimes a cuticle on the underside of the leaf as well.

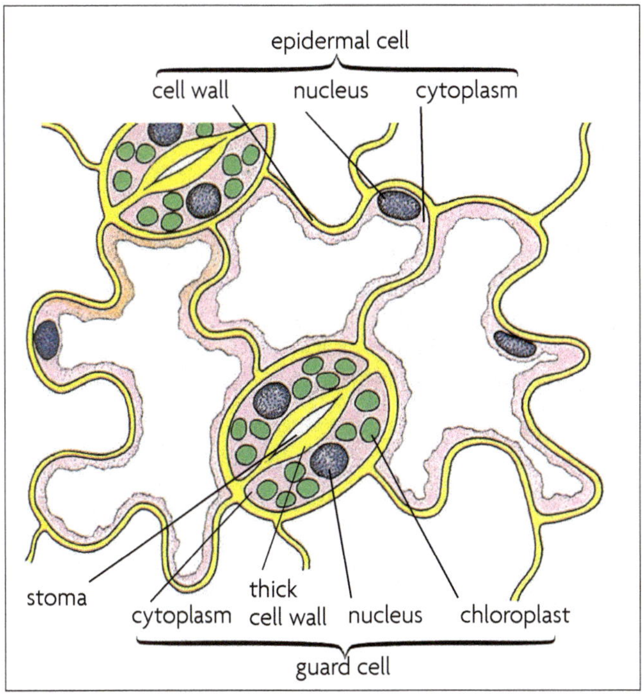

Figure 4.5 Surface view of the lower epidermis of a leaf.

In the lower epidermis, there are small openings called **stomata** (singular: stoma). Each stoma is surrounded by a pair of sausage-shaped **guard cells** (Figures **4.5** and **4.6**) which can open or close the hole (Figure **8.13**, page **155**). Guard cells, unlike other cells in the epidermis, do contain chloroplasts.

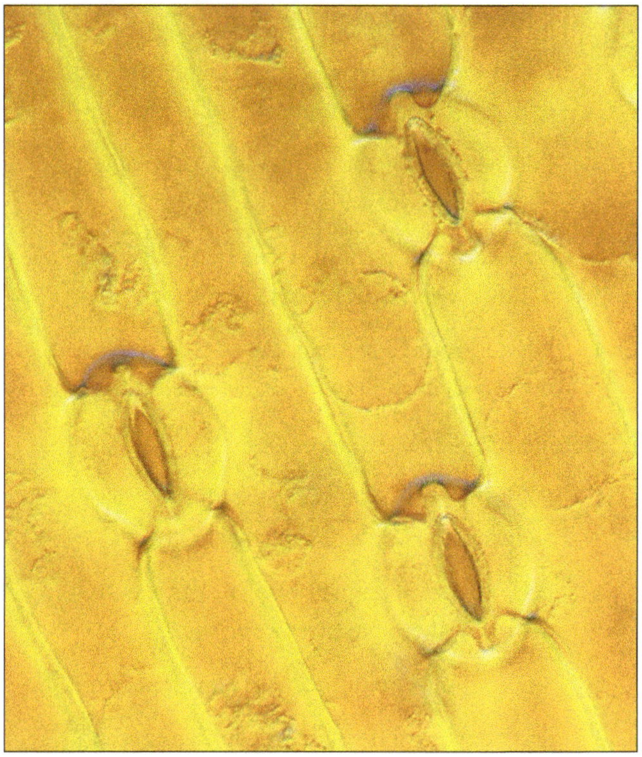

Figure 4.6 The lower surface of a leaf, showing the closely fitting cells of the epidermis. The oval openings are stomata, and the two curved cells around each stoma are guard cells.

The middle layers of the leaf are called the **mesophyll** ('meso' means middle, and 'phyll' means leaf). These cells all contain chloroplasts. The cells nearer to the top of the leaf are arranged like a fence or palisade, and they form the **palisade layer**. The cells beneath them are rounder, and arranged quite loosely, with large **air spaces** between them. They form the **spongy layer** (Figures **4.3** and **4.4**).

Running through the mesophyll are veins. Each vein contains large, thick-walled **xylem vessels** (section **7.31**) for carrying water, and smaller, thin-walled **phloem tubes** (section **7.32**) for carrying away sucrose and other substances that the leaf has made.

Investigation 4.1
Looking at the epidermis of a leaf

SBA skills
Observation/Recording/Reporting *Drawing*

Using a piece of epidermis

1. Using forceps, carefully peel a small piece of epidermis from the underside of a leaf.
2. Put the piece of epidermis into a drop of water on a microscope slide.
3. Spread it out carefully, trying not to let any part of it fold over. Cover it with a coverslip.
4. Look at your slide under the microscope, and make a labelled drawing of a few cells.

Making a nail varnish impression

1. Paint the underside of a leaf with transparent nail varnish. Leave to dry thoroughly.
2. Peel off part of the nail varnish, and mount it in a drop of water on a microscope slide.
3. Spread it out carefully, and cover with a coverslip.
4. Look at your slide under the microscope, and make a labelled drawing of the impressions made by a few cells.
5. Repeat with the upper surface of a leaf.

Questions

1. On which surface of the leaf did you find most stomata?
2. Which of these two techniques for examining the epidermis of a leaf do you consider **(a)** is easier and **(b)** gives you better results?
3. There are two kinds of cell in the lower epidermis of a leaf. What are they, and what are their functions?

FACT! The largest leaves of any plant belong to the raffia palm, which grows on the Mascarene Islands in the Indian Ocean, and also to the Amazonian bamboo palm. They both have leaves up to 19.8 m long.

Questions

4.9 What is another name for a leaf stalk?

4.10 Which kind of cells make the cuticle on a leaf?

4.11 What is the function of the cuticle?

4.12 What are stomata?

4.13 What are guard cells?

4.14 List three kinds of cells in a leaf which contain chloroplasts, and one kind which does not.

4.8 Leaves are adapted to obtain carbon dioxide, water and sunlight.

Carbon dioxide Carbon dioxide is obtained from the air. There is not very much available, because only about 0.04% of the air is carbon dioxide. Therefore the leaf must be very efficient at absorbing it. The leaf is held out into the air by the stem and the leaf stalk, and its large surface area helps to expose it to as much air as possible.

The cells which need the carbon dioxide are the mesophyll cells, inside the leaf. The carbon dioxide can get into the leaf through the stomata. It does this by diffusion, which is described in Chapter **2**. Behind each stoma is an air space (Figure **4.3**) which connects up with other air spaces between the spongy mesophyll cells. The carbon dioxide can therefore diffuse to all the cells in the leaf. It can then diffuse through the cell wall and cell membrane of each cell, and into the chloroplasts.

Water Water is obtained from the soil. It is absorbed by the root hairs (section **7.36**), and carried up to the leaf in the xylem vessels. It then travels from the xylem vessels to the mesophyll cells by osmosis, which was described in Chapter **2**. The path it takes is shown in Figures **4.7** and **4.8**.

Sunlight The position of a leaf and its broad, flat surface help it to obtain as much sunlight as possible. If you look up through the branches of a tree, you will see that the leaves are arranged so that they do not cut off light from one another more than necessary. Plants that live in shady places often have particularly big leaves.

The cells that need the sunlight are the mesophyll cells. The thinness of the leaf allows the sunlight to penetrate right through it, and reach all the cells. To help this the epidermal cells are transparent, with no chloroplasts.

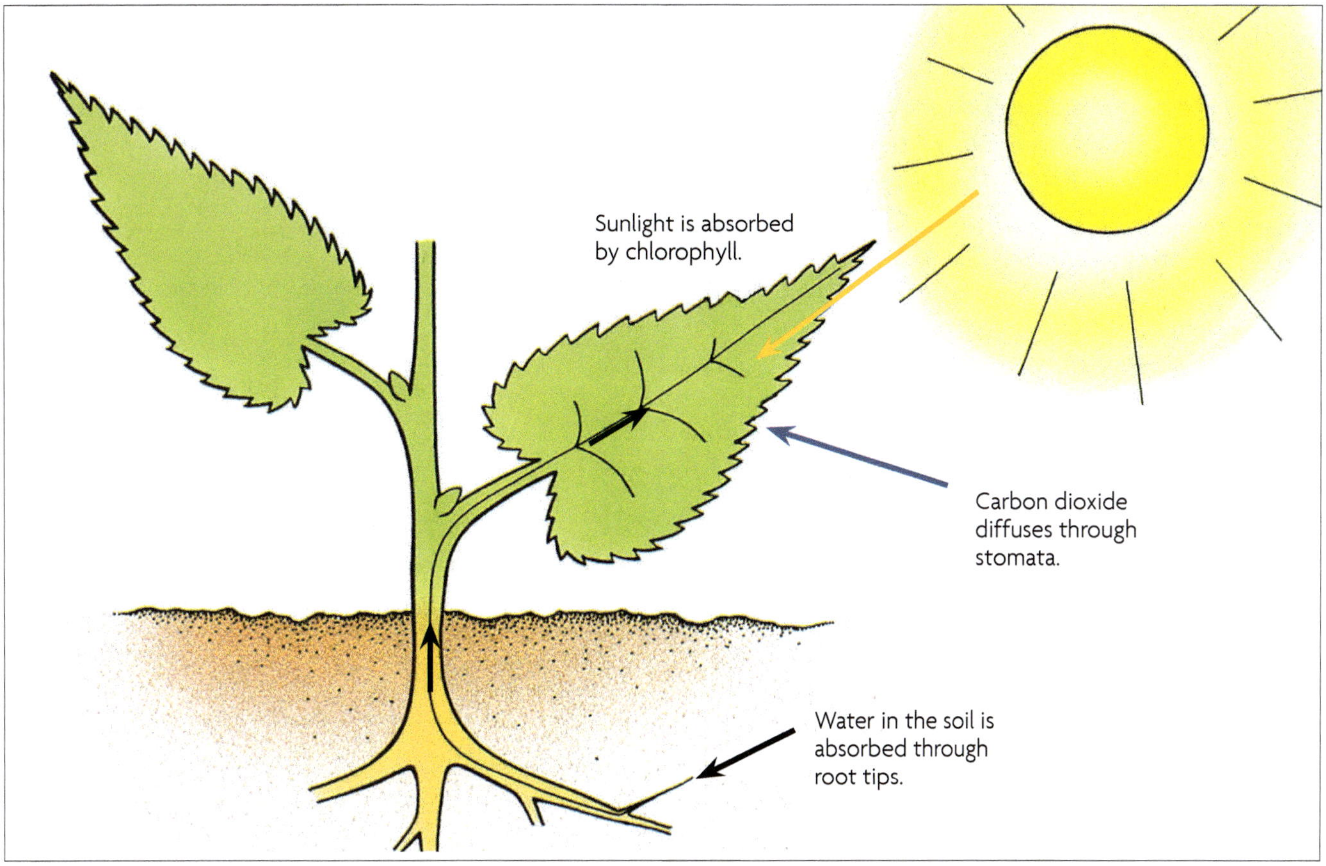

Figure 4.7 How the materials for photosynthesis get into a leaf.

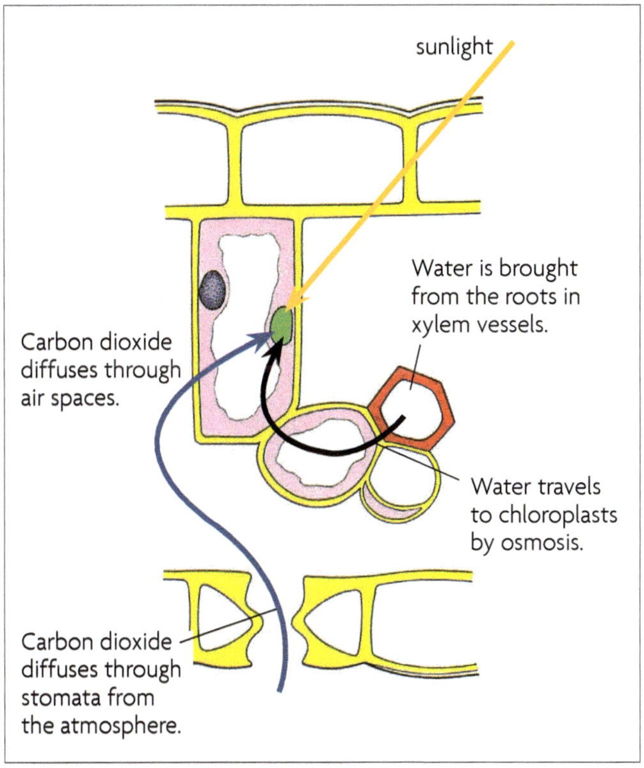

Figure 4.8 How the raw materials for photosynthesis get into a palisade cell.

In the mesophyll cells, the chloroplasts are arranged to get as much sunlight as possible, particularly those in the palisade cells. The chloroplasts can lie broadside on to do this, but in strong sunlight, they often arrange themselves end on. This reduces the amount of light absorbed. Inside them, the chlorophyll is arranged on flat membranes (see Figure **4.9**) to expose as much as possible to the sunlight.

Table **4.1** (overleaf) sums up the adaptations of leaves for photosynthesis.

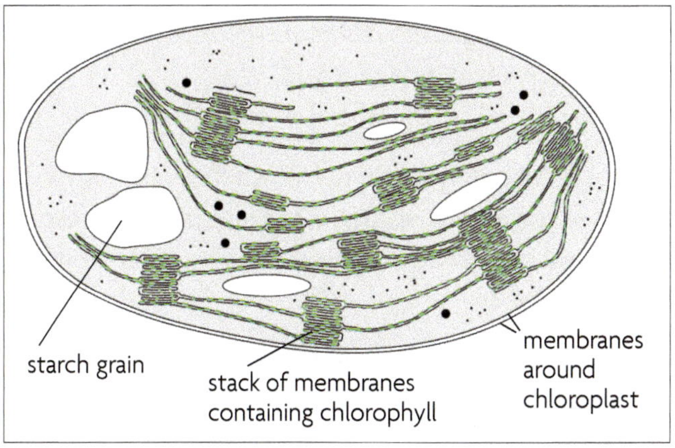

Figure 4.9 The structure of a chloroplast.

Table 4.1 Adaptations of leaves for photosynthesis

Adaptation	Function
supported by stem and petiole	to expose as much of the leaf as possible to the sunlight and air
large surface area	to expose as large an area as possible to the sunlight and air
thin	to allow sunlight to penetrate to all cells; to allow CO_2 to diffuse in and O_2 to diffuse out as quickly as possible
stomata in lower epidermis	to allow CO_2 to diffuse in and O_2 to diffuse out
air spaces in spongy mesophyll	to allow CO_2 and O_2 to diffuse to and from all cells
no chloroplasts in epidermal cells	to allow sunlight to penetrate to the mesophyll layer
chloroplasts containing chlorophyll present in the mesophyll layer	to absorb energy from sunlight, so that CO_2 will combine with H_2O
palisade cells arranged end on	to keep as few cell walls as possible between sunlight and the chloroplasts
chloroplasts inside palisade cells often arranged broadside on	to expose as much chlorophyll as possible to sunlight
chlorophyll arranged on flat membranes inside the chloroplasts	to expose as much chlorophyll as possible to sunlight
xylem vessels within short distance of every mesophyll cell	to supply water to the cells in the leaf, some of which will be used in photosynthesis
phloem tubes within short distance of every mesophyll cell	to take away sucrose and other organic products of photosynthesis

Questions

4.15 What are the raw materials needed for photosynthesis?

4.16 What percentage of the air is carbon dioxide?

4.17 How does carbon dioxide get into a leaf?

4.18 How does a leaf obtain its water?

4.19 Give two reasons why the large surface area of leaves is advantageous to the plant.

4.20 Leaves are thin. What purpose does this serve?

Uses of glucose

4.9 Glucose is used in different ways.

One of the first carbohydrates to be made in photosynthesis is glucose. There are several things that may then happen to it (Figure **4.10**).

Used for energy Energy may be released from glucose in the leaf. All cells need energy, which they obtain by the process of respiration (section **6.1**). Some of the glucose which a leaf makes will be broken down by respiration, to release energy.

Stored as starch Glucose may be turned into starch and stored in the leaf. Glucose is a simple sugar (section **3.3**). It is soluble in water, and quite a reactive substance. It is not, therefore, a very good storage molecule. First, being

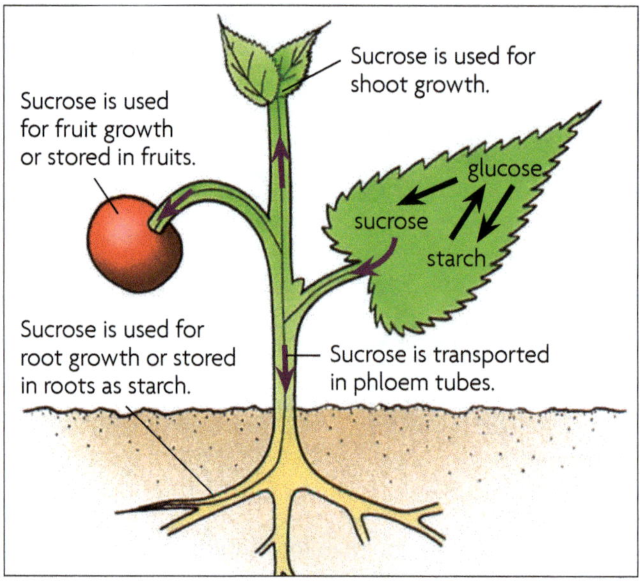

Figure 4.10 The products of photosynthesis.

reactive, it might get involved in chemical reactions where it was not wanted. Secondly, it would dissolve in the water in and around the plant cells, and might be lost from the cell. Thirdly, when dissolved, it would increase the concentration of the solution in the cell, which could damage the cell.

The glucose is therefore converted into starch to be stored. Starch is a polysaccharide, made of many glucose molecules joined together. Being such a large molecule, it is not very reactive, and not very soluble. It can be made into granules which can be easily stored inside the chloroplasts.

Used to make proteins and other organic substances Glucose may be used to make other organic substances. The plant can use glucose as a starting point for making all the other organic substances it needs. These include sucrose and cellulose. Plants also make lipids, especially oils.

With the addition of minerals containing nitrogen and sulfur, amino acids can be made. These are then joined together to make proteins. The plant also makes other substances such as chlorophyll and vitamins.

The mineral substances required are all obtained from the soil. They are absorbed through the root hairs. Some of the most important ones are listed in Table **4.2**. Water culture investigations (Figure **4.11**) can show which minerals a plant needs, and what happens to the plant if it does not have them (Figure **4.12** overleaf).

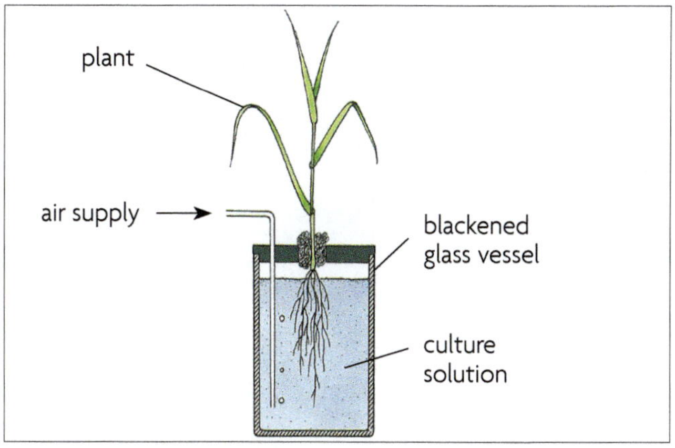

Figure 4.11 Apparatus for water culture experiments. Several plants can be grown like this, in identical conditions. Some (the controls) are given a culture solution containing all the minerals needed by plants. Others have a solution with one mineral missing. By comparing each plant with the control plants, the effect of a lack of each mineral can be seen.

Changed to sucrose for transport A molecule has to be small and soluble to be transported easily. Glucose has both of these properties, but it is also rather reactive. It is therefore converted to the complex sugar sucrose to be transported to other parts of the plant. Sucrose molecules are also quite small and soluble, but less reactive than glucose. They dissolve in the sap in the phloem vessels, and can be distributed to whichever parts of the plant need them (Figure **4.10**).

The sucrose may later be turned back into glucose again, to be broken down to release energy, or turned into starch and stored, or used to make other substances which are needed for growth.

Table 4.2 Mineral salts required by plants

Element	Mineral salt	Why it is needed	Deficiency effect
nitrogen	nitrates or ammonium salts	to make proteins	poor growth, yellowing
sulfur	sulfates	to make proteins	poor growth, yellowing leaves
phosphorus	phosphates	to make ATP and DNA	poor growth, especially of roots
magnesium	magnesium salts	to make chlorophyll	yellowing between veins of leaves
calcium	calcium salts	to make cell walls	death of growing tips
potassium	potassium salts	to keep correct salt balance in cells	yellowing in young leaves

Note: All of these mineral salts are obtained from the soil, through the root hairs.

Figure 4.12 These stunted, yellow maize seedlings are suffering from nitrogen deficiency.

Questions

4.21 Why is glucose not very good for storage in a leaf?

4.22 What substances does a plant need to be able to convert glucose into proteins?

4.23 Why do plants need magnesium?

4.24 How do parts of the plant such as the roots, which cannot photosynthesise, obtain food?

Investigation 4.2
Which kind of fertilizer helps plants grow best?

SBA skills

Observation/Recording/Reporting *Drawing*
Analysis/Interpretation

1 Collect five containers with drainage holes in the base. Almost fill each one with dry, clean sand. Label the containers A to E.

2 Collect five seedlings. It is important that they look healthy, and have an intact root system.

3 Carefully plant each seedling in a pot of sand.

4 Decide how much water you will need to thoroughly wet the sand in the pot. (You could try this out on a spare pot.) Measure this quantity of distilled water, and pour this slowly into pot A.

5 Measure out the same quantity of each of the four fertilizer solutions your teacher will provide. Pour each of them into a different pot. Make a careful record of which solution you used with each pot.

6 Make drawings of your five seedlings as they appear now.

7 Each day, water your plants with the correct liquid – either distilled water or the appropriate fertilizer solution. Write notes on the appearance of each seedling every few days. Keep your experiment running until you can see clear differences between the seedlings. The length of time this will take will depend on the types of seedlings you have used, and the conditions where they are growing, especially the temperature and the light.

8 Make drawings of each seedling at the end of your experiment.

9 Describe the differences between the seedlings. Use your results to determine which kind of fertilizer produced the healthiest-looking seedling.

Questions

1 Explain why it was important to have one seedling that was not given any fertilizer.

2 Suggest why clean sand was used in the pots, rather than soil.

3 Why was it important to give each seedling the same volume of liquid?

4 Look carefully at the list of ingredients of each of the fertilizers you used. Can you suggest why the seedlings grew differently in the different fertilizers?

Photosynthesis investigations

4.10 Investigations need controls.

If you do Investigations **4.4**, **4.5** and **4.6**, you can find out for yourself which substances a plant needs for photosynthesis. In each investigation, the plant is given everything it needs, except for one substance. Another plant is used at the same time. This is a **control**. The control is given everything it needs, including the substance being tested for. (Sometimes the control is a leaf, or even a part of a leaf, from the experimental plant. The important thing is that the control has all the substances it needs, while the experimental plant – or leaf – is lacking one substance.)

Both plants (or leaves) are then treated in exactly the same way. Any differences between them at the end of the investigation, therefore, must be because of the substance being tested.

At the end of the investigation, test a leaf from your experimental plant and your control to see if they have made starch. By comparing them, you can find out which substances are necessary for photosynthesis.

4.11 Plants for photosynthesis investigations must be destarched.

It is very important that the leaves you are testing should not have any starch in them at the beginning of the investigation. If they did, and you found that the leaves contained starch at the end of the investigation, you could not be sure that they had been photosynthesising. The starch might have been made before the investigation began.

So, before doing any of these investigations, you must destarch the plants. The easiest way to do this is to leave them in a dark cupboard for at least 24 hours. The plants cannot photosynthesise while they are in the cupboard because there is no light. So they use up their stores of starch. To be certain that they are thoroughly destarched, test a leaf for starch before you begin your investigation.

4.12 Iodine solution can stain starch in leaves.

Iodine solution is used to test for starch. A blue-black colour shows that starch is present. However, if you put iodine solution onto a leaf which contains starch, it will not immediately turn black. This is because the starch is inside the chloroplasts in the cells (Figure **4.9**, page **59**). The iodine solution cannot get through the cell membranes to reach the starch and react with it.

Investigation 4.3
Testing a leaf for starch

SBA skills
Observation/Recording/Reporting

1 Take a leaf from a healthy plant, and drop it into boiling water in a water bath. Leave for about 30 s.

2 Remove the leaf, which will be very soft, and drop it into a tube of alcohol in the water bath. Leave it until all the chlorophyll has come out of the leaf.

3 The leaf will now be brittle. Remove it from the alcohol, and dip it into boiling water again to soften it.

4 Spread out the leaf on a white tile, and cover it with iodine solution. A black colour shows that the leaf contains starch.

Questions

1 Why was the leaf put into boiling water?

2 Why did the alcohol become green?

3 Why was the leaf put into alcohol after being put into boiling water?

Another difficulty is that the green colour of the leaf and the brown iodine solution can look black together.

Therefore before testing a leaf for starch, you must break down the cell membranes, and get rid of the green colour (chlorophyll). The way this is done is described in Investigation **4.3**. The cell membranes are first broken down by boiling water, and then the chlorophyll is removed by dissolving it out with alcohol.

Investigation 4.4
To see if light is needed for photosynthesis

SBA skills

Observation/Recording/Reporting
Drawing
Manipulation/Measurement
Analysis/Interpretation

1 Take a healthy bean plant, growing in a pot. Leave it in a cupboard for a few days, to destarch it.

2 Test one of its leaves for starch, to check that it does not contain any.

3 Using a folded piece of black paper or aluminium foil, a little larger than a leaf, cut out a shape (see diagram). Fasten the paper or foil firmly over both sides of a leaf on your plant, making sure that the edges are held firmly together. Don't take the leaf off the plant!

4 Leave the plant near a warm, sunny window for a few days.

5 Remove the cover from your leaf, and test it for starch.

6 Make a labelled drawing of the appearance of your leaf after testing for starch.

Questions

1 Why was the plant destarched before the beginning of the experiment?

2 Why was part of the leaf left uncovered?

3 What do your results tell you about light and photosynthesis?

Investigation 4.5
To see if chlorophyll is needed for photosynthesis

SBA skills

Observation/Recording/Reporting
Manipulation/Measurement
Analysis/Interpretation

1 Destarch a plant with variegated (green and white) leaves.

2 Leave your plant in a warm, sunny spot for a few days.

3 Test one of the leaves for starch.

4 Make a drawing of your leaf before and after testing.

Questions

1 What was the control in this investigation?

2 What do your results tell you about chlorophyll and photosynthesis?

Investigation 4.6
To see if carbon dioxide is needed for photosynthesis

SBA skills

Observation/Recording/Reporting
Manipulation/Measurement
Analysis/Interpretation

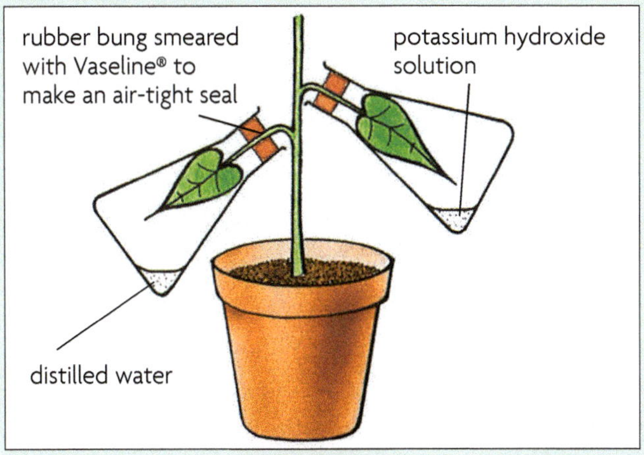

1 Destarch a plant.

2 Set up your apparatus as shown in the diagram. Take special care that no air can get into the flasks. Leave the plant in a warm sunny window for a few days.

3 Test each treated leaf for starch.

Questions

1 Why was potassium hydroxide put in with one leaf, and water with the other?

2 Which was the control?

3 Why was Vaseline® put around the tops of the flasks?

4 What do your results suggest about carbon dioxide and photosynthesis?

Investigation 4.7
To show that oxygen is produced in photosynthesis

SBA skills

Observation/Recording/Reporting
Manipulation/Measurement
Analysis/Interpretation

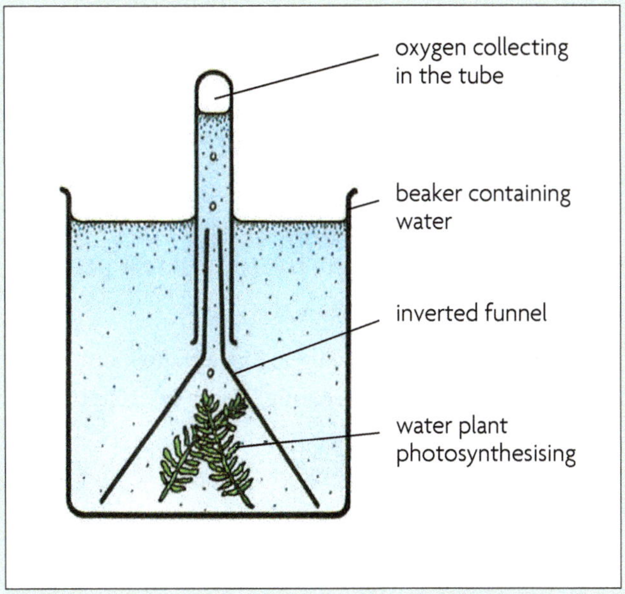

1 Set up the apparatus shown in the diagram. Make sure that the test tube is completely full of water.

2 Leave the apparatus near a warm, sunny window for a few days.

3 Carefully remove the test tube from the top of the funnel, allowing the water to run out, but not allowing the gas to escape.

4 Light a wooden splint, and then blow it out so that it is just glowing. Carefully put it into the gas in the test tube. If it bursts into flame, then the gas is oxygen.

Questions

1 Why was this investigation done under water?

2 This investigation has no control. Try to design one.

Investigation 4.8
Investigating the effect of light intensity on photosynthesis

SBA skills

Observation/Recording/Reporting *Planning/Design*
Manipulation/Measurement
Analysis/Interpretation

If you did Investigation **4.7**, you may have noticed that the plant seemed to produce more bubbles in bright sunlight than when it was in the shade. This could mean that the rate of photosynthesis is affected by light intensity.

1 Write down a hypothesis that you will investigate. The hypothesis should be one sentence, and it should describe the relationship that you think exists between light intensity and the rate of photosynthesis.

You can vary light intensity by moving a light source closer to the plant. The shorter the distance between the light and the plant, the greater the light intensity.

You can use a water plant in your investigation.

2 Once you have an idea about how you will do your experiment, write it down as a list of points. Then think through it again, and make improvements to your plan. Once you are fairly happy with it, show your teacher. You must not try to do your experiment until your teacher says that you may begin.

- What apparatus and other materials will you need for your experiment?
- What will you vary in your experiment? How will you vary it?
- What will you keep the same in all the tubes or beakers in your experiment? How will you do this?
- What will you measure in your experiment? How will you measure it? When will you measure it? Will you do repeat measurements and calculate a mean?
- How will you record your results? (You can sketch out a results chart, ready to fill in.)
- How will you display your results? (You can sketch the axes of the graph you plan to draw.)
- What will your results be if your hypothesis is correct? (You can sketch the shape of the graph you think you will get.)

Once you have approval from your teacher, you should do your experiment. Most scientific researchers find that they want to make changes to their experiment once they actually begin doing it. This is a good thing to do. Make careful notes about all the changes that you make.

Finally, write up your experiment in the usual way, including:

- a heading, and the hypothesis that you tested
- a diagram of the apparatus that you used, and a full description of your method
- a neat and carefully headed table of results, including means if you decided to do repeats
- a neat and carefully headed line graph of your results
- a conclusion, in which you say whether or not your results support your hypothesis
- a discussion, in which you use what you know about photosynthesis to try to explain the pattern in your results
- an evaluation, in which you explain the main limitations that you feel might have affected the reliability of your data.

4.13 Many factors affect photosynthesis.

If a plant is given plenty of sunlight, carbon dioxide and water, the limit on the rate at which it can photosynthesise is its own ability to absorb these materials, and make them react. However, quite often plants do not have unlimited supplies of these materials, and so their rate of photosynthesis is not as high as it might be.

Sunlight In the dark, a plant cannot photosynthesise at all. In dim light, it can photosynthesise slowly. As light intensity increases, the rate of photosynthesis will increase, until the plant is photosynthesising as fast as it can. At this point, even if the light becomes brighter, the plant cannot photosynthesise any faster (Figure **4.13**).

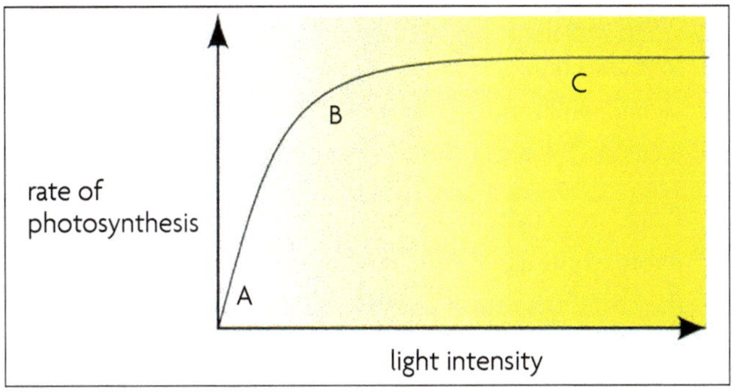

Figure 4.13 The effect of light intensity on the rate of photosynthesis.

Over the first part of the curve in Figure **4.13**, between A and B, light is a **limiting factor**. The plant is limited in how fast it can photosynthesise because it does not have enough light. You can see this because when the plant is given more light it photosynthesises faster.

Between B and C, however, light is not a limiting factor. You can show this because, even if more light is shone on the plant, it still cannot photosynthesise any faster. It already has as much light as it can use.

Carbon dioxide Carbon dioxide can also be a limiting factor (Figure **4.14**). The more carbon dioxide a plant is given, the faster it can photosynthesise up to a point, but then a maximum is reached.

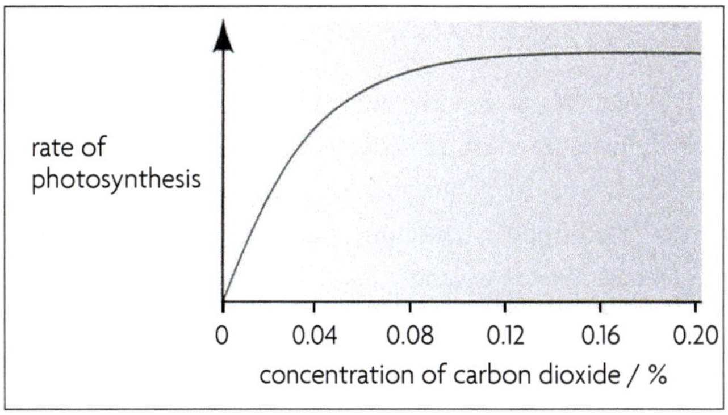

Figure 4.14 The effect of carbon dioxide concentration on the rate of photosynthesis.

Temperature The chemical reactions of photosynthesis can only take place very slowly at low temperatures (section **11.8**), so a plant can photosynthesise faster on a warm day than a cold one.

Stomata The carbon dioxide which a plant uses diffuses into the leaf through the stomata. If the stomata are closed, then photosynthesis cannot take place. Stomata often close if the weather is very hot and sunny, to prevent too much water being lost (Figure **8.13**). This means that on a really hot day photosynthesis may slow down.

4.14 The process of photosynthesis is vital to all living things.

Photosynthesis is of importance, not only to green plants, but to all living organisms. It is the basic energy reaction which brings the energy of the Sun into ecosystems (sections **1.9** and **17.15**). The flow of energy in ecosystems is one-way. So there is constant need for replenishment from the energy source, and therefore constant need for photosynthesis.

Photosynthesis is also essential for maintaining a constant global level of oxygen and carbon dioxide (section **1.20**). The oxygen given off is available for respiration. Carbon dioxide produced by respiration and from the combustion of fuels is used in photosynthesis, which helps to stop the levels of carbon dioxide in the atmosphere from rising too high.

Questions

4.25 What is meant by a limiting factor?

4.26 Name two factors which may limit the rate of photosynthesis of a healthy plant.

4.27 Why do plants sometimes stop photosynthesising on a very hot, dry day?

Key ideas

- Plants are autotrophic, making their own organic materials by photosynthesis. Animals and fungi are heterotrophic, obtaining organic materials that have been made by plants.
- Photosynthesis takes place in chloroplasts in the leaves of plants. The balanced equation is:

$$6CO_2 + 6H_2O \xrightarrow[\text{chlorophyll}]{\text{sunlight}} C_6H_{12}O_6 + 6O_2$$

- In the light-dependent stage of photosynthesis, energy from light is used to split water into hydrogen and oxygen. In the light-independent stage, hydrogen and carbon dioxide are combined to form glucose.
- Photosynthesis takes place in the cells of the mesophyll layer, especially the palisade mesophyll. Leaves are thin and have a large surface area, to speed up the supply of carbon dioxide to the palisade cells and to maximise the amount of sunlight that hits the leaf and can be absorbed by chlorophyll. Stomata and air spaces allow carbon dioxide to diffuse quickly from the air to the chloroplasts. Xylem vessels bring water, and phloem tubes take away the products of photosynthesis.
- Some of the glucose that is made is used in respiration, to provide energy to the plant cells. Some is stored as starch. Some is used to make cellulose for cell walls. Some is transported around the plant in the form of sucrose, in the phloem tubes. Some is combined with nitrate or ammonium ions to make proteins. Some is used to make other substances such as lipids.
- When testing a leaf for starch, it must first be boiled to break down cell membranes and allow iodine solution to make contact with any starch inside the cells. Hot alcohol will remove chlorophyll from the leaf, making it easier to see any colour changes.
- Plants need light and carbon dioxide for photosynthesis. If either of these are in short supply, they limit the rate of photosynthesis and are said to be limiting factors. The rate of photosynthesis is also affected by temperature.

End-of-chapter questions

1 Copy and complete this table.

	Obtained from	Used for
Nitrates		
Water		
Magnesium		
Carbon dioxide		

2 Explain how each of the following helps a leaf to photosynthesise.

a There is an air space behind each stoma.
b The epidermal cells of a leaf do not have chloroplasts.
c Leaves have a large surface area.
d The veins in a leaf branch repeatedly.
e A leaf containing starch does not turn black immediately when you put iodine solution onto it.
f Chloroplasts have many membranes in them.

3 Which carbohydrate does a plant use for each of these purposes? Explain why.

a transport
b storage

4 Describe how a carbon atom in a carbon dioxide molecule in the air could become part of a starch molecule in a cassava root. Mention all the structures it would pass through, and what would happen to it at each stage.

5 Read the following passage carefully, then answer the questions, using both the information in the passage and your own knowledge.

White light is made up of all the colours of the rainbow. Sea water acts as a light filter which screens off some of the light energy, starting at the red end of the spectrum. As sunlight travels downwards through the water, first the red light is lost, then green and yellow and finally blue. In very clear water, the blue light can penetrate to a maximum of 1000 m. Below this, all is dark.

(*continues on page* **69**)

(... *continued*)

The upper layers of the sea contain a large community of microscopic floating organisms called plankton, many of which are tiny plants known as phytoplankton. These act as a gigantic solar cell, which feeds all the animals of the sea and supplies both them and the atmosphere above with oxygen.

Nearer the shore, larger plants are found. Seaweeds grow on rocky shores, brown and green ones high on the shore, and red ones lower down, where they are covered with deep water when the tide is in. The colours of the seaweeds are due to their light-absorbing pigments, not all of which are chlorophyll.

a Why are no green plants found below the upper few hundred metres of the sea?
b Some living organisms are found in the permanently dark depths of the oceans. What might they feed on?
c What are phytoplankton?
d Explain as fully as you can the last sentence of paragraph 2, 'These act as ... with oxygen.'
e Chlorophyll is a green pigment. Which colours of light does it **(i)** absorb, and **(ii)** reflect?
f What colour light would you expect the pigment of red seaweeds to absorb?
g Why are red seaweeds normally found lower down the shore than green ones?

6 An experiment was performed to find out how fast a plant photosynthesised as the concentration of CO_2 in the air around it was varied. The results were as follows.

CO_2 concentration / % by volume in air	Rate of photosynthesis in arbitrary units	
	at low light intensity	at high light intensity
0	0	0
0.02	20	33
0.04	29	53
0.06	35	68
0.08	39	79
0.10	42	86
0.12	45	89
0.14	46	90
0.16	46	90
0.18	46	90
0.20	46	90

a Plot these results on a graph, drawing one line for low and one for high light intensity, both on the same pair of axes.
b What is the CO_2 concentration of normal air?
c What is the rate of photosynthesis at this CO_2 concentration in a high light intensity?
d Market gardeners often add carbon dioxide to the air in greenhouses. What is the advantage of doing this?
e Up to what values does CO_2 concentration act as a limiting factor at high light intensities?

5 How animals feed

In this chapter, you will find out:

- what is meant by a balanced diet
- the different types of nutrients we should eat, and foods that are good sources of them
- that different people need different amounts of energy in their diet
- some problems that can be caused by eating an unbalanced diet
- why we need to digest the food that we eat
- the structure of the alimentary canal, and the functions of each of its parts
- how digested food is absorbed and assimilated
- how fungi digest and absorb their food.

Diet

5.1 Animals are heterotrophic.

Animals get their food from other organisms – from plants or other animals. They cannot make their own food as plants do. They are **heterotrophic** (section **4.2**).

The food an animal eats every day is called its **diet**. Most animals need seven types of nutrients in their diets. These are:

carbohydrates	minerals
proteins	water
fats	roughage
vitamins	

A diet which contains all of these things, in the correct amounts and proportions, is called a **balanced diet**.

5.2 A balanced diet provides the right amount of energy.

Every day, a person uses up energy. The amount you use partly depends on how old you are, which sex you are and what job you do. A few examples are shown in Figure **5.1**.

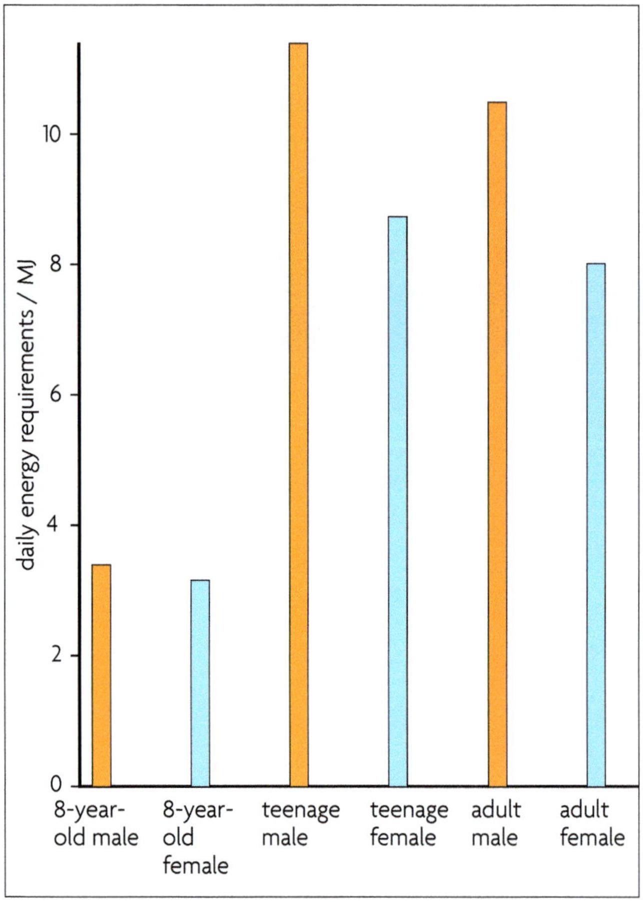

Figure 5.1 Daily energy requirements.

The energy you use each day comes from the food you eat. If you eat too much food, some of the extra will probably be stored as fat. If you eat too little, you may not be able to obtain as much energy as you need. This will make you feel tired.

All food contains some energy. Scientists have worked out how much energy there is in a particular kind of food. You can look up this information. A few examples are given in Table **5.1**. You may remember that one gram of fat contains about twice as much energy as one gram of protein or carbohydrate. This is why fried foods should be avoided if you are worried about putting on weight.

Pregnant women need a little more energy each day than other women of the same age, to supply the growing fetus.

People who weigh 20% more than the average for their age and height are said to be **obese**. Obesity is caused by eating more food than you require for normal activity and may be a result of lack of exercise or eating too much.

Obese people are more likely to suffer from heart disease and diabetes. They are unlikely to live as long as people of average body mass.

5.3 Diets should contain a variety of food.

As well as providing you with energy, food is needed for many other reasons. To make sure that you eat a balanced diet you must eat food containing carbohydrate, lipid and protein. You also need each kind of vitamin and mineral, roughage and water. If you miss out on any of these things, your body will not be able to work properly.

Table **5.2** (overleaf) and Table **5.3** (page 73) give some of the most important vitamins and minerals you need.

Many people eat too many carbohydrates. This is partly because they are cheap, and partly because they are 'satisfying' foods; that is, they make you feel full. The staple foods of many countries are carbohydrate foods. Rice, the staple food of China, is largely a carbohydrate food. So are white (Irish) potatoes, the staple food for much of Europe.

There is no single staple food in the Caribbean. The carbohydrate foods used are mainly underground storage stems and roots, such as yams, eddoes, dasheens and sweet potatoes. In addition, much rice is eaten.

Roughage, or fibre, is food that cannot be digested. It goes right through the digestive system from one end to the other, and is egested in the faeces (section **5.23**).

Table 5.1 Energy content of some different kinds of food

Food	kJ / 100 g	Food	kJ / 100 g
Breakfast foods		**Main meals**	
cornflakes	1567	stewed steak	932
oatmeal	1698	roast chicken	599
boiled egg	612	ham	1119
brown bread	948	fish (sea water)	340
white bread	991	fish (dried, salt)	1016
milk	272	sardines	906
sugar	1682	fried liver	1016
marmalade	1035	cheddar cheese	1682
unsweetened fruit juice	143	cottage cheese	402
Desserts		baked beans	270
pawpaw	160	cabbage	66
bananas	326	carrots	98
melon	96	lettuce	36
oranges	150	peas	161
canned peaches	373	boiled white (Irish) potatoes	339
ice cream	698	french fries	1065
custard	496	tomatoes	60
Snacks		rice	1536
chocolate	2214	spaghetti	1612
fruit yogurt	405		
plain biscuits	1925		
chocolate biscuits	2197		
roast peanuts	2364		

Table 5.2 Vitamins

Vitamin	Foods that contain it	Why it is needed	Deficiency disease
A	butter, egg yolk, cod liver oil, carrots	to keep the cells lining the gas exchange system healthy; to make a pigment in the rod cells of the retina of the eye, needed for seeing in dim light	infections of cells lining the gas exchange system; night blindness
B (There are many different B vitamins, but they usually occur together)	wholemeal bread, yeast extract, liver, brown rice	involved in many chemical reactions in the body, such as respiration	beri-beri, which is common in S.E. Asia where polished (not brown) rice is the staple food; this disease causes muscular weakness and paralysis
C	citrus fruits (such as oranges, limes), Barbados (West Indian) cherries, raw vegetables	to make the stretchy protein collagen, found in skin and other tissues; keeps tissues in good repair	scurvy, which causes pain in joints and muscles, and bleeding from gums and other places; this used to be a common disease of sailors, who had no fresh vegetables for long voyages
D	butter, egg yolk (and can be made by the skin when sunlight falls on it)	helps calcium to be absorbed, for making bones and teeth	rickets, in which the bones become soft and deformed; this disease was common in young children in industrial areas, who rarely got out into the sunshine

Roughage helps to keep the alimentary canal working properly. Food moves through the alimentary canal (section **5.13**) because the muscles contract and relax to squeeze it along. This is called **peristalsis** (Figure **5.9**, page **79**). The muscles are stimulated to do this when there is food in the alimentary canal. Soft foods do not stimulate the muscles very much. The muscles work more when there is harder, less digestible food, like roughage, in the alimentary canal. Roughage keeps the digestive system in good working order, and helps to prevent constipation.

All plant foods, such as fruit and vegetables, contain roughage. This is because the plant cells have cellulose cell walls. Humans cannot digest cellulose.

One common form of roughage is the outer husk of cereal grains, such as oats, wheat and barley. This is called bran. Some of this husk is also found in wholemeal bread. Brown or unpolished rice is also a good source of roughage.

5.4 Incorrect diets may lead to disease.

There is some evidence that people who do not eat a balanced diet are more likely to suffer from colds and other infections. There are also diseases caused by deficiencies in diet. Some of these are described in Tables **5.2** and **5.3**.

One example of a deficiency disease is **anaemia**. People suffering from anaemia feel tired and often complain of 'loss of energy'. This is because their blood has fewer red blood cells and less haemoglobin than is required to supply their cells with oxygen (section **7.16**).

One cause of anaemia is a deficiency of iron in the diet. A person with anaemia may be advised to eat more iron-rich foods. Liver, leafy green vegetables and dried pulses (peas and beans) are good sources of iron. Anaemia may also be caused by a deficiency of the vitamin B_{12}. Meat, liver and yeast are good sources of this vitamin.

Energy protein malnutrition (EPM) is caused by a diet that does not contain enough energy, or enough protein. EPM is most often seen in children after breastfeeding has stopped. These young children show reduced growth and feel tired. Their diets do not supply enough energy for normal life functions. Thus, their bodies have to use proteins as energy sources. This means that they do not have enough protein for growth.

Table 5.3 Minerals

Mineral element	Foods that contain it	Why it is needed	Deficiency disease
calcium, Ca	milk and other dairy products, bread	for bones and teeth; for blood clotting	brittle bones and teeth; poor blood clotting
phosphorus, P	milk	for bones and teeth	brittle bones and teeth
fluorine, F	fluoride toothpaste; some drinking water	makes tooth enamel resistant to decay	bad teeth
iodine, I	seafood, table salt	for making the hormone thyroxine	goitre, a swelling in the neck; a reduced metabolic rate
iron, Fe	liver, red meat, egg yolk, dark green vegetables	for making haemoglobin, the red pigment in blood which carries oxygen	anaemia, in which there are not enough red blood cells so the tissues do not get enough oxygen delivered to them

All these minerals are found in food in the form of ions. For example, calcium is in the form of calcium ions, and phosphorus is found as phosphates.

5.5 Diet control may improve health.

Some diseases can be controlled by being very careful about diet. **Diabetes mellitus** is a disease in which the body is not able to control the level of glucose in the blood. You can read more about diabetes in section **16.4**. Many people with diabetes are able to remain healthy by taking great care over their diet. They need to eat small amounts of carbohydrates regularly, but to avoid eating too much carbohydrate.

Hypertension (high blood pressure) is a common problem (section **7.12**). There is some evidence that a low-salt diet can help this condition, and a person with hypertension is often advised to have a low-salt diet. Cooking salt is sodium chloride. It is the sodium which is the problem. Potassium chloride can sometimes be used as a substitute.

Obese people may be advised to control the energy content of their diet. The energy content of some foods is given in Table **5.1** (page **71**).

5.6 Some people are vegetarians.

Vegetarians eat mainly foods derived from plants. Their diet is made up of vegetables, fruits, nuts, pulses and grains. Their reasons for having this type of diet may be ethical, religious or nutritional. The ethical and religious reasons may be based upon a belief that there should be no direct destruction of animal life to feed people. Many people, however, simply do not like the idea of eating meat, perhaps because they are aware that it comes from dead animals. Vegetarians do eat milk, cheese and eggs. Vegans do not eat any food that comes from animals, including honey.

It is possible to be perfectly healthy on a vegetarian diet, but care is needed to make sure that the diet contains suitable amounts of each kind of nutrient. Plant-based foods are generally rich in carbohydrates, lipids (usually in the form of oils), vitamins, minerals and roughage (fibre). However, they do not contain vitamin B_{12}, so vegetarians should either take vitamin B_{12} tablets regularly, or eat foods that have been fortified with extra vitamin B_{12}. A vegetarian diet also needs to include plenty of protein-containing foods, such as pulses.

A vegetarian diet can be a very healthy one. It is likely to contain very few saturated fats, which can contribute to the development of heart disease. It can also reduce the risk of developing high blood pressure, gall stones, kidney stones and obesity.

Special care, however, should be taken if parents are giving a growing child a vegetarian diet. It is very important to ensure that the child has a wide range of foods in the diet, with plenty of protein, minerals and vitamins.

Questions

5.1 Which vitamin prevents rickets?

5.2 Plant foods contain a lot of roughage. Explain why.

5.3 Describe how food is moved along the alimentary canal.

5.4 Why do you need iron in your diet?

5.5 Why do some people not eat meat?

5.6 What is meant by a balanced diet?

Investigation 5.1
To find out which of three sets of food would provide the most balanced meal

SBA skills

Observation/Recording/Reporting

Analysis/Interpretation *Planning/Design*

You are provided with three groups of foods for a meal. Design and carry out an investigation to help you to decide which group would provide the most balanced meal.

Group 1: carrot; Irish potato; saltfish.

Group 2: gungo (pigeon) peas; rice with coconut milk.

Group 3: cornmeal; green plantain; pumpkin.

You will need to:

1. State the principles underlying your investigation.
2. Sequence the steps in the procedure you want to carry out.
3. Select the apparatus, reagents and any other materials you need.
4. Make a table showing the data you will collect.
5. Show how the data is used to solve the problem.
6. Discuss the limitations of the procedure(s) you have used.

Questions

1. What reasonable deductions about the nutrients in the meals can you make from the results you obtain?
2. What other nutrients would you add to improve the meal you have selected, and why?

Digestion

5.7 Digestion makes nutrients easier to absorb.

The alimentary canal of a mammal is a long tube running from one end of its body to the other (Figure **5.2**). Before food can be of any use to the animal, it has to get out of the alimentary canal and into the bloodstream. This is called **absorption**. To be absorbed, molecules of food have to get through the walls of the alimentary canal. They need to be quite small to be able to do this.

The food that is eaten by mammals usually contains some large molecules (section **5.8**). Before these molecules can be absorbed, they must be broken down into small ones. This is called **digestion**.

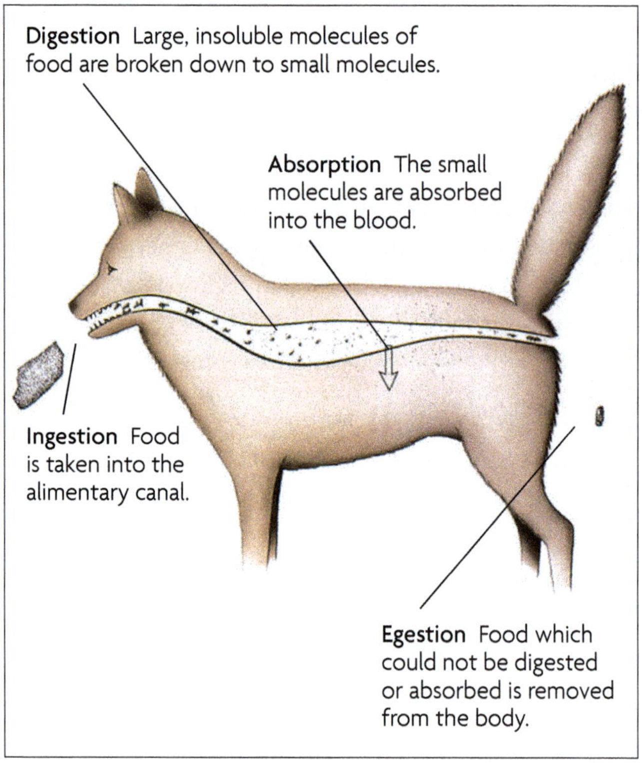

Digestion Large, insoluble molecules of food are broken down to small molecules.
Absorption The small molecules are absorbed into the blood.
Ingestion Food is taken into the alimentary canal.
Egestion Food which could not be digested or absorbed is removed from the body.

Figure 5.2 How an animal deals with food.

5.8 Not all foods need digesting.

Figure 5.3 shows what happens to the three kinds of nutrients that need to be digested – lipids, proteins and carbohydrates. Look at one column at a time, and work down it, to follow what happens to that type of food as it passes through the alimentary canal.

Large carbohydrate molecules, such as polysaccharides, have to be broken down into simple sugars (monosaccharides). Proteins are broken down to amino acids. Fats are broken down to fatty acids and glycerol.

Simple sugars, water, vitamins and minerals are small molecules, and they can be absorbed just as they are. They do not need to be digested.

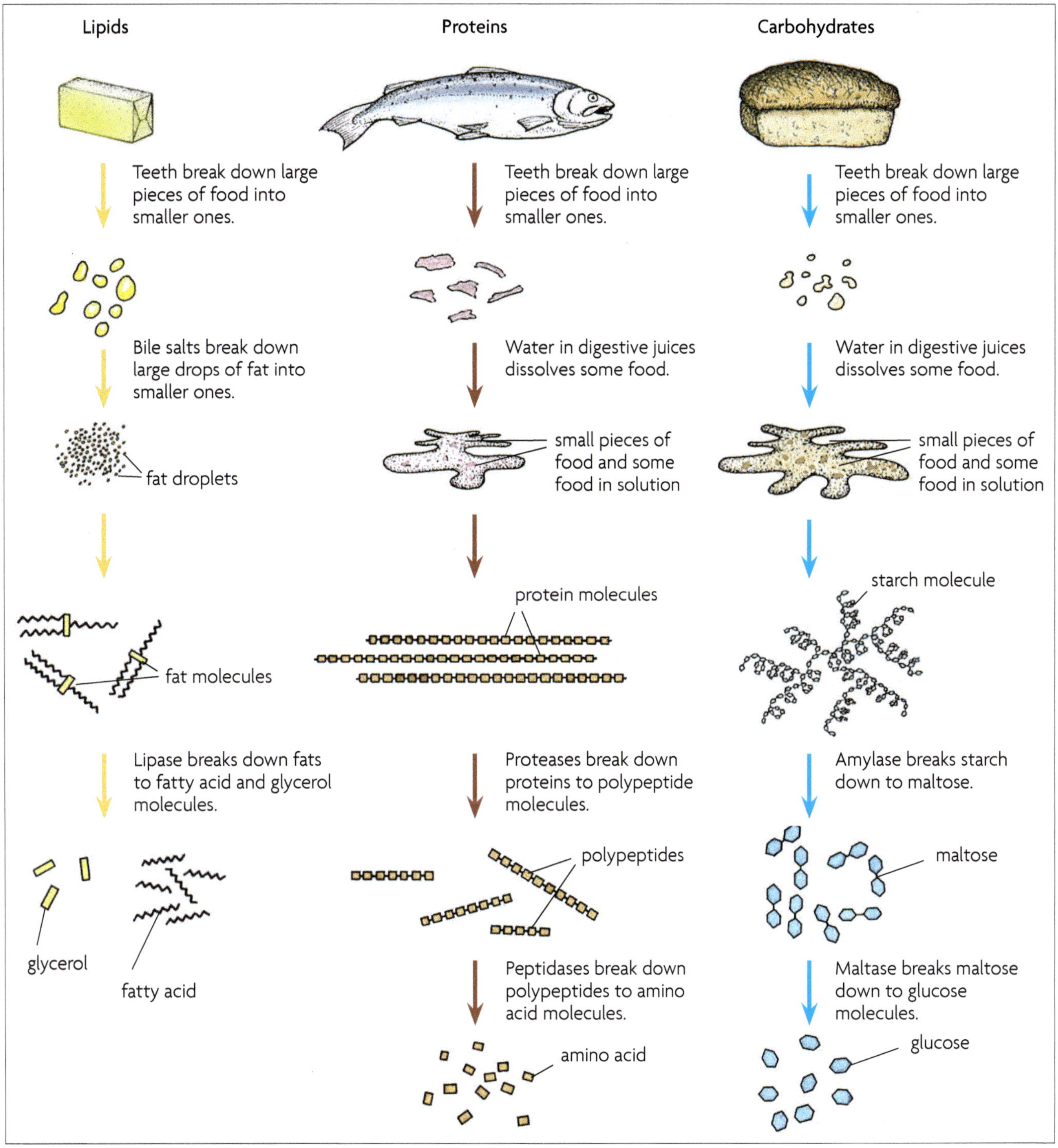
Lipids
Proteins
Carbohydrates
Teeth break down large pieces of food into smaller ones.
Teeth break down large pieces of food into smaller ones.
Teeth break down large pieces of food into smaller ones.
Bile salts break down large drops of fat into smaller ones.
Water in digestive juices dissolves some food.
Water in digestive juices dissolves some food.
fat droplets
small pieces of food and some food in solution
small pieces of food and some food in solution
protein molecules
starch molecule
fat molecules
Lipase breaks down fats to fatty acid and glycerol molecules.
Proteases break down proteins to polypeptide molecules.
Amylase breaks starch down to maltose.
polypeptides
maltose
glycerol
fatty acid
Peptidases break down polypeptides to amino acid molecules.
Maltase breaks maltose down to glucose molecules.
amino acid
glucose

Figure 5.3 Digestion.

5.9 Digestion may be mechanical and chemical.

Often the food an animal eats is in quite large pieces. These need to be broken up by teeth, and by churning movements of the alimentary canal. This is called **mechanical digestion**.

Once any pieces of food have been ground up, the large molecules present are then broken down into small ones. This is called **chemical digestion**. It involves a chemical change from one sort of molecule to another. Enzymes are involved in this process (Chapter 3). Figure 5.3 summarises how mechanical and chemical digestion work together to produce small molecules the body can use.

Questions

5.7 What is digestion?

5.8 Name two groups of food that do not need to be digested.

5.9 What does digestion change each of these kinds of food into: **(a)** polysaccharides, **(b)** proteins, **(c)** fats?

5.10 What is meant by chemical digestion?

Digestion in humans – teeth

5.10 Teeth are important for the ingestion and mechanical digestion of food.

Teeth help with the ingestion and mechanical digestion of food. They can be used to bite off pieces of food. They then chop, crush or grind them into smaller pieces. This gives the food a larger surface area, which makes it easier for the enzymes to work on the food. It also helps to dissolve soluble parts of the food.

The structure of a tooth is shown in Figure 5.4. The part of the tooth which is embedded in the gum is called the **root**. The part which can be seen is the **crown**. The crown is covered with **enamel**. Enamel is the hardest substance made by animals. It is very difficult to break or chip it. However, it can be dissolved by acids. Bacteria will feed on sweet foods left on the teeth. This makes acids, which dissolve the enamel and decay sets in.

Under the enamel is a layer of **dentine**, which is rather like bone. Dentine is quite hard, but not as hard as enamel. It has channels in it which contain living cytoplasm.

In the middle of the tooth is the **pulp cavity**. It contains nerves and blood vessels. These supply the cytoplasm in the dentine with food and oxygen.

The root of the tooth is covered with **cement**. This has **fibres** growing out of it. These attach the tooth to the jawbone, but allow it to move slightly when biting or chewing.

5.11 Mammals have different types of teeth.

Most mammals have four kinds of teeth (Figures 5.5 and 5.6). **Incisors** are the sharp-edged, chisel-shaped teeth at the front of the mouth. They are used for biting off pieces of food. **Canines** are the more pointed teeth

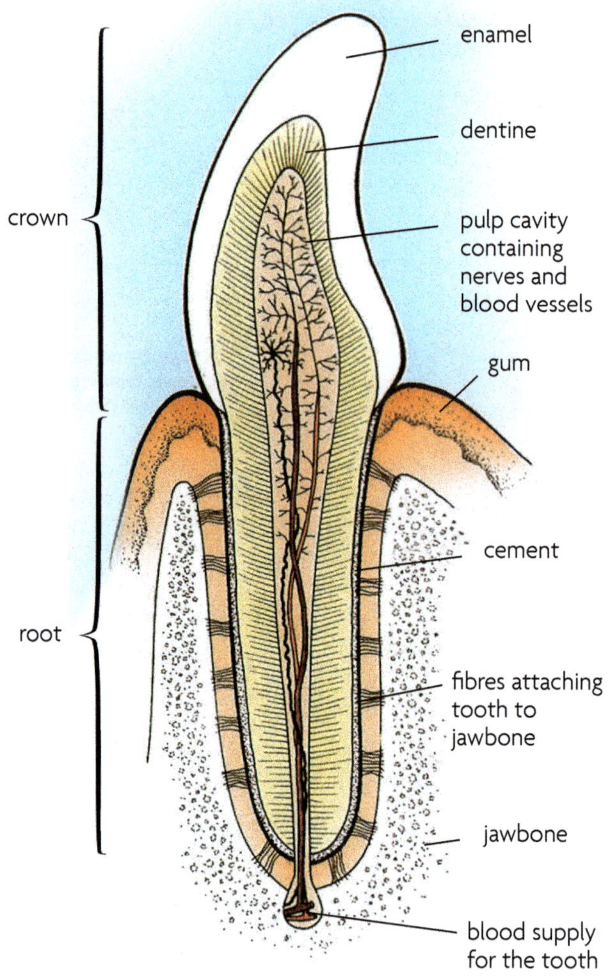

Figure 5.4 Longitudinal section of an incisor tooth.

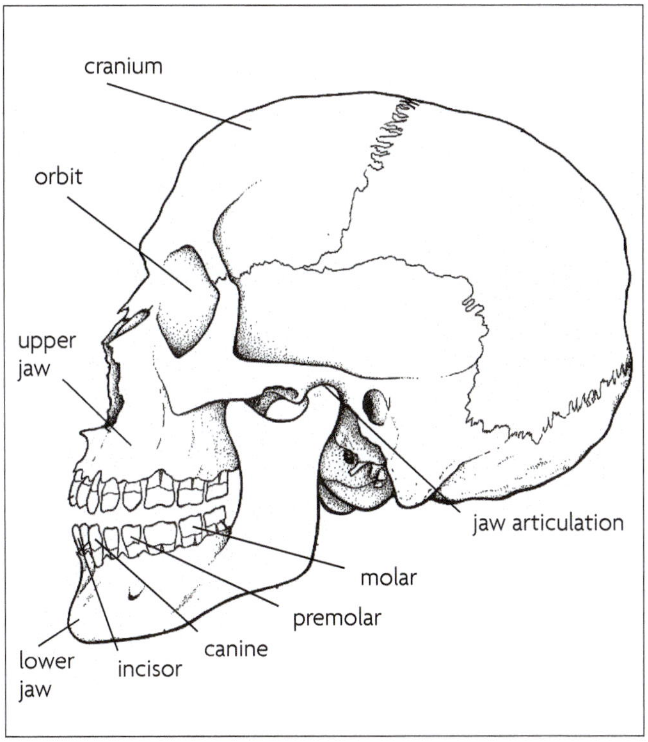
cranium
orbit
upper jaw
jaw articulation
molar
premolar
canine
lower jaw
incisor

Figure 5.5 A human skull, showing the different types of teeth.

at either side of the incisors. **Premolars** and **molars** are the large teeth towards the back of the mouth. They are used for chewing food. The ones right at the back are sometimes called wisdom teeth. They do not grow until much later than the others. Animals other than mammals have teeth that are all the same (Figure 5.7).

5.12 Mammals have two sets of teeth in their life.

Mammals also differ from other animals in having two sets of teeth. The first set is called the **milk teeth** or **deciduous teeth**. In humans, these start to grow through the gum, one or two at a time, when a child is about five months old. By the age of 24 to 30 months, most children have a set of 20 teeth.

This first set of teeth begins to fall out when the child is about seven years old. The teeth that replace them are called permanent teeth. These are made up of 20 teeth that replace the first set that has fallen out, and also 12 new teeth. There are therefore 32 permanent teeth altogether. Most people have all their permanent teeth by about 17 years of age.

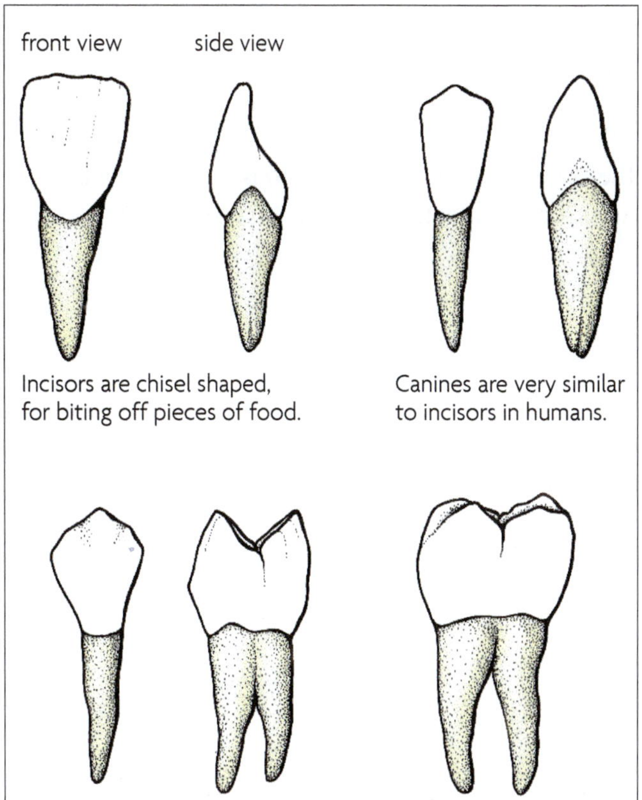
front view
side view
Incisors are chisel shaped, for biting off pieces of food.
Canines are very similar to incisors in humans.
Premolars have wide surfaces, for grinding food.
Molars, like premolars, are used for grinding.

Figure 5.6 Types of human teeth.

Figure 5.7 This skull belonged to a Komodo dragon, a reptile. Unlike those of mammals, reptiles' teeth are all the same type.

Questions

5.11 Explain how sugary foods can cause tooth decay.

5.12 What are incisors, and what are they used for?

5.13 Describe two ways in which mammals' teeth differ from those of other animals.

Digestion in humans – the alimentary canal

5.13 The alimentary canal is a muscular tube.

The **alimentary canal** (Figure **5.8**) is a long tube which runs from the mouth to the anus. It is part of the **digestive system**. The digestive system also includes the **liver** and the **pancreas**.

The wall of the alimentary canal contains muscles, which contract and relax to make food move along. This movement is called **peristalsis** (Figure **5.9**).

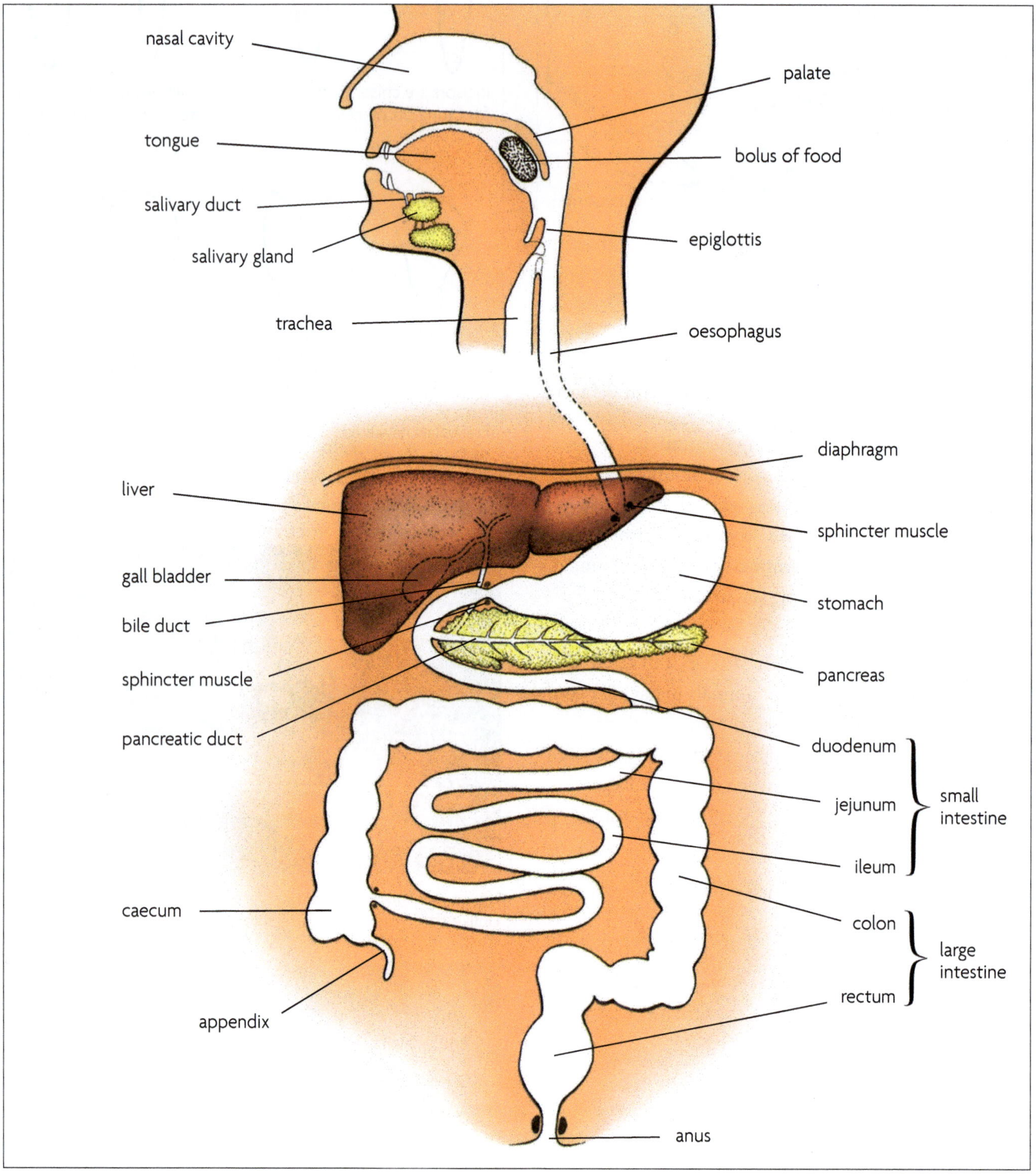

Figure 5.8 The human digestive system.

Sometimes, it is necessary to keep the food in one part of the alimentary canal for a while, before it is allowed to move to the next part. Special muscles can close the tube completely in certain places. They are called **sphincter muscles**.

To help the food to slide easily through the alimentary canal, it is lubricated with mucus. Mucus is made in goblet cells which occur along the alimentary canal.

Each section of the alimentary canal has its own part to play in the digestion, absorption, and egestion of food.

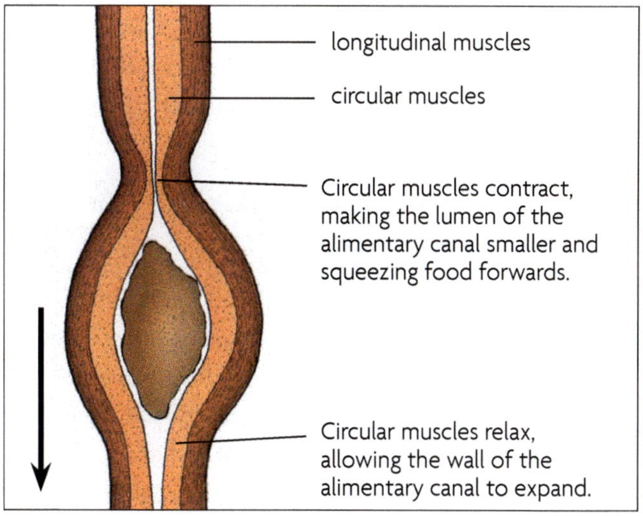

longitudinal muscles
circular muscles
Circular muscles contract, making the lumen of the alimentary canal smaller and squeezing food forwards.
Circular muscles relax, allowing the wall of the alimentary canal to expand.

Figure 5.9 Peristalsis.

Investigation 5.2
Observing the digestive system of a mammal

SBA skills

Observation/Recording/Reporting *Drawing*

Your teacher may be able to show you a dissection of a small mammal such as a mouse or rat. Watch carefully as the dissection is done. Make notes in pencil on some rough paper as you watch.

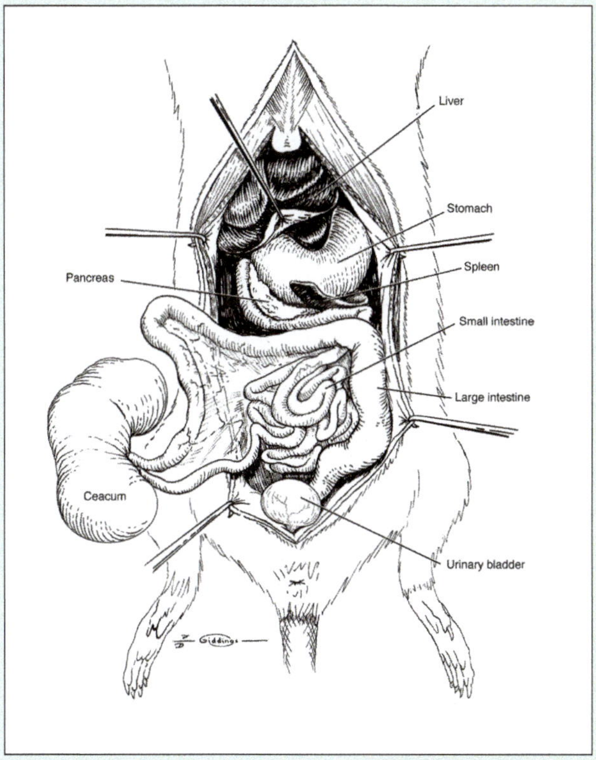

Liver
Stomach
Spleen
Pancreas
Small intestine
Large intestine
Ceacum
Urinary bladder

After the dissection has finished, you may be able to make a drawing of the alimentary canal inside the animal's body. It will look very complicated, so your task is to simplify your drawing so that it is easy to understand. Don't try to draw every detail. Concentrate on showing the overall shape and structure of each part, and their positions relative to each other. Don't put on any labels until you are happy with your drawing.

You should also write a description of what you have seen. You might like to use these questions to help you to think of what to write.

- What colour was the alimentary canal? How would you describe the feel of it (if you were allowed to touch it)?
- Which parts of the alimentary canal were widest? Which were narrowest? Which were longest?
- Could you see the liver and the pancreas? What did they look like? Why are they not actually part of the alimentary canal?
- Could you see the small and large intestines? Why are they given these names? Could you see any faeces in the rectum?
- Did the mammal have a fairly large caecum? If so, find out what this is used for.

5.14 In the mouth, food is mixed with saliva.

Food is ingested using the teeth, lips and tongue. The teeth then bite or grind the food into smaller pieces, increasing its surface area.

The tongue mixes the food with saliva, and forms it into a **bolus**. The bolus is then swallowed.

Saliva is made in the salivary glands. It is a mixture of water, **mucus** and the enzyme **amylase**. The water helps to dissolve substances in the food, allowing us to taste them. The mucus helps the chewed food to bind together to form a bolus, and lubricates it so that it slides easily down the oesophagus when it is swallowed. Amylase begins to digest starch in the food to maltose. Usually, it does not have time to finish this because the food is not kept in the mouth for very long. However, if you chew something starchy (such as a piece of bread) for a long time, you may be able to taste the sweet maltose that is produced.

5.15 The oesophagus carries food to the stomach.

There are two tubes leading down from the back of the mouth. The one in front is the **trachea** or windpipe, which takes air down to the lungs. Behind the trachea is the **oesophagus**, which takes food down to the stomach.

When you swallow, a piece of cartilage covers the entrance to the trachea. It is called the **epiglottis**, and it stops food from going down into the lungs.

The entrance to the stomach from the oesophagus is guarded by a ring of muscle called a **sphincter**. This muscle relaxes to let the food pass into the stomach.

5.16 The stomach stores food and digests proteins.

The **stomach** has strong, muscular walls. The muscles contract and relax to churn the food and mix it with the enzymes and mucus. The mixture is called **chyme**.

Like all parts of the alimentary canal, the stomach wall contains **goblet cells** which secrete mucus. It also contains other cells which produce enzymes called **pepsin** and **rennin**, and others which make **hydrochloric acid**. These are situated in pits in the stomach wall (Figure **5.10**).

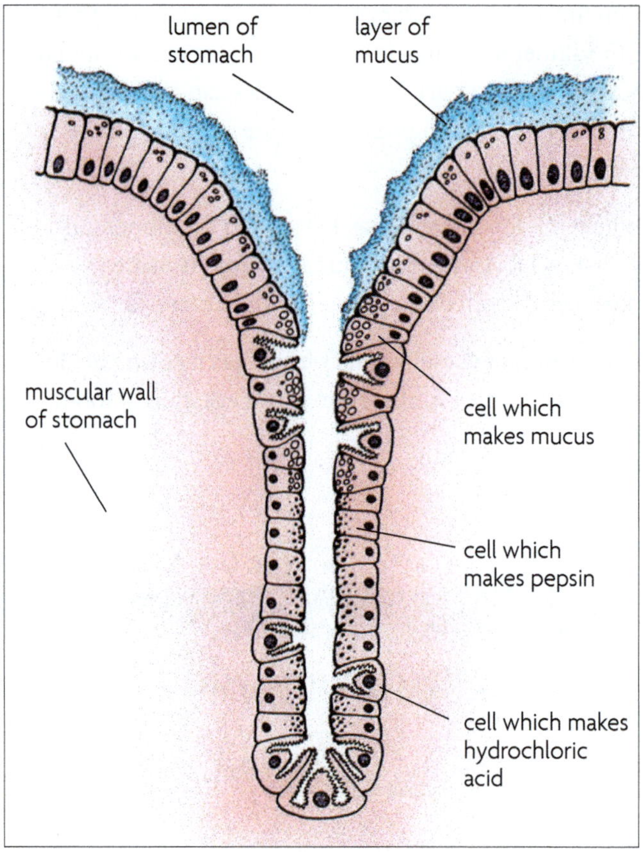

Figure 5.10 A gastric pit. 'Gastric' means 'to do with the stomach'.

Pepsin is a protease. It begins to digest proteins by breaking them down into polypeptides. Pepsin works best in acid conditions. The acid also helps to kill any bacteria in the food.

Rennin is only produced in the stomach of young mammals. It causes milk that they get from their mothers to clot. The milk proteins are then broken down by pepsin.

The stomach can store food for quite a long time. After one or two hours, the sphincter at the bottom of the stomach opens and lets the chyme into the duodenum.

5.17 The small intestine is very long.

The **small intestine** is the part of the alimentary canal between the stomach and the colon. It is about 5 m long. It is called the small intestine because it is quite narrow.

Different parts of the small intestine have different names. The first part, nearest to the stomach, is the **duodenum**. The middle section is the **jejunum**. The last part, nearest to the colon, is the **ileum**.

5.18 Pancreatic juice flows into the duodenum.

Several enzymes are secreted into the duodenum. They are made in the **pancreas**, which is a cream-coloured gland, lying just underneath the stomach. A tube called the **pancreatic duct** leads from the pancreas into the duodenum. **Pancreatic juice**, which is a fluid made by the pancreas, flows along this tube.

This fluid contains many enzymes. One is **amylase**, which breaks down starch to maltose. Another is **trypsin**, which is a protease and breaks down proteins to polypeptides. Another is **lipase**, which breaks down lipids (fats) to fatty acids and glycerol.

These enzymes do not work well in acid environments, but the chyme which has come from the stomach contains hydrochloric acid. Pancreatic juice contains **sodium hydrogencarbonate** which partially neutralises the acid.

5.19 Bile helps digest fats.

As well as pancreatic juice, another fluid flows into the duodenum. It is called **bile**. Bile is a yellowish green, watery liquid. It is made in the liver, and then stored in the **gall bladder**. It flows to the duodenum along the **bile duct**.

Bile does not contain any enzymes. It does, however, help to digest fats. It does this by breaking up the large drops of fat into very small ones, making it easier for the lipase in the pancreatic juice to digest them. This is called **emulsification**, and is done by salts in the bile called **bile salts**.

Bile also contains yellowish **bile pigments**. These are made by the liver when it breaks down old red blood cells. The bile pigments are made from haemoglobin. The pigments are not needed by the body, so they are eventually excreted in the faeces.

5.20 Digestion is completed in the small intestine.

As well as receiving enzymes made in the pancreas, the small intestine makes some enzymes itself. They are made by cells in its walls.

The inner wall of all three parts of the small intestine – the duodenum, jejunum and ileum – is covered with millions of tiny projections. They are called **villi**. Each villus is about 1 mm long (Figure **5.11** and Figures **5.12**, **5.13** and **5.14** overleaf). Cells covering the villi make enzymes. The enzymes do not come out into the lumen of the small intestine, but stay close to the cells which make them. These enzymes complete the digestion of food.

Maltase breaks down maltose to glucose. **Sucrase** breaks down sucrose to glucose and fructose. **Lactase** breaks down lactose to glucose and galactose. These three enzymes are all **carbohydrases**. There are also **proteases**, which finish breaking down any polypeptides into amino acids. **Lipase** completes the breakdown of fats to fatty acids and glycerol.

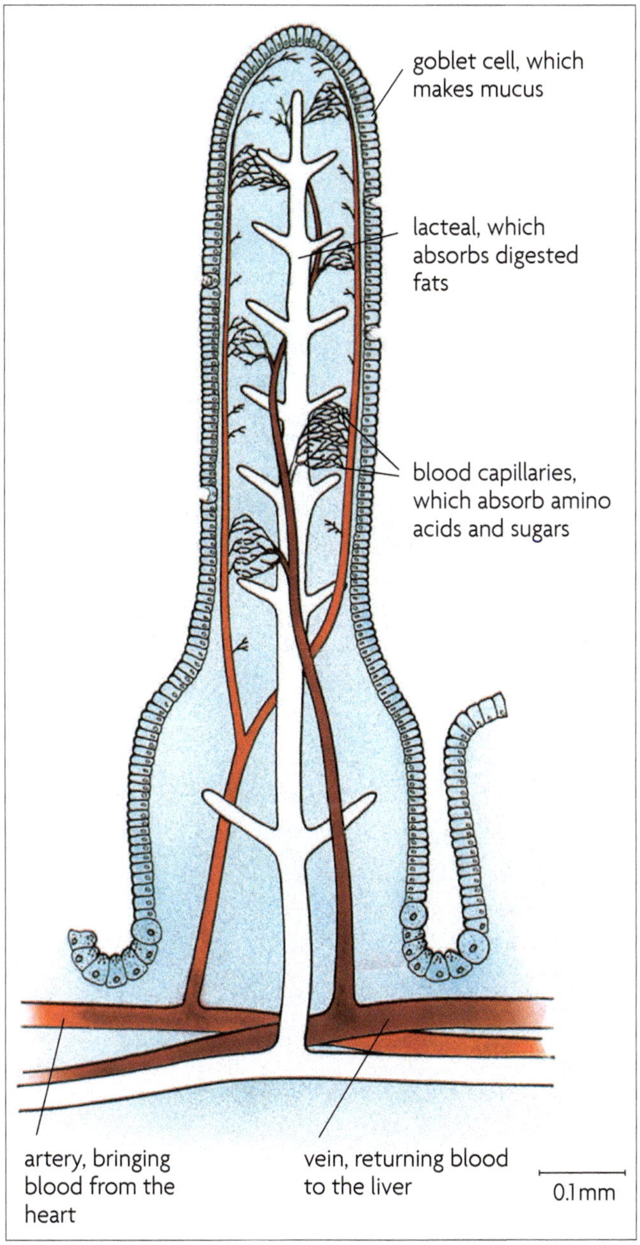

Figure 5.11 Longitudinal section through a villus.

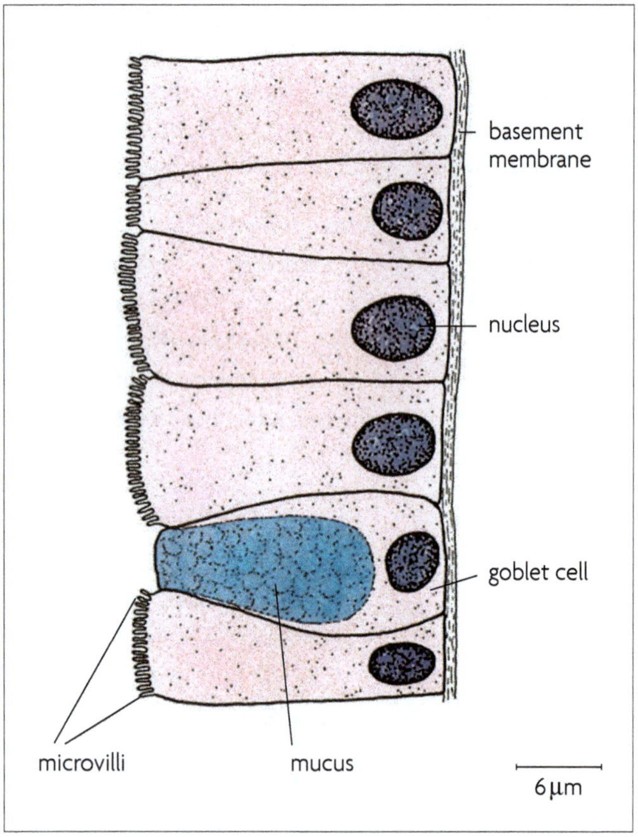

Figure 5.12 Detail of the surface of a villus.

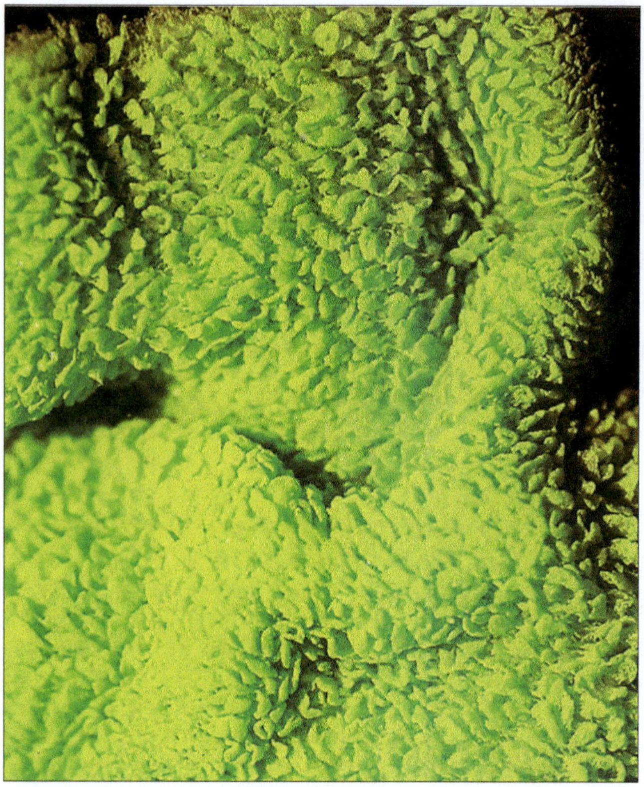

Figure 5.13 This micrograph shows thousands of villi covering the inner wall of the small intestine. It is magnified about 20 times.

5.21 Digested food is absorbed in the small intestine.

By now, most carbohydrates have been broken down to simple sugars, proteins to amino acids, and fats to fatty acids and glycerol.

These molecules are small enough to pass through the wall of the small intestine and into the blood. This is called **absorption**. The small intestine is especially adapted to allow absorption to take place very efficiently. Some of its features are listed in Table **5.4**.

Water, mineral salts and vitamins are also absorbed in the small intestine.

Table **5.5** (page **84**) gives a summary of digestion in the human alimentary canal.

Table 5.4 How the small intestine is adapted for absorbing digested nutrients

Feature	How this helps absorption take place
It is very long, about 5 m in an adult.	This gives plenty of time for digestion to be completed, and for digested food to be absorbed as it slowly passes through.
It has villi. Each villus is covered with cells which have even smaller projections on them, called microvilli.	This gives the inner surface of the small intestine a very large surface area. The larger the surface area, the faster nutrients can be absorbed.
Villi contain blood capillaries.	Monosaccharides, amino acids, water, minerals and vitamins pass into the blood, to be taken to the liver and then round the body.
Villi contain lacteals, which are part of the lymphatic system.	Lipids are absorbed into lacteals.
Villi have walls only one cell thick.	The digested nutrients can easily cross the wall to reach the blood capillaries and lacteals.

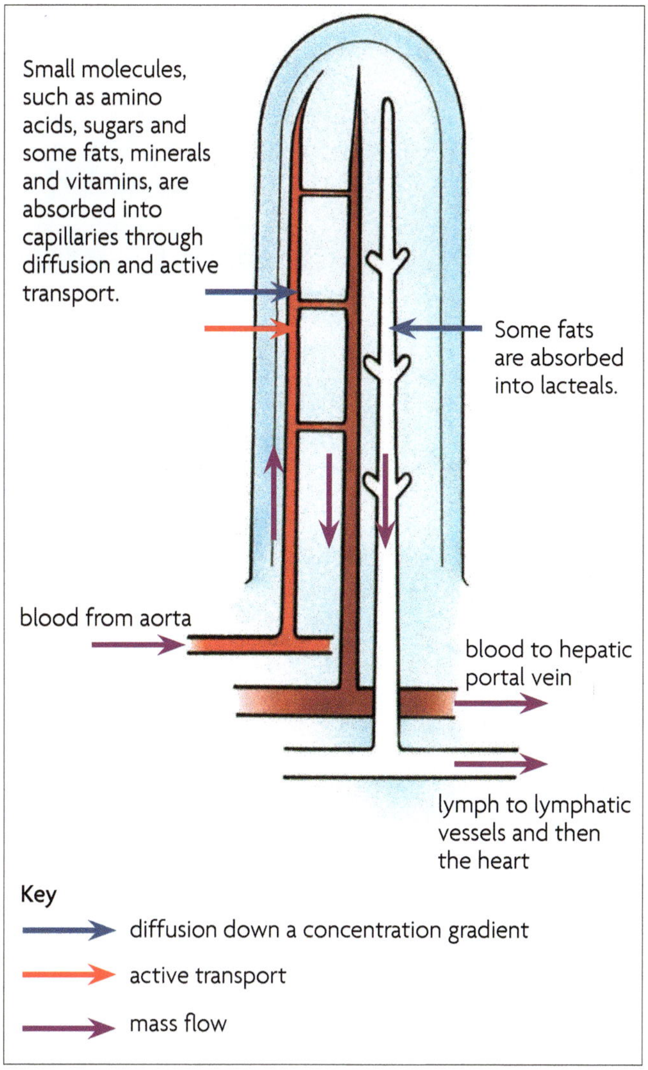

Figure 5.14 Absorption of digested nutrients into a villus.

5.22 The colon absorbs water.

Not all the food that is eaten can be digested, and this undigested food cannot be absorbed in the small intestine. It travels on, through the caecum, past the appendix and into the **colon**. In humans, the caecum and appendix have no function. In the colon, more water and salt are absorbed.

The colon and rectum are sometimes called the **large intestine,** because they are wider tubes than the duodenum and ileum.

5.23 The rectum temporarily stores undigested food.

By the time the food reaches the **rectum**, most of the substances which can be absorbed have gone into the blood. All that remains is indigestible food (roughage), bacteria, and some dead cells from the inside of the alimentary canal. This mixture forms the **faeces**, which are passed out at intervals through the **anus**. This process is called **egestion**.

5.24 Most absorbed food goes straight to the liver.

After they have been absorbed into the blood, the nutrients are taken to the liver, in the **hepatic portal vein** (Figure **5.15**). The liver processes some of it, before it goes any further (Table **8.1**, page **149**). Some of these nutrients can be broken down, some converted into other substances, some stored and the remainder left unchanged.

The nutrients, dissolved in the blood plasma, are then taken to other parts of the body where they may become assimilated as part of a cell.

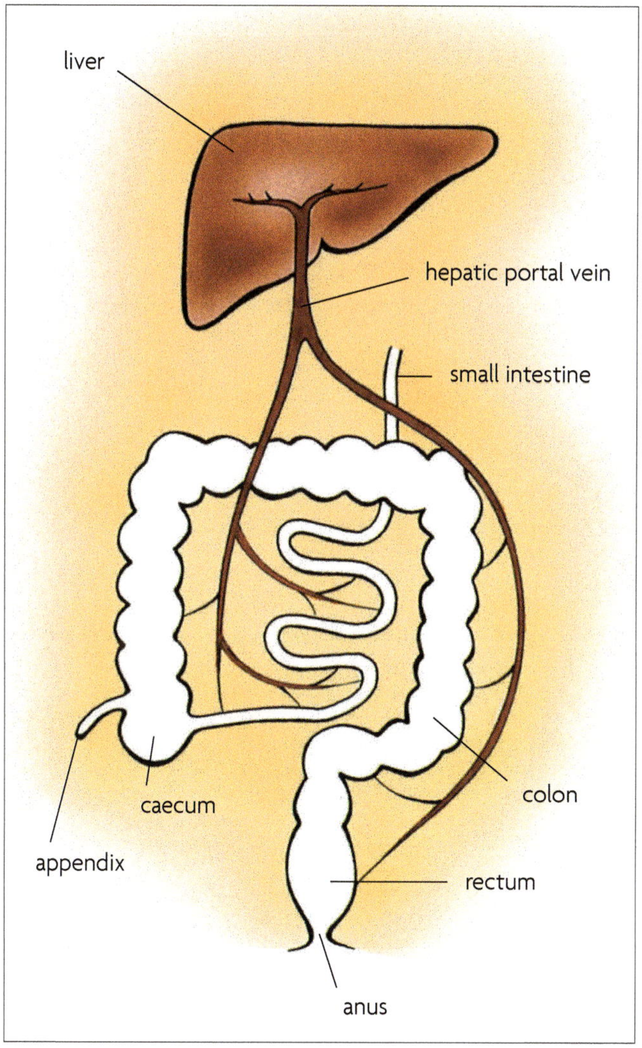

Figure 5.15 The hepatic portal vein transports absorbed nutrients from the small intestine to the liver.

Table 5.5 Summary of digestion in the human alimentary canal

Part of the canal	Juices secreted	Where made	Enzymes in juice	Substrate	Product	Other substances in juice	Functions of other substances in juice
mouth	saliva	salivary glands	amylase	starch	maltose		
oesophagus	none						
stomach	gastric juice	in pits in wall of stomach	pepsin	proteins	polypeptides	hydrochloric acid	acid environment for pepsin; kills bacteria in food
			rennin (only in young mammals)	milk protein	curdled milk protein		
duodenum	pancreatic juice	pancreas	amylase	starch	maltose	sodium hydro-gencarbonate	reduces acidity of chyme for enzymes
			trypsin	proteins	polypeptides		
			lipase	lipids	fatty acids and glycerol		
	bile	liver, stored in gall bladder	none			bile salts	emulsify fats
						bile pigments	excretory products
ileum	no juice secreted; enzymes remain in or on the cells covering the villi	by cells covering the villi	maltase	maltose	glucose		
			sucrase	sucrose	glucose and fructose		
			lactase	lactose	glucose and galactose		
			peptidase	polypeptides	amino acids		
			lipase	lipids	fatty acids and glycerol		

All of the digestive juices contain water and mucus. The water is used for the digestion (hydrolysis) of large molecules to small ones. It is also a solvent for the nutrients and enzymes. Mucus acts as a lubricant. It also forms a covering over the inner surface of the alimentary canal, preventing enzymes from digesting the cells.

Questions

5.14 What is a sphincter muscle?

5.15 Name two places in the alimentary canal where sphincter muscles are found.

5.16 In which parts of the alimentary canal is mucus secreted? Explain why.

5.17 Name two parts of the alimentary canal where amylase is secreted. What does it do?

5.18 What is the epiglottis?

5.19 Why do the walls of the stomach secrete hydrochloric acid?

5.20 Which two parts of the alimentary canal make up the small intestine?

5.21 Which two digestive juices are secreted into the duodenum?

Questions

5.22 How do bile salts help in digestion?

5.23 Name three enzymes made by the cells covering the villi in the small intestine and explain what they do.

5.24 **(a)** In which part of the alimentary canal is digested food absorbed? **(b)** Describe three ways in which this part is adapted for absorption.

5.25 In which part of the alimentary canal is water absorbed?

5.26 What do faeces contain?

Digestion in fungi

5.25 Fungi feed saprophytically.

Moulds and mushrooms belong to the kingdom Fungi. Fungi have cells that have cell walls, but these are not made of cellulose like those of plants. They do not have chlorophyll, so they cannot photosynthesise. Fungi, like animals, are heterotrophic. They cannot make their own food, and feed on organic substances made by plants, or from animals that have eaten plants.

A common mould is the bread mould *Mucor* (Figure 5.16). *Mucor* grows on many kinds of non-living organic material, such as bread. It consists of threads of **hyphae**, which make up a **mycelium**.

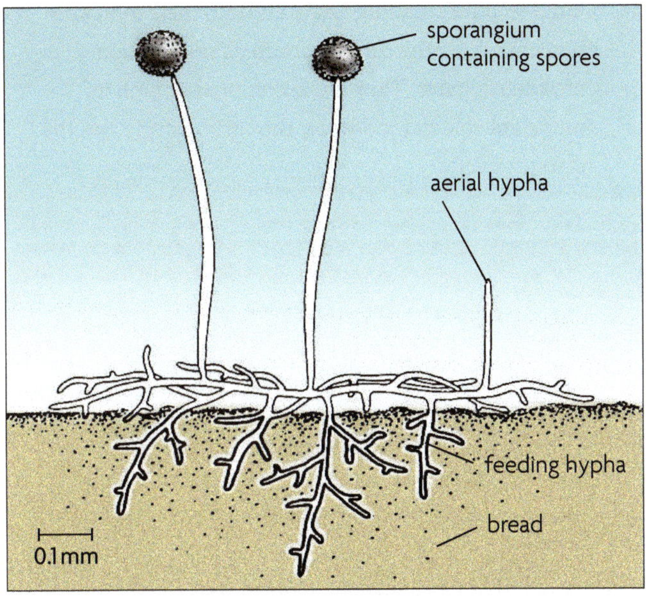

Figure 5.16 *Mucor*. The network of hyphae is called a mycelium. The fungus reproduces by producing spores, which are spread around on air currents or the feet and bodies of flies.

Mucor feeds on the substances on which it grows – for example, bread. The tips of the hyphae secrete enzymes, which digest the bread. These enzymes are very similar to those produced in the human alimentary canal.

The starch in the bread is broken down to glucose, which is soluble, and diffuses into the hyphae. Proteins in the bread are broken down to amino acids, and fats to fatty acids and glycerol. All of these are absorbed by the hyphae. The hyphae then grow forward into the space made by the dissolved bread (Figure 5.17).

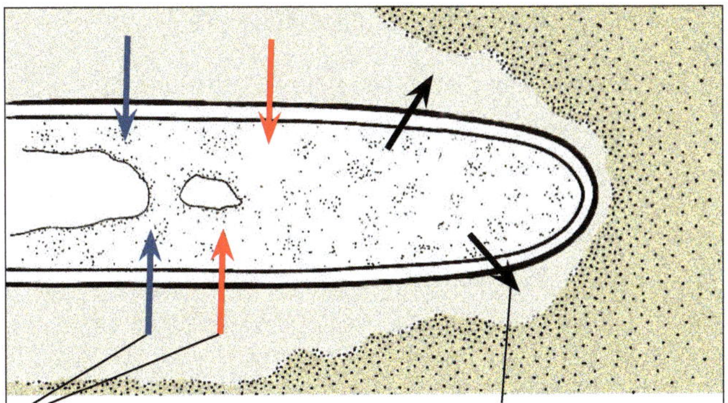

The dissolved and digested bread contains small molecules, such as glucose and amino acids. They are absorbed into the hypha.
Enzymes are secreted to digest the bread.

Figure 5.17 How a fungal hypha digests and absorbs nutrients.

This type of nutrition is called **saprophytism**. Most fungi feed in this way, and so do many bacteria. It is the way in which dead organisms and waste materials (such as faeces) are decayed by decomposers, and is very important because it helps to release nutrients from them which would not otherwise be available to other organisms. Fungi are important components of the carbon cycle (section **1.20**) and the nitrogen cycle (section **1.22**).

Questions

5.27 In what ways are the cells of fungi like those of plants? In what ways are they different?

5.28 Explain what is meant by the term saprophytism.

5.29 Suggest how the branching network of hyphae making up the fungal mycelium helps to speed up the digestion and absorption of nutrients.

5.30 Outline the role of fungi in a food web.

Key ideas

- A balanced diet contains some of each group of nutrients – carbohydrates, fats, proteins, minerals, vitamins, water and roughage – in suitable proportions, and the correct amount of energy.
- Eating food containing more energy than you can use up causes weight increase, which can lead to obesity. Children who do not get enough food may suffer from energy protein malnutrition, in which they do not grow properly and have little energy.
- A vegetarian diet can be a very healthy one, but care needs to be taken to get plenty of protein and vitamin B_{12}.
- Digestion is the breakdown (hydrolysis) of large molecules of food into small ones, so that they can be absorbed through the wall of the alimentary canal.
- Mechanical digestion breaks down large pieces of food to small ones. It is done by the teeth, and the muscles in the wall of the alimentary canal. Chemical digestion breaks down large molecules to small ones. It is done by enzymes.
- Mammals have four types of teeth – incisors, canines, premolars and molars – each with their own functions.
- Digestion begins in the mouth, as teeth grind food into smaller pieces, and amylase digests starch to maltose.
- Protein digestion begins in the stomach, where pepsin digests proteins to polypeptides. Rennin is present in young mammals, and clots milk protein. Hydrochloric acid kills bacteria and provides a low pH for the action of pepsin.
- Pancreatic juice flows into the duodenum. It contains enzymes that digest starch, proteins and lipids, and also sodium hydrogencarbonate to partly neutralise the food coming from the stomach.
- Bile also flows into the duodenum. It contains bile salts which emulsify fats, making it easier for lipase to digest them.
- The lining of the small intestine is covered with villi, giving it a very large surface area which helps to speed up absorption. Cells on the surface of the villi make enzymes, which complete the digestion of food. The villi contain blood capillaries to absorb glucose, amino acids, water, vitamins and minerals, and lacteals to absorb fatty acids and glycerol.
- The absorbed nutrients are carried to the liver in the hepatic portal vein. Some are used in the liver, some are stored, and some are sent on in the blood to be delivered to cells all over the body.
- The colon absorbs more water from the food. In the rectum, the undigested food is formed into faeces, which are eventually egested through the anus.
- Fungi feed by secreting enzymes onto their food and then absorbing the soluble products of digestion into their hyphae. They are decomposers, with an important role in food webs, the carbon cycle and the nitrogen cycle.

End-of-chapter questions

1 With the aid of examples wherever possible, explain the differences between each of the following pairs of terms:
   a autotrophic; heterotrophic
   b monosaccharide; disaccharide
   c inorganic; organic
   d enamel; dentine
   e digestion; absorption
   f maltose; maltase
   g substrate; product.

2 a What is meant by a balanced diet?
   b Using Table 5.1 and Figure 5.1, plan menus for one day which would provide a balanced diet for **(i)** a teenage boy, and **(ii)** a pregnant woman. For each food you include, state how much energy, and which types of nutrients it contains.

3 Describe what would happen to a piece of steak, containing only protein, and a chip, containing starch and fat, as they passed through your alimentary canal.

6 Respiration

In this chapter, you will find out:

- how respiration in all living cells releases energy from food
- the equations for aerobic respiration and anaerobic respiration
- about ATP and its use as energy currency in cells
- how we use respiration by yeast in baking and brewing
- the features required by all gas exchange surfaces
- how gas exchange happens in an amoeba, a human, a fish and a flowering plant
- the structure and functions of the human gas exchange system
- the differences between inspired air and expired air
- about the effects of exercise on breathing rate
- about the effects of cigarette smoking on health.

Respiration as energy release

6.1 Respiration releases energy from food.

Every cell in every living organism needs energy (Figure **6.1**). Cells get their energy from food. The energy is released from the food by a process called **respiration**.

The process can be summarised like this:

sugar + oxygen ⟶ carbon dioxide + water + energy

The sugar which is normally used is glucose, $C_6H_{12}O_6$. The balanced equation for respiration is this:

$$C_6H_{12}O_6 + 6O_2 \longrightarrow 6CO_2 + 6H_2O + \text{energy}$$

The carbon dioxide and water are by-products. The reaction produces energy for the cell.

Most cells need a good supply of glucose for respiration. Glucose is one of the first substances that green plants make in photosynthesis (section **4.4**). It is also produced when animals digest their food (section **5.8**).

Figure 6.1 What are these young people using energy for?

Investigation 6.1

To show that carbon dioxide is produced by a respiring mammal

SBA skills

Observation/Recording/Reporting
Analysis/Interpretation

1 Set up the apparatus shown in the diagram.

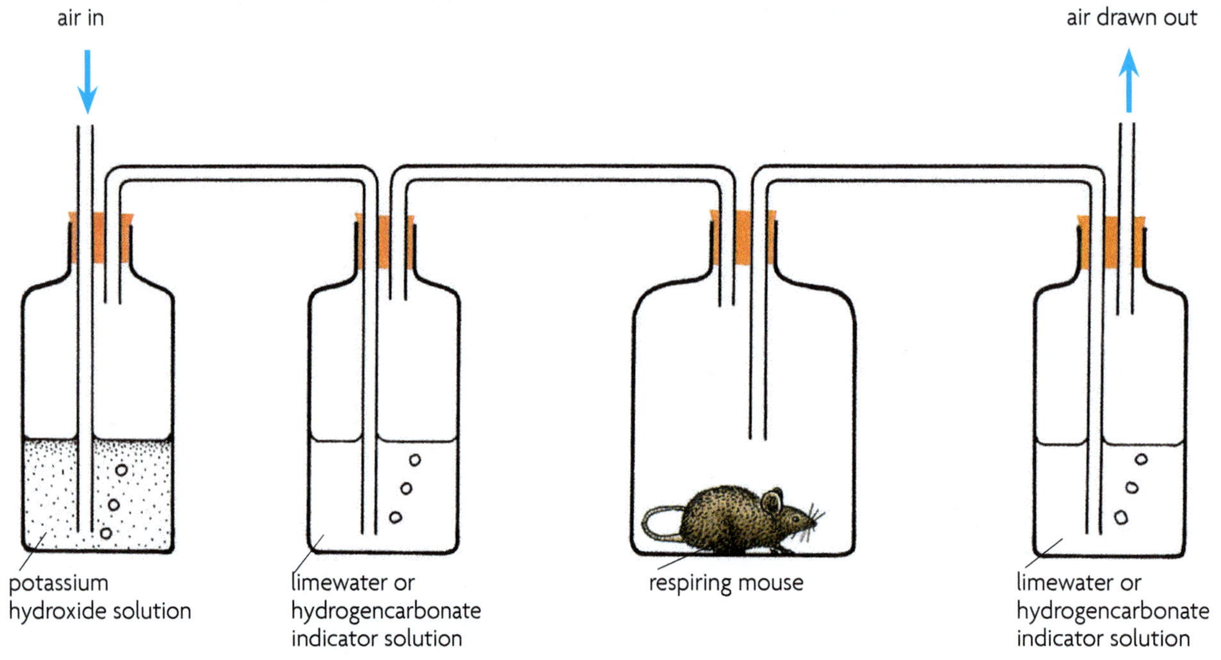

2 Note the colour of the hydrogencarbonate indicator solution or limewater in each flask.

3 Turn on the pump, to draw air through the apparatus. Leave it running until one of the solutions has changed colour.

Hydrogencarbonate indicator solution changes from red to yellow when carbon dioxide is bubbled through it. Limewater changes from clear to milky white.

Questions

1 Potassium hydroxide solution absorbs carbon dioxide. Why was the air bubbled through this solution before it reached the mouse?

2 Why was the air bubbled through limewater or hydrogencarbonate indicator solution before reaching the mouse?

3 Which solution changed colour? What does this show?

Investigation 6.2

To measure the rate of uptake of oxygen during respiration in a small invertebrate

SBA skills

Observation/Recording/Reporting
Manipulation/Measurement
Analysis/Interpretation

1 Copy out the results table, ready to fill it in.

Time in minutes	0	1	2	3	4	5
Distance travelled by oil drop in B, in cm						
Distance travelled by oil drop in A, in cm						
Distance B – A						

2 Set up both pieces of apparatus shown in the diagram. Make sure that the connections between capillary tube, bung and chamber are airtight. Vaseline will help to seal them.

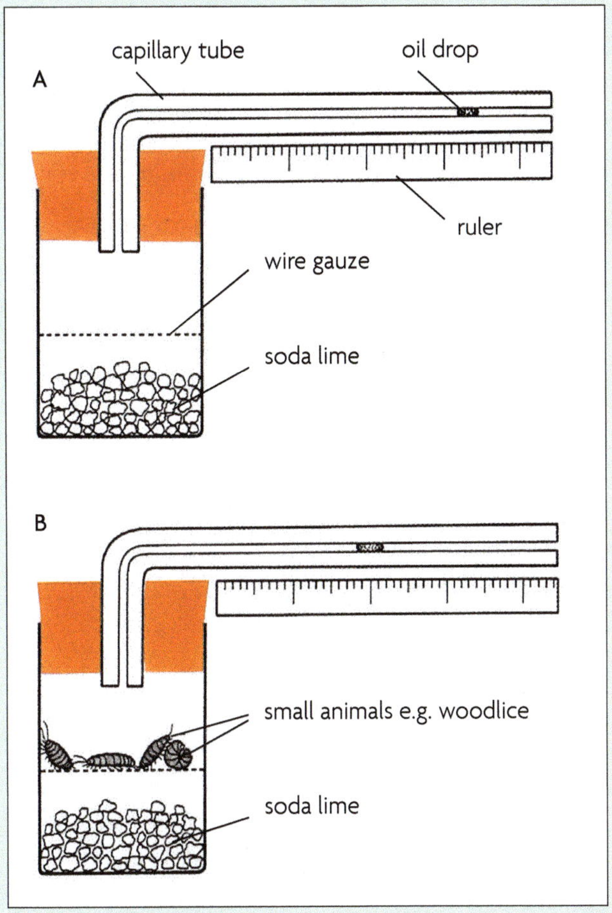

3 Dip the end of the capillary tube of each apparatus into oil, so that a drop is introduced into it.

4 Watch the movement of the oil drop in apparatus **A**. This should move quite quickly at first, as the soda lime absorbs any carbon dioxide already in the apparatus.

5 When the oil drop in apparatus **A** slows down or stops, set your stopwatch to time 0, and record the position of the oil drop in both pieces of apparatus.

6 At suitable time intervals, note both time and distance travelled by both oil drops. Record these results in your results table.

7 Plot a graph of the distance travelled in **B** minus distance travelled in **A**, against time. Put time on the *x*-axis.

Questions

1. What gas is absorbed by soda lime?
2. Why does the oil drop in apparatus **A** move quickly at first?
3. Why does the oil drop in **A** slow down or stop?
4. Why does the oil drop carry on moving in apparatus **B**, when the oil drop stops in **A**?
5. Why does the CO_2 breathed out by the woodlice not cause the oil drop in **B** to move to the right?
6. What is the purpose of apparatus **A**?
7. What might cause the oil drop to move in apparatus **A** after its first rapid movement?
8. How could another similar apparatus be used to work out the amount of CO_2 breathed out by the woodlice?

Investigation 6.3
Comparing the energy content of two kinds of food

SBA skills

Observation/Recording/Reporting *Planning/Design*
Manipulation/Measurement
Analysis/Interpretation

You know that food contains energy. We can change this energy into heat energy by burning the food. We can measure the amount of heat energy that is produced by measuring the temperature change in a known volume of water.

The diagram shows the apparatus you can use. You will also need a thermometer.

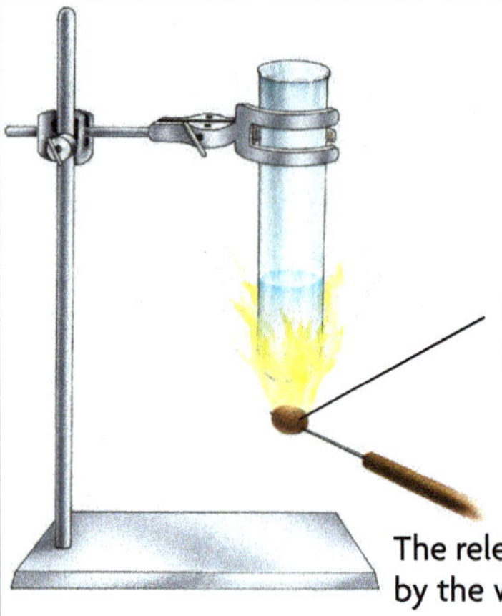

combustion of a piece of food
The released energy is absorbed by the water and this raises the temperature of the water.

In order to calculate the energy that is released as heat when you burn the food, you need to know:

- the volume of water in the tube
- the initial temperature of water in the tube
- the final temperature of water in the tube.

You can then calculate the amount of heat energy that went into the water using this formula:

heat energy in J = temperature change in °C × volume of water in cm^3 × 4.2

Your task is to design and carry out an investigation to compare the amount of energy in two kinds of food. Suitable foods could be: plain popcorn and popcorn soaked in oil; white bread and brown bread; a peanut and a cashew nut. Your teacher will suggest which foods you can use.

1 Decide on a hypothesis you will investigate. The hypothesis should be one sentence, and should state which of the two foods you predict contains the more energy.

2 Plan how you will carry out your investigation. Then think through it again, and make improvements to your plan. Once you are fairly happy with it, show your teacher. You must not try to do your experiment until your teacher says that you may begin.

- What apparatus and other materials will you need for your experiment?
- What will you vary in your experiment? How will you vary it?
- What will you try to keep the same in your experiment? How will you do this?
- What will you measure in your experiment? How will you measure it? When will you measure it? Will you do repeat measurements and calculate a mean?
- How will you record your results? (You can sketch out a results chart, ready to fill in.)
- How will you use your results to calculate the amount of energy in the food?
- What will your results be if your hypothesis is correct?

Once you have approval from your teacher, you should do your experiment. Most scientific researchers find that they want to make changes to their experiment once they actually begin doing it. This is a good thing to do. Make careful notes about all the changes that you make.

Finally, write up your experiment, including:

- a heading, and the hypothesis that you tested
- a diagram of the apparatus that you used, and a full description of your method
- a neat and carefully headed table of results, including means if you decided to do repeats
- a conclusion, in which you say whether or not your results support your hypothesis
- a discussion, in which you use what you know about the energy content of different nutrients (look back at page 71) to try to explain the pattern in your results
- an evaluation, in which you explain the main limitations that you feel might have affected the reliability of your data.

6.2 In respiration, glucose is oxidised in stages.

When glucose is oxidised or combined with oxygen in the laboratory, a great deal of heat energy is released (Figure **6.2**). In living cells, if all the energy from glucose were set free at one time, the cells would get so hot that they would die. Instead, in respiration, the sugar is oxidised gradually in a series of small, controlled reactions. These reactions are controlled by enzymes (sections **3.14** to **3.17**), and the energy is released gradually in small quantities.

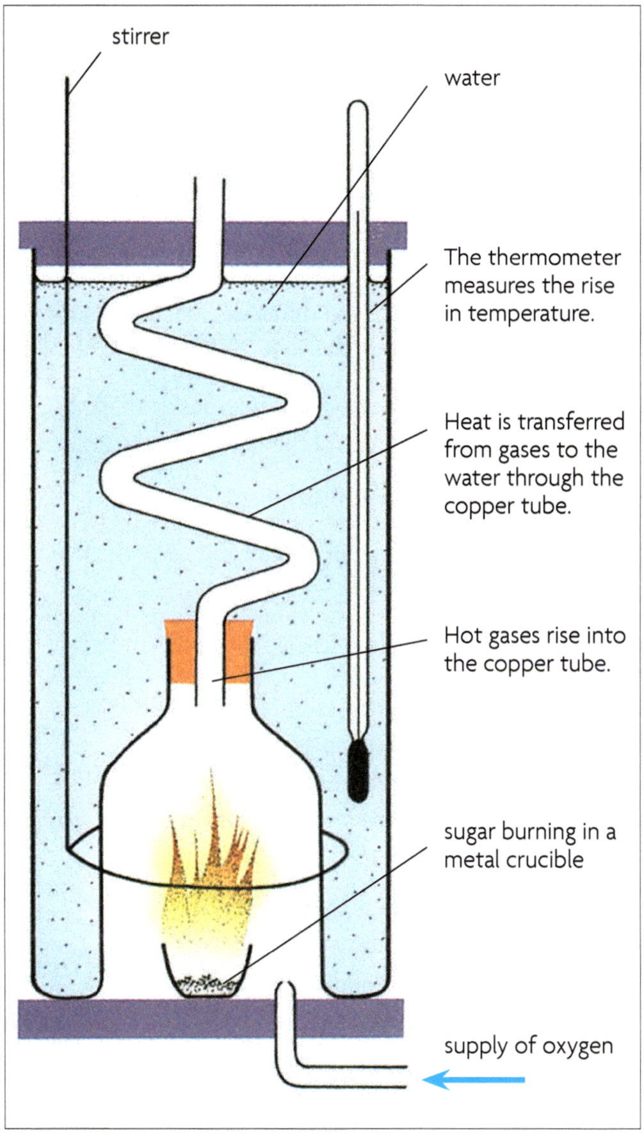

Figure 6.2 Apparatus for measuring the energy released when sugar is oxidised.

6.3 ATP is the energy currency in a cell.

Respiration is going on in all living cells all the time, so they are continually releasing energy from glucose. They immediately use this energy to make a substance called **ATP** (Figure **6.3**).

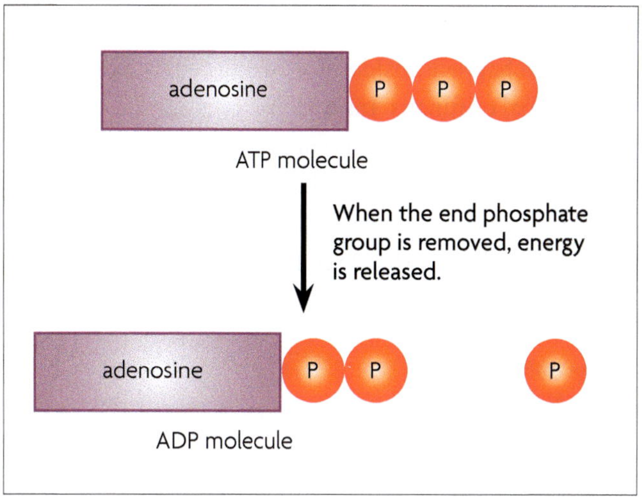

Figure 6.3 ATP and ADP.

The cells contain a substance called **ADP** (adenosine diphosphate). Each molecule of ADP has two phosphate groups firmly attached. The energy from respiration is used to add another phosphate group to each molecule to make ATP.

ADP + phosphate + energy ⟶ ATP

This third phosphate group is easily separated from the other two. When it is, energy is quickly released, and ADP is formed (Figure **6.3**).

ATP ⟶ ADP + phosphate + energy

So ATP is used as a little package of energy, keeping energy when it is not needed, and releasing it when it is. The molecule represents the basic energy unit of the cell. Only a small amount of energy is released when one molecule of ATP is broken down. When larger amounts of energy are needed, more ATP molecules are used. So ATP is sometimes called the energy 'coin' or 'currency' of the cell.

Using energy in small packages prevents waste. It allows only what is needed at the time to be used. ATP is used for all the reactions in the cell which require energy. This makes things simpler and more efficient in cell metabolism.

6.4 Respiration produces heat.

The energy released by respiration is not all stored as ATP. Some of it does escape as heat. In fact, many animals use the heat from respiration to keep their bodies warm (section **11.10**).

6.5 ATP is made inside mitochondria.

Respiration happens inside every living cell, whether plant, animal or fungus. Inside these cells are **mitochondria**. Mitochondria are called the 'power-houses' of a cell, because it is there that most ATP is made. The more energy a cell needs, the more mitochondria it has. Muscle cells and liver cells, for example, contain large numbers of mitochondria.

FACT!

A resting human uses about 40 kg of ATP in one day. During strenuous exercise, a person may use as much as 0.5 kg of ATP a minute.

Questions

6.1 In respiration, sugar is oxidised. What does this mean?

6.2 What is special about the way that oxidation happens inside cells?

6.3 What is the purpose of respiration?

6.4 What is the energy released in respiration used for?

6.5 In which part of a cell does respiration take place?

6.6 Why do liver cells contain so many mitochondria?

Investigation 6.4
Investigating heat production by germinating peas

SBA skills

Observation/Recording/Reporting

Analysis/Interpretation

1 Soak some peas (or beans) in water for a day, so that they begin to germinate.

2 Boil a second set of peas, to kill them.

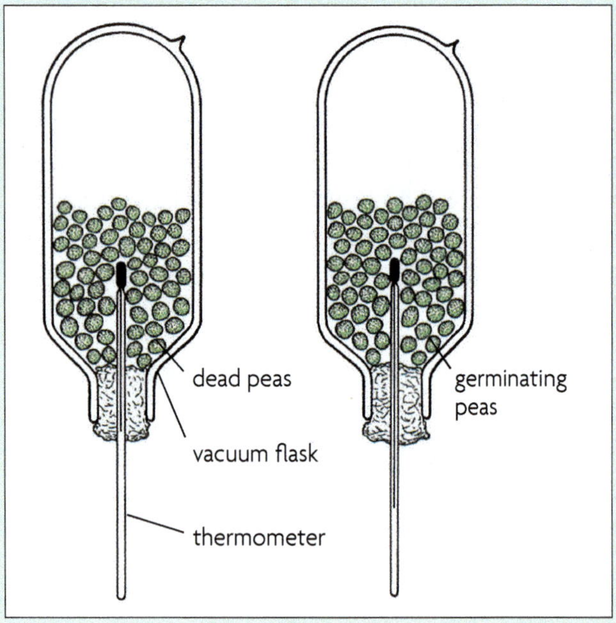

3 Wash both sets of peas in dilute disinfectant, so that any bacteria and fungi on them are killed.

4 Put each set of peas into a vacuum flask as shown in the diagram. Do not fill the flasks completely.

5 Note the temperature of each flask.

6 Support each flask upside down, and leave them for a few days.

7 Note the temperature of each flask at the end of your experiment.

Questions

1 Which flask showed the higher temperature at the end of the experiment? Explain your answer.

2 Why is it important to kill any bacteria and fungi on the peas?

3 Why should the flasks not be completely filled with peas?

4 Carbon dioxide is a heavy gas. Why were the flasks left upside down, with porous cotton wool plugs in them?

5 Not all of the energy produced by the respiring peas is given off as heat. What happens to the rest of it?

6.6 Respiration sometimes occurs without oxygen.

The process described so far in this chapter releases energy from sugar by combining it with oxygen. It is called **aerobic respiration**, because it uses air (which contains oxygen).

It is possible, though, to release energy from sugar without using oxygen. It is not such an efficient process and not much energy is released, but the process is used by some organisms. It is called **anaerobic respiration** ('an' means without).

Yeast, a single-celled fungus, can respire anaerobically. It breaks down sugar to alcohol.

sugar ⟶ alcohol + carbon dioxide + energy

$$C_6H_{12}O_6 \longrightarrow 2C_2H_5OH + 2CO_2 + \text{energy}$$

As in aerobic respiration, carbon dioxide is made and the energy is used to make ATP. Plants can also respire anaerobically like this, but only for short periods of time (Table **6.1**, page **94**).

Some of the cells in your body, particularly muscle cells, can also respire anaerobically for a short time. They make lactic acid instead of alcohol and no carbon dioxide is produced. This is described in section **6.21**.

Investigation 6.5
Investigating the production of carbon dioxide by anaerobic respiration

SBA skills

Observation/Recording/Reporting *Planning/Design*
Analysis/Interpretation

1. Boil some water, to drive off any dissolved air.
2. Dissolve a small amount of sugar in the boiled water, and allow it to cool.
3. When it is cool, add yeast and stir with a glass rod.
4. Set up the apparatus as in the diagram. Add the liquid paraffin by trickling it gently down the side of the tube, using a pipette.
5. Set up an identical piece of apparatus, but use boiled yeast instead of living yeast.
6. Leave your apparatus in a warm place.

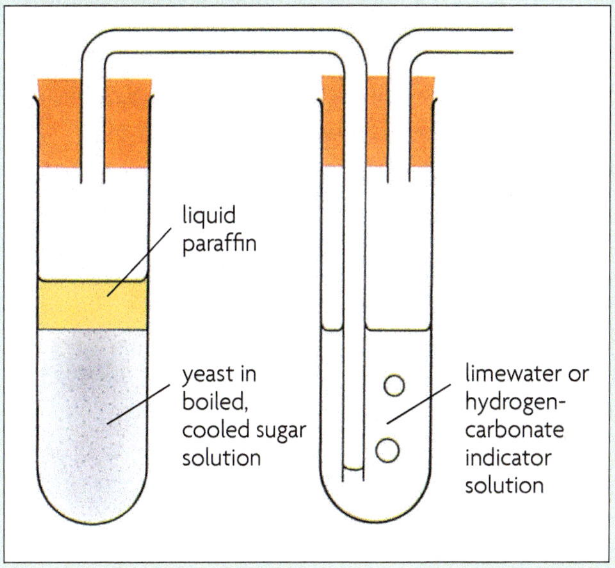

7. Observe what happens to the limewater after half an hour.

Questions

1. Why is it important to boil the water?
2. Why must the sugar solution be cooled before adding the yeast?
3. What is the liquid paraffin for?
4. What happened to the limewater or hydrogencarbonate indicator solution in each of your pieces of apparatus? What does this show?
5. What new substance would you expect to find in the sugar solution containing living yeast at the end of the experiment?
6. Describe a method you could use to compare the rate of carbon dioxide production by yeast using aerobic and anaerobic respiration. Remember to describe the variables you will change, those you will control and how, and how you will collect, record and analyse your results.

6.7 Yeast is used for baking and brewing.

Breaking down sugar to alcohol and carbon dioxide, which is the way in which yeast respires anaerobically, is called **fermentation**. Fermentation is used to make drinks such as beer, rum and wine.

Brewing and rum making To make beer, yeast is dissolved in a warm liquid containing the sugar maltose. The maltose comes from germinating barley seeds. The yeast respires, breaking down the maltose and making alcohol and carbon dioxide. The carbon dioxide makes the beer fizzy.

Rum is made in a similar way, but the sugar comes from cane juice or molasses.

Bread making When making bread, flour is mixed with water to make a dough. Flour contains starch and some of this breaks down to the sugar maltose when the flour is moistened. Yeast is added to the dough and breaks down the sugar as it respires.

There is air in the dough, so the yeast respires aerobically at first, until the oxygen is used up. It makes carbon dioxide, and bubbles of this gas get caught in the dough, making it rise. The yeast is killed when the bread is cooked.

Table 6.1 A comparison of aerobic and anaerobic respiration

Aerobic respiration	Anaerobic respiration
uses oxygen	does not use oxygen
no alcohol or lactic acid made	alcohol (in yeast and plants) or lactic acid (animals) is made
large amount of energy released from each molecule of glucose	much less energy released from each molecule of glucose
carbon dioxide made	carbon dioxide is made by yeast and plants, but not by animals

Questions

6.7 What is anaerobic respiration?

6.8 Name on organism which can respire anaerobically.

6.9 What is fermentation?

6.10 Why does bread not taste of alcohol after baking?

Gas exchange

6.8 Gas exchange occurs at special surfaces.

If you look back at the respiration equation in section **6.1**, you will see that two substances are needed. They are glucose and oxygen. The way in which cells obtain glucose is described in Chapters **4** and **5**. Animals get sugar from carbohydrates which they eat. Plants make theirs by photosynthesis.

Oxygen is obtained in a different way. Animals and plants get their oxygen directly from their surroundings.

If you look again at the respiration equation you can see that carbon dioxide is made. This is a waste product and it must be removed from the organism. In organisms, there are special areas where the oxygen enters and carbon dioxide leaves. One gas is entering, and the other leaving, so these are surfaces for **gas exchange**. These surfaces have to be permeable. They have other characteristics which help the process to be quick and efficient.

1 They should be thin to allow gases to diffuse across them quickly.
2 They should be close to an efficient transport system to take gases to and from the exchange surface.
3 They should be kept moist, to stop the cells dying.
4 They should have a large surface area, so that a lot of oxygen can diffuse across at the same time.
5 They should have a good supply of oxygen, brought by breathing movements.

6.9 *Amoeba* exchanges gases through its surface membrane.

Amoeba is a single-celled organism that lives in water. Gas exchange takes place through its cell surface membrane (Figure **6.4**).

Oxygen dissolves in water, so there are usually oxygen molecules in the water around *Amoeba*. Inside the cell, however, oxygen is being used up in respiration. Therefore, there is a higher concentration of oxygen molecules outside the cell, but a lower concentration inside. So oxygen diffuses into the cell, across the cell surface membrane, down a concentration gradient. Carbon dioxide diffuses in the opposite direction.

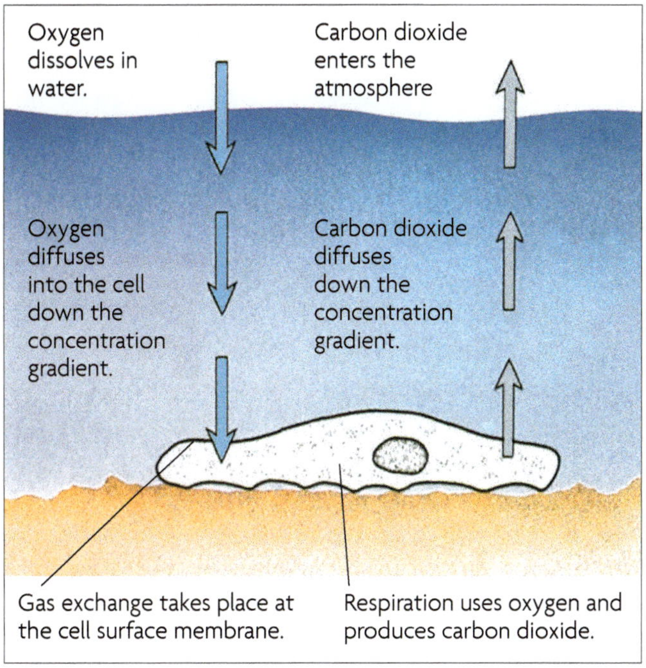

Figure 6.4 Gas exchange in an amoeba.

6.10 Larger organisms need transport systems.

Amoeba is a very small organism made of only one cell. Oxygen can quickly diffuse into the centre of the cell because it does not have far to go.

This method would not work, though, for a large organism like a human. It would take too long for oxygen to diffuse from the air to every cell in your body. Some sort of transport system is needed to get the oxygen all around the body as quickly as possible. In humans this is the blood system.

6.11 Large objects have a small surface area to volume ratio.

Large organisms have another problem with gas exchange. The larger their volume, the more oxygen they need. This oxygen has to get through their gas exchange surface. The amount that can get into their body depends on the area of this surface.

So, the need for oxygen increases with an organism's volume, but the supply of oxygen increases with the surface area available for gas exchange. This is a problem because, as an organism gets larger, its surface area and volume increase by different amounts.

Imagine a cube-shaped organism (Figure **6.5**), where the outer surface is used for gas exchange. A good way to compare the surface area to the volume is to divide the surface area by the volume. This is called the surface area to volume ratio. For the small cube, this is 6. For the medium-sized cube it is 0.6, and for the large cube only 0.06. So, the larger the organism is, the smaller is its surface area to volume ratio.

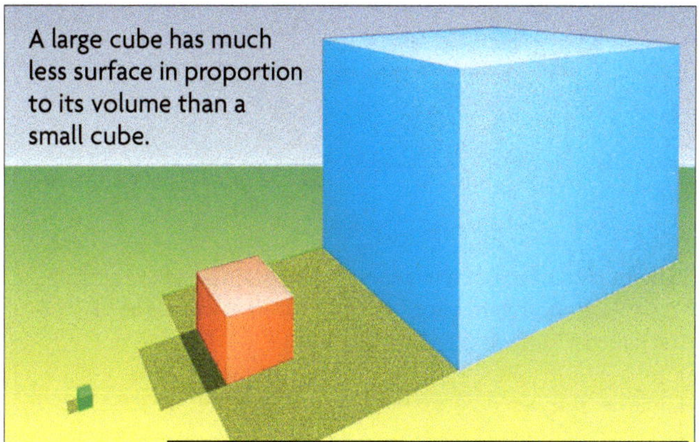

	Length of side / cm	Surface area / cm^2	Volume / cm^3	$\frac{\text{Surface area}}{\text{Volume}}$
Small cube	1	6	1	6.00
Medium cube	10	600	1000	0.60
Large cube	100	60 000	1 000 000	0.06

Figure 6.5 Surface area to volume ratio.

A small organism like *Amoeba*, which has a large surface area compared to its volume, can use its body surface for gas exchange. But a large organism cannot use its ordinary body surface alone, because it is not extensive enough. Large organisms need special surfaces, which provide the large areas required for gas exchange. Specialised parts of their surface are highly divided or folded to provide this extra area for gas exchange (Figures **6.6** and **6.7**, page **96**). Sometimes, these surfaces are tucked inside the body for protection. This also helps to prevent too much water evaporating from organisms which live on land.

6.12 Surfaces for gas exchange are thin and moist.

Gas exchange surfaces contain living cells. These must be kept moist, even though they may be exposed to quite dry air. This is no problem in an aquatic animal, but

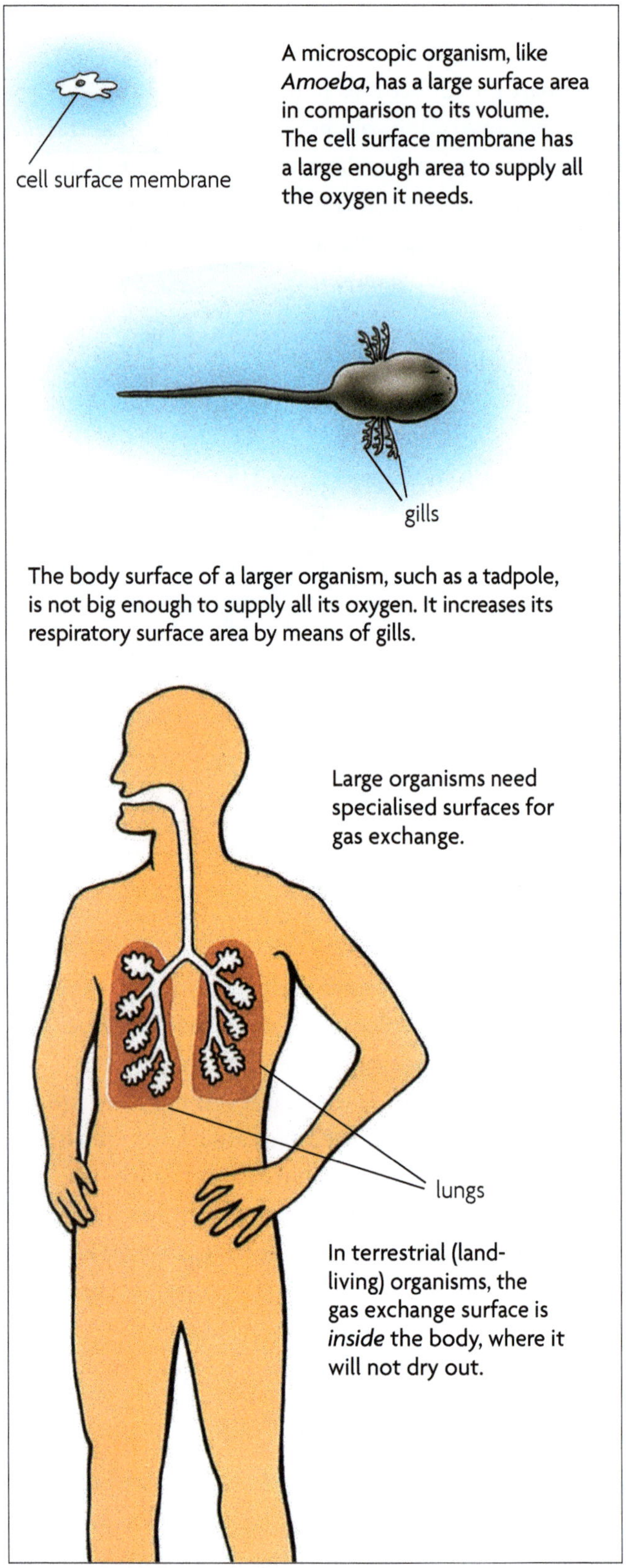

A microscopic organism, like *Amoeba*, has a large surface area in comparison to its volume. The cell surface membrane has a large enough area to supply all the oxygen it needs.
cell surface membrane
gills
The body surface of a larger organism, such as a tadpole, is not big enough to supply all its oxygen. It increases its respiratory surface area by means of gills.
Large organisms need specialised surfaces for gas exchange.
lungs
In terrestrial (land-living) organisms, the gas exchange surface is *inside* the body, where it will not dry out.

Figure 6.6 Large organisms need specialised surfaces for gas exchange.

Figure 6.7 These Mexican axolotls live in water. Their external gills provide a large surface area for gas exchange.

it is a problem that must be solved by every terrestrial organism. Your lungs, for example, contain cells which make a liquid to keep the gas exchange surface wet (Figure **6.12**, page **99**).

A surface for gas exchange should also be as thin as possible. The thinner it is, the more quickly oxygen can diffuse across it. This means that these surfaces are often very delicate.

Questions

6.11 Why is gas exchange necessary in living organisms?

6.12 How does gas exchange take place in *Amoeba*?

6.13 Explain, as briefly as you can, why large organisms need special gas exchange surfaces.

6.14 Why are the gas exchange surfaces of most terrestrial (land living) animals inside their bodies?

6.15 Many animals have a ventilation (breathing) mechanism. How does this help gas exchange?

6.16 Why must gas exchange surfaces be kept moist?

Gas exchange in humans

6.13 The structure of the breathing system.

Figure **6.8** shows the structures which are involved in gas exchange in a human. The most important are the two **lungs**. Each lung is filled with many tiny air spaces called air sacs or **alveoli**. It is here that oxygen diffuses into the blood. Because they are so full of spaces, lungs feel very light and spongy to touch. The lungs are supplied with air through the windpipe or **trachea**.

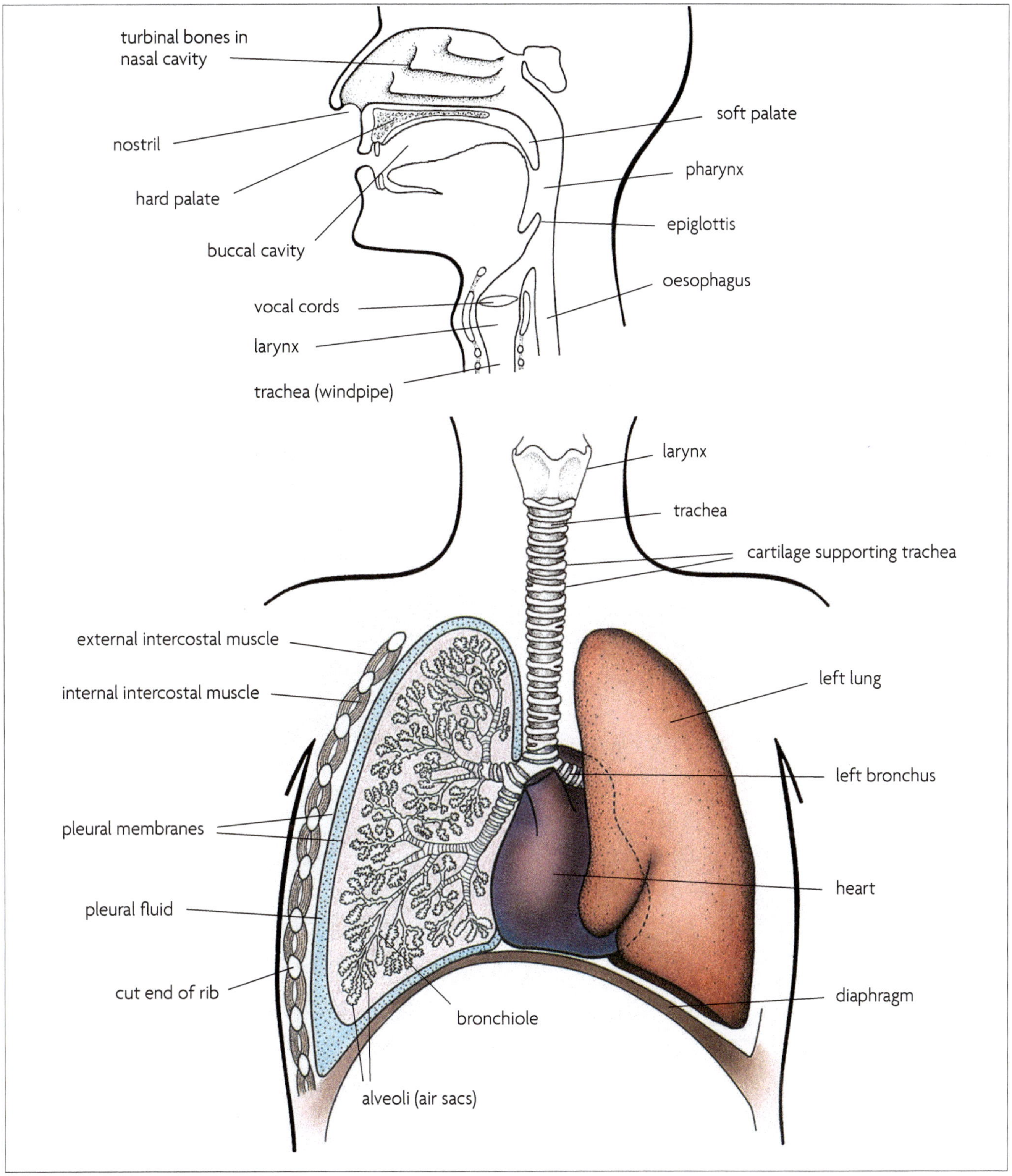

Figure 6.8 The human gas exchange system.

6.14 The path taken by air to the lungs.

The nose and mouth Air can enter the body through either the nose or mouth. The nose and mouth are separated by the **palate** (Figure **6.8**, page **97**), so you can breathe through your nose even when you are eating.

It is better to breathe through your nose, because the structure of the nose allows the air to become warm, moist and filtered before it gets to the lungs. Inside the nose are some thin bones called turbinal bones which are covered with a thin layer of cells. Some of these cells make a liquid containing water and mucus which evaporates into the air in the nose and moistens it (Figure **6.9**).

Other cells have very tiny hair-like projections called **cilia**. The cilia are always moving and bacteria or particles of dust get trapped in them and in the mucus. Cilia are found all along the trachea and bronchi, too. They waft the mucus, containing bacteria and dust, up to the back of the throat, so that it does not block up the lungs. Cilia in the nose also waft mucus into the oesophagus where it is swallowed.

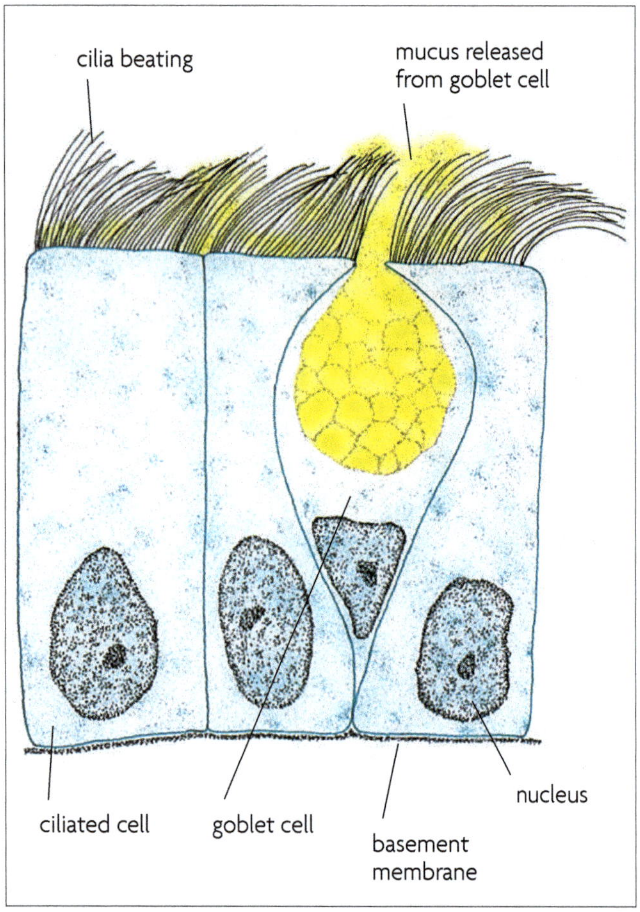

Figure 6.9 Part of the lining of the respiratory passages.

The trachea The air then passes into the windpipe or **trachea**. At the top of the trachea is a piece of cartilage called the **epiglottis**. This closes the trachea and stops food going down the trachea when you swallow. This is a reflex action that happens automatically when a bolus of food touches the soft palate.

Just below the epiglottis is the voice box or **larynx**. This contains the **vocal cords**. The vocal cords can be tightened by muscles so that they make sounds when air passes over them. The trachea has rings of cartilage around it which keep it open.

The bronchi The trachea goes down through the neck and into the thorax. The thorax is the upper part of your body from the neck down to the bottom of the ribs and diaphragm. In the thorax the trachea divides into two. The two branches are called the right and left **bronchi**. One bronchus goes to each lung and then branches out into smaller tubes called **bronchioles**.

The alveoli At the end of each bronchiole are many tiny air sacs or alveoli (Figure **6.10**). This is where gas exchange takes place.

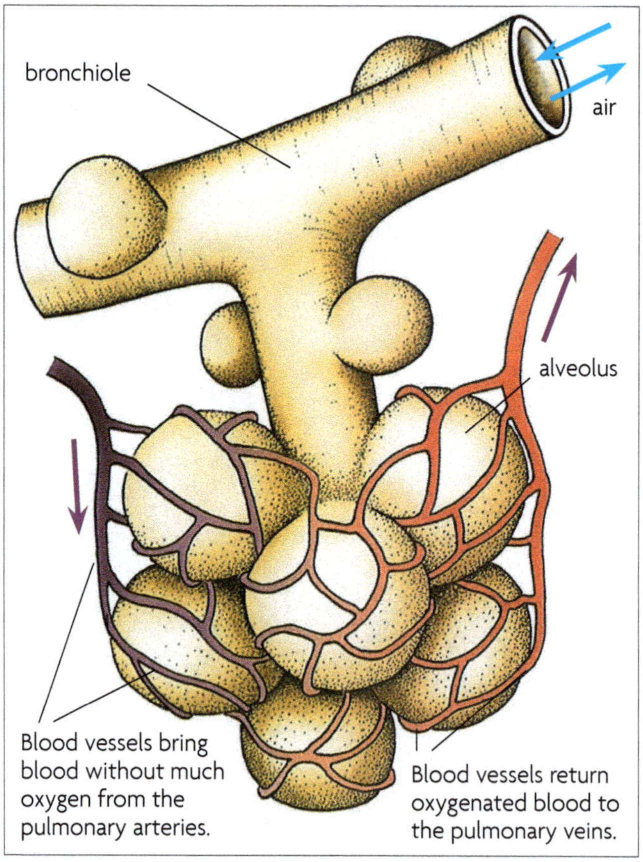

Figure 6.10 Alveoli.

6.15 Alveolar walls are the surface for gas exchange.

The walls of the alveoli are the gas exchange surface. Tiny blood vessels, called capillaries, are closely wrapped around the outside of the alveoli (Figure **6.10**). Oxygen diffuses across the walls of the alveoli into the blood (Figures **6.11** and **6.12**). Carbon dioxide diffuses the other way.

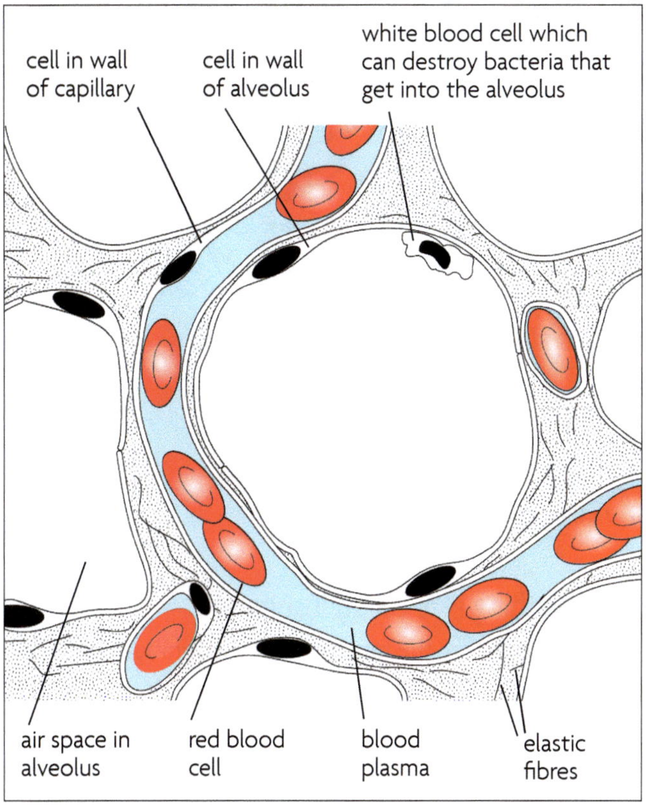

Figure 6.11 Section through part of the lung, magnified.

The walls of the alveoli have several features which make them an efficient gas exchange surface.

- They are very thin. They are only one cell thick. The capillary walls are also only one cell thick. An oxygen molecule only has to diffuse across this small thickness to get into the blood.
- They have an excellent transport system. Blood is constantly pumped to the lungs along the pulmonary artery. This branches into thousands of capillaries which take blood to all parts of the lungs. Carbon dioxide in the blood can diffuse out into the air spaces in the alveoli and oxygen can diffuse into the blood. The blood is then taken back to the heart in the pulmonary vein, ready to be pumped to the rest of the body.

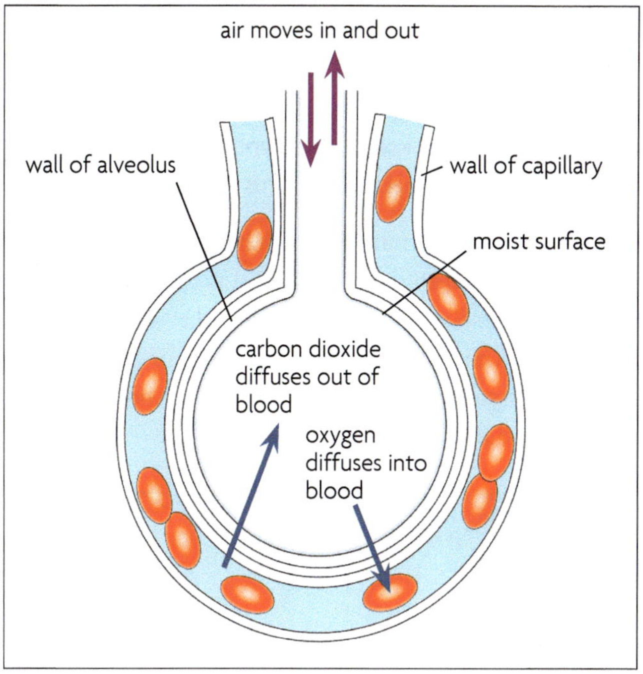

Figure 6.12 Gas exchange in an alveolus.

The way in which the blood carries oxygen and carbon dioxide is explained in section **7.20**.

- They are moist. Special cells in the alveoli secrete a watery liquid. This covers the surface of the cells in the alveoli and prevents them from drying out.
- They have a large surface area. In fact, the surface area is enormous! The total surface area of all the alveoli in your lungs is over 100 m^2.
- They have a good supply of oxygen. Your breathing movements keep your lungs well supplied with oxygen.

Questions

6.17 Why is it better to breathe through your nose than through your mouth?

6.18 What is the function of the cilia in the respiratory passages?

6.19 What is the larynx?

6.20 Where does gas exchange take place in a human?

6.21 How many cells does an oxygen molecule have to pass through, to get from an alveolus into the blood?

6.16 Ribs and diaphragm move during breathing.

To make air move in and out of the lungs, you must keep changing the volume of your thorax. First, you make it large so that air is sucked in. Then you make it smaller again so that air is squeezed out. This is called **breathing**.

There are two sets of muscles which help you to breathe. One set is in between the ribs. This set is called the **intercostal** muscles (Figure **6.13**). The other set is in the **diaphragm**. The diaphragm is a large sheet of muscle and elastic tissue which stretches across your body, underneath the lungs and heart.

Investigation 6.6
Examining lungs

SBA skills

Observation/Recording/Reporting

Examine some ox lungs obtained from a butcher's shop or abattoir.

Questions

1 What colour are the lungs? Why are they this colour?

2 Push them gently with your finger. What do they feel like? Why do they feel like this?

3 What is covering the surface of the lungs? What is its name, and why is it there?

4 Find the two tubes leading down to the lungs. Which one is the oesophagus? Follow it along, and notice that it goes right past the lungs. Where is it going to?

5 The other tube is the trachea. What does it feel like? Why does it feel like this?

6 What is the name of the wide part at the top of the trachea? What is its function?

7 If the lungs have not been badly cut, take a long glass tube (such as a burette tube) and push it down through the trachea. Hold the trachea tightly against it, and blow down it. What happens?

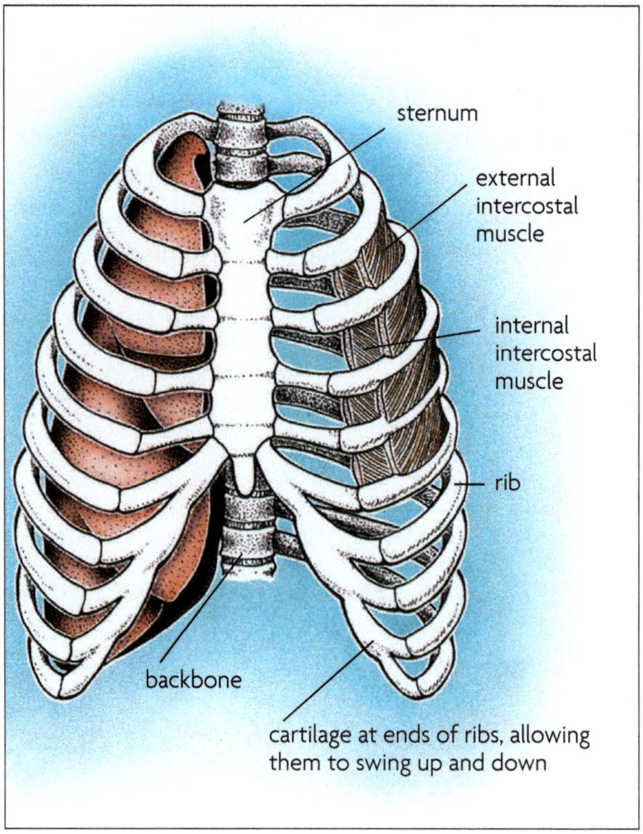

Figure 6.13 The rib cage.

6.17 Breathing in is called inspiration.

When breathing in, the muscles of the diaphragm contract. This pulls the diaphragm downwards, which increases the volume in the thorax (Figure **6.14**). At the same time, the external intercostal muscles contract. This pulls the rib cage upwards and outwards (Figure **6.15**). Together, these movements increase the volume of the thorax.

As the volume of the thorax increases, the pressure inside it falls below atmospheric pressure. Extra space has been made and something must come in to fill it up. Air therefore rushes in along the trachea and bronchi into the lungs.

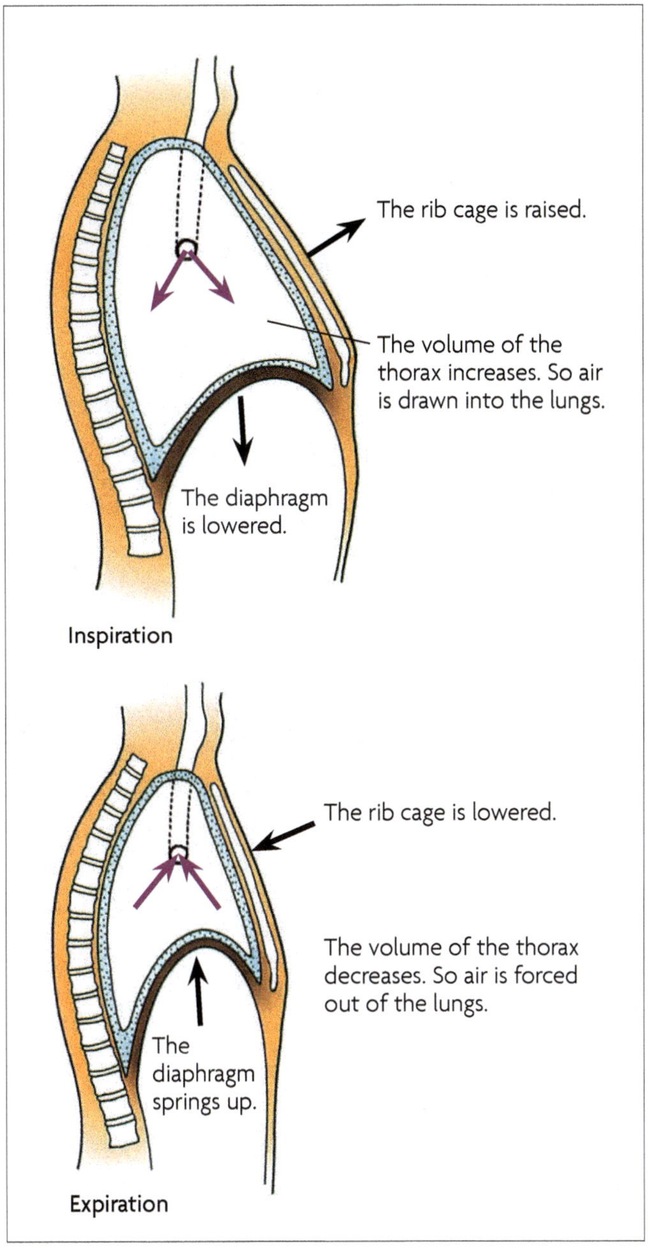

Figure 6.14 How the thorax changes shape during breathing.

6.18 Breathing out is called expiration.

When breathing out, the muscles of the diaphragm relax. The diaphragm springs back up into its domed shape because it is made of elastic tissue. This decreases the volume in the thorax. The external intercostal muscles also relax. The rib cage drops down again into its normal position. This also decreases the volume of the thorax (Figure **6.14**).

As the volume of the thorax decreases, the pressure inside it increases. Air is squeezed out through the trachea into the nose and mouth, and on out of the body.

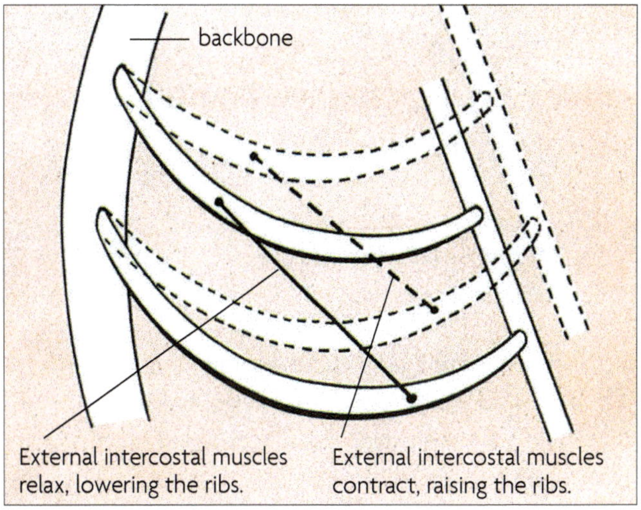

Figure 6.15 How the external intercostal muscles raise the ribs.

6.19 Internal intercostal muscles can force air out.

Usually, you breathe out by relaxing the external intercostal muscles and the muscles of the diaphragm, as explained in section **6.18**.

Sometimes, though, you breathe out more forcefully – when coughing, for example. Then the internal intercostal muscles contract strongly, making the rib cage drop down even further. The muscles of the abdomen wall also contract, helping to squeeze extra air out of the thorax.

6.20 Pleural membranes help with breathing.

Each lung is covered with a thin, smooth membrane. Another similar membrane lines the inside of the rib cage. These are called the **pleural membranes** (Figure **6.8**, page **97**).

The pleural membranes make a liquid called **pleural fluid**. This fills the space between the two membranes. As the lungs inflate and deflate, the pleural fluid helps to lubricate them so that they do not rub against the rib cage too much. Also, as the rib cage expands, the pleural fluid ensures that the lungs adhere closely to the moving ribs.

Sometimes, in a car accident for example, the thorax becomes punctured so that the air gets in between the pleural membranes. If this happens, then the lungs will not work and they collapse.

The pleural membranes also help to keep the two lungs separate from one another. If one lung is punctured in an accident so that is collapses, the other pleural cavity will still be airtight, so the other lung can work normally.

Investigation 6.7
Using a syringe to show how the diaphragm works

SBA skills
Observation/Recording/Reporting
Analysis/Interpretation

1 Use the apparatus in the diagram. Begin with the plunger in as far as it will go. Put your thumb tightly over the hole, and pull the plunger outwards.

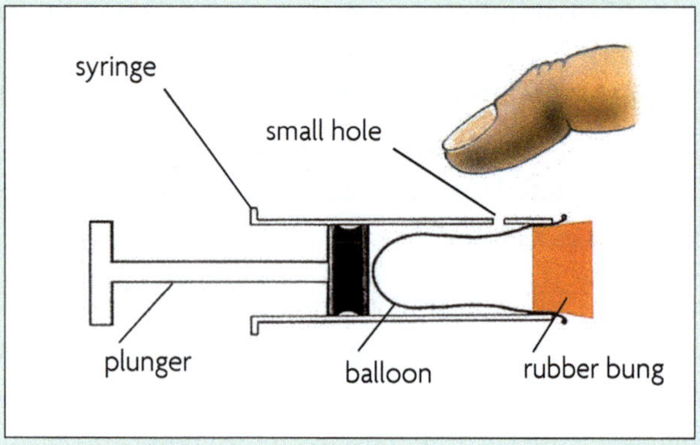

2 Repeat this, but this time do not cover the hole with your thumb.

Questions

1 What does the balloon represent?
2 What does the plunger represent?
3 What happens to the balloon when you cover the hole and pull the plunger? Explain why.
4 What happens to the balloon when you pull the plunger without covering the hole? Explain why.
5 In what ways is this a misleading demonstration of the mechanism of breathing?

Tables **6.2** and **6.3** compare the composition of inspired and expired air, and the differences between respiration, gas exchange and breathing.

Investigation 6.8
Comparing the carbon dioxide content of inspired air and expired air

SBA skills
Observation/Recording/Reporting
Analysis/Interpretation

You can use either limewater or hydrogencarbonate indicator solution for this experiment. Limewater changes from clear to cloudy when carbon dioxide dissolves in it. Hydrogencarbonate indicator solution changes from red to yellow.

1 Set up the apparatus as in the diagram.

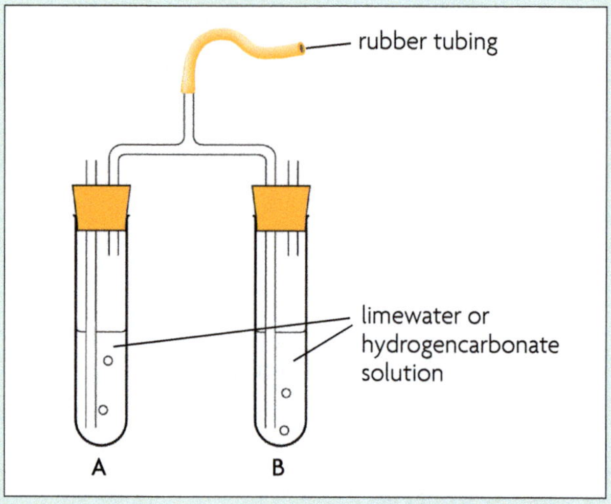

2 Breathe in and out gently through the rubber tubing.

Do not breathe too hard. Keep doing this until the liquid in one of the tubes changes colour.

Questions

1 In which tube did bubbles appear when you breathed out? Explain why.
2 In which tube did bubbles appear when you breathed in? Explain why.
3 What happened to the liquid in tube **A**?
4 What happened to the liquid in tube **B**?
5 What do your results tell you about the relative amounts of carbon dioxide in inspired air and expired air?

Table 6.2 A comparison of inspired and expired air

	Inspired air	Expired air	Reason for difference
Oxygen	21%	16%	oxygen is absorbed across the gas exchange surface, then used by cells in respiration
Carbon dioxide	0.04%	4%	carbon dioxide is made inside respiring cells, and diffuses out across the gas exchange surface
Argon and other noble gases	1%	1%	
Water content (humidity)	variable	always high	gas exchange surfaces are made of living cells, so must be kept moist; some of this moisture evaporates into the air
Temperature	variable	always warm	air is warmed as it passes through the respiratory passages

Table 6.3 The differences between respiration, gas exchange and breathing

Respiration A series of chemical reactions which happen in all living cells, in which food is broken down to release energy, usually by combining it with oxygen.

Gas exchange The exchange of gases across a respiratory surface. For example, oxygen is taken into the body, and carbon dioxide is removed from it. Gas exchange also takes place during photosynthesis and respiration of plants.

Breathing Muscular movements which keep the respiratory surface supplied with oxygen.

6.21 Exercise can create an oxygen debt.

All the cells in your body need oxygen for respiration and all of this oxygen is supplied by the lungs. The oxygen is carried by the blood to every part of the body.

Sometimes, cells may need a lot of oxygen very quickly. Imagine you are running in a race. The muscles in your legs are using up a lot of energy. To produce this energy, the mitochondria in the muscles will be combining oxygen with glucose as fast as they can, to make ATP which will provide the energy for the muscles.

A lot of oxygen is needed to work as hard as this. You breathe deeper and faster to get more oxygen into your blood. Your heart beats faster to get the oxygen to the leg muscles as quickly as possible. Eventually a limit is reached. The heart and lungs cannot supply oxygen to the muscles any faster. But more energy is still needed for the race. How can that extra energy be found?

Extra energy can be produced by anaerobic respiration. Some glucose is broken down without combining it with oxygen.

glucose ⟶ lactic acid + energy

As explained in section **6.6**, this does not release very much energy, but a little extra might make all the difference.

When you stop running, you will have quite a lot of lactic acid in your muscles and your blood. This lactic acid must be broken down by combining it with oxygen. So, even though you do not need the energy any more, you go on breathing hard. You are taking in extra oxygen to break down the lactic acid.

While you were running, you built up an **oxygen debt**. You 'borrowed' some extra energy, without 'paying' for it with oxygen. Now, as the lactic acid is combined with oxygen, you are paying off the debt. Not until all the lactic acid has been used up, does your breathing rate and rate of heart beat return to normal (Figure **6.16**, overleaf).

Figure 6.16 These athletes will pay back their oxygen debts after the race.

Investigation 6.9

Investigating how breathing rate changes with exercise

SBA skills

Observation/Recording/Reporting

Analysis/Interpretation

1. Read through what you are going to do, and then draw a results chart in which you can record your results.
2. Sit quietly for two minutes, to make sure you are completely relaxed.
3. Count how many breaths you take in one minute. Record it in your table.
4. Wait one minute, then count breaths again, and record.
5. Now do some vigorous exercise, such as stepping up and down onto a chair, for exactly two minutes. At the end of this time, sit down. Immediately count your breaths in the next minute, and record.
6. Continue to record your breaths per minute every other minute, until they have returned to near the level before you started to exercise.
7. Draw a graph of your results, putting time on the *x*-axis.

Questions

1. Why does your breathing rate rise so quickly during exercise?
2. Why did your breathing rate not go back to normal as soon as you finished exercising? (Hint: think about anaerobic respiration.)

Questions

6.22 What is breathing?

6.23 Which muscles help in breathing?

6.24 Where are the pleural membranes?

6.25 Give two functions of pleural fluid.

Investigation 6.10

Investigating how recovery time varies with fitness

SBA skills

Observation/Recording/Reporting *Planning/Design*

Analysis/Interpretation

When we exercise vigorously, our breathing rate increases. When the exercise finishes, it takes a while for the breathing rate to return to normal. In general, the time taken for breathing rate to return to normal is less for a fit person than for an unfit person.

1 Decide on a hypothesis you will investigate. The hypothesis should be one sentence, and should describe the relationship you predict will exist between a person's fitness and the time their breathing rate takes to return to normal after exercise.

2 Plan how you will carry out your investigation. Then think through it again, and make improvements to your plan. Once you are fairly happy with it, show your teacher. You must not try to do your experiment until your teacher says that you may begin.

- What apparatus and other materials will you need for your experiment?
- What will you vary in your experiment? How will you vary it?
- What will you try to keep the same in your experiment? How will you do this?
- What will you measure in your experiment? How will you measure it? When will you measure it? Will you do repeat measurements and calculate a mean?
- How will you record your results? (You can sketch out a results chart, ready to fill in.)
- How will you display your results? (You can sketch the axes of the graph you plan to draw.)
- What will your results be if your hypothesis is correct? (You can sketch the shape of the graph you think you will get.)

Once you have approval from your teacher, you should do your experiment. Most scientific researchers find that they want to make changes to their experiment once they actually begin doing it. This is a good thing to do. Make careful notes about all the changes that you make.

Finally, write up your experiment in the usual way, including:

- a heading, and the hypothesis that you tested
- a full description of your method
- a neat and carefully headed table of results, including means if you decided to do repeats
- a neat and carefully headed line graph of your results
- a conclusion, in which you say whether or not your results support your hypothesis
- a discussion, in which you use what you know about aerobic and anaerobic respiration to try to explain the pattern in your results
- an evaluation, in which you explain the main limitations that you feel might have affected the reliability of your data.

The effects of smoking on health

6.22 Tobacco smoke contains irritants and carcinogens.

Everyone knows that smoking damages your health, but still people do it. It is especially worrying that so many young people smoke cigarettes. Young people in the Americas and Caribbean are more likely to smoke cigarettes than young people in any other part of the world (Figure **6.17**, overleaf).

Figure **6.18** (overleaf) shows the main components of tobacco smoke. There are, in fact, many more substances in tobacco smoke, and researchers are still finding out more about them, and the damage that each of them can do to the smoker's health.

One public health concern is that these dangers exist for both smokers and non-smokers. The possible damage is just as real for non-smokers who are in a smokers' environment. They breathe in smoke from burning

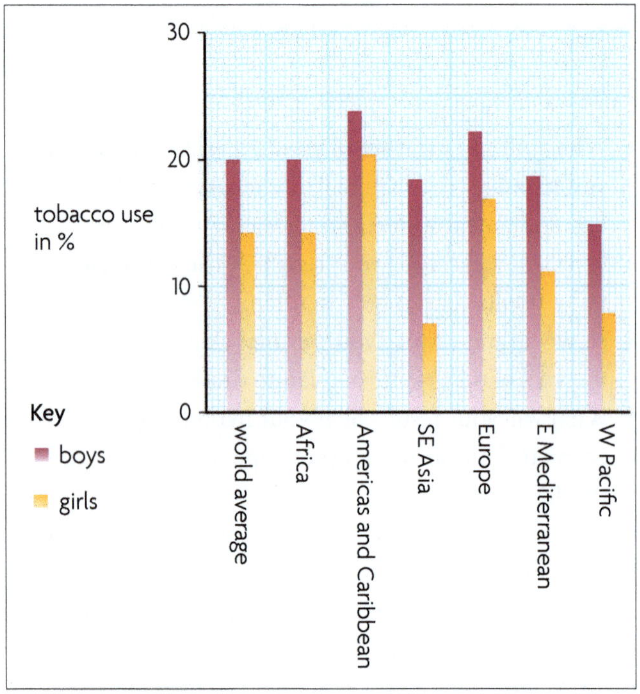

Figure 6.17 Cigarette smoking by 13–14-year-old students in different parts of the world.

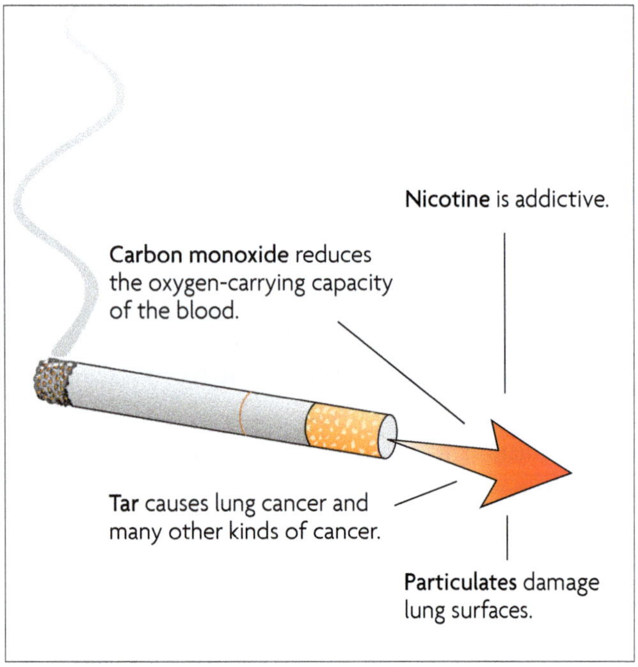

Figure 6.18 Some of the substances in tobacco smoke.

cigarettes, and from smoke exhaled by smokers. This is termed passive smoking. In many countries, smoking is now banned in all public places. It is also very strongly recommended that parents do not smoke anywhere near their children.

6.23 The effects of cigarette smoking on health.

Nicotine is an addictive drug. This is why smokers often find it extremely difficult to give up. Nicotine damages the circulatory system, making blood vessels get narrower. This can increase blood pressure, leading to hypertension. Smokers have a much greater chance of developing heart disease than non-smokers.

Tar contains many different chemicals, some of which are **carcinogens** – that is, they can cause cancer. The chemicals can affect the behaviour of some of the cells in the respiratory passages and the lungs, causing them to divide uncontrollably. The cells divide over and over again, forming a lump or **tumour**. If this tumour is **malignant**, this is **cancer**. Cells may break away from the first tumour and spread to other parts of the body, where new tumours will grow. Almost everyone who gets lung cancer is a smoker, or has lived or worked in an environment where they have been breathing in other people's cigarette smoke. Smoking cigarettes increases the risk of developing many different kinds of cancer.

Carbon monoxide is a poisonous gas which affects the blood. The carbon monoxide diffuses from the lungs into the blood, and combines with haemoglobin inside the red blood cells. This means that less oxygen can be carried. The body cells are therefore deprived of oxygen. This is not good for anyone, but it is especially harmful for a baby growing in its mother's uterus. When the mother smokes, the baby gets all the harmful chemicals in its blood. The carbon monoxide can prevent it from growing properly.

Particulates are little particles of carbon and other materials that are present in cigarette smoke. They get trapped inside the lungs. White blood cells try to remove them, and secrete chemicals that are intended to get rid of these invading particles. Unfortunately, the chemicals secreted by the white blood cells often do serious damage to the lungs themselves. Often, this causes the delicate walls of the alveoli to break down (Figure **6.19**). There is therefore less surface area across which gas exchange can take place. The person is said to have **emphysema**. They will find it difficult to get enough oxygen into their blood. A person with emphysema may not be able to do anything at all active, and eventually they may not even have the energy to walk.

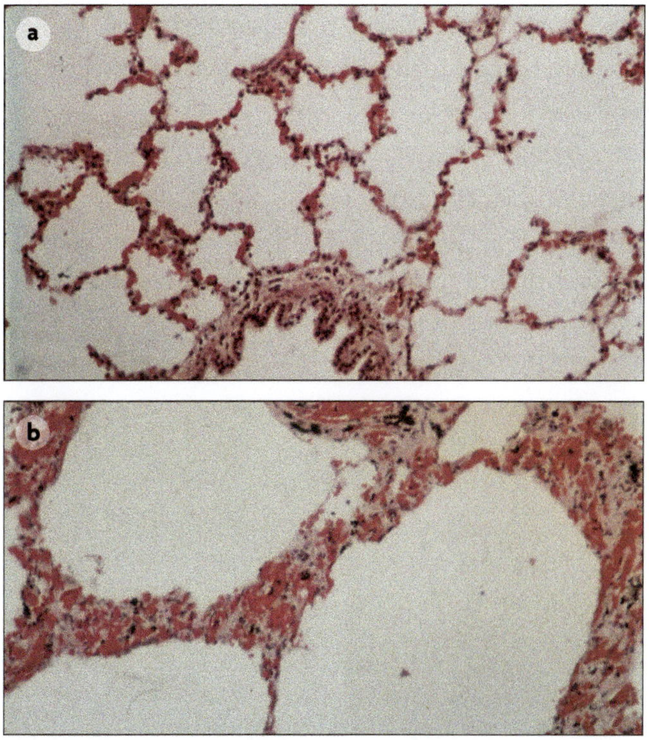

Figure 6.19 **a** Healthy lung tissue with many small air spaces. **b** Lung tissue with emphysema – air spaces are fewer, larger and have thicker walls between.

Several of the chemicals in cigarette smoke harm the cells lining the respiratory passages. You may remember that these clean the air as it passes through, stopping bacteria and dust particles from getting down to the lungs. Figure **6.20** shows how smoking affects this cleaning mechanism.

Gas exchange in fish

6.24 Fish absorb oxygen through gills.

Fish use oxygen which is dissolved in water, just as *Amoeba* does. The surface of their **gills** is the surface for gas exchange.

Figure **6.21** shows the structure of a fish's gills. A fish has several gills. These have spaces in between them called **gill pouches**. The gill pouches open to the outside. In bony fish, the opening is covered by a piece of skin and bone called the **operculum**.

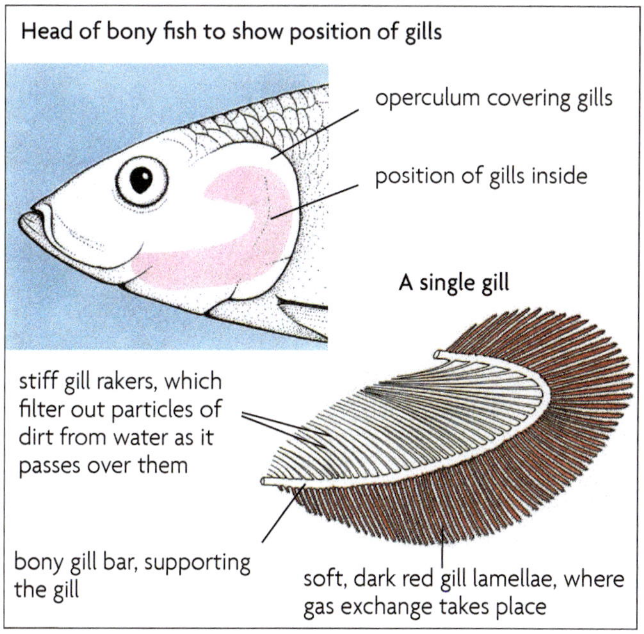

Figure 6.21 The gills of a bony fish.

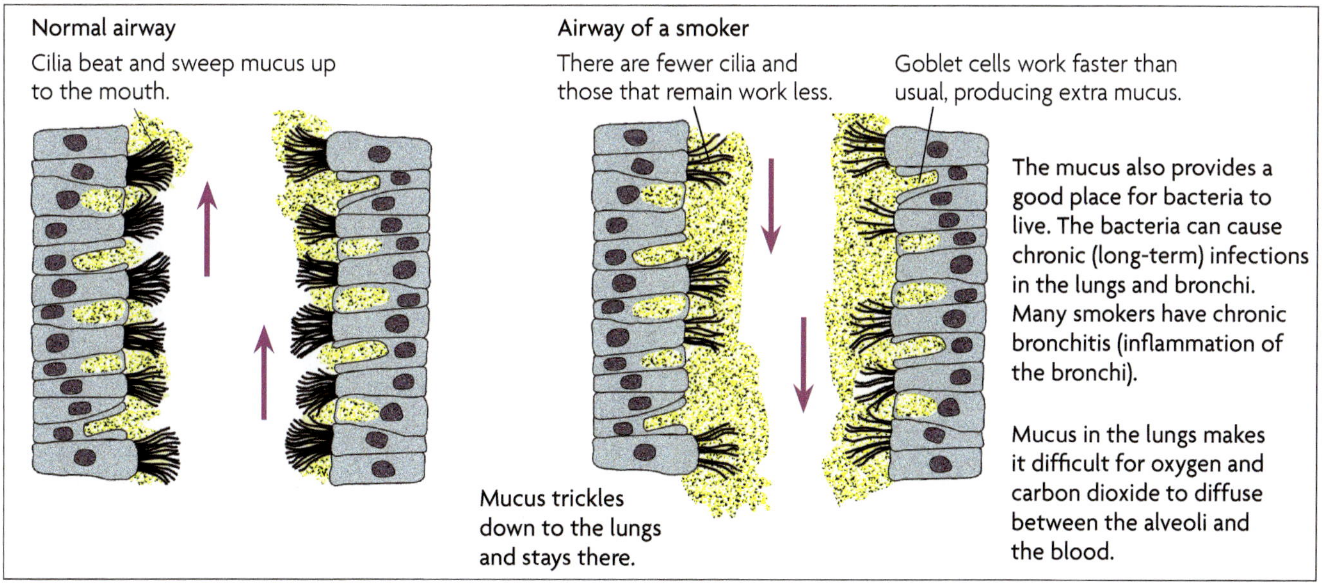

Normal airway
Cilia beat and sweep mucus up to the mouth.
Airway of a smoker
There are fewer cilia and those that remain work less.
Goblet cells work faster than usual, producing extra mucus.
The mucus also provides a good place for bacteria to live. The bacteria can cause chronic (long-term) infections in the lungs and bronchi. Many smokers have chronic bronchitis (inflammation of the bronchi).
Mucus in the lungs makes it difficult for oxygen and carbon dioxide to diffuse between the alveoli and the blood.
Mucus trickles down to the lungs and stays there.

Figure 6.20 How smoking damages the cells lining the bronchi and bronchioles.

Each gill is supported by a piece of bone called a **gill bar**. On the outer surface of the gill bar are many thin, soft flaps of tissue. These are the gill **lamellae** and it is here that gas exchange takes place. Because they are so finely divided, they have a very large surface area. They are thin and have a good blood supply.

On the other side of each gill bar are the **gill rakers**. These trap particles of dirt and stop them from clogging up the lamellae.

6.25 Some fish make breathing movements.

Oxygen is brought to the gills as water flows over them. Water flows in through the mouth, over the gills and out through the gill slits.

Some fish swim fast with their mouths open. This makes water pass over their gills. Some fresh-water fish lie in fast-running water, facing upstream. Fish that cannot swim fast, or that live in still water, have to make breathing movements. These are explained in Figure **6.22**.

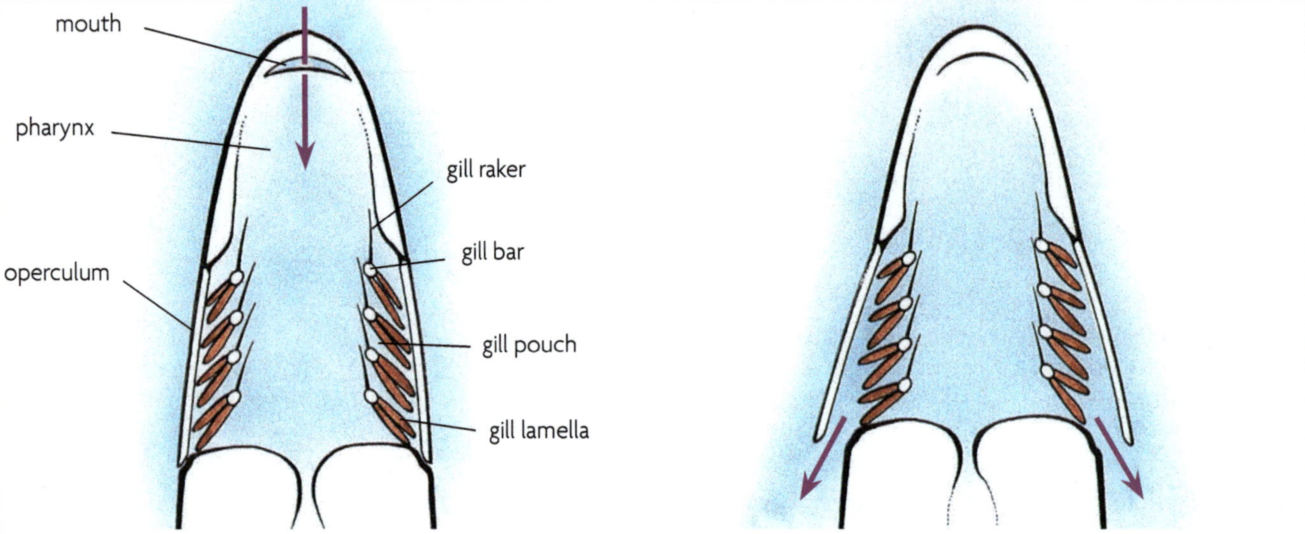

In inspiration, the mouth opens and the floor of the pharynx is pulled down. This increases the space inside the pharynx. Water therefore flows into the pharynx through the mouth.

In expiration, the mouth closes and the floor of the pharynx goes up. This squeezes water out past the gills.

Figure 6.22 Breathing movements in a fish.

Investigation 6.11
Investigating the structure of gills

SBA skills

Observation/Recording/Reporting *Drawing*
Analysis/Interpretation

1. Examine a dead fish. Find the operculum. Using a seeker, lift it up gently. Notice the gills lying underneath. What colour are they? Why are they this colour?
2. Gently push a seeker into the fish's mouth, and out under the operculum. What normally travels along this path?
3. Using scissors, cut the operculum neatly where it joins the body. Using forceps and scissors, cut out one gill, as close to its ends as possible.
4. Put the gill into a small dish containing water. Make a drawing of it. Label the gill bar, gill lamellae and gill rakers. What is the function of each of these?
5. Take the gill out of the water, and lay it on a dry tile. What difference is there between the position of the gill lamellae now, and when they were floating in the water? Can you think of one reason why a fish cannot breathe out of the water?

Gas exchange in flowering plants

6.26 Plants respire and photosynthesise.

Green plants photosynthesise. They make glucose by combining water and carbon dioxide.

$$\text{carbon dioxide} + \text{water} \xrightarrow[\text{chlorophyll}]{\text{sunlight}} \text{glucose} + \text{oxygen}$$

$$6CO_2 + 6H_2O \xrightarrow[\text{chlorophyll}]{\text{sunlight}} C_6H_{12}O_6 + 6O_2$$

This needs energy which comes from sunlight. The energy is trapped by chlorophyll. The glucose which is made contains some of this energy.

When the plant needs energy, it releases it from the glucose in the same way that an animal does – that is, by respiration.

$$\text{glucose} + \text{oxygen} \longrightarrow \text{carbon dioxide} + \text{water} + \text{energy}$$

$$C_6H_{12}O_6 + 6O_2 \longrightarrow 6CO_2 + 6H_2O + \text{energy}$$

At first sight, this reaction looks like photosynthesis going 'backwards'. In some ways it is. The photosynthesis reaction makes glucose and the respiration reaction breaks it down. However, the reactions are really very different. In photosynthesis, the energy that goes into the reaction is light energy which is trapped by the chloroplast. In respiration, the energy which comes out is chemical energy. This process occurs in the mitochondrion.

As in animals, the energy which is released during respiration is used to make ATP. The ATP can then be used whenever the plant needs energy (Figure **6.23**).

6.27 Plants, like animals, need energy.

Plants do not need as much energy as animals. They are not so active, partly because they do not have to move to find their food. However, all living cells need some energy. Plant cells need energy for growth, reproduction, for transporting food material between cells and inside cells and many other reasons. They need energy all the time. So all living plant cells, like animal cells, are always respiring (Figure **6.24**).

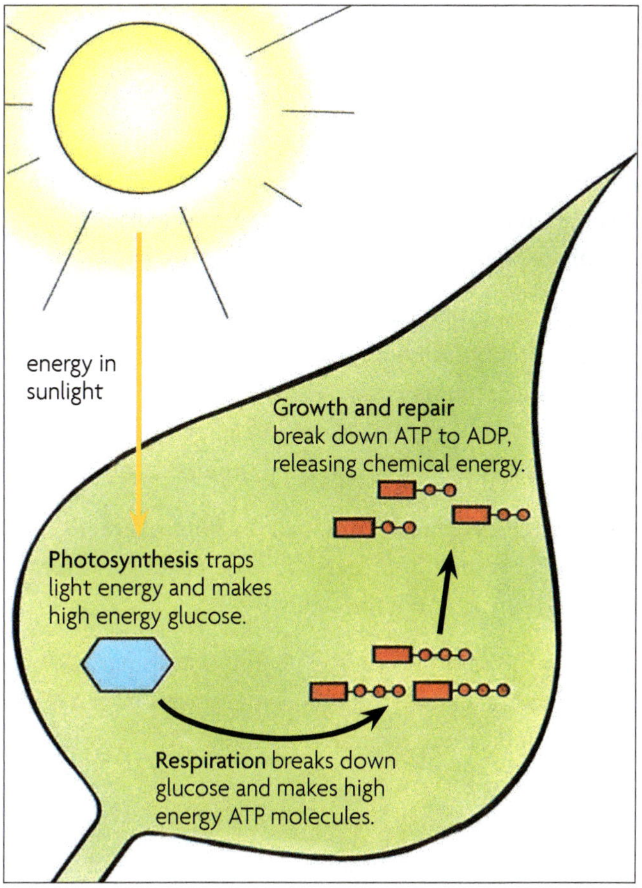

Figure 6.23 How the energy in sunlight is changed to useful energy in a plant.

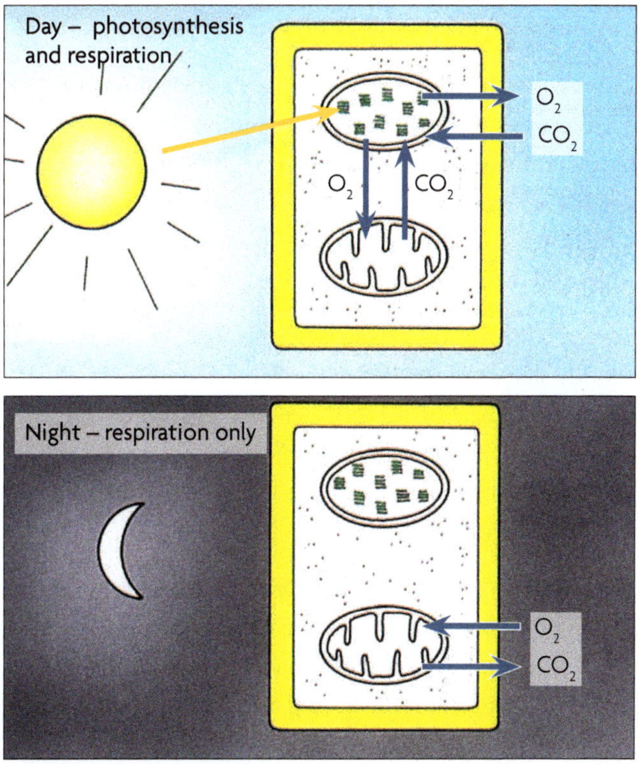

Figure 6.24 Photosynthesis and respiration in plants.

6.28 The balance between photosynthesis and respiration.

Some plant cells, however, also photosynthesise. The cells in a leaf have chloroplasts and they use carbon dioxide and release oxygen during the daytime. At the same time, respiration is happening inside the mitochondria (Figure **6.24**, page **109**).

In the daytime, photosynthesis is going on much faster than respiration. All of the carbon dioxide that the plant makes by respiration is used up by the chloroplasts in photosynthesis. Even this is not enough, and the plant takes in extra carbon dioxide from the air.

Some of the oxygen which is made by photosynthesis is used up for respiration. There is a lot left over, however, and this diffuses out of the cell.

At night, the chloroplasts stop photosynthesising. The mitochondria, however, continue to respire. Oxygen is used up, and carbon dioxide is released.

6.29 Plants get oxygen by diffusion.

Plants have a branching shape, so they have quite a large surface area in comparison to their volume. Therefore, diffusion alone can supply all their cells with as much oxygen as they need for respiration. Diffusion occurs in the leaves, stems and roots of plants.

Leaves In the daytime, leaves are photosynthesising. This supplies plenty of oxygen for respiration. At night, oxygen diffuses into the leaves through the stomata (Figure **4.3**, page **56**). It dissolves in the thin layer of moisture around the cells and diffuses in across their cell walls and membranes.

Stems The stems of herbaceous plants have stomata. Woody stems are covered with a layer of cork cells which make up the bark. These cells will not let air through, so the cork cells are packed loosely in places, to let oxygen diffuse into the cells underneath. These places are called **lenticels** (Figure **6.25**).

Roots Roots get their oxygen from the air spaces in the soil. If the soil is waterlogged for very long, they become short of oxygen. Under these conditions the roots will respire anaerobically, producing alcohol (section **6.6**). This may kill the plant.

Investigation 6.12
The effect of animals and plants on the carbon dioxide concentration in water

SBA skills

Observation/Recording/Reporting
Manipulation/Measurement
Analysis/Interpretation

1 Read through the investigation, then draw a results chart in which you can write your results.

2 Take four clean tubes, and put an equal quantity of hydrogencarbonate indicator into each. Note the colour of the solution, and write it in your results table.

3 Put water snails and water plants into each tube as shown in the diagram.

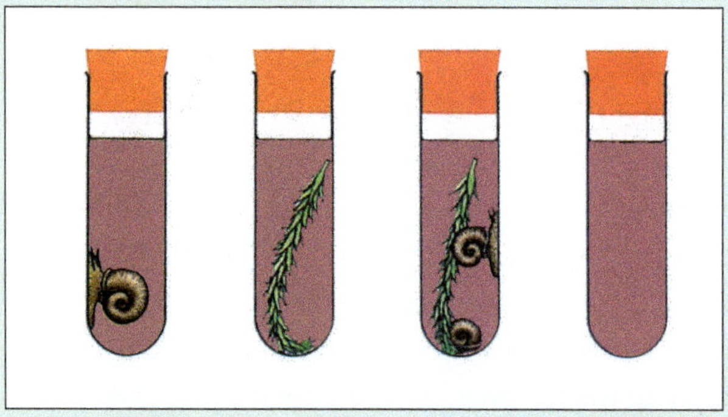

4 Stopper each tube firmly with a rubber bung.

5 Leave all four tubes in a light place for 30–45 minutes.

Questions

1 Remembering that animals and plants respire, and that plants also photosynthesise in the light, explain the differences in the colour of the hydrogencarbonate indicator solution in each tube.

2 What would you expect to happen to the animals and/or the plants in each tube if you left them for a long time?

3 What would happen to the colour of the solution in each of your four tubes if you left them in the dark?

The roots of plants that normally grow in swampy habitats have special adaptations which allow air into the roots. For example, the red mangrove, *Rhizophora mangle*, has stilt roots which have many lenticels (section 17.37 and Figure 17.20).

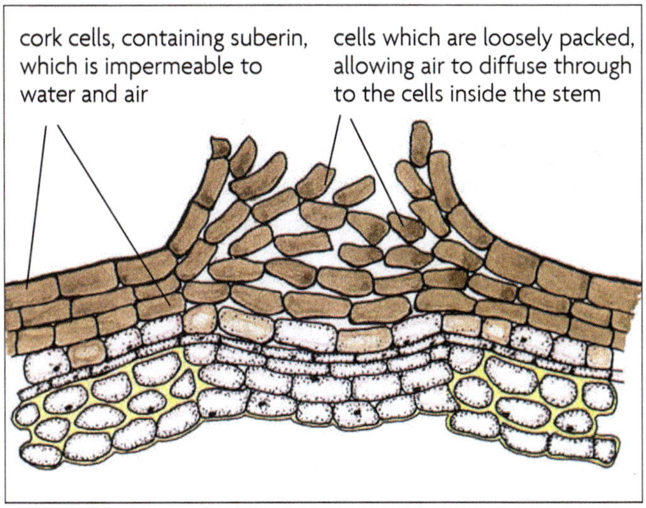

Figure 6.25 Section through a lenticel in a woody stem. Lenticels are also present in some roots.

Table **6.4** compares gas exchange in living organisms.

Questions

6.26 Why is respiration not really like 'photosynthesis backwards'?

6.27 Why do plants need energy?

6.28 In which parts of a plant cell does **(a)** respiration, and **(b)** photosynthesis happen?

6.29 At what times of day do plant cells respire?

6.30 At what times of day do plant cells photosynthesise?

6.31 Why do plants not need a transport system to carry oxygen around their bodies?

Table 6.4 Comparison of gas exchange in living organisms

Organism	Gas exchange surface	How it is kept moist	How it is supplied with oxygen	Transport system in the organism	How its surface area is increased
Amoeba	cell surface membrane	surrounded by water	water current, diffusion	diffusion only	not necessary as the organism is small
mammal	alveoli in lungs	cells in alveoli secrete fluid	breathing movements by diaphragm muscles and intercostal muscles	blood containing haemoglobin	many alveoli create a very large surface area
fish	lamellae of gills	surrounded by water	water currents and breathing movements	blood containing haemoglobin	each gill divided into many thin lamellae, which are then further subdivided
flowering plant	surface of cells inside the leaf, stem and roots	cell walls in leaf soak up water brought by xylem vessels	by diffusion through stomata (in leaves) and air spaces	no transport system for gases – rely on diffusion only	leaf is very thin and has a large surface area compared to its volume; roots are thin and branching

Key ideas

- Respiration is a series of metabolic reactions that takes place in every living cell. The purpose of respiration is to release energy from glucose, so that the cell can make use of the energy.
- Some of the energy released by respiration is used to make ATP, the energy currency of the cell. Some of it is released as heat.
- In aerobic respiration, the glucose is combined with oxygen, forming carbon dioxide and water. These reactions take place inside mitochondria.
- In anaerobic respiration, the glucose is broken down without being combined with oxygen. In plants and fungi, this produces alcohol and carbon dioxide. In animals (including humans) it produces lactic acid.
- Muscles respire aerobically when they are working so fast that they cannot be supplied with oxygen quickly enough. The lactic acid that is made is transported to the liver, and later is broken down by combining it with oxygen. This extra oxygen is breathed in after the exercise has stopped, and it is known as the oxygen debt.
- At gas exchange surfaces, oxygen diffuses into the body and carbon dioxide diffuses out. In an amoeba, the gas exchange surface is its cell surface membrane. In a human, it is the alveoli in the lungs. In a plant, it is its leaves. In a fish, it is the lamellae of its gills.
- All gas exchange surfaces need to be thin, have a large surface area, be kept moist, and have a good supply of oxygen. In larger animals, a transport system is needed to carry away the carbon dioxide and bring oxygen.
- The air we breathe in travels down the trachea and bronchi, through the bronchioles and into the alveoli. Some of these tubes are lined with goblet cells which make mucus, and ciliated cells. The mucus traps dirt, bacteria and other particles and the cilia sweep the mucus up and away from the lungs.
- Air is drawn into the lungs by the contraction of the external intercostal muscles and the muscles in the diaphragm. These muscle contractions increase the volume of the thorax, which decreases the pressure. Air flows down the pressure gradient and into the lungs.
- Cigarette smoke contains addictive nicotine, several different carcinogenic chemicals, carbon monoxide and particulates, all of which do significant harm to a person's health.

End-of-chapter questions

1 Match each of these words with its definition listed below: operculum, stoma, alveolus, lenticel, lamellae, fermentation, mitochondrion, cilia.

  a A type of anaerobic respiration which makes alcohol and carbon dioxide.
  b A bony covering over a fish's gills.
  c An air sac inside a mammal's lungs.
  d Small hair-like projections from a cell.
  e A small hole on the surface of a leaf, through which gases diffuse.
  f The part of a cell where glucose is oxidised.
  g Finely divided parts of a fish's gills.
  h Part of a woody stem through which gas exchange takes place.

2 Which of these descriptions applies to aerobic respiration, which to anaerobic respiration, and which to both?

  a lactic acid or alcohol made
  b carbon dioxide made
  c energy released from glucose
  d heat produced
  e ATP made
  f glucose oxidised

3 a What is meant by a gas exchange surface?
  b Describe, with the aid of diagrams, how the gas exchange surfaces of (i) a fish, and (ii) a human are kept supplied with oxygen.
  c List three properties which these two types of gas exchange surface have in common.

4 Describe an investigation you could do to see if germinating seeds give off carbon dioxide. Include a labelled diagram of your apparatus, a control, and explain what you think your results would be.

5 Construct a table to compare the processes of respiration and photosynthesis in a green plant.

6 Describe two processes in which anaerobic respiration is of commercial value to humans.

7 Explain the term 'oxygen debt'. How is such a debt repaid?

8 Previously, aircraft designated smoking and non-smoking sections in their seating plans. Now, the trend is not to allow smoking anywhere on the aircraft. Discuss the possible reasons for this change in policy.

7 Transport and storage

In this chapter, you will find out:

- why large organisms need transport systems
- which substances are transported in animals and plants
- about the structure and function of the human circulatory system, including the heart and blood vessels
- about the structure and functions of blood
- about the structure and functions of xylem vessels and phloem tubes in plants
- about transpiration and how to measure its rate, and the factors that affect it
- how roots take up water and mineral ions
- how, why and where animals and plants store nutrients.

7.1 Large organisms need transport systems.

Living organisms need to supply all their cells with food, water and oxygen. In section **6.9**, we saw that it is relatively easy for small organisms to get these requirements by relying on diffusion. Small organisms like *Amoeba* have a large surface area to volume ratio, and gases can easily diffuse in and out through their cell surface membrane.

Large organisms such as ourselves, however, have a small surface area to volume ratio. Large organisms need a transport system to get these materials to all cells.

In many animals, like the vertebrates, this transport system is a blood system made up of a network of tube-like vessels. Larger plants, like the ferns, the pines and the flowering plants, also have a system of interconnecting vessels. These systems are sometimes called a **vascular system**. They all need to have some mechanism to push fluid along the tubes. For example, in the vertebrates, there is a pump, the heart (section **7.4**). In plants, the force of the transpiration stream pulls water through the water vessels to all parts of the plant (section **7.39**).

Transport in mammals

7.2 Mammals have double circulatory systems.

The main transport system of a mammal is its blood system, also known as the **circulatory system**. It is a network of tubes, called **blood vessels**. A pump, the **heart**, keeps blood flowing through the vessels.

Figure **7.1** illustrates the general layout of the human blood system. The arrows show the direction of blood flow. If you follow the arrows, beginning at the lungs, you can see that blood flows into the left-hand side of the heart, and then out to the rest of the body. It is brought back to the right-hand side of the heart, before going back to the lungs again.

This is called a **double circulatory system**, because the blood travels through the heart twice on one complete journey around the body.

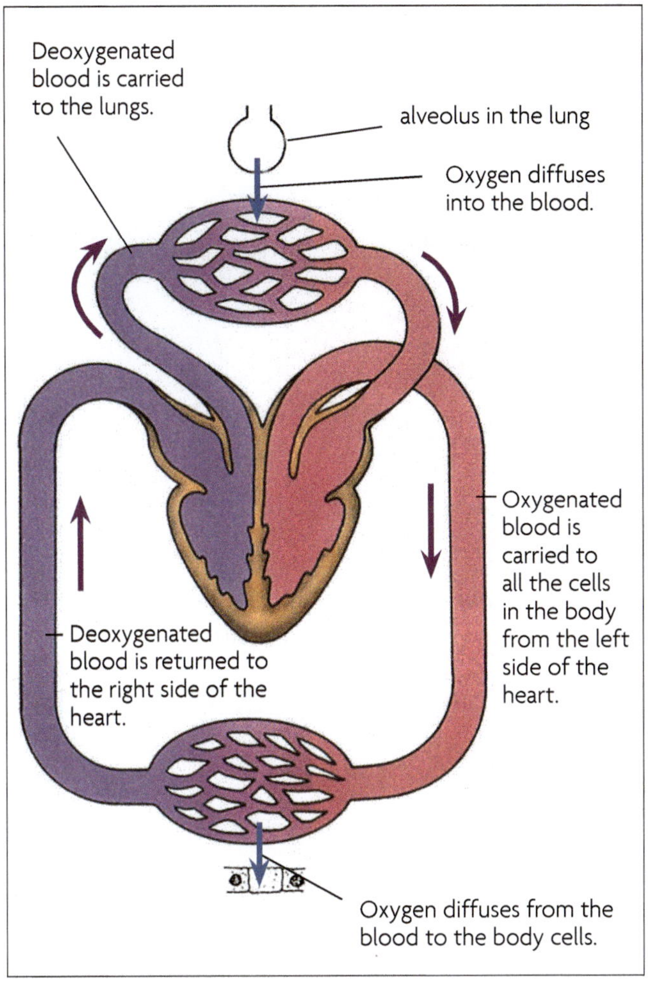

Deoxygenated blood is carried to the lungs.
alveolus in the lung
Oxygen diffuses into the blood.
Oxygenated blood is carried to all the cells in the body from the left side of the heart.
Deoxygenated blood is returned to the right side of the heart.
Oxygen diffuses from the blood to the body cells.

Figure 7.1 The general layout of the circulatory system of a human, as seen from the front.

7.3 Oxygenated and deoxygenated blood.

The blood in the left-hand side of the heart has come from the lungs. It contains oxygen, which was picked up by the capillaries surrounding the alveoli. It is called **oxygenated blood**.

This oxygenated blood is then sent around the body. Some of the oxygen in it is taken up by the body cells, which need oxygen for respiration. When this happens the blood becomes **deoxygenated**. The deoxygenated blood is brought back to the right-hand side of the heart. It then goes to the lungs, where it becomes oxygenated once more.

Questions

7.1 Why do large organisms need transport systems?

7.2 What is a double circulatory system?

7.3 What is oxygenated blood?

7.4 Where does blood become oxygenated?

7.5 Which side of the heart contains oxygenated blood?

The heart

7.4 The structure of the heart.

The function of the heart is to pump blood around the body. It is made of a special type of muscle called **cardiac muscle** (Figure **9.12**, page **166**). This muscle contracts and relaxes regularly, throughout life.

Figure 7.2 (overleaf) is a section through a heart. It is divided into four chambers. The two upper chambers are called **atria**. The two lower chambers are **ventricles**. The chambers on the left-hand side are completely separated from the ones on the right-hand side by a **septum**.

If you look at Figure 7.2, you will see that blood flows into the heart at the top, into the atria. Both of the atria receive blood. The left atrium receives blood from the **pulmonary veins**, which come from the lungs. The right atrium receives blood from the rest of the body, arriving through the **venae cavae** (singular: vena cava).

From the atria, the blood flows into the ventricles. The ventricles then pump it out of the heart. They do this by contracting the muscle in their walls. The strong cardiac muscle contracts with considerable force, squeezing inwards on the blood inside the heart and pushing it out. The blood in the left ventricle is pumped into the **aorta**, which takes the blood around the body. The right ventricle pumps blood into the **pulmonary artery**, which takes it to the lungs.

The function (job) of the ventricles is quite different from the function of the atria. The atria simply receive blood, either from the lungs or the body, and supply it to the ventricles. The ventricles pump blood out of the heart and all round the body. To help them to do this, the ventricles have much thicker, more muscular walls than the atria.

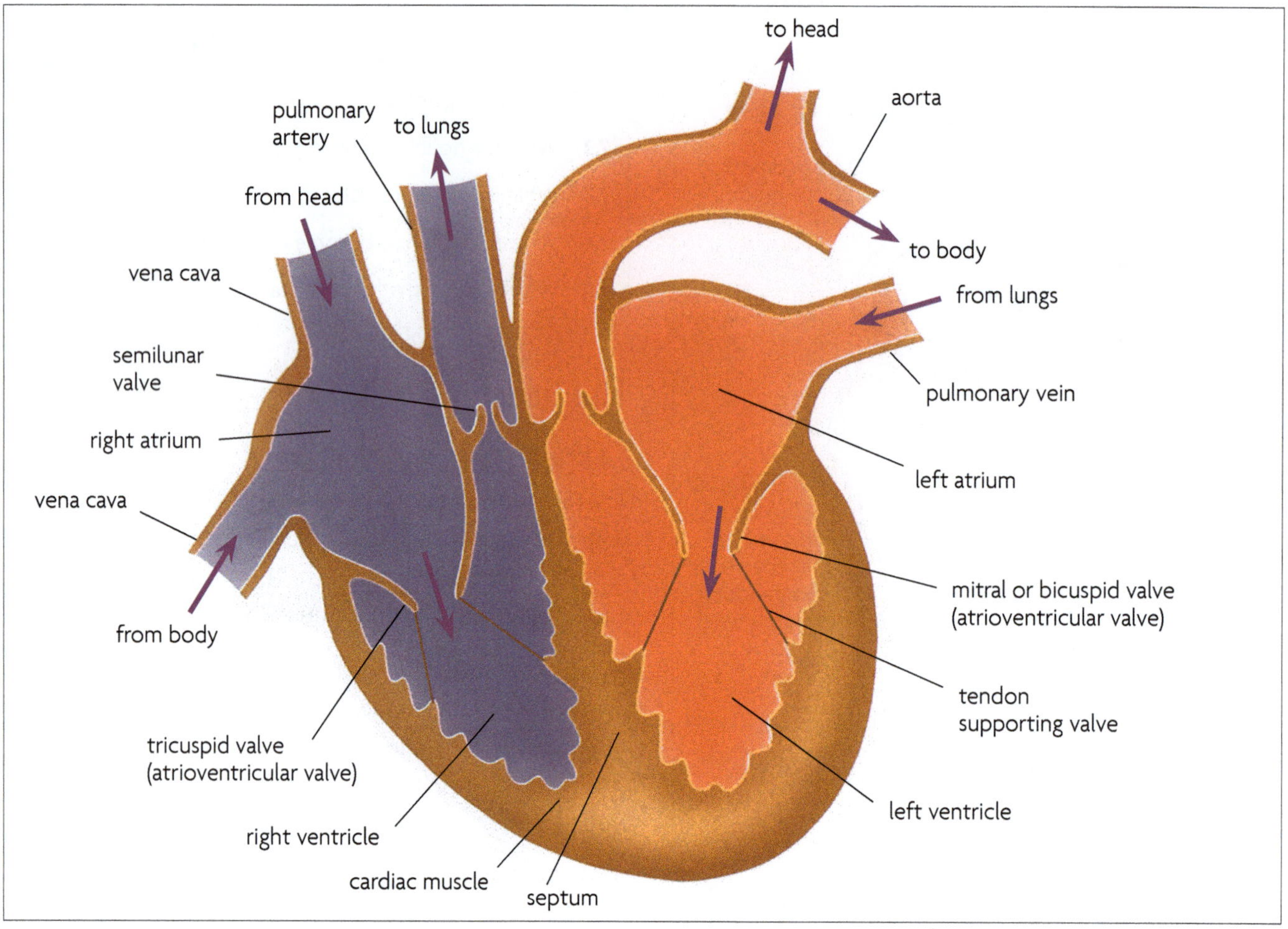

Figure 7.2 Vertical section through a human heart.

There is also a difference in the thickness of the walls of the right and left ventricles. The right ventricle pumps blood to the lungs, which are very close to the heart. The left ventricle, however, pumps blood all around the body. The left ventricle has an especially thick wall of muscle to enable it to do this.

7.5 Coronary arteries supply heart muscle.

In Figure 7.3, you can see that there are blood vessels on the outside of the heart. They are called the **coronary arteries**. These vessels supply blood to the heart muscles.

It may seem odd that this is necessary, when the heart is full of blood. However, the muscles of the heart are so thick that the food and oxygen in the blood inside the heart would not be able to diffuse to all the muscles quickly enough. The heart muscle needs a constant supply of nutrients and oxygen, so that it can keep contracting and relaxing. The coronary arteries supply this.

If a coronary artery gets blocked, for example by a blood clot, the cardiac muscles run short of oxygen. They cannot respire, so they cannot obtain energy to allow

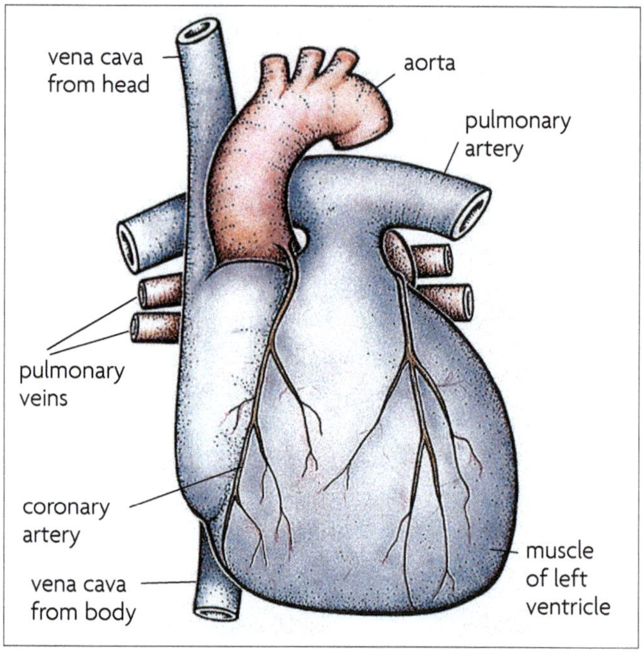

Figure 7.3 External appearance of a human heart.

them to contract. The heart therefore stops beating. This is called a **heart attack** or **cardiac arrest**.

7.6 The pacemaker triggers the heart beat.

The heart beats as the cardiac muscles in its walls contract and relax. When they contract, the heart becomes smaller, squeezing blood out. This is called **systole**. When they relax, the heart becomes larger, allowing the blood to flow into the atria and ventricles. This is called **diastole**. Figure 7.4 illustrates this.

The heart beat begins in the wall of the right atrium, then spreads throughout the heart. A group of specialised muscle cells begins and maintains the heart beat. The cells are together known as the **sinoatrial node** or **pacemaker**. In humans, if the pacemaker becomes defective, it may sometimes be replaced by an artificial one. The X-ray photograph in Figure 7.5 shows an artificial pacemaker in position next to someone's heart. Section 11.17 explains how the rate of the heart beat is regulated.

7.7 Blood flows one way through heart valves.

There is a valve between the left atrium and the left ventricle, and another between the right atrium and ventricle. These are called **atrioventricular valves** (Figure 7.4).

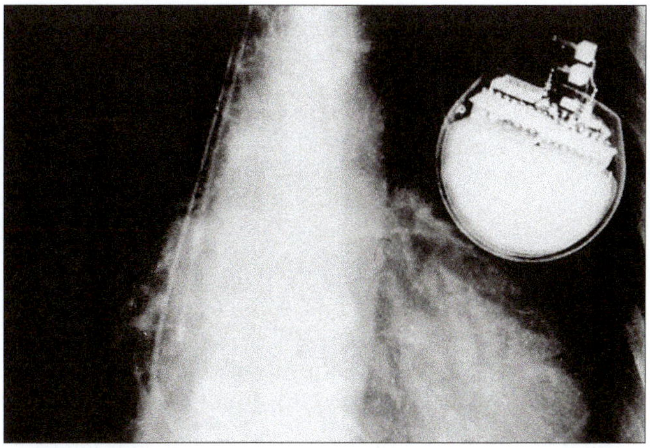

Figure 7.5 This X-ray photograph shows an artificial pacemaker in position next to someone's heart.

The valve on the left-hand side of the heart is made of two parts and is called the **bicuspid valve**, or the **mitral valve**. The valve on the right-hand side has three parts, and is called the **tricuspid valve**.

The function of these valves is to stop blood flowing from the ventricles back to the atria. This is important, so that when the ventricles contract, the blood is pushed up into the arteries, not back into the atria. As the ventricles contract, the pressure of the blood pushes the valves upwards. The **tendons** attached to them stop them from going up too far.

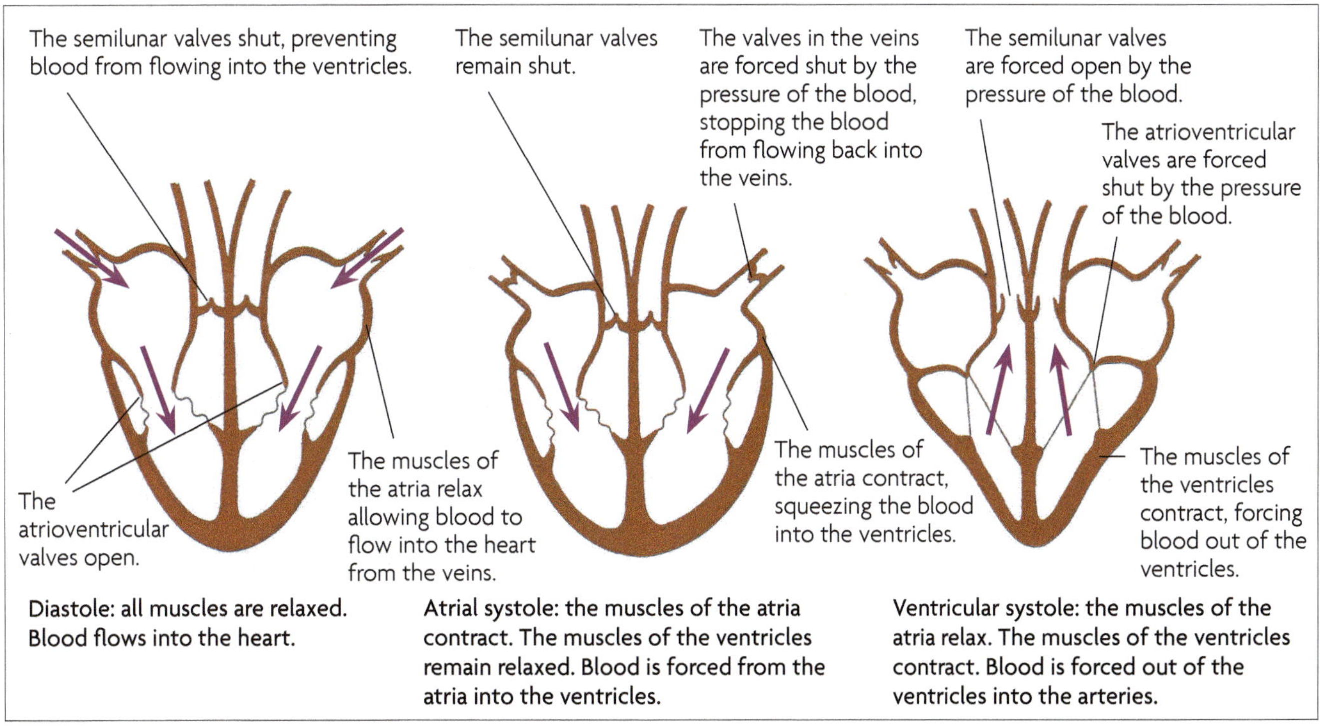
The semilunar valves shut, preventing blood from flowing into the ventricles.
The atrioventricular valves open.
The muscles of the atria relax allowing blood to flow into the heart from the veins.
Diastole: all muscles are relaxed. Blood flows into the heart.
The semilunar valves remain shut.
The valves in the veins are forced shut by the pressure of the blood, stopping the blood from flowing back into the veins.
The muscles of the atria contract, squeezing the blood into the ventricles.
Atrial systole: the muscles of the atria contract. The muscles of the ventricles remain relaxed. Blood is forced from the atria into the ventricles.
The semilunar valves are forced open by the pressure of the blood.
The atrioventricular valves are forced shut by the pressure of the blood.
The muscles of the ventricles contract, forcing blood out of the ventricles.
Ventricular systole: the muscles of the atria relax. The muscles of the ventricles contract. Blood is forced out of the ventricles into the arteries.

Figure 7.4 How the hearts pumps blood.

Investigation 7.1
To find the effect of exercise on the rate of heart beat

SBA skills

Observation/Recording/Reporting

Analysis/Interpretation

The best way to measure the rate of your heart beat is to take your pulse. Use the first two fingers of your right hand and rest them on the inside of your left wrist. Feel for the tendon near the outside of your wrist. If you rest your fingers lightly just over this tendon, you can feel the artery in your wrist pulsing as your heart pumps blood through it.

Perform the experiment as explained in Investigation **6.9**, this time counting the number of pulse beats per minute.

Questions

1 Why does your heart beat faster during exercise?

2 Why does the heart not return to its normal rate of beating as soon as you finish exercising?

Questions

7.6 What kind of muscle is found in the heart?

7.7 Which parts of the heart receive blood from **(a)** the lungs, and **(b)** the body?

7.8 Which parts of the heart pump blood into **(a)** the pulmonary artery, and **(b)** the aorta?

7.9 Why do the ventricles have thicker walls than the atria?

7.10 Why does the left ventricle have a thicker wall than the right ventricle?

7.11 What is the function of the coronary artery?

7.12 What is **(a)** systole, and **(b)** diastole?

7.13 Where are the atrioventricular valves?

7.14 What is their function?

7.15 Why are these valves supported by tendons?

7.16 What is the sinoatrial node?

Blood vessels

7.8 There are three kinds of blood vessels.

There are three main kinds of blood vessels: **arteries**, **capillaries** and **veins** (Figure **7.6**). Arteries carry blood away from the heart. They divide again and again, and eventually form very tiny vessels called capillaries. The capillaries gradually join up with one another to form large vessels called veins. Veins carry blood towards the heart. These vessels are compared in Table **7.1**, page **120**.

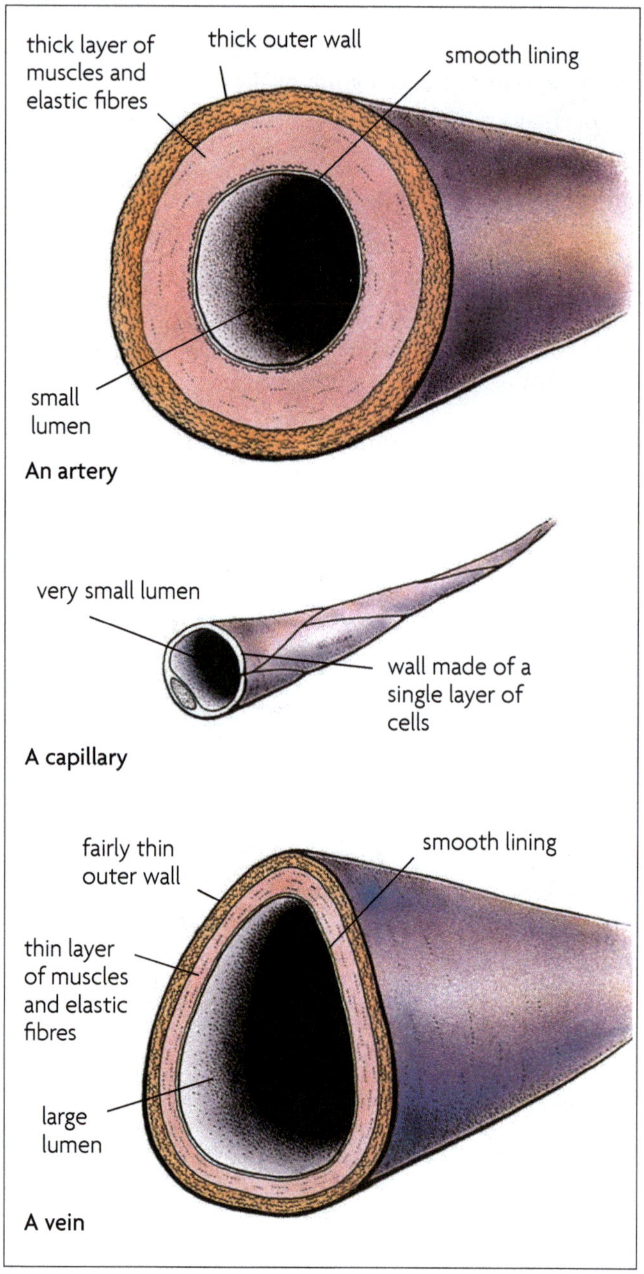

Figure 7.6 Sections through the three types of blood vessels.

7.9 Arteries have thick elastic walls.

When blood flows out of the heart, it enters the arteries. The blood is then at very high pressure, because it has been forced out of the heart by the contraction of the muscular ventricles. Arteries therefore need very strong walls to withstand the high pressure of the blood flowing through them.

The blood does not flow smoothly through the arteries. It pulses through, as the ventricles contract and relax. The arteries have elastic tissue in their walls which can stretch and recoil with the force of the blood. This helps to make the flow of blood smoother. You can feel your arteries stretch and recoil when you feel your pulse in your wrist.

The blood pressure in the arteries of your arm can be measured using a **sphygmomanometer** (Figure 7.7).

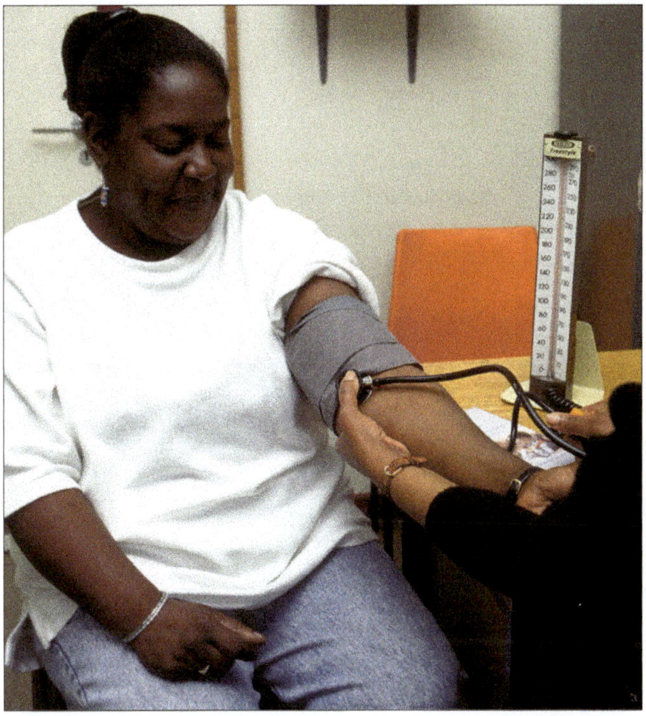

Figure 7.7 A sphygmomanometer being used to measure blood pressure.

7.10 Capillaries are very narrow, with thin walls.

The arteries gradually divide to form smaller and smaller vessels (Figures **7.8** and **7.9**). These are the capillaries. The capillaries are very small and penetrate to every part of the body. No cell is very far away from a capillary.

The function of the capillaries is to take nutrients, oxygen and other materials to all the cells in the body, and to take away their waste materials. To do this, their walls must be very thin so that substances can get in and out of them easily. The walls of the smallest capillaries are only one cell thick (Figure **7.6**).

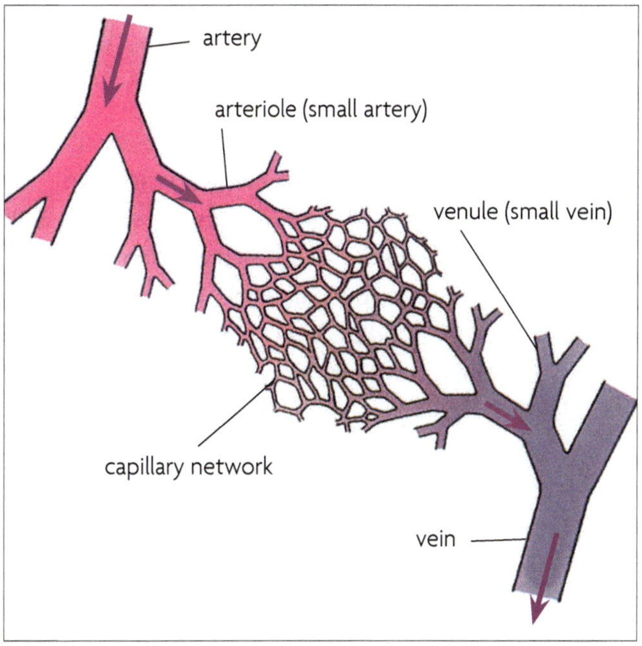

Figure 7.8 A capillary network.

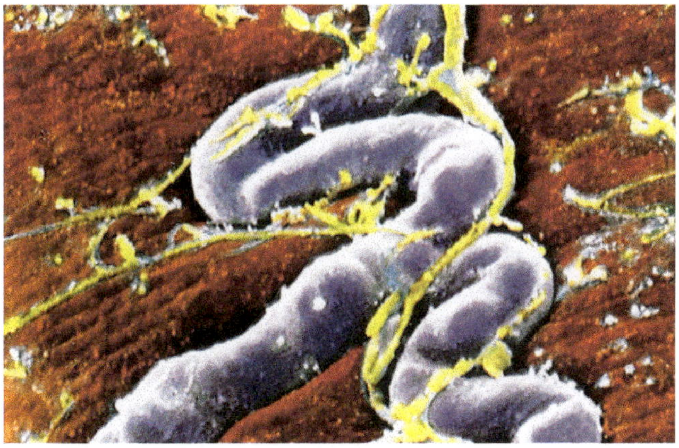

Figure 7.9 A capillary, shown in blue, snakes its way through muscle tissue (×600).

7.11 Veins have one-way valves.

The capillaries gradually join up again to form veins. By the time the blood gets to the veins, it is at a much lower pressure than it was in the arteries. The blood flows more slowly and smoothly now. There is no need for veins to have such thick, strong, elastic walls.

If the veins were narrow, this would slow down the blood even more. To help keep the blood moving easily through them, the space inside the veins, called the **lumen**, is much wider than the lumen of the arteries.

Veins have valves in them to stop the blood flowing backwards (Figure 7.10). Valves are not needed in the arteries, because the force of the heart beat keeps blood moving forwards through them.

Blood is also kept moving in the veins by the contraction of muscles around them (Figure 7.10). The large veins in your legs are squeezed by your leg muscles when you walk. This helps to push the blood back up to your heart. If a person is confined to bed for a long time, then there is a danger that the blood in these veins will not be kept moving. A clot may form in them, called a **thrombosis**. If the clot is carried to the lungs, it could get stuck in the arterioles. This is called a **pulmonary embolism**, and it may prevent the circulation reaching part of the lungs. In serious cases this can cause death.

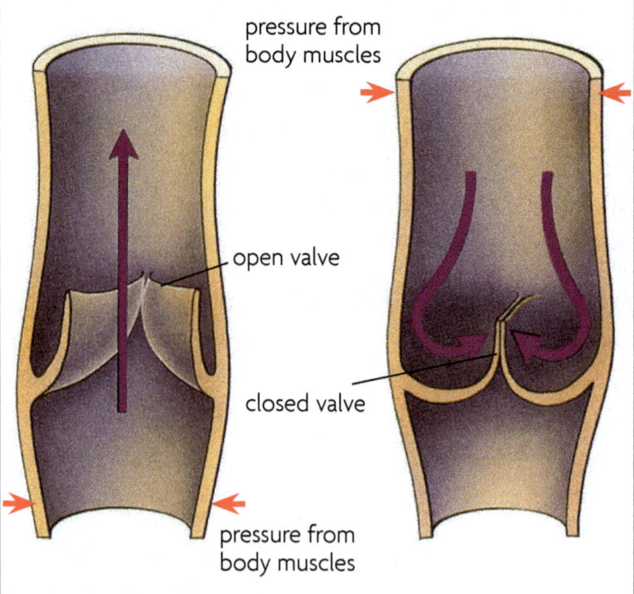

The valves are like pockets set in the wall of the vein.

Figure 7.10 Valves in a vein.

FACT!

The body adjusts to changes in blood volume so quickly that there is no detectable change in the volume of the blood when the standard 450 cm^3 is taken in a blood donation clinic (450 cm^3 is about one tenth of an adult's total blood volume).

Table 7.1 Arteries, veins and capillaries

	Function	Structure of wall	Width of lumen	Reasons for structure
Arteries	carry blood away from the heart	thick and strong, containing muscles and elastic tissues	relatively narrow; it varies with heart beat, as it can stretch and recoil	strength and elasticity needed to withstand the pulsing of the blood as it is pumped through the heart
Capillaries	supply all cells with their requirements, and take away waste products	very thin, only one cell thick	very narrow, just wide enough for a red blood cell to pass through	no need for strong walls, as most of the blood pressure has been lost; thin walls and narrow lumen bring blood into close contact with body tissues
Veins	return blood to the heart	quite thin, containing far less muscle and elastic tissue than arteries	wide; contains valves	no need for strong walls, as most of the blood pressure has been lost; wide lumen offers less resistance to blood flow; valves prevent backflow

7.12 Hypertension is a serious problem.

High blood pressure or **hypertension** is one of the major health problems in the Caribbean. More than one in five of the adults in the region have this condition. Hypertension often causes death by heart attacks and strokes.

Hypertension may cause damage to the smooth lining of the blood vessels. It can cause narrowing and increased hardening of the arteries all over the body, especially in the heart, brain and kidneys. As a result, the heart has to work harder and eventually, as the muscles stretch too much or get too thick, the enlarged heart muscle itself is not supplied with enough blood. At this stage, the heart is no longer able to function properly.

As pressure increases in the brain, damage occurs to the blood vessels and they may rupture. This causes a **stroke**, with bleeding in the brain, and the result may be paralysis of one side of the body, loss of speech or even death.

In the kidneys, hypertension causes narrowing and hardening of the arteries. This reduces the amount of fluid that can be filtered (section **8.11**). The result is that waste products build up in the body and disease may result. In extreme cases, the kidneys may fail completely leading to further complications.

Hypertension may be associated with the deposition of cholesterol into the walls of the arteries. Plaques (deposits of fatty material) accumulate in the artery walls, like rust on the inside of an iron pipe. This condition is called **atherosclerosis**, or hardening of the arteries. When the walls of the arteries become thickened with fat there is less space for the blood to flow through. Moreover, the plaques reduce the elasticity of the artery walls, so they can no longer stretch easily when blood pulses through them.

If the arteries that supply blood to the heart itself become clogged with plaques then the blood flow to portions of the heart muscle is reduced. When one of these vessels becomes completely blocked, there is a temporary stop in the blood supply to that part of the heart. This results in that part of the heart muscle becoming damaged and we say that a heart attack has occurred.

Many people have heart attacks without knowing that they have taken place. But once an attack has happened the heart is permanently damaged. People who have had a heart attack must be careful not to over-exert their hearts.

As we get older, even if our blood pressure is normal, some hardening of the arteries will take place. People with untreated or undetected high blood pressure develop this condition early and may suffer from its consequences at an earlier age.

Medical researchers believe that certain factors make a person more likely to develop hypertension. These factors include the following.

Stress When people are excited or scared their blood pressure normally rises. In some people, blood pressure fails to return to normal immediately after the stressful conditions are over. The blood pressure of people whose jobs are extremely stressful may be kept at a high level for long periods of time.

Genes People whose parents have high blood pressure are more likely to develop hypertension.

Diet There is good evidence that a salt-rich diet is associated with high blood pressure. Large amounts of fatty foods may also lead to atherosclerosis, and, therefore, to hypertension and heart disease.

Obesity All of the body's cells require substances carried to them in the blood. Therefore, as body weight increases the circulatory system also increases in size and the heart is made to work harder to pump more blood.

Smoking The drug nicotine causes blood vessels to constrict and as a result blood pressure rises. The heart also has to work harder to pump increased volumes of blood through damaged lungs.

It is obvious from this list that good health habits reduce the occurrence of hypertension. Regular exercise (such as aerobics, jogging or running) can also be beneficial.

7.13 Each organ has its own blood supply.

Figures 7.11 and 7.12 illustrate the positions of the main arteries and veins in the body.

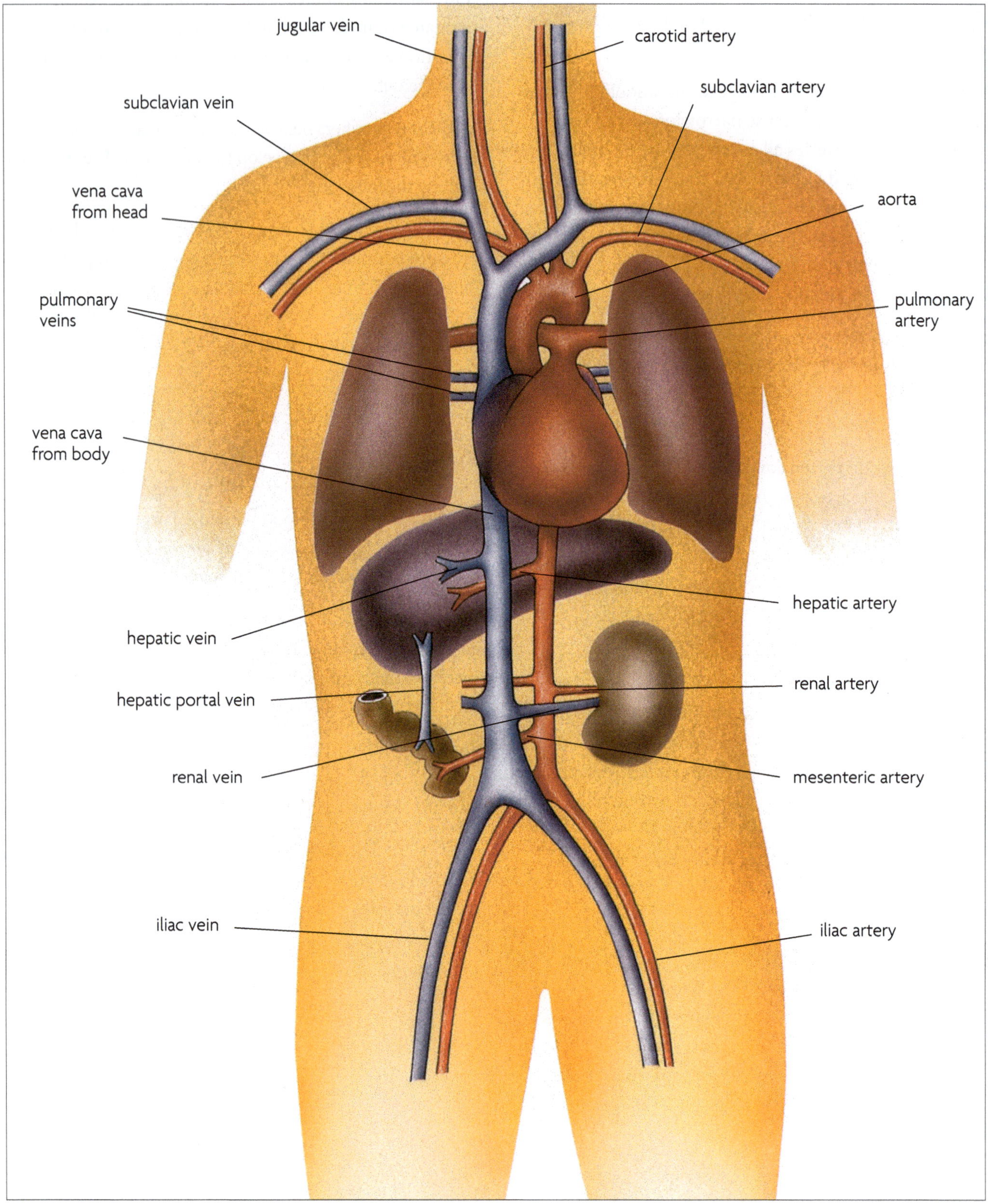

Figure 7.11 The main arteries and veins in the human body.

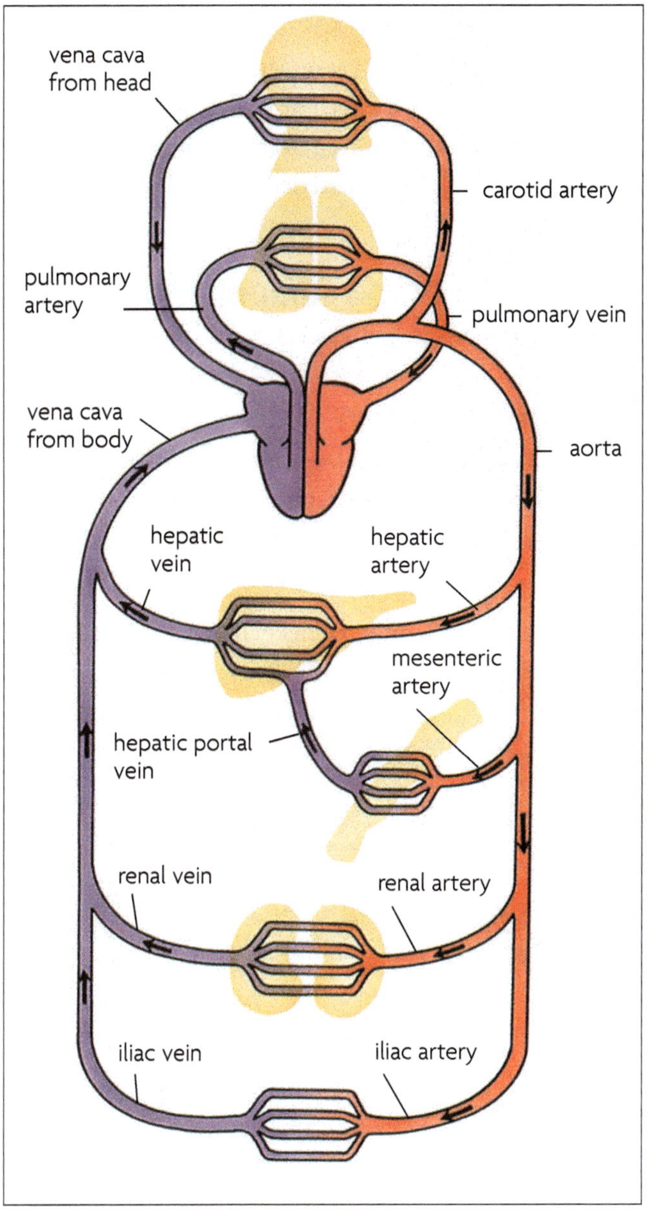

Figure 7.12 Plan of the main blood vessels in the human body.

Each organ of the body, except the lungs, is supplied with oxygenated blood from an artery. Deoxygenated blood is taken away by a vein. The artery and vein are named according to the organ with which they are connected. For example, the blood vessels of the kidneys are the **renal** artery and vein.

All arteries, other than the pulmonary artery, branch from the aorta. All the veins, except the pulmonary veins and hepatic portal vein, join up to one of the two venae cavae.

The liver has two blood vessels supplying it with blood. The first is the **hepatic artery**, which supplies oxygen. The second is the **hepatic portal vein**. This vein brings blood from the digestive system (Figure 5.15), so that the liver can process the food which has been absorbed, before it travels to other parts of the body. All the blood leaves the liver in the **hepatic vein**.

Questions

7.17 Which blood vessels carry blood **(a)** away from, and **(b)** towards the heart?

7.18 Why do arteries need strong walls?

7.19 Why do arteries have elastic walls?

7.20 What is the function of capillaries?

7.21 Why do veins have a large lumen?

7.22 How is blood kept moving in the large veins of the legs?

7.23 What is unusual about the blood supply to the liver?

7.24 What is hypertension?

7.25 What are plaques?

7.26 What factors can lead to hypertension?

7.27 What advice would you give an obese smoker who suffers from hypertension?

Blood

7.14 Blood consists of cells floating in plasma.

The liquid part of blood is called **plasma**. Floating in the plasma are cells. Most of these are **red blood cells**. A much smaller number are **white blood cells**. There are also small fragments formed from special cells in the bone marrow, called **platelets** (Figures 7.13 and 7.14 overleaf).

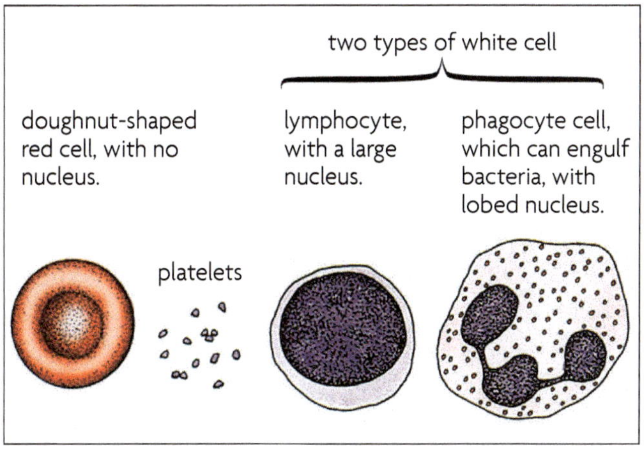

Figure 7.13 Blood cells.

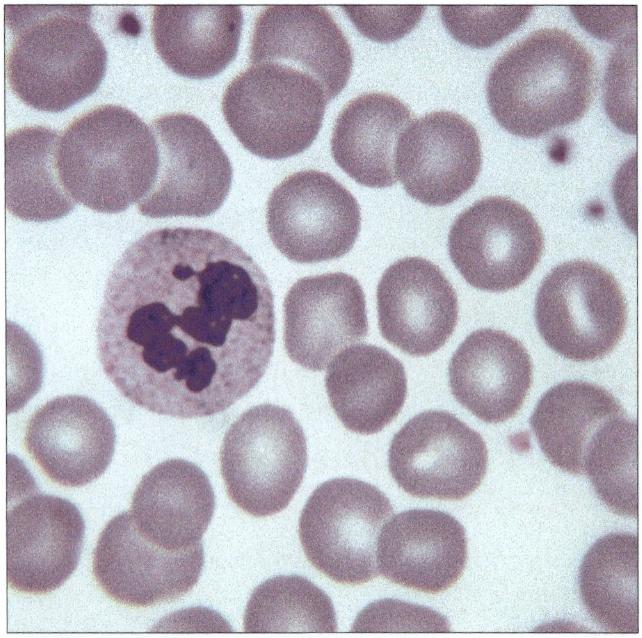

Figure 7.14 Blood seen through a microscope. The large cell is a white cell. The others are all red cells. There are also a few platelets (magnification ×1700).

7.15 Plasma is a complex solution.

Plasma is mostly water. Many substances are dissolved in it. Glucose, amino acids, salts, hormones, blood proteins, and antibodies are all dissolved in the plasma. More details about the substances carried in blood plasma are provided in Table 7.2.

Functions of blood components

These are summarised in Table 7.3.

7.16 Red blood cells carry oxygen.

Red blood cells are made in the bone marrow of some bones, including the ribs, vertebrae and some limb bones. They are produced at a very fast rate – about 9000 million per hour!

Red cells have to be made so quickly because they do not live for very long. Each red cell only lives for about four months. One reason for this is that they do not have a nucleus (Figure 7.13, page 123).

Table 7.2 Some of the main components of blood plasma

	Source	Destination	Notes
Water	Absorbed in small intestine and colon.	All cells.	Excess is removed by the kidneys.
Plasma proteins (including fibrinogen and antibodies)	Fibrinogen is made in the liver. Antibodies are made by lymphocytes.	Remain in the blood.	Fibrinogen helps in blood clotting. Antibodies kill bacteria.
Lipids including cholesterol and fatty acids	Absorbed in the ileum. Also derived from fat reserves in the body.	To the liver, for breakdown. To adipose tissue, for storage. To respiring cells, as an energy source.	Breakdown of fats yields energy – heart muscle depends largely on fatty acids for its energy supply. High cholesterol levels in the blood increase the risk of developing heart disease.
Carbohydrates, especially glucose	Absorbed in the ileum. Also produced by the breakdown of glycogen in the liver.	To all cells, for energy release by respiration.	Excess glucose is converted to glycogen and stored in the liver.
Excretory substances, e.g. urea	Produced by amino acid deamination in the liver.	To kidneys for excretion.	
Mineral ions, e.g. Na^+, Cl^-	Absorbed in the ileum and colon.	To all cells.	Excess ions are excreted by the kidneys.
Hormones	Secreted into the blood by endocrine glands.	To all parts of the body.	Hormones only affect their target cells. Hormones are broken down by the liver, and their remains are excreted by the kidneys.
Dissolved gases, e.g. carbon dioxide	Carbon dioxide is released by all cells as a waste product of respiration.	To the lungs for excretion.	Most carbon dioxide is carried as hydrogencarbonate ions (HCO_3^-) in the blood plasma.

Red cells are red because they contain the pigment **haemoglobin**. This carries oxygen. Haemoglobin is a protein, and contains iron. It is this iron that readily combines with oxygen where the gas is in good supply. It just as readily gives it up where the oxygen supply is low, as in active tissues.

But haemoglobin will combine with carbon monoxide in preference to oxygen. If this happens, oxygen can no longer be transported. This can cause a person to lose consciousness.

Recovery requires the administration of oxygen, as well as carbon dioxide. The oxygen is to flush out the carbon monoxide, and the carbon dioxide is to stimulate breathing (section **11.18**). People can die from carbon monoxide in the exhaust gases of cars. Tobacco smoke also contains carbon monoxide.

Old red blood cells are broken down in the liver, spleen and bone marrow. Some of the iron from the haemoglobin is stored, and used for making new haemoglobin. Some of it is turned into bile pigment and excreted.

7.17 White blood cells fight infection.

White cells are made in the bone marrow and in the lymph nodes (section **7.26**). White cells do have a nucleus, which is often quite large and lobed (Figure **7.13**, page **123**). They can move around, like an amoeba, and can squeeze out through the walls of blood capillaries into all parts of the body. Their function is to fight infection, and to clear up any dead body cells.

7.18 Platelets help blood clot.

Platelets are small fragments of cells, with no nucleus. They are made in the red bone marrow, and they are involved in blood clotting (Figure **16.17**, page **301**).

Questions

7.28 List five components of plasma.

7.29 Where are red blood cells made?

7.30 What is unusual about red blood cells?

7.31 What is haemoglobin?

7.32 Why is carbon monoxide so dangerous to humans?

7.33 Where are white blood cells made?

7.34 What are platelets?

Table 7.3 Components of blood

	Structure	Functions
Plasma	water, containing many substances in solution	1 liquid medium in which cells and platelets can float 2 transports CO_2 in solution 3 transports nutrients in solution 4 transports urea in solution 5 transports hormones in solution 6 transports heat 7 transports substances needed for blood clotting 8 transports antibodies
Red cells	biconcave discs with no nucleus, containing haemoglobin	1 transport oxygen 2 transport small amount of CO_2
White cells	variable shapes, with nucleus	1 engulf and destroy bacteria (phagocytosis) 2 make antibodies
Platelets	small fragments of cells, with no nucleus	help in blood clotting

7.19 Blood has many functions.

Blood has three main functions. These are transport, defence against disease, and regulation of body temperature.

7.20 Many substances are transported by blood.

Transport of oxygen In the lungs, oxygen diffuses from the alveoli into the blood (section **6.15**). The doughnut shape of the red blood cells (Figure **7.15**) increases the surface area for diffusion, so that oxygen can diffuse into and out of the cells very rapidly. In the lungs, oxygen diffuses into the red blood cells, where it combines with the haemoglobin (Hb) to form **oxyhaemoglobin** (oxyHb).

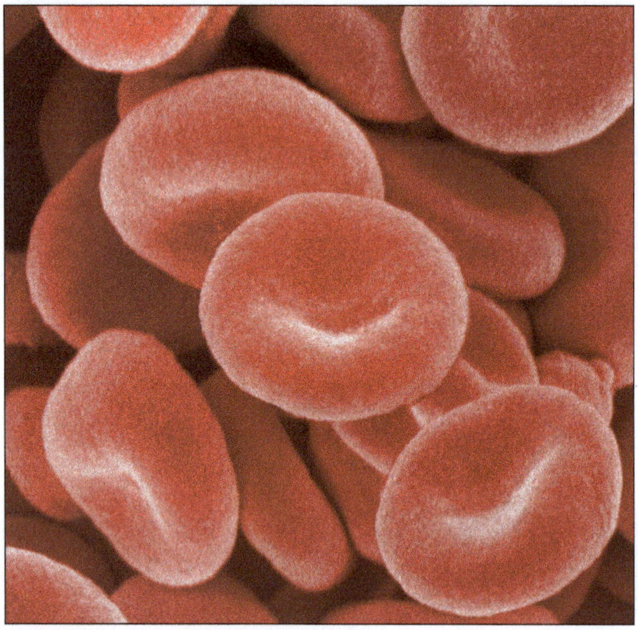

Figure 7.15 Scanning electron micrograph of red blood cells (magnification ×4500).

The blood is then taken to the heart in the pulmonary veins and pumped out of the heart in the aorta.

Arteries branch from the aorta to supply all parts of the body with oxygenated blood. When it reaches a tissue which needs oxygen, the oxyHb gives up its oxygen, to become Hb again.

Because capillaries are so narrow, the oxyHb in the red blood cells is taken very close to the tissues which need the oxygen. The oxygen only has a very short distance to diffuse. OxyHb is bright red, whereas Hb is purplish-red. The blood in arteries is therefore a brighter red colour than the blood in veins.

Transport of carbon dioxide Carbon dioxide is made by all the cells in the body as they respire. The carbon dioxide diffuses through the walls of the capillaries into the blood.

Most of the carbon dioxide is carried by the blood plasma in the form of hydrogencarbonate ions, HCO_3^-. A small amount is carried by Hb in the red cells.

Blood containing carbon dioxide is returned to the heart in the veins, and then to the lungs in the pulmonary arteries. The carbon dioxide diffuses out of the blood and is passed out of the body on expiration.

Transport of food materials Digested food is absorbed in the ileum (section **5.21**). It includes amino acids, fatty acids and glycerol, monosaccharides (such as glucose), water, vitamins and minerals. These all dissolve in the plasma in the blood capillaries in the villi.

These capillaries join up to form the hepatic portal vein. This takes the dissolved food to the liver. The liver processes the food (Table **8.1**, page **149**) and returns some of it to the blood.

The food is then carried, dissolved in the blood, to all parts of the body.

Transport of urea Urea, a waste substance (section **8.7**), is made in the liver. It dissolves in the blood plasma, and is carried to the kidneys. The kidneys excrete it in the urine.

Transport of hormones Hormones are made in **endocrine** glands (section **11.1**). The hormones dissolve in the blood plasma, and are transported all over the body.

Transport of heat Some parts of the body, such as the muscles, make a great deal of heat. The blood transports the heat to all parts of the body. This helps to keep the rest of the body warm.

FACT!

Large quantities of blood are sometimes needed during operations. A 50-year-old haemophiliac, who underwent open heart surgery in Chicago in 1970, needed 1080 litres of blood.

7.21 Blood defends the body.

The ways in which the blood defends the body are described in sections **16.19** to **16.23**. They include blood clotting, phagocytosis and production of antibodies.

7.22 Blood helps to regulate temperature.

The capillaries in the skin help to keep your body temperature constant at about 36.8 °C. This is described in section **11.10**.

Questions

7.35 Why is blood in arteries a brighter red than the blood in veins?

7.36 Which vessel transports digested food to the liver?

7.37 How is urea transported?

7.38 Outline two functions of blood other than transport.

Lymph and tissue fluid

7.23 Tissue fluid is leaked plasma.

Capillaries leak! The cells in their walls do not fit together exactly, so there are small gaps between them. Plasma can therefore leak out from the blood.

White blood cells can also get through these gaps. They are able to move, like an amoeba, and can squeeze through, out of the capillaries. Red blood cells cannot get out. They are too large and cannot change their shape very much.

So plasma and white cells are continually leaking out of the blood capillaries. The fluid formed in this way is called **tissue fluid**. It surrounds all the cells in the body (Figure 7.16).

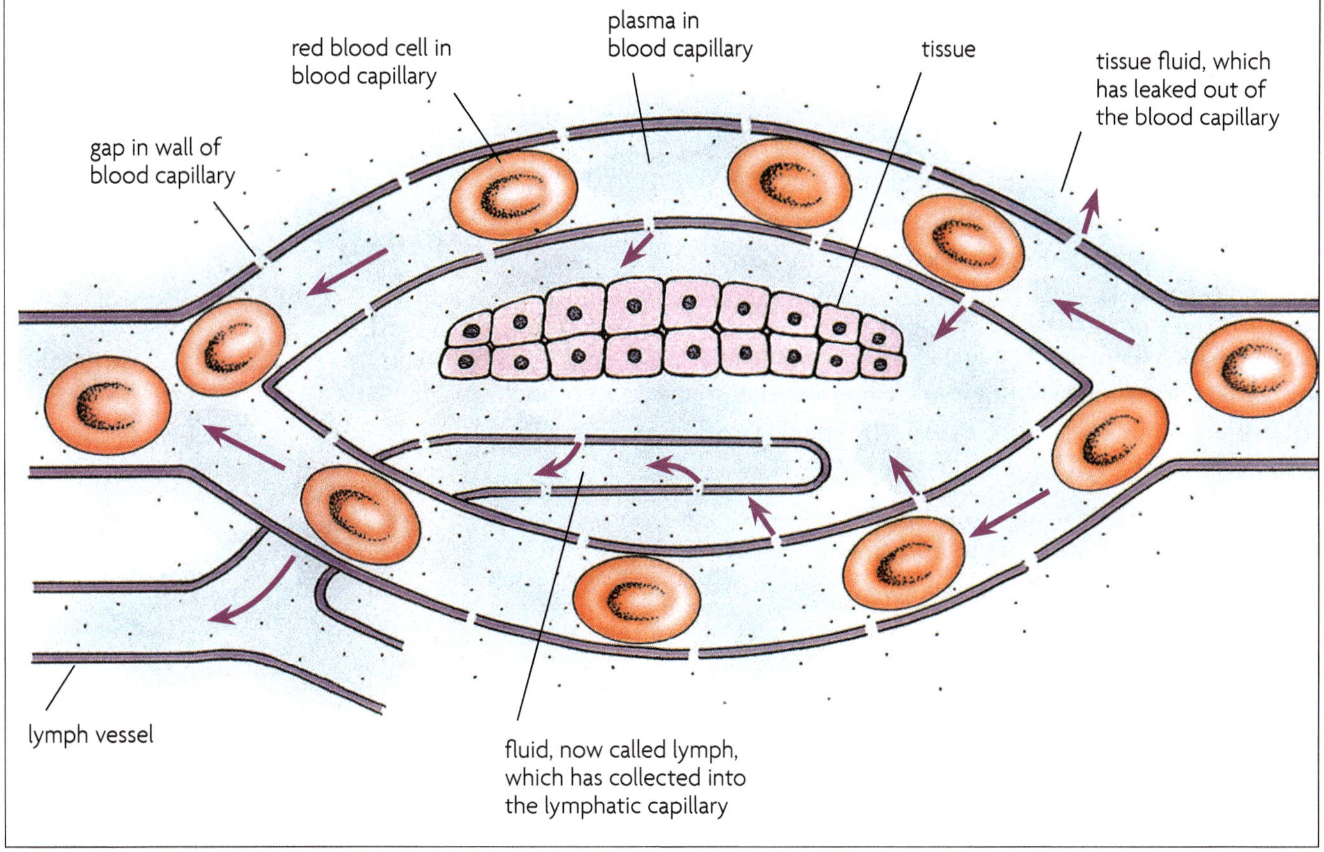

Figure 7.16 Part of a capillary network, to show how tissue fluid and lymph are formed.

7.24 The functions of tissue fluid.

Tissue fluid is very important. It supplies cells with all their requirements. These requirements, such as oxygen and food materials, diffuse from the blood, through the tissue fluid, to the cells. Waste products, such as carbon dioxide, diffuse in the opposite direction.

The tissue fluid is the immediate environment of every cell in your body. It is easier for a cell to carry out its functions properly if its environment stays constant. For example, this means it should stay at the same temperature, and at the same osmotic concentration.

Several organs in the body work to keep the composition and temperature of the blood constant, and therefore the tissue fluid as well. This process is called **homeostasis**, and is described in section **11.7**.

7.25 Lymph is drained tissue fluid.

The plasma and white cells that leak out of the blood capillaries must eventually be returned to the blood. In the tissues, as well as blood capillaries, are other small vessels. They are lymphatic capillaries (Figure 7.17). The tissue fluid slowly drains into them. The fluid is now called **lymph**.

The lymphatic capillaries gradually join up to form larger lymphatic vessels (Figure 7.17). These carry the lymph to the **subclavian veins** which bring blood back from the arms (Figure 7.18). Here the lymph enters the blood again.

The lymphatic system has no pump to make the lymph flow. Lymph vessels do have valves in them, however, to make sure that movement is only in one direction. Lymph flows much more slowly than blood. Many of the larger lymph vessels run within or very close to muscles, and when the muscles contract they squeeze inwards on the lymph and force it to move along the vessels.

7.26 Lymph nodes contain white blood cells.

On its way from the tissues to the subclavian vein, lymph flows through several **lymph nodes**. Some of these are shown in Figure 7.18.

Lymph nodes contain large numbers of white cells. Most bacteria or toxins in the lymph can be destroyed by these cells (section **16.22**).

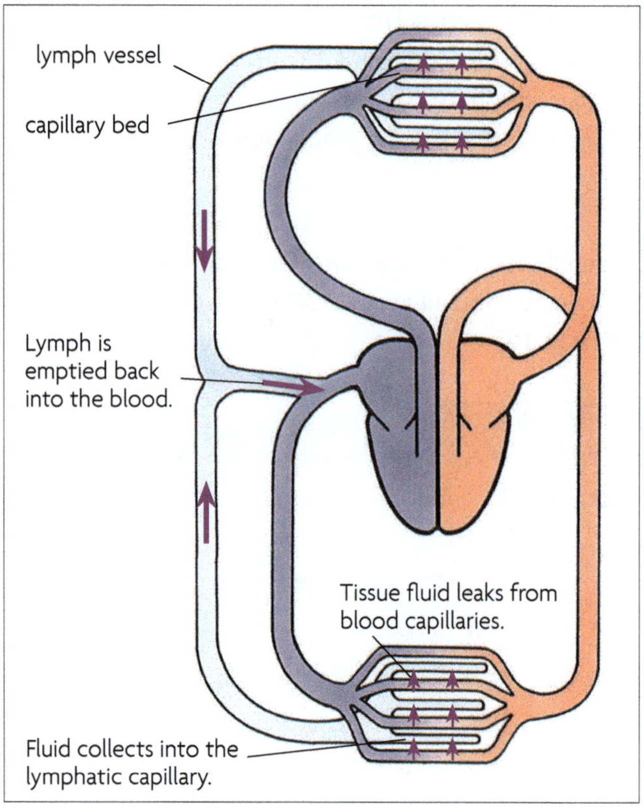

Figure 7.17 The relationship between the blood circulation and the lymph circulation.

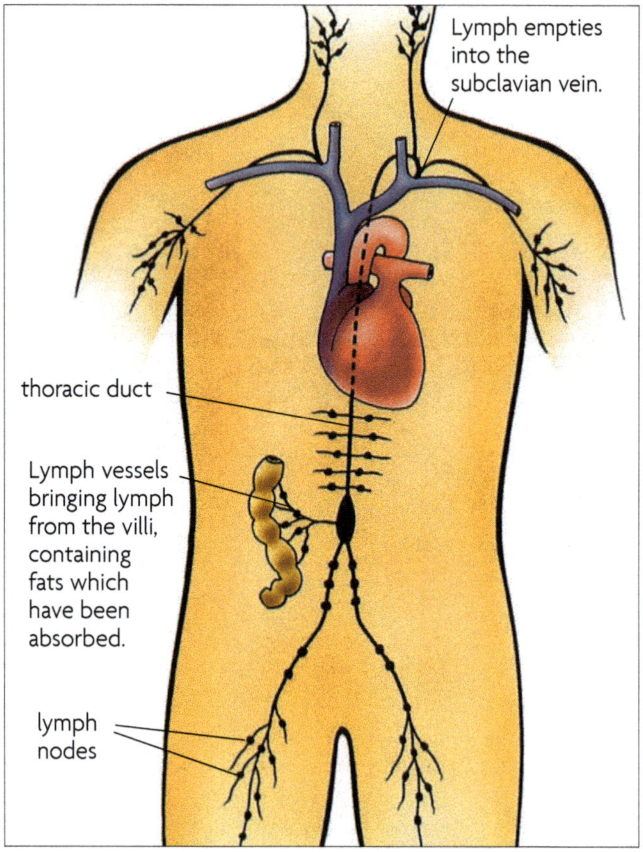

Figure 7.18 The main lymph vessels and lymph nodes.

Questions

7.39 What is tissue fluid?

7.40 Give two functions of tissue fluid.

7.41 What is lymph?

7.42 Why do lymphatic capillaries have valves in them?

7.43 Name two places where lymph nodes are found.

7.44 What happens inside lymph nodes?

FACT!

A human being contains about 70 cm^3 of blood per kilogram of bodyweight. For an adult, this is about 4 or 5 litres of blood, in total.

Storage in mammals

7.27 Organisms store food that is not immediately needed.

Sometimes the food available for use in the cells is not immediately needed. So it is stored for future use, in special sites. Food is often stored as **polysaccharides**, which are carbohydrates. It may also be stored as **lipids** (oils and fats). In mammals, the polysaccharide is **glycogen**, and the lipid is fat. In plants, the polysaccharide is **starch**, and the lipid is oil. These food stores are reserves of energy. Lipids provide much more energy than carbohydrates of equal mass.

Polysaccharides and lipids are insoluble in water. Therefore they do not affect the osmotic concentration of the cell fluids. When energy is needed, they are converted by enzymes to soluble substances. These are then transported to where they are needed.

7.28 In mammals, food reserves are found in the liver, in muscle and beneath the skin.

Mammals store glycogen in the liver, and in muscle. Both are centres of high metabolic activity. Glycogen is built up of glucose, which is released for respiration as needed.

Fat is mostly stored beneath the skin. In cold countries, some mammals store extra fat for hibernation. Some aquatic mammals, for example the seal, have a thick layer of fat beneath the skin. This is called blubber. It acts as an insulator. The water produced when fat is oxidised in respiration is very important for desert animals. An extreme case is the kangaroo rat, which does not drink. It relies solely on the water from respiration.

7.29 Some types of vitamins and minerals are also stored.

The liver is perhaps the main storage organ in vertebrates. In addition to glycogen, it also stores the fat-soluble vitamins A, D, E and K. Some fish liver oils are especially rich in vitamins A and D. The liver stores some of the water-soluble vitamins of the B group, especially nicotinic acid, B_{12}, and folic acid. Vitamin B_{12} and folic acid are needed in the bone marrow for the formation of the red blood cells.

The iron from the breakdown of red blood cells is also stored in the liver. This is later used for making new red blood cells. Potassium is also stored in the liver.

The vessels of the liver, together with the hepatic portal vein, provide an emergency reservoir of blood. This reservoir is not static. Blood is in continual movement through it.

Questions

7.45 Why are polysaccharides and lipids useful storage materials?

7.46 Why do you think cod liver oil is commonly recommended for young children?

7.47 Name three different kinds of substances stored in the liver.

7.48 Inuit people traditionally ate a lot of blubber in their diet. Where does this come from?

7.49 Metabolic water is very important to desert animals. Why?

Transport in flowering plants

7.30 Plants have two transport systems – phloem and xylem.

Transport systems in plants are less elaborate than in mammals. Plants are less active than mammals, and so their cells do not need to be supplied with materials so quickly. Also, the branching shape of a plant means that all the cells can get their oxygen for respiration, and carbon dioxide for photosynthesis, directly from the air, by diffusion.

Plants have two transport systems. The **xylem vessels** carry water and minerals, while the **phloem tubes** carry organic nutrients which the plant has made.

7.31 Xylem helps to support plants.

A xylem vessel is like a long drainpipe (Figures **7.19** and **7.20**). It is made of many hollow, dead cells, joined end to end. The end walls of the cells have disappeared, so a long, open tube is formed. Xylem vessels run from the roots of the plant, right up through the stem. They branch out into every leaf.

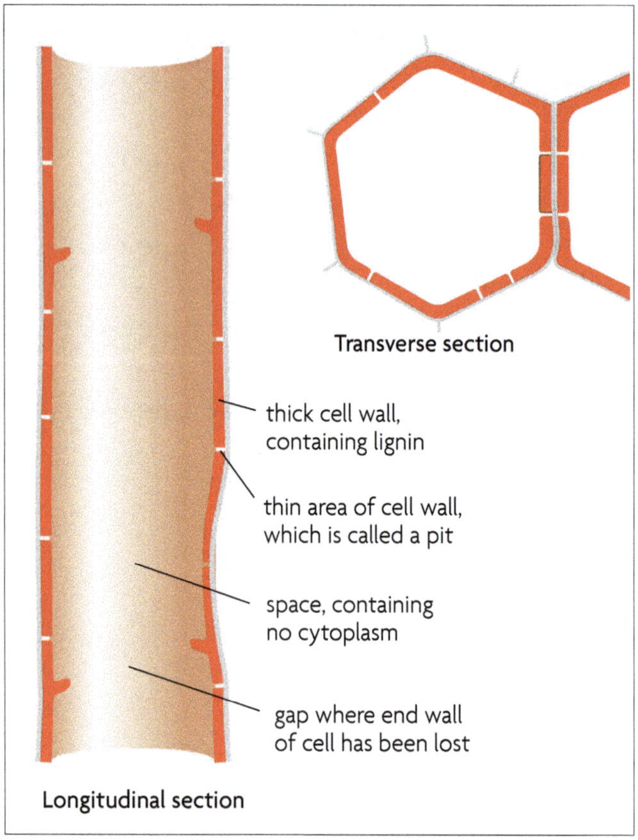

Figure 7.19 Xylem vessels.

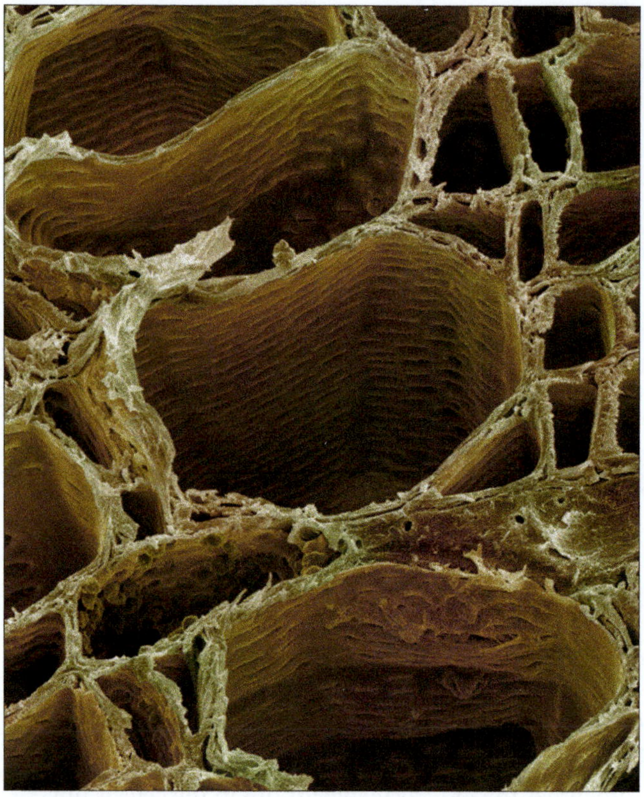

Figure 7.20 This is a scanning electron micrograph of xylem vessels (magnification ×1800).

Xylem vessels contain no cytoplasm or nuclei. Their walls are made of cellulose and **lignin**. Lignin is very strong, so xylem vessels help to keep plants upright. Wood is made almost entirely of lignified xylem vessels.

7.32 Phloem contains sieve tube elements.

Like xylem vessels, phloem tubes are made of many cells joined end to end. However, their end walls have not completely broken down. Instead, they form **sieve plates** (Figures 7.21 and 7.22), which have small holes in them. The cells are called sieve tube elements. Sieve tube elements contain cytoplasm, but no nucleus. They do not have lignin in their cell walls.

Each sieve tube element has a companion cell next to it. The companion cell does have a nucleus, and also contains many other organelles. Companion cells probably supply sieve tube elements with some of their requirements.

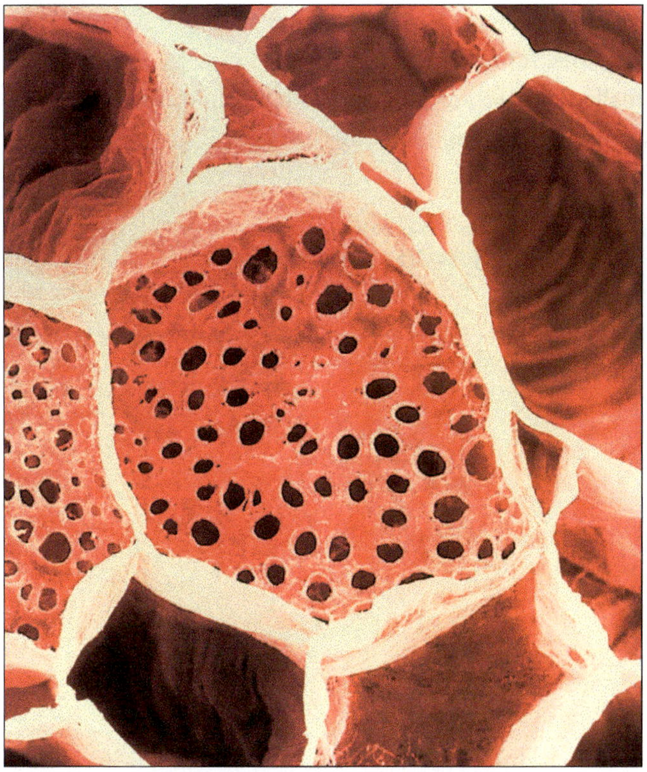

Figure 7.21 This scanning electron micrograph shows a sieve plate in a sieve tube (magnification ×1300).

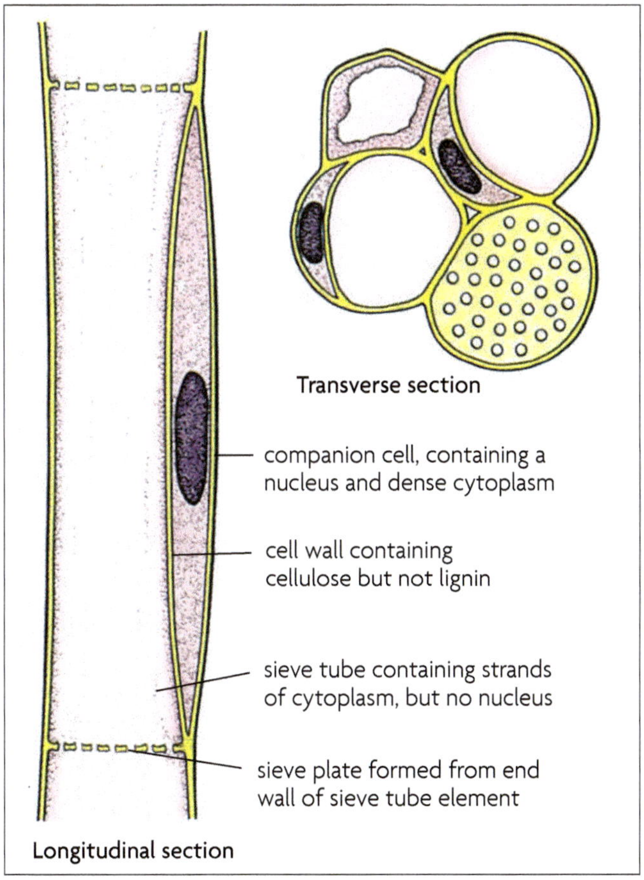

Figure 7.22 Phloem tubes.

7.33 Vascular bundles contain xylem and phloem.

Xylem vessels and phloem tubes are usually found close together. A group of xylem vessels and phloem tubes is called a **vascular bundle**.

The positions of vascular bundles in roots and shoots are shown in Figures **7.23** and **7.24**. In a root, vascular tissue is found at the centre, whereas in a shoot vascular bundles are arranged in a ring near the outside edge. They help to support the plant (section **9.16**).

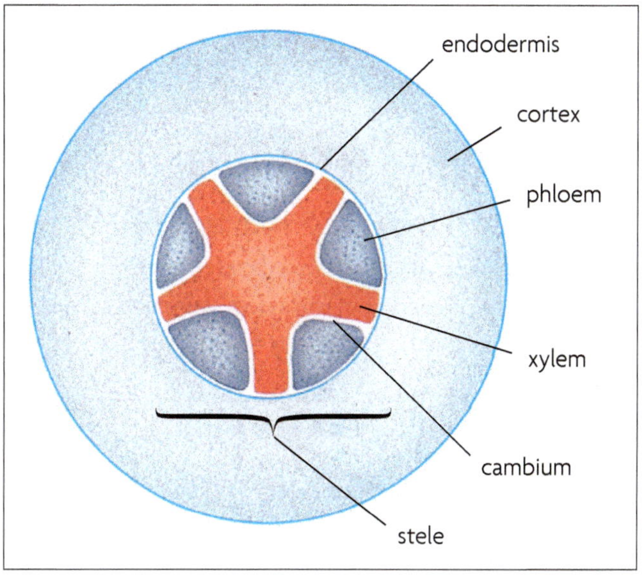

Figure 7.23 Transverse section of a root.

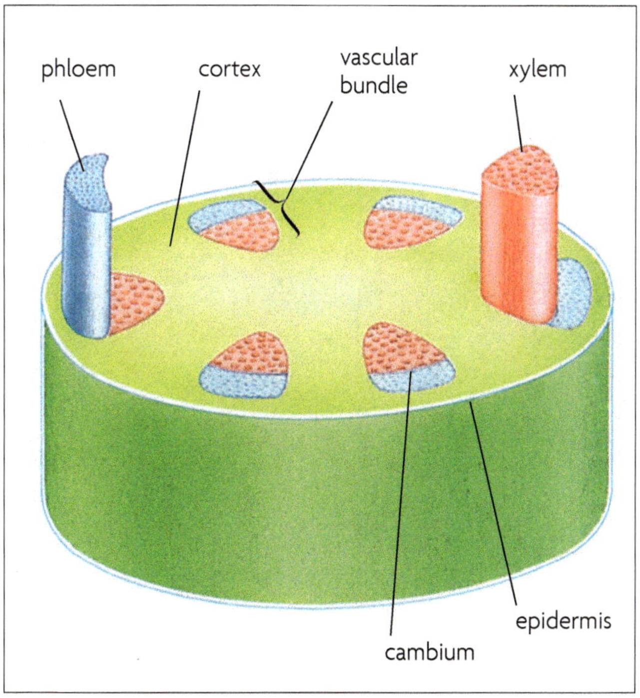

Figure 7.24 Transverse section of a stem.

Questions

7.50 Why do plants not need such elaborate transport systems as mammals?

7.51 What do xylem vessels carry?

7.52 What do phloem tubes carry?

7.53 What substance makes up the cell walls of xylem vessels?

7.54 Give three ways in which phloem tubes differ from xylem vessels.

7.55 What is a vascular bundle?

The transport of water

7.34 Most plants have either fibrous or tap roots.

Plants take in water from the soil, through their root hairs. The water is carried in the xylem vessels to all parts of the plant.

There are several different types of root system. Plants such as grasses have **fibrous root systems** (Figure 7.25). There are many roots of similar size, which may have lateral or side roots branching from them.

Figure 7.25 Fibrous root system of a wheat plant.

Crotalaria (Figure 7.26) and carrots (Figure 7.27) have **tap roots**. A tap root is a single main root, again with smaller lateral roots growing from it. Tap roots are often swollen with stored food.

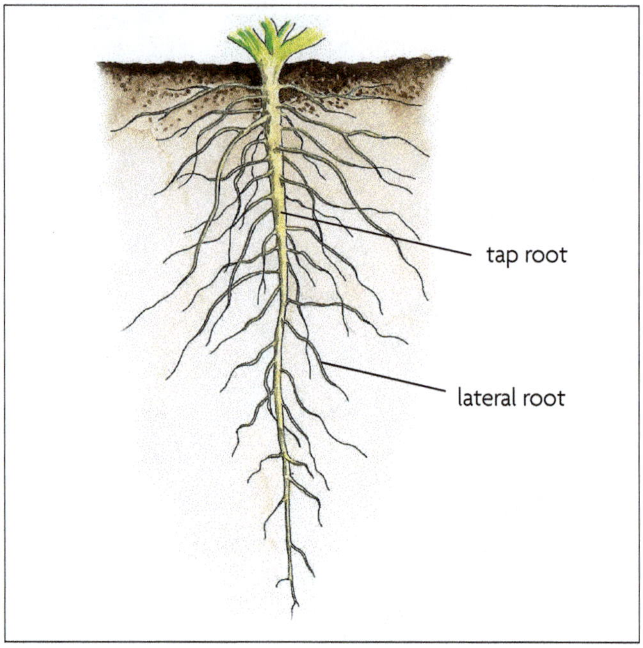

Figure 7.26 Tap root of a *Crotalaria* plant.

Figure 7.27 Swollen tap root of carrot.

If roots grow straight out of a stem, they are called **adventitious roots**. Ivy has adventitious roots, which attach it to walls or trees (Figure 7.28).

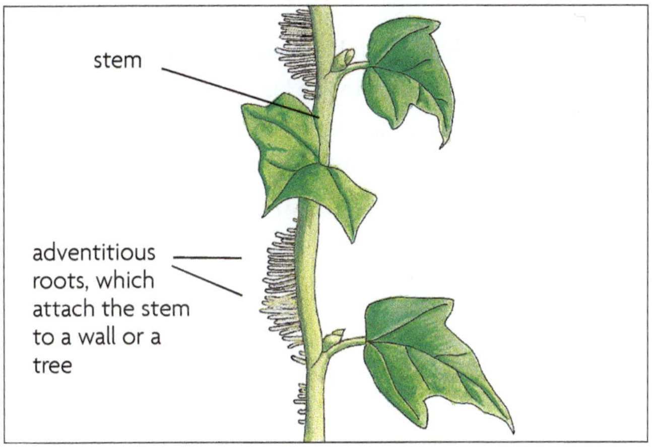

stem
adventitious roots, which attach the stem to a wall or a tree

Figure 7.28 Adventitious roots of ivy.

FACT!

The longest roots measured were produced by a rye plant (a grass). It had over 600 km of roots in only 0.051 m^3 of soil.
The deepest roots which have ever been measured belonged to a fig tree growing in southern Africa. They went down to a depth of 120 m.

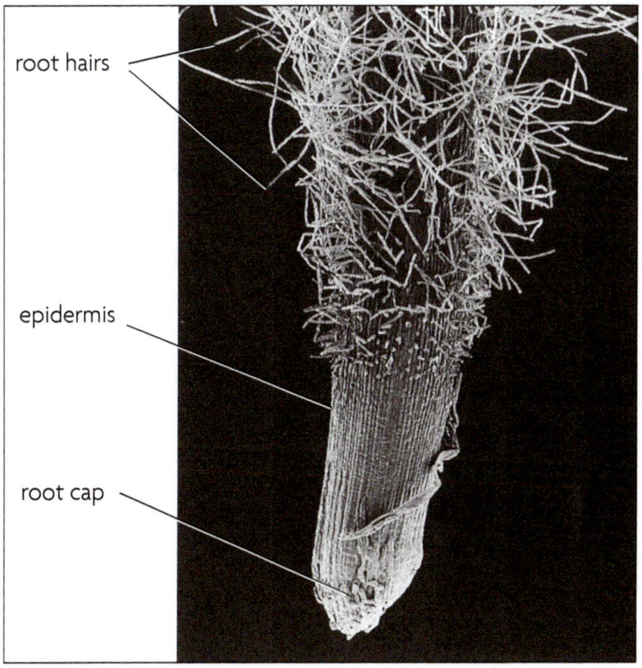

root hairs
epidermis
root cap

Figure 7.29 A root tip (magnification ×50).

7.35 The structure of a root.

Figure 7.29 shows the end of a root, magnified. At the very tip is a **root cap**. This is a layer of cells which protects the root as it grows through the soil. The rest of the root is covered by a layer of cells called the **epidermis**.

The root hairs are a little way up from the root tip. Each root hair is a long epidermal cell (Figure 7.30). Root hairs do not live for very long. As the root grows, they are replaced by new ones.

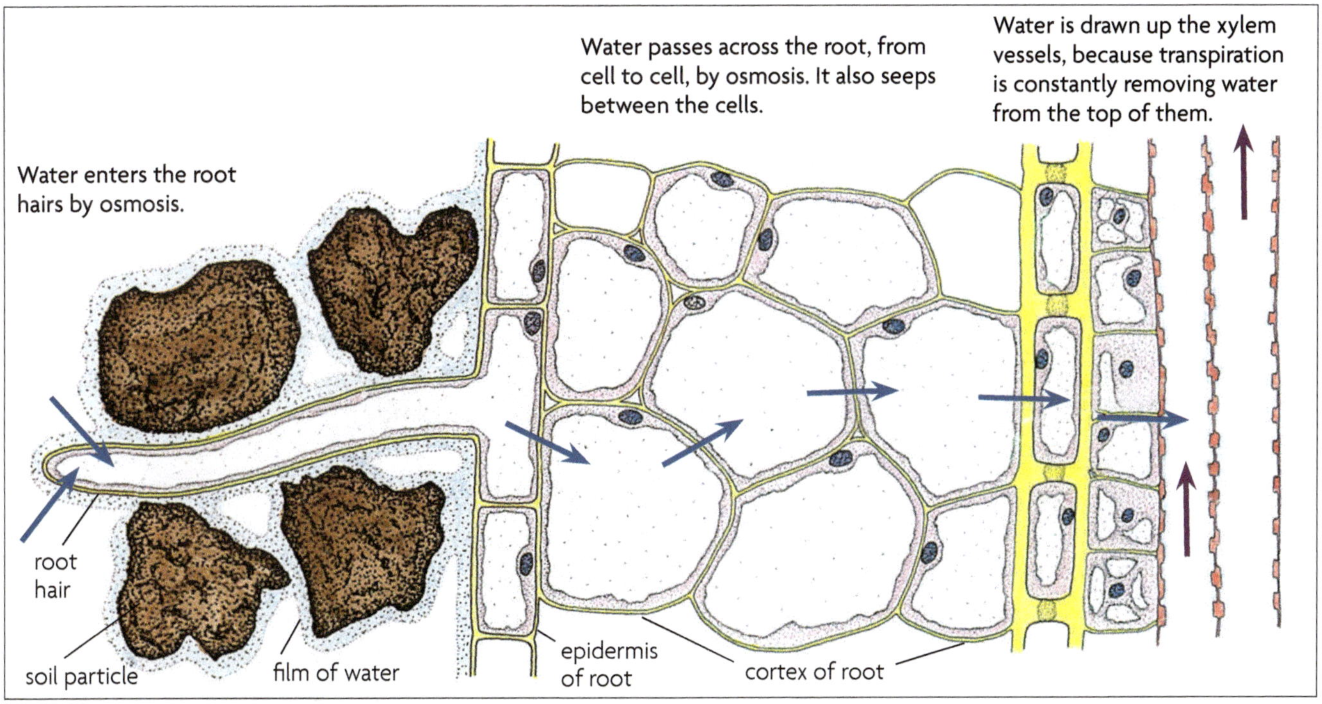

Water passes across the root, from cell to cell, by osmosis. It also seeps between the cells.
Water is drawn up the xylem vessels, because transpiration is constantly removing water from the top of them.
Water enters the root hairs by osmosis.
root hair
soil particle
film of water
epidermis of root
cortex of root

Figure 7.30 How water is absorbed by a plant.

7.36 Root hairs absorb water by osmosis.

The function of root hairs is to absorb water and minerals from the soil. Water gets into a root hair by **osmosis**. The cytoplasm and cell sap inside it are quite concentrated solutions. The water in the soil is normally a more dilute solution. Water therefore diffuses into the root hair, down its concentration gradient, through the partially permeable cell surface membrane.

7.37 Absorbed water enters the xylem.

The root hairs are on the edge of the root. The xylem vessels are in the centre. Before the water can be taken to the rest of the plant, it must travel to these xylem vessels.

The path it takes is shown in Figure **7.30**. It travels by osmosis through the cortex, from cell to cell. Some of it may also just seep through the spaces between the cells, or through the cell walls, never actually entering a cell at all.

7.38 Water is sucked up the xylem.

Water moves up xylem vessels in the same way that a drink moves up a straw when you suck it. When you suck a straw, you are reducing the pressure at the top of the straw. The liquid at the bottom of the straw is at a higher pressure, so it flows up the straw into your mouth.

The same thing happens with the water in xylem vessels. The pressure at the top of the vessels is lowered, while the pressure at the bottom stays high. Water therefore flows up the xylem vessels.

How is the pressure at the top of the xylem vessels reduced? It happens because of **transpiration**.

7.39 Transpiration is evaporation from the parts of the plant above the ground.

Transpiration is the evaporation of water from a plant. Most of this evaporation takes place from the leaves.

If you look back at Figure **4.5** (page **57**), you will see that there are openings on the surface of the leaf called **stomata**. There are usually more stomata on the underside of the leaf, in the lower epidermis. The cells inside the leaf are each covered with a thin film of moisture. This is necessary, so that gas exchange can take place.

Some of this film of moisture evaporates from the cells, and this water vapour diffuses out of the leaf through the stomata. Water from the xylem vessels in the leaf will travel to the cells by osmosis to replace it.

Water is constantly being taken from the top of the xylem vessels, to supply the cells in the leaves. This reduces the effective pressure at the top of the xylem vessels, so that water flows up them. This process is known as the **transpiration stream** (Figure **7.31**).

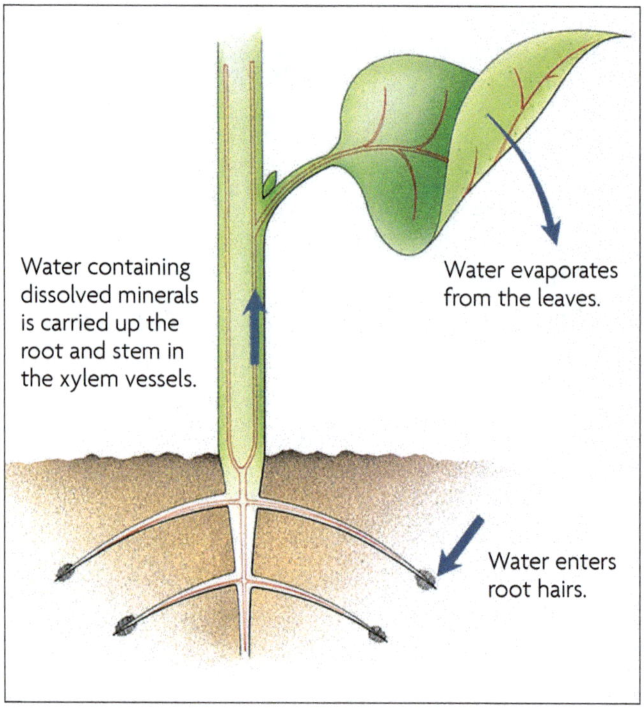

Figure 7.31 The transpiration stream.

7.40 Xylem vessels act like fine capillary tubes.

If you place a glass tube into a beaker of water, the water will rise a little way up the tube. This is due to attraction between the water molecules and the glass molecules. The narrower the glass tube the higher the water will rise. Xylem vessels are very narrow and the attraction of water molecules to those of the cell wall is great. This helps to keep a continuous column of water from the roots to the leaves.

7.41 A potometer compares transpiration rates.

It is not easy to measure how much water is lost from the leaves of a plant. It is much easier to measure how fast the plant takes up water. The rate at which a plant takes up water depends on the rate of transpiration – the faster a plant transpires, the faster it takes up water.

Figure **7.32** illustrates apparatus which can be used to compare the rate of transpiration in different conditions. It is called a **potometer**. By recording how fast the air/water meniscus moves along the capillary tube you can compare how fast the plant takes up water in different conditions.

There are many different kinds of potometer, so yours may not look like this. The simplest kind is just a long glass tube which you can fill with water. A piece of rubber tubing slid over one end can enable you to fix the cut end of a shoot into it, making an airtight connection. This works just as well as the one in Figure **7.32**, but is much harder to refill with water.

7.42 Conditions that affect transpiration rate.

Temperature On a hot day, water will evaporate quickly from the leaves of a plant. Transpiration increases as temperature increases.

Humidity Humidity means the moisture content of the air. The higher the humidity, the less water will evaporate from the leaves. This is because there is not much of a diffusion gradient for the water between the air spaces inside the leaf, and the wet air outside it. Transpiration decreases as humidity increases.

Wind speed On a windy day, water evaporates more quickly than on a still day. Transpiration increases as wind speed increases.

Light intensity In bright sunlight, a plant may open its stomata to supply plenty of carbon dioxide for photosynthesis. More water can therefore evaporate from the leaves.

Water supply If water is in short supply, then the plant will close its stomata. This will cut down the rate of transpiration. Transpiration decreases when water supply decreases below a certain level.

Transpiration is useful to plants, because it keeps water moving up the xylem vessels and evaporation helps to cool the leaves. But if the leaves lose too much water, the roots may not be able to take up enough to replace it. If this happens, the plants **wilts**. Many plants have other ways of cutting down their rate of transpiration, and these are described in section **8.22**.

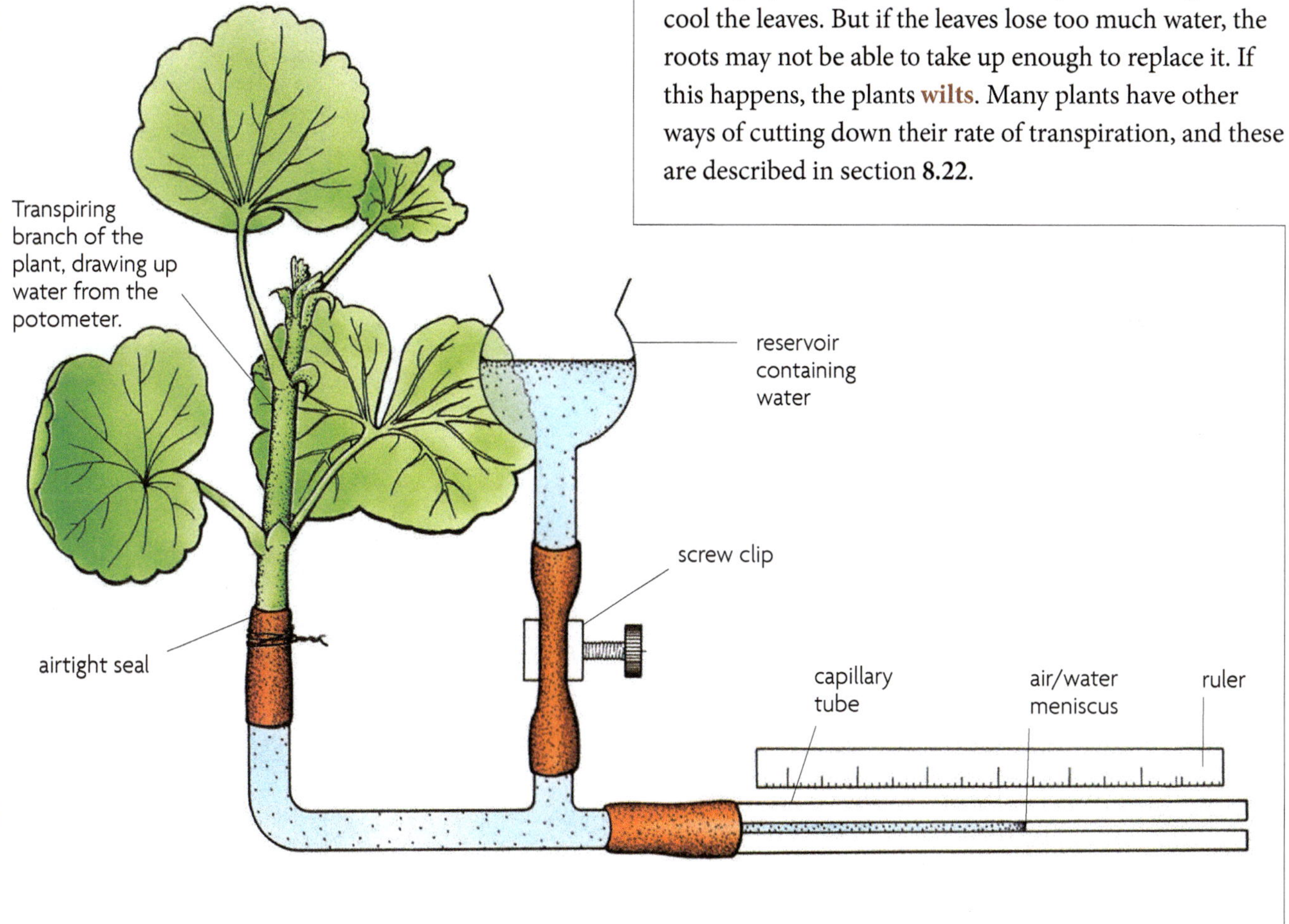

Figure 7.32 A potometer.

Investigation 7.2
To see which part of a stem transports water and solutes

SBA skills

Observation/Recording/Reporting
Manipulation/Measurement
Analysis/Interpretation
Drawing
Planning/Design

1 Take a plant, such as *Impatiens*, with a root system intact. Wash the roots thoroughly.

2 Put the roots of the plant into eosin solution. Leave overnight.

3 Set up a microscope.

4 Remove the plant from the eosin solution, and wash the roots thoroughly.

5 Use a razor blade to cut across the stem of the plant about half-way up. Take great care when using a razor blade and do not touch its edges.

6 Now cut very thin sections across the stem. Try to get them so thin that you can see through them. It does not matter if your section is not a complete circle.

7 Choose your thinnest section, and mount it in a drop of water on a microscope slide. Cover with a coverslip.

8 Observe the section under a microscope. Compare what you can see with Figure **7.24** (page **131**). Make a labelled drawing of your section.

Questions

1 Which part of the stem contained the dye? What does this tell you about the transport of water and solutes (substances dissolved in water) up a stem?

2 Why was it important to wash the roots of the plant:
  a before putting it into the eosin solution, and
  b before cutting sections?

3 Design an experiment to investigate the effect of one factor (for example light intensity, temperature, wind speed) on the rate at which the dye is transported up the stem. Remember to write down your hypothesis, and to think about variables. When you have completed your plan, ask your teacher to check it for you. Then carry out your experiment and record and display your results. Write down your conclusions, and discuss them in the light of your knowledge about transport in plants. You should also evaluate the reliability of your results and suggest how you could improve your experiment if you were able to do it again.

Investigation 7.3
To see which surface of a leaf loses most water

SBA skills

Observation/Recording/Reporting
Analysis/Interpretation

Cobalt chloride paper is blue when dry and pink when wet. Use forceps to handle it.

1 Use a healthy, well-watered potted plant, with leaves which are not too hairy. Fix a small square of blue cobalt chloride paper onto each surface of one leaf, using clear sticky tape. Make sure there are no air spaces around the paper.

2 Leave the paper on the leaf for a few minutes.

Questions

1 Which piece of cobalt chloride paper turned pink first? What does this tell you about the loss of water from a leaf?

2 Why does this surface lose water faster than the other?

3 Why is it important to use forceps, not fingers, for handling cobalt chloride paper?

Investigation 7.4
To measure the rate of transpiration of a potted plant

SBA skills

Observation/Recording/Reporting

Analysis/Interpretation

1 Use two similar well-watered potted plants. Enclose one plant entirely in a polythene bag, including its pot. This is the control.

2 Enclose only the pot of the second plant in a polythene bag. Fix the bag firmly around the stem of the plant, and seal with Vaseline®.

3 Place both plants on balances, and record their masses.

4 Record the mass of each plant every day, at the same time, for at least a week.

5 Draw a graph of your results.

Questions

1 Which plant lost mass? Why?

2 Do you think this is a good method of measuring transpiration rate? How could it be improved?

Investigation 7.5
Using a potometer to compare rates of transpiration under different conditions

SBA skills

Observation/Recording/Reporting

Manipulation/Measurement

Analysis/Interpretation

1 Set up the potometer as in Figure 7.32 (page 135). The stem of the plant must fit exactly into the rubber tubing, with no air gaps. Vaseline® will help to make an air-tight seal.

2 Fill the apparatus with water, by opening the clip.

3 Close the clip again, and leave the apparatus in a light, airy place. As the plant transpires, the water it loses is replaced by water taken up the stem. Air will be drawn in at the end of the capillary tube.

4 When the air/water meniscus reaches the scale, begin to record the position of the meniscus every two minutes.

5 When the meniscus reaches the end of the scale, refill the apparatus with water from the reservoir as before.

6 Now repeat the investigation, but with the apparatus in a different situation. You could try each of these:

- a blowing it with a fan
- b putting it in a cupboard
- c putting it in a refrigerator.

7 Draw graphs of your results.

Questions

1 Under which conditions did the plant transpire **(a)** most quickly, and **(b)** most slowly?

2 You have been using the potometer to compare the rate of uptake of water under different conditions. Does this really give you a good measurement of the rate of transpiration? Explain your answer.

Uptake of mineral salts

7.43 Root hairs absorb minerals by active transport.

As well as absorbing water by osmosis, root hairs absorb mineral salts. These are in the form of ions (Table **4.2**, page **61**) dissolved in the water in the soil. They travel to the xylem vessels along with the water which is absorbed, and are transported to all parts of the plant.

These minerals are usually present in the soil in quite low concentrations. The concentration inside the root hairs is higher. In this situation the mineral ions would normally diffuse out of the root hair into the soil. Root hairs can, however, take up mineral salts against their concentration gradient. It is the cell surface membrane which does this. Special carrier molecules in the cell membrane of the root hair carry the mineral ions across the cell membrane into the cell, against their concentration gradient. This is called **active transport**.

7.44 In active transport particles enter a cell against the concentration gradient.

In diffusion and osmosis, molecules move down a concentration gradient. They are going from an area where there are many of one type of molecule, to an area where are few of the same type. In some situations, in order for substances to enter the cell, molecules or ions (electrically charged particles) need to move *against* a concentration gradient. That is, they are moving from an area where they are scarce, to one in which they are in better supply. This type of movement needs energy from respiration, which why it is known as active transport. Movement is usually in one direction only, so it is a kind of pumping action (Figure 7.33).

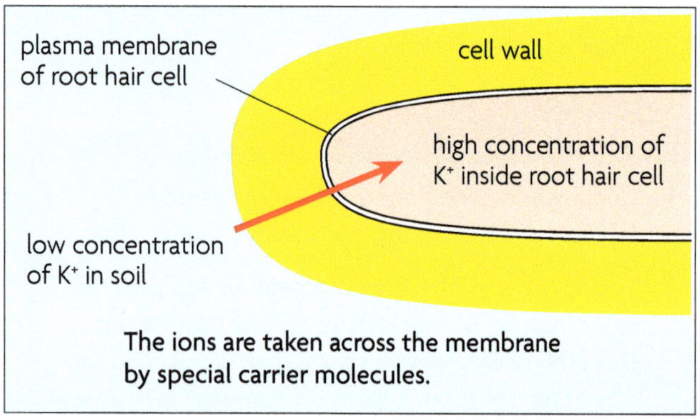

Figure 7.33 Active transport.

In plants, this kind of movement occurs when mineral ions move from the soil into a plant root. Sometimes also, sugar is actively 'pushed' into the phloem for transport around the plant (section **7.45**).

In animal cells, active transport keeps sodium and potassium at the right levels inside cells. Fluid outside the cell has a low concentration of potassium ions, K^+, and a high concentration of sodium ions, Na^+. But inside the cell, the level of potassium must be kept high, and the level of sodium low. So potassium is actively pumped into the cell, and sodium out of it.

Transport of manufactured food

7.45 Phloem translocates organic foods.

Leaves make carbohydrates by photosynthesis. They also use some of these carbohydrates to make amino acids, proteins, oils and other organic substances.

Some of the organic food material, especially sugar, that the plant makes is transported in the phloem tubes. It is carried from the leaves to whichever part of the plant needs it. This is called **translocation**. The sap inside the phloem tubes therefore contains a lot of sugar, particularly **sucrose** (Figure **7.34**).

Questions

7.56 What are adventitious roots?

7.57 What is the function of a root cap?

7.58 Explain how water goes into root hairs. How does this process differ from the way in which minerals enter?

7.59 What is transpiration?

7.60 What are stomata?

7.61 What is a potometer used for?

7.62 Explain how **(a)** temperature, and **(b)** light affect the rate of transpiration.

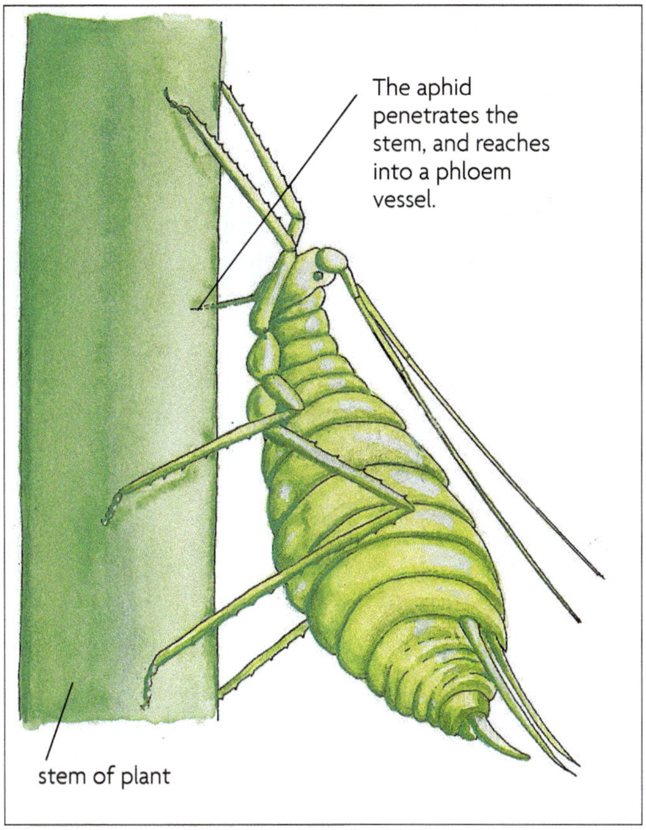

Figure 7.34 Aphids feed on the sugary sap that is flowing in a plant's phloem tubes. These are close to the surface of a stem, so the stylet of an aphid can easily reach into them.

Storage in plants

7.46 Plants store food for many reasons.

The food produced by photosynthesis is not all used straight away. Sugars and amino acids are stored for short periods in cell vacuoles. Starch may also be stored temporarily in leaves. Later it is broken down into sugars and translocated to the places where it is needed in the plant. Food is also stored for longer periods of time.

Some plants (such as maize and peanut) grow, flower, produce fruit and die in a single year. They are called **annuals**. Others, including many weeds, complete their life cycles in a considerably shorter period of time. Since they live for such a short period of time, they are called **ephemerals**. Annuals and ephemerals do not have specialised storage organs but, like all other flowering plants, they have food stores in their seeds (section **7.56**).

Some other plants, such as century plants (*Agave* spp.), like annuals, die after flowering but may live for several years first. They accumulate stored food until they have enough reserves to produce their flowering structures. In *Agave barbadensis* the flower stalk is about eight metres tall.

Perennial plants are those that live from year to year. Trees and shrubs are called woody perennials. Those that shed their leaves in the dry season are said to be **deciduous**. Flamboyante (*Delonix regia*) is a deciduous woody perennial. Plants like citrus and mango, which shed their leaves throughout the year, are said to be **evergreens**.

Herbaceous perennials grow more slowly in the dry season. In some, the above-ground part of the plant may die off. The plants survive the dry season as underground structures. These plants have perennating organs that allow them to store food for rapid growth when conditions improve.

In the temperate regions, the season which is unfavourable for growth is winter, when temperatures are too low. In these areas, deciduous woody perennials shed their leaves in autumn or fall as the temperature falls. Herbaceous perennials die back at this time too.

7.47 Modified stems are used for storage.

Some plants have underground stems which are modified as perennating storage organs. These are **rhizomes**, **stem tubers** and **corms**. The stems of sugarcane are also modified for storage.

7.48 Rhizomes are horizontal underground stems.

In plants which produce rhizomes, the main part of the stem remains below ground and grows horizontally (Figure 7.35, overleaf). Rhizomes look like roots but have the features of stems. They have scale leaves or scars where leaves were attached. Buds grow in the axils of these leaves and adventitious roots are seen.
A cross section of a rhizome shows that the arrangement of tissues is typical of a stem.

FACT! Sweet potatoes are known as yams in the southern states of the USA.

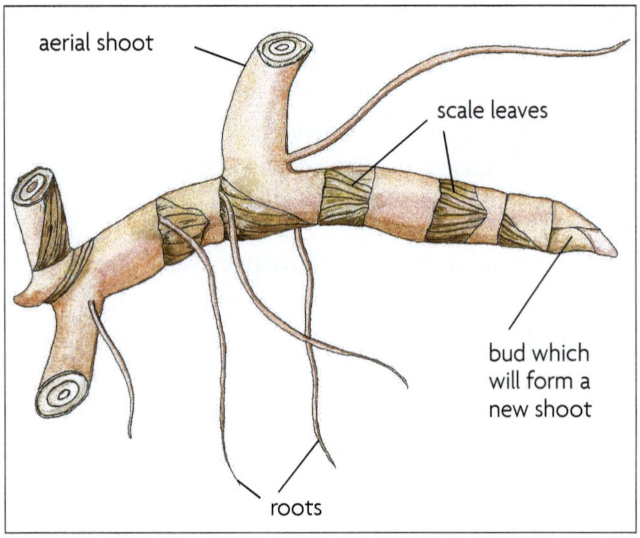

Figure 7.35 Rhizome of *Canna* lily.

Ginger is another example of a plant with a swollen rhizome. Slender rhizomes are found in many grasses. An example is *Cynodon dactylon* which is known as devil's grass when it is a weed and Bahama or Bermuda grass when it is used to make a lawn. The rhizomes of khus khus grass (*Vetiveria zizanoides*) produce a valuable oil which is used in the perfume industry.

7.49 Stem tubers are produced by underground stems.

Stem tubers are the swollen ends of slender rhizomes. Irish potatoes (Figure 7.36) and yams are examples of stem tubers. They can be seen to be stem structures from the distribution of the vascular bundles in a stained cross section. They also have the stem features of leaf scars, with their associated buds, and a terminal bud. At the end of the adverse season, green shoots grow from the buds.

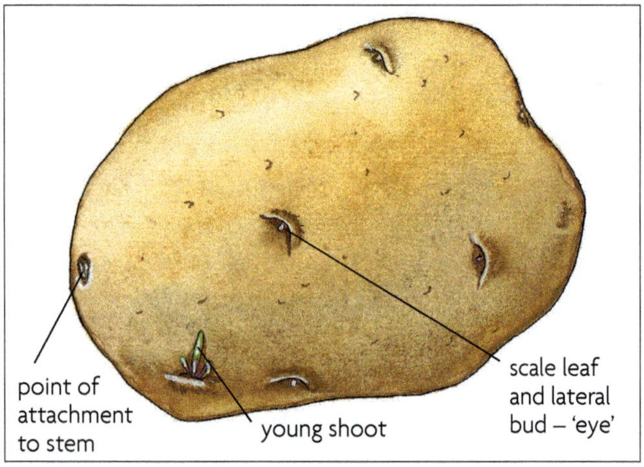

Figure 7.36 Tuber of Irish potato.

Irish potatoes and yams are grown for food. Humans have developed the plants to give bigger tubers with increased nutritional value.

7.50 A corm is a modified stem.

A corm is a short, swollen underground stem (Figure 7.37). It looks like a short, upright rhizome. The leaf bases form a protective scaly covering.

Figure 7.37 A corm of *Colocasia* sp. (coco).

At the end of the perennating period, regrowth is from the lateral buds between the leaves. Dasheen (*Colocasia*), *Caladium* and garlic produce corms and can be propagated from them.

7.51 Roots are storage organs too.

The primary function of roots is the absorption of water and mineral nutrients. Even the slender ones may have a small amount of food stored temporarily in them. This happens when sugar is translocated to the roots faster than it is used. The storage is in the cortical cells.

Roots may also be modified for storage. The specialised storage structures are root tubers and swollen tap roots.

FACT!

The largest Irish potato tuber grown weighed 33 kg. A giant yam, *Dioscorea elephantipes*, grown in southern Africa, had a tuber weighing 365 kg.

7.52 Root tubers are modified roots.

Root tubers are formed on herbaceous perennials with fibrous root systems. They are swollen ends of roots (Figure **7.38**). Root tubers can be distinguished from stem tubers since they do not have leaf scars, scale leaves or buds. A stained cross section shows vascular bundles in a root arrangement. The absence of buds means that regrowth of the plant does not occur from the root tuber. Cassava cannot be propagated from its root tubers, and stem cuttings are used. The root tubers of sweet potato are an exception and new shoots can develop from adventitious buds on them. Thus, sweet potatoes can be propagated from their tubers.

Figure 7.38 Sweet potato tubers.

7.53 Biennials use swollen tap roots for storage.

Biennial plants take two years to complete their life cycle. In the first year, they grow vegetatively and store food for the second year's growth. In the second year, rapid growth of new shoots occurs. These produce flowers, fruits and seeds and the plant dies. Storage is in a swollen main root or tap root (Figure **7.27**, page **132**).

Carrots, beets and radishes use tap roots for storage. When we grow these plants, they are harvested at the end of the first growing season. At this stage, the storage in the tap root is at its peak. If we leave them later, they begin to use their food stores to develop new shoots on which flowers will develop.

7.54 Storage also occurs in leaves.

The products of photosynthesis are often stored temporarily in leaves before translocation to other parts of the plant. This explains positive starch tests in photosynthesis investigations.

Leaves are sometimes modified as food or water storage organs. Bulbs are condensed underground shoots and look like a large bud (Figure **7.39**). They have two types of leaves. The outer ones are dry and protect the inner, thick fleshy ones. The fleshy leaves are modified for storage. *Zephyranthes* species (crocus, Barbados snowdrop and rain lily) and onions have bulbs as their perennating organs. Most plants have starch as their carbohydrate storage compound. Onions store sugars in their bulbs.

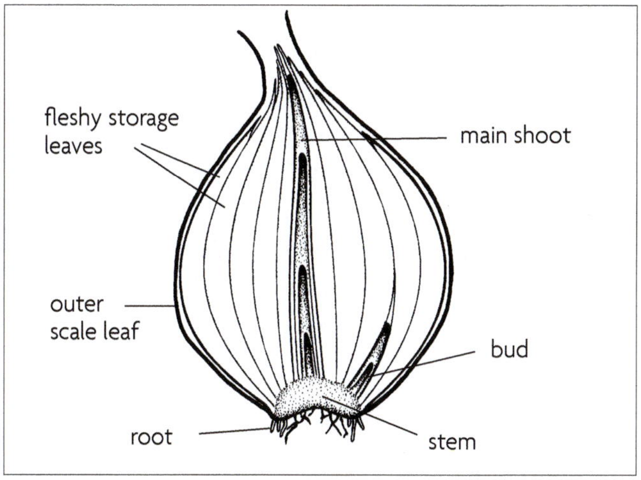

Figure 7.39 Longitudinal section through an onion bulb.

Succulents have fleshy leaves modified for water storage (Figure **8.18**). Succulents are found in dry areas, such as deserts, or grow in soils where it is difficult to obtain water. These soils include those of salt marshes, beach environments and the frozen soils of the tundra.

7.55 Some plants have stems above ground modified for storage.

The stems of sugar cane are swollen and store sucrose (Figure **7.40**, overleaf). Sugar cane is an important crop. The stems are squeezed to extract their cell sap. This juice is processed to give crystals of sugar.

In cacti, the leaves are reduced to spines and the stems are green. Photosynthesis occurs in the stems. The small leaves are an adaptation to reduce water loss by transpiration. The stems of cacti are modified for water storage.

Figure 7.40 A crop of sugar cane.

7.56 Food substances are stored in seeds.

A seed contains a young plant, the **embryo**. When the conditions for germination are provided, the embryo develops into a seedling (sections **12.5** to **12.7**). To grow, the embryo requires food. It cannot make its own food until it has green leaves and can photosynthesise. The mother plant provides a food store in the seed. In some plants, such as corn and castor oil, the food is in the **endosperm**. This type of storage is called endospermic. In non-endospermic plants, storage is in the seed leaves, or **cotyledons**.

Table **7.4** gives the proportions of the major food types stored in some seeds. The values are percentages of air-dried seeds.

The food stored in seeds is required for the early growth of seedlings. A young seedling needs simple materials to make more complex molecules. It also needs food substances which can be used in respiration to provide energy. In Table **7.4**, the lowest value for protein is 9%. There is no substitute for amino acids which are needed to make enzymes and other proteins. Fats and carbohydrates can both be used in respiration. Compare the amount of each of these in castor oil and pigeon pea.

7.57 Fruits are storage organs too.

Fruits often store carbohydrates. A few, like the avocado (*Persea americana*) and ackee (*Blighia sapida*), store lipids. Succulent fruits especially are a source of food for animals. The animals, such as birds, bats, monkeys and humans, often carry the fruits away from the parent plant and eat them. The indigestible seeds are discarded and may germinate. So new plants grow away from the parent plant (section **13.41**).

Questions

7.63 What are the storage structures in each of the following: *Caladium*, carrot, cassava, devil's grass, sweet potato, yam?

7.64 How can you tell whether a tuber is a modified root or a modified stem?

7.65 Name two plants which do not store starch.

7.66 How is the tuber of sweet potato unusual?

Table 7.4 Food storage in seeds

Plant species	Percentage of storage substance in dry seeds		
	Carbohydrates	Proteins	Lipids
castor oil (*Ricinus communis*)	0	18	64
corn or maize (*Zea mays*)	74	10	5
peanut (*Arachis hypogaea*)	22	25	45
pigeon pea (*Cajanus cajan*)	63	22	2
rice (*Oryza sativa*)	75	9	2
sunflower (*Helianthus annuus*)	2	25	47

Key ideas

- Large organisms have a small surface area to volume ratio, and so need a transport system to deliver requirements such as oxygen and nutrients to their cells.
- Mammals have a double circulatory system, in which blood is moved through vessels by the regular contraction and relaxation of cardiac muscles in the wall of the heart.
- Blood enters the atria of the heart, flows through open valves into the ventricles, and is then forced out into the arteries during systole.
- The ventricles have thicker walls than the atria, and the left ventricle has a thicker wall than the right ventricle, to allow them to produce a greater force when the muscles contract, necessary so that they can push the blood further.
- Arteries are thick-walled, elastic vessels that carry pulsing, high-pressure blood away from the heart. They split into capillaries, which are tiny vessels with walls only one cell thick. Capillaries take blood close to every cell in the body, so that the cells are supplied with oxygen and nutrients and have their waste products removed. Capillaries join up to form veins. Veins are thin-walled vessels with valves, which carry low-pressure blood back to the heart.
- Blood contains red cells, white cells and platelets floating in plasma. Plasma transports many different substances in solution. Red cells contain the iron-containing protein haemoglobin, which transports oxygen. White cells fight against bacteria. Platelets help the blood to clot.
- Fluid leaks out of capillaries to fill the spaces between all the body cells, where it is called tissue fluid. It is collected into lymph vessels which carry it back to the bloodstream.
- In plants, xylem vessels transport water and mineral ions from the roots upwards to the leaves. Phloem tubes transport sucrose and other organic nutrients from the leaves where they are made to all parts of the plant.
- Xylem vessels are made of dead, empty cells with strong lignin in their walls. As well as transporting water, they help to support the plant.
- Water is drawn up xylem vessels by the evaporation of water from the leaves, called transpiration. Transpiration happens fastest when it is hot, dry, windy and sunny.
- Water enters root hairs by osmosis, and then moves across the cortex of the root into the xylem.
- Root hairs take up mineral ions by active transport, using energy supplied by respiration to move them against their concentration gradient.
- Phloem is made of living cells with sieve plates at their ends. A companion cell is associated with each phloem tube.
- Most organisms store nutrients for times when they are in short supply. In humans, lipids are stored underneath the skin, and glycogen (a polysaccharide carbohydrate) is stored in the liver. Plants store food in seeds, stems, rhizomes, leaves, stem tubers, root tubers, corms and bulbs. It is often in the form of starch, but seeds also contain a lot of protein and often lipid as well.

End-of-chapter questions

1 Using Figure 7.11 (page 122) to help you, list in order the blood vessels and parts of the heart which:
   a a glucose molecule would travel through on its way from your digestive system to a muscle in your leg
   b a carbon dioxide molecule would travel through on its way from the leg muscle to your lungs.

2 Explain the difference between each of the following pairs:
   a blood, lymph
   b diastole, systole
   c artery, vein
   d deoxygenated blood, oxygenated blood
   e atrium, ventricle
   f hepatic vein, hepatic portal vein
   g red blood cell, white blood cell
   h xylem, phloem
   i diffusion, active transport.

3 Arteries, veins, capillaries, xylem vessels and phloem tubes are all tubes used for transporting substances in mammals and flowering plants. Describe how each of these tubes is adapted for its particular function.

4 a What is meant by a double circulatory system?
   b Copy this diagram of a section through a heart.
   c Fill in the labels **A** to **F**, and draw in arrows to show the direction of blood flow through it.

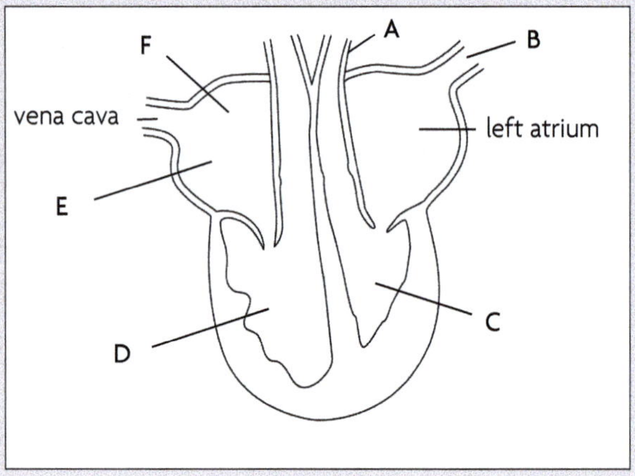

   d In an unborn child, the lungs do not work. The baby gets its oxygen from the mother, to which it is connected by the umbilical cord. This cord contains a vein, which carries the oxygenated blood to the baby's vena cava.
      i Which chamber of the heart does oxygenated blood enter in an adult person?
      ii Which chamber of the heart does oxygenated blood enter in an unborn baby?
      iii In an unborn child, there is a hole in the septum between the left and right atria. What purpose do you think this has?
      iv As soon as the baby takes its first breath, this hole closes up. Why is this important?

5 An experiment was performed where a solution of human haemoglobin was exposed to samples of air containing different amounts of oxygen (measured in kilopascals, kPa). At each oxygen concentration, the haemoglobin sample was tested to see how much oxygen it had absorbed.

   If it had absorbed as much oxygen as it could possibly carry, it was said to be 100% saturated. If it only carried half this amount, it was 50% saturated, and so on. The graph overleaf shows the results obtained.

   a What is the approximate percentage saturation of human haemoglobin with oxygen, at an oxygen tension of
      i 2 kPa
      ii 6 kPa?
   b If haemoglobin which had been exposed to an oxygen tension of 6 kPa was then exposed to an oxygen tension of 2 kPa, would it absorb or give up oxygen?
   c In the lungs, the oxygen tension is usually about 13 kPa. In the muscles, it is around 4 kPa. Explain why.
   d Using the information in part **(c)**, and your answer to part **(b)**, explain how haemoglobin transports oxygen from the lungs to a muscle.
   e What would be the disadvantage of having haemoglobin which absorbed a lot of oxygen at low oxygen tensions?

(*continues on page* **145**)

(... *continued*)

f The lugworm, *Arenicola*, lives in burrows on muddy beaches. There is often only very little oxygen available. *Arenicola* is not a very active animal. The blood of *Arenicola* contains haemoglobin, which behaves rather differently from human haemoglobin (see the graph). Can you explain why this type of haemoglobin suits *Arenicola*'s way of life better than human haemoglobin would?

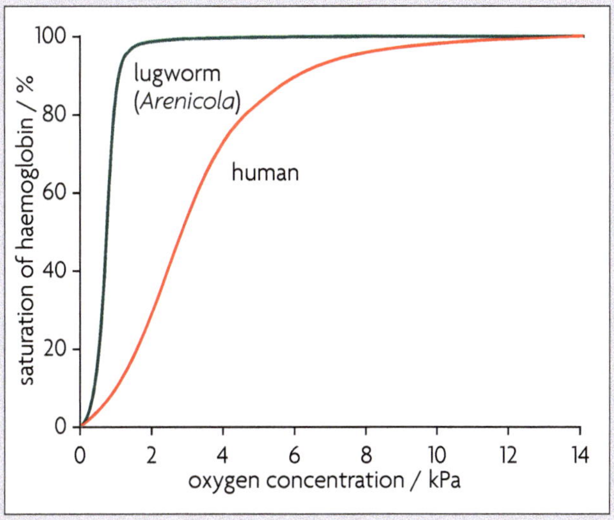

6 Why do plants store the products of photosynthesis?

7 The essential food substances are carbohydrates, proteins and fats. Some seeds only have two of these.

Suggest how it is possible for seedlings to survive with just two of these essential nutrient types.

8 Horticulturists often get new plants of *Hibiscus*, crotons and other species by circumposing. In practice, this means ringing a portion of stem just beneath a node. Fine soil is then affixed to this portion of the stem. After about three weeks, roots develop at the point of ringing, and the new plant can be cut off. How does it help the plant for roots to develop where the stem has been ringed?

8 Excretion and osmoregulation

In this chapter, you will find out:

- that all organisms must excrete the waste products of their metabolism
- the main excretory products of animals and plants, and the organs which excrete them
- how the liver makes urea
- about the structure and function of the kidneys, including their role in osmoregulation
- how xerophytic plants are adapted to conserve water.

8.1 Waste products of metabolism are excreted.

All living cells have a great many metabolic reactions going on inside them. The reactions of respiration (section **6.2**) for example, provide energy for the cell. The reactions of photosynthesis (section **4.4**) provide plant cells with sugars.

However, these reactions often produce other substances as well, which the cells do not need. If allowed to remain in the cells, these substances may become poisonous or toxic. Respiration, for example, produces not only energy, but also water and carbon dioxide.

Animal cells need the energy, and may be able to make use of the water. They do not, however, need the carbon dioxide. The carbon dioxide is a waste product.

During daylight hours, plant cells can use the carbon dioxide that they produce in respiration for photosynthesis, so it is not a waste product for them at that time. However, at night, when they cannot photosynthesise but continue to respire, carbon dioxide *is* a waste product.

A waste product like carbon dioxide, which is made in a cell as a result of a metabolic reaction, is called an **excretory product.** The removal of excretory products is called **excretion**.

8.2 Egestion is not excretion.

Many animals have another kind of waste material to get rid of. Almost always, some of the food that an animal eats cannot be digested. Humans, for example, cannot digest cellulose. The cellulose in our food goes straight through the alimentary canal, and out of the anus as part of the faeces.

This cellulose is not an excretory product. It has never been involved in any metabolic reaction in your cells. It has not even been inside a cell – it has simply passed, unchanged, through your digestive system. So getting rid of undigested cellulose in faeces is not excretion. It is called **egestion**.

Excretion in plants

8.3 Excretory products of plants fall into two main groups.

Plants are not as metabolically active as animals, and so size for size, do not produce as great quantities of waste products (Figure **8.1**). There are two main ways in which plants get rid of these products. Some actually leave the plant; others are kept in the plant, but they are put in a 'safe place' where they do not interfere with the functioning of the cells.

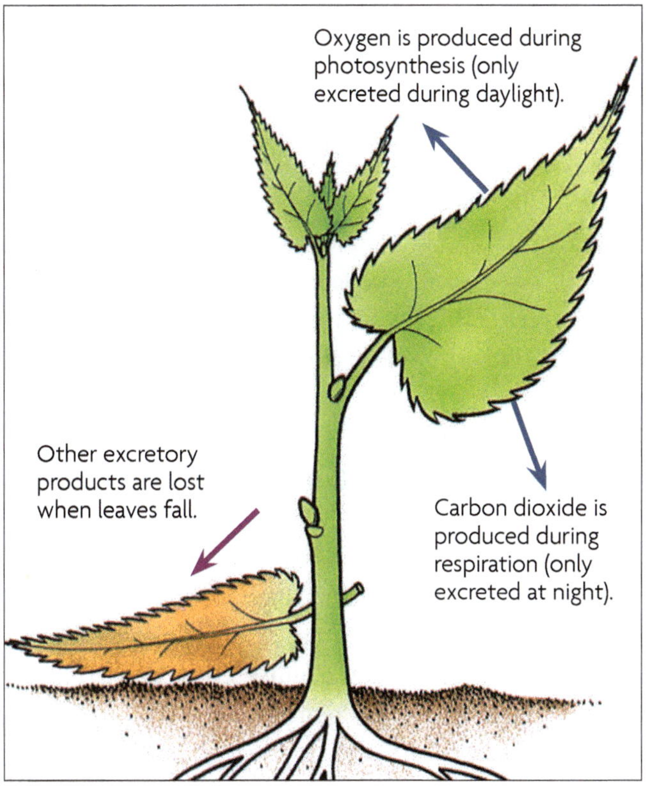

Oxygen is produced during photosynthesis (only excreted during daylight).
Other excretory products are lost when leaves fall.
Carbon dioxide is produced during respiration (only excreted at night).

Figure 8.1 Excretory products of plants.

8.4 Some excretory products leave the plant.

Carbon dioxide Like all cells, plant cells are always respiring. Respiration produces carbon dioxide as a waste product.

If this carbon dioxide is not used by the chloroplasts for photosynthesis (section **6.28**), it is excreted through the stomata by diffusion. As we have seen, this happens at night, when the plant is not photosynthesising. During the day, plants photosynthesise more than they respire, so they do not excrete carbon dioxide.

Oxygen During daylight, plants produce oxygen as a by-product of photosynthesis.

$$6CO_2 + 6H_2O \xrightarrow[\text{chlorophyll}]{\text{sunlight}} C_6H_{12}O_6 + 6O_2$$

Some of this oxygen is used by the plant for respiration, but there is often much left over. This is excreted through the stomata.

Other substances Leaves often change to brilliant colours before they fall. These colours are due to waste **pigments** which the plants lose in this way. Sometimes these leaves also contain crystals of **calcium oxalate**.

8.5 Some excretory products remain in the plant.

Since a build-up of waste products can become poisonous, any which remain in the plant must be in a form in which they do not affect the metabolic processes taking place in the plant cells. Some are changed into insoluble substances like calcium oxalate, oils and **alkaloids**, and kept in living cells. Calcium oxalate is usually in the form of crystals. It is the oils in citrus, pimento, eucalyptus, cinnamon and many other plants that give them their characteristic smell. The white milky substances which ooze from oleander (*Nerium oleander*), *Allamanda, Euphorbia* spp. and *Echites* spp. contain alkaloids. Alkaloids are nitrogen compounds. Some of them are poisonous – for example, strychnine. Many are used in medicine – for example, quinine, codeine and morphine.

Other waste substances are taken to structures in the plant which are dead, but kept on the plant as they are still useful. The tannins in the bark of many trees like the mangroves, and the dyes in the 'heartwood' of others like logwood, are examples of these types of substances. In these dead structures, the waste substances serve to preserve and protect them, making the structures less likely to rot or, in the case of bark, to be eaten.

Many oils, tannins and dyes are of commercial value to us. Pimento and citrus oils are among the useful oils.

Questions

8.1 What is meant by an excretory product?

8.2 Explain the difference between excretion and egestion.

8.3 Why do plants have relatively less waste to excrete than animals?

8.4 What are the main excretory products of plants?

8.5 How do plants deal with these excretory products?

Excretion in animals

8.6 Excretory products of animals.

The carbon dioxide from respiration is excreted from the lungs, gills or other gas exchange surface (Figure **8.2**). Animals also produce **nitrogenous waste**. This is formed from excess proteins and amino acids. Animals are not able to store these in their bodies, so any that are surplus to requirements are broken down to form a nitrogen-containing excretory product.

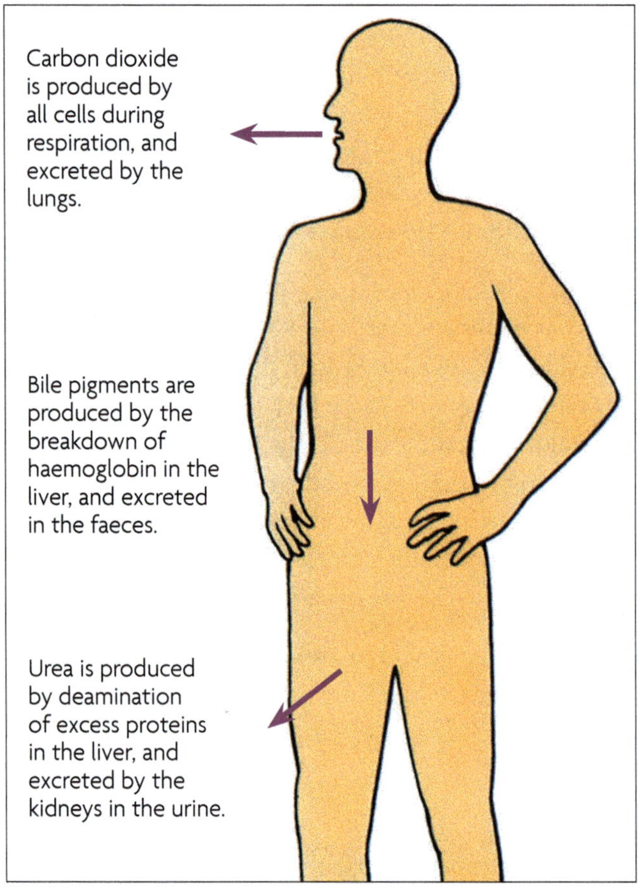

Carbon dioxide is produced by all cells during respiration, and excreted by the lungs.
Bile pigments are produced by the breakdown of haemoglobin in the liver, and excreted in the faeces.
Urea is produced by deamination of excess proteins in the liver, and excreted by the kidneys in the urine.

Figure 8.2 Excretory products of mammals.

In *Amoeba* this nitrogenous waste compound is **ammonia** which is very soluble and very poisonous. We have seen that an amoeba is small, with a large surface area for its size, so the ammonia can easily diffuse across the membrane into the water in which it lives.

Where this large volume of water is not available, and the surface area is smaller in relation to the size of the animal, the nitrogenous waste must be a less poisonous compound than ammonia.

In mammals, this substance is mainly **urea**, though there are small amounts of **uric acid** as well. In insects, reptiles and birds, the compound is uric acid, which does not dissolve in water and is the least poisonous of the three nitrogen compounds mentioned.

Plants do not have the problem of getting rid of excess proteins. This is because they make their own proteins, and so they only make as much as is needed. There is, of course, some waste produced in these reactions – for example, the alkaloids – but the amounts are relatively small. Plants are also able to store protein, for example in seeds.

8.7 In mammals, excess proteins are converted to urea.

When you eat proteins, digestive enzymes in your stomach, duodenum and ileum break them down into amino acids. The amino acids are absorbed into the blood capillaries in the villi in your ileum (section **5.21**). The blood capillaries all join up to the hepatic portal vein, which takes the absorbed food to the liver.

The liver allows some of the amino acids to carry on, in the blood, to other parts of your body. But if you have eaten more than you need, then some of them must be got rid of.

It would be very wasteful to excrete the extra amino acids just as they are. They contain energy which, if it is not needed straight away, might be needed later.

So enzymes in the liver split up each amino acid molecule (Figures **8.3** and **8.4**). The part containing the energy is kept, turned into carbohydrate and stored. The rest, which is the part that contains nitrogen, is turned into **urea**. This process is called **deamination**.

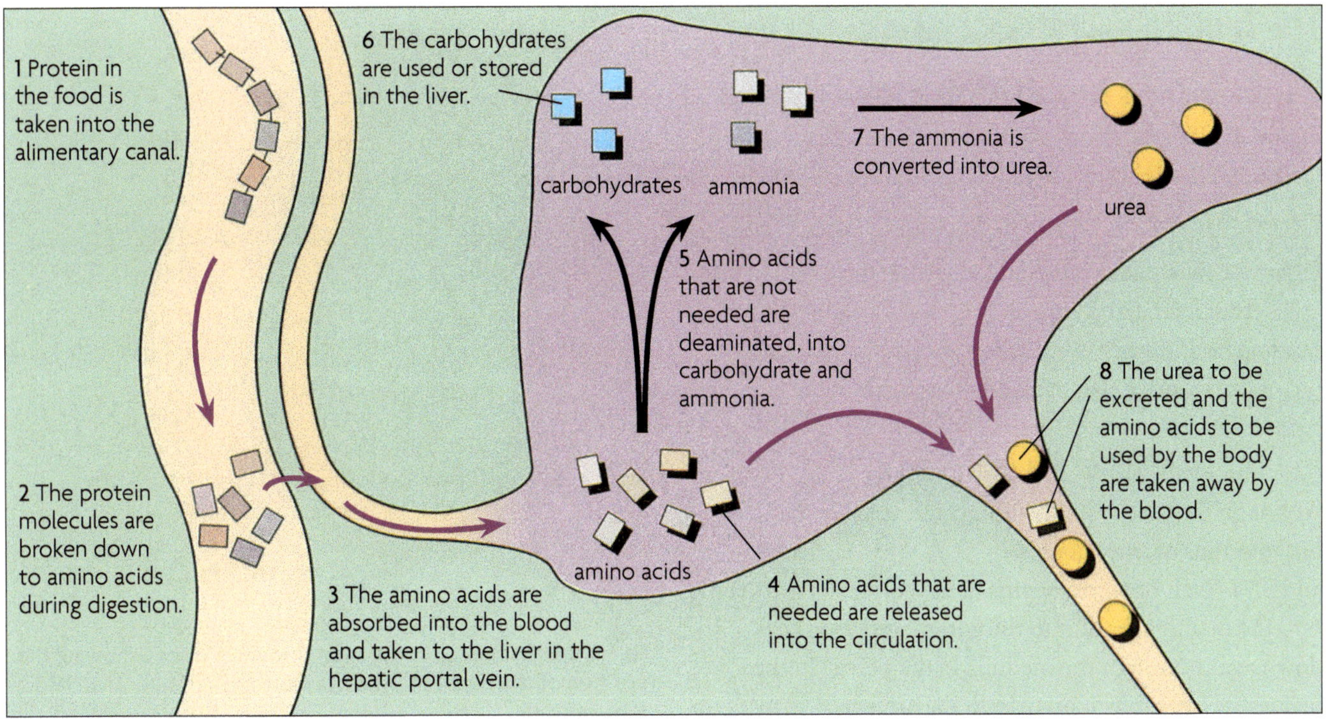

1 Protein in the food is taken into the alimentary canal.
6 The carbohydrates are used or stored in the liver.
carbohydrates
ammonia
7 The ammonia is converted into urea.
urea
5 Amino acids that are not needed are deaminated, into carbohydrate and ammonia.
8 The urea to be excreted and the amino acids to be used by the body are taken away by the blood.
2 The protein molecules are broken down to amino acids during digestion.
amino acids
3 The amino acids are absorbed into the blood and taken to the liver in the hepatic portal vein.
4 Amino acids that are needed are released into the circulation.

Figure 8.3 How urea is made.

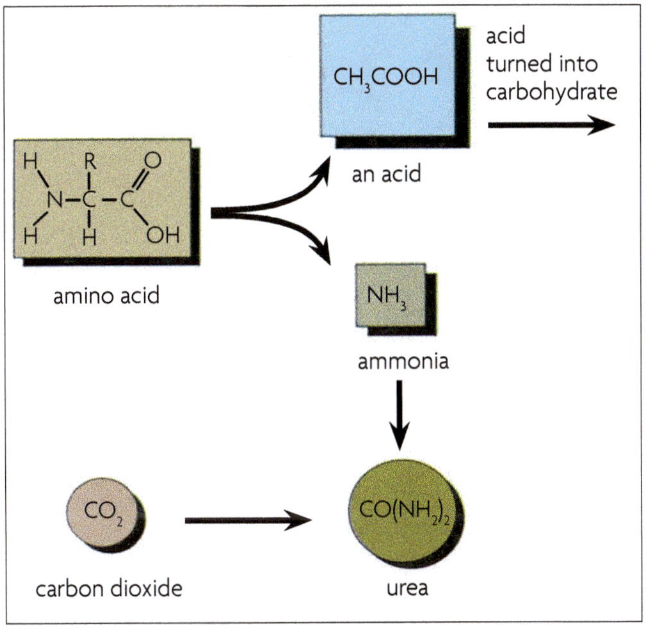

CH3COOH
acid turned into carbohydrate
an acid
amino acid
NH3
ammonia
CO2
carbon dioxide
CO(NH2)2
urea

Figure 8.4 Deamination and urea formation.

The urea dissolves in the blood plasma, and is taken to the kidneys to be excreted. A small amount is also excreted in sweat.

The liver has many other functions, as well as deamination. One of the more important ones is storage. Table 8.1 lists some of the functions.

Table 8.1 Some functions of the liver

1	Converts excess amino acids into urea and carbohydrate, in a process called deamination.
2	Controls the amount of glucose in the blood, with the aid of the hormones insulin and glucagon.
3	Stores carbohydrate as the polysaccharide glycogen.
4	Makes bile.
5	Breaks down old red blood cells, storing the iron and excreting the remains of the haemoglobin as bile pigments.
6	Breaks down harmful substances such as alcohol.
7	Stores vitamins A, B, D, E and K.
8	Stores potassium.
9	Makes cholesterol, which is needed to make and repair cell membranes.

Questions

8.6 What are the main excretory products of animals?

8.7 What processes produce these products?

8.8 What happens to the excess protein you eat?

The human excretory system

8.8 The kidneys are part of the excretory system.

Figure **8.5** illustrates the position of the two kidneys in the human body. They are at the back of the abdomen, behind the intestines.

Figure **8.6** illustrates a longitudinal section through a kidney. It has three main parts – the **cortex**, **medulla** and **pelvis**. Leading from the pelvis is a tube, called the **ureter**. The ureter carries urine that the kidney has made to the **bladder**.

8.9 The kidneys are full of tubules.

Although they seem solid, kidneys are actually made up of thousands of tiny tubules, or **nephrons** (Figures **8.6** and **8.7**). Each nephron begins in the cortex, loops down into the medulla, back into the cortex, and then goes down again through the medulla to the pelvis. In the pelvis, the nephrons join up with the ureter.

8.10 Urine is made by filtration and selective reabsorption.

The function of the kidneys is to take unwanted substances from the blood and to pass them on to the bladder, to be excreted. The way they do this is shown in Figure **8.8**.

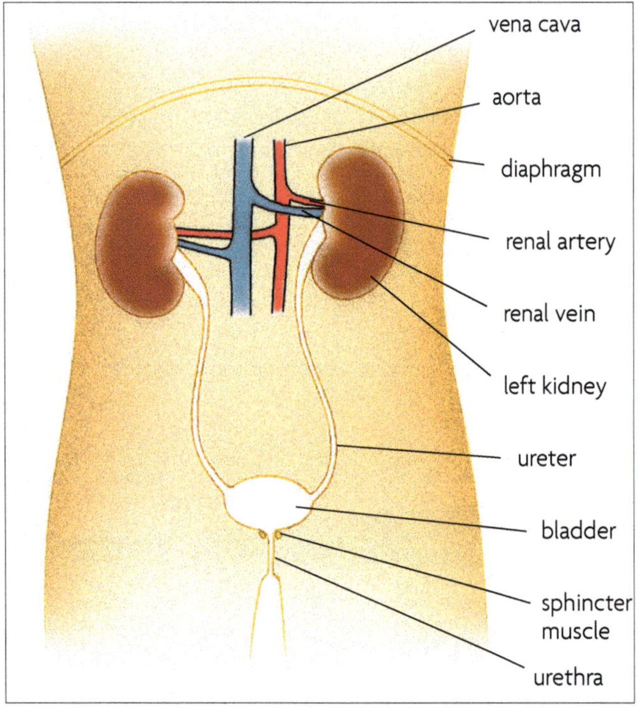

Figure 8.5 The human excretory system.

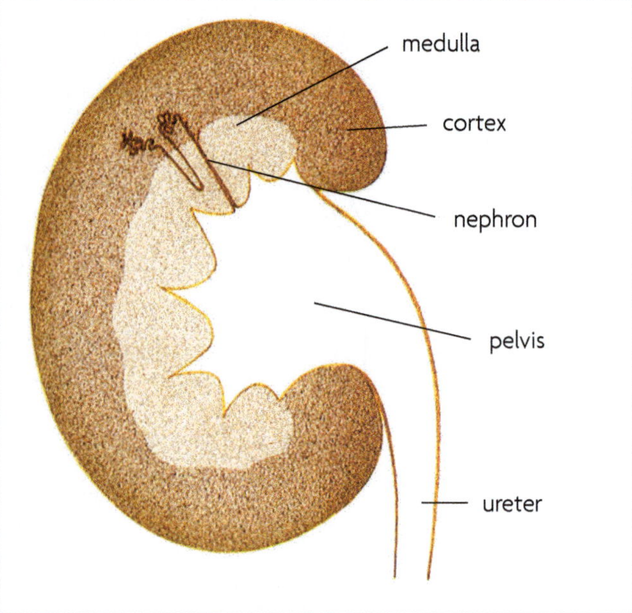

Figure 8.6 A longitudinal section through a kidney showing the position of the nephron (which is drawn much larger than its relative size).

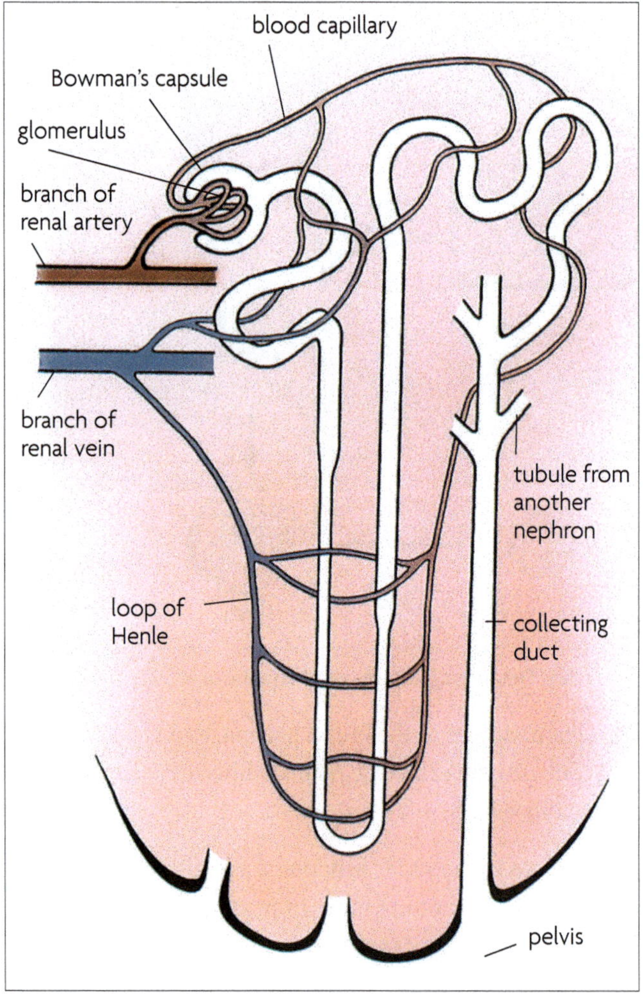

Figure 8.7 A nephron.

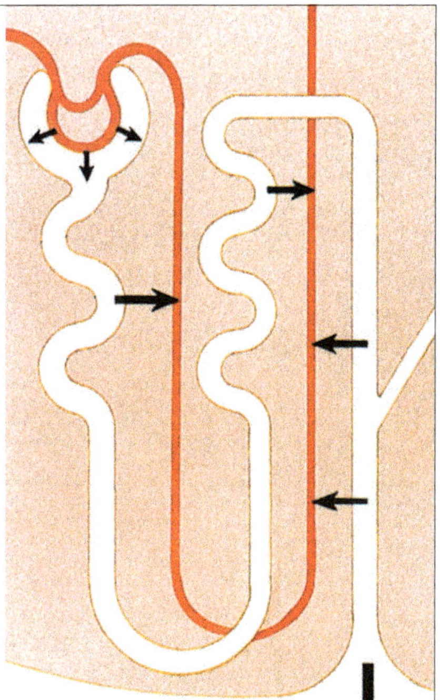

Filtration Small molecules, such as water, glucose, salts and urea, are squeezed out of the blood into a Bowman's capsule.
Reabsorption Any useful substances, such as water and glucose, are taken back into the blood.
The remaining liquid, called urine, flows into the ureter.

Figure 8.8 How urine is made.

Blood is brought to the **Bowman's capsule** in a branch of the renal artery. Small molecules, including water and most of the things dissolved in it, are squeezed out of the blood into the Bowman's capsule. Any useful substances are then taken back into the blood again. The liquid left in the tubule, called **urine**, goes into the ureter and is taken to the bladder.

8.11 Filtration happens in Bowman's capsules.

There are thousands of Bowman's capsules in the cortex of each kidney. Each one is shaped like a cup. It has a tangle of blood capillaries, called a **glomerulus**, in the middle.

The blood vessel bringing blood to each glomerulus is quite wide, but the one taking blood away is narrow. This means that the blood in the glomerulus cannot get away easily. Quite a high pressure builds up, squeezing the blood in the glomerulus against the capillary walls.

These walls have small holes in them. So do the walls of the Bowman's capsules. Any molecules small enough to go through these holes will be squeezed through, into the space in the Bowman's capsule.

Only small molecules can go through. These include **water, salt, glucose** and **urea**. Most protein molecules are too big, so they stay in the blood, along with the blood cells.

8.12 Useful substances are reabsorbed.

The fluid in the Bowman's capsule is a solution of glucose, salts and urea, dissolved in water. Some of the substances in this fluid are needed by the body. All of the glucose, some of the water and some of the salts, need to be kept in the blood.

Wrapped around each kidney tubule are blood capillaries. They reabsorb these useful substances from the fluid in the kidney tubule.

The remaining fluid continues on its way along the tubule. By the time it gets to the collecting duct, it is mostly water, with urea and salts dissolved in it. It is called urine.

The tubules are extremely efficient at reabsorbing water. Over 99% of the water entering the tubules is reabsorbed. In humans, the two kidneys filter about 170 litres of water per day, yet only about 1.5 litres of urine are produced in the same period.

8.13 The bladder stores urine.

The urine from all the nephrons in the kidneys flows into the ureters. The ureters take it to the bladder.

The bladder stores urine. It has stretchy walls, so that it can hold quite large quantities.

Leading out of the bladder is a tube called the **urethra**. There is a sphincter muscle at the top of the urethra, which is usually tightly closed. When the bladder is full, the sphincter muscle opens, so that the urine flows along the urethra and out of the body.

Adult mammals can consciously control this sphincter muscle. In young mammals, it opens automatically when the bladder gets full.

8.14 Dialysis does the work of damaged kidneys.

Sometimes, a person's kidneys stop working properly. This might be because of an infection. Complete failure of the kidneys allows urea and other waste products to build up in the blood, and will cause death if not treated.

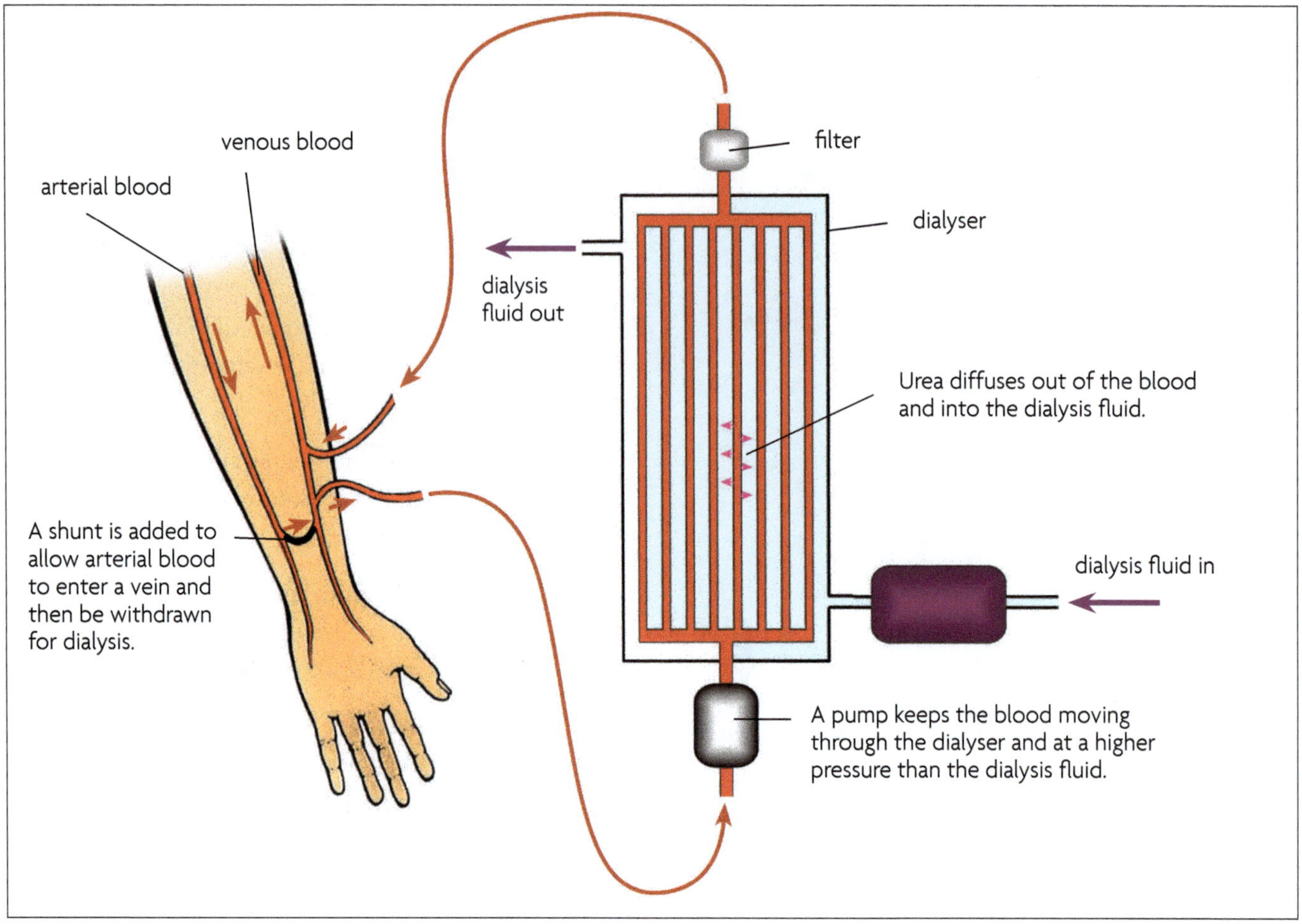

Figure 8.9 How kidney dialysis works.

The best treatment is a kidney transplant, but this is not easy to arrange, because the 'tissue type' of the donor and the recipient must be a close match, or the recipient's body will reject the transplanted kidney. The donated kidney usually comes from a healthy person who has died suddenly, for example in a car accident.

The usual treatment for a person with kidney failure is to have several sessions a week using a **dialysis** unit (Figure 8.9), sometimes called a kidney machine. The person's blood flows through the machine and back into their body. Inside the machine, the blood is separated from a special fluid by a partially permeable membrane (like Visking tubing). This fluid contains water, glucose, salts and other substances that should be present in the blood.

As the patient's blood passes through the tubes, the substances in the fluid diffuse through the membrane, down their concentration gradients. For example, there is no urea in the dialysis fluid, so urea diffuses out of the patient's blood and into the fluid. The amount of other substances in the blood can be regulated by controlling their concentrations in the dialysis fluid.

Patients need to be treated on a dialysis unit two or three times a week, and the treatment lasts for several hours.

Questions

8.9 What is a nephron?

8.10 Which blood vessels bring blood to the kidneys?

8.11 What is a glomerulus?

8.12 How is a high blood pressure built up in a glomerulus?

8.13 Why is this high blood pressure needed?

8.14 Name two substances found in the blood which you would not find in the fluid inside a Bowman's capsule.

8.15 List three substances which are reabsorbed from the nephron into the blood.

8.16 What is urine?

Osmoregulation

8.15 All organisms need water.

Living organisms are mostly water. You are about 60% water. A cucumber is 95% water.

Water is very important to living organisms, for many reasons. One of the most important reasons is that water is a solvent. It dissolves salts, sugars, proteins and many other substances. Cytoplasm contains all of these things, dissolved in water.

Unless these substances are dissolved in water, they will not behave in the way they should. Metabolic reactions could not take place, and the cell would die.

Too much water can also be dangerous. Figure **2.10** (page **32**) shows what happens to an animal cell if it has too much water.

8.16 How organisms gain water.

By osmosis Plants take in water from the soil, by osmosis, through the cell surface membrane of their root hairs. Animals that live in fresh water also take in water by osmosis through their cell surface membranes.

In food Most animals drink water, and also get a lot of water from the food they eat.

By respiration If you look at the respiration equation (section **6.1**) you will see that six molecules of water are made for every molecule of glucose that is broken down in respiration. Because this water is made as a result of a metabolic reaction, it is called metabolic water.

Metabolic water is not very important to most organisms. Some desert animals, though, depend on it to keep their cells supplied with water (section **7.28**).

8.17 How organisms lose water.

By evaporation Organisms living on land lose water by evaporation from the surface of their bodies. In plants, this is called transpiration.

In animals, most of the water evaporates from their moist gas exchange surfaces. If they do not have waterproof coverings to their skins, then water will evaporate from there, too. Mammals also lose water when sweat evaporates.

In urine Nitrogenous excretory products, like urea, have to be dissolved in water, so that they can be passed out of the body.

By osmosis Fish which live in the sea have body fluids which are more dilute than sea water, so they lose water by osmosis.

8.18 Organisms keep the composition of their body fluids constant.

To continue to survive in their surroundings, organisms must have ways of keeping the fluids inside their bodies at about the same concentration all the time. This is called **osmoregulation**. To do this they must balance the amount of water and salts coming into their bodies, and the amount going out.

8.19 Terrestrial organisms can lose water easily by evaporation.

All terrestrial organisms face the problem of desiccation or drying out because it is easy for them to lose water from the surface of their bodies by evaporation into the air. Mechanisms for osmoregulation are, therefore, very much linked with means for conserving or saving water. Two important ways in which this is done are by the development of waterproof coverings, and the storage or reabsorption of water already in the body.

8.20 Terrestrial animals can control their water loss.

In mammals the cornified layer of the skin (Figure **11.8**, page **204**) is waterproof, except where there are pores from the sweat glands. This reduces water loss from the body by evaporation into the air.

In humans, the kidneys have an important part to play in regulating the amount of water in the body. They do this by controlling how much water is lost in the urine. Figure **8.10** (overleaf) summarises how this happens.

In the **hypothalamus** in the brain, there are cells which can sense the amount of water in the blood which flows past them. If there is not enough water, then these cells cause the **pituitary gland** to secrete a hormone called **ADH** (anti-diuretic hormone). The ADH dissolves in the blood and is taken to the kidneys.

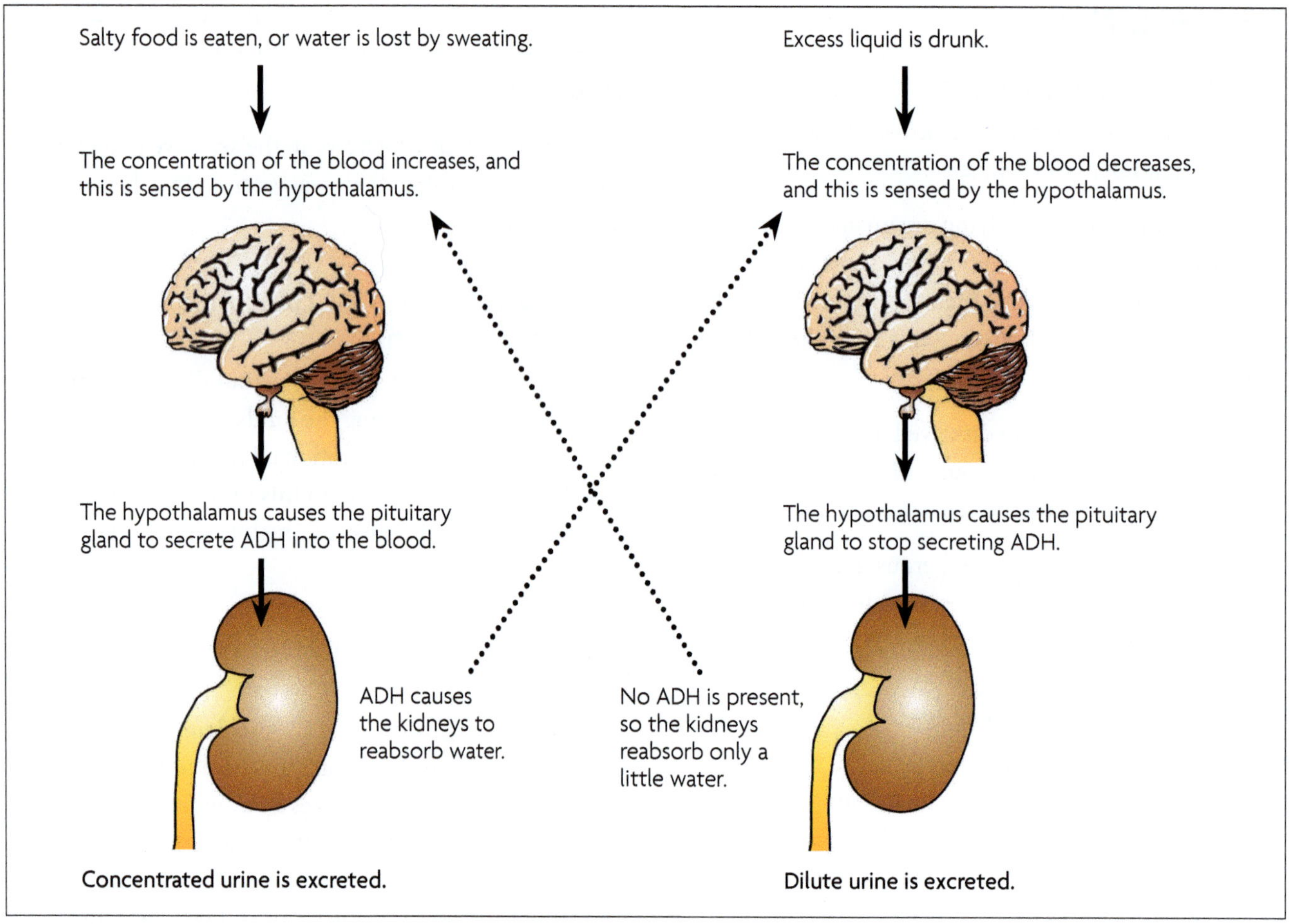

Salty food is eaten, or water is lost by sweating.
The concentration of the blood increases, and this is sensed by the hypothalamus.
The hypothalamus causes the pituitary gland to secrete ADH into the blood.
ADH causes the kidneys to reabsorb water.
Concentrated urine is excreted.
Excess liquid is drunk.
The concentration of the blood decreases, and this is sensed by the hypothalamus.
The hypothalamus causes the pituitary gland to stop secreting ADH.
No ADH is present, so the kidneys reabsorb only a little water.
Dilute urine is excreted.

Figure 8.10 The roles of the kidneys and hypothalamus in osmoregulation.

When the ADH arrives at the kidneys, it has an effect on the nephrons. It makes the capillaries around them reabsorb more water from the urine. The water goes back into the blood, instead of going down the ureter to the bladder. There will be less urine, and it will be concentrated.

If there is too much water in the blood, the hypothalamus secretes less ADH. A large amount of urine is made, containing a lot of water.

Desert mammals need to use additional mechanisms besides the kidneys and the skin. The camel, for example, can go without water for many days because its tissues can tolerate a high degree of water loss without dying.

For other desert animals, the water formed in respiration is very important in maintaining the water balance of the cells. The kangaroo rat, in addition to producing a very concentrated urine and losing very little water from its skin, makes such good use of the water from respiration in its cells that it does not need to drink.

8.21 Negative feedback helps in homeostasis

Water is just one example of something that is kept fairly constant in the body. Later, we will see how the body also regulates temperature and the concentration of glucose in the blood. These are all part of **homeostasis**, which is the maintenance of constant internal conditions in the body. Homeostasis is usually carried out through **negative feedback**.

The mechanism by which the water content of the body is kept constant is a good example of negative feedback (Figures **8.11** and **8.12**). If the water content rises too high, this is detected by sensors, and these bring about actions that get rid of the extra water and return the water content to normal. If the water content falls too low, then the sensors again detect the change and bring about actions that reduce the loss of any more water. You will meet more examples of negative feedback in Chapter **11**.

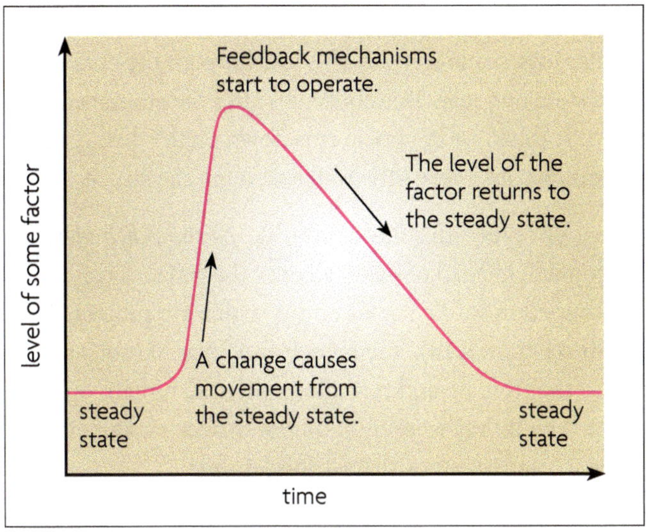

Figure 8.11 Negative feedback.

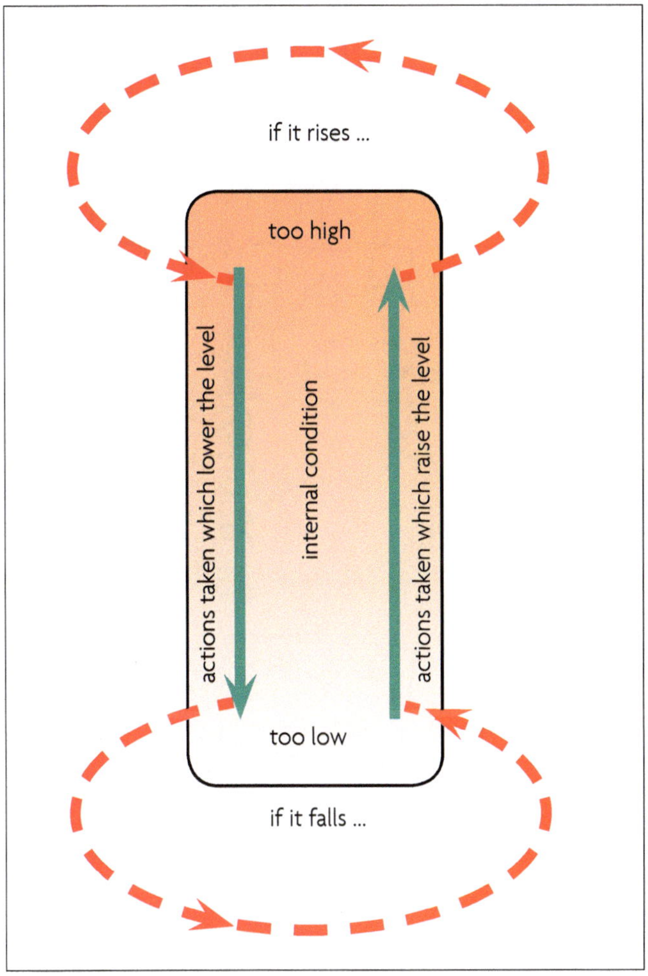

Figure 8.12 'Actions taken which raise the level' and 'actions taken which lower the level'.

8.22 Many terrestrial plants can cut down on water loss.

Evaporation from the parts of plants above ground will always take place. The rate of loss is greater when the stomata are open. When there is enough water available in the soil for roots to absorb water as fast as it is lost, evaporation from the leaves and stems provides a kind of pull. This ensures that water gets to the cells of even the highest branches. When water is in short supply, uncontrolled transpiration will upset the water balance of the plant. It is in short supply in the dry seasons in most tropical areas. In desert and semi-desert regions water is scarce throughout the year.

Terrestrial plants have a variety of ways which help them to maintain enough water in their cells. Plants which have become adapted to survive in very dry places are called **xerophytes**.

Closing stomata Plants lose most water through their stomata. If they close their stomata, then transpiration will slow right down. Figure **8.13** shows how they do this.

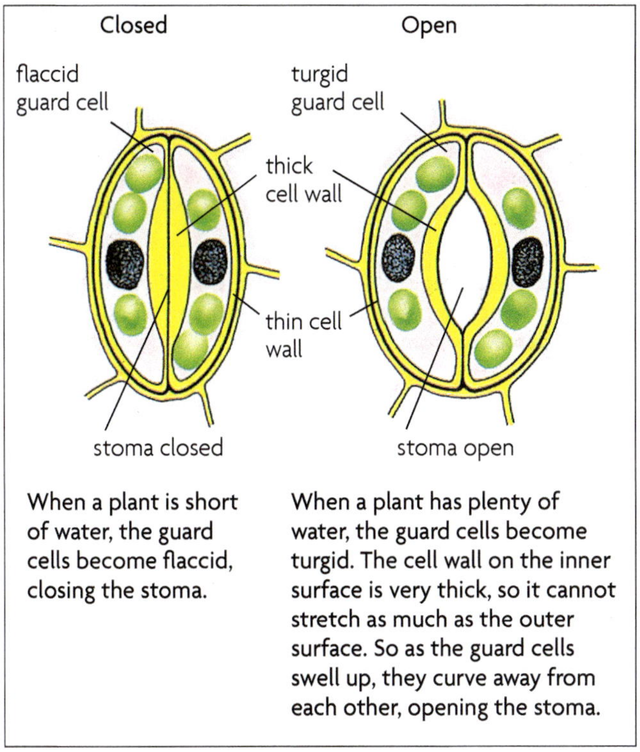

Closed
Open
flaccid guard cell
turgid guard cell
thick cell wall
thin cell wall
stoma closed
stoma open
When a plant is short of water, the guard cells become flaccid, closing the stoma.
When a plant has plenty of water, the guard cells become turgid. The cell wall on the inner surface is very thick, so it cannot stretch as much as the outer surface. So as the guard cells swell up, they curve away from each other, opening the stoma.

Figure 8.13 How stomata are opened and closed.

However, if its stomata are closed, then the plant cannot photosynthesise, because carbon dioxide cannot diffuse into the leaf. Plants only close their stomata when they really need to, such as when it is very hot and dry, or when they could not photosynthesise anyway, such as at night.

Reducing the surface area Most evaporation takes place from the surface of the leaves. Reducing leaf size, therefore, reduces water loss. In some plants – for example, the conifers – the leaves are narrow, but still perform photosynthesis. In other plants the leaves are reduced to spines, as in *Opuntia* and other cacti (Figure **8.14**), or scales, as in *Casuarina* (Figure **8.15**). These leaves do not photosynthesise. The stems of these plants take over the function of photosynthesis, but they have fewer stomata.

Figure 8.14 The leaves of the prickly pear (*Opuntia*) are reduced to spines. This and a thick waxy cuticle help in reducing water loss from the leaves.

Figure 8.15 A branch of *Casuarina equisetifolia*.

Waxy cuticles Although stomata are the main source of water loss, some water is also lost through the cuticle of the stem and leaf. This continues after the stomata are closed. A thick, waxy cuticle cuts down on this loss. Cacti, for example, lose very little water through the cuticle.

Stomata in pits In some plants, like *Nerium oleander*, the stomata, instead of being all over the leaf surface, are grouped in sunken areas or pits which are protected by hairs (Figure **8.16**). The hairs trap a layer of moist air next to the stomata and this allows them to remain open longer than if they were right on the surface, so the plant is able to photosynthesise for a longer time.

Figure 8.16 A stoma in a pit of a leaf of *Nerium oleander*.

Rolling leaves Marram grass (*Ammophila arenaria*) can roll up its leaves when water is in short supply (Figure **8.17**). The stomata are enclosed inside the leaf, so hardly any water is lost through them.

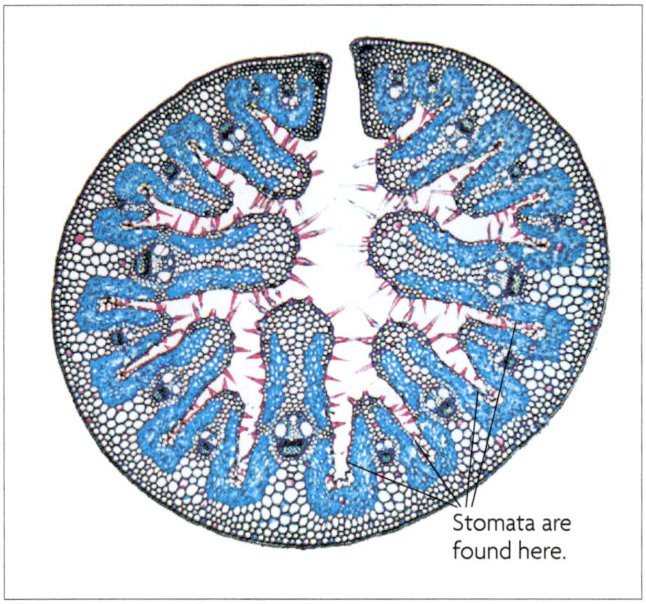

Figure 8.17 A cross section of a marram grass leaf in dry conditions, when it is rolled up.

8.23 Some plants store water.

Some plants of dry areas store water in leaves or stems. They are called **succulents**. Good examples are the cacti, *Agave* spp. (sisal, century plant) (Figure **8.18**), *Aloe vera* (aloes) and *Sempervivum*. This water helps the plant to survive when there is a really severe shortage. Therefore, many plants that store water also show many of the characteristics listed in section **8.22**. Can you name some plants which show any of these combinations?

Figure 8.18 *Agave* plants are grown to produce sisal. Their tough, swollen leaves store water and help to adapt the plant for growing in very dry soils.

8.24 Long roots can reach deep water supplies.

As well as having adaptations to reduce water loss, many plants that live in dry areas have roots that are adapted to reach water even when the ground is quite dry. They may have roots that grow very deep into the soil, able to reach down to the water table where water may still be found even after a very long period without rain (Figure **8.19**).

Figure 8.19 The roots of this tree in the Moroccan desert go down very deep into the dry ground to reach water.

Other plants have a different strategy. They may have roots that spread out very widely, near the surface of the soil, to quickly absorb large quantities of water if it does eventually rain.

8.25 Some plants can tolerate drying out.

Lichens (Figure **8.20**) and some mosses are able to withstand severe water loss without dying. The plants become dormant, stopping almost all metabolic activity. When water is again available, the cells become active. These plants are often found growing on bare surfaces and barks of trees.

Figure 8.20 Lichen can grow on bare stone, such as a grave stone.

8.26 In a few plants the cell fluids are very concentrated.

Plants that live where the soil solution is very concentrated, as in marshy areas or near the sea, often have a much more concentrated fluid inside their cells than most other plants (Figure **8.21**). Otherwise the roots would not be able to absorb water by osmosis. Some of these plants are succulents – the water stored helps to dilute cell fluids if this becomes necessary. Others, like the black mangrove (*Avicennia germinans*), have glands which can secrete excess salts so that they are removed from the plant (Figure **8.22**).

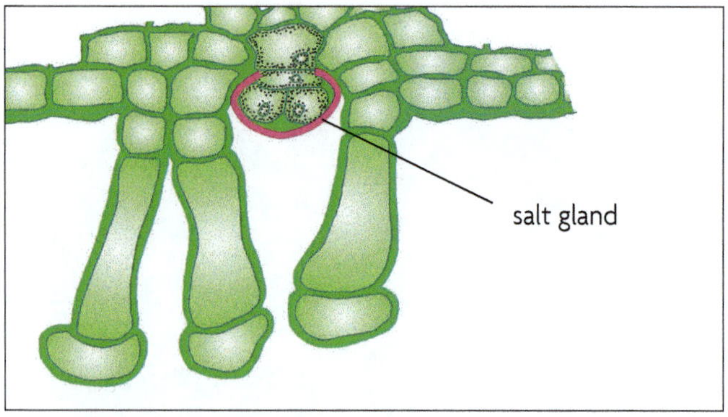

Figure 8.22 Salt gland from the lower epidermis of a leaf of *Avicennia*.

Figure 8.21 *Borrichia arborescens* (sea daisy) is adapted for growing in salty soil close to the sea.

Questions

8.17 What is osmoregulation?

8.18 What is metabolic water?

8.19 Describe three ways in which humans lose water from their bodies.

8.20 What is the name of the hormone which causes the kidneys to retain water, and which organ secretes it?

8.21 What sort of urine, and how much, would be produced by a person who had been playing tennis on a hot day? Explain your answer.

8.22 Explain how the structure of guard cells enables them to open or close a stoma.

Key ideas

- Excretion is the removal from the body of waste products of metabolism. The main excretory products of mammals are carbon dioxide and urea. The main excretory product of plants is oxygen. Some plants also excrete calcium oxalate. Water may also be considered to be an excretory product.
- Plants excrete oxygen through the stomata of their leaves and stems. They may also excrete substances by dropping their leaves. Animals excrete carbon dioxide from the lungs and urea from their kidneys.
- Urea is produced in the liver from excess amino acids. It is transported in solution in blood plasma to the kidneys, where it is excreted in urine.
- Urine is made in the nephrons of each kidney. First, blood is filtered. Then any substances to be retained in the blood are reabsorbed. The fluid that is left in the nephron flows into the ureters and then to the bladder, before leaving the body as urine through the urethra.
- The kidneys help in osmoregulation. The hypothalamus senses the amount of water in the blood. If it is too low, ADH is secreted which causes the kidneys to reabsorb a lot of water from urine. If it is too high, then less ADH is secreted, causing the kidneys not to reabsorb water. This is part of homeostasis, the maintenance of constant internal conditions. The mechanism by which it is done is an example of negative feedback.
- Plants that live in dry conditions are called xerophytes. They have several adaptations to conserve water, including thick cuticles, leaves that store water and sunken stomata. They may also have very long or wide-spreading roots to obtain water.

End-of-chapter questions

1 Explain the difference between each of the following pairs of terms:
  a excretion, egestion
  b urine, urea
  c ureter, urethra
  d osmosis, osmoregulation
  e ADH, ATP.

2 Explain the following:
  a There is no glucose in normal urine.
  b Plants have no special structures for excreting nitrogenous waste material.

3 a What is meant by osmoregulation?
  b Why is osmoregulation necessary for living cells?
  c Describe how osmoregulation is carried out in a named mammal, including the role of negative feedback.

4 a What are the main ways in which water is:
    i gained
    ii lost by terrestrial animals?
  b How do terrestrial plants lose water?
  c List three ways in which terrestrial plants keep water loss to a minimum.

5 a What is the main nitrogenous waste product excreted by human kidneys?
  b Where is this waste product formed?
  c Briefly describe how this waste product is formed.
  d Which blood vessels deliver this waste product to the kidneys?
  e Name two substances found in the blood plasma which are not found in the urine of a healthy person.
  f For each of the substances named in **(e)**, explain how the structure and function of the kidney ensures that they are not lost in the urine.

9 Support and movement

In this chapter, you will find out:

- the structure and functions of the human skeleton
- the similarities and differences in vertebrae from different areas of the vertebral column
- the different types of joints, and how synovial joints allow movement
- what antagonistic muscles do
- how plants can move parts of their bodies.

9.1 Skeletons support organisms.

All living organisms are held in shape, or supported, in some way. Many of them have special structures that do this. These structures are called **skeletons**.

The human skeleton, made of bone and cartilage, is only one kind of skeleton. Because it is inside the body, it is called an **endoskeleton** ('endo-' means inside). Earthworms and plants also have endoskeletons, although they are very different. Insects have a skeleton on the outside of their bodies, called an **exoskeleton** ('exo-' means outside).

Support and movement in humans

9.2 The human skeleton has several functions.

Our skeleton is made mostly of bone, and also a softer, more flexible material called cartilage. The skeleton has several different functions (Table **9.1**).

Support Bones support the body. The vertebral column, pectoral girdle (shoulder bones), pelvic girdle (hip bones), and leg bones are especially important.

Movement The bones provide strong, firm attachments against which muscles can contract, which enables us to move.

Protection The cranium protects the brain, the vertebrae protect the spinal cord, and the rib cage protects the heart and lungs.

Making blood cells Many bones, especially the ribs and leg bones, have soft **marrow** in their centres. This is where red and white blood cells are made.

9.3 The mammalian skeleton has a main axis and appendages.

The skeleton of a mammal is made up of two main parts. The main **axis** of support includes the skull and vertebral column. Attached to this are the limbs or **appendages**, which are connected to the main axis by girdles. The simple diagram in Figure **9.1** illustrates this.

The direction of the axis is usually horizontal, with the limbs beneath. One important development in humans is walking upright, with the axis vertical. The powerful

Table 9.1 Functions of the human skeleton

Function	Example
support	vertebral column pectoral girdle pelvic girdle leg bones
movement	leg and arm bones vertebral column
protection	skull ribs vertebral column
making red and white blood cells	marrow in leg bones and ribs

muscles of the buttocks enable us to walk like this. One consequence of this is that the forelimbs do not have to be used for movement, so it has been possible for human arms and hands to be used in a great variety of ways.

Figure **9.2** shows the main bones in the human skeleton. The structure of the vertebral column is shown in Figure **9.3**, and the bones of the pelvic and pectoral girdles and the arms are shown in Figure **9.4** (pages **162** and **163**).

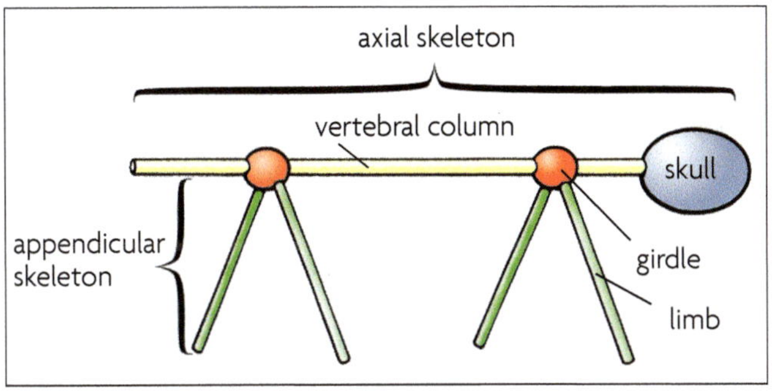

Figure 9.1 General plan of a mammalian skeleton.

FACT!

There are 206 bones in the human body. The longest is the femur and the smallest is the stapes in the middle ear.

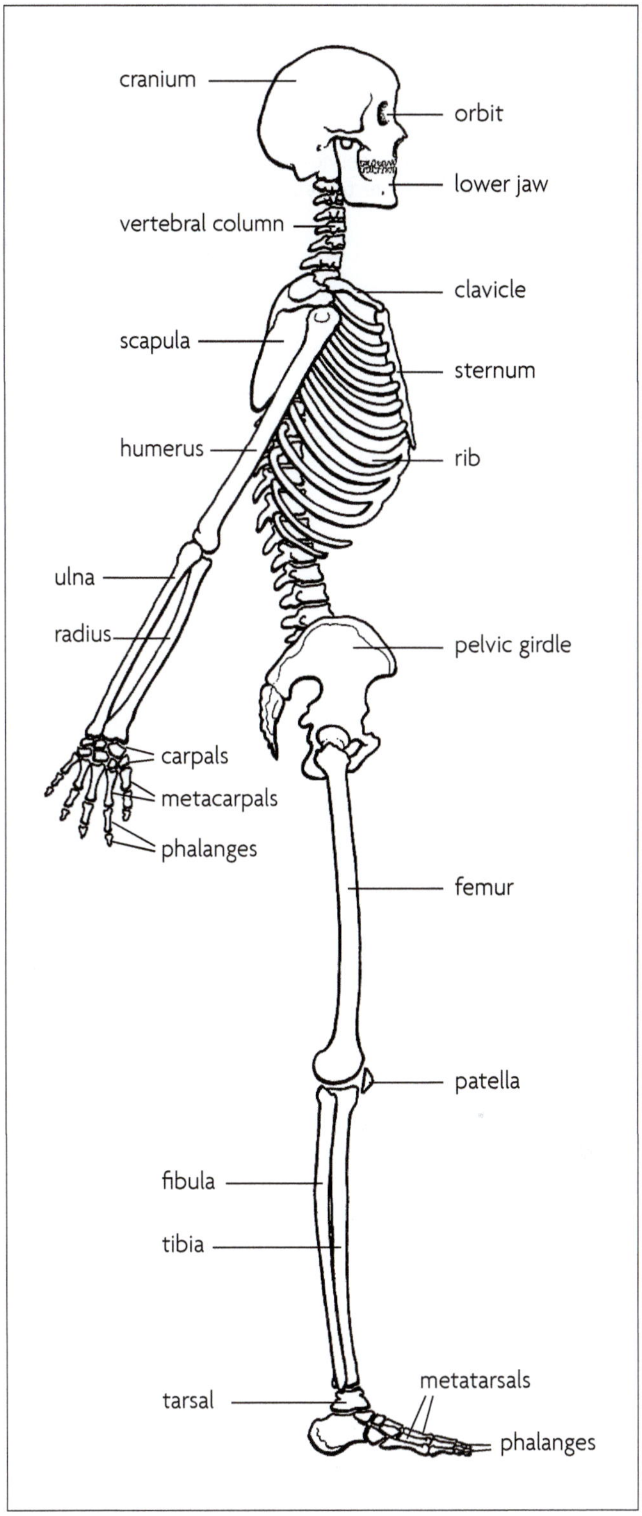

Figure 9.2 The human half-skeleton.

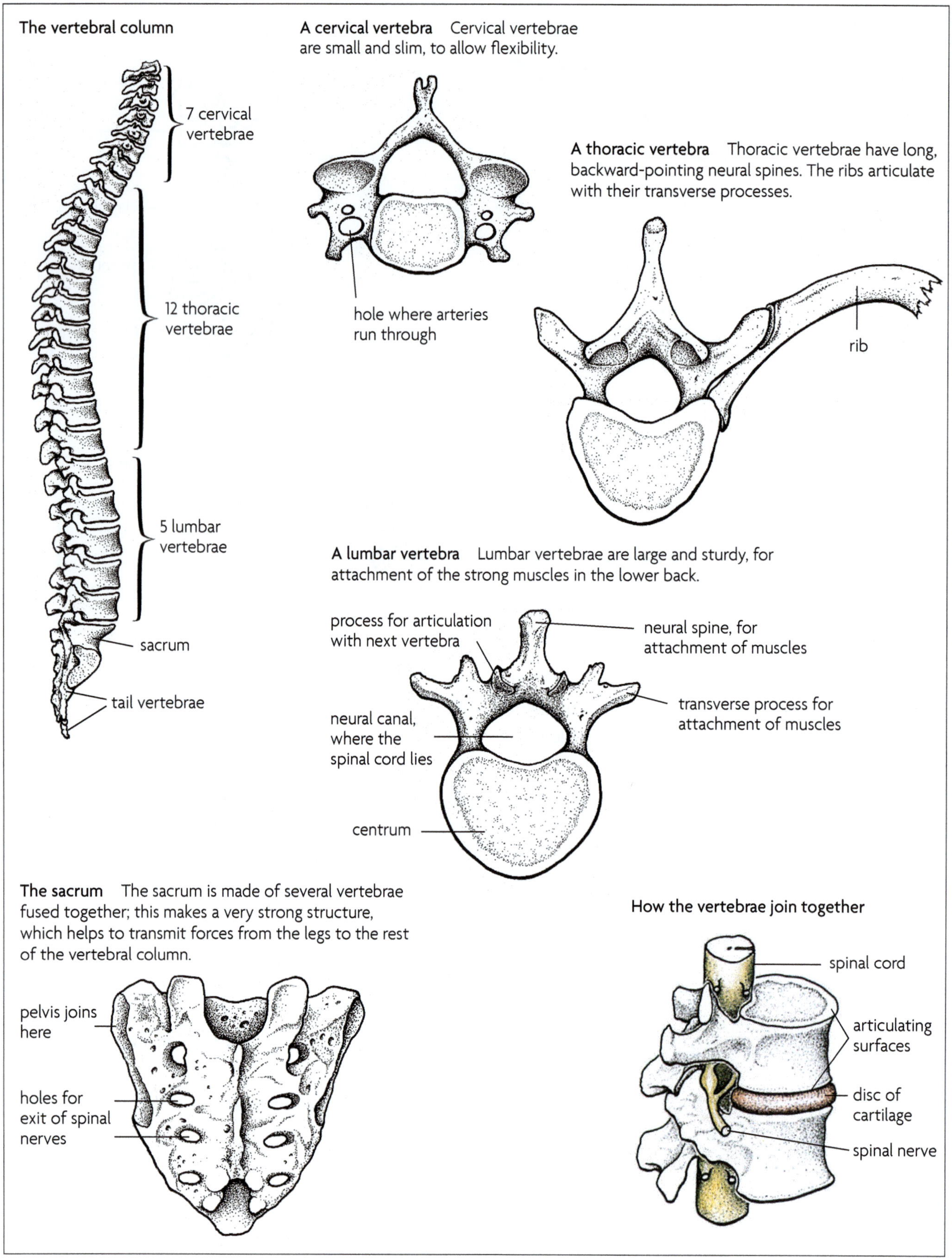
The vertebral column
7 cervical vertebrae
12 thoracic vertebrae
5 lumbar vertebrae
sacrum
tail vertebrae
A cervical vertebra Cervical vertebrae are small and slim, to allow flexibility.
hole where arteries run through
A thoracic vertebra Thoracic vertebrae have long, backward-pointing neural spines. The ribs articulate with their transverse processes.
rib
A lumbar vertebra Lumbar vertebrae are large and sturdy, for attachment of the strong muscles in the lower back.
process for articulation with next vertebra
neural spine, for attachment of muscles
transverse process for attachment of muscles
neural canal, where the spinal cord lies
centrum
The sacrum The sacrum is made of several vertebrae fused together; this makes a very strong structure, which helps to transmit forces from the legs to the rest of the vertebral column.
pelvis joins here
holes for exit of spinal nerves
How the vertebrae join together
spinal cord
articulating surfaces
disc of cartilage
spinal nerve

Figure 9.3 The vertebral column.

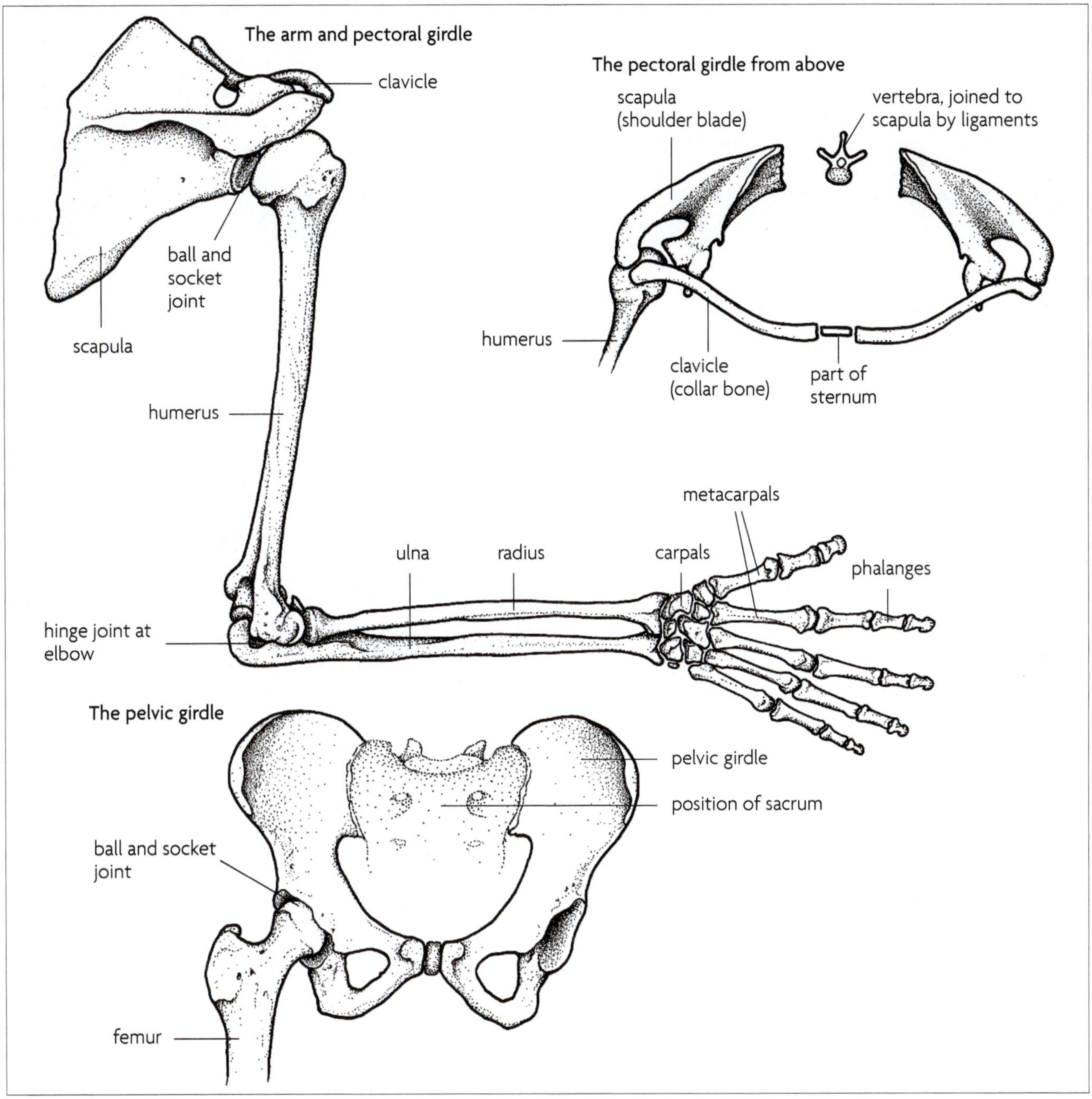

Figure 9.4 Limbs and girdles.

9.4 Bone is made of protein and minerals.

Most of the human skeleton, like that of other mammals, is made of **bone**. Bone is mostly made of mineral substances such as **calcium phosphate**, with small amounts of magnesium salts. This makes it very hard. Bone also contains **collagen** fibres (Figure **9.5**, overleaf) which give it elasticity. Collagen is a protein. Bone contains living cells, which are supplied with food and oxygen by blood vessels. The cells are arranged in rings around the blood vessels (Figure **9.6**, overleaf).

9.5 The structure of a bone.

Figure **9.7** (overleaf) shows a leg bone, cut in half lengthways. The hardest bone, called **compact bone**, is on the outside. Underneath this is a layer of **spongy bone**, which has spaces in it. This stops the bone from being too heavy. In the centre is the **bone marrow**. This is very soft, and has a good supply of blood. Red blood cells, white blood cells and platelets are made here. The ends of the bone are covered with a layer of **cartilage**.

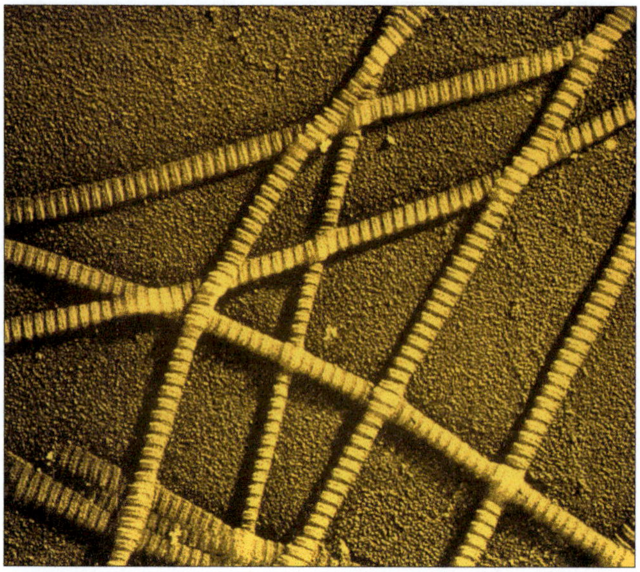

Figure 9.5 Collagen is a protein that forms long, strong, stretchy fibres. This photo was taken using a scanning electron microscope.

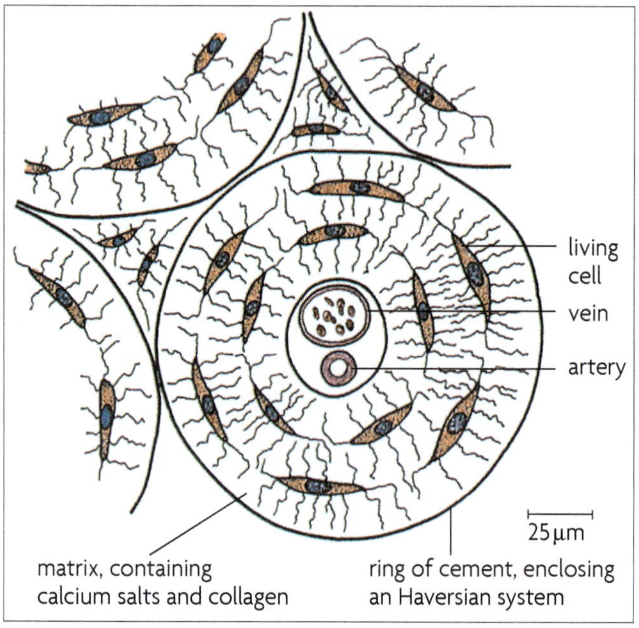

Figure 9.6 A piece of living bone as it would appear seen with a light microscope.

9.6 Cartilage has less mineral content than bone.

Cartilage (Figure **9.8**) is much softer than bone. This is because it does not contain very many mineral salts, but, like bone, it contains collagen.

Cartilage is found on the ends of bones where they meet one another at a joint. It allows the bones to move easily over each other because it is exceptionally smooth. There is also cartilage in the pinnae of your ears and in the end of your nose.

Figure 9.7 A section through the upper end of a femur (thigh bone) showing an outer layer of compact bone which surrounds a layer of spongy bone.

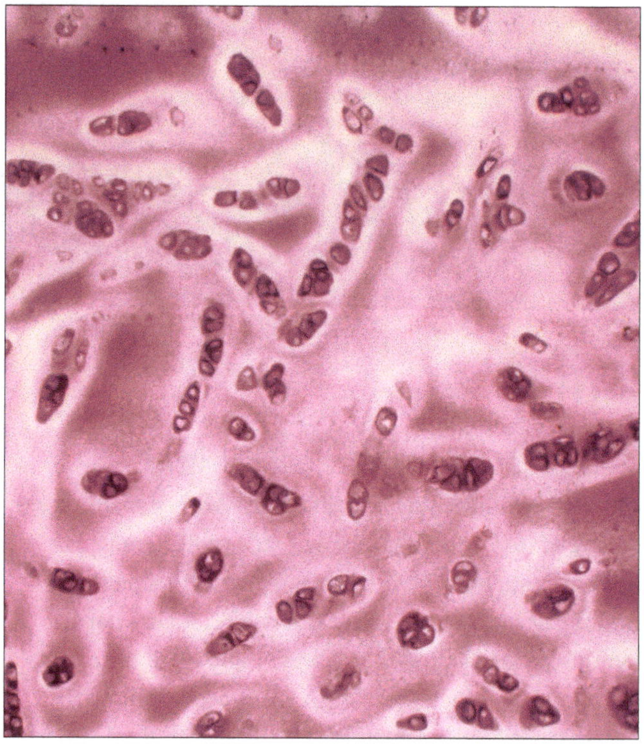

Figure 9.8 Light micrograph of cartilage. The dark, roundish structures are cells. They are surrounded by the smooth matrix they have made.

Questions

9.1 What is an endoskeleton? Give an example of an organism which has one.

9.2 What is an exoskeleton? Give an example of an organism which has one.

9.3 What are the two main constituents of bone?

9.4 Give one similarity and one difference between bone and cartilage.

9.5 What runs through the centre of the vertebral column?

9.6 Why do vertebrae have transverse processes?

9.7 How can you tell the difference between a cervical vertebra and a lumbar vertebra?

9.8 Which vertebrae have ribs joined to them?

9.9 Why does the sacrum need to be very strong?

9.10 What is the correct name for **(a)** the shoulder blade, and **(b)** the collar bone?

9.7 Bones are joined in different ways.

Wherever two bones meet each other, a **joint** is formed. There are two main kinds of joint.

Fibrous joints Sometimes two bones are joined quite firmly together by fibres. The bones in the cranium of the skull are joined like this. The joints are called **sutures**. The bones are held so tightly together in an adult human that they cannot move at all.

There are also fibrous joints between the vertebrae (Figure **9.3**, page **162**). The bones are joined by cartilage with fibres in it, called **intervertebral discs**. The cartilage is quite soft in the middle, so the bones can move a little. Although any one joint between two vertebrae only allows a slight movement, the sum total of all these movements makes the backbone quite supple.

Synovial joints Synovial joints are found where two bones need to move freely. The elbow joint and shoulder joint are examples of synovial joints.

Figure **9.9** shows the structure of a typical synovial joint. The two bones are held together by ligaments. Ligaments are very strong, but can stretch when the bones move.

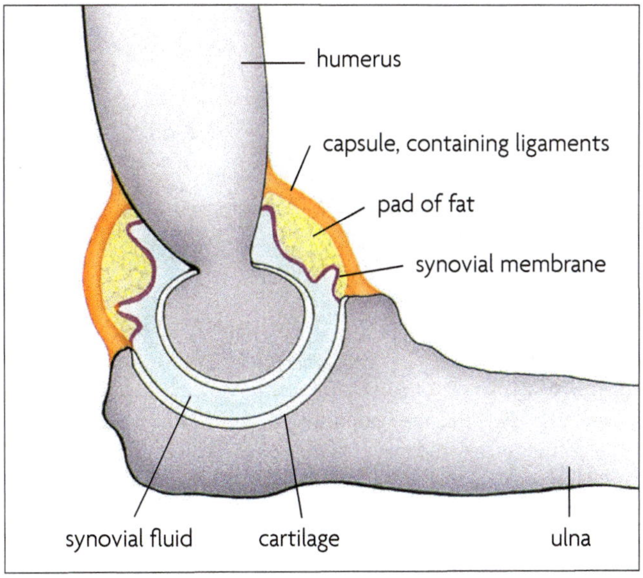

Figure 9.9 Section through the elbow joint.

9.8 Tendons and ligaments help joints to function.

Tendons are strong cords that attach your muscles to your bones (Figure **9.10**). If you hold your hand out palm upwards and tip it downwards, you will see the strong tendons in your wrist. You can also feel your Achilles tendon at the back of your ankle.

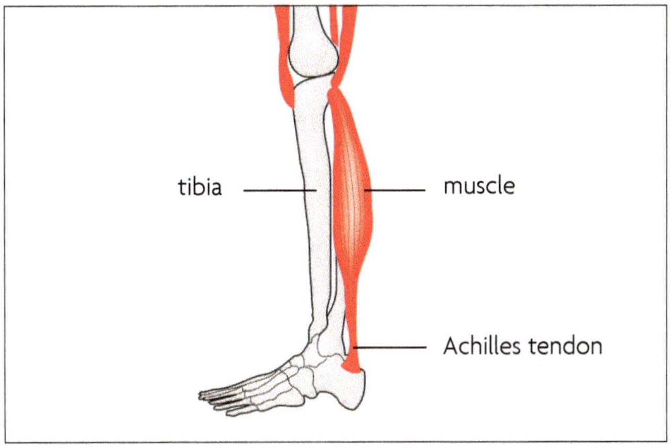

Figure 9.10 The Achilles tendon attaches the strong leg muscles to the heel bone.

As we will see in section **9.11**, when a muscle contracts it pulls on a bone and makes it move. The tendons transmit the force from the muscle to the bone. They do not stretch. If they did, your muscles could pull very hard and just stretch the tendon, rather than making the bones move.

Ligaments are also strong cords, but they are stretchy. They attach one bone to another at a joint (Figure **9.11**, overleaf). They have to be a bit stretchy, so that the bones can move.

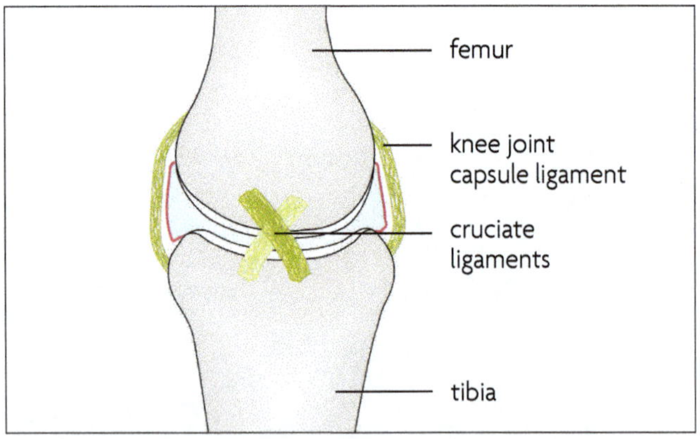

Figure 9.11 The cruciate ligaments help keep the femur and tibia connected at the knee joint.

Questions

9.11 What is meant by a fibrous joint?

9.12 Where can you find sutures in the human skeleton?

9.13 What is an intervertebral disc?

9.14 What is meant by a synovial joint?

9.15 What are ligaments?

9.16 Describe two features of the elbow joint which help it to move smoothly.

9.9 There are three kinds of muscle in mammals.

Figure **9.12** shows the three types of muscle that are found in the human body.

Cardiac muscle **Cardiac muscle** is only found in the heart. It makes up the walls of the atria and ventricles.

Smooth muscle **Smooth muscle** is found in organs such as the walls of the alimentary canal, the bladder and blood vessels. The muscle is also called involuntary muscle, because you do not have conscious control over it.

Striated muscle All of the muscles attached to your bones are **striated muscle**. They are sometimes called skeletal muscles, or voluntary muscles, as they are normally under conscious control.

'Striated' means striped, and you can see why this kind of muscle – and also cardiac muscle – has this name if you look at Figure **9.12**.

FACT! Muscles make up about 40% of your body weight.

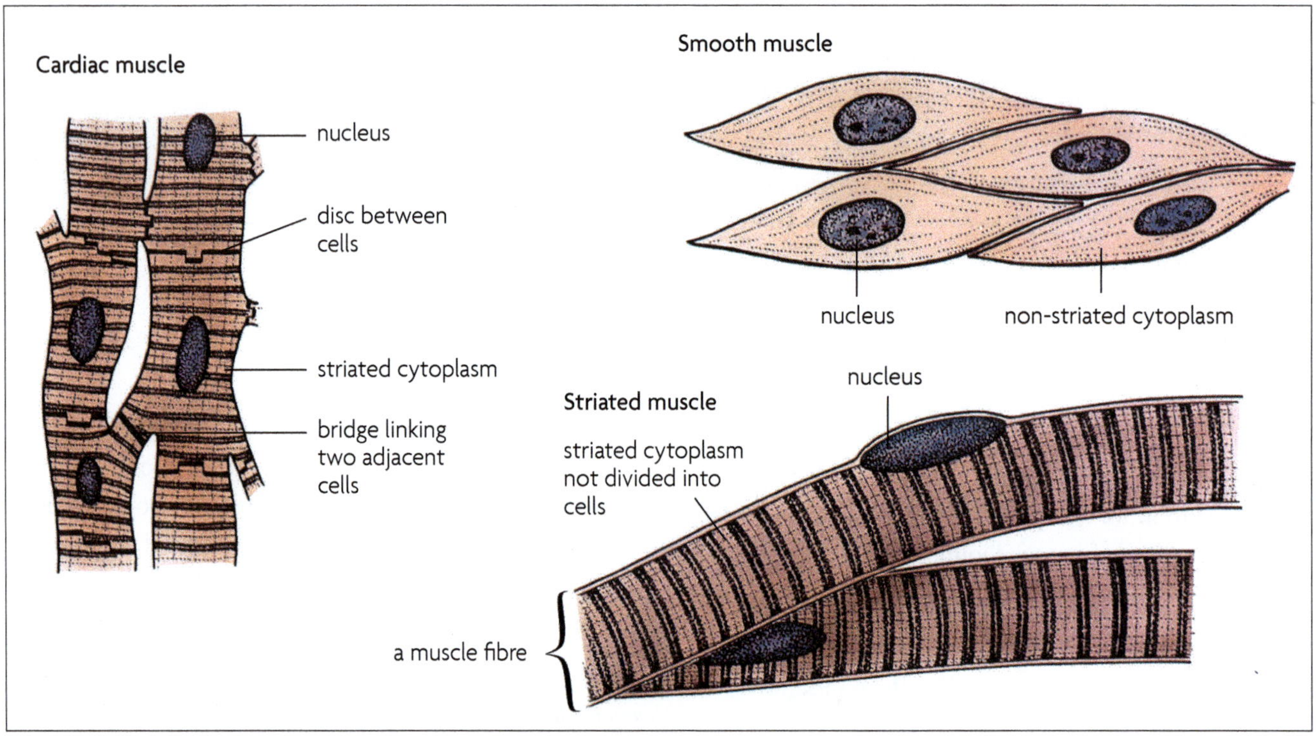

Figure 9.12 The microscopic appearance of the three types of muscle.

9.10 Each kind of muscle contracts in a different way.

Muscles cause movement by getting shorter, which is called **contraction**. They need energy to do this. They get their energy from respiration, and so muscles must have a good blood supply to bring nutrients (especially glucose) and oxygen to them. As in every cell, they use these substances to make ATP, which is the source of energy for the work they do.

All of the three types of muscle can contract, but they do it in slightly different ways. Cardiac muscle contracts and relaxes rhythmically all through your life. It never tires. It does not need conscious messages from your brain to make it contract – it will do it anyway. Nervous impulses from the brain can, however, alter its rate of contraction.

Smooth muscle, too, can contract of its own accord. For example, the muscles in the wall of the alimentary canal do this during peristalsis. In other places, however, smooth muscle needs to be stimulated by nerves, in the same way as striated muscle.

The contractions of smooth muscle are much slower than those of cardiac muscle. Smooth muscle contracts and relaxes slowly and rhythmically.

Striated muscle only contracts when electrical impulses are sent to it along nerves. Striated muscle can contract quickly, and very strongly. But is gets tired more quickly than smooth or cardiac muscle.

Skeletal muscle contains a dark red pigment called **myoglobin**, which can combine with oxygen in a similar way to haemoglobin. But myoglobin does not give up its oxygen as easily as haemoglobin does. It will only release oxygen when there is very little in the cell. Therefore, myoglobin acts as a store of oxygen which is only used when the oxygen in the oxyhaemoglobin has been used up. This is likely to happen, for example, when you do vigorous exercise.

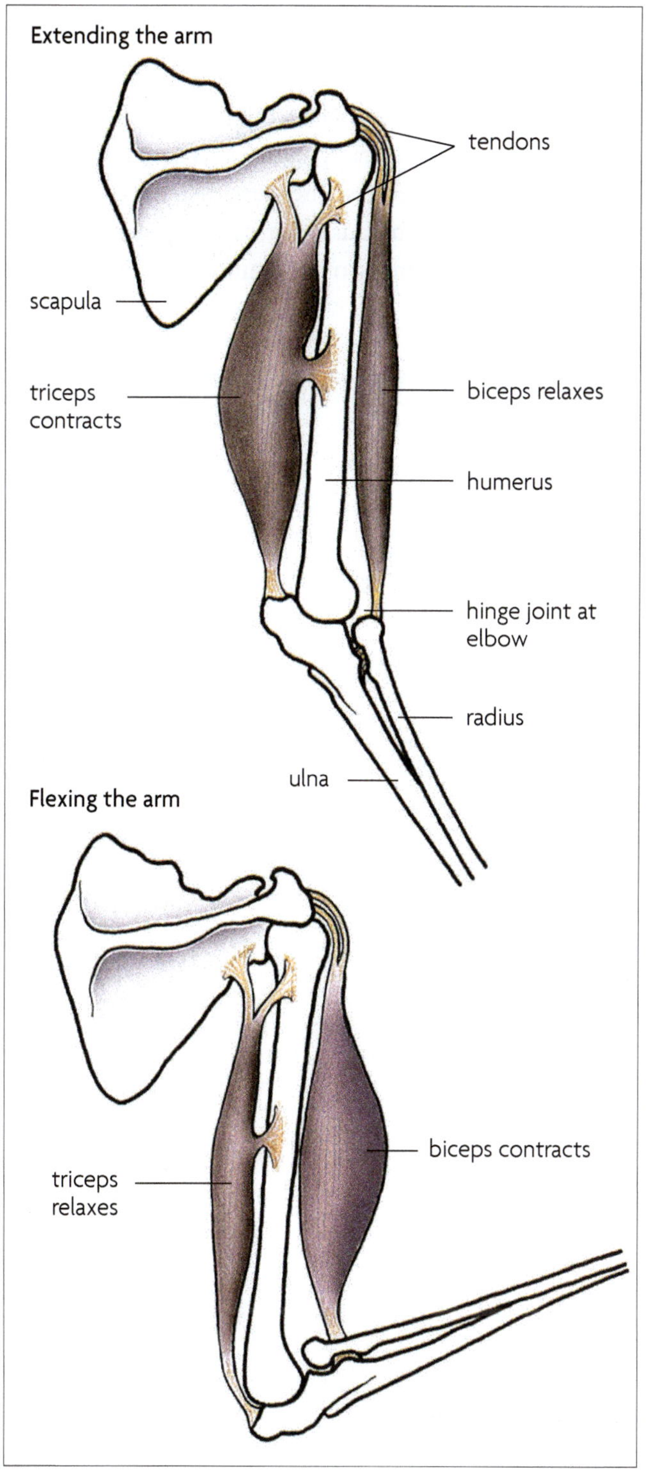

Figure 9.13 Movement at the elbow joint.

9.11 Movements of the forearm.

Figure **9.13** shows the bones and two of the muscles in your arm. The arm can bend at the elbow, which is a hinge joint.

The **biceps muscle** is attached to the scapula at the top and the radius at the bottom. When it contracts, it pulls the radius and ulna up towards the scapula, so the arm bends. This is called flexing your arm, so the biceps is a **flexor muscle**.

But muscles can only pull, not push. The biceps cannot push your arm back down again. Another muscle is needed to pull it down. The **triceps muscle** does this.

When it contracts, the triceps straightens or extends your arm. It is called an **extensor muscle**.

The flexor and extensor muscles work together. When the biceps contracts, the triceps relaxes. When the triceps contracts, the biceps relaxes. The muscles are said to be **antagonistic muscles** because, in a way, they work against each other. There are many other examples of antagonistic muscles in your body.

9.12 Ageing causes changes in muscle and bone.

As we get older, some muscle fibres are replaced by connective tissue like collagen (Figure **9.5**, page **164**). This makes muscle weaker.

Bone contains collagen fibres (section **9.4**). As we age, collagen tends to become thicker, and not as elastic. This helps to make bone more brittle. Also, with ageing, we tend to lose calcium more easily than it is replaced.

Investigation 9.1
Using a model arm to investigate the action of the biceps muscle

SBA skills

Observation/Recording/Reporting

Manipulation/Measurement

Analysis/Interpretation

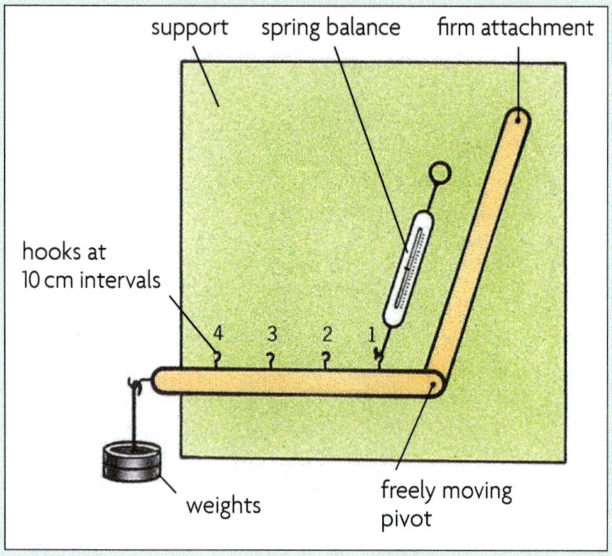

1 Read the instructions, then construct a results table.

2 Hang a 1 newton weight on the hook at the end of the 'forearm' on the model.

3 Attach a spring balance to hook 1. Pull upwards with the spring balance, parallel to the 'humerus', until the 'forearm' is exactly horizontal. Take the reading on the spring balance, and fill it in on the results table.

4 Repeat with the balance pulling on hooks 2, 3 and 4.

5 Replace the 1 newton weight with a 5 newton weight, and repeat steps 3 and 4.

Questions

1 What does the spring balance represent?

2 At which position was the force needed to lift the weight greatest?

3 Which position most closely represents the actual position of attachment of the biceps to the radius?

4 The biceps muscle cannot shorten by a very large amount. Since it is attached in this position, what can you suggest about the force the muscle must be able to exert?

The forces acting on the forearm when lifting a weight can be shown diagrammatically like this.

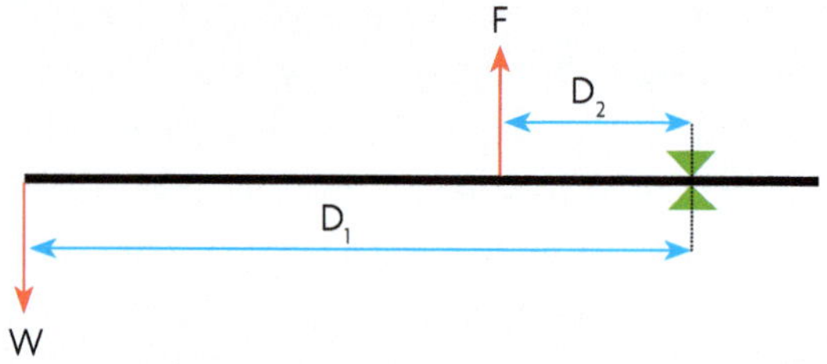

When the arm is horizontal and not moving,

$$W \times D_1 = F \times D_2$$

5 What does W stand for?

6 What does F stand for?

Therefore, bones become less dense and weaker. More women than men tend to have difficulty with weakening bones. This is because, after menopause, the hormone oestrogen is no longer produced. Oestrogen helps to maintain the strength of the bones.

9.13 Cilia can cause movement.

Muscles are not the only things that can move in the human body. Some cells have microscopic threads on them, called cilia (Figure **6.9**, page **98**).

Ciliated cells are found in the tubes of the respiratory system. There are cilia in your trachea and bronchi, for example. They beat rhythmically, wafting mucus up towards the back of your mouth. The mucus traps bacteria and particles of dirt in the air you breathe in (section **6.14**).

9.14 Some blood cells move like *Amoeba*.

Another type of movement that happens inside the human body is amoeboid movement. White blood cells move like this (Figure **9.14**). They can pass out of the blood capillaries into every part of the body, where they destroy bacteria and other unwanted cells (section **7.17**).

Figure 9.14 This is a white blood cell, crawling over a surface. The cell spreads out 'arms' of cytoplasm and uses them to pull itself along.

Questions

9.17 Which kinds of muscle will contract without a conscious message from the brain?

9.18 What are the special features of striated muscle?

9.19 What is meant by **(a)** a flexor muscle, and **(b)** an extensor muscle? Give an example of each.

9.20 What are tendons? How do they differ from ligaments?

Support and movement in plants

9.15 Plants have skeletons.

We have seen that the human skeleton helps with support and movement. Plants, though, do not move very much; their skeletons serve mainly for support.

9.16 Xylem forms wood and supports plants.

Plant stems, roots and leaves contain xylem (section **7.30**). Xylem is made of cells which have very strong walls containing lignin. These lignified xylem vessels help to support the stem (section **7.31**).

The larger and taller the plant, the more support it needs. Trees are supported by the wood in their trunks and branches, which is made almost entirely of xylem.

9.17 Cell turgor supports herbaceous plants.

In parts of plants where there is not much xylem, another means of support is needed.

When a plant has plenty of water, the contents of each cell press outwards on the cell wall (Figure **2.12**, page **33**). This makes the cells firm, or **turgid**. They press against each other, holding the plant firm and upright. This is particularly important in leaves, and in **herbaceous** plants which do not have woody stems. If a plant loses too much water, then the cells lose their turgor and the plant wilts (Figure **9.15**, overleaf).

9.18 Movement in plants.

Most animals are able to move their entire body from place to place. This is called **locomotion**. Plants cannot do this. Usually only parts of plants move. Some of these movements involve growth, but there are also other types of plant movement.

The leaves become soft and floppy, because their cells have lost their turgor.
The stem is still firm and upright, because it is supported by xylem vessels and other lignified cells.

Figure 9.15 A wilting shoot.

Plants do not need to move their whole bodies because they feed by photosynthesis. They simply have to stay in one place and absorb carbon dioxide and water, allowing sunlight to fall onto their leaves. Most animals, however, need to move to find their food. Herbivores move from place to place in search of nutritious vegetation to eat, and to escape from their predators. Carnivores move to find, chase and kill their prey.

Reproduction may also involve movement. Animals move to find a mate. Gametes are an organism's reproductive cells – you will read more about them in Chapter **13**. In animals, the male gamete is the **sperm** cell. Sperm cells move actively, swimming in search of a female gamete (egg). Female gametes do not move actively. They wait to be found by a sperm.

In flowering plants, the male gametes are inside the pollen grains. Neither the plant nor the gametes are able to move, but instead rely on insects or the wind to carry pollen grains from one flower to another. In some primitive plant-like organisms, such as seaweeds (actually classified as Protoctista rather than plants), the male gametes do swim from plant to plant.

Growth movements These are in response to particular directional stimuli – gravity, light, chemicals, water, touch – and are controlled by hormone-like substances produced in the plant. They are described in more detail in Chapter **10**.

Non-growth movements These are of several types.

1 Folding of leaves, as a result of turgor changes in response to contact or shock, as in *Mimosa pudica* (Shamey Lady, Sensitive Plant, Shame Bush) (Figure **9.16**).
2 'Sleep' movements – regular movements in response to changes in light and temperature. These are illustrated by the closing of petals of the Four o' clock (*Portulaca* sp.), some varieties of *Hibiscus*, Morning Glory (*Ipomoea purpurea*), and of the leaves of several members of the Mimosaceae in the evenings.

Figure 9.16 The leaves of *Mimosa pudica* **a** before and **b** after shock. The plant in the foreground in **b** has closed its leaves.

3 'Feeding' movements of insectivorous plants. These plants grow in situations of low nitrogen availability, and have developed mechanisms for trapping and digesting insects in order to obtain the nitrogen they need. The sundew (*Drosera* spp.) is a good example (Figure **9.17**). The leaf blades are covered with sticky hairs. If a small insect lands on the leaf, it is held by some of the hairs while the leaf folds over and forms a trap it cannot escape from. The leaf produces juices which digest the insect protein. This is absorbed by the leaf cells. After digestion the leaf unfolds, releasing the insect skeleton.

4 Mechanical movements resulting from changes in humidity, as in the dehiscence or 'bursting' of some fruits to scatter their seeds. In many legumes, drying out causes the pods to curl and split – for example in gungo beans (congo peas, pigeon peas, *Cajanus cajan*) and Barbados Pride (*Caesalpinia pulcherrima*). In Duppy Gun (Minnie Roots, *Ruellia tuberosa*) a drop of moisture on the mature fruit causes it to burst forcefully.

Figure 9.17 The insect-eating sundew lives in boggy soils where there is very little nitrate available. This one has caught an insect on its sticky hairs, which will hold it firmly while juices containing enzymes digest it.

Key ideas

- The human skeleton supports, protects, allows movement and makes blood cells.
- The skeleton is made of hard, strong bone and softer, more flexible cartilage.
- The vertebral column is made up of many vertebrae, which join with each other at articulating surfaces. They are separated by discs made of cartilage. Each vertebra has a hole in the middle in which the spinal cord lies. Transverse processes serve for the attachment of muscles. Vertebrae from different areas of the vertebral column all have the same basic structure, but the relative sizes and shapes of the various parts differ.
- A joint is a place where two bones meet. Fibrous joints do not allow much, if any, movement. Synovial joints allow movement between the bones. The bones are connected to each other by ligaments, and to muscles by tendons. Cartilage and synovial fluid help to reduce friction between the ends of the moving bones.
- Muscles are able to contract (shorten) but they cannot lengthen again by themselves. Two muscles generally work together so that when one contracts it lengthens the other. Muscles like this are said to be antagonistic. At the elbow joint, contraction of the biceps bends the elbow joint, while contraction of the triceps straightens it.
- Plants do not move as much as animals, and do not locomote – that is, move their whole body from place to place. Animals need to move to feed, whereas plants do not. Animals also move to reproduce, but plants use the wind, insects or birds to move their male gametes from one plant to another.

End-of-chapter questions

1 Match each word below with its definition:
collagen, cartilage, ligament, tendon,
flexor, extensor, lignin.

  a a structure which holds two bones together at a joint, allowing movement between them
  b a muscle which pulls two bones closer together when it contracts
  c the protein found in bone
  d a muscle which pulls two bones away from one another when it contracts
  e the strong substance found in the walls of xylem vessels
  f a strong but flexible substance, found on the ends of movable bones
  g a structure which attaches a muscle to a bone

2 a What is meant by antagonistic muscles? Give one example.
  b Make a large, labelled diagram to show the position of one pair of antagonistic muscles in a named mammal, including the structure of the joint whose movement they cause.
  c Describe how these muscles cause flexing of the joint you have shown.

3 Discuss **(a)** any similarities and **(b)** differences you can identify between the mechanism(s) for support in a large tree and a human being.

4 Movement in animals often involves going from one place to another. To what extent does this apply to movement in plants? Discuss other purposes served by movement in plants.

10 Coordination

In this chapter, you will find out:

- how receptors and effectors help organisms to respond to stimuli
- how some invertebrate animals respond to changes in their environment
- about the structure and function of the nervous system of a human
- what is meant by a reflex action, and how it is brought about
- about the structure and function of the eye, including some common visual defects
- how plants respond by growth to stimuli such as light and gravity.

10.1 Organisms detect changes around them.

All living organisms are sensitive to their environment. This means that they can detect changes in the environment. The changes they detect are called **stimuli** (singular: stimulus) and they **respond** to these stimuli in various ways which have the effect of helping them to survive.

This capacity of living cells to respond to stimuli is sometimes known as **irritability**.

Response and coordination in animals

10.2 Nerves and hormones allow communication.

Changes in an organism's environment are sensed by specialised cells called **receptors**. The organism responds using **effectors**. Muscles are effectors, and may respond to a stimulus by contracting. Glands can also be effectors. For example, if you smell good food cooking, your salivary glands may respond by secreting saliva.

Animals need fast and efficient communication systems between their receptors and effectors. This is partly because most animals move in search of food. Many animals need to be able to respond very quickly to catch their food, or to avoid predators.

To make sure that the right effectors respond at the right time, there needs to be some kind of communication system between receptors and effectors. If you touch something hot, pain receptors on your fingertips need to send an impulse to your arm muscles to tell them to contract. The way in which receptors pick up stimuli, and then pass information on to effectors, is called **coordination**.

Most animals have two methods of sending information from receptors to effectors. The fastest is by means of **nerves**. The receptors and nerves make up the animal's **nervous system**. A slower method, but still a very important one, is by means of chemicals called **hormones**. Hormones are part of the **endocrine system**.

10.3 How invertebrates deal with change in their environment.

The response of many simple multicellular invertebrates – such as millipedes, earthworms, woodlice, insect larvae and adult ants – to stimuli, is a movement of the whole organism. You can observe this for yourself by carrying out Investigation **10.1**.

In small, simple, unicellular organisms like an amoeba, there are usually no specialised structures set aside for receiving, passing on and responding to stimuli. Whole or parts of these organisms may respond in definite ways to certain stimuli. An amoeba, for example, responds to contact with food (other single-celled organisms) by enclosing it with the nearest pseudopodia ('false feet') to form a food vacuole.

Some organisms move directly towards or away from a stimulus. Fly larvae, for example, are able to sense the *direction* from which light is coming and move away from it. Woodlice, however, do not respond to light and dark like this. If they find themselves in a light place, they move more quickly and turn less than if they are in a dark place. Once they arrive (by chance) in a dark place, they move more slowly and turn more frequently. This results in a tendency to stay in dark places and move out of light ones.

Investigation 10.1
Do woodlice prefer light or dark?

SBA skills

Observation/Recording/Reporting

Analysis/Interpretation

Choice chambers can be used to investigate how woodlice respond to light and dark. A simple choice chamber can be constructed from two plastic Petri dishes shown below. To make this choice chamber for yourself, make an opening in the side of the top half of each dish by using a hot metal rod. While the plastic is still soft, join the dishes by pushing together the holes you have made in the dishes. (Alternatively, use glue.)

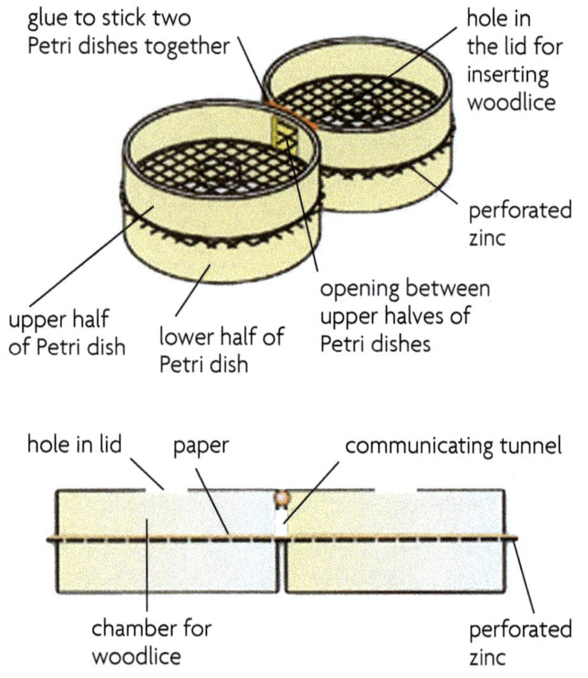

This creates a choice chamber connected by a tunnel so that the animals under investigation can move from one chamber to the other.

The lower halves of the dishes are used to produce the two different environments. In this investigation, one chamber will be light and one chamber will be dark.

1. Put perforated zinc (or window mesh) across the lower halves of two Petri dishes.
2. Cover one dish with black plastic or black cloth. Label this dish chamber X. Leave the other dish in the light and label this dish chamber Y.
3. Collect some woodlice or other suitable invertebrates, such as millipedes.
4. Place the same number of woodlice in each chamber.
5. Count and record the number of woodlice in each chamber at one-minute intervals for 10 minutes.
6. From your results, work out whether the woodlice move towards or away from light.

Questions

1. Why is the apparatus described as a choice chamber?
2. What conclusions can you draw from your results about the response of woodlice to light and dark?
3. From your observations of the woodlice, would you say that they moved directly towards a particular part of the dish? Explain your answer.
4. How could you improve the reliability of your results?

Investigation 10.2
The response of an invertebrate to humidity

SBA skills

Observation/Recording/Reporting
Planning/Design
Analysis/Interpretation

You are going to plan this investigation for yourself. Your teacher will tell you which organisms you can use. Good choices are woodlice or millipedes.

This is the hypothesis you will test:

> Woodlice/Millipedes move towards more humid areas.

You can use choice chambers for your investigation. You can make one side humid by placing some wet filter paper in the base. You can make the other side dry by placing some dry calcium chloride in the base – this will absorb water vapour from the air.

Remember to think carefully about variables. Record, display and analyse your results, summarise your conclusions and discuss the main sources of error.

10.4 A nerve net is a simple nervous system.

As organisms get larger and more complex, the need arises for some means of carrying sensations from one part of the organism to another, so that it can act as a unit. This is done by means of a **nervous system**.

One such simple nervous system is found in the sea anemone and other members of the jellyfish or cnidarian group of animals. Sense cells act as receptors, receiving stimuli. This sets up an electrical impulse which passes through special conducting cells or **neurones** which link up with each other to form a **nerve net**. Eventually the stimulus reaches muscle cells which respond by contracting. The muscle cells are said to be effectors.

The conducting cells or neurones have a number of thin fibres leading out from their cell bodies along which sensations can pass. In the sea anemone, and its relatives, electrical impulses can travel in any direction along these fibres (Figures **10.1a** and **10.1b**).

10.5 More active animals need a more efficient nervous system.

A simple nerve net like this works perfectly well for the sea anemone. But an active animal, particularly one with such complex behaviour as a human, needs a more elaborate system. Like the neurones in the sea anemone, mammalian neurones contain the same basic parts as any animal cell. Each has a nucleus, cytoplasm and a cell membrane. But their structure is specially adapted to be able to carry electrical impulses very quickly (Figure **10.2**, overleaf).

To enable them to do this, they have long, thin fibres of cytoplasm stretching out from the cell body. These are called **nerve fibres**. Nerve fibres carrying impulses into the cell body are called **dendrons** or **dendrites**. Usually there is one nerve fibre taking impulses away from the cell body. This is called the **axon**. In many neurones, the axon is the longest fibre. Axons may be more than a metre long.

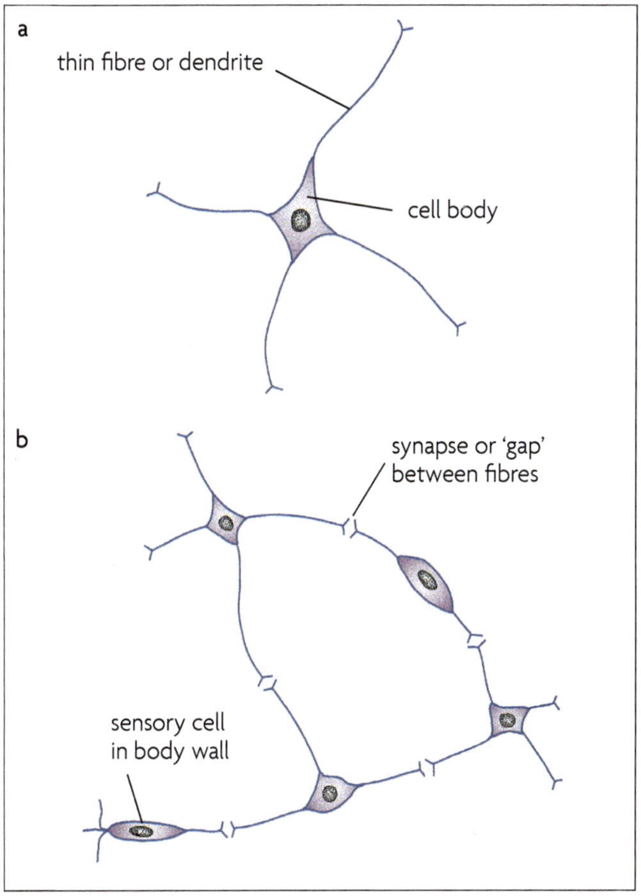

Figure 10.1 **a** Single neurone from the nerve net of the sea anemone. **b** The neurones in a nerve net.

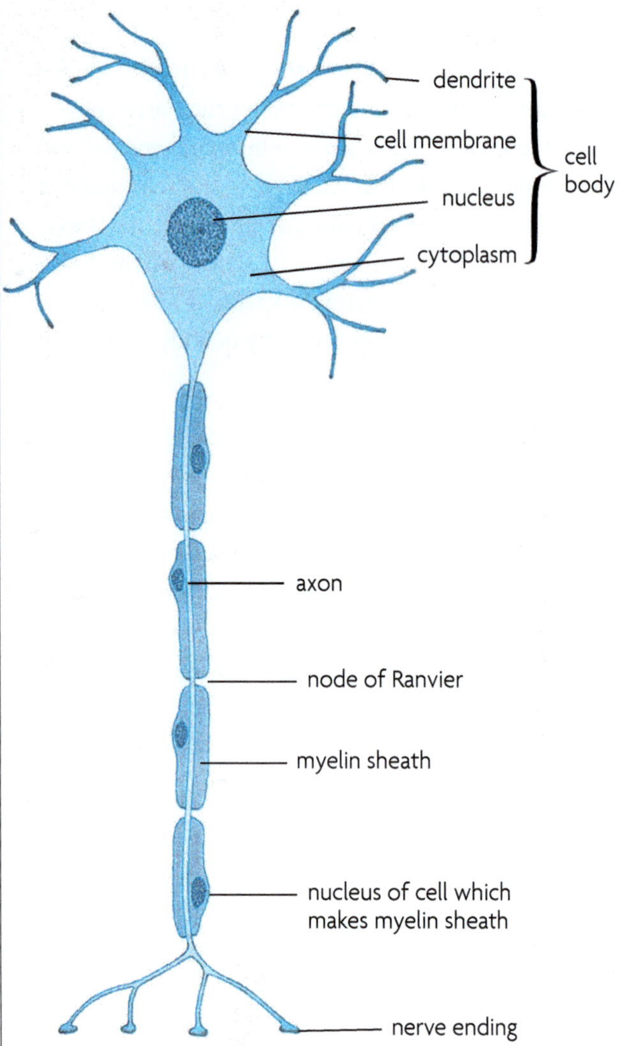

Figure 10.2 A vertebrate motor neurone.

The dendrites pick up electrical impulses from other neurones lying nearby. They pass the impulse to the cell body, and then along the axon. The axon might then pass it on to another neurone. So, unlike what happens in the sea anemone, the electrical impulses can pass in one direction only. This helps to make the system more precise.

Another difference between the mammalian nervous system and that of the sea anemone is that most mammalian nerve fibres are wrapped in a layer of fat and protein called **myelin**. Every now and then there are narrow gaps in the myelin sheath. Myelin insulates the nerve fibres, so that they can carry impulses much faster. A myelinated axon in a cat's body can carry impulses at up to 100 metres per second. An axon without myelin can only carry impulses at about 5 metres per second.

FACT!

A nerve impulse can travel through some parts of your nervous system at a speed of 288 km/h.

Another difference between a mammal's nervous system and that of a sea anemone is that fibres do not run through the body on their own. They are usually in groups of several hundred, called a **nerve**. Figure **10.3** shows a cross section through a nerve.

Figure 10.3 A nerve consists of a group of nerve fibres.

10.6 A central nervous system sorts out information.

Perhaps the most important difference between the human nervous system and the sea anemone's simple nerve net is that humans have a **brain** and **spinal cord**. These make up the **central nervous system**, or CNS (Figure **10.4**). Like the rest of the nervous system, the CNS is made up of neurones. Its function is to coordinate the messages travelling through the nervous system.

When a receptor detects a stimulus, it sends an electrical impulse to the brain or spinal cord. The brain or spinal cord receives the impulse, and 'decides' which effectors need to react to the stimulus. It then sends the impulse on, along the appropriate nerve fibres, to the appropriate effector.

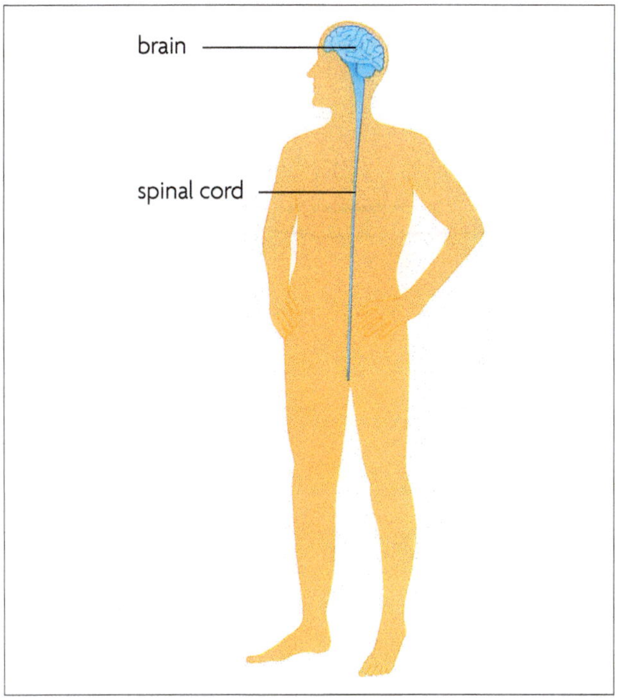

Figure 10.4 The human central nervous system.

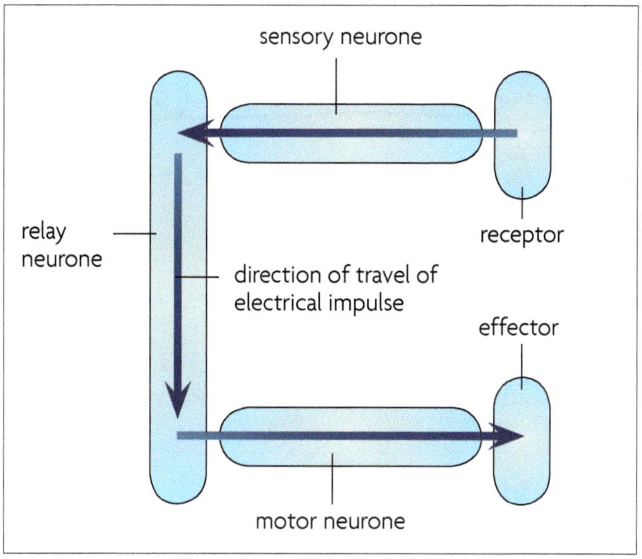

Figure 10.5 Schematic diagram of a reflex arc.

How the nervous system works

10.7 A reflex arc is a basic pathway in the nervous system.

Figure **10.5** illustrates the most basic way in which electrical impulses may be sent from receptors through the nervous system to effectors. The arrangement of sensory neurone, relay neurone and motor neurone is called a **reflex arc** (Figure **10.6**). The structures of a motor neurone and a sensory neurone are compared in Figure **10.7** (overleaf). The way in which these structures fit around and inside the vertebrae is shown in Figure **10.8** (overleaf).

When, for example, your hand touches a hot plate, the high temperature picked up by the sensory receptor in your finger causes it to send an electrical impulse along a sensory neurone to the spinal cord.

In the spinal cord, the electrical impulse is passed on to several other neurones. Only one is shown in Figure **10.6**. These neurones are called **relay neurones**, because they relay the message on to other neurones. The relay

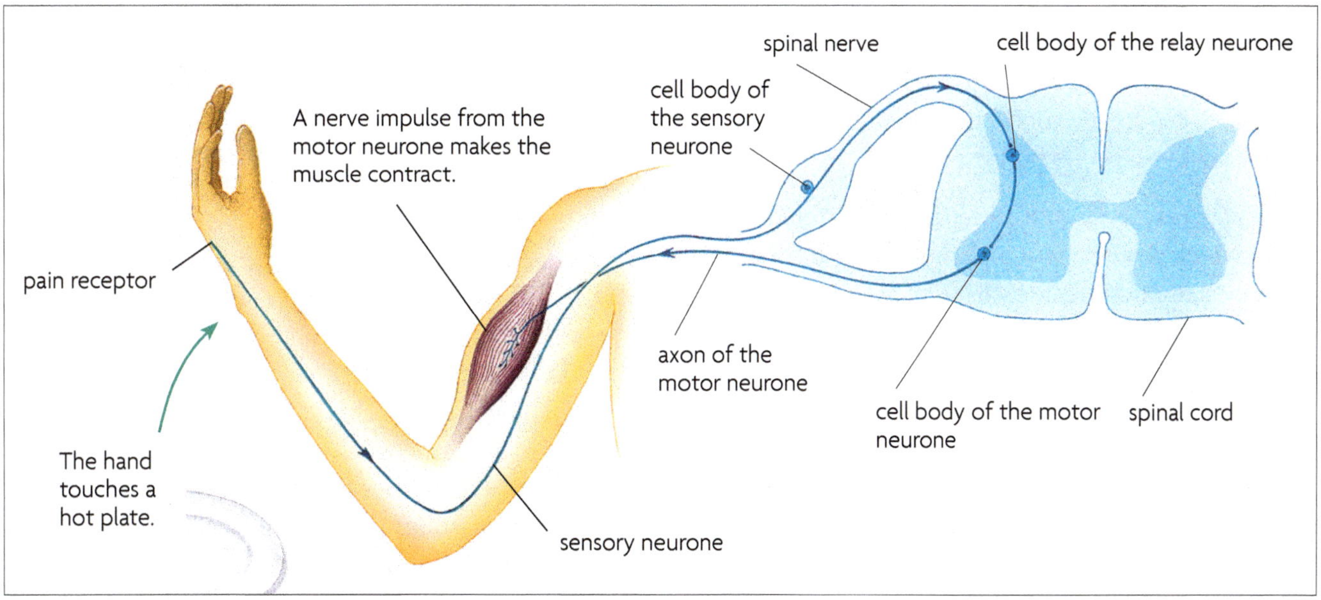

Figure 10.6 A reflex arc.

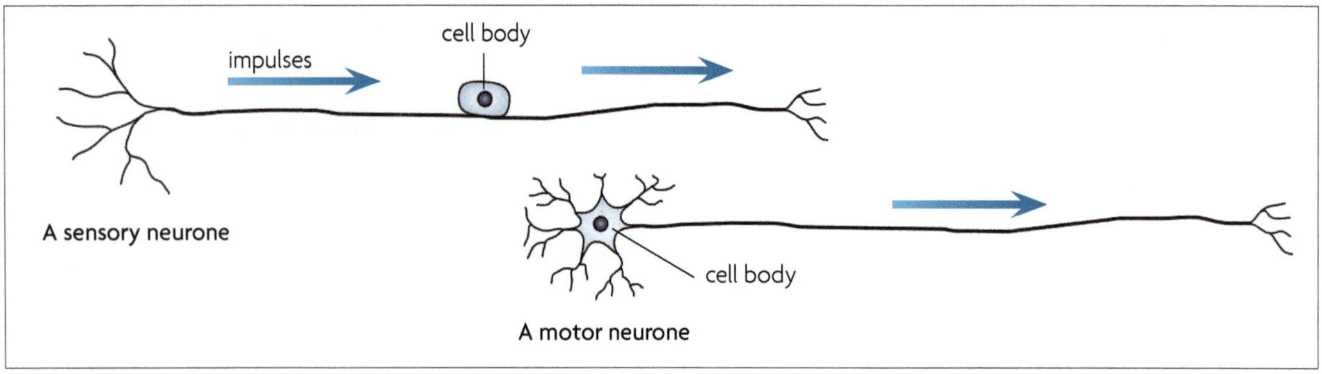

Figure 10.7 The structure of motor and sensory neurones.

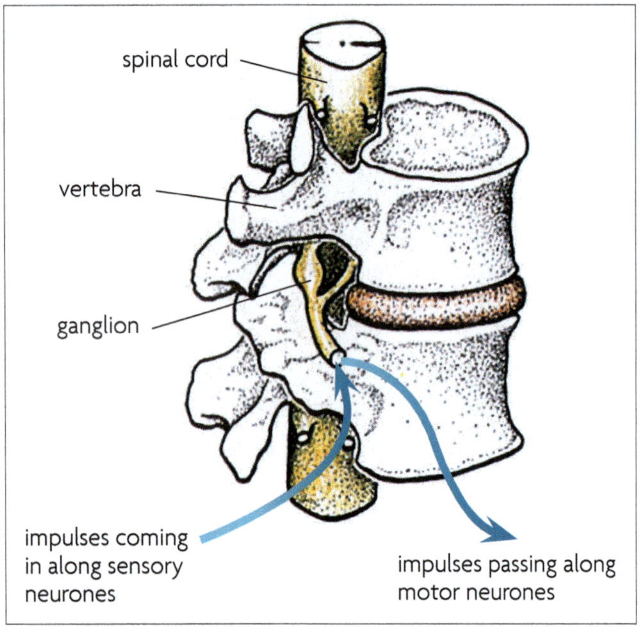

Figure 10.8 The route taken by nerve impulses into and out of the spinal cord.

neurones pass the impulse on to the brain. They also pass it on through a motor neurone to the muscles in your arm, which are the effectors in this case. The muscles then contract and your arm is pulled away.

This sort of reaction is called a **reflex action**. You do not need to think about it. Your brain is made aware of it, but you only consciously realise what is happening after the message has been sent on to your muscles.

Reflex actions are very useful, because the impulse gets from the receptor to the effector as quickly as possible. You do not waste time in thinking about what to do.

Reflexes such as this one, which involve the spinal cord, are called **spinal reflexes**. Figure **10.9** shows another example of a spinal reflex. But not all reflex actions

Figure 10.9 The knee jerk reflex is an example of a spinal reflex. A sharp tap just below the knee stimulates a receptor. This sends impulses along a sensory neurone into the spinal cord. The impulse then travels along a motor neurone to the thigh muscle, which quickly contracts and raises the lower leg.

involve the spinal cord. Some of them involve the brain – but not the 'conscious' parts of it. For example, if you see something flying towards your eye, you will blink. A nerve impulse has gone from your eye to the brain and back into the muscles of the eyelid, all before you have had time to think about it. This is called a **cranial reflex**. You can investigate another cranial reflex if you do Investigation **10.7** (page **186**).

Investigation 10.3
To measure reaction time

SBA skills

Observation/Recording/Reporting
Analysis/Interpretation

The time taken for a nerve impulse to travel from a receptor, through your CNS and back to an effector is very short. It can be measured, but only with special equipment. However, you can get a reasonable idea of the time it takes if you use a large number of people and work out an average time.

1 Get as many people as possible to stand in a circle, holding hands.

2 One person lets go of his or her neighbour with the left hand, and holds a stopwatch in it. When everyone is ready, this person simultaneously starts the stopwatch, and squeezes his or her neighbour's hand with the right hand.

3 As soon as each person's left hand is squeezed, he or she should squeeze his or her neighbour with the right hand. The message of squeezes goes all round the circle.

4 While the message is going round, the person with the stopwatch puts it into the right hand, and holds his or her neighbour's hand with the left hand. When the squeeze arrives, he or she should stop the watch.

5 Keep repeating this, until the message is going round as fast as possible. Record the time taken, and also the number of people in the circle.

6 Now try again, but this time make the message of squeezes go the other way around the circle.

Questions

1 Using the fastest time you obtained, work out the average time it took for one person to respond to the stimulus they received.

2 Did people respond faster as the experiment went on? Why might this happen?

3 Did the message go as quickly when you changed direction? Explain your answer.

4 If you have access to the internet, find a site that allows you to measure your reaction time and try it out. Do you think the website gives you more reliable results than the 'circle' method? Compare the results you obtain, and discuss the advantages and disadvantages of each method.

10.8 Some reflex actions are learned.

Sometimes our response in a reflex action is changed by previous experience. We may not be aware of these changes, but they mean that some 'learning' has taken place. Many of our actions are complicated sets of these learned reflex actions. Riding a bicycle, playing the piano and typing are all examples of these. This type of reflex action is called a conditioned reflex.

10.9 A complex CNS allows complex behaviour.

Why is the central nervous system needed? Would it not be much quicker if pain receptors in your hand could just send a nerve impulse straight to your arm muscles to tell them to move your hand away from a hot plate, rather than all the way to the spinal cord and back? Yes, it would, but that system would not be good enough for animals which need to be able to vary their behaviour under different circumstances.

With a central nervous system it is possible to give a modified, more 'intelligent' response. Say, for example, that you started to pick up the hot plate before you knew it was hot. If you just pulled your hand away, you would drop the plate and break it.

When the message from your fingers saying 'hot plate' arrives at your CNS, there is already another message there saying 'but don't drop it'.

The CNS will 'consider' the two messages together. It will probably send a nerve impulse to your muscles to tell them to put the plate down gently, not to drop it.

The function of the CNS is to collect up all the information from all the receptors in your body, and from your memory. This information will be added together before impulses are sent to effectors. In this way, the best action can be taken in a particular set of circumstances.

10.10 Brain functions are localised.

The brain and spinal cord both help to receive impulses from receptors, and pass them on to effectors. But the brain does much more than this.

Figures **10.10** and **10.11** show the structure of the human brain. It is surrounded by three membranes or **meninges**, which help to protect it.

The **cerebrum** is the largest part of the brain. It is made of two **cerebral hemispheres**. Mammals have much larger cerebral hemispheres than any other kind of animal. Humans have the largest ones of all, compared with the size of the rest of the brain.

Conscious thought and memory take place in the cerebrum. Different parts of the cerebrum have different functions. For example, some areas deal with sight, others with speech. An area near the front determines your personality.

The **hypothalamus** lies underneath the front part of the cerebrum. This is the part of the brain which controls osmoregulation and temperature regulation.

The **cerebellum** is in control of coordination of body movements and posture.

The **medulla oblongata** controls heart rate and breathing (sections **11.17** and **11.18**).

The pituitary gland is not actually a part of the brain, but is just attached to it. It produces several hormones which are concerned with growth, sexual reproduction and water balance in the body.

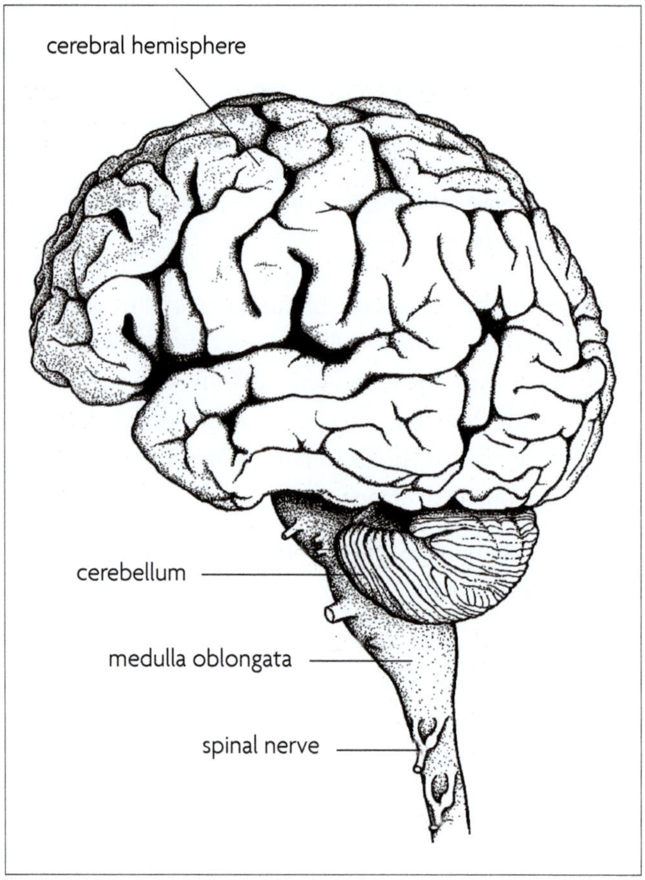

Figure 10.10 External view of a human brain.

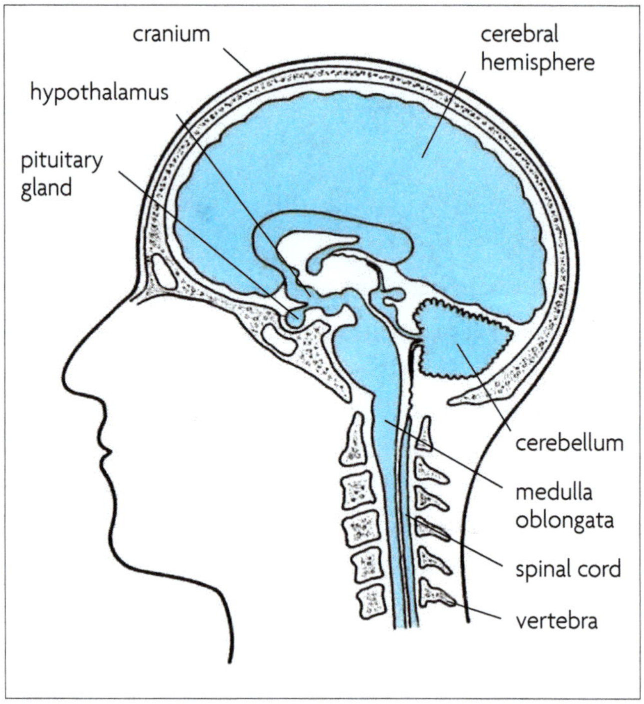

Figure 10.11 Section through a human head, to show the brain.

FACT!

Your brain contains about 100 000 000 000 neurones. After the age of 18, you will lose about 1000 of these every day.
The animal with the heaviest brain is the sperm whale. Its brain weighs about 9.2 kg.

10.11 The responses of the internal organs are special.

We have no conscious control over the actions of the vital internal organs like the alimentary canal and the heart. The motor neurones which go to these internal visceral organs are together known as the **autonomic nervous system** ('auto' means self). This system is made up of two sets of nerves. Many organs, like the heart, breathing muscles, pupil of the eye and alimentary canal are supplied by both sets. One set tends to bring impulses in times of stress, and these cause an increase in the rate of heart beat and breathing, opening up the bronchi of the lungs, slowing down digestion and dilating the pupil of the eye. Impulses brought along the other set of nerves will, in general, have the opposite effect on these organs.

Many of the nerve impulses within the autonomic nervous system originate in the medulla of the brain.

Questions

10.1 Give two examples of effectors.

10.2 What are the two main communication systems in an animal's body?

10.3 List three ways in which neurones are similar to other cells.

10.4 List three ways in which neurones are specialised to carry out their function of transmitting electrical impulses very quickly.

10.5 What is a nerve?

10.6 What is the function of the central nervous system?

10.7 Where are the cell bodies of each of these types of neurone found: **(a)** sensory neurone, **(b)** relay neurone, and **(c)** motor neurone?

10.8 What is the value of reflex actions?

10.9 Describe two reflex actions, other than the ones described in section 10.7.

The receptors

10.12 Receptors are often part of a sense organ.

The parts of the organism's body that detect stimuli, the receptors, may be specialised cells or just the endings of sensory neurones. In animals, the receptors are often part of a **sense organ** (Figure **10.12**). Your eye, for example, is a sense organ, and the rod and cone cells in the retina are receptors. They are sensitive to light.

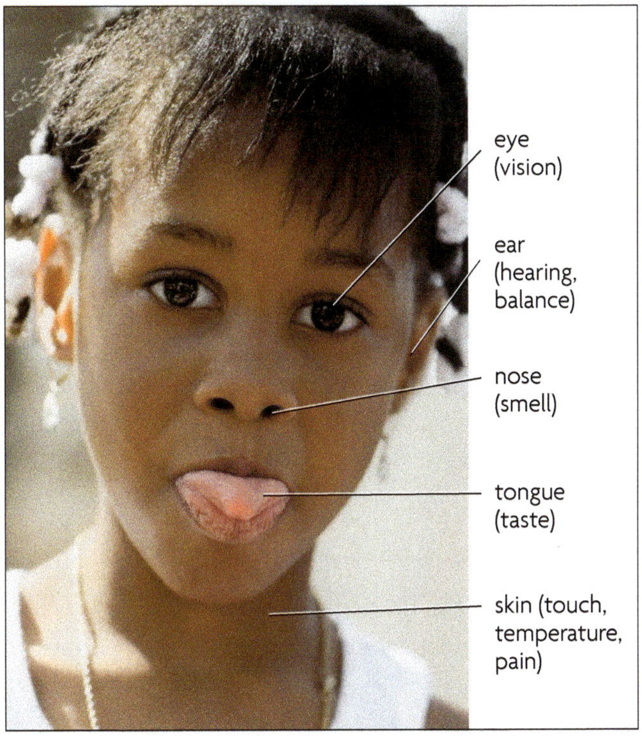

Figure 10.12 Sense organs.

10.13 Skin contains receptive nerve endings.

One of the functions of skin is to pick up various kinds of information about your environment. Figure **11.8** (page **204**) shows a section through human skin. If you look at this, you will see that there are several sorts of nerve endings in the dermis. These nerve endings are receptors for touch, heat, cold, pressure and pain.

If you do Investigation **10.4**, you can find out which parts of your skin contain the most touch receptors.

Investigation 10.4

To find out which part of the skin contains the most touch receptors

SBA skills

Observation/Recording/Reporting
Manipulation/Measurement
Analysis/Interpretation

This investigation tests the skin on the back of the hand, the palm of the hand, and the forehead. You could try different parts of the body if you like.

1 Read the instructions below, and then draw a suitable results table, ready to fill in your results.

2 Set two pins in plasticine at exactly 2 cm apart, with the sharp ends pointing out. Keep checking that the points stay 2 cm apart all the time you use them.

3 Ask your partner to close his or her eyes. Touch your partner gently on the back of the hand with either one or two pins.

Ask your partner to tell you how many pins are touching the hand.

Put a tick in the first space in your table if your partner is right, and a cross if your partner is wrong.

4 Repeat this nine more times.

5 Now repeat steps 3 and 4, still keeping the pins exactly 2 cm apart, but this time touching the skin on the palm of the hand.

6 Repeat on the forehead.

7 Now adjust the pins to 1 cm apart. Test the back of the hand, the palm of the hand and the forehead as before.

8 Adjust the pins to 0.5 cm apart, and test as before.

9 If there is time, test again with the pins 0.2 cm apart.

10 Use your results to draw a histogram. The diagram shows how you can do this.

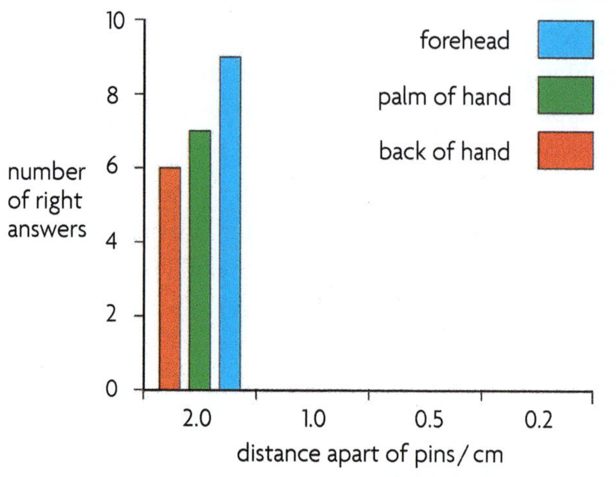

Questions

1 Why does it get more difficult to tell how many pins are touching your skin, as the pins get closer together?

2 Which of the three parts of the body you tested had the most touch receptors?

3 Why do you think this part of the body needs to be so sensitive?

10.14 Some receptors detect chemicals.

The nose and tongue both contain receptors which respond to chemical stimuli. They are sensitive to chemicals in the air, or in food.

On the tongue, these receptor cells are in small groups, called taste buds. The taste buds do not all respond to the same kinds of chemical. Try Investigation **10.5**, to find out which parts of your tongue can taste which kinds of flavour.

Investigation 10.5
To find out which parts of the tongue can taste which flavours

SBA skills
Observation/Recording/Reporting
Analysis/Interpretation

The five tastes you are going to test are sweet, sour, bitter, salty and umami (savoury).

1 Construct a results table, ready to fill in your results.

2 Arrange a communications system between yourself and your partner, so that he or she can tell you which flavour can be tasted without moving the tongue.

3 Put a cotton wool stick into each of the five kinds of solution. Each stick must be put back into its own solution as soon as you finish using it.

4 Ask your partner to shut his or her eyes, and put out his or her tongue. Choose one cotton wool stick, and touch it onto one of the areas of the tongue shown in the diagram. Do not let your partner put his or her tongue back into their mouth yet.

5 Ask your partner to indicate what flavour has been put on his or her tongue. Don't say whether they are right or not. Your partner can now put their tongue back into their mouth and moisten it ready for the next test. Fill in the result in the appropriate space in the table, with a tick or a cross.

6 Repeat with each flavour on each part of the tongue, in a random order. If there is time, do each test twice.

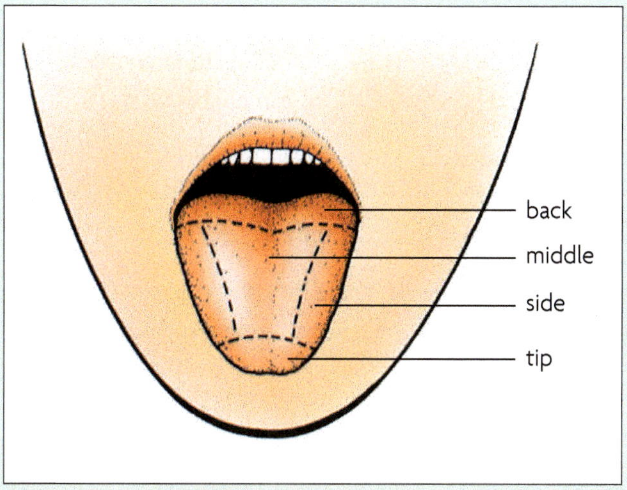

Questions

1 Why must your partner not be allowed to put their tongue into their mouth before telling you what flavour they can taste?

2 Why is it best to do the tests in a random order?

3 Copy the drawing of the tongue, and show on it which parts of the tongue are most sensitive to sweet, sour, bitter, salty and umami tastes.

The eye

10.15 The eye is well protected.

The part of the eye that contains the receptor cells is the **retina** (Figure **10.13**). This is the part which is actually sensitive to light. The rest of the eye simply helps to protect the retina, or to focus light onto it.

Each eye is set in a bony socket in the skull, called the **orbit**. Only the very front of the eye is not surrounded by bone (Figure **10.14**).

The front of the eye is covered by a thin, transparent membrane called the **conjunctiva**, which helps to protect the parts behind it. The conjunctiva is always kept moist by a fluid made in the **tear glands**. This fluid contains an enzyme called **lysozyme**, which can kill bacteria.

The fluid is washed across your eye by your **eyelids** when you blink. The eyelids, eyebrows and eyelashes also help to stop dirt from landing on the surface of your eyes.

Even the part of the eye inside the orbit is protected. There is a very tough coat surrounding it called the **sclera**.

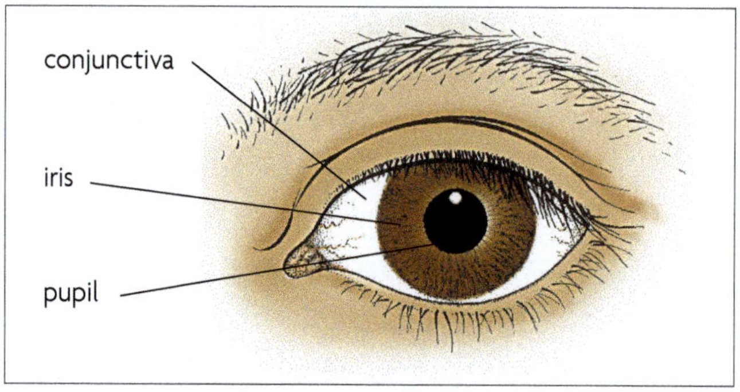

Figure 10.14 The eye from the front.

10.16 Cells in the retina are receptive to light.

The retina is at the back of the eye. It contains two sorts of receptor cells. **Rods** are sensitive to quite dim light, but only let you see in black and white. **Cones** give colour vision, but only in bright light (Figure **10.15**).

When light falls on a receptor cell in the retina, the cell sends an electrical impulse along the optic nerve to the brain. The brain sorts out all the messages from each receptor cell, and builds up an image.

The closer together the receptor cells are, the clearer the image the brain will get. The part of the retina where the receptor cells are packed most closely together is called the **fovea**. This is the part of the retina where

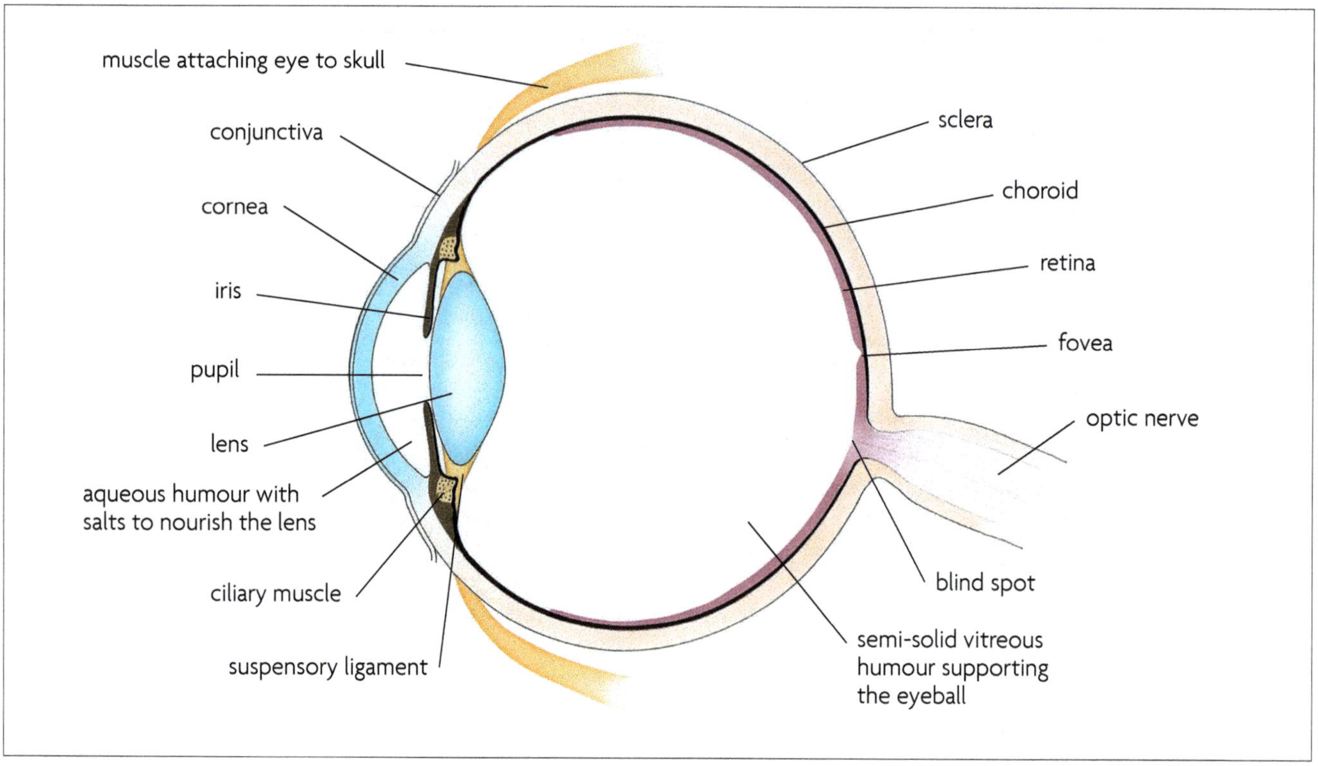

Figure 10.13 Section through a human eye (seen from above).

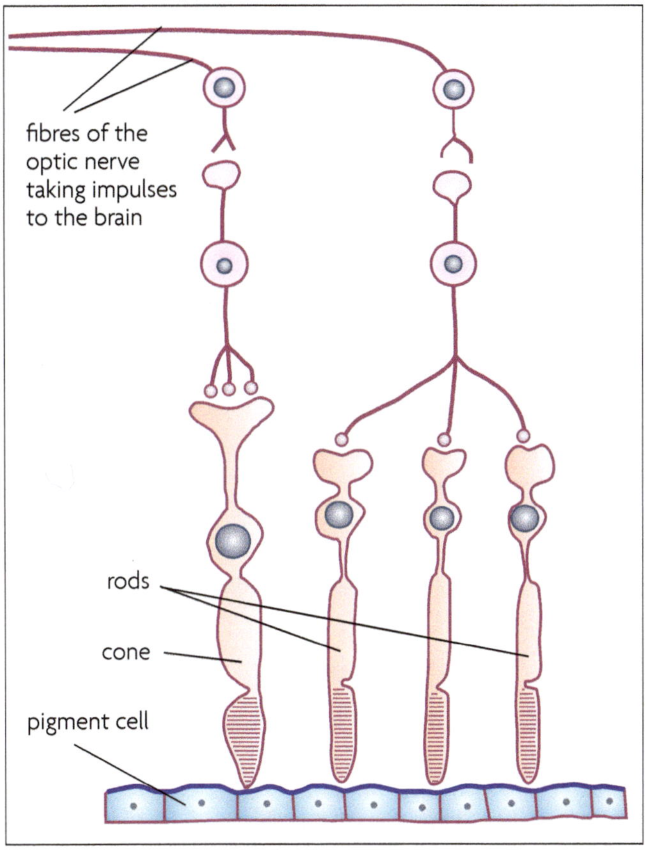

Figure 10.15 A small part of the retina, showing rods and a cone.

light is focused when you look straight at an object. All the receptor cells in the fovea are cones. The rods are scattered further out on the retina.

There are no receptor cells where the optic nerve leaves the retina. This part is called the **blind spot**. If light falls on this place, no impulses will be sent to the brain. Try Investigation **10.6**.

Behind the retina is a black layer called the **choroid**. The choroid absorbs all the light after it has been through the retina, so it does not get scattered around the inside of the eye. The choroid is also rich in blood vessels which nourish the eye.

10.17 The iris adjusts how much light enters the eye.

In front of the lens is a circular piece of tissue called the **iris**. The iris contains pigments, which absorb light and stop it getting through to the retina.

In the middle of the iris is a gap called the **pupil**. The size of the pupil can be adjusted. The wider the pupil is, the more light can get through to the retina. In strong light, the iris closes in, and makes the pupil small. This stops too much light getting in and damaging the retina.

To allow it to adjust the size of the pupil, the iris contains muscles. Circular muscles lie in circles around the pupil. When they contract, they make the pupil constrict, or get smaller. Radial muscles run outwards from the edge of the pupil. When they contract, they make the pupil dilate, or get larger (Figure **10.16**).

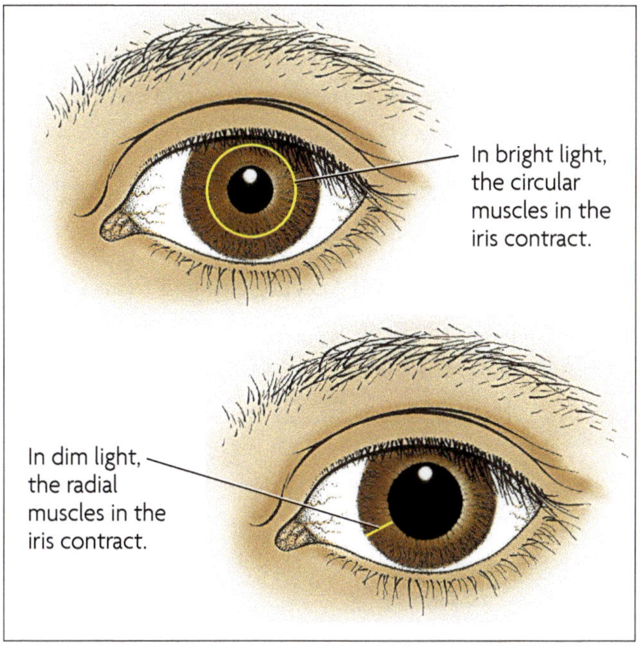

Figure 10.16 The iris reflex.

Investigation 10.6
Can you always see the image?

Hold this page about 45 cm from your face. Close the left eye, and look at the cross with your right eye. Gradually bring the page closer to you. What happens? Can you explain it?

These responses of the iris are examples of a **cranial reflex**. Although the nerve impulses go into the brain, we do not need to think consciously about what to do. The response is fast and automatic. Like many reflex actions, this is very advantageous: it prevents damage to the retina that could be caused by very bright light falling onto it.

10.18 How the eye focuses light.

For the brain to see a clear image, there must be a clear image focused on the retina. Light rays must be bent, or refracted, so that they focus exactly onto the retina. The humours inside the eye are clear so that light can pass through them easily.

The cornea is responsible for most of the bending of the light. The lens makes fine adjustments.

Figure **10.17** shows how the cornea and lens focus light onto the retina. The image on the retina is upside down. The brain interprets this so that you see it the right way up.

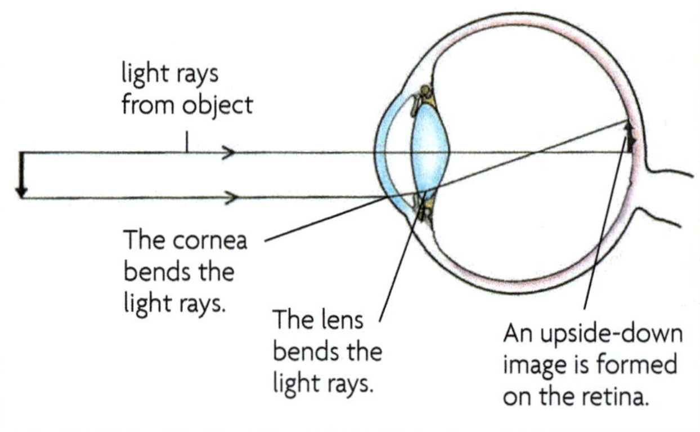

Figure 10.17 How an image is focused onto the retina.

10.19 The lens adjusts the focusing.

Not all light rays need bending the same amount to focus them onto the retina. Light rays coming from a nearby object are going away from one another, or diverging. They will need to be bent inwards quite strongly (Figure **10.18**).

Light rays coming from an object in the distance will be almost parallel to one another. They will not need bending so much (Figure **10.19**).

The shape of the lens can be adjusted to bend light rays more. The fatter it is, the more it will bend them. The thinner it is, the less it will bend them. The adjustment in the shape of the lens, to focus light coming from different distances, is called **accommodation**.

Figure **10.20** shows how the shape of the lens is changed. It is held in position by a ring of **suspensory ligaments**. The tension on the suspensory ligaments, and thus the shape of the lens, is altered by means of the **ciliary muscle**. When it contracts, the suspensory ligaments are

Investigation 10.7
Observing the effect of light on the pupil

SBA skills

Observation/Recording/Reporting

Analysis/Interpretation

Work with a partner for this, or observe your own eyes. Sit in a darkened room and look directly forward. Bring a torch near to one eye and watch the pupil. Explain your observations.

Investigation 10.8
Examining the form and structure of a mammalian eye

SBA skills

Observation/Recording/Reporting

Drawing

Obtain and examine the eye of a mammal.

1 Note on the outside the remnants of the muscles which held the eye into the bony socket in the head. There are six of these. Make a labelled drawing of the eye as it looks from the outside.

2 With a very sharp blade, cut carefully down through the eye, beginning at the centre of the cornea. Identify the internal structures, and note the positions of the fovea (yellow spot) and the blind spot. Make a labelled drawing of what you can see.

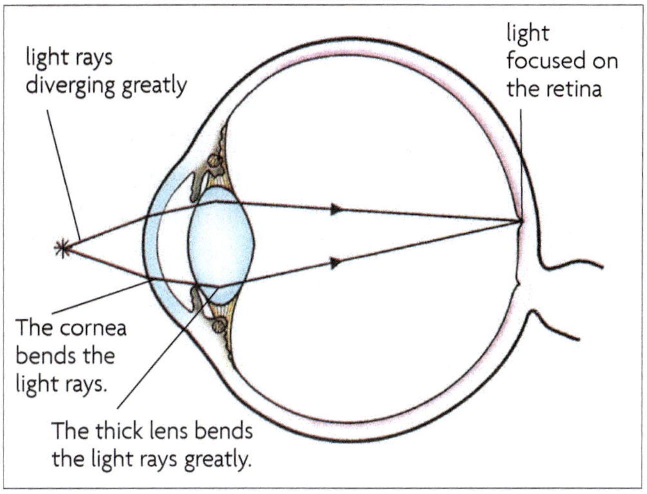

Figure 10.18 Focusing on a nearby object.

loosened. When it relaxes, they are pulled tight. When the suspensory ligaments are tight, the lens is pulled thin. When they are loosened, the lens gets fatter.

10.20 The focusing mechanism may be faulty in some individuals.

Long sight In some people the eyeball is shorter from back to front than is usual; in others, the lens is too flat. Light from a distant object can be focused onto the retina. However, the light from a close object is focused at a point that would be behind the retina, because the rays are not bent enough. Wearing convex or converging lenses can help these people to overcome this defect, which is known as long sight (Figure **10.21**, overleaf).

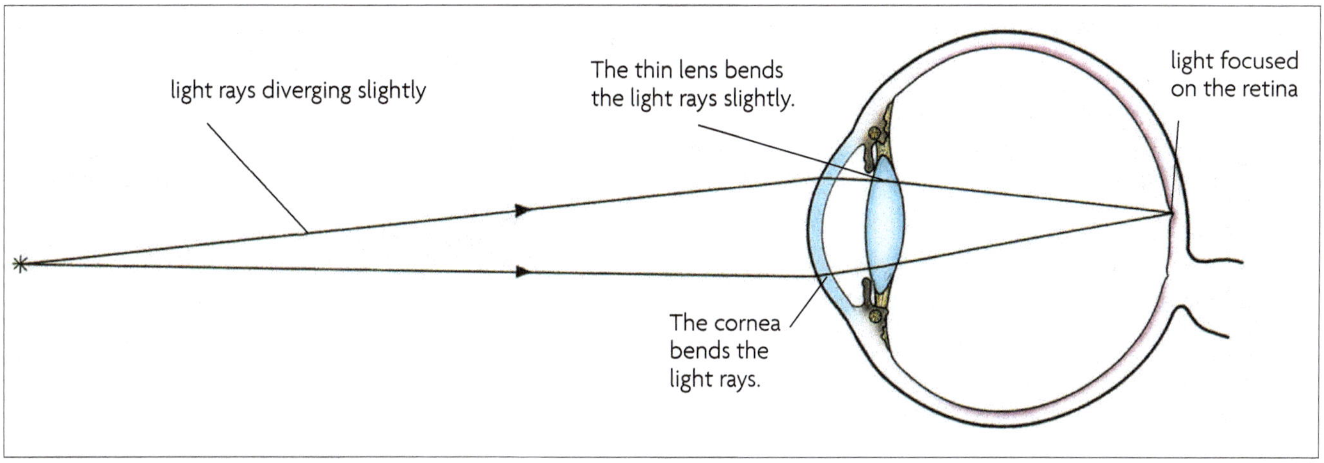

Figure 10.19 Focusing on a distant object.

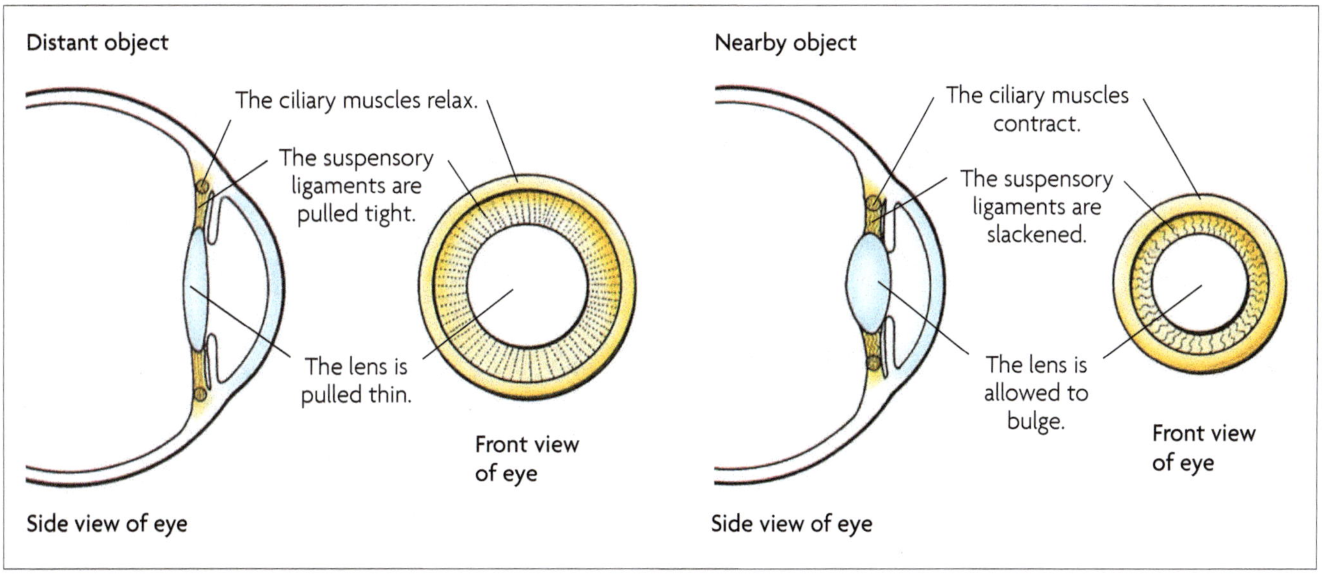

Figure 10.20 How the shape of the lens is changed.

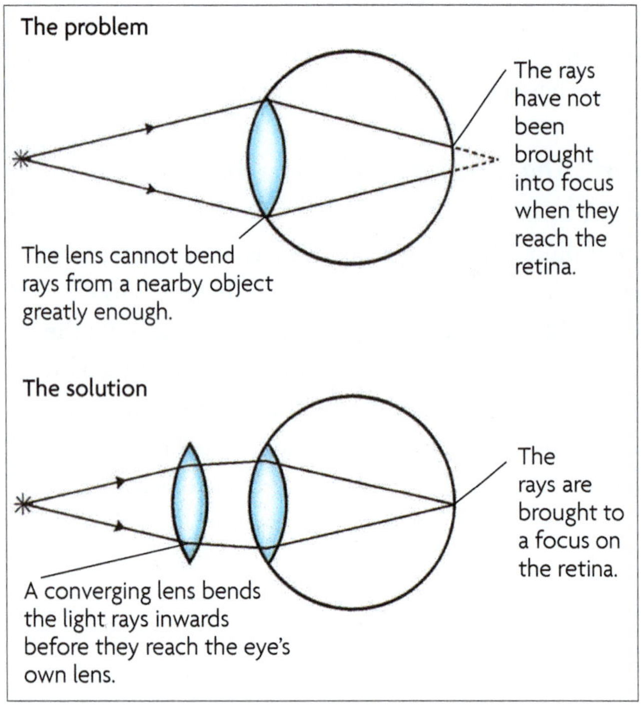

The problem
The rays have not been brought into focus when they reach the retina.
The lens cannot bend rays from a nearby object greatly enough.
The solution
The rays are brought to a focus on the retina.
A converging lens bends the light rays inwards before they reach the eye's own lens.

Figure 10.21 Long sight and its correction.

Short sight If the lens is too curved, or the eyeball is too deep from cornea to retina, the rays from a distant object are bent more than necessary. The image is thus formed in the jelly in front of the retina, and is blurred by the time the light reaches the retina. Persons with this defect are said to be short sighted (Figure **10.22**). Wearing concave or diverging lenses helps the individual to see far objects clearly.

Astigmatism In this defect, the surface of the lens and/or the cornea is irregularly curved. As a result, light rays reaching the eye may be in focus in one plane, but not in others. The condition is known as astigmatism and may be corrected by wearing cylindrical lenses which work along one axis only. If the person is long or short sighted, in addition, the spectacles will need to be a combination of cylindrical and spherical surfaces.

10.21 Ageing has some effects on vision.

With increasing age, the lens loses some of its elasticity, and the ciliary muscles become weaker. As a result, accommodation becomes increasingly difficult. As with long sight, converging lenses will help to give clear vision of near objects.

In some cases the lens becomes opaque, a condition known as **cataract**. Light cannot pass through to the retina, and so the person is unable to see. The condition may be helped by surgery. The lens is removed and an artificial lens put in its place, either by wearing spectacles, contact lenses or actually inserting a lens inside the eye.

In **glaucoma**, too much fluid gathers in front of the lens. This increases pressure within the eye, damaging the optic nerve so vision becomes poorer.

Among patients with diabetes, cataract and glaucoma are common and may occur at an earlier age than in non-diabetics.

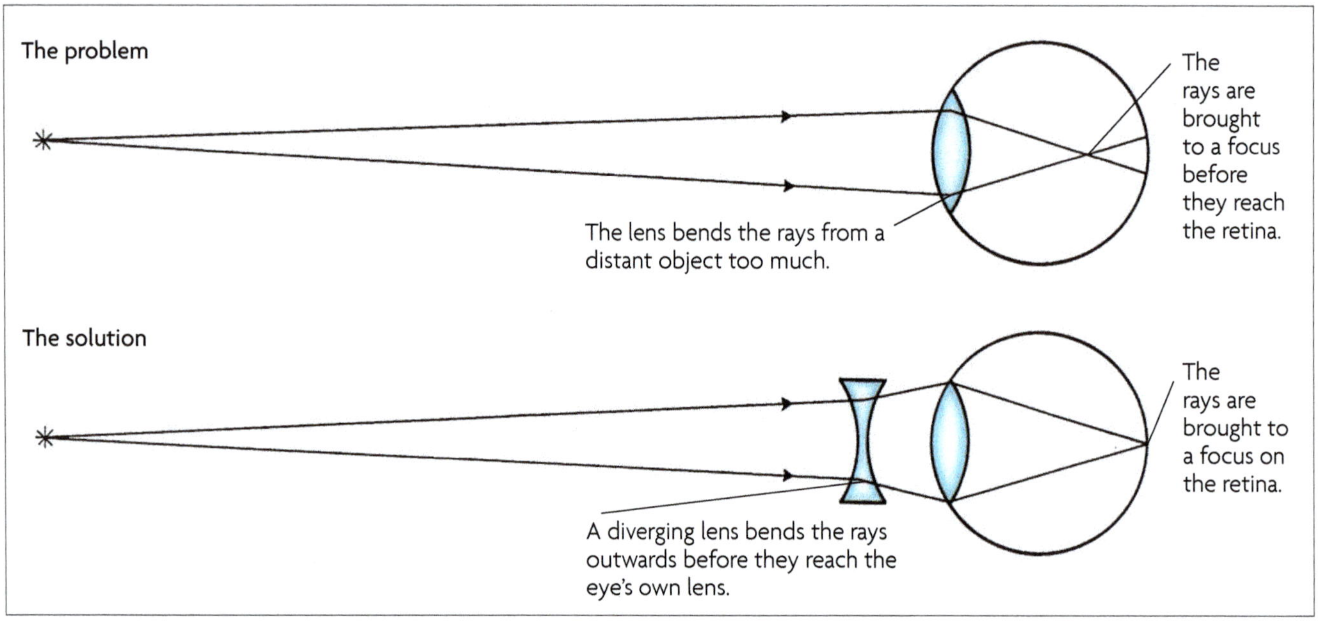

The problem
The rays are brought to a focus before they reach the retina.
The lens bends the rays from a distant object too much.
The solution
The rays are brought to a focus on the retina.
A diverging lens bends the rays outwards before they reach the eye's own lens.

Figure 10.22 Short sight and its correction.

10.22 Having two eyes is an advantage.

The images of an object sent to the retina from the two eyes are slightly different. The brain is able to interpret these differences so that we can appreciate size, shape and distance of the object. Thus we get a three-dimensional picture of the object. The fields seen by the two eyes overlap somewhat, but two eyes allow a wide range of vision.

The ear

10.23 The structure of the ear.

The ear has two functions. First, it is sensitive to sound. It also contains receptor cells which are sensitive to the position and movement of your head. These cells help with balance.

Figure **10.23** illustrates the structure of the human ear. The outer ear and the middle ear both contain air. The inner ear is filled with fluid.

10.24 The cochlea is sensitive to sound waves.

The cells that are sensitive to sound waves are inside the cochlea. Sound waves need to be made stronger, or amplified, before these cells will respond to them.

First, the sound waves make the air in the outer ear vibrate. This makes the eardrum vibrate. The vibrations are passed along the chain of tiny bones – the malleus, incus and stapes – until it reaches the oval window. The oval window transmits the vibrations to the perilymph, inside the cochlea.

The cochlea contains cells with tiny hairs, which are embedded in a plate of jelly. As the fluid inside the cochlea vibrates, the hairs are pulled and pushed against the jelly plate. This makes the hair cells send impulses along the auditory nerve to the brain.

The hair cells in different parts of the cochlea respond to different frequencies of vibration. The ones nearest to the

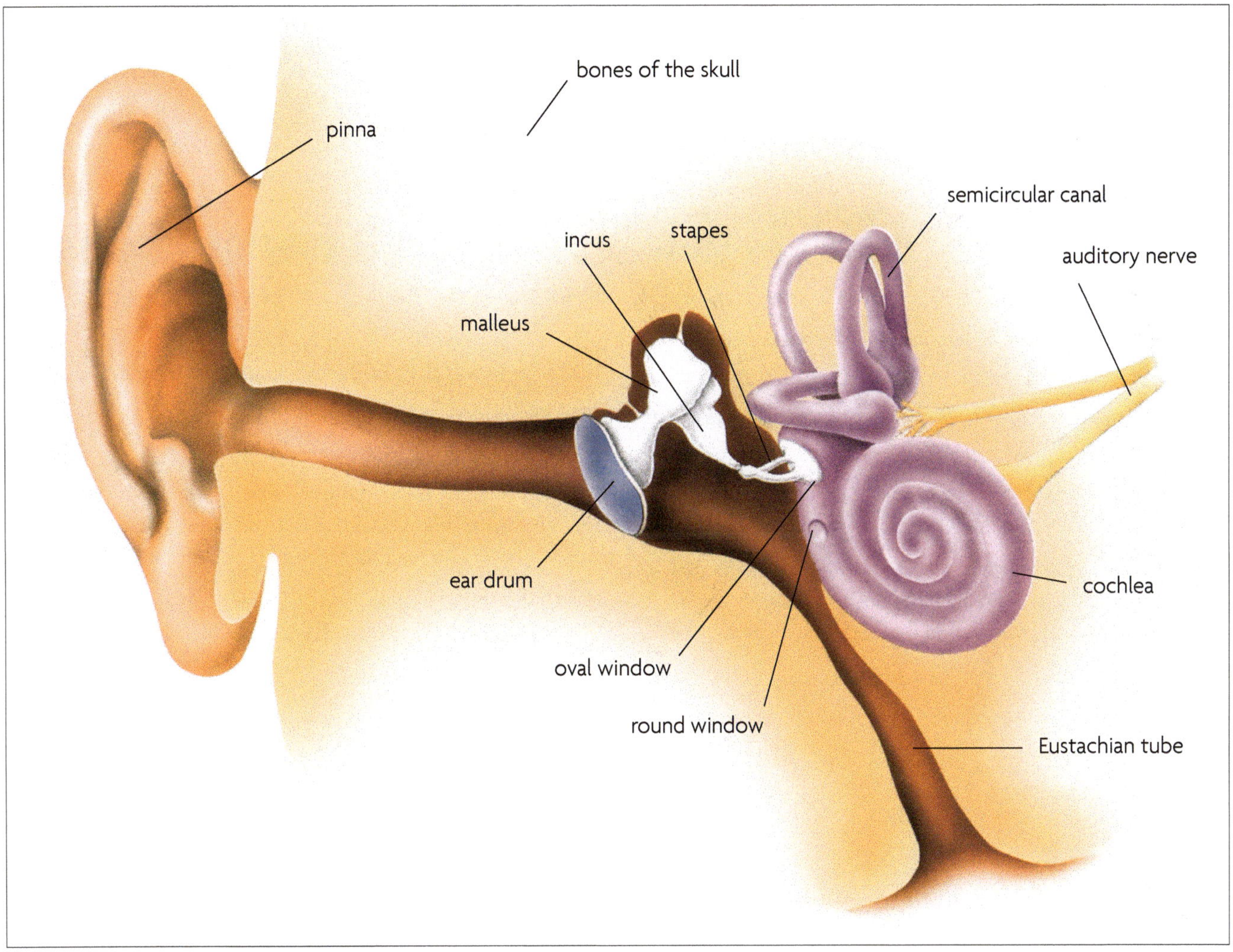

Figure 10.23 The human ear.

oval window respond to high frequencies (high pitched sounds). Low frequency sounds are picked up by the cells nearest the middle of the coil. Frequent exposure to loud sounds, such as loud music, damages the hair cells and can cause partial hearing loss or even deafness.

10.25 The semicircular canals help you keep your balance.

The three semicircular canals are sensitive to movements of the head. Like the cochlea, they are filled with fluid. Each semicircular canal has a swelling near one end of it, called an ampulla. Each one contains hair cells with their hairs embedded in a plate of jelly. When you move your head, the heavy cupula moves too. It pulls on the hairs, so the hair cells send impulses along a nerve to the brain.

Each ear has three semicircular canals, all at right angles to one another. By comparing the impulses from each one, your brain can tell exactly how your head is moving, and so enable you to keep your balance. Usually, impulses from your eyes help with this as well. If the information from your eyes and ears does not match, such as when you are reading a book while travelling in a car, then you may feel sick.

Coordination and response in plants

10.26 Some plant responses result in growth.

In section **9.18**, we saw that plants are able to respond to their environment, although usually with much slower responses that those of animals.

In general, plants respond to stimuli by changing their rate or direction of growth. They may grow either towards or away from a stimulus. Growth towards is said to be a positive response, and growth away from is a negative response to a particular stimulus.

These responses are called **tropisms**. A tropism is a growth response by a plant, in which the direction of the growth is affected by the direction of the stimulus.

Two important stimuli for plants are light and gravity. Shoots normally grow towards light. Roots do not usually respond to light, but a few grow away from it.

Shoots tend to grow away from the pull of gravity, while roots normally grow towards it.

Questions

10.10 What is a stimulus?

10.11 Name two parts of the body which contain receptors of chemical stimuli.

10.12 Which part of the eye contains cells which are sensitive to light?

10.13 Your brain can build up a very clear image when light is focused onto the fovea. Explain why it can do this.

10.14 If you look straight at an object when it is nearly dark, you may find it difficult to see it. It is easier to see if you look just to one side of it. Explain why this is.

10.15 What is the choroid, and what is its function?

10.16 List, in order, the parts of the eye through which light passes to reach the retina.

10.17 Name two parts of the eye which refract light rays.

10.18 What is meant by accommodation?

10.19 **a** What do the ciliary muscles do when you are focusing on a nearby object?

b What effect does this have on **(i)** the suspensory ligaments, and **(ii)** the lens?

10.20 Many older people use two pairs of glasses, or wear bifocal spectacles. Can you explain this?

Investigation 10.9
To find out how shoots respond to light

SBA skills

Observation/Recording/Reporting *Drawing*
Analysis/Interpretation

1 Label three Petri dishes A, B and C. Line each with moist cotton wool or filter paper, and put about six peas or beans in each.

2 Leave all three dishes in a warm place for a day or two, until the seeds begin to germinate. Check that they do not dry out.

3 Now put dish **A** into a light-proof box with a slit in one side, so that the seedlings get light from one side only.

4 Put dish **B** onto a clinostat (see diagram) in a light place. The clinostat will slowly turn the seedlings around, so that they get light from all sides equally. If you do not have a clinostat, arrange to turn the dish by hand three or four times per day to achieve a similar effect.

5 Put dish C into a completely light-proof box.

6 Leave all the dishes for a week, checking that they do not dry out.

7 Make labelled drawings of one seedling from each dish.

Questions

1 How did the seedlings in **A** respond to light from one side? What is the name for this response?

2 Why was dish **B** put onto a clinostat, and not simply left in a light place?

3 Explain what happened to the seedlings in dish **C**.

4 What was the control in this experiment?

Investigation 10.10
To find out how roots respond to gravity

SBA skills

Observation/Recording/Reporting
Analysis/Interpretation
Planning/Design

You are going to design this investigation yourself. You can use similar techniques to those in Investigation **10.9**. This is the hypothesis you are going to test:

Roots grow towards gravity.

When you have written your plan, get it checked by your teacher before you try to carry it out. Write it up in the usual way, including a discussion and evaluation.

Investigation 10.11
To find out which part of a shoot is sensitive to light

SBA skills

Observation/Recording/Reporting
Manipulation/Measurement
Analysis/Interpretation

1 Germinate several maize grains in three pots, labelled **A**, **B** and **C**. Space the seeds well out from each other. The seeds will grow shoots called coleoptiles (Figure **10.24**).

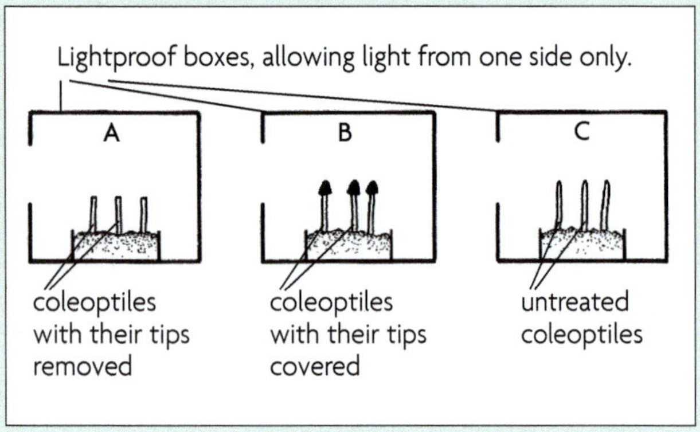

2 Cut the tips from each coleoptile in pot **A**.

3 Cover the tips of each coleoptile in pot **B** with foil.

4 Measure the length of each coleoptile in each pot. Find the average length of the coleoptiles in each pot and record it.

5 Put pots **A**, **B** and **C** into light-proof boxes with light shining in from one side. Leave them for one or two days.

6 Find the new average length of the coleoptiles in each pot and record it. Compare it with the original average length, to see whether the coleoptiles have grown or not.

7 Draw a results table and record your results fully.

Questions

1 Explain why some coleoptiles grew, and some did not.

2 Which coleoptiles grew towards the light, and which did not? Explain why.

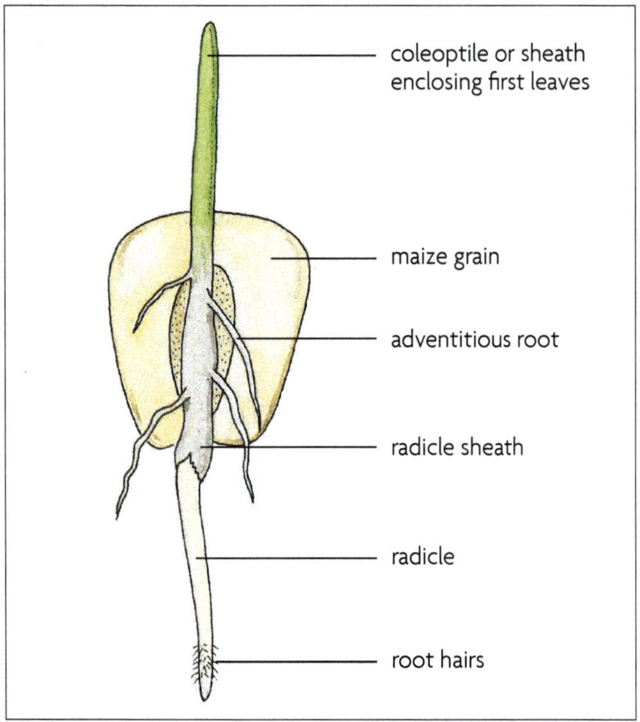

Figure 10.24 A maize seedling.

10.27 These growth movements aid plant survival.

It is very important to the plant that its roots and shoots grow in appropriate directions. Shoots must grow upwards, away from gravity and towards the light, so that the leaves are held out into the sunlight. The more light they have, the better they can photosynthesise. Flowers, too, need to be held up in the air, where insects, birds or the wind can pollinate them.

Roots, though, need to grow downwards, into the soil in order to anchor the plant in the soil, and to absorb water and minerals from between the soil particles.

10.28 How a shoot responds to light.

In section **10.2** we saw that for an organism to respond to a stimulus, there must be a receptor to pick up the stimulus, an effector to respond to it, and some kind of communication system in between. In mammals, the receptor is often part of a sense organ, and the effector is a muscle or gland. Messages are sent between them along nerves, or sometimes by means of hormones.

Plants, however, do not have complex sense organs, muscles or nervous systems. So how do they manage to respond to stimuli like light and gravity?

Figure **10.25** shows an experiment that can be done to find out which part of a shoot picks up the stimulus of light shining onto it. The sensitive region is the tip of the shoot. This is where the receptor is.

If you are able to do Investigation **10.12**, you will probably find that the part of the shoot which responds to the stimulus is the part just below the tip. This is the effector.

These two parts of the shoot must be communicating with one another somehow. They do it by means of chemicals called **hormones**.

Animals also have hormones, and some of these are described in Chapter **11**.

10.29 Differences in auxin concentration cause growth movements.

One kind of plant hormone is called **auxin**. Auxin is being made all the time by the cells in the tip of a shoot. The auxin diffuses downwards from the tip, into the rest of the shoot.

Auxin makes the cells just behind the tip get longer. The more auxin there is, the faster they will grow. Without auxin, they will not grow (Figure **10.25**).

When light shines onto a shoot from all around, auxin is distributed evenly around the tip of the shoot. The cells all grow at about the same rate, so the shoot grows straight upwards. This is what normally happens in plants growing outside.

When, however, light shines onto a shoot from one side, the auxin at the tip concentrates on the shady side (Figure **10.26**). This makes the cells on the shady side grow faster than the ones on the bright side, so the shoot bends towards the light.

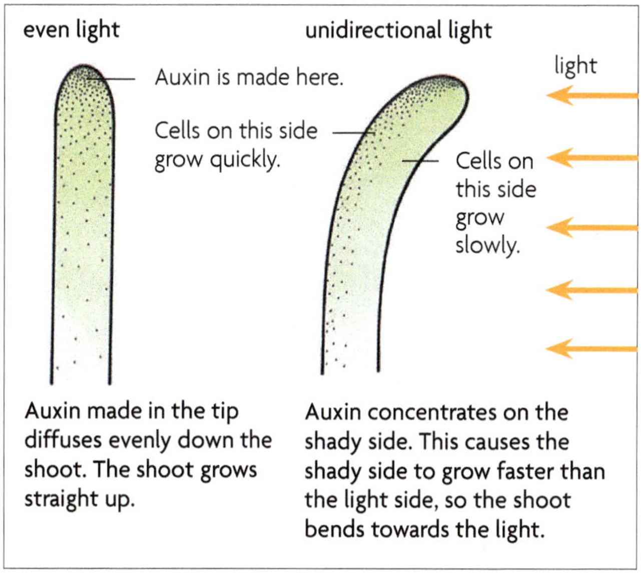

Figure 10.26 Auxin and phototropism.

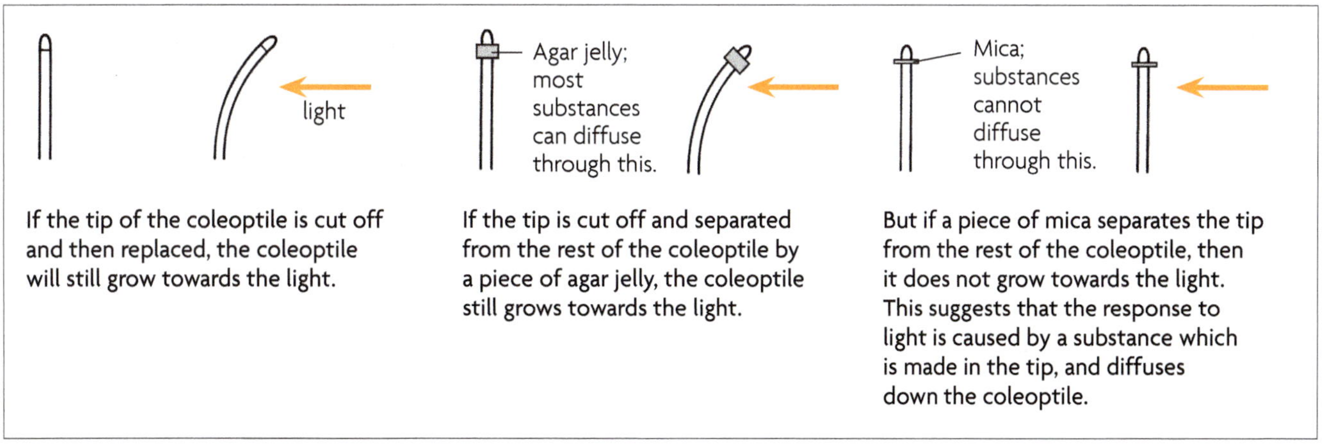

Figure 10.25 An experiment investigating the method by which shoots respond to light.

If a potted *Coleus* plant is placed on its side in a dark room overnight, the shoot will be seen to bend upwards (Figure **10.27**). Since there was no light, we can presume the result to be a response to gravity. (What other precaution should we take to be sure of this?)

Figure 10.27 Auxin and the response to gravity in a *Coleus* plant.

With the stem in the horizontal position, auxin tended to collect on the lower side of the stem, causing faster growth there. Therefore the stem curved upward.

In the same way, in the bean seedlings shown in Figure **10.28**, auxin has tended to build up on the lower surface of the root. The effect, however, is the opposite from that in the *Coleus* shoot. This amount of auxin slows down the growth on this side, and so the radicle bends downwards.

Figure 10.28 The response to gravity in a root.

10.30 Plants become etiolated in the dark.

If you did Investigation **10.9**, you will probably have found that the seedlings which had no light looked very different from the others. In darkness, auxin is also distributed evenly around the tip, and the shoot grows rapidly upwards. But chloroplasts do not develop properly in darkness. Therefore plants without light become yellow

Investigation 10.12
To find out how auxin affects shoots

SBA skills

Observation/Recording/Reporting
Manipulation/Measurement
Analysis/Interpretation

In this experiment, you will use a kind of auxin called indoleacetic acid, or IAA. When you put it onto a shoot, you need to mix it with lanolin, so that it will stick on.

1 Germinate some maize grains in three pots, labelled **A**, **B** and **C**.

2 Mix some IAA with a little warm lanolin. Gently smear the mixture down one side only of each coleoptile in pot **A**. Put the IAA on the same side of each coleoptile. Put a label in the pot to show which side of the coleoptiles the IAA was put on.

3 Leave pot **C** untreated.

4 Do the same with the coleoptiles in pot **B**, but use pure lanolin with no IAA in it.

5 Put all three pots onto clinostats in a light place, and leave them for a day.

Questions

1 What has happened to the coleoptiles in pots **A**, **B** and **C**? Explain why.

2 What was the reason for smearing the coleoptiles in pot **B** with lanolin?

3 Why were all the pots put onto clinostats?

and spindly. They grow very tall and thin, and have smaller leaves, which are often further apart than in a normal plant. Plants like this are said to be etiolated.

If these plants reach the light, chlorophyll will develop, and the plants will begin to grow normally. If they do not reach light, they will die because they cannot photosynthesise.

Questions

10.21 What part of the shoot is sensitive to light?

10.22 What part of the shoot responds to light?

10.23 How do these parts communicate with each other? How is this like or unlike a similar system in the mammal?

10.24 How does the normal response of a shoot to light help the plant?

10.25 How does a main root respond to gravity?

10.26 Describe three features of an etiolated shoot.

Key ideas

- All organisms are able to sense changes in their environment, called stimuli, and respond to them. The part of the body that senses the stimulus is a receptor, and the part that responds is an effector.
- Invertebrates respond to some stimuli by moving towards or away from them, or by altering their speed of movement or rate of turning. Choice chambers can be used to investigate these responses.
- The human nervous system contains specialised cells called neurones. The brain and spinal cord make up the central nervous system, which coordinates stimuli and responses.
- Reflex actions are fast, automatic responses to a stimulus. They involve a series of neurones making up a reflex arc. A sensory neurone takes the impulse to the CNS and a motor neurone takes it from the CNS to an effector.
- Reflex actions in which the route runs through the spinal cord are known as spinal reflexes. If the route runs through the brain, it is a cranial reflex. The knee-jerk reflex is a spinal reflex. The iris reflex is a cranial reflex.
- In the brain, the cerebrum controls conscious thought, language and emotions. The cerebellum coordinates body movements. The medulla controls the rate of heart beat and the rate and depth of breathing movements, sending impulses along motor neurones in the autonomic nervous system.
- Receptors are generally found within sense organs. The receptors in the eye are rod and cone cells, found in the retina.
- The cornea and lens focus light rays onto the fovea, the part of the eye where cone cells are most densely packed.
- The shape of the lens is changed by the contraction or relaxation of the ciliary muscle. When focusing on a distant object, the muscle relaxes so that the suspensory ligaments are pulled taut and the lens is pulled into a thin shape. When focusing on a near object, the muscle contracts and the lens falls into its natural, more rounded shape.
- A person with short sight cannot make the lens thin enough to focus light from distant objects onto the retina. This can be corrected with glasses with a concave lens. A person with long sight cannot make the lens thick enough, and needs to wear glasses with a convex lens.
- Plants may respond to a stimulus by growing towards or away from it. This is called tropism.

End-of-chapter questions

1 Explain the difference between each of the following pairs of terms, giving examples whenever they make your answer clearer:

a cornea, conjunctiva
b choroid, sclera
c neurone, nerve
d receptor, effector
e sensory neurone, motor neurone
f cerebrum, cerebellum
g negative geotropism, positive geotropism.

2 If you walk from a brightly lit street into a dark room, your pupils will rapidly dilate.

a What type of action is this?
b Using each of the following words at least once, but not necessarily in this order, explain how this reaction is brought about.
synapse, receptor, motor neurone, sensory neurone, relay neurone, radial muscles
c As well as the muscles in the iris, the eye also contains muscles in the ciliary body. What is their function?

3 a Make a large, labelled diagram of a nerve cell or neurone.
b List three ways in which this cell is similar to other animal cells.
c List three ways in which this cell differs from other animal cells, explaining how each of these differences enables it to perform its function efficiently.

4 From your general observations, how do you think leaves respond to light? Try to explain your observations in terms of the use of the response to the survival of the plant.

5 In tropical forests, many trees tend to be very tall and thin, and there are many climbing plants. Can you suggest a reason for this?

6 This graph shows the effect of different concentrations of auxin on the growth of roots and shoots. Use the graph to explain the responses of roots and shoots to gravity.

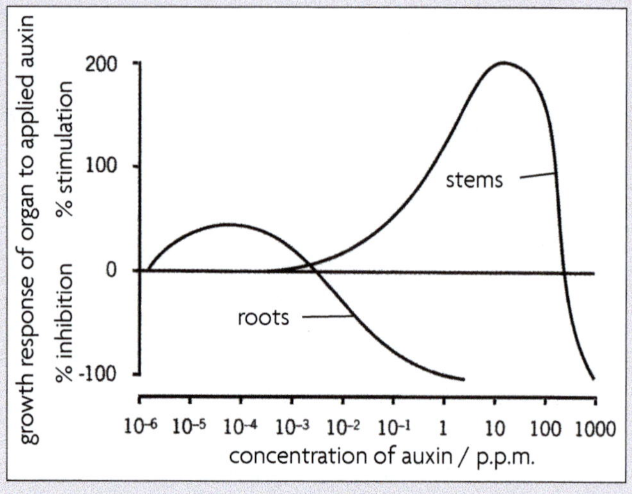

7 In section 10.26, the statement is made that in general plants respond more slowly than animals. Describe one plant reaction you know which is fast.

11 Hormones and homeostasis

In this chapter, you will find out:

- about the main glands in the human endocrine system, and the hormones that they secrete
- how insulin and glucagon help to keep the blood glucose concentration constant
- the meaning of the term homeostasis, and how negative feedback mechanisms help homeostasis to be achieved
- how humans control the internal temperature of the body
- the structure and functions of skin.

Hormones

11.1 Endocrine glands make hormones.

In Chapter **10**, we saw how nerves can carry electrical impulses very quickly from one part of an animal's body to another. But animals also use chemicals to transmit information from one part of the body to another.

The chemicals are called **hormones**. Hormones are made in special glands called **endocrine glands**. Figure **11.1** (overleaf) shows the positions of the most important endocrine glands in the human body.

Endocrine glands have a good blood supply. They have blood capillaries running right through them. When the endocrine gland makes a hormone, it releases it directly into the blood (Figure **11.2**, overleaf).

Other sorts of gland do not do this. The salivary glands, for example, do not secrete saliva into the blood. Saliva is secreted into the salivary duct, which carries it into the mouth. Endocrine glands do not have ducts, so they are sometimes called **ductless glands**.

Once the hormone is in the blood, it is carried to all parts of the body, dissolved in the plasma. Although the blood is carrying so many hormones, each affects only certain parts of the body. These are called its **target organs**.

11.2 Adrenaline prepares the body for action.

There are two adrenal glands, one above each kidney. They make a hormone called **adrenaline**. When you are frightened, excited or keyed up, your brain sends impulses along a nerve to your adrenal glands. This makes them secrete adrenaline into the blood.

Adrenaline has several effects which are designed to help you to cope with danger. For example, it makes your heart beat faster, supplying oxygen to your brain and muscles more quickly. This gives them more energy for fighting or running away.

The blood vessels in your skin and digestive system contract so that they carry very little blood. This makes you go pale, and gives you 'butterflies in your stomach'. As much blood as possible is needed for your brain and muscles in the emergency.

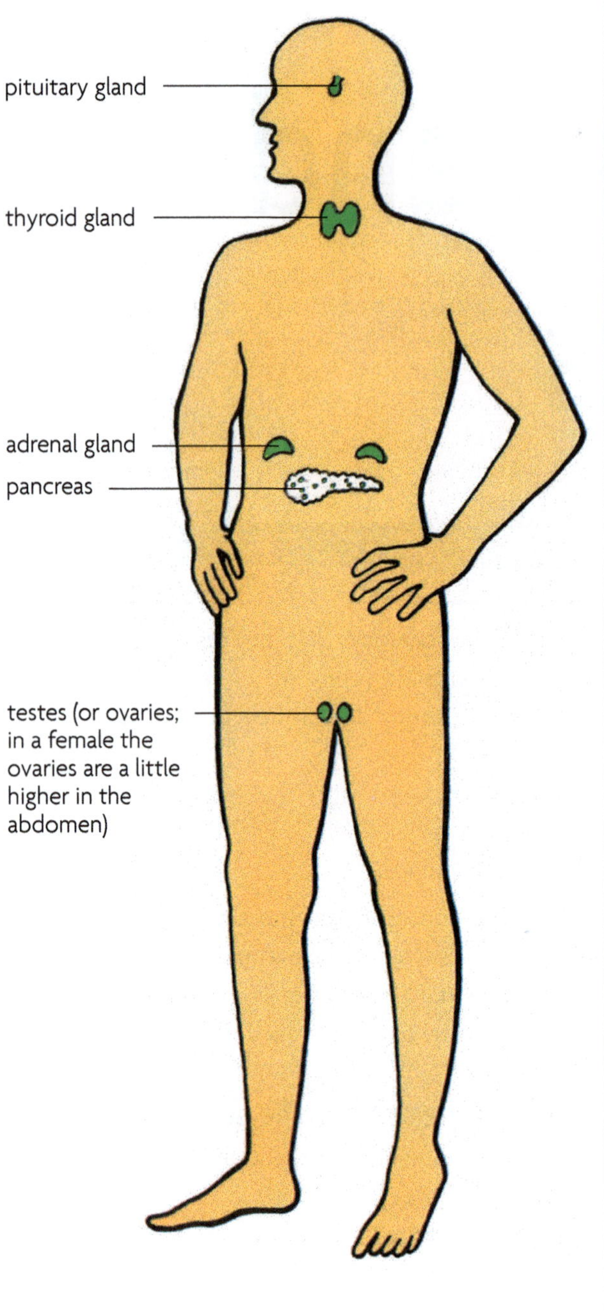

Figure 11.1 The main endocrine glands.

All of this is very useful if you really have to fight an enemy. It is also useful if you are an athlete at the start of a race. But it does not help at all if you are on your way to the dentist, or watching a horror film.

Like most hormones, adrenaline breaks down very quickly after it is released, so its effects do not last long. If you need to go on feeling frightened, then your brain will keep telling the adrenal glands to secrete more adrenaline.

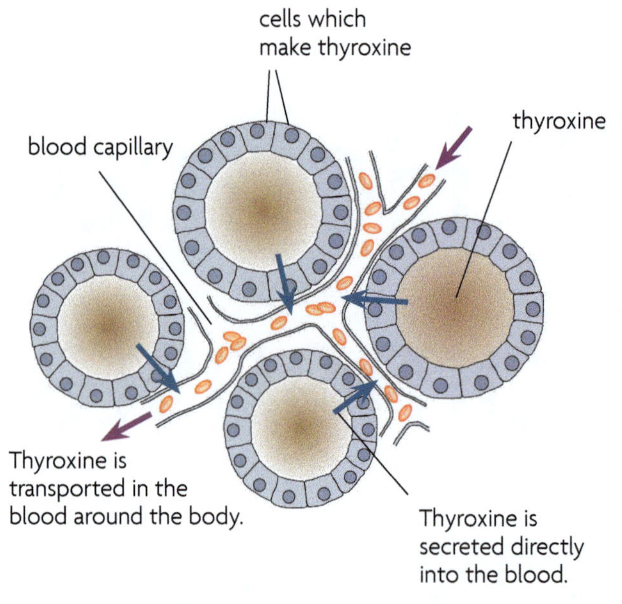

Figure 11.2 Section through the thyroid gland.

11.3 The thyroid regulates metabolism and growth.

The thyroid gland secretes **thyroxine**. Thyroxine is secreted almost all the time, but in quite small amounts. Thyroxine helps to control the metabolic rate, mostly by regulating the speed at which cells oxidise glucose in respiration. This is particularly important in children. If a child does not have enough thyroxine, he or she will not grow properly, and the brain will not develop. A child like this is called a cretin. Cretinism can be cured by giving injections of thyroxine.

Adults who are short of thyroxine are sluggish, and tend to be overweight. Too much thyroxine makes a person overactive, thin and edgy.

Thyroxine contains iodine. A lack of iodine in a diet will mean that the thyroid gland cannot make enough thyroxine. To compensate for this, the thyroid gland may get bigger, forming a swelling or goitre (Figure **11.3**).

11.4 Insulin regulates blood sugar levels.

The control of the concentration of glucose in the blood is a very important part of homeostasis – the control of conditions inside the body (section **11.7**) . Cells need a steady supply of glucose to allow them to respire; without this, they cannot release the energy they need. Brain cells are especially dependent on glucose for respiration, and die quite quickly if they are deprived of it.

On the other hand, too much glucose in the blood is not good either, as it can cause water to move out of cells and into the blood by osmosis. This leaves the cells with too little water for them to carry out their normal metabolic processes.

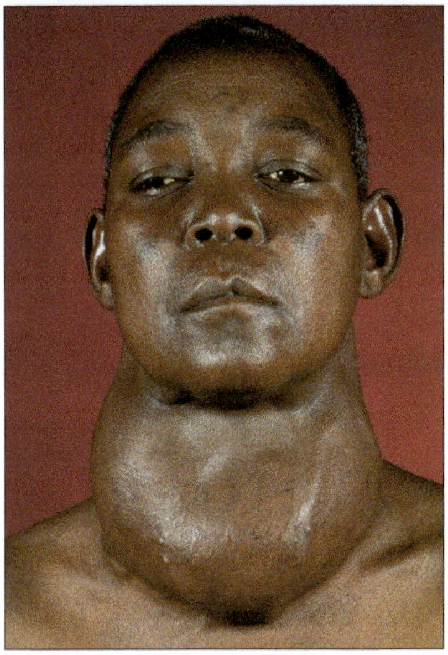

Figure 11.3 This man has a goitre, a swelling of the thyroid gland.

The control of blood glucose concentration is carried out by the **pancreas** and the **liver**.

The pancreas is two glands in one. Most of it is an ordinary gland with a duct. It makes pancreatic juice, which flows along the pancreatic duct into the duodenum (section **5.18**).

Scattered through the pancreas, however, are groups of cells called **islets of Langerhans**. These cells do not make pancreatic juice. They make two hormones called **insulin** and **glucagon**. These hormones help the liver to control the amount of glucose in the blood. Insulin has the effect of lowering blood sugar, and glucagon does the opposite.

If you eat a meal which gives a lot of glucose, the level in the blood goes up. The islets of Langerhans detect this, and secrete insulin into the blood. When insulin reaches the liver, it causes the liver to absorb glucose from the blood. Some is used for respiration, but some is stored in the liver as the insoluble polysaccharide, **glycogen**.

If the blood sugar level falls too low, the pancreas secretes glucagon. This causes liver cells to break down glycogen to glucose, and release it into the blood (Figure **11.4**).

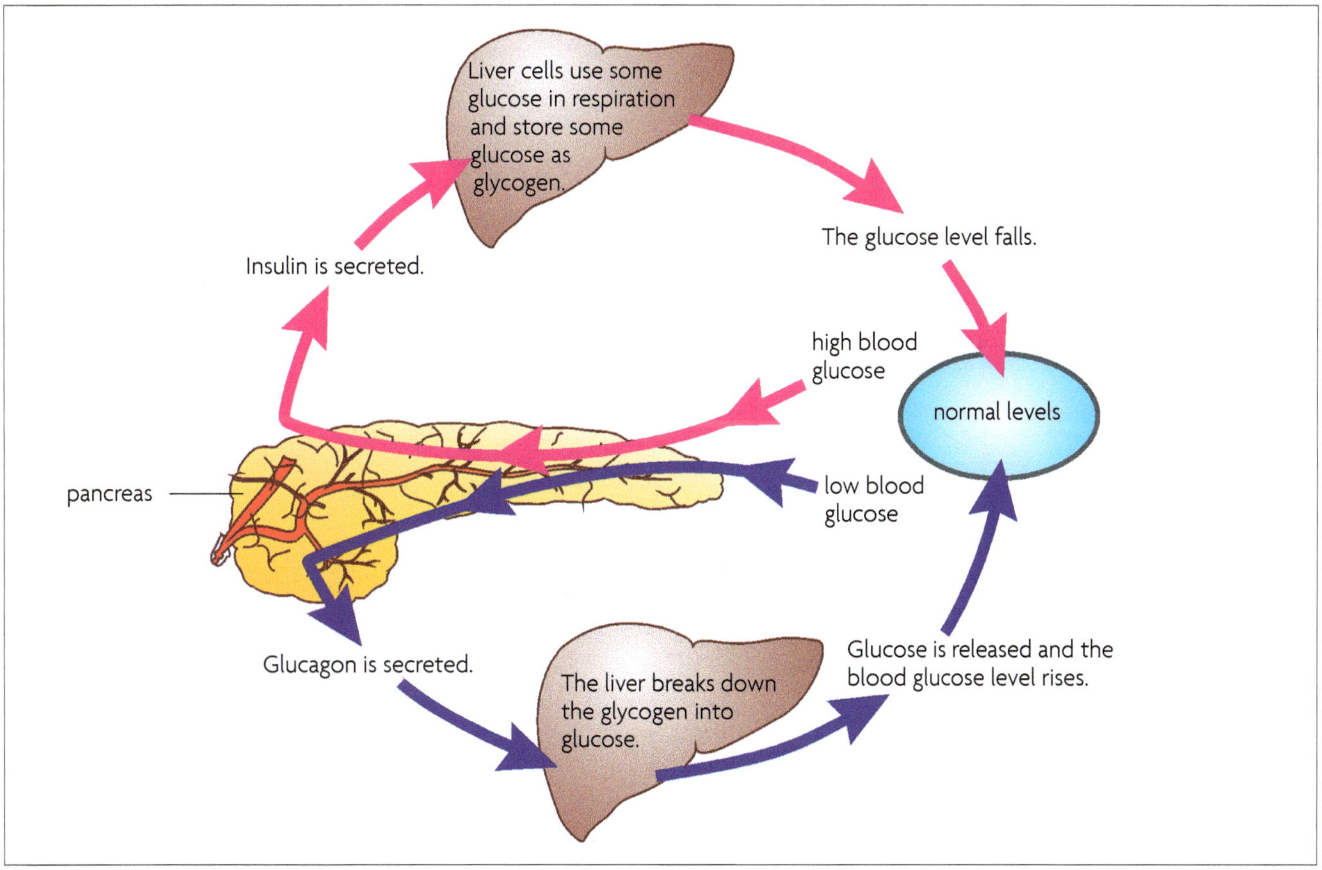

Figure 11.4 How blood glucose concentration is regulated.

Table 11.1 Mammalian endocrine glands and hormones

Hormone	Gland which secretes it	When secreted	Function	Other points
adrenaline	adrenal glands	in small amounts all the time; in large amounts when frightened or excited	prepares the body for fight or flight	
thyroxine	thyroid gland	throughout life	controls metabolic rate	thyroxine contains iodine
insulin	islets of Langerhans in the pancreas	when blood glucose levels go too high	causes liver and muscles to take up glucose from the blood and convert it to glycogen	lack of insulin, or failure of the liver and muscles to respond to it, causes diabetes
glucagon	islets of Langerhans in the pancreas	when blood glucose levels go too low	causes liver and muscles to convert glycogen to glucose	
testosterone	testes	in small quantities throughout life; in larger quantities from puberty onward	controls development of male sex organs and secondary sexual characteristics	
oestrogen	ovaries	in small quantities throughout life; in larger quantities from puberty onward, particularly when a follicle is developing in an ovary	controls development of female sex organs and secondary sexual characteristics; causes lining of uterus to become thick and spongy	
FSH	pituitary gland	at certain stages of the menstrual cycle	helps an egg to develop in an ovary	
LH	pituitary gland	at certain stages of the menstrual cycle	causes an egg to be released from an ovary	
progesterone	ovaries	after ovulation	maintains lining of uterus	
	placenta	during pregnancy		if placenta does not secrete enough progesterone, a miscarriage may occur
ADH	pituitary gland	when quantity of water in the blood gets too low	causes kidneys to reabsorb water from urine	
thyroid stimulating hormone	pituitary gland	throughout life	causes thyroid gland to secrete thyroxine	
growth hormone	pituitary gland	throughout life	stimulates growth	lack of growth hormone may cause dwarfism; too much causes gigantism

11.5 Sex hormones.

The **ovaries** and **testes** are the organs in which gametes are made. They are called **gonads**. As well as making gametes, the gonads also act as endocrine glands.

The testes secrete male sex hormones called **androgens**. The most important androgen is **testosterone**. Testosterone and other androgens regulate the development of the male sex organs. They also control the development of the male secondary sexual characteristics (section **13.23**).

The ovaries secrete female sex hormones called **oestrogens**. They regulate the development of the female sex organs, and the female secondary sexual characteristics.

The female sex hormones have an important role in regulating the menstrual cycle (section **13.22**).

11.6 The pituitary gland controls other glands.

The **pituitary gland** is in the centre of the head. It is attached to the hypothalamus.

The pituitary gland secretes a large number of hormones. For example, when receptor cells in the hypothalamus sense that there is not enough water in the blood, they send messages along nerves to the pituitary gland. The pituitary gland then secretes **ADH**. ADH stops the kidneys allowing too much water to leave the body in the urine (section **8.20**).

Many of the hormones secreted by the pituitary gland control the other endocrine glands. **Thyroid stimulating hormone**, for example, makes the thyroid gland secrete thyroxine.

The pituitary gland also secretes **growth hormone**. Growth hormone stimulates the growth of the body, partly by causing proteins to be built up in cells. Sometimes, not enough growth hormone is secreted during childhood. If this happens, the child may develop into a dwarf.

The pituitary gland secretes hormones that interact with the female sex hormones to control the menstrual cycle and reproduction. They are called **FSH** (follicle stimulating hormone) and **LH** (luteinising hormone).

Table **11.1** provides a summary of the endocrine glands and their hormones.

Questions

11.1 How do endocrine glands differ from other glands?

11.2 Describe three effects of adrenaline, and explain the value of each one.

11.3 Why is it important that adrenaline is broken down very quickly in your body?

11.4 Why do you need iodine in your diet?

11.5 Where are the islets of Langerhans?

11.6 Explain what happens when you eat a meal containing a lot of carbohydrate.

11.7 Which female hormone is secreted by a follicle as it develops inside an ovary?

11.8 What effect does this hormone have?

11.9 Which hormone is secreted by an ovary after ovulation?

11.10 What effect does this hormone have?

11.11 Name one other structure which secretes this hormone.

11.12 The pituitary gland is sometimes called 'the master gland'. Suggest why this is.

Homeostasis

11.7 Homeostasis is the maintenance of a constant internal environment.

In sections **8.20** and **8.21**, we saw how mammals control the water content of the body. In section **11.4**, the control of blood glucose level was described. These are examples of **homeostasis**. Homeostasis keeps the conditions surrounding the cells in the body almost constant. This enables the cells to work to their best ability, no matter what changes are going on in the environment *outside* the body.

You may remember that the control of water content involves a hormone called ADH. Hormones are also involved in the control of blood glucose concentration. However, the control of internal temperature is largely under the control of the nervous system.

Homeostasis is generally carried out through a **negative feedback** mechanism. The general features of negative feedback were described in section **8.21**.

Temperature regulation

11.8 Reactions go faster at higher temperatures.

Most chemical reactions happen faster when the temperature is higher. At higher temperatures molecules move around faster, which makes them collide more frequently and therefore react together more rapidly. Usually, a rise of 10 °C will double the rate of a chemical reaction (Figure **11.5a**).

You will remember that chemical reactions, called **metabolic reactions**, take place continuously inside the bodies of living organisms. These reactions are also affected by temperature.

Most of the chemical reactions happening inside a living organism are controlled or catalysed by **enzymes** (Chapter **3**) which are very sensitive to heat. Once the temperature gets to about 40 °C, they begin to be damaged. When this happens to an enzyme, it cannot catalyse its reaction so well, so the reaction slows down. At higher temperatures, it will stop completely because the enzymes are destroyed (Figure **11.5b**).

11.9 Ectothermic animals cannot completely control their body temperature.

Invertebrate animals, and also fish, amphibians and reptiles, have very little control over their body temperature. If their environment is cold, their bodies are cold, and so their metabolism slows down. Because the chemical reactions in the cells have slowed down, all their activities are slow. The animals become very sluggish.

If the environment is warm, the animals' cells become warm, and their metabolism speeds up. The animals become more active. If it gets too hot, though, their enzymes may be damaged, which could kill the animals.

Animals like this, whose internal body temperatures change with the temperature of their environment, are often called **poikilothermic** animals. They are also known as **ectothermic** animals, because their temperature is controlled from the outside ('ecto' means outside).

Many of these animals can behave in ways that help them to regulate their body temperature. For example, a lizard can often be seen basking in the sun on a rock (Figure **11.6**). Its body is warmed by the sun and by the rock. If it gets too hot in the sun, the animal can move into the shade.

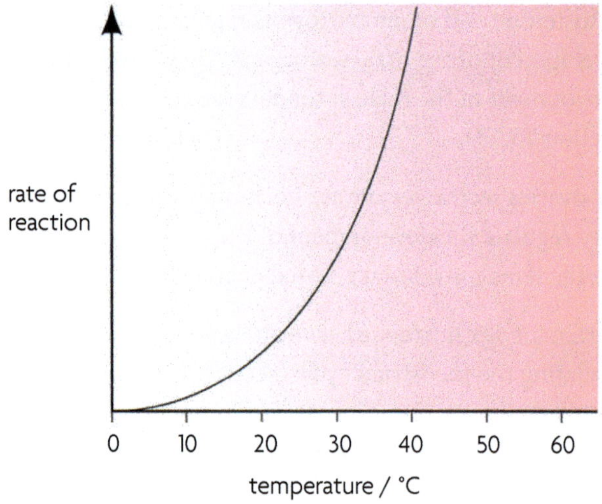

a No enzyme involved
The rate of reaction doubles with every 10 °C rise in temperature. This is because the molecules which are reacting move faster and have more energy at higher temperatures.

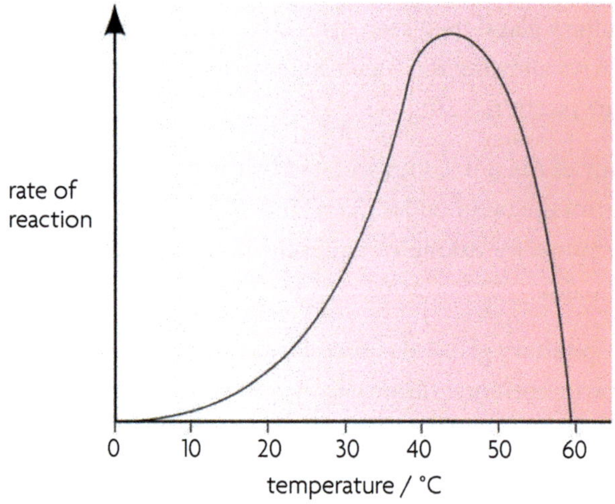

b Enzyme-catalysed reaction
Between 0 and 40 °C, the rate of reaction rises in just the same way as in graph **a** for just the same reasons. But at 40 °C, the enzyme begins to be damaged, so the reaction slows down. By 60 °C, the enzyme is completely destroyed. 40 °C is the **optimum** temperature for this enzyme – the temperature at which the rate of reaction is greatest.

Figure 11.5 How temperature affects metabolic reactions.

Figure 11.6 This lizard is basking on a hot rock to raise its body temperature. This helps it to warm up quickly in the morning, so that it can become active.

11.10 Endothermic animals can keep their body temperature constant.

Some animals – including ourselves – are very good at controlling their body temperature. They can keep their temperature almost constant, even though the temperature of their environment changes.

Animals that can do this are called **homeothermic** animals. They are also termed **endothermic** because they get their heat energy from within themselves ('endo' means within). Mammals and birds are homeothermic (Figure **11.7**).

Being homeothermic has great advantages. If the internal body temperature can be kept at around 37 °C, then enzymes can always work very efficiently, no matter what the outside temperature is. Metabolism can keep going, even when it is cold outside. In cold weather, or at night, a homeothermic animal can be active when a poikilothermic animal is too cold to move.

But there is a price to pay. The energy to keep warm has to come from somewhere. Homeothermic animals get their heat energy from food, by respiration. Because of this, homeothermic animals have to eat far more food than poikilothermic ones.

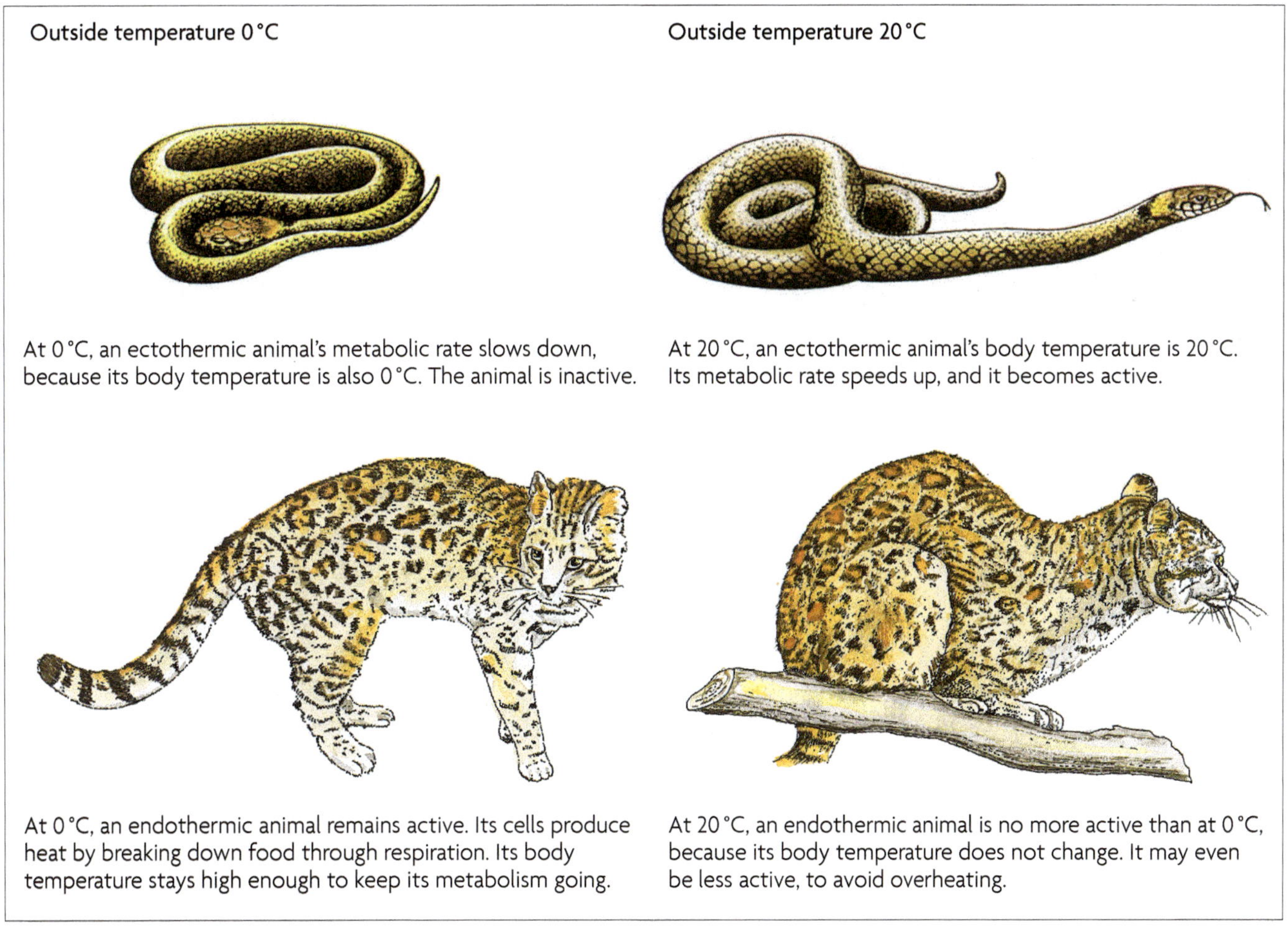

Outside temperature 0 °C
Outside temperature 20 °C
At 0 °C, an ectothermic animal's metabolic rate slows down, because its body temperature is also 0 °C. The animal is inactive.
At 20 °C, an ectothermic animal's body temperature is 20 °C. Its metabolic rate speeds up, and it becomes active.
At 0 °C, an endothermic animal remains active. Its cells produce heat by breaking down food through respiration. Its body temperature stays high enough to keep its metabolism going.
At 20 °C, an endothermic animal is no more active than at 0 °C, because its body temperature does not change. It may even be less active, to avoid overheating.

Figure 11.7 Ectothermic and endothermic animals.

11.11 Skin has two layers.

One of the most important organs involved in temperature regulation in mammals is the skin. You have already investigated the role of the skin as a sense organ, but it also helps to control the rate at which heat is lost from the body. Figure **11.8** shows a section through human skin.

Human skin is made up of two layers. The top layer is called the epidermis, and the lower layer is the dermis.

11.12 The epidermis protects the deeper layers.

All the cells in the epidermis have been made in the layer of cells at the base of it, called the **Malpighian layer**. These cells are always dividing by a type of cell division called **mitosis** (section **12.3**). The new cells that are made gradually move towards the surface of the skin. As they go, they die, and fill up with a protein called **keratin**.

The top layer of the skin is made up of these dead cells. It is called the **cornified layer**.

The cornified layer protects the softer, living cells underneath, because it is hard and waterproof. It is always being worn away, and replaced by cells from beneath. On the parts of the body which get most wear, for example the soles of the feet, it grows thicker.

Some of the cells in the epidermis contain a dark brown pigment, called **melanin**. Melanin absorbs the harmful ultraviolet rays in sunlight, which would damage the living cells in the deeper layers of the skin.

Here and there, the epidermis is folded inwards, forming a **hair follicle**. A hair grows from each one. Hairs are made of keratin.

Each hair follicle has a **sebaceous gland** opening from the side of it. These glands make an oily liquid called sebum. Sebum keeps the hair and skin soft and supple.

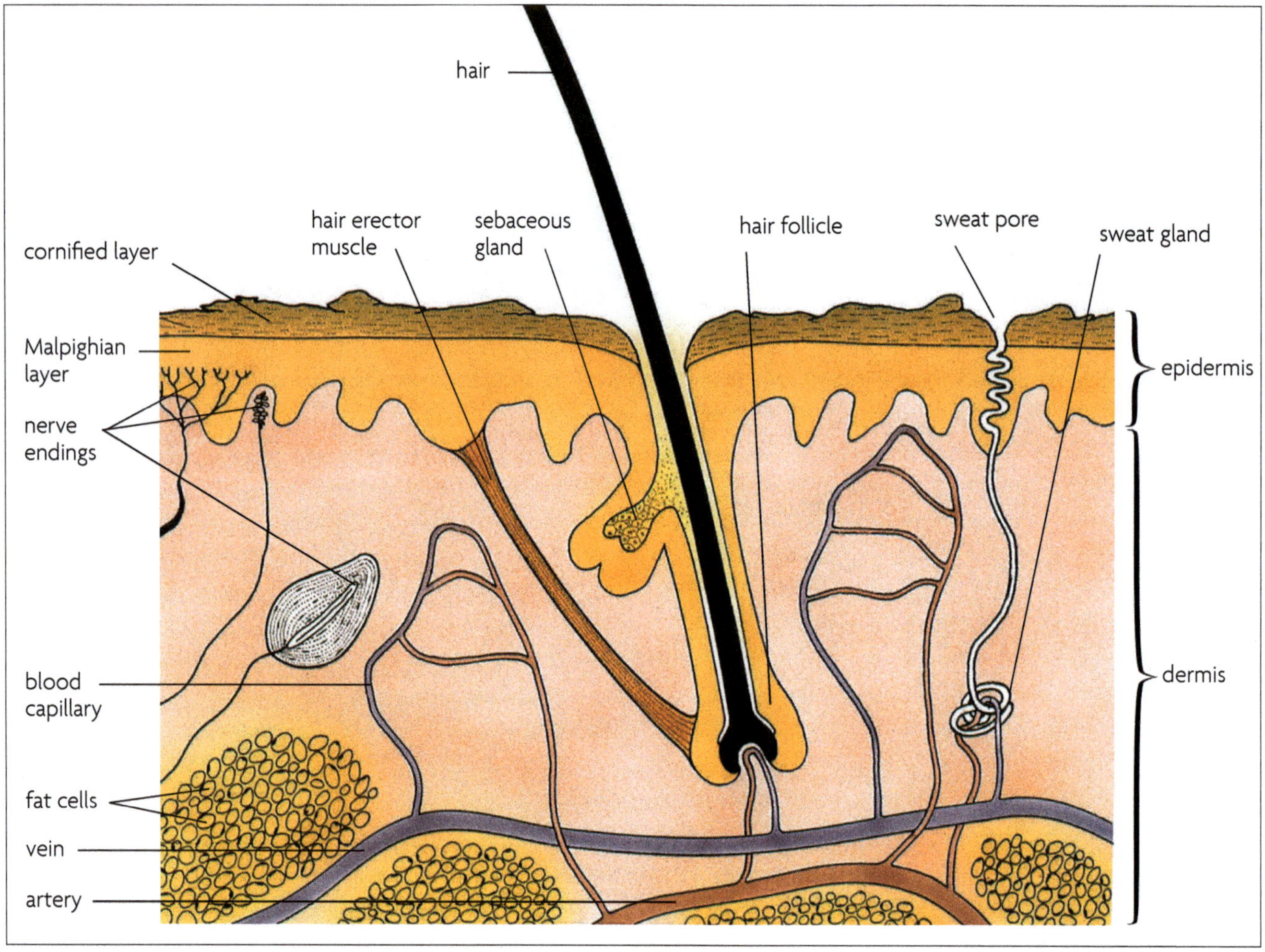

Figure 11.8 A section through human skin.

11.13 The dermis has many functions.

Most of the dermis is made of connective tissue. This tissue contains elastic fibres and collagen fibres. As a person gets older, the fibres lose their elasticity, so the skin becomes loose and wrinkled.

The dermis also contains **sweat glands**. These secrete a liquid called sweat. Sweat is mostly water, with small amounts of salts and urea dissolved in it. It travels up the sweat ducts, and out onto the surface of the skin through the sweat pores. As we will see, sweat helps in temperature regulation.

The dermis contains blood vessels, and nerve endings. As we have seen, these nerve endings are sensitive to touch, pain, pressure and temperature, so they help to keep you aware of changes in your environment.

Underneath the dermis is a layer of fat, called **adipose tissue**. This is made up of cells which contain large drops of oil. This layer helps to insulate your body, and also acts as a food reserve (section **7.28**).

11.14 The hypothalamus coordinates temperature control.

You may remember that the hypothalamus is at the centre of the negative feedback mechanism that keeps the water content of the body approximately constant. The hypothalamus is also involved in the maintenance of a constant internal temperature. The hypothalamus coordinates the activities of the parts of the body that can bring about temperature changes.

The hypothalamus acts like a thermostat. It can sense the temperature of the blood running through it. If it is above or below 37 °C, then the hypothalamus sends electrical impulses, along nerves, to the parts of the body which have the function of regulating your body temperature.

11.15 When cold the body produces and saves heat.

If your body temperature drops below 37 °C, nerve impulses from the hypothalamus cause the following things to happen (Figure **11.9**).

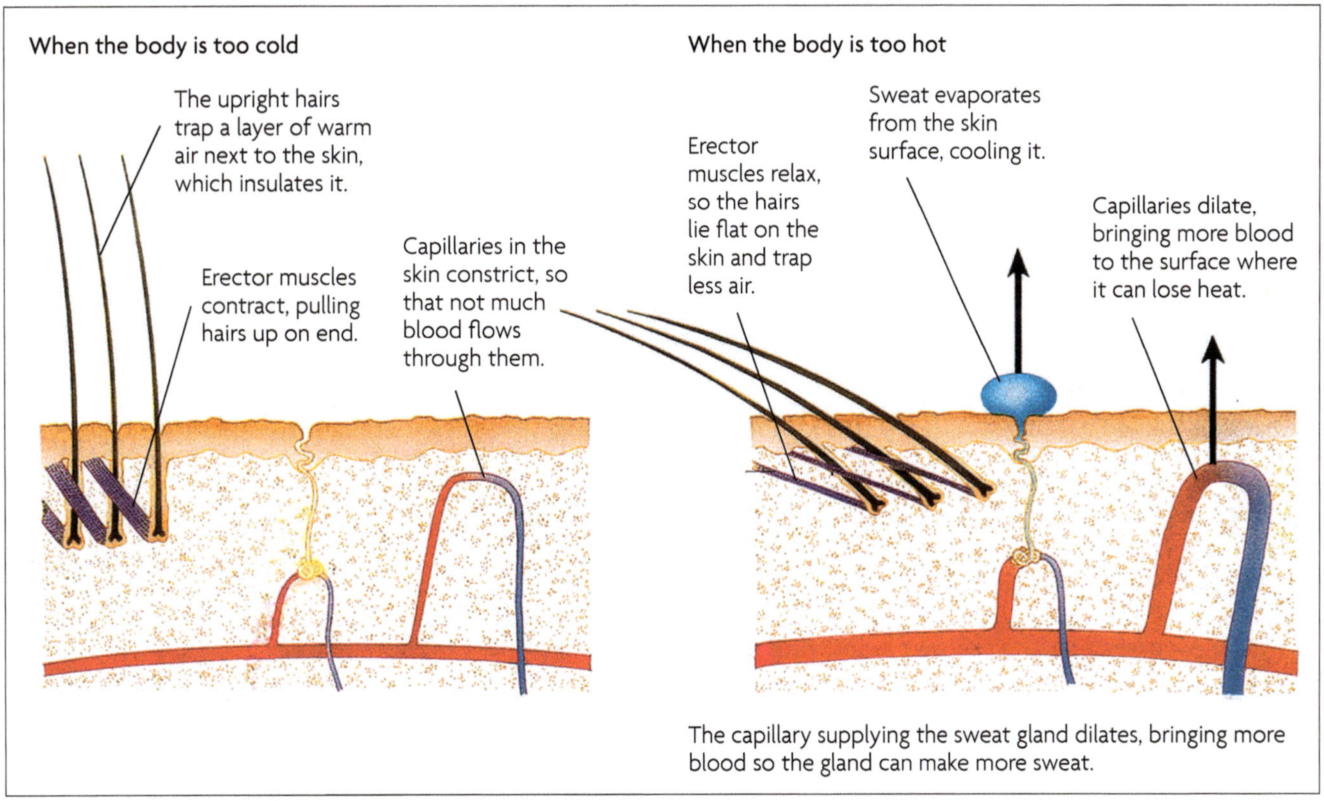

When the body is too cold
The upright hairs trap a layer of warm air next to the skin, which insulates it.
Erector muscles contract, pulling hairs up on end.
Capillaries in the skin constrict, so that not much blood flows through them.
When the body is too hot
Erector muscles relax, so the hairs lie flat on the skin and trap less air.
Sweat evaporates from the skin surface, cooling it.
Capillaries dilate, bringing more blood to the surface where it can lose heat.
The capillary supplying the sweat gland dilates, bringing more blood so the gland can make more sweat.

Figure 11.9 How skin helps with temperature regulation.

Muscles work Muscles in some parts of the body contract and relax very quickly. This also produces heat. It is called shivering. The heat generated in the muscles warms the blood as it flows through them. The blood distributes this heat all over the body.

Metabolism may increase The speed of chemical reactions, for example in the liver, may increase. This also releases more heat.

Hair stands up The erector muscles in the skin contract, pulling the hairs up on end. In humans this does not do anything very useful – it just produces 'goose pimples'. In a hairy animal though, like a cat, it traps a thicker layer of warm air next to the skin. This prevents the skin from losing more warmth. It acts as an insulator.

Blood system conserves heat The arterioles that supply the blood capillaries near to the surface of the skin become narrower, or constricted. This is called **vasoconstriction**. Only a very little blood can flow in them. The blood flows through the deep-lying capillaries instead. Because these are deep under the skin, the blood does not lose so much heat to the air.

11.16 When hot the body loses more heat.

Hair lies flat The erector muscles in the skin relax, so that the hairs lie flat on the skin.

Blood system loses heat The arterioles supplying the capillaries near the surface of the skin get wider, or become dilated (Figure **11.9**, page **205**). This is called **vasodilation**. More blood therefore flows through them. Because a lot of blood is so near the surface of the skin, heat is readily lost from the blood into the air.

Sweat The sweat glands secrete sweat. The sweat lies on the surface of the hot skin. The water in it then evaporates, taking heat from the skin with it, thus cooling the body.

Figure **11.10** summarises the mechanism that controls body temperature.

FACT!

The highest body temperature a person has ever had and survived is 46.5 °C.

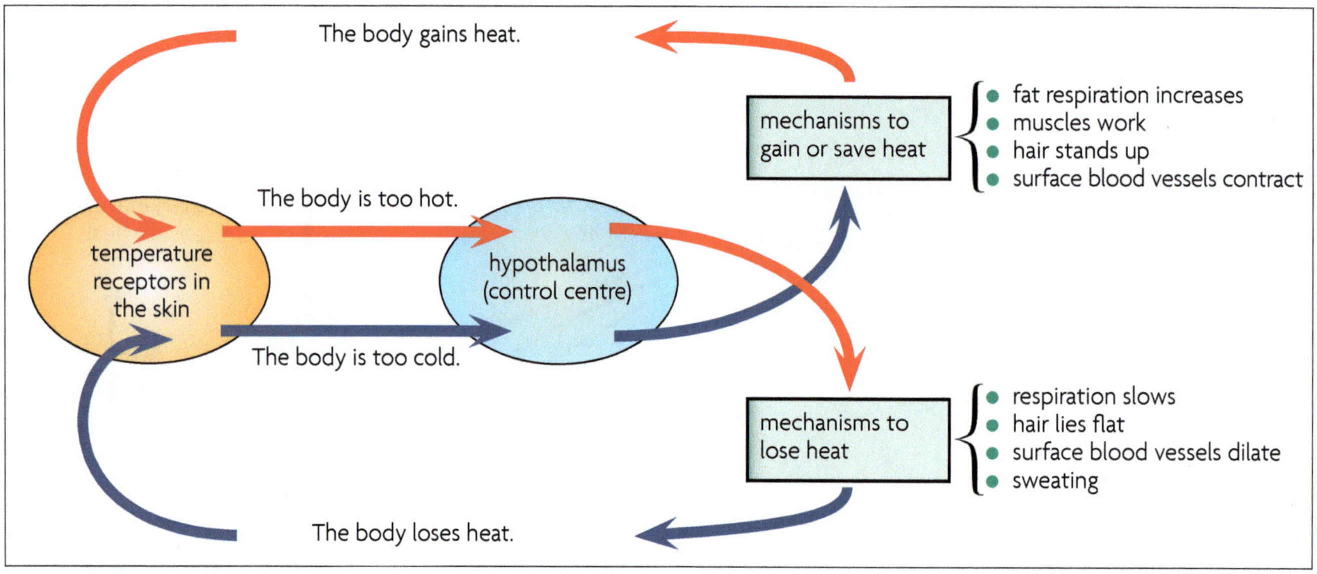

Figure 11.10 Maintaining body temperature in a steady state.

Questions

11.13 In which part of the skin are new cells produced?

11.14 What is keratin?

11.15 What is melanin?

11.16 What do sebaceous glands make?

11.17 Which part of the brain controls your body temperature?

11.18 Why do you get 'goose pimples' when you are cold?

Investigation 11.1

Experiment to investigate the effect of size on rate of cooling

SBA skills

Observation/Recording/Reporting
Manipulation/Measurement
Analysis/Interpretation

Temperature regulation is an important part of homeostasis. We lose heat from our bodies to the air around us. Cells produce more heat to prevent the body temperature from dropping.

In this investigation, you will use containers of hot water to represent a human body. The experiment will test this hypothesis:

> A large body cools more slowly than a small one.

1 Take two test tubes or other containers, identical except that one is large and one is small. You will also need two thermometers.

2 Read through what you are going to do. Draw a results chart in which you can write your results as you go along. Remember to put the units in your table headings.

3 Now collect some hot water. Pour water into each of your containers until they are almost full. Immediately take the temperature of each one and record your results for time 0.

4 Take readings every 2 minutes for at least 14 minutes.

5 Draw a line graph to display your results.

Questions

1 a State two variables that were kept constant in this experiment.

b Why was it important to keep these variables constant?

2 a Calculate the number of °C by which the large container cooled during your experiment.

b Calculate the number of °C by which the small container cooled during your experiment.

3 Do your results support the hypothesis that you were testing? Explain your answer.

Investigation 11.2

Investigating the effect of evaporation on the rate of cooling

SBA skills

Observation/Recording/Reporting
Manipulation/Measurement
Planning/Design
Analysis/Interpretation

Sweating helps to cool the body. You are going to plan and carry out an experiment to test this hypothesis:

> Evaporation of water from the surface of a hot object causes it to cool faster.

You can use a technique similar to the one you used in Investigation 11.1. You will need to use two or three test tubes all the same size. You will also need to use some water-absorbent material, which you can wrap round one or more of the tubes.

1 What are you going to vary in your experiment? How will you do this?

2 Make a list of the things that you will keep the same in your experiment.

3 What will you measure? How will you measure it, and how often?

4 How will you display your results?

5 Predict the results you will obtain, if the hypothesis is correct.

Now get your plan checked by your teacher, before you carry it out.

Control of heart rate and breathing rate

11.17 Centres in the brain regulate the rate at which the heart beats.

Without the constant supply of oxygen and food carried by the blood, the body tissues will die. Therefore, the rate at which the heart beats and pumps blood out to the tissues must be kept at a certain level.

The heart beat starts in the right atrium in the **sinoatrial node**, sometimes known as the pacemaker (section **7.6**). From here, the beat spreads throughout the whole heart (Figure **11.11**). The heart beat is felt in the arteries as the pulse beat (Investigation **7.1**).

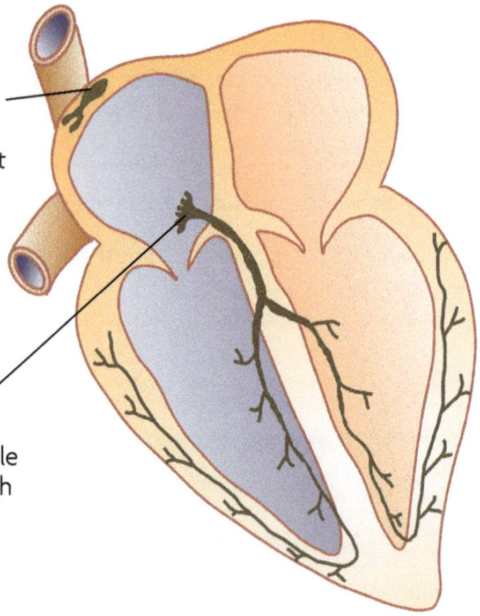

Figure 11.11 Section through a heart, showing the pathway along which the heart beat spreads.

A part of the brain known as the **medulla oblongata** (section **10.10** and Figure **10.11**, page **180**) controls the rate at which the heart beats. The walls of a blood vessel stretch as blood flows through the vessel. Special cells in the walls of major blood vessels near the heart register the stretch in their walls. This information is carried by nerve cells to the medulla which uses it to speed up or slow down the rate as necessary (section **10.11**). Figure **11.12** illustrates the process.

Maintaining the steady state of the heart beat is so important that there is more than one mechanism for the purpose. There is also a response to the level of carbon dioxide in the blood. A high level causes the rate to be speeded up and a low level slows it down.

11.18 Breathing rate is also regulated by the medulla oblongata.

In the medulla oblongata is a breathing centre which regulates inspiration and expiration (sections **6.17** to **6.19**). One section of this centre controls inspiration, and another expiration. They work together to keep the body supplied with oxygen, and remove the carbon dioxide.

In the bronchi and bronchioles, there are certain sense cells or receptors which register stretch when you breathe in. They send more and more messages to the expiration centre as inspiration continues. These messages stimulate the expiration centre, causing it to inhibit the action of the inspiration centre until inspiration stops. This allows expiration to take place. During expiration, the sense cells register no stretch. This inactivates the expiration centre and allows inspiration to take place. Then the cycle is repeated.

Other stimuli may modify this rhythm – for example, the level of carbon dioxide in the blood. If this level increases, as it does when you exercise, sense cells in the aorta and carotid artery detect the change. They send nerve impulses to the inspiration centre directly, speeding up the rate of breathing. This control of breathing by stretch and chemical receptors is another example of negative feedback. The process is illustrated in Figure **11.13**.

When you consciously hold your breath for singing or speech, for example, you are voluntarily overriding the normal control.

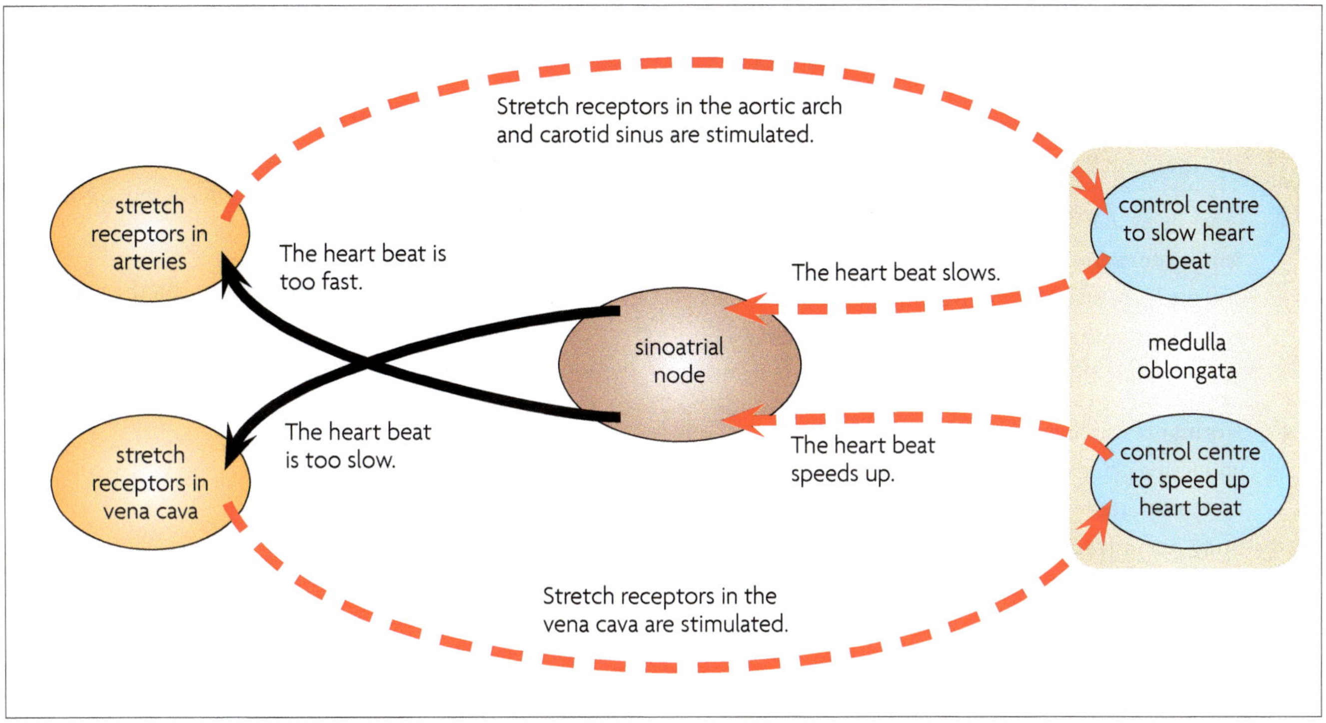

Figure 11.12 How the rate of heart beat is regulated.

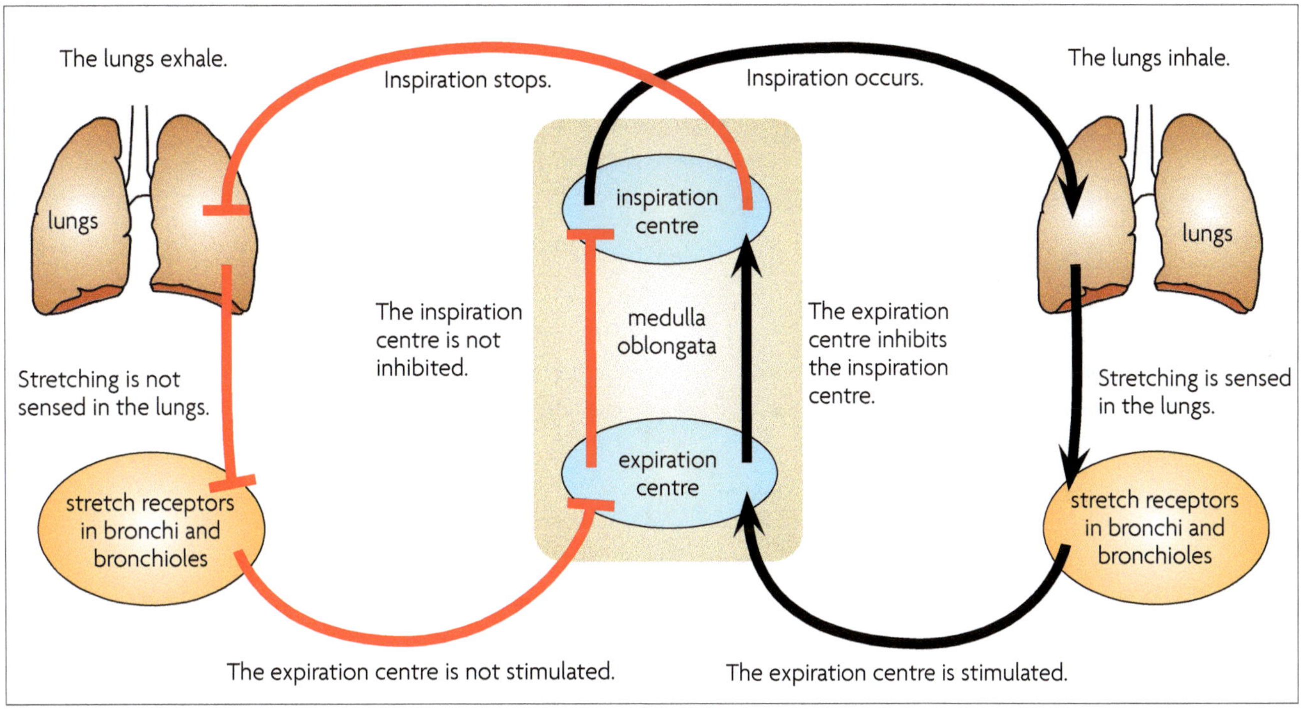

Figure 11.13 How breathing rate is controlled.

Key ideas

- Homeostasis is the maintenance of a constant internal environment. It is achieved using negative feedback.
- Organisms that can control their internal body temperature are called endotherms. Mammals and birds are endotherms. All other animals are ectotherms, meaning that they have only limited ways of controlling their temperature.
- Hormones are chemicals that are secreted by endocrine glands directly into the blood. They are transported in blood plasma to all parts of the body, but only have an effect on their target organs. Endocrine glands include the thyroid, adrenals, pancreas, gonads and pituitary.
- The control of body temperature in humans involves the hypothalamus, the skin and muscles. When the body becomes too hot, sweating and vasodilation increase the rate of heat loss from the skin. When the body becomes too cold, shivering increases heat production, and vasoconstriction reduces the rate of heat loss from the skin.
- The pancreas, working in conjunction with the liver, controls blood glucose concentration. When this rises too high, the pancreas secretes insulin which causes the liver to remove glucose from the blood and convert it to glycogen. When blood glucose concentration falls too low, the pancreas secretes glucagon which causes the liver to convert glycogen to glucose.
- The adrenal glands secrete adrenaline in stressful, exciting or dangerous conditions. Adrenaline affects various target organs, including the heart, preparing the body for fight or flight.

End-of-chapter questions

1 Explain the differences between each of the following pairs of terms:
  a ectothermic, endothermic
  b dilate, constrict
  c epidermis, dermis
  d sebaceous gland, sweat gland.

2 Explain why endothermic animals eat more food in proportion to their weight than ectothermic animals.

3 An investigation was performed, to find how the rate of a chemical reaction was affected by temperature. The results are shown on the graph.
  a Is this reaction catalysed by an enzyme? Give reasons for your answer.
  b What is the optimum temperature for this reaction?
  c Suggest one reaction which might give results like this.
  d Use your answers to (b) and (c) to explain the advantages to an organism of being endothermic rather than exothermic.

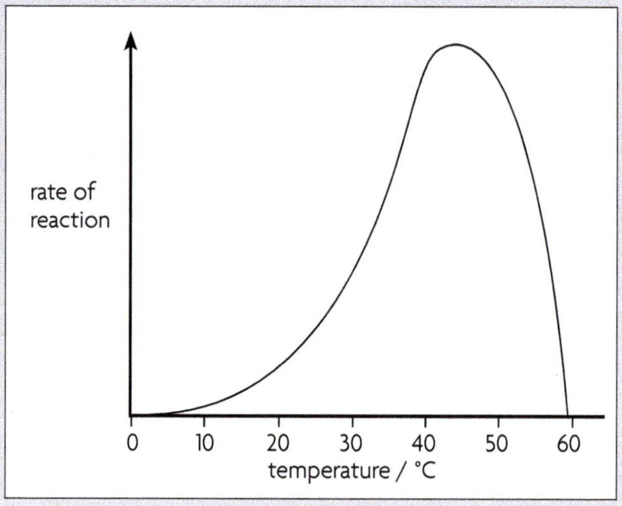

(*continues on page* **211**)

(*... continued*)

4 In an investigation, a number of newly hatched birds were kept at a temperature of 20 °C. Each day, their body temperature and the amount of oxygen they used were measured. The average temperature and oxygen consumption for each day were plotted on a graph.

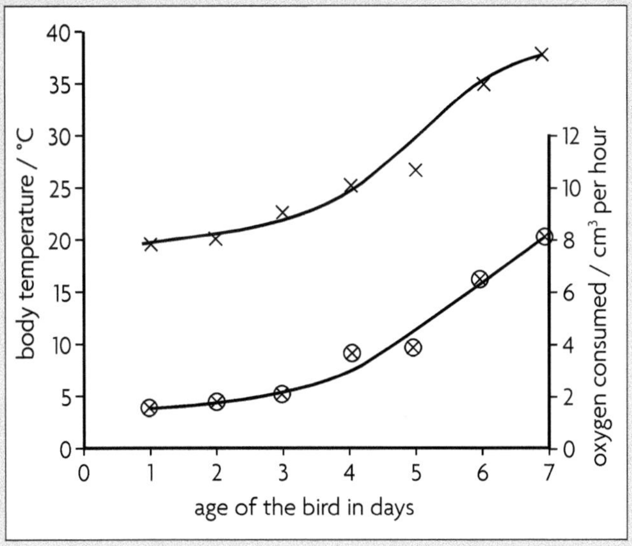

a What is (i) the body temperature, and (ii) the oxygen consumption of a three-day-old bird, when the air temperature is 20 °C?

b Adult birds are homeothermic, keeping their body temperature at around 38 °C. At what age do young birds become able to maintain this body temperature?

c Using the information provided by the graph, and your own knowledge of how homeothermic animals maintain their body temperature, explain why one-day-old birds consume less oxygen than seven-day-old birds.

d What would you expect to happen to (i) the body temperature, and (ii) the oxygen consumption of a one-day-old bird, if the air temperature was raised to 25 °C? Explain your answer.

5 Explain how the principle of negative feedback operates in controlling each of the following. (You will need to look back to an earlier chapter to find information about one of these.)

a the internal body temperature

b the water content of the blood

c the glucose concentration of the blood

d the rate at which the heart beats

12 Growth

In this chapter, you will find out:

- about how cell growth and cell division result in the growth of the body
- how cells divide by mitosis
- how plants grow from a seed
- the conditions that are needed for seeds to germinate
- about some of the plant growth substances that help to control their growth
- about the patterns of growth in humans
- about the hormones that affect growth in humans
- several different ways of measuring growth.

Growth and cell division

12.1 Growth does not just mean getting bigger.

All living organisms are said to grow: but what exactly is growth?

Growth does not simply mean getting bigger. Puffer fish, for example, swallow water when a predator attacks them. They swell up, and get much larger. This often frightens the predator away, and the fish shrinks back to its normal size again. This is not growth, because the fish only got bigger for a very short time.

An organism can be said to be growing if it gets bigger, and stays bigger. Growth is permanent increase in size.

12.2 Growth usually involves cell division.

When an organism grows, the cells it is made of get bigger. However, a cell can only grow to a certain size. If it gets too big, then its surface area to volume ratio (section **6.12**) becomes so small that gas exchange cannot take place fast enough.

Because of this, growth also involves the division of cells to make new ones. This in itself does not make the organism any bigger, because the two new cells are the same size as the one big cell which divided to form them. However, the new cells can then grow bigger.

The way in which cells divide to provide new cells for growth is called **mitosis**.

12.3 In growth, cells divide by mitosis.

Mitosis is the way in which any cell, plant or animal, divides when an organism is growing, or repairing a damaged part of its body.

The nucleus of a cell contains **chromosomes** (Figure **12.1**).

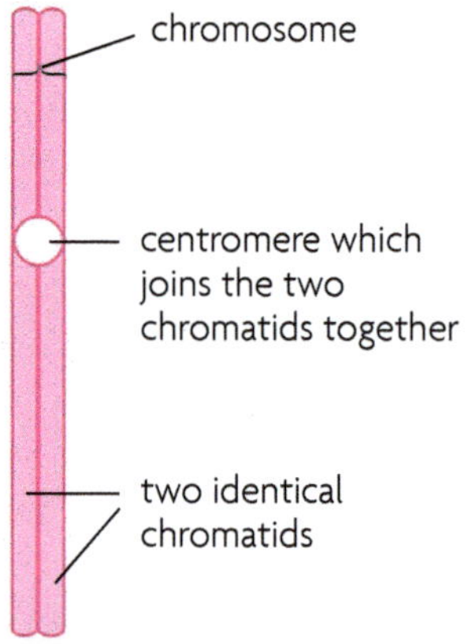

Figure 12.1 A chromosome just before division.

Chromosomes have **genes** on them, which give instructions to the cell about what sorts of proteins to make. When a cell divides, it is very important that the two new cells each get a complete set of chromosomes from their parent cell.

Mitosis is a method of cell division which makes two new cells with exactly the same number and kinds of chromosomes as the original cell. This is shown in Figures **12.2** and **12.3** (overleaf). After step 6 (late telophase) each daughter cell grows to the size of the original mother cell.

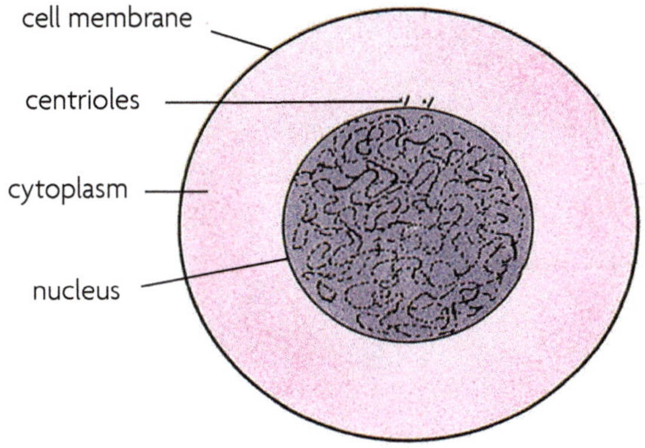

1 Interphase When a cell is not dividing, no chromosomes can be seen clearly in the nucleus. They are there, but are so long and thin that they are invisible.

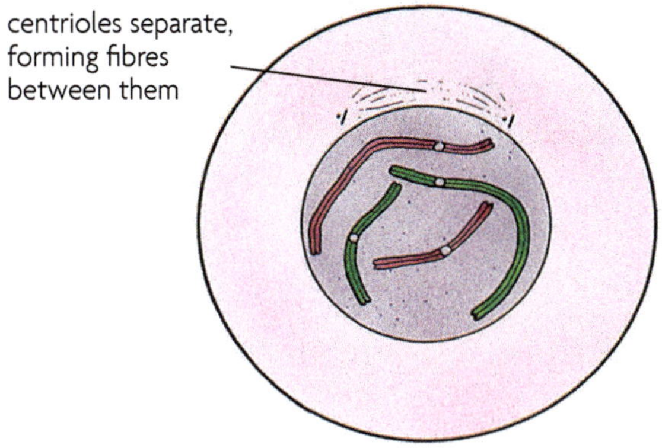

2 Prophase The chromosomes get short and fat, so they can now be seen with a light microscope. Each chromosome contains two chromatids.

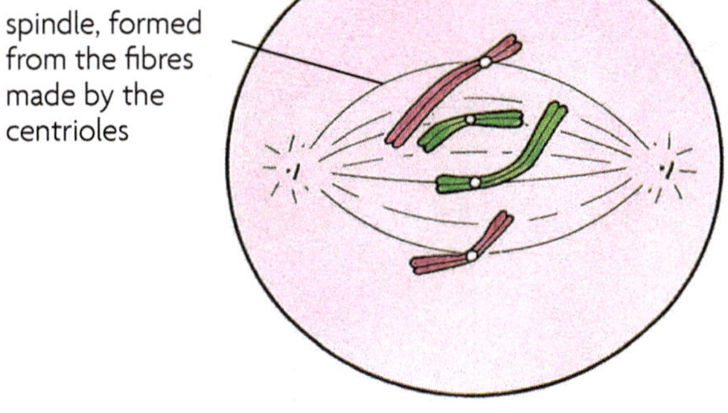

3 Metaphase The nuclear membrane vanishes. The chromosomes line up on the equator of the spindle.

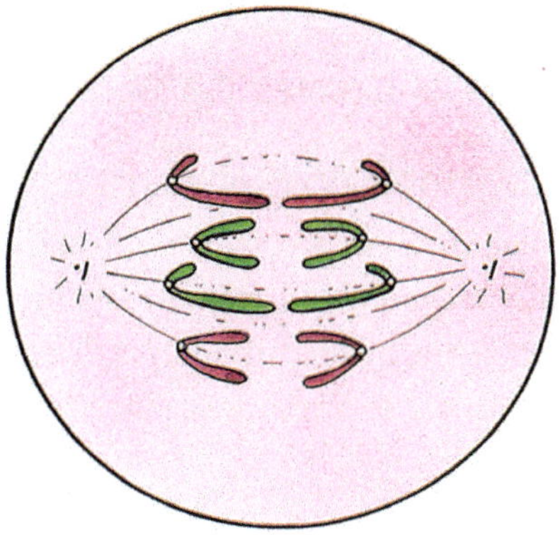

4 Anaphase The centromere of each chromosome splits, so the two chromatids separate. The chromatids move away from each other, along the spindle fibres.

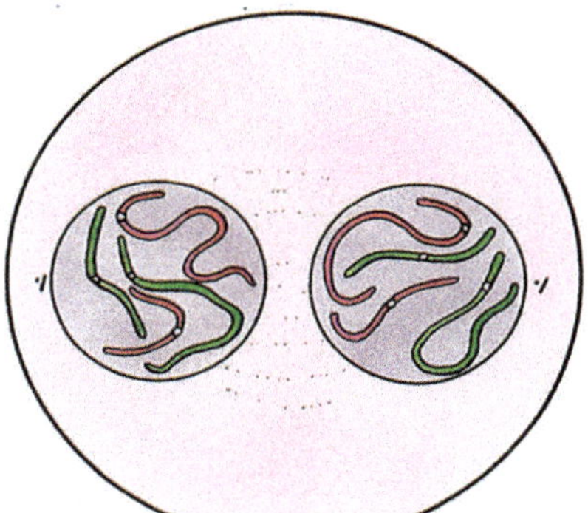

5 Telophase The chromatids arrive at opposite ends of the cell, and form into groups. A nuclear membrane appears round each group. The spindle fibres fade away.

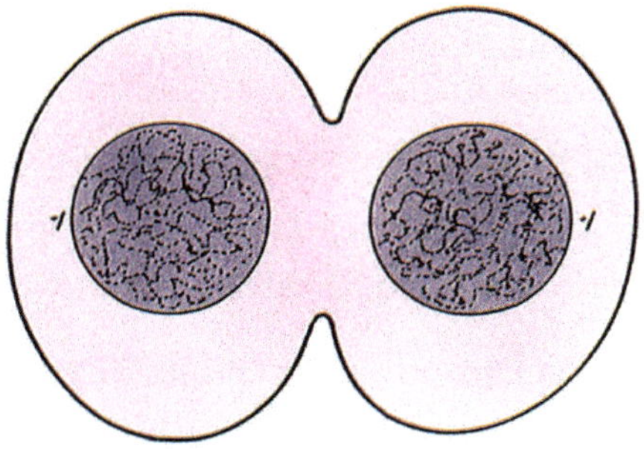

6 Late telophase The chromosomes become long and thin again, so that they are invisible. The cytoplasm divides, forming two daughter cells. Each cell now goes into interphase again. Each of the two cells and the original mother cell, shown in **1**, have the same genes.

Figure 12.2 Mitosis in an animal cell with four chromosomes. You do not need to remember the names of the different stages, just the sequence in which the events take place.

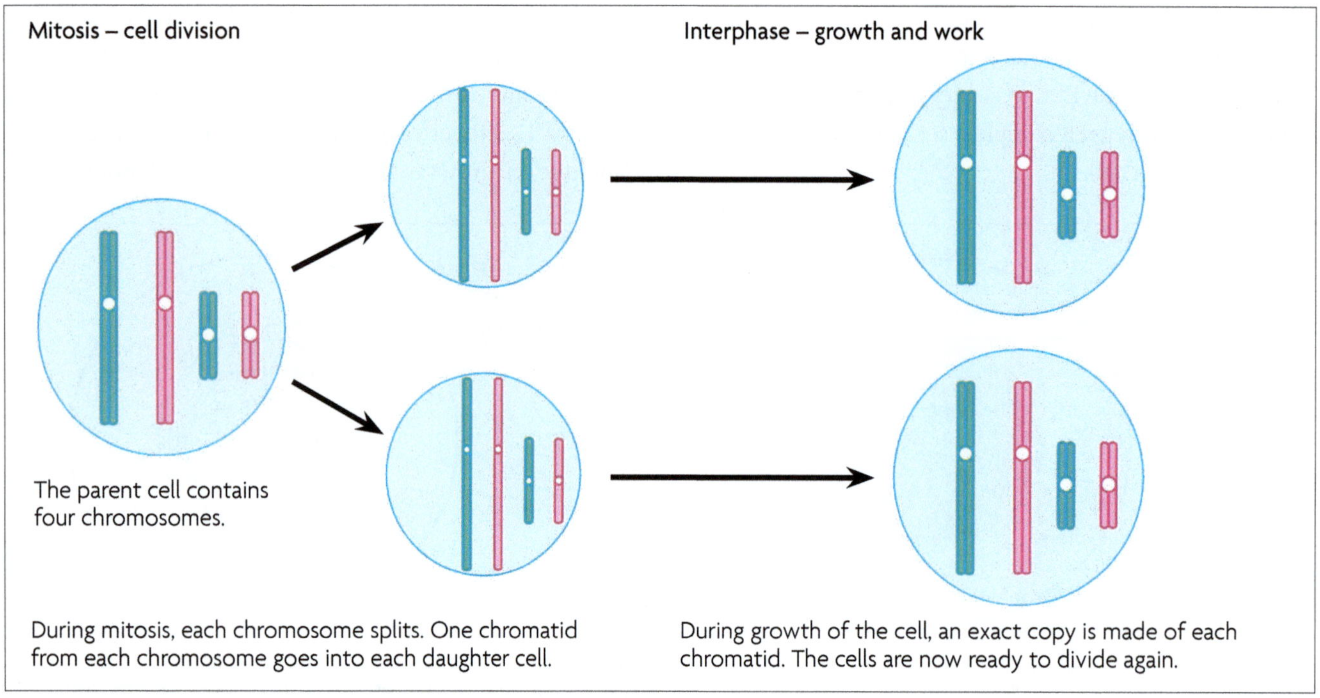

Mitosis – cell division
Interphase – growth and work
The parent cell contains four chromosomes.
During mitosis, each chromosome splits. One chromatid from each chromosome goes into each daughter cell.
During growth of the cell, an exact copy is made of each chromatid. The cells are now ready to divide again.

Figure 12.3 Chromosomes during the life of a cell dividing by mitosis.

Growth in flowering plants

12.4 Only some parts of plants can grow.

In animals, most cells can divide by mitosis. All the parts of an animal's body can grow. In a plant, though, not all cells can divide by mitosis. Only the cells in certain places can do this. These places are called **meristems**.

Figure **12.4** shows where the meristems are in a typical plant. Most of them are at the tips of shoots, and just behind the tips of roots. Because of this, most plants grow in a branching shape. Animals, however, because all the parts of their bodies can grow, usually grow into a more compact shape.

Figure 12.4 The main meristems of a plant.

12.5 A flowering plant grows from a seed.

Many plants begin their life as a seed. The way in which a seed is formed is explained in section **13.40**.

A seed contains an **embryo** plant. The embryo consists of a **radicle**, which will grow into a root, and a **plumule**, which will grow into a shoot (Figure **12.5**).

There is also food for the embryo. In a bean seed, the food is stored in two cream-coloured **cotyledons**. These contain starch and protein. The cotyledons also contain enzymes.

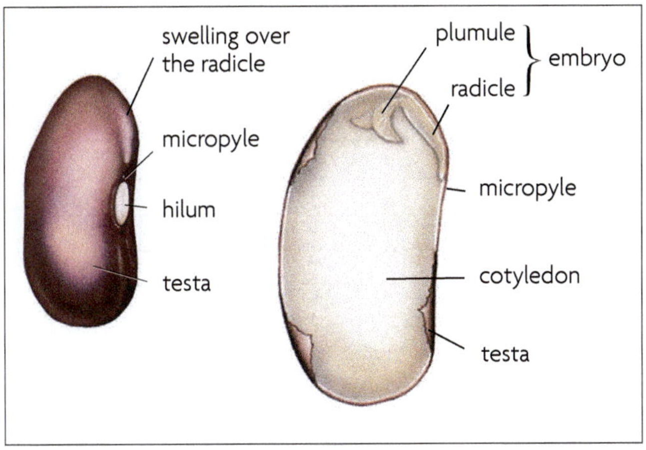

Figure 12.5 Structure of a bean seed.

Surrounding the cotyledons is a tough, protective covering called the **testa**. The testa stops the embryo from being damaged and it prevents bacteria and fungi from entering the seed.

The testa has a tiny hole in it called the **micropyle**. Near the micropyle is a scar, the **hilum,** where the seed was joined onto the pod.

12.6 Uptake of water begins seed germination.

A seed contains hardly any water. When it was formed on the plant, the water in it was drawn out, so that it became dehydrated. Without water, almost no metabolic reactions can go on inside it. The seed is inactive or **dormant**. This is very useful, because it means that the seed can survive harsh conditions, such as cold or drought, which would kill a growing plant.

A seed must be in certain conditions before it will begin to germinate. You can find out what they are if you do Investigation **12.1**.

When a seed germinates, it first takes up water through the micropyle. As the water goes into the cotyledons, they swell. Eventually, they burst the testa (Figure **12.6**).

Once there is sufficient water, the enzymes in the cotyledons become active. **Amylase** begins to break down the stored starch molecules to maltose. **Proteases** break down the protein molecules to amino acids.

Maltose and amino acids are soluble, so they dissolve in the water. They diffuse to the embryo plant, which uses these foods for growth. The way in which the embryo plant grows is shown in Figure **12.6**.

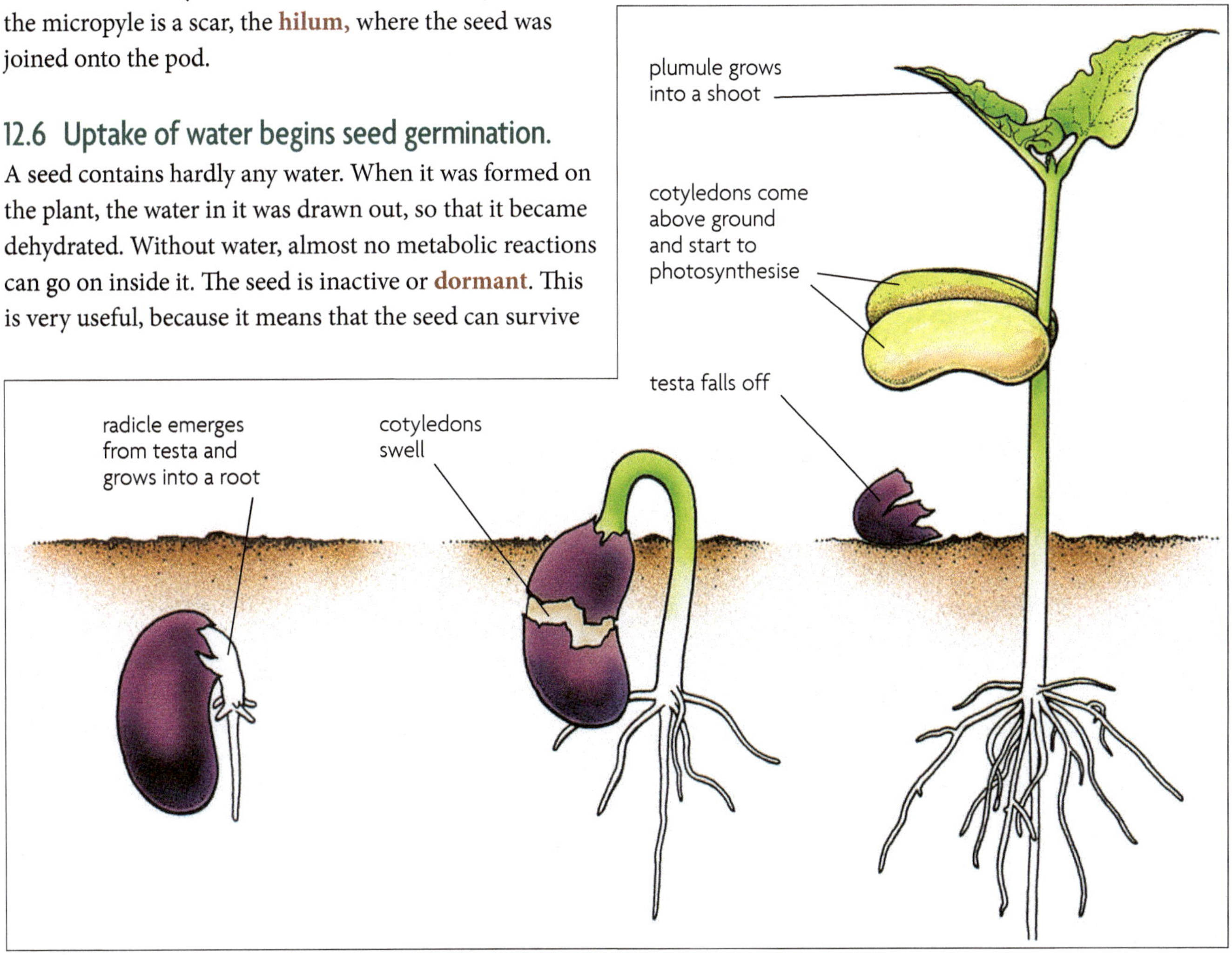

Figure 12.6 Stages in germination of one type of bean seed.

Investigation 12.1

To find the conditions necessary for the germination of tomato seeds

SBA skills

Observation/Recording/Reporting

Analysis/Interpretation

1 Set up five tubes as shown in the diagram. Pyrogallol absorbs oxygen.

	Tube				
	A	B	C	D	E
water	✓	✓	✓	✓	
warmth					
oxygen					
light					
Did seeds germinate?					

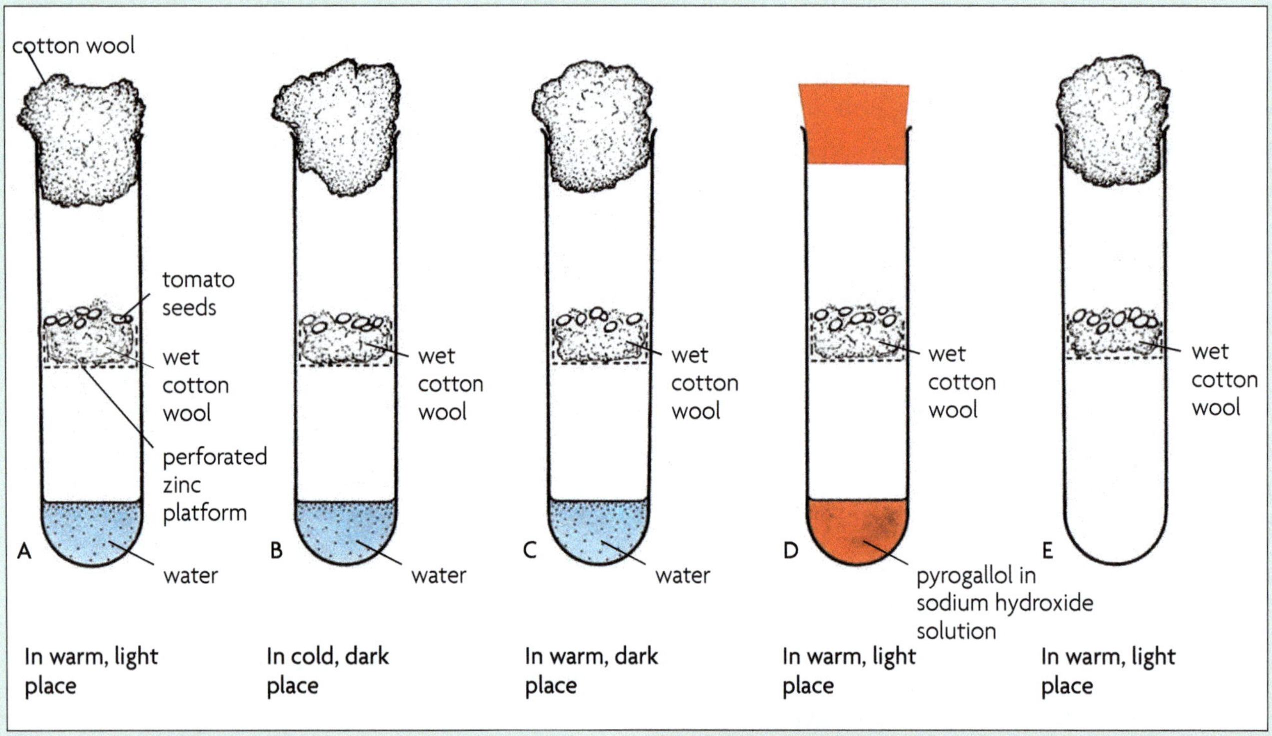

2 Put tubes A, D and E in a warm place in the laboratory, in the light.

3 Put tube B in a refrigerator.

4 Put tube C in a warm, dark cupboard.

5 Copy the results table and fill it in to show what conditions the seeds in each tube have. The first line has been done for you.

Questions

1 What three conditions do tomato seeds need for germination?

2 Read sections 12.6 and 12.7, and then explain why each of these conditions is needed for successful germination.

12.7 During germination, enzymes digest food stores.

When a seed first begins to germinate, it increases in mass. This is because it absorbs water from the soil.

As soon as it begins to grow, it starts to use its food stores. The stored protein is broken down to amino acids, which are used to make new protein molecules for cell membranes and cytoplasm. The stored starch is broken down to maltose and then to glucose. Some of the glucose will be made into cellulose, to make cell walls for the new cells.

All this requires energy. The seed, like all living organisms, gets its energy by breaking down glucose, in respiration. Quite a lot of the glucose from the stored starch will be used up in respiration, so the seed loses mass.

After a few days, the plumule of the seed grows above the surface of the ground. The first leaves open out and begin to photosynthesise. The plant can now make its own food faster than it is using it up. Its mass begins to increase.

Figure 12.7 summarises the changes in mass of an annual plant, such as a bean, from germination until death.

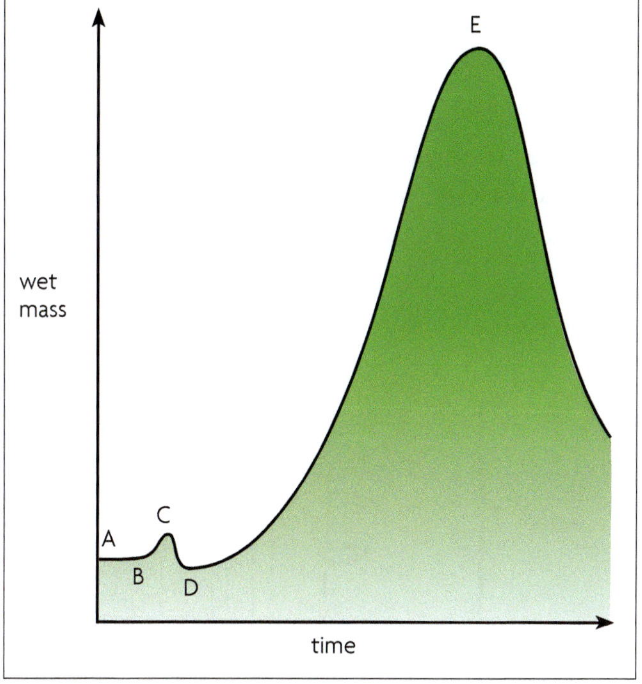

Figure 12.7 Growth curve for an annual plant. Can you explain what is happening at points A, B, C, D and E?

Questions

12.1 What is a meristem?

12.2 List three places where meristems may be found on a growing plant.

12.3 What do the cotyledons of a bean seed contain?

12.4 What does dormant mean?

12.5 What is the advantage of dormancy?

12.6 What activates the enzymes in the cotyledons of a germinating seed?

12.7 What do the enzymes do?

Investigation 12.2
To find the effect of storage time on the germination rate of seeds

SBA skills

Observation/Recording/Reporting *Planning/Design*
Analysis/Interpretation

Many seeds are able to survive in a dormant state for years. However, the percentage of seeds that germinate does tend to become less as the seeds age.

You are going to design and carry out in investigation to test this hypothesis:

> The older a batch of seeds is, the lower the percentage of the seeds that will germinate.

Remember to think about variables – what you will change, what you will keep the same and what you will measure. Think also about how you will record and display your results.

When you have written your plan, check it with your teacher before carrying out your experiment.

Analyse your results. Do they support or disprove your hypothesis? Discuss the main sources of error in your experiment, and suggest how you could improve it if you were able to do it again.

12.8 Plants grow lengthways by cell division and elongation.

During germination, the radicle and plumule grow lengthways, quickly becoming the root and shoot of the young plant. Roots and shoots continue to grow throughout the life of the plant.

Figure **12.8** shows how the cells are arranged near the tip of a root. The very tip of the root is covered by a **root cap**. This protects the root as it grows through the soil.

Just behind the tip is an area where the cells are very small. They are small because they are young; they have been made by other cells dividing. These small cells go on dividing, making many new cells. This part of the root is called the **region of cell division** or **root meristem**. It always remains just behind the root tip, no matter how long the root grows.

A little way up from these dividing cells, the cells are larger. The further up the root you look, the larger the cells are. These larger cells have grown from the small cells made in the region of cell division.

This part of the root is called the **region of cell elongation**.

Shoots grow in a very similar way. There is a region of cell division at the tip (there is no need for a protective layer at the tip), and a region of cell elongation behind it.

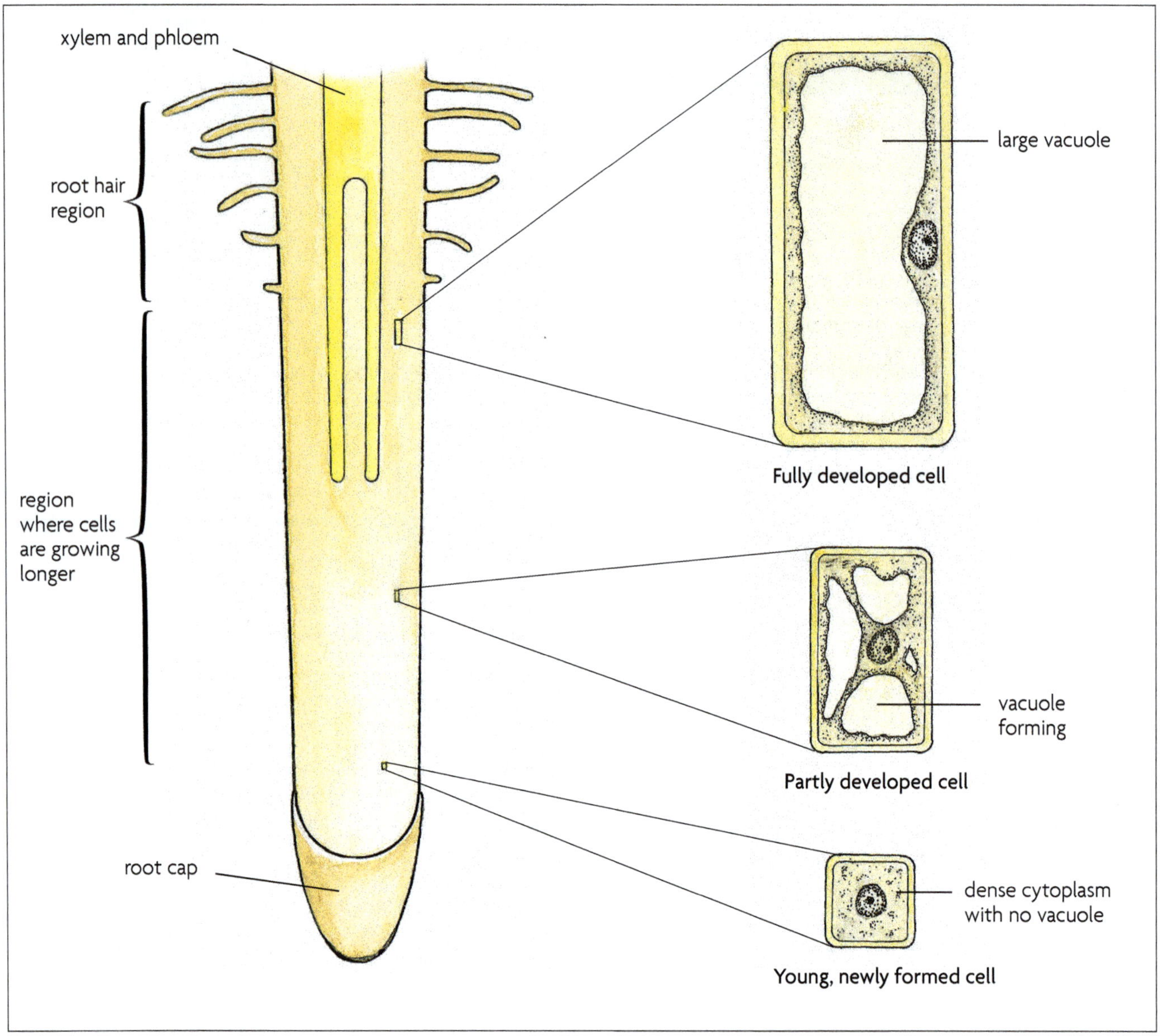

Figure 12.8 Longitudinal section through a root tip.

Investigation 12.3
To find out which part of a root is the growing region

SBA skills

Observation/Recording/Reporting *Drawing*
Manipulation/Measurement
Analysis/Interpretation

1 Germinate some bean seeds, by soaking them in water and leaving them in a gas jar supported by wet blotting paper. Leave them until their radicles (young roots) are about 4 cm long.

2 Copy the results table shown on the right.

3 Choose a bean seedling with a really straight, healthy-looking radicle. Carefully remove it from the gas jar, without damaging the radicle. Dry the radicle gently, by patting it with blotting paper.

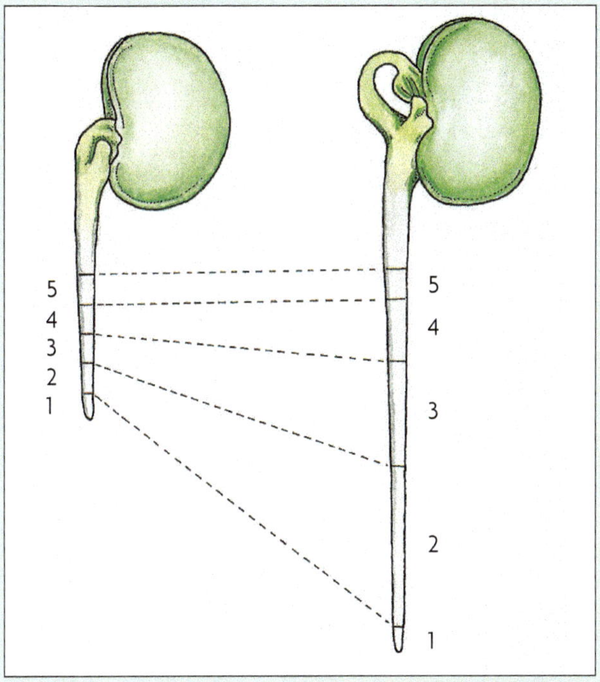

interval (numbered from bottom)	1	2	3	4	5
initial distance apart in mm					
final distance apart in mm					
increase in distance apart					

4 Using Indian ink, mark the radicle all the way along, at exactly equal intervals (see left-hand diagram). The size of interval you choose will depend on the length of your radicle. Record this distance in your results table.

5 Carefully replace the bean in the gas jar, as before. Leave it for several days.

6 Remove the bean again, and measure the distances between your markings. Fill in these results in the table.

7 Calculate the increase in distance between each pair of marks.

8 Draw a graph of your results. Put the number of the interval on the bottom axis, and the increase in distance on the vertical axis.

Questions

1 Which part of the bean radicle grew most quickly?

2 What was happening to the cells in this region?

3 Were there any parts of the bean radicle that did not grow? Explain why.

Questions

12.8 Why does a seed increase in mass at the beginning of germination?

12.9 Why does a seed decrease in mass for a time, once germination is under way?

12.10 What is a root cap, and what is its function?

12.11 In which part of a root are new cells formed?

12.12 Apart from size, what difference is there between a newly formed cell in a root, and a mature cell?

12.9 Roots and stems grow wider.

When a young plant first begins to grow, its shoots and roots mainly grow longer. This is called **primary growth**. Some plants, such as trees, have stems and roots which also grow much wider. This is called **secondary growth**.

Figure **12.9a** shows a section through a young stem of a plant. Between the xylem and phloem tissue of the vascular bundles, there is a very narrow band of **cambium**. The cells in the cambium can divide; they are meristematic cells.

As they divide, they make two sorts of new cells. The ones towards the middle of the stem become **xylem** cells. The ones towards the outside of the stem become **phloem** cells.

As more and more xylem cells are made, the cambium and phloem get pushed outwards. The circumference of the stem gets larger and larger. The epidermis can no longer cover it.

Underneath the epidermis another layer of meristematic cells is formed. They are called the **cork cambium**. They divide to make cork cells (Figure **12.9b**).

Cork cells have a waterproof substance called **suberin** in their cell walls. No water can get to the inside of the cell through the suberin, and so the cell contents die. Cork cells are therefore hollow.

A thick layer of cork cells builds up, to replace the old epidermis. It makes up the bark of the tree. The bark protects the cells underneath it from damage, and stops bacteria and fungi from getting in. It also prevents too much water being lost from the tree trunk by evaporation, and it insulates the tree. The hollow cork cells are rather like expanded polystyrene, and make an excellent insulating material.

Figure **12.9c** shows the final structure of the trunk of a tree. Almost all of it is xylem tissue, called **wood**. The phloem and cambium are found in a thin, soft layer between the cork and the wood.

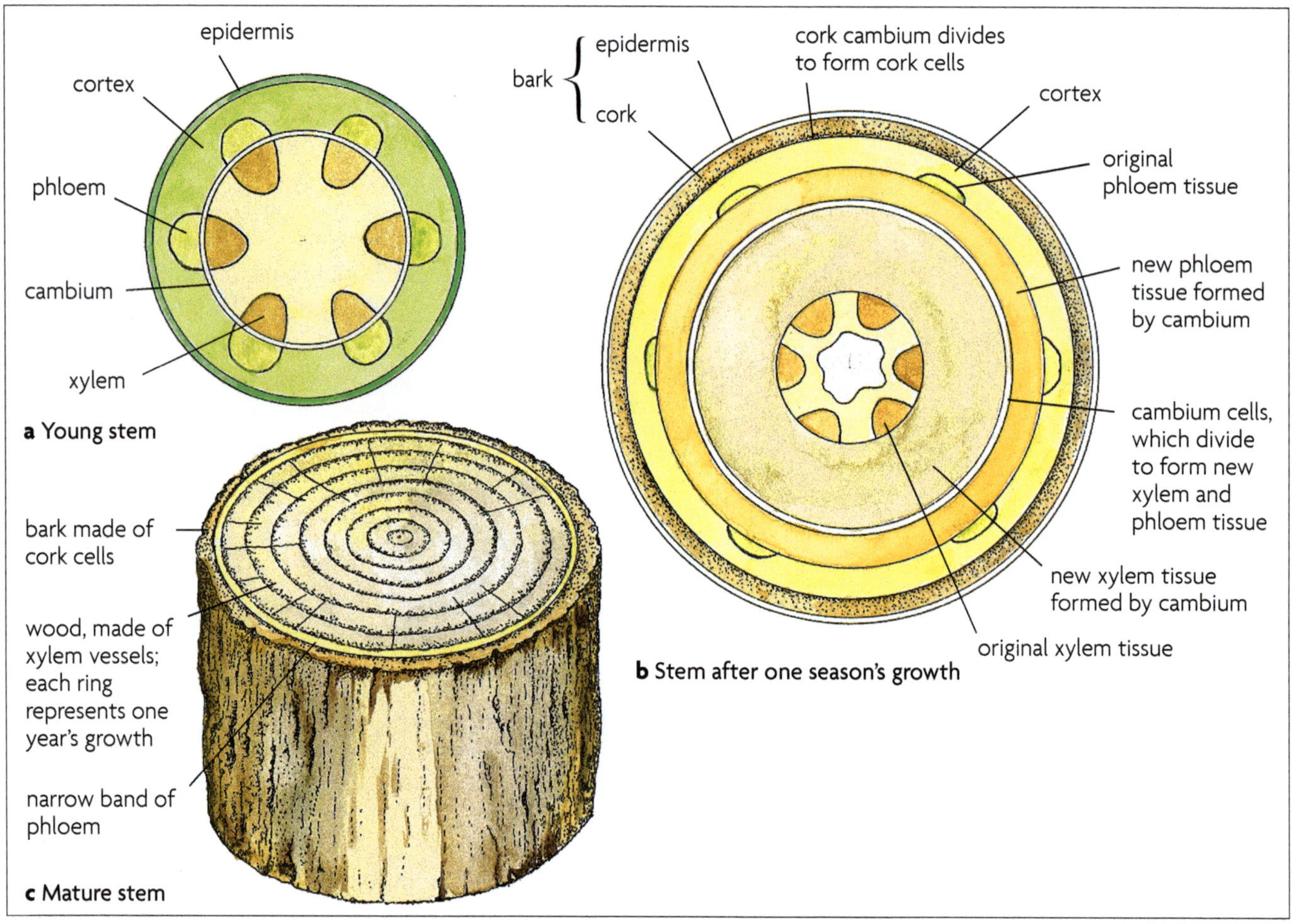

Figure 12.9 Secondary growth.

12.10 Seasonal growth shows as rings in wood.

The secondary growth of a tree is faster at some times of year than at others. In temperate countries, during the spring, a lot of new large xylem vessels are made. They are needed to supply water to the expanding buds. In summer, not so many new xylem vessels form, and they are smaller. In autumn and winter, there is almost no growth.

You can see these different types of xylem vessel on a cross section of a tree trunk (Figure **12.10**). Each year's growth forms a ring. Nearest the inside of the ring is the spring wood, with the summer wood towards the outside. The number of rings tells you the age of the tree.

Figure 12.10 Section of a tree trunk. The dark outer layer is the bark, with a thin layer of phloem beneath. The rest is wood, made of xylem.

In tropical countries with well-defined wet and dry seasons, large xylem cells may be made at the start of the wet season, and rings may be found in some trees. When there is more than one rainy season, more than one growth ring may be formed during a single year.

12.11 Plant growth substances.

The meristems (places where cells are dividing) in plants produce a number of different chemicals called **plant growth substances**. They are sometimes also known as **plant hormones**.

We have already seen (section **10.29**) how the plant growth substance **auxin** affects the growth of shoots and roots. Auxin is produced by the meristems in shoots and roots, and diffuses down the shoot and up the root. In shoots, it speeds up the elongation of cells, so the parts of the shoot with most auxin grow fastest. In roots, it slows down growth.

Plants also produce another growth substance called **gibberellin**. This also makes stems grow faster. Some varieties of plants do not produce gibberellin, and they do not grow tall. If gibberellin is applied to them, then their stems elongate rapidly (Figure **12.11**).

Figure 12.11 Gibberellin has made the internodes (shown by brackets) of these wheat stems grow longer.

Questions

12.13 Explain the difference between primary and secondary growth.

12.14 Which tissue is responsible for secondary growth in a stem or root?

12.15 What does cork cambium do?

12.16 What is suberin?

12.17 List four functions of bark.

12.18 What is wood made of?

12.18 Where is auxin made, and where does it have its effect?

12.19 What is the effect of gibberellin on plant growth?

Growth in animals

12.12 Mammals grow rapidly when young.

Figure **12.12** shows a growth curve for a human. The curve is quite smooth, showing that growth takes place fairly steadily until a person is about 20 years old. There is a growth spurt at adolescence.

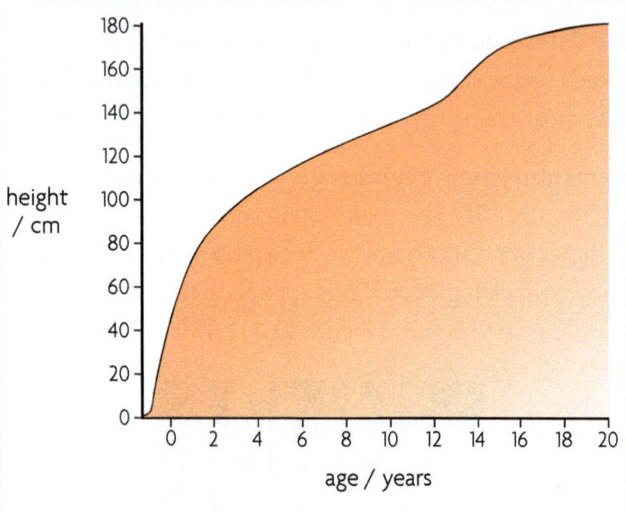

Figure 12.12 Growth curve of a human.

12.13 Growth is controlled by hormones.

The rate at which a person grows is controlled by a number of different hormones. The most important of these is **growth hormone**, which is secreted by the **pituitary gland**.

The sex hormones, **testosterone** and **oestrogen**, also affect growth. The increase in their secretion at puberty causes some parts of the body to grow at a greater rate than they have done up to now. This brings about the development of the secondary sexual characteristics, described in section **13.23**.

FACT!

The fastest growth rate that has been measured in the animal kingdom is shown by the blue whale calf. It puts on 26 tonnes of mass in 22¾ months – 10¾ months in its mother's body, and the first 12 months after birth.

Measuring growth

12.14 There are many ways of measuring growth.

Whatever way you choose to measure the growth of an animal or plant, you must take your measurements regularly. This might be every hour, or at the same time every day, or at the same time every week. The time interval you choose will depend on how fast the organism grows.

There are different sorts of measurement you could make. Each has its advantages (Table **12.1**, page **224**).

12.15 Height is a quick measurement of growth.

Height and length are quick and easy ways to measure growth in many organisms, such as humans and plants. They also have the advantage that they do not damage the animal or plant. However, they do not take into account any sideways growth, nor do they include the roots of a plant unless you uproot it.

Sometimes, the length of a certain part of an animal's body can be measured, instead of its entire length. It is quick and easy, for example, to measure the length of a mouse's tail, and this does give a reasonable idea of its overall size.

12.16 Fresh mass measures all the body contents.

Increase in mass gives a better estimate of the overall increase in size of an organism than height or length do. It does, however, take a little longer to measure. If you measure the mass of a complete plant, you must uproot it, which may kill it, and will certainly slow down its growth.

Fresh mass includes all the water in the organism. Since the amount of water in the organism will vary from time to time, fresh mass is not a very accurate method.

FACT!

The slowest growth rate that has been measured in the animal kingdom is shown by the deep-sea clam, *Tindaria callistiformis*. It can take 100 years to grow 8 mm.

12.17 Dry mass is the most accurate method.

To get rid of any fluctuations in mass which are simply due to changes in water content, **dry mass** can be measured. All of the water is removed from the plant. It is dried gently in a cool oven, until all the water has evaporated from its tissues. To check that the water has all been lost, the mass of the dried remains is found. The material is returned to the oven for a little longer, and the mass found again. When the two measurements are the same, then all the water has gone. This is called drying to constant mass.

12.18 Using the dry mass method.

There is one very obvious disadvantage to the dry mass method of measuring growth. It kills the organism you are measuring! How can you measure growth if you kill the organism whenever you measure it?

The answer is to use a large number of organisms. If you wanted to measure growth of a plant, for example, using the dry mass method, you may need to grow several hundred plants. They would need to be as identical as possible – all from the same pure-breeding stock (section **14.16**), all planted at exactly the same time, and all grown under identical conditions.

Each day, you could take a sample of these (the larger the sample the better) and measure their dry mass. If the average dry mass is then worked out for each day, you will get a very good idea of how any one plant increases its dry mass.

Since large numbers of organisms are required to measure changes in dry mass, it should not be used to follow the growth of organisms in nature. You may upset the balance of nature by removing the food source of organisms at higher trophic levels.

Investigation 12.4
Measuring the rate of growth of a plant

SBA skills

Observation/Recording/Reporting *Drawing*
Manipulation/Measurement *Planning/Design*
Analysis/Interpretation

You are going to compare the rate of growth of seedlings in two different temperatures.

Your teacher will tell you which kinds of plants you can use. When you know this, you need to decide how you will measure their rate of growth. Suitable methods might be:

- measuring the height of the plant
- growing many different plants, and uprooting some each day to measure their mass
- counting the number of leaves on the plant
- measuring the surface area of the leaves.

1 Decide on the hypothesis you will test.

2 Write up your plan. Think about the variable you will change, those you will keep the same, and what you will measure. Decide when you will take your measurements, exactly how you will take them and how you will record them. You might like to take photographs as well as making measurements.

3 Display your results. Use them to draw a conclusion. Was your hypothesis supported or not?

4 Discuss your findings. How do they relate to what you know about the effect of temperature on living organisms? How reliable do you think your results are? What were your main sources of error? How would you improve your experiment if you could do it again?

Questions

12.20 Give one advantage of using height or length as a method for measuring growth.

12.21 Why is fresh mass not a very accurate method for measuring growth?

12.22 What is meant by drying to constant mass?

Table 12.1 Some methods of measuring growth

Method	Advantages	Disadvantages	Suitable organisms
height or length	quick, easy, does not damage organism, can be used in the field	only measures growth in one dimension	small plants, most animals
length of one part of the body	quick, easy, does not damage organism, can be used in the field	only measures growth in one part of the body	many small animals, such as mammals and birds
fresh mass	gives a better measurement of overall size than height or length; fairly quick for small animals	plants must be uprooted, and roots cleared of soil; difficult for large animals without special equipment; fluctuations in water content may affect results	most animals; small plants
dry mass	gives best measurement of the amount of living material in an organism	time consuming; kills individual, so large numbers are needed; may upset balance of nature	plants; invertebrates, such as insects and slugs

Key ideas

- Growth is permanent increase in size.
- Growth involves cell growth and cell division. The type of cell division that is used is mitosis. It produces new cells with exactly the same number of chromosomes and the same genes as the original cell.
- The growing regions of plants are called meristems. The main ones are just behind the tip of the shoot, in lateral buds, and just behind the tip of the root.
- A bean seed contains an embryo plant, including a plumule that will develop into a shoot, a radicle that will develop into a root, and a food store in the cotyledons.
- Germination begins when the seed takes up water. This activates enzymes which digest the food stores. In the early stages of germination, the cells in the seed get the energy they need by respiration using these food stores. Once they are above the ground, they can begin to photosynthesise.
- Lengthways growth in a plant is known as primary growth. Widthways growth is called secondary growth.
- Plant growth is controlled by plant growth substances, including auxin and gibberellin.
- Mammals, unlike plants, do not grow all of their lives. In humans, there are growth spurts shortly after birth and during puberty. Once adult, the person stops growing.
- Mammalian growth is controlled by several hormones, including growth hormone, thyroxine, testosterone and oestrogen.
- Growth can be measured in many different ways, including length or height, wet mass or dry mass.

End-of-chapter questions

1 Explain the difference between each of the following pairs of terms: **(a)** fresh mass, dry mass, **(b)** primary growth, secondary growth, **(c)** radicle, plumule.

2 For a named seed:
   - a List three conditions which need to be fulfilled before the seed will germinate.
   - b What are the main food reserves in this seed?
   - c In which part of the seed are these food reserves found?
   - d How are these food reserves mobilised when germination begins?
   - e With the aid of diagrams, describe how the radicle of this seed grows in length.

3 a Use the following table to plot a growth curve for a pea plant.
   - b Explain exactly how these results would have been obtained.
   - c Explain the reasons for the shape of the curve.

Time in weeks from planting of seed	Dry weight in g
0	1.4
0.5	0.8
1	1.6
1.5	2.5
2	5.2
3	21.5
4	31.6
5	41.3
6	49.0
7	53.2
8	61.1
9	63.4
10	66.5
11	65.2
12	67.4
13	66.5
14	66.4
15	67.2
16	66.0
17	53.2

4 Use the table below to plot growth curves for **(a)** a human male, and **(b)** a human female. Plot both curves on the same axes.
   - a At which age does growth appear to stop?
   - b At which age is the difference in height between male and female **(i)** least, and **(ii)** greatest?
   - c How much does the female grow between the ages of 9 and 17?
   - d What is the average rate of growth per year for the female between the ages of 9 and 17?
   - e Do you think that height is a good way of measuring human growth? Give reasons for your answer.

Age in years	Height in centimetres	
	Male	Female
0	53.0	53.0
1	61.0	61.0
2	71.5	71.5
3	91.5	86.5
4	99.0	91.5
5	104.5	96.0
6	108.5	101.0
7	114.0	111.0
8	122.0	119.0
9	124.5	124.0
10	124.5	127.5
11	127.0	130.0
12	129.5	132.0
13	131.5	134.0
14	137.0	137.0
15	142.0	142.0
16	147.0	147.0
17	155.0	152.5
18	162.5	157.0
19	170.0	160.0
20	172.5	161.5
21	175.0	162.0
22	175.0	162.0
23	175.0	162.0
24	175.0	162.0

13 Reproduction

In this chapter, you will find out:

- how asexual and sexual reproduction differ from each other
- some examples of organisms that reproduce asexually
- how reproduction takes place in humans
- about the menstrual cycle, and how it is controlled by hormones
- about various methods of birth control, including their advantages and disadvantages
- how flowering plants reproduce
- about the function of fruits in dispersing seeds, and some examples of different methods of dispersal.

13.1 Reproduction may be sexual or asexual.

Living organisms may be killed by other organisms, or die of old age. New organisms have to be produced to replace those that die. This is **reproduction**.

Each species reproduces in a different way. However, there are only two basic types – **asexual reproduction**, and **sexual reproduction**.

Asexual reproduction

13.2 Mitosis takes place in asexual reproduction.

Asexual reproduction involves only one parent. The parent organism simply produces new cells by mitosis, which grow into a new organism. Because mitosis produces new cells genetically identical to the parent cell (section **12.3**), the new organism is exactly like its parent. A group of genetically identical organisms is called a **clone**.

13.3 *Amoeba* reproduces asexually.

Amoeba reproduces by binary fission (Figure **13.1**). This happens when the cell gets so large that its surface area to volume ratio is too small to allow gas exchange to occur easily. In good conditions, division will take place every two to three days.

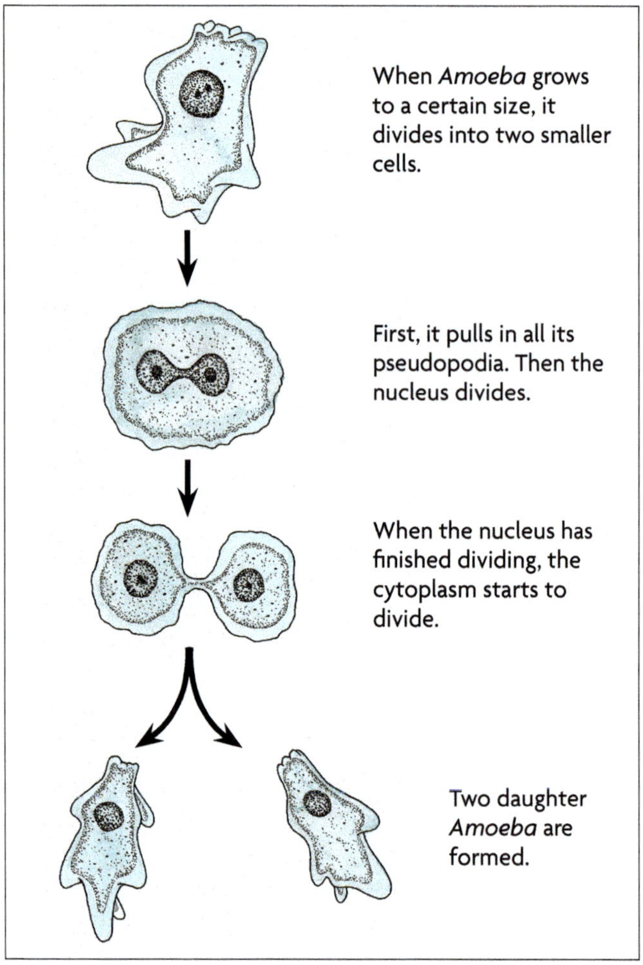

When *Amoeba* grows to a certain size, it divides into two smaller cells.
First, it pulls in all its pseudopodia. Then the nucleus divides.
When the nucleus has finished dividing, the cytoplasm starts to divide.
Two daughter *Amoeba* are formed.

Figure 13.1 An amoeba reproducing by binary fission.

13.4 Some plants reproduce by vegetative propagation.

Many flowering plants can produce offspring by a form of asexual reproduction called **vegetative propagation**. New plants are formed from an outgrowth of the old one. Some examples of the outgrowths are **runners** (Figure **13.2**) and **plantlets** (Figure **13.3**). Not surprisingly, many storage organs are also organs of vegetative propagation (Figure **7.36**, page **140**).

Gardeners and farmers often use artificial methods of vegetative propagation to increase their stock of a plant. The advantage of this method is that the new plants will be just like their parent. **Cuttings** (Figure **13.4**) are the commonest method, because many young plants can be quickly produced from just one parent plant.

Sugar cane plants are grown from stem cuttings. The stem is cut into sections with two or three buds and these are planted. The new plants grow from the buds. These plants

In summer, the parent plant grows long stems called runners. New plants grow from the buds along each runner. The new plants get food and water from the parent plant until they have grown their own roots. After several months, the connection to the parent plant dies away. Several new plants may grow from just one runner. Strawberry plants will grow and produce fruit at altitudes over 250 m in the Caribbean.

Figure 13.2 Asexual reproduction of a strawberry runner.

Buds develop in notches in the leaf margin, forming new plants.

Figure 13.3 Asexual reproduction along the leaf margin of *Bryophyllum* sp. (leaf of life).

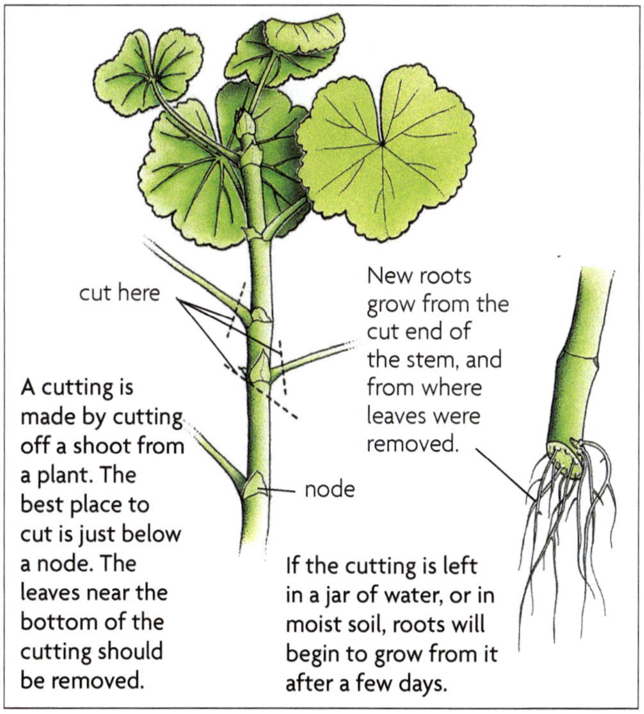

cut here
A cutting is made by cutting off a shoot from a plant. The best place to cut is just below a node. The leaves near the bottom of the cutting should be removed.
node
New roots grow from the cut end of the stem, and from where leaves were removed.
If the cutting is left in a jar of water, or in moist soil, roots will begin to grow from it after a few days.

Figure 13.4 Propagating a plant by cuttings.

are genetically identical to the plant from which they are cut. All the plants in many fields are identical and are ready to harvest at the same time.

Grafting is used if you want to grow more of a plant with good flowers or fruit, but do not want it to grow on its own roots. This might be because its own root system is too weak, not allowing it to grow, or it may be too strong, tending to make an enormous tree.

A piece of the plant is grafted onto a rootstock from another sort of tree (Figure 13.5). After a while, the two will grow together. The new plant will have all the features of its parent, but its size will be governed by the rootstock it has been grafted onto.

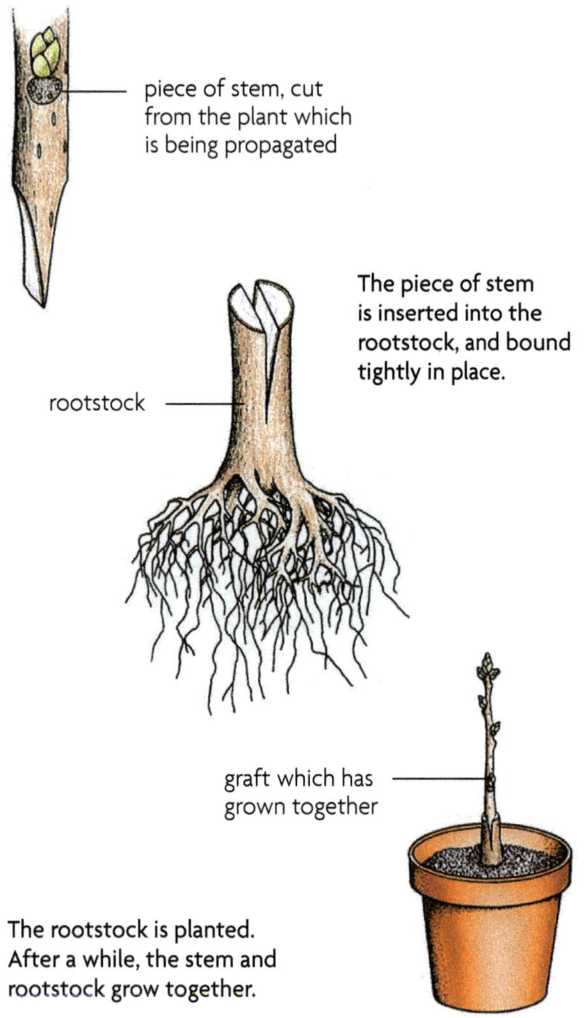

Figure 13.5 Propagating a plant by grafting.

Many fruit trees, including citrus and mango, are grafted onto rootstocks.

Tissue culture is another artificial means of vegetative propagation used for some plants. It involves the growth of plant material – for example, cell, tissue or organ – in a suitable medium, under sterile conditions in a laboratory. It has the advantage of producing clones as desired, free of disease organisms; permitting all-year propagation; allowing the propagation of species which cannot otherwise be obtained by vegetative reproduction. The technique has been used for propagating bananas in the Caribbean.

Investigation 13.1
Cloning of sugar cane

SBA skills

Observation/Recording/Reporting

Analysis/Interpretation

1. Cut a sugar cane stem into sections, each with a single bud.
2. Cut another cane into sections with two buds each.
3. Cut a third cane into sections with three buds each.
4. Plant your cuttings and cover with a shallow depth of soil.
5. Water regularly to keep the soil moist.
6. After three or four weeks, record the proportion of cuttings, of each type, that have produced new plants. Also record the number of plants produced by each cutting.

Questions

1. Why do you think that farmers are normally advised to plant three-bud cuttings?
2. On the basis of your results, do you think that this is good advice?

13.5 Some organisms may reproduce by parthenogenesis.

Sometimes, an egg will develop into a new organism without being fertilised. This is called **parthenogenesis**.

Aphids (greenfly) can reproduce in this way. When they have plenty of food, the female aphids produce large numbers of eggs. The eggs are not fertilised. They stay inside the female's body, where they grow into young aphids. The young are then born, fully developed (Figure **13.6**). Drone bees are also produced from unfertilised eggs.

Figure 13.6 An aphid (greenfly) reproducing by parthenogenesis.

Questions

13.1 What kind of cell division is involved in asexual reproduction?

13.2 What is vegetative propagation?

13.3 Give two reasons why gardeners often use cuttings to produce new plants.

13.4 What is a clone?

13.5 What is parthenogenesis?

Sexual reproduction

13.6 Sexual reproduction involves fertilisation.

In sexual reproduction, the parent organism produces sex cells called **gametes**. Eggs and sperm are examples of gametes. Two of these gametes join and their nuclei fuse together. This is called **fertilisation**. The new cell which is formed by fertilisation is called a **zygote**. The zygote divides again and again, and eventually grows into a new organism.

13.7 Gametes have half the normal number of chromosomes.

Gametes are different from ordinary cells, because they contain only half as many chromosomes as usual. This is so that when two of them fuse together, the zygote they form will have the correct number of chromosomes.

Humans, for example, have 46 chromosomes in each of their body cells. But human egg and sperm cells only have 23 chromosomes each. When an egg and sperm fuse together at fertilisation, the zygote which is formed will therefore have 46 chromosomes, the normal number (Figure **13.7**, overleaf).

The 46 chromosomes in an ordinary human cell are of 23 different kinds. There are two of each kind. The two chromosomes of one kind are called **homologous chromosomes**. A cell which has the full number of chromosomes, with two of each kind, is called a **diploid cell**.

An egg or sperm, though, only has 23 chromosomes, one of each kind. It is called a **haploid cell**. Gametes are always haploid. When two gametes fuse together, they form a diploid zygote.

13.8 Gametes are made by meiosis.

Gametes are made by ordinary body cells dividing. For example, human sperm are made when cells in a testis divide.

Because gametes need to have only half as many chromosomes as their parent cell, division by mitosis will not do. When gametes are being made, cells divide in a different way, called **meiosis**. This process is shown in Figures **13.8** to **13.10** (pages **231** and **232**).

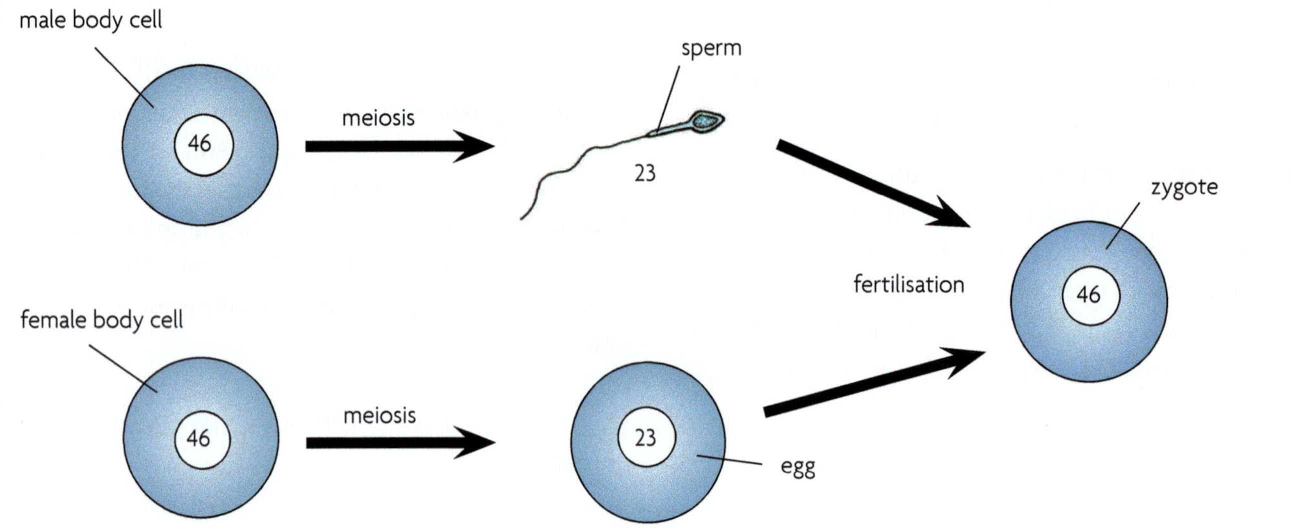

male body cell
46
meiosis
sperm
23
zygote
fertilisation
46
female body cell
46
meiosis
23
egg
The cells in a human body each contain 46 chromosomes.
In sexual reproduction, cells in testes and ovaries divide by meiosis, producing gametes, with half the number of chromosomes.
When the male and female gametes join together, a zygote is formed which has the full number of chromosomes.

Figure 13.7 Sexual reproduction.

In flowering plants and animals, meiosis only happens when gametes are being made. Meiosis produces new cells with only half as many chromosomes as the parent cell.

13.9 Male gametes move – female ones stay still.

In many organisms, there are two different kinds of gamete. One kind is quite large, and does not move much. This is called the female gamete. In humans, the female gamete is the **egg**.

The other sort of gamete is smaller, and usually moves actively in search of the female gamete. This is called the male gamete. In humans, the male gamete is the **sperm**. In flowering plants, the male gamete is found inside the pollen grain. It does not move by itself, but is carried to the female gamete by a pollen tube (Figure **13.39**, page **248**).

Often, one organism can only produce one kind of gamete. Its sex is either male or female, depending on what kind of gamete it makes. All mammals, for example, are either male or female.

Sometimes, though, an organism can produce both sorts of gamete. Earthworms and slugs, for example, can produce both eggs and sperms. An organism which produces both male and female gametes is a **hermaphrodite**. Many flowering plants are also hermaphrodite.

Questions

13.6 What is a gamete?

13.7 What is a zygote?

13.8 Why do gametes contain only half the normal number of chromosomes?

13.9 What is meant by a diploid cell?

13.10 Name one part of your body where you have diploid cells.

13.11 What is meant by a haploid cell?

13.12 Give one example of a haploid cell.

13.13 When do cells divide by meiosis?

13.14 What is the purpose of meiosis?

13.15 What does hermaphrodite mean?

13.16 Give one example of a hermaphrodite organism.

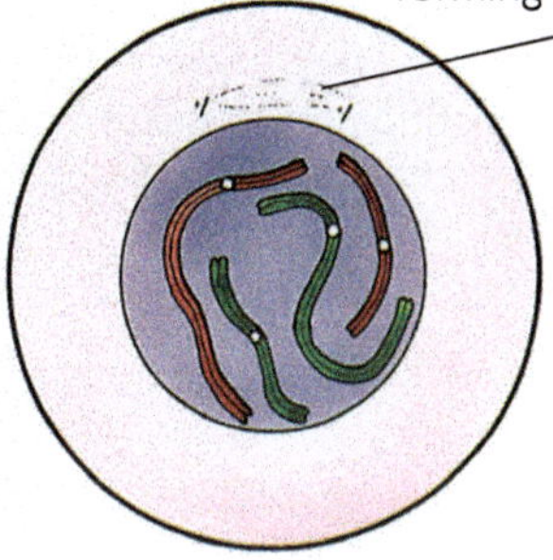

1 Early prophase I The chromosomes get short and fat, so they can be seen with a light microscope. Each chromosome contains two chromatids, just as in mitosis.

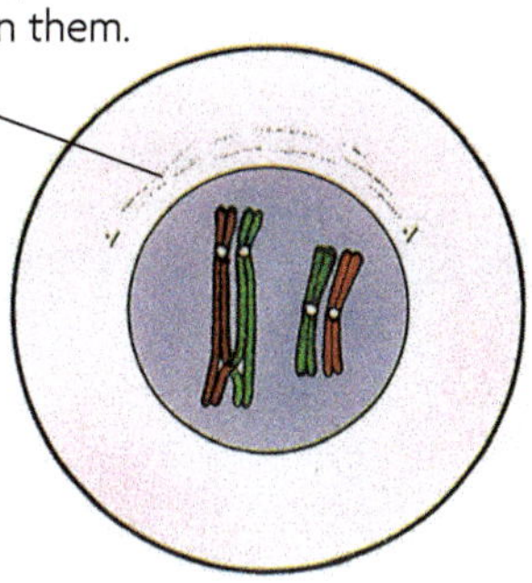

2 Late prophase I Homologous chromosomes come together, forming two bivalents. Chromatids of homologous chromosomes may break and rejoin with each other, forming crossover points.

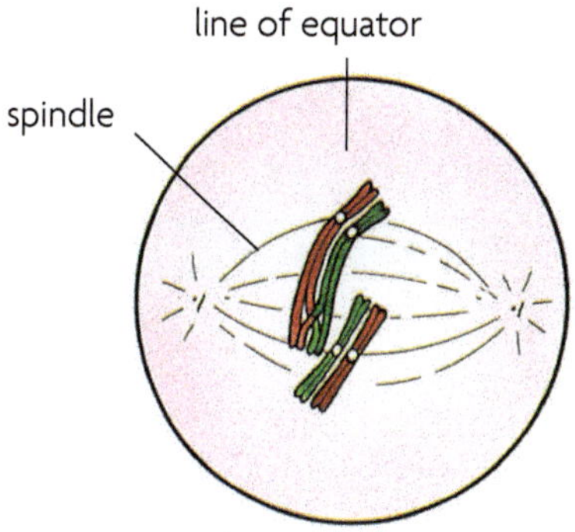

3 Metaphase I The bivalents line up on the equator.

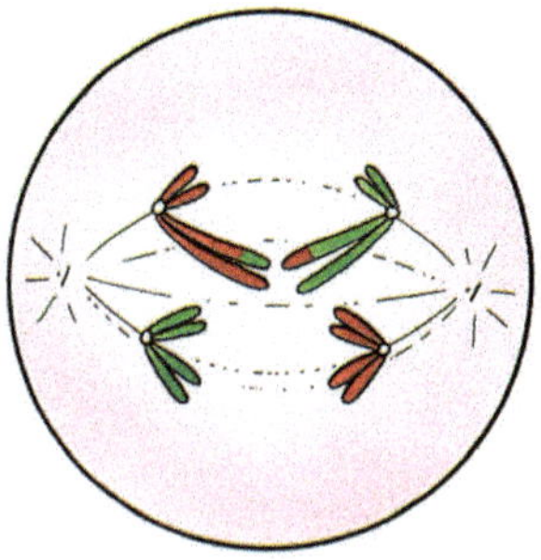

4 Anaphase I The bivalents separate, and the homologous chromosomes move away from one another along the spindle fibres. Notice that the centromeres do not split, so the two chromatids of each chromosome are still joined together.

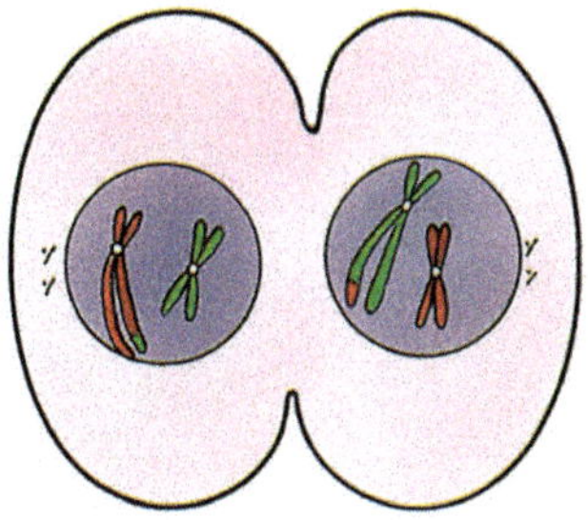

5 Telophase I The chromosomes arrive at opposite ends of the cell. A nuclear membrane forms round each group. The spindle fibres fade away. The centrioles divide, and so does the cytoplasm.

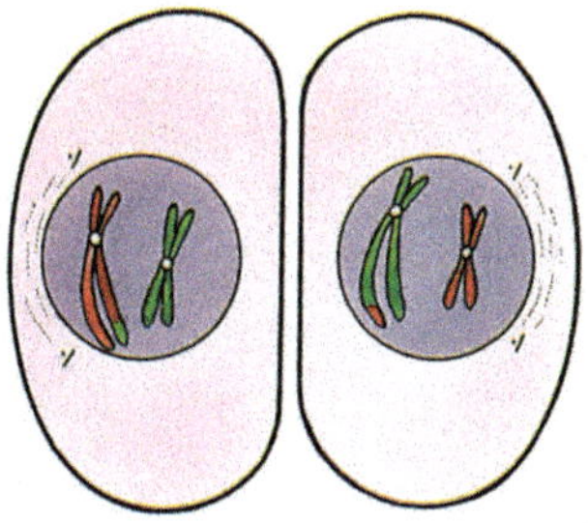

6 Prophase II The centrioles begin to form new spindles at right angles to the first one.

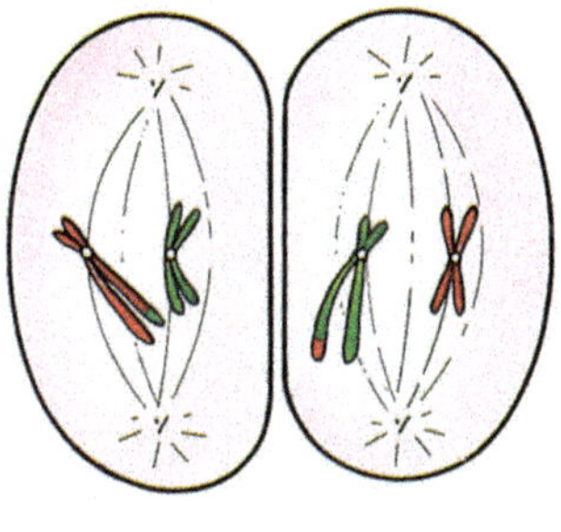

7 Metaphase II The chromosomes line up on the equators of the spindles.

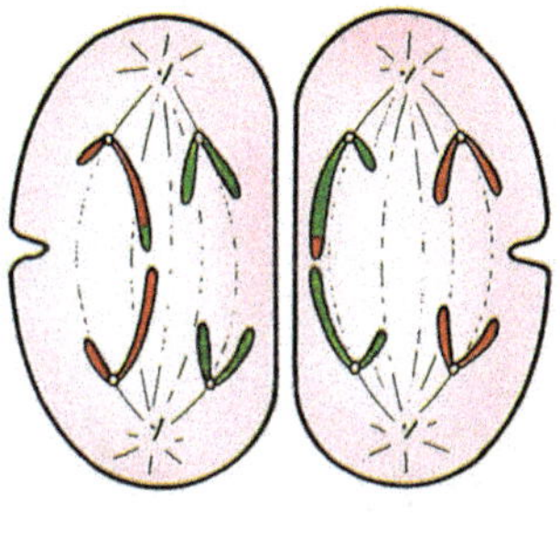

8 Anaphase II The centromeres of each chromosome split, so the two chromatids separate. The chromatids move away from each other, along the spindle fibres.

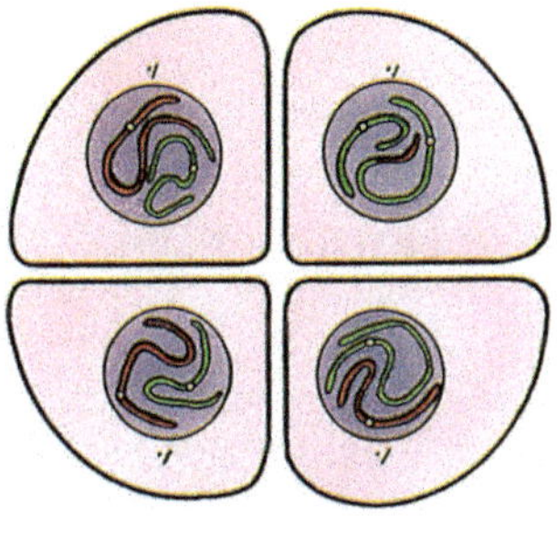

9 Telophase II The chromatids arrive at opposite ends of the cell, and nuclear membranes form around them. The cytoplasm divides.
Four daughter cells have been formed, each with half the number of chromosomes of the parent cell. Each of these cells is called a gamete.

Figure 13.8 Meiosis in an animal cell with four chromosomes (two pairs). In meiosis, the cell divides twice. In the first division, shown in diagrams **1** to **5**, the homologous chromosomes separate from their partners. In the second division, each individual chromosome splits into two. You do not need to learn the names of the different stages.

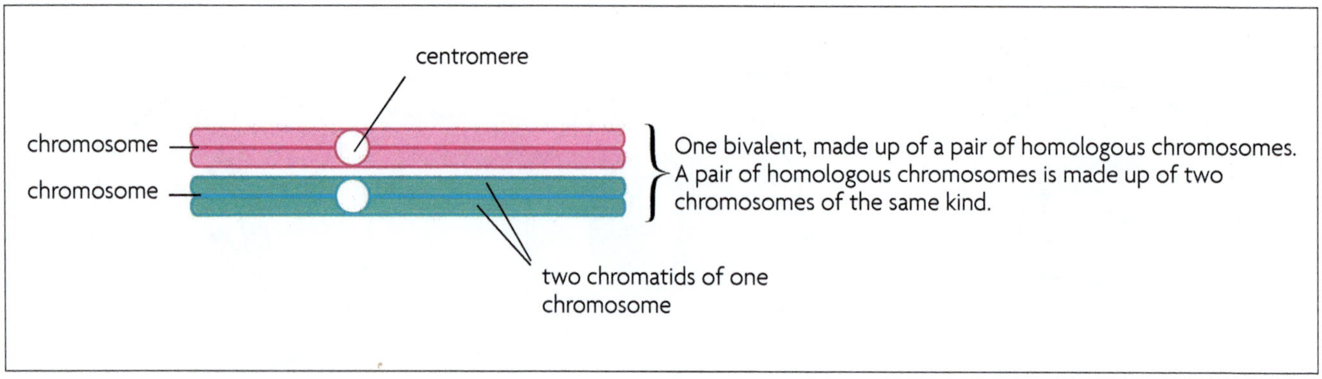

centromere
chromosome
chromosome
One bivalent, made up of a pair of homologous chromosomes. A pair of homologous chromosomes is made up of two chromosomes of the same kind.
two chromatids of one chromosome

Figure 13.9 A pair of homologous chromosomes.

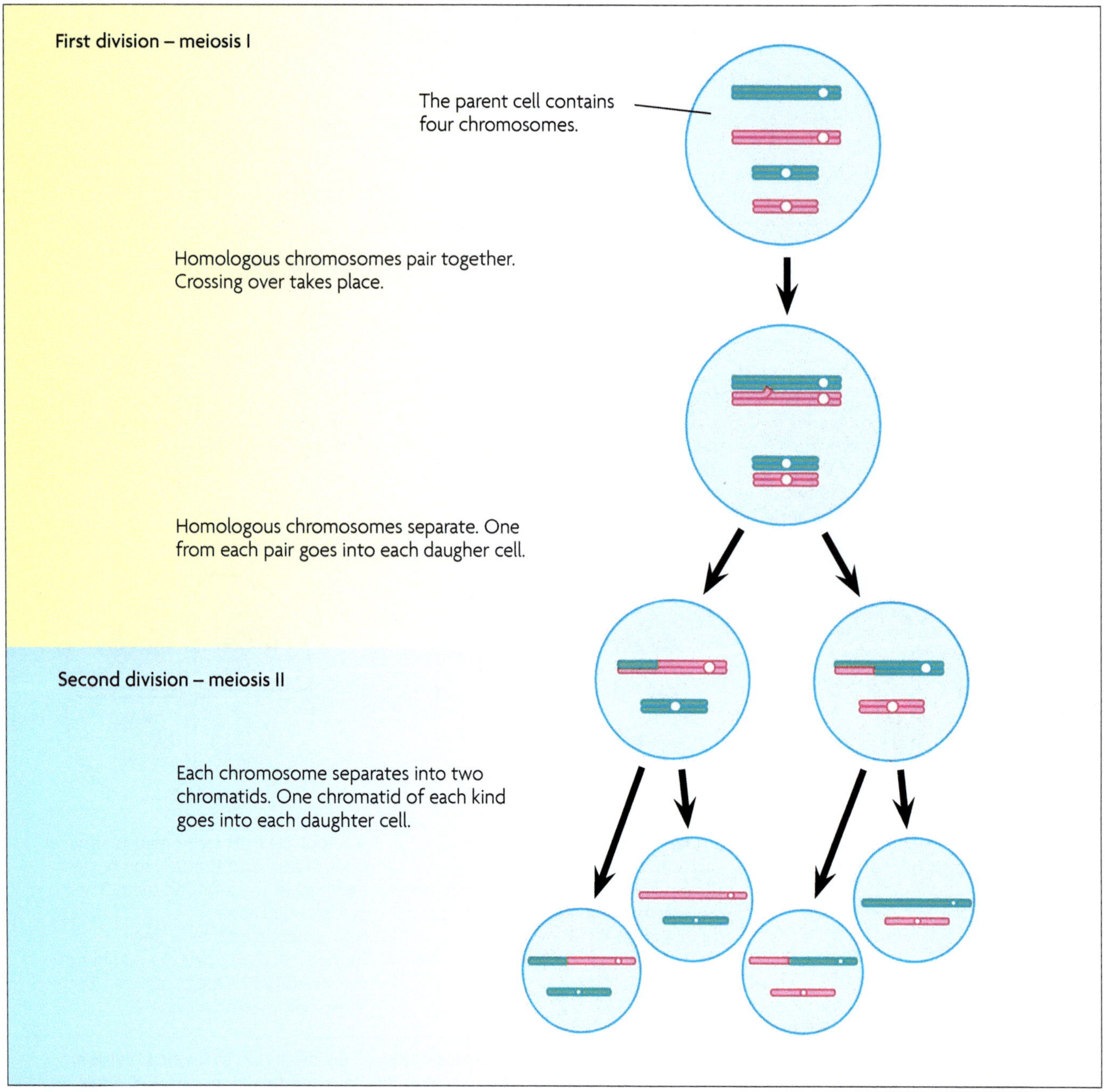

Figure 13.10 Summary of chromosome behaviour during meiosis.

Sexual reproduction in a mammal

13.10 The female reproductive organs.

Figure **13.11** shows the reproductive organs of a woman. The female gametes, called eggs are made in the two **ovaries**. Leading away from the ovaries are the **oviducts**, sometimes called **Fallopian tubes**. They do not connect directly to the ovaries, but have a funnel-shaped opening just a short distance away.

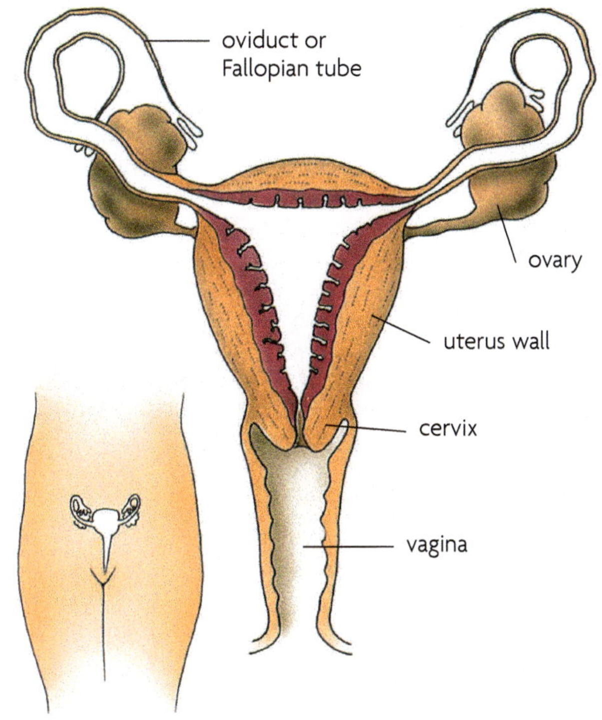

Figure 13.11 The female reproductive organs.

The two oviducts lead to the womb or **uterus**. This has very thick walls, made of muscle. It is quite small – only about the size of a clenched fist – but it can stretch a great deal when a woman is pregnant.

At the base of the uterus is a narrow opening, guarded by muscles. This is the neck of the womb, or **cervix**. It leads to the **vagina**, which opens to the outside.

The opening from the bladder, called the **urethra**, runs in front of the vagina, while the **rectum** is just behind it. The three tubes open quite separately to the outside.

13.11 The male reproductive organs.

Figure **13.12** shows the reproductive organs of a man. The male gametes, called spermatozoa or **sperm**, are made in

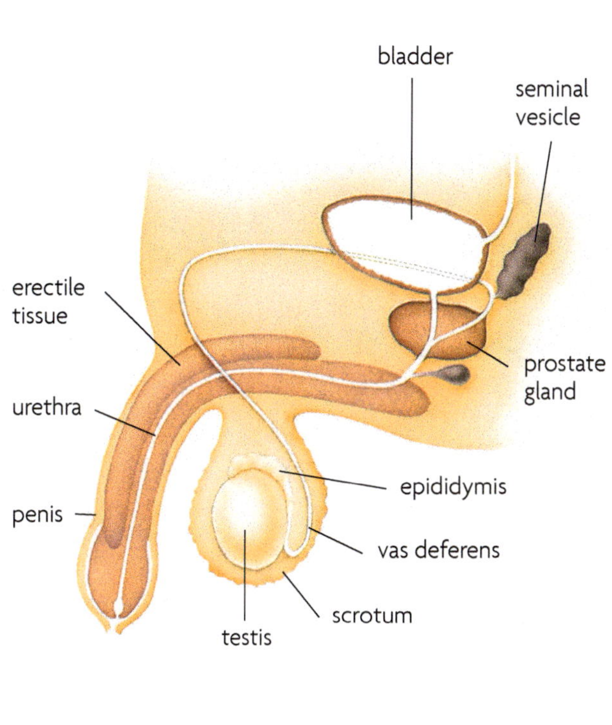

Figure 13.12 The male reproductive organs.

two **testes**. These are outside the body, in two sacs of skin called the **scrotum**.

The sperm are carried away from each testis in a tube called the **sperm duct** or **vas deferens**. The vasa deferentia from the testes join up with the urethra just below the bladder. The urethra continues downwards and opens at the tip of the **penis**. The urethra can carry both urine and sperm at different times.

Where the vasa deferentia join the urethra, there is a gland called the **prostate gland**. This makes a fluid which the sperm swim in. Just behind the prostate gland are the **seminal vesicles**, which also secrete fluid.

13.12 Ovaries make eggs.

Figure **13.13** (overleaf) shows a section through a human ovary. The eggs are made from cells in the outside layer, or **epithelium,** of the ovary. A small space, filled with liquid, forms around each one. The space and the cell inside is called a **follicle**.

This has happened inside a girl's ovaries before she is born. At birth, she will already have many thousands of follicles inside her ovaries.

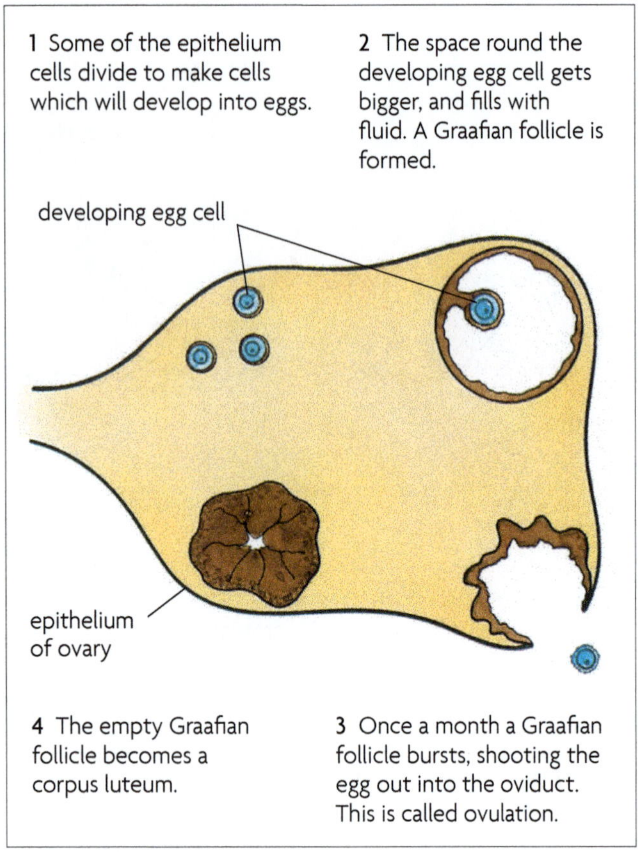

1 Some of the epithelium cells divide to make cells which will develop into eggs.
2 The space round the developing egg cell gets bigger, and fills with fluid. A Graafian follicle is formed.
developing egg cell
epithelium of ovary
4 The empty Graafian follicle becomes a corpus luteum.
3 Once a month a Graafian follicle bursts, shooting the egg out into the oviduct. This is called ovulation.

Figure 13.13 How eggs are made.

When she reaches puberty (section **13.23**), some of these follicles will begin to develop. Usually, only one develops at a time. The cell inside the follicles grows bigger, and so does the fluid-filled space around it. The follicle moves to the edge of the ovary.

It is now called a **Graafian follicle**. It is a little more that 1 cm across, and bulges from the outside of the ovary.

The cell inside it undergoes meiosis. Only one of the cells which are made becomes an egg (Figure **13.14**). The follicle bursts, and the egg shoots out of the ovary. This is called **ovulation**. In humans, it happens once a month.

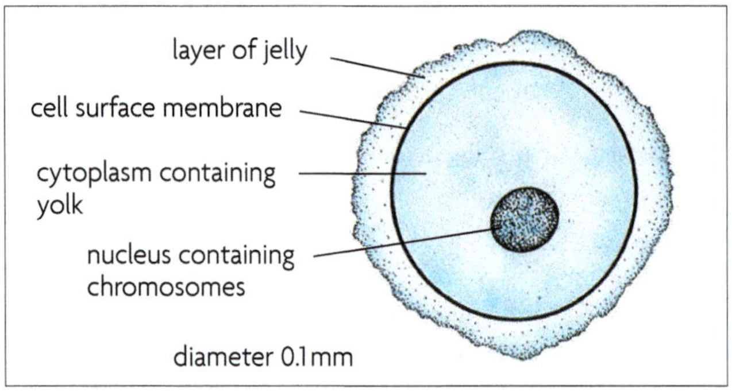

Figure 13.14 An egg.

13.13 Testes make sperm.

Figure **13.15** shows a section through a testis. It contains thousands of very narrow, coiled tubes or tubules. These are where the sperm are made. Sperm develop from cells in the walls of the tubules, which divide by meiosis. Sperm are made continually from puberty onwards. Figure **13.16** shows the structure of a sperm.

Sperm production is very sensitive to heat. If they get too hot, the cells in the tubules will not develop into sperm. This is why the testes are outside the body, where they are cooler than they would be inside.

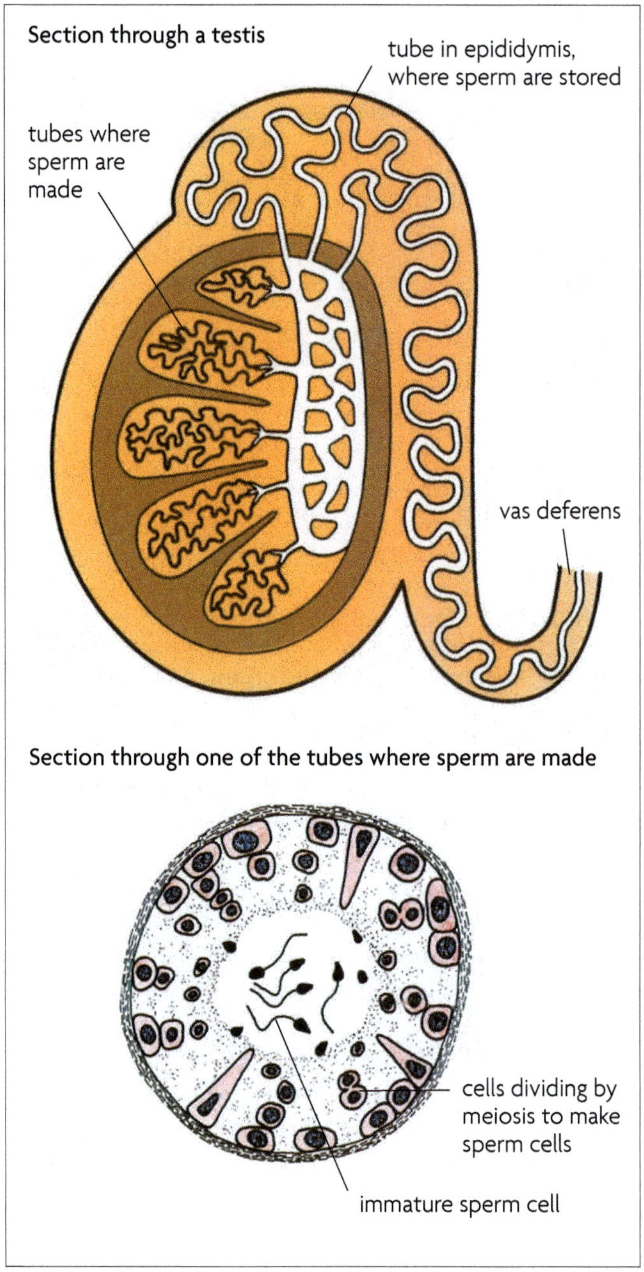

Figure 13.15 How sperm are made.

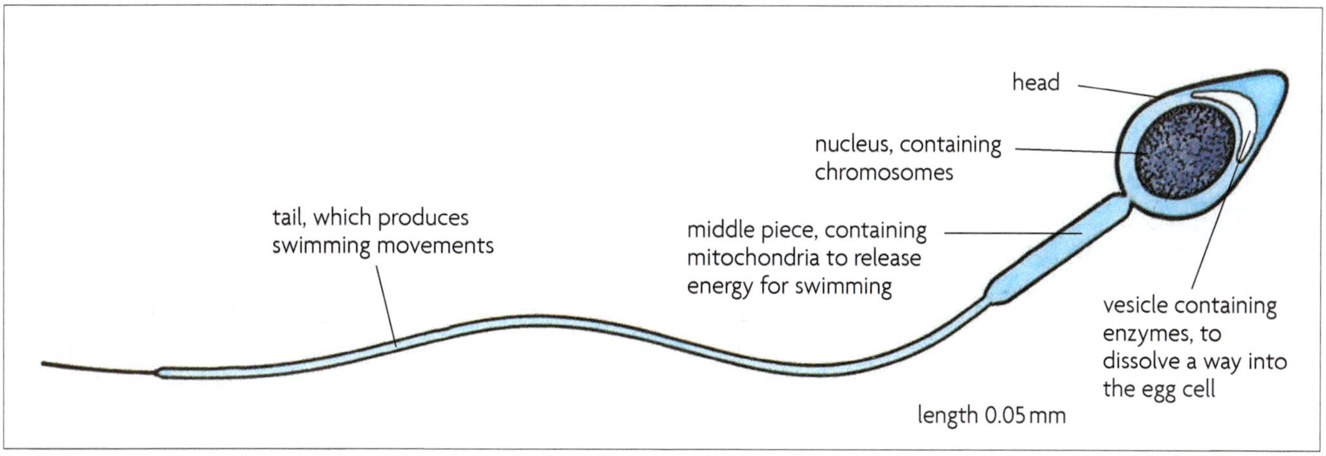

Figure 13.16 A sperm cell.

13.14 Mating introduces sperm into the vagina.

After ovulation, the egg is caught in the funnel of the oviduct. The funnel is lined with cilia (section **6.14**) which beat rhythmically, wafting the egg into the entrance of the oviduct.

Very slowly, the egg travels towards the uterus. Cilia lining the oviduct help to sweep it along. Muscles in the wall of the oviduct also help to move it, by **peristalsis** (Figure **5.9** on page **79** shows peristalsis in the alimentary canal).

If the egg is not fertilised by a sperm within 8–24 hours after ovulation, it will die. By this time, it has only travelled a short way along the oviduct. So a sperm must reach an egg while it is quite near the top of the oviduct if fertilisation is to be successful.

When the man is sexually excited, blood is pumped into spaces inside the penis, so that it becomes erect. To bring the sperm as close as possible to the egg, the man's penis is placed inside the vagina of the woman. This is called **sexual intercourse**.

Sperm are pushed out of the penis into the vagina. This happens when muscles in the walls of the tubes containing the sperm contract rhythmically. The wave of contraction begins in the testes, travels along the vasa deferentia, and into the penis. The sperm are squeezed along, and out of the man's urethra into the woman's vagina. This is called **ejaculation**.

The fluid containing the sperm is called **semen**. Ejaculation deposits the semen at the top of the vagina, near the cervix.

13.15 Fertilisation happens in the oviduct.

The sperm are still quite a long way from the egg. They swim, using their tails, up through the cervix, through the uterus, and into the oviduct (Figures **13.17** and **13.18**, overleaf).

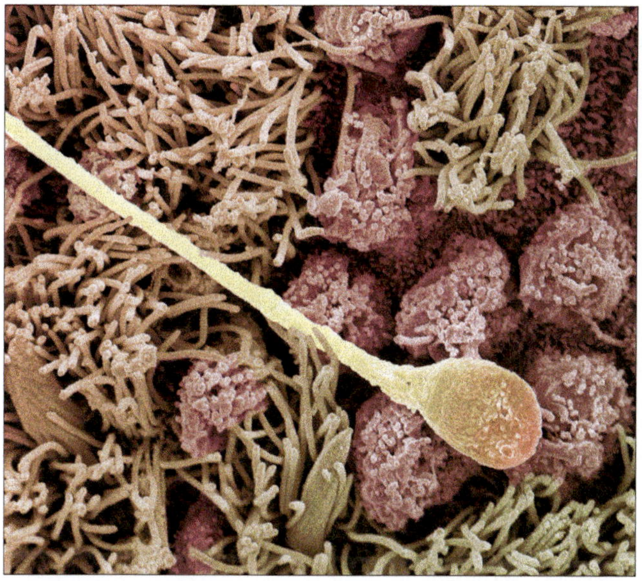

Figure 13.17 This sperm cell is swimming over the surfaces of the ciliated cells in the oviduct.

Sperm can only swim at a rate about 4 mm per minute, so it takes quite a while for them to get as far as the oviducts. Many will never get there at all. But one ejaculation deposits about a million sperm in the vagina, so there is a good chance that some of them will reach the egg.

One sperm enters the egg. Only the head of the sperm goes in; the tail is left outside. The nucleus of the sperm fuses with the nucleus of the egg. This is **fertilisation** (Figure **13.19**).

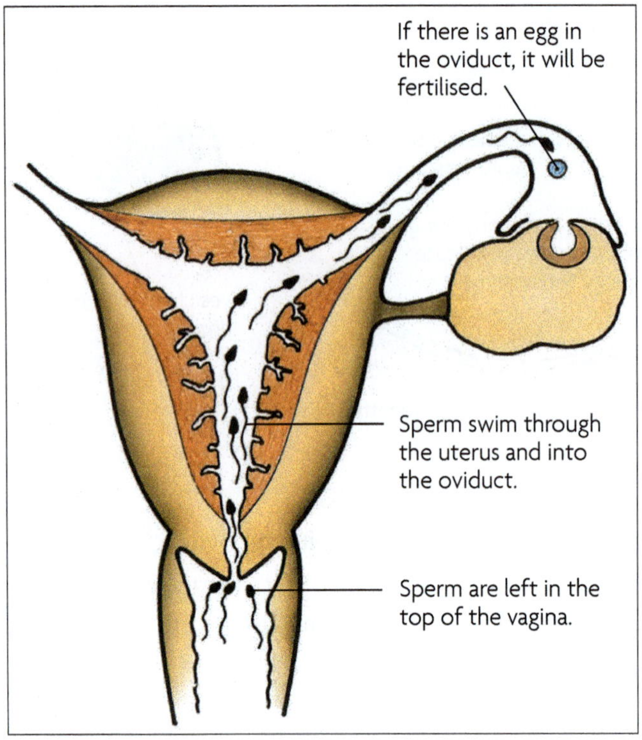
If there is an egg in the oviduct, it will be fertilised.
Sperm swim through the uterus and into the oviduct.
Sperm are left in the top of the vagina.

Figure 13.18 How sperm get to the egg (sperm and egg drawn to different scale).

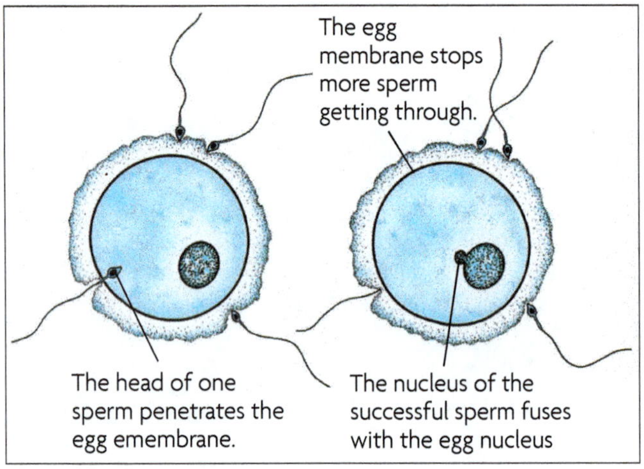
The egg membrane stops more sperm getting through.
The head of one sperm penetrates the egg emembrane.
The nucleus of the successful sperm fuses with the egg nucleus

Figure 13.19 Fertilisation.

As soon as the successful sperm enters the egg, the egg membrane becomes impenetrable, so that no other sperm can get in. The unsuccessful sperm will all die.

13.16 The zygote implants in the uterus wall.

When the sperm nucleus and the egg nucleus have fused together, they form a zygote. The zygote continues to move slowly down the oviduct. As it goes, it divides by mitosis. After several hours, it has formed a ball of cells. This is called an **embryo**. The embryo obtains food from the yolk of the egg.

FACT! Length for length, a sperm swimming up the uterus travels as fast as a nuclear submarine.

It takes several hours for the embryo to reach the uterus, and by this time it is a ball of 16 or 32 cells. The uterus has a thin, spongy lining, and the embryo sinks into it. This is called **implantation** (Figure 13.20).

13.17 The embryo's life-support system is its placenta.

The cells in the embryo, now buried in the soft wall of the uterus, continue to divide. As the embryo grows, a **placenta** also grows, which connects it to the wall of the uterus (Figure 13.21). The placenta is soft and dark red, and has finger-like projections called villi. The villi fit closely into the uterus wall.

The placenta is joined to the embryo by the **umbilical cord**. Inside the cord are two arteries and a vein. The arteries take blood from the embryo into the placenta, and the vein returns the blood to the embryo.

In the placenta are capillaries filled with the embryo's blood (Figure 13.22). In the wall of the uterus are large spaces filled with the mother's blood. The embryo's and mother's blood do not mix. They are separated by the wall of the placenta. But they are brought very close together, because the wall of the placenta is very thin.

Oxygen and food materials in the mother's blood diffuse across the placenta into the embryo's blood, and are then carried along the umbilical cord to the embryo. Carbon

Questions

13.17 What is the name for the narrow opening between the uterus and the vagina?

13.18 Where is the prostate gland, and what is its function?

13.19 What is a Graafian follicle?

13.20 Explain how ovulation happens.

13.21 Where are sperm made?

13.22 How does an egg travel along the oviduct?

13.23 What is semen?

13.24 Where does fertilisation take place?

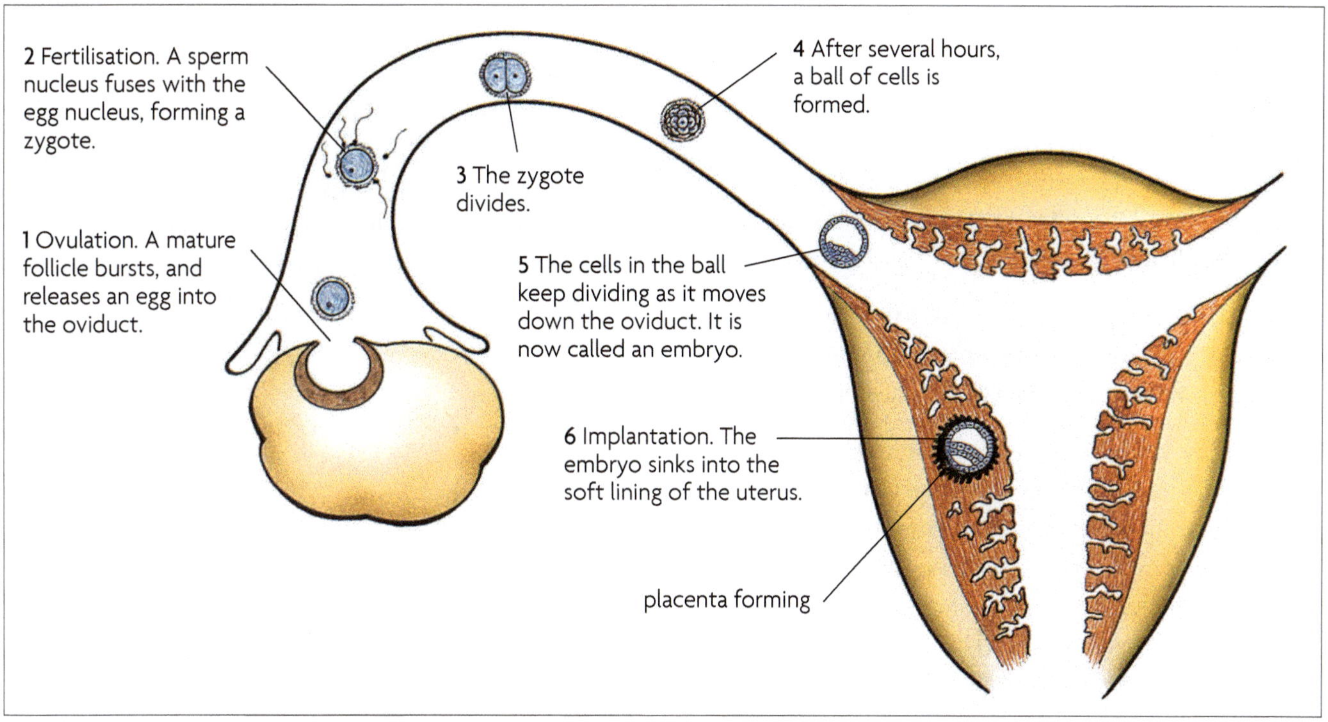

2 Fertilisation. A sperm nucleus fuses with the egg nucleus, forming a zygote.
3 The zygote divides.
4 After several hours, a ball of cells is formed.
1 Ovulation. A mature follicle bursts, and releases an egg into the oviduct.
5 The cells in the ball keep dividing as it moves down the oviduct. It is now called an embryo.
6 Implantation. The embryo sinks into the soft lining of the uterus.
placenta forming

Figure 13.20 Stages leading to implantation.

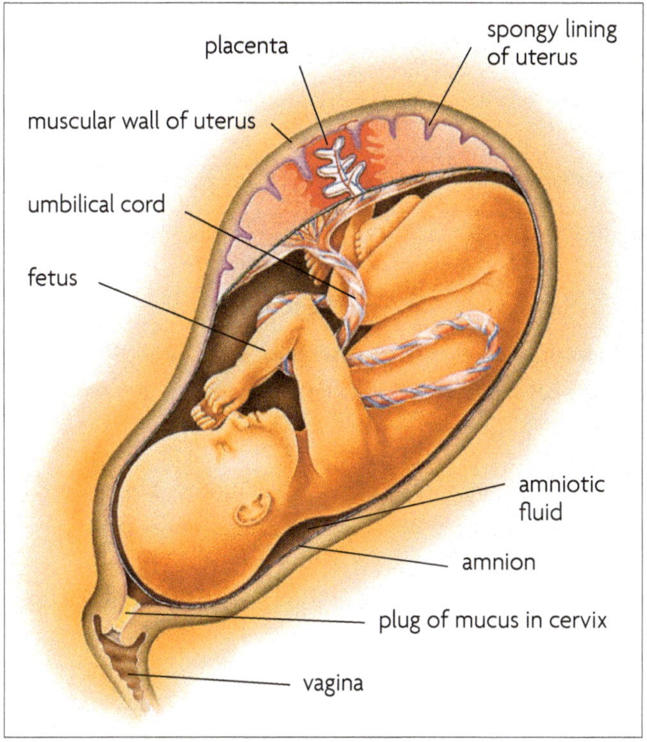

Figure 13.21 Side view of fetus in the uterus.

dioxide and waste materials diffuse the other way, and are carried away in the mother's blood. As the embryo grows, the placenta grows too. By the time the baby is born, the placenta will be a flat disc, about 12 cm in diameter, and 3 cm thick.

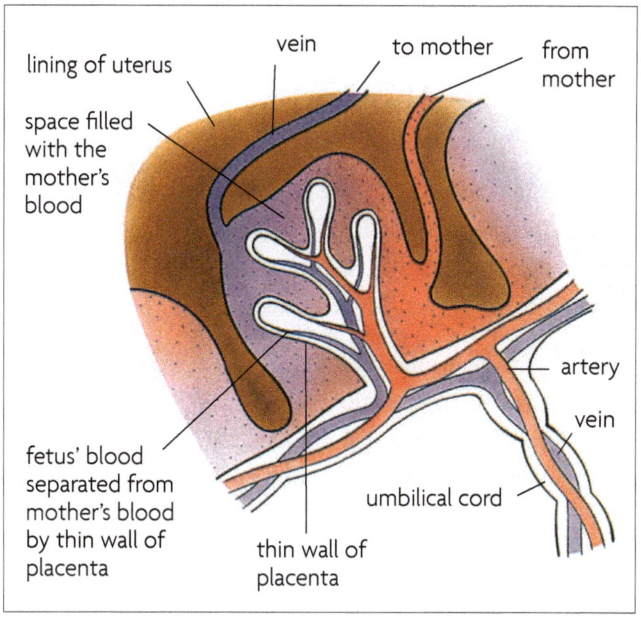

Figure 13.22 Part of the placenta.

13.18 An amnion protects the embryo.

The embryo is surrounded by a strong membrane, called the **amnion**. Inside the amnion is a liquid called **amniotic fluid**. This fluid helps to support the embryo, and to protect it.

13.19 A baby develops during gestation.

No-one fully understands how the cells in the ball which embedded itself in the wall of the uterus become arranged to form a baby. The cells gradually divide and grow. By eleven weeks after fertilisation, they have become organised into all the different organs. By this stage the embryo is called a **fetus**.

After this, the fetus just grows. It takes nine months before it is ready to be born. This length of time between fertilisation and birth is called the **gestation period**.

The fetus is entirely dependent on materials passed to and from the mother's blood by way of the placenta. So the mother has to be careful about the substances that reach her blood. For example, if she smokes, harmful nicotine and carbon monoxide enter the bloodstream. The exact mechanism is not known, but there is evidence which suggests that smoking may result in premature birth and a baby of reduced birthweight.

13.20 Muscular contractions cause birth.

A few weeks before birth, the fetus usually turns over in the uterus, so that it is lying head downwards. Its head lies just over the opening of the cervix.

Birth begins when the strong muscles in the wall of the uterus start to contract. This is called **labour**. To begin with, the contractions of the muscles slowly stretch the opening of the cervix (Figure **13.23**).

After several hours, the cervix is wide enough for the head of the baby to pass through. Now, the muscles start to push the baby down through the cervix and the vagina. This part of the birth happens quite quickly.

The baby is still attached to the uterus by the umbilical cord and the placenta. Now that it is in the open air, it can breathe for itself, so the placenta is no longer needed. The placenta falls away from the wall of the uterus, and passes out through the vagina. It is called the **afterbirth**.

The umbilical cord is cut, and clamped just above the point where it joins the baby. This is completely painless, because there are no nerves in the cord. The stump of the cord forms the baby's navel.

FACT!

The mammal with the longest gestation period is the Asian elephant – it is 609 days on average, but may last as long as 760 days

The contractions of the muscles of the uterus are sometimes painful. They feel rather like cramp. However, there is now no need for any mother to suffer really bad pain. She can help herself a lot by preparing her body with exercises before labour begins, by breathing in a special way during labour, and she can also be given pain-killing drugs if she needs them.

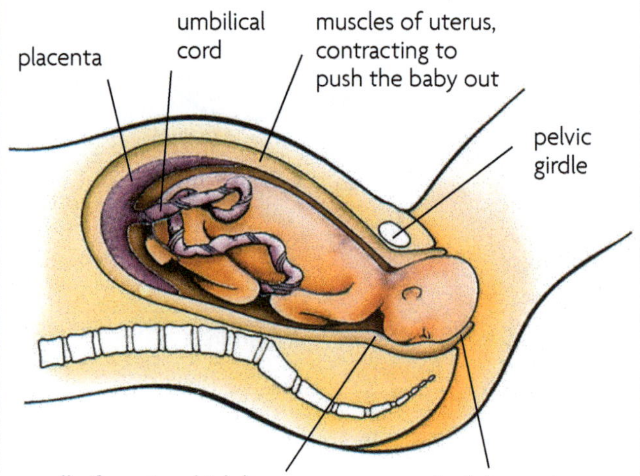

Figure 13.23 Birth.

13.21 Mammals care for their young.

Although it has been developing for nine months, a human baby is very helpless when it is born. Usually both parents help to care for it.

During pregnancy, the glands in the mother's breasts will have become larger. Soon after the birth of the baby, they begin to make milk. This is called **lactation**. Lactation happens in all mammals, but not in other animals (Figure **13.24**).

Milk contains all the nutrients that the baby needs. It also contains antibodies (section **16.22**) which will help the baby to resist infection.

As well as being fed, the baby needs to be kept warm. Because it is so small, a baby has a large surface area in relation to its volume (Figure **6.5**, page **95**), so it loses heat very quickly.

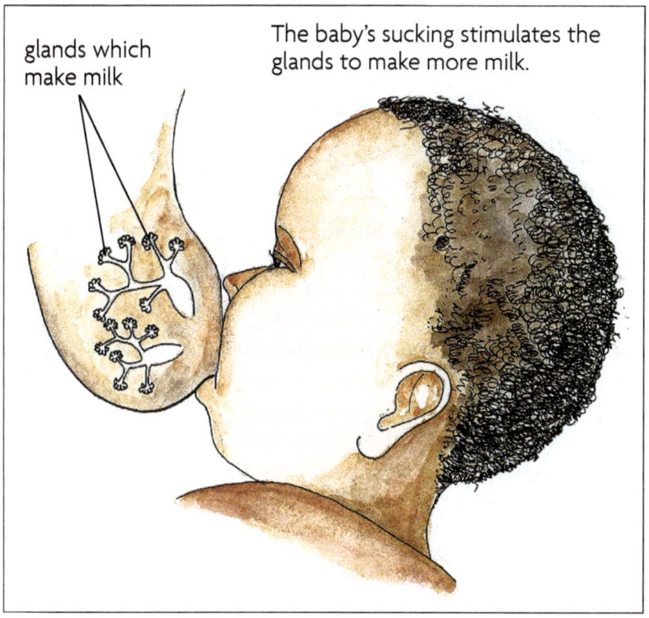

glands which
make milk
The baby's sucking stimulates the
glands to make more milk.

Figure 13.24 Lactation.

It is extremely important that a young baby is cared for emotionally, as well as physically. Babies need a lot of close contact with their parents.

Most mammals care for their young by feeding them and keeping them warm. In humans, parental care also involves teaching the baby and young child how to look after itself, and how to live in society. This continues into its 'teens' – a much longer time than for any other animal.

FACT!

The most children one woman has ever had is 69. A Russian woman who lived between 1707 and 1782 had sixteen pairs of twins, seven sets of triplets and four sets of quadruplets, all born between 1725 and 1765.

13.22 The menstrual cycle is controlled by hormones.

Usually, one egg is released into the oviduct every month in an adult woman. Before the egg is released, the lining of the uterus becomes thick and spongy, to prepare itself for a fertilised egg. It is full of tiny blood vessels, ready to supply the embryo with food and oxygen if it should arrive.

If the egg is not fertilised, it is dead by the time it reaches the uterus. It does not sink into the spongy wall, but continues onwards, down through the vagina. As the spongy lining is not needed now, it gradually disintegrates. It, too, is slowly lost through the vagina. This is called **menstruation**, or a period. It usually lasts for about five days.

After menstruation, the lining of the uterus builds up again, so that it will be ready to receive the next egg, if it is fertilised.

The menstrual cycle is controlled by hormones. Female sex hormones are called **oestrogens**. They regulate the development of the female sex organs, and the female secondary sexual characteristics.

Questions

13.25 What is formed when an egg and sperm fuse together?

13.26 What kind of cell division takes place in the growth of an embryo?

13.27 From where does the very young embryo obtain its food?

13.28 What is implantation?

13.29 What is a fetus?

13.30 How is the fetus connected to the placenta?

13.31 Describe two ways in which the structure of the placenta helps diffusion between the mother's and the fetus's blood to take place quickly.

13.32 List two substances which pass from the mother's blood into the fetus's blood.

13.33 What is the function of the amnion?

13.34 How long is the gestation period in humans?

13.35 Describe what happens to each of the following during the birth of a baby:
a muscles in the uterus wall
b the cervix
c the placenta.

13.36 Why must babies be kept warm?

Figures **13.25** and **13.26** illustrate what happens during the human menstrual cycle. First, a follicle develops inside an ovary. The developing follicle secretes a hormone called **oestrogen**. The oestrogen makes the lining of the uterus grow thick and spongy.

When the follicle is fully developed, ovulation takes place. The follicle stops secreting oestrogen. It becomes a **corpus luteum**. The corpus luteum starts to secrete another hormone, called **progesterone**.

Progesterone keeps the uterus lining thick and spongy, and well supplied with blood, in case the egg is fertilised. If it is not fertilised, then the corpus luteum gradually disappears. Progesterone is not secreted any more, and so the lining of the uterus breaks down. Menstruation happens. A new follicle starts to develop in the ovary, and the cycle begins again.

But if the egg is fertilised, the corpus luteum does not degenerate so quickly. It carries on secreting progesterone until the embryo sinks into the uterus wall, and a placenta develops. Then the placenta secretes progesterone and carries on secreting it all through the pregnancy. The progesterone maintains the uterus lining, so that menstruation does not happen during the pregnancy.

13.23 Sexual maturity is reached at puberty.

The time when a person approaches sexual maturity is called **adolescence**. Sperm production begins in a boy and ovulation in a girl.

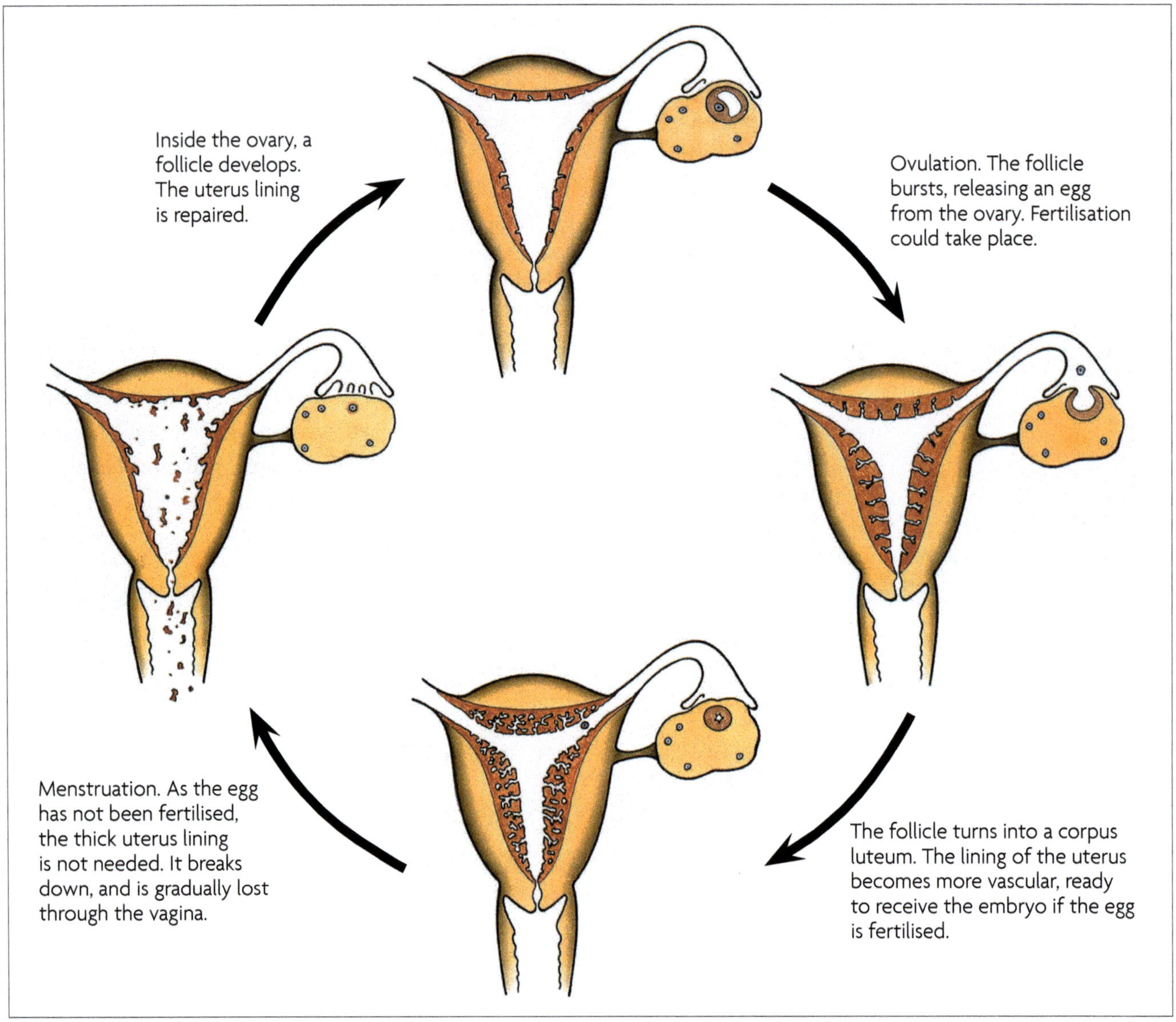

Figure 13.25 The menstrual cycle.

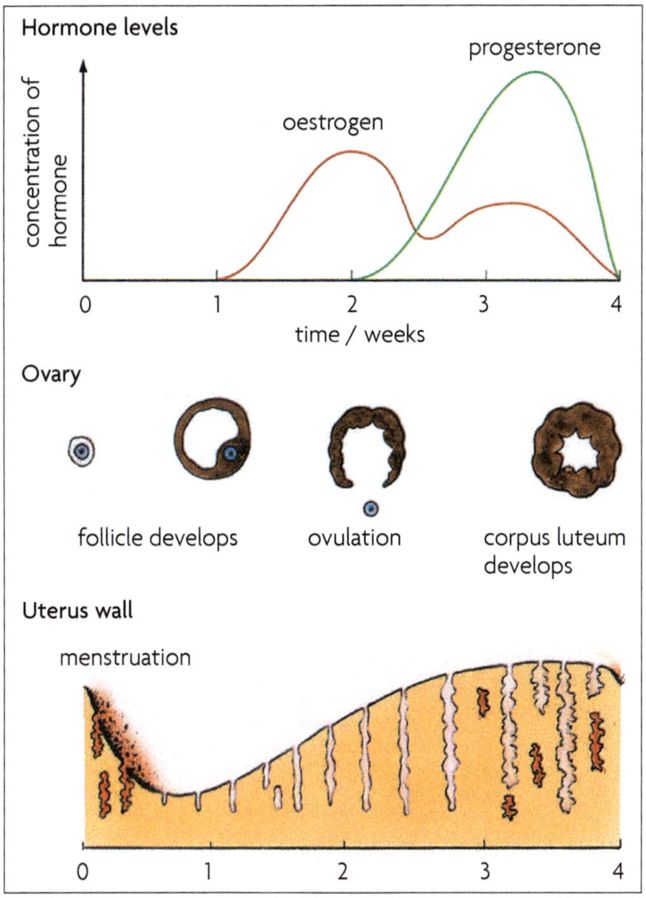

Figure 13.26 Hormones and the menstrual cycle.

During adolescence, the **secondary sexual characteristics** develop. In boys, these include growth of facial and pubic hair, breaking of the voice, and muscular development. In girls, pubic hair begins to grow, the breasts develop, and the pelvic girdle becomes broader.

These changes are brought about by hormones. As we have seen, the male hormones are called androgens of which the most important is testosterone, and the female hormones are called oestrogens.

The point at which sexual maturity is reached is called **puberty**. This is often several years earlier for girls than for boys.

13.24 Sexual maturity brings with it social responsibility.

The changes taking place at puberty bring with them more awareness of ourselves as boys and girls, and increased attraction between the sexes is a normal and natural outcome. Sexual maturity does not, however, mean adulthood, because our emotional development is not complete. In spite of this, it is a time for taking on added social responsibility. Young people need to be concerned about several issues relating to sexual functions:

- birth control
- responsible versus irresponsible parenthood
- the dangers of promiscuity including its association with cervical cancer
- sexually transmitted diseases and their effects.

13.25 Some diseases are spread by sexual intercourse.

Sexually transmitted diseases (STDs) are passed on by sexual intercourse. There are more than a dozen STDs. These occur most frequently in people aged between 14 and 24 years. Anyone having sex with an infected partner may become infected.

The chance of becoming infected increases with the number of sexual partners. Actually, the type of partner one chooses is more important than the number. Individuals who are indiscriminate in their choice of partners, or have sex with casual acquaintances, run a high risk of infection. This is because their partners are also less selective in choosing partners. Indiscriminate sex is more likely to lead to infection than sex with a steady partner in a loving relationship.

Gonorrhoea, syphilis, herpes genitalis and AIDS are all sexually transmitted diseases. They are discussed more fully in Chapter **16**.

Questions

13.37 Why does the uterus wall become thick and spongy before ovulation?

13.38 What happens if the egg is not fertilised?

13.39 What is meant by **(a)** adolescence, and **(b)** puberty?

13.40 What are androgens?

13.41 List two effects of androgens.

13.42 What are STDs?

13.43 How are sexually transmitted diseases avoided?

Birth control

13.26 Family planning is important.

Many Caribbean countries have organisations to advise people about family planning matters. The number of children people have should be manageable. This allows children to be given proper care, enough food and adequate attention. One of the main functions of a family planning centre is to advise people about methods of birth control.

13.27 Birth control prevents pregnancy.

There are many methods of birth control and new ones are being developed all the time. The main objective of birth control is to prevent a sperm fertilising an egg. Some methods work by preventing the egg and sperm from meeting, other methods work by preventing the egg from leaving the ovary, by changing the environment of the uterus or by restricting mating times. What methods a couple use will depend upon their own circumstances and also their personal beliefs.

13.28 There are several ways of preventing the egg and sperm meeting.

A man may cover his penis, when it becomes erect, with a thin rubber sheath or **condom**. The sperm are caught in the end of the condom when they are ejaculated, and so do not reach the egg. A woman may also wear a condom (Figure 13.27). Female condoms are thin sheaths of rubber or polyurethane with rings at both ends. They are inserted into the vagina before intercourse, with the open end outside the vagina. A woman may also use a **diaphragm** or rubber cap which fits over the cervix and covers the entrance to the uterus. Both mechanisms act as barriers and prevent sperm in her vagina from reaching the uterus.

When a couple decide to have no more children, one of the partners may be **sterilised** (Figure 13.28). This means having surgery to prevent eggs or sperm from leaving the body. The operation for the male is called a vasectomy. It is a simple procedure involving cutting and tying the sperm duct from each testis. A woman can be sterilised by cutting and tying the two oviducts. This is, however, a more difficult and complicated operation.

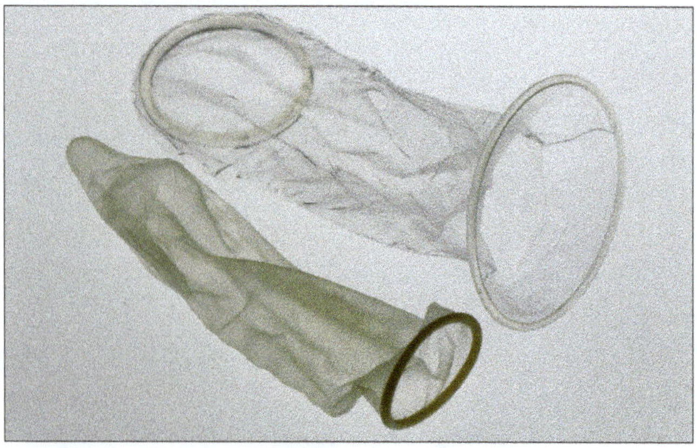

Figure 13.27 Condoms also give protection against sexually transmitted diseases.

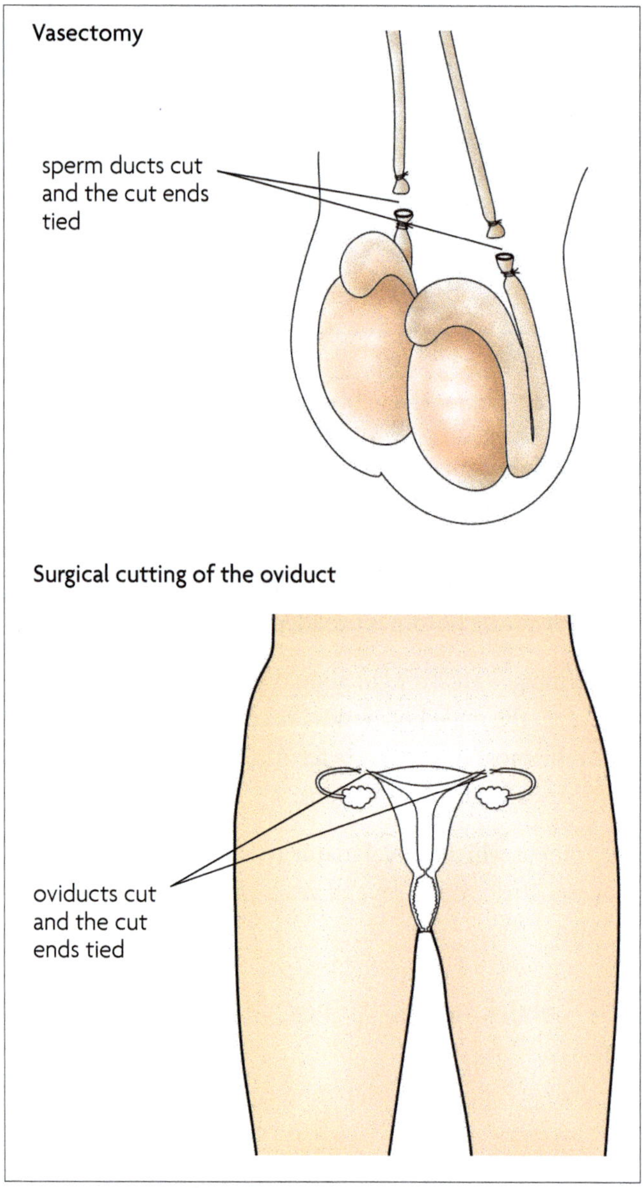

Figure 13.28 Surgical methods of birth control.

13.29 The pill prevents the egg from leaving the ovary.

Contraceptive pills contain hormones similar to those produced during the menstrual cycle. These hormones prevent the release of the egg from the ovary. There are many different kinds of contraceptive pill. Each individual woman has to find the type which suits her. The pill is a very reliable form of contraception, provided the instructions on the packet are followed closely.

13.30 The coil changes the environment of the uterus.

The **coil** is a small spring-shaped structure made of plastic or copper (Figure **13.29**). It must be inserted by a doctor because it fits inside the uterus, and may remain in place for up to five years. As it fits inside the uterus, it is called an intra-uterine device (**IUD**). The coil interrupts the preparation of the uterus for the fertilised egg and so prevents implantation. The coil is a reliable method of birth control.

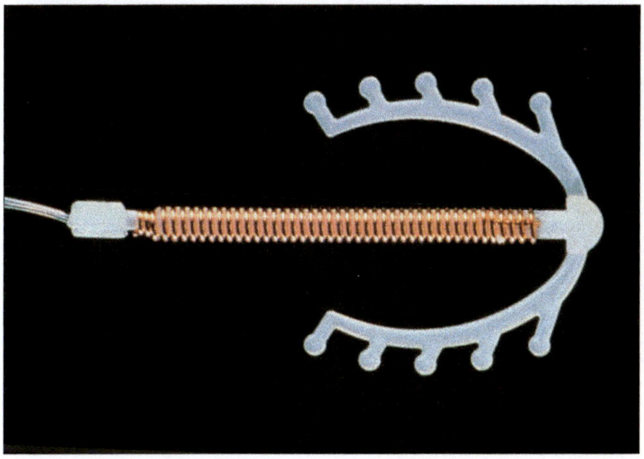

Figure 13.29 An intra-uterine device or IUD.

13.31 The 'safe period' method is not reliable.

The use of the 'safe period' (sometimes called the rhythm method) is one of the most common methods of birth control. It depends on a detailed knowledge of the female's menstrual cycle. However, it is not a very reliable method. Fertilisation can only take place after ovulation and while the egg is still in the female reproductive system. This means that it is unsafe to have intercourse on the three or four days either side of the ovulation time. However, the length of the menstrual cycle may vary. It is this that makes this method of birth control unreliable.

Some women are able to predict when ovulation is expected to happen by keeping careful record of their temperature. Figure **13.30** shows how this changes throughout one cycle. You can see that the temperature rises over about three days during the period in which ovulation occurs.

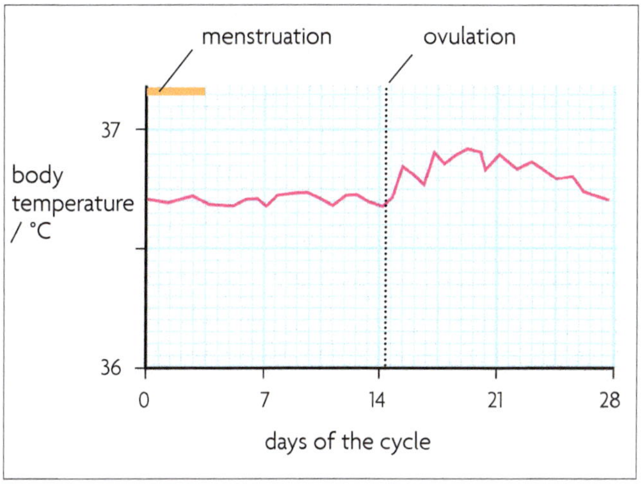

Figure 13.30 Body temperature through the menstrual cycle.

13.32 New methods are being discovered all the time.

Injectable hormone contraceptives now exist. They have similar effects to the 'pill', but are taken by the woman at intervals of many weeks. Another type of contraceptive has been produced called the 'morning-after pill'. It is taken by mouth and prevents implantation of the fertilised egg. A woman may also now have capsules of synthetic progesterone placed under the skin (usually of the inner upper arm). This is believed to be effective for up to five years. However, the long-term effects of these newer methods of birth control are not yet fully understood.

Sexual reproduction in flowering plants

13.33 Flowers are for sexual reproduction.

Many flowering plants can reproduce in more than one way. Often, they can reproduce asexually, by vegetative propagation (section **13.4**) and also sexually, by means of flowers.

The function of a flower is to make gametes, and to ensure that fertilisation will take place. Figure **13.31** illustrates the structure of a flower. Figure **13.32** shows flowers of Pride of Barbados which makes both male and female gametes, so it is a hermaphrodite flower. Most, but not all, flowers are hermaphrodite.

On the outside of the flower are the **sepals**. The sepals protect the flower while it is a bud. Sepals are normally green.

Just inside the sepals are the **petals**. These are brightly coloured. The petals attract insects or birds to the flower. The petals of some flowers have lines running from top to bottom. These lines are called **guide-lines**, because they guide insects to the base of the petal. Here, there is a gland called a **nectary**. The nectary makes a sugary liquid called nectar, which insects feed on.

Inside the petals are the **stamens**. These are the male parts of the flower. Each stamen is made up of a long **filament**, with an **anther** at the top. The anthers contain **pollen grains**, which contain the male gametes.

The female part of the flower is in the centre. It consists of one or more **carpels.** A carpel contains an **ovary**. Inside the ovary are many **ovules**, which contain the female gametes. At the top of the ovary is the **style**, with a **stigma** at the tip. The function of the stigma is to catch pollen grains. The female parts of different kinds of flower vary. One of the differences is the arrangement of the ovules in the ovary. Figure **13.33** shows one arrangement.

Figure 13.32 Pride of Barbados flower.

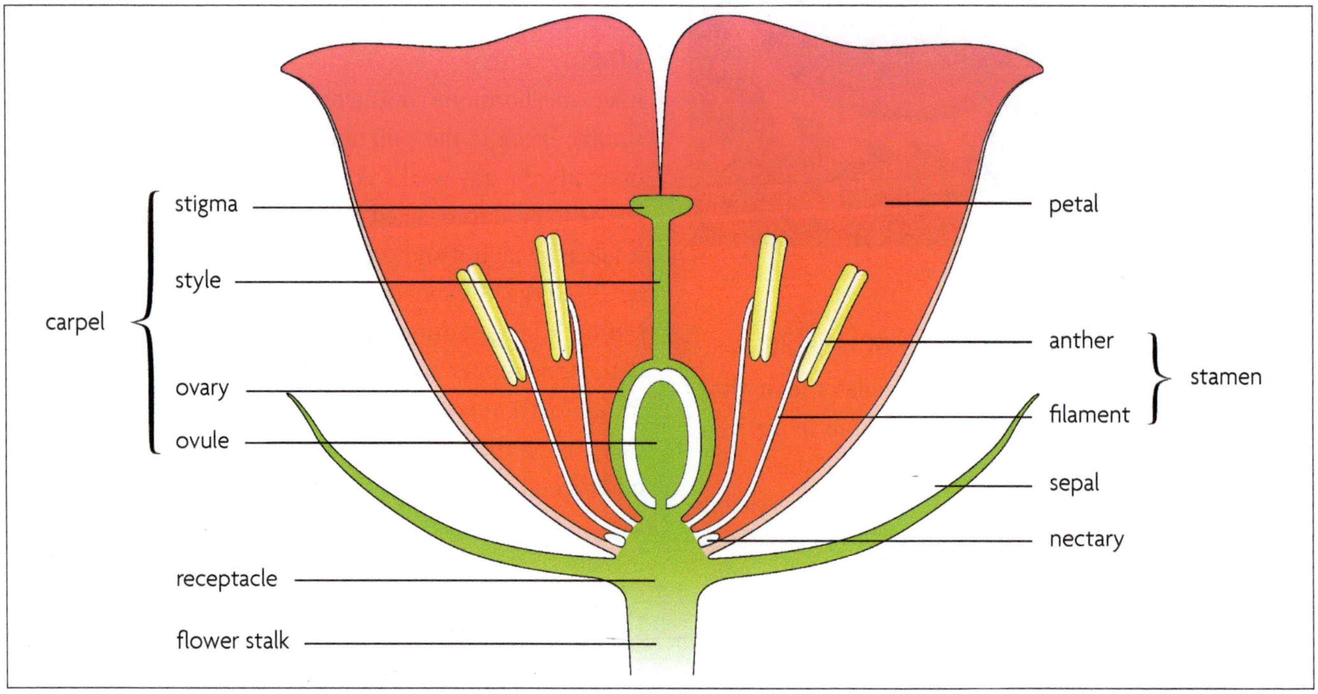

Figure 13.31 A generalised flower.

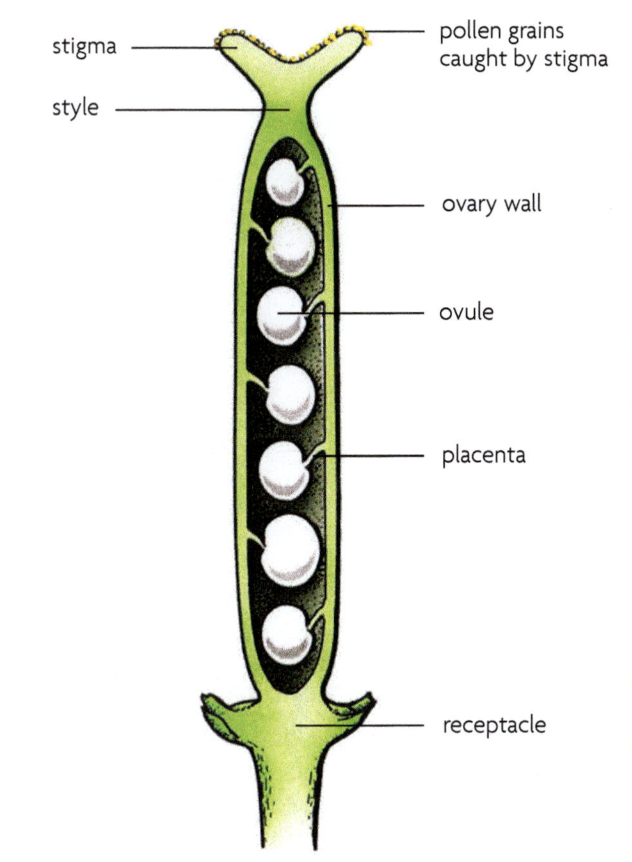

Figure 13.33 Section through the female part of a flower showing a linear arrangement of ovules.

13.34 Pollen grains contain male gametes.

The male gametes are inside the pollen grains, which are made in the anthers.

Figure **13.34a** (overleaf) illustrates a young anther, as it looks before the flower bud opens. You can see in Figure **13.34b** that the anther has four spaces or pollen sacs inside it. Some of the cells around the edge of the pollen sacs divide by meiosis to make pollen grains. When the flower bud opens, the anthers split open (Figure **13.34c**). Now the pollen is on the outside of the anther.

The pollen looks like a fine powder. It is often yellow. Under the microscope, you can see the shape of individual grains (Figure **13.35**, overleaf). Pollen grains from different kinds of flowers have different shapes. Each grain is surrounded by a hard coat, so that it can survive in difficult conditions if necessary. The coat protects the male gametes that are inside the grains, as the pollen is carried from one flower to another.

Investigation 13.2
Investigating the structure of a flower

SBA skills

Observation/Recording/Reporting *Drawing*

During this investigation, make large, labelled drawings of the structures that you observe.

1. Take an open, fresh-looking flower. Can you suggest two ways in which the flower advertises itself to insects?
2. Gently remove the sepals from the outside of the flower. Look at the sepals on a flower bud, near the top of the stem. What is the function of the sepals?
3. Now remove the petals from your flower. Make a labelled drawing of one of them, to show the markings. What is the function of these markings?
4. Find the stamens. If you have a young flower, there will be pollen on the anthers at the top of the stamens. Dust some onto a microscope slide, and look at it under a microscope. Draw a few pollen grains.
5. Now remove the stamens. What do you think is the function of the filaments?
6. Using a hand lens, try to find the nectaries at the bottom of the flower. What is their function?
7. The carpel is now all that is left of the flower. Find the ovary, style and stigma. Look at the stigma under a binocular microscope or a lens. What is its function, and how is it adapted to perform it?
8. Using a sharp razor blade, make a clean cut lengthways through the ovary, style and stigma. You have made a longitudinal section. Find the ovules inside the ovary. How big are they? What colour are they? About how many are there?

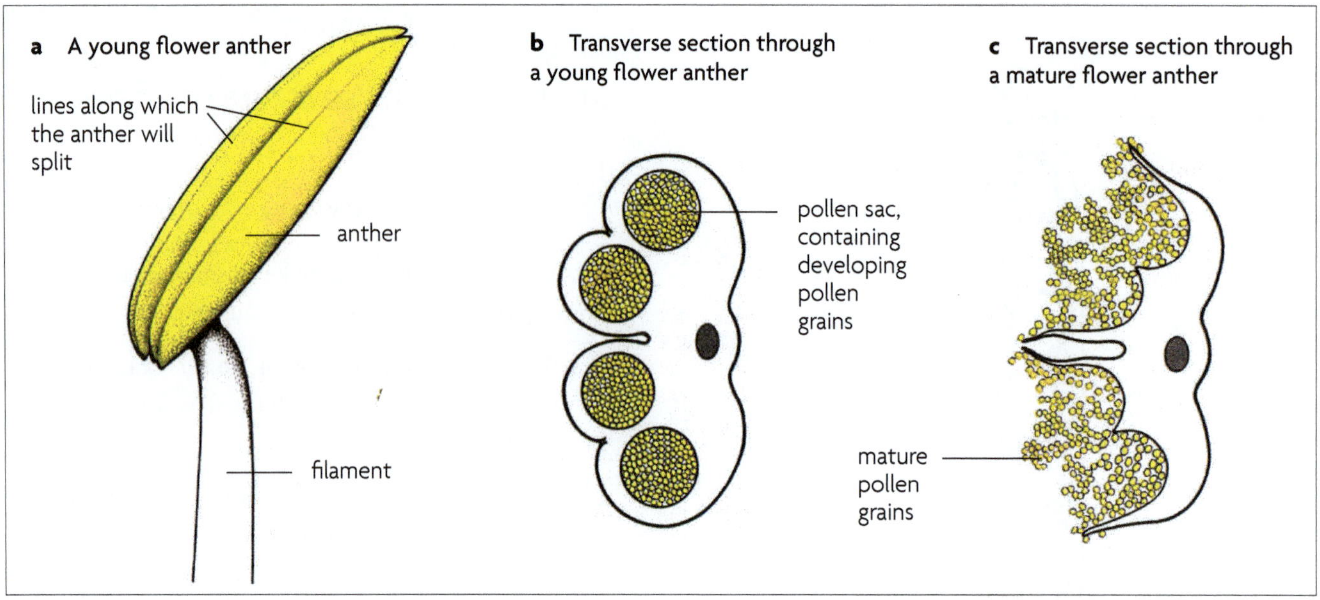

Figure 13.34 How pollen is made.

Figure 13.35 a These pollen grains are from a flower of a melon plant. They have been magnified about 600 times. **b** This photo of an anther of a rape plant was taken using a scanning electron microscope. You can see the pollen grains bursting out of a split in the anther.

13.35 Each ovule contains a female gamete.

The female gametes are inside the ovules, in the ovary. They have been made by meiosis. Each ovule contains just one gamete.

13.36 Pollen must be carried from anther to stigma.

For fertilisation to take place, the male gametes must travel to the female gametes. The first stage of this journey is for pollen to be taken from the anther where it was made, to a stigma. This is called **pollination**.

Pollination is often carried out by insects (Figure 13.36). Insects such as honey bees come to the flowers, attracted by their colour and strong sweet scent. The bee follows the guide-lines to the nectaries, brushing past the anthers as it goes. Some of the pollen will stick to its body.

The bee will probably then go to another flower, looking for more nectar. Some of the pollen it picked up at the first flower will stick onto the stigma of the second flower when the bee brushes past it. The stigma is sticky, and many pollen grains get stuck on it. If the second flower is from the same species of plant as the first, pollination has taken place.

Birds are also important pollinators. Flowers that are pollinated by birds are often red, and have a strong landing platform for the bird to rest on as it reaches inside the flower to get nectar (Figure 13.37).

Figure 13.36 The bee has come to the flower to collect nectar. Pollen will get stuck to its body, and the bee will then carry this to the next flower it visits.

Figure 13.37 Hummingbirds act as pollinators. Many bird-pollinated flowers are red.

13.37 Flowers can be self- or cross-pollinated.

Sometimes, pollen is carried to the stigma of the same flower, or to another flower on the same plant. This is called **self-pollination**.

If pollen is taken to a flower on a different plant of the same species, this is called **cross-pollination**. If pollen lands on the stigma of a *different species* of plant, it usually dies.

13.38 Some flowers are wind-pollinated.

In some plants, it is the wind which carries the pollen between flowers. Figure **13.38** (overleaf) shows a grass flower, which is an example of a wind-pollinated flower.

Table **13.1** (overleaf) compares insect-pollinated and wind-pollinated flowers.

Investigation 13.3
Pollination

SBA skills

Observation/Recording/Reporting *Planning/Design*
Manipulation/Measurement
Analysis/Interpretation

You are going to design and carry out an investigation to test this hypothesis:

> Bees visit yellow flowers more often than flowers of other colours.

You will need to carry out this investigation outdoors. It will be much easier to control variables if you make artificial flowers rather than using real ones. You can make them using coloured plastic to make 'petals', surrounding a central area where you can put a little pot of sugar solution. You will need to do your experiment on a sunny day, when there are plenty of bees flying.

Remember to think about controlling variables. Think carefully about exactly how you will count the bee visits, how you will record them and how you will display your results.

Write a simple conclusion from your results, and then discuss the results in the light of what you know about pollination. (You might also be interested in finding out about how bees see colour.) Evaluate your experiment, and suggest improvements you could make.

Table 13.1 A comparison between insect-pollinated and wind-pollinated flowers

Insect-pollinated, e.g. *Crotalaria*	Wind-pollinated, e.g. sugarcane
large, conspicuous petals, often with guide-lines	small, inconspicuous petals, or no petals at all
often strongly scented	no scent
often have nectaries at the base of petals	no nectaries
anthers inside flower, where insect has to brush past them to reach nectar	anthers dangling outside the flower, where they catch the wind
stigma inside flower, where insect has to brush past it to reach nectar	stigmas large and feathery and dangling outside the flower, where pollen in the air may land on it
sticky or spiky pollen grains, which stick to insects	smooth, light pollen, which can be blown in the wind
quite large quantities of pollen made, because some will be eaten or will be delivered to the wrong kind of flower	very large quantities of pollen made, because most will be blown away and lost

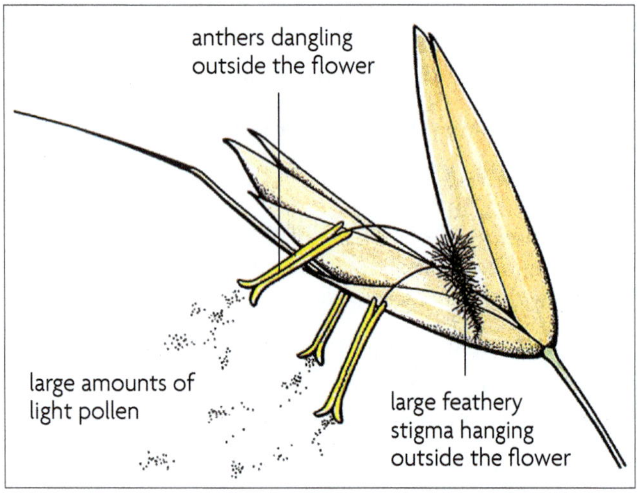

Figure 13.38 An example of a wind-pollinated flower.

13.39 Pollen tubes take male gametes to ovules.

After pollination, the male gamete inside the pollen grain on the stigma still has not reached the female gamete. The female gamete is inside the ovule, and the ovule is inside the ovary.

If it has landed on the right kind of stigma, the pollen grain begins to grow a tube. You can try growing some pollen tubes, in Investigation 13.4. The pollen tube grows down through the style and the ovary, towards the ovule (Figure 13.39). It secretes enzymes to digest a pathway through the style.

The ovule is surrounded by several layers of cells called the **integuments**. At one end, there is a small hole in the integuments, called the micropyle. The pollen tube grows through the micropyle, into the ovule.

The male gamete travels along the pollen tube, and into the ovule. It fuses with the female gamete. **Fertilisation** has now taken place.

One pollen grain can only fertilise one ovule. If there are many ovules in the ovary, then many pollen grains will be needed to fertilise them all.

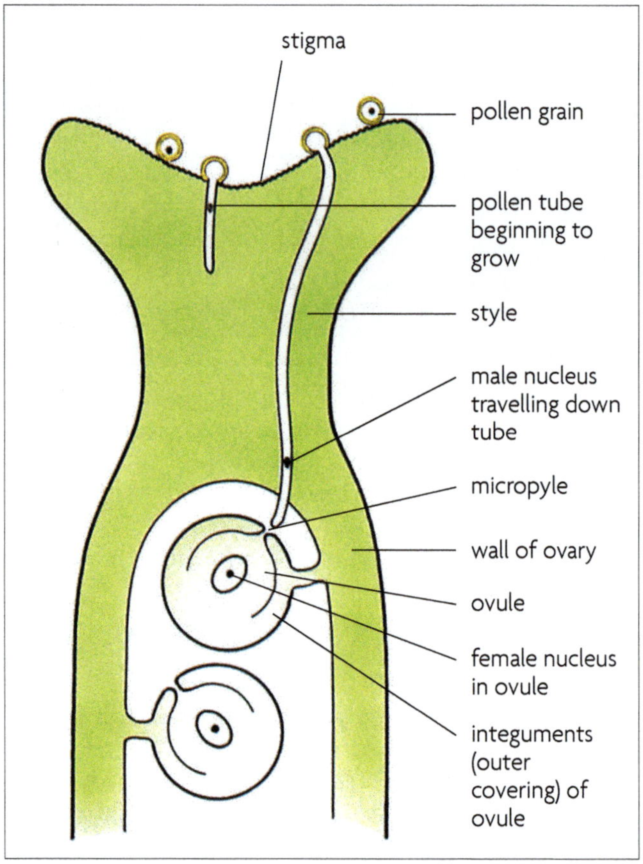

Figure 13.39 Fertilisation in a flower.

13.40 Fertilised ovules become seeds.

Once the ovules have been fertilised, many of the parts of the flower are not needed any more. The sepals, petals and stamens have all done their job. They wither, and fall off.

Inside the ovary, the ovules start to grow. Each ovule now contains a **zygote**, which was formed at fertilisation. The zygote divides by mitosis to form an **embryo plant**. The structure of the embryo is shown in Figure **12.5** (page **215**).

The ovule is now called a **seed**. The integuments of the ovule become hard and dry, to form the **testa** of the seed. Water is withdrawn from the seed, so that it becomes dormant (section **12.6**).

The ovary also grows. It is now called a **fruit**. The wall of the fruit is called a **pericarp**.

13.41 Fruits protect and disperse seeds.

The function of the fruit is to protect the seeds inside it until they are ripe, and then to help disperse the seeds.

Dispersal of seeds is important, because it prevents too many plants growing close together. If this happens, they compete for light, water and nutrients, so that none of them can grow properly. Dispersal also allows the plant to colonise new areas.

Fruits and seeds are dispersed by animals and water and through the air. Some examples are shown in Figures **13.40** to **13.43** (pages **250** and **251**).

Investigation 13.4
Growing pollen tubes

SBA skills

Observation/Recording/Reporting
Manipulation/Measurement
Analysis/Interpretation

When a stigma is ripe, it secretes a fluid which stimulates pollen grains on it to grow tubes. The fluid contains sugar. In this investigation, you can try germinating different kinds of pollen grains in different concentrations of sugar solution.

It is best if the class is divided into groups. Each group should use sugar solution of just one concentration.

1. Collect four cavity slides. Using your finger, make a neat ring of Vaseline® around the outer edge of each cavity.
2. Stick a label on each slide. Write your initials on it, and the concentration of sugar solution your group is using.
3. Fill the cavity in each slide with sugar solution.
4. Choose one flower of each kind which has pollen on its anthers. Dust pollen from one flower onto the solution on one of your slides. Gently lower a cover slip over it, without squashing the Vaseline® ring. Write the name of the flower on the label.
5. Repeat step 4 with the other three flowers.
6. Place each slide in a warm incubator, and leave for at least an hour.
7. Set up a microscope. Examine each of your slides under the microscope. Look carefully for pollen tubes. Record your results in a table, and collect results from groups using other concentrations of sugar solution.

Questions

1. Why was a ring of Vaseline® put around the cavity in each slide?
2. In which solution did each of the four types of pollen germinate best?
3. Can you suggest why pollen dies if it lands on an unripe stigma, or a stigma of the wrong sort of flower?
4. Why do pollen grains grow tubes?

Figure 13.40 Coconuts are dispersed through water.

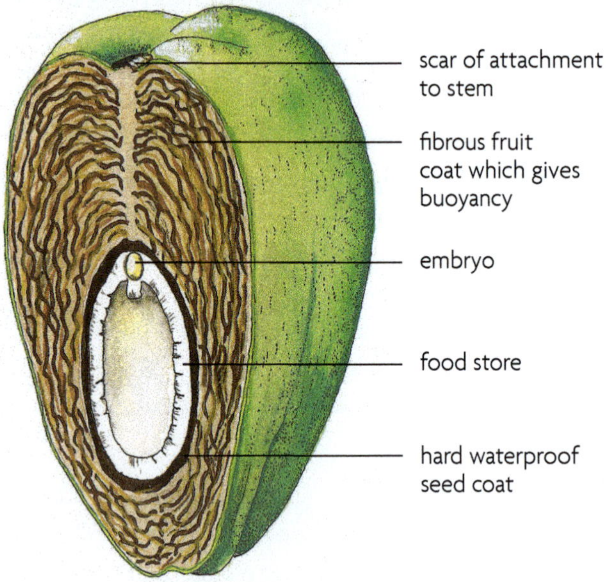

Figure 13.41 Longitudinal section of a coconut fruit.

FACT!

The plant with the largest seed is the Coco de Mer, which grows on the Seychelles islands in the Indian Ocean. The seeds (coconuts) weigh up to 18 kg.
The plants with the smallest seeds are epiphytic orchids. Some kinds have 1 235 000 seeds to the gram.

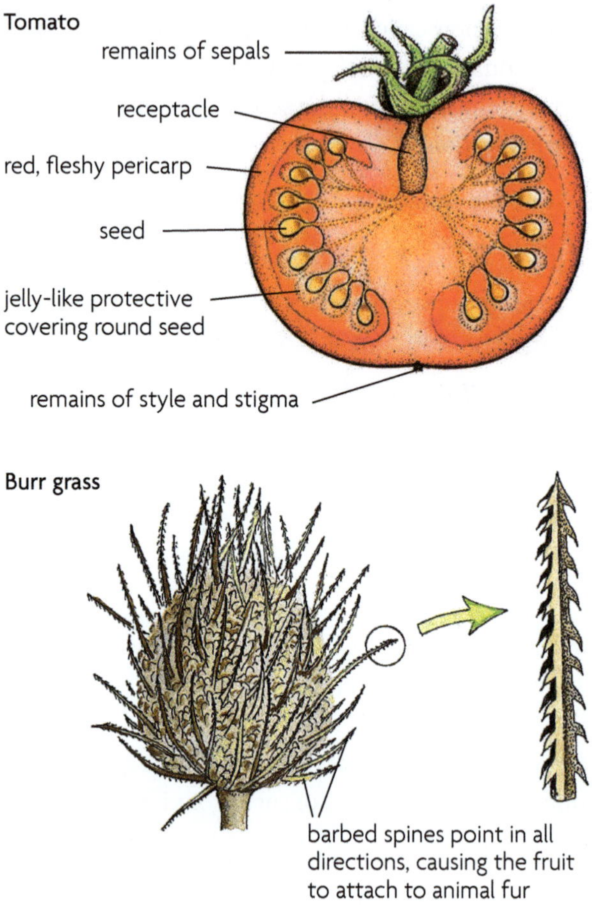

Figure 13.42 Fruits dispersed by animals.

Questions

13.44 What is the function of a flower?

13.45 In which part of a flower are male gametes made?

13.46 In which part of a flower are female gametes made?

13.47 What is pollination?

13.48 Why do wind-pollinated flowers usually produce more pollen than insect-pollinated ones?

13.49 After pollination, how does the male gamete reach the ovule?

13.50 What is a micropyle?

13.51 What happens to each of the following once a flower's female gametes have been fertilised?

a petals
b stamens
c zygote
d ovule
e integuments of the ovules
f ovary

Figure 13.43 Fruits dispersed through the air.

13.42 Fruits are ovaries after fertilisation.

Plants have an enormous variety of fruits, all adapted to disperse their seeds as effectively as possible. It is important to remember that, in biology, the word 'fruit' has a very particular meaning. Most people use the word to mean sweet fruits eaten as snacks or dessert. The fruits of tomato, pepper and beans are commonly called vegetables.

The biological definition of a fruit is an ovary after fertilisation, containing seeds. Barbados cherries, plums and oranges are true fruits, but so also are tomatoes. You can tell a fruit because it contains one or more seeds, and it has two scars - one where it was attached to the plant, and one where the style and stigma were attached to it.

Sometimes, it is not easy to tell a fruit from a seed. A seed, though, only has one scar, called the hilum, where it was joined to the fruit.

Sexual and asexual reproduction

13.43 Sexual reproduction produces variation.

This chapter has described some methods of asexual reproduction and sexual reproduction. Now that you know something about them, we can look in more detail at some of the important differences between them.

In asexual reproduction, some of the parent's cells divide by mitosis. This makes new cells that are genetically identical with the parent cell. They are clones. Asexual reproduction does not produce variation.

But in sexual reproduction, some of the parent's cells divide by meiosis. The new cells that are made are called gametes, and they have only half as many chromosomes as the parent cell. When two sets of chromosomes in the two gametes combine at fertilisation, a new combination of genes is produced. So sexual reproduction produces offspring that are genetically different from their parents.

13.44 Sexual and asexual reproduction each have their advantages.

Is it useful or not to have genetic variation among offspring? This depends on the circumstances.

Sometimes, it is a good thing not to have any variation. If a plant, for example, is growing well in a particular place, then it must be well adapted to its environment. If it's offspring all inherit the same genes, then they will be equally well adapted and are likely to grow well. This is especially true if there is plenty of space for them in that area; if it is getting crowded, then it may not be a good thing for the parent to produce new offspring that grow all around it.

Questions

13.52 Give two functions of a fruit.

13.53 List three different ways in which seeds may be dispersed, giving one example for each.

13.54 Give two differences between fruits and seeds.

13.55 Which of the following are fruits, and which are not? **(a)** orange, **(b)** tomato, **(c)** potato, **(d)** cabbage, **(e)** bean pod, **(f)** cucumber, **(g)** tamarind.

13.56 A navel orange is a seedless fruit. Can you explain why it is seedless?

Another advantage of asexual reproduction is that a single organism can reproduce on its own. It does not need to wait to be pollinated, or to find a mate. This can be good if there are not many of those organisms around – perhaps there is only a single one growing in an isolated place. In that case, asexual reproduction is definitely the best option. Do remember, though, that even a single plant may be able to reproduce sexually, by using self-pollination.

However, if the plant is not doing very well in its environment, or if a new disease has come along to which it is not resistant, then it could be an advantage for its offspring to be genetically different from it. There is a good chance that at least some of the offspring may be better adapted to that environment, or be resistant to that disease.

In flowering plants, sexual reproduction produces seeds, which are likely to be dispersed over a wide area. This spreads the offspring far away from the parents, so that they are less likely to compete with them. It also allows them to colonise new areas.

You will find out more about variation, and its importance for evolution, in Chapter **15**.

Key ideas

- Asexual reproduction involves cell division by mitosis, producing a group of genetically identical individuals called a clone.
- Sexual reproduction involves the production of genetically different gametes by meiosis. A male gamete fertilises a female gamete, producing a zygote which is genetically different from its parents.
- In humans, the male gametes are sperm and are made in the testes. During sexual intercourse, semen containing sperm passes out of the penis and into a woman's vagina.
- The female gametes are eggs and are made in the ovaries. After sexual intercourse, sperm swim through the cervix and uterus into the oviducts, where they may meet an egg. One sperm may fertilise the egg to produce a zygote.
- The zygote travels to the uterus and implants in the lining, growing into an embryo attached to the uterus wall via an umbilical cord and placenta. The placenta brings its blood very close to the mother's blood, so that nutrients and waste products can diffuse between them. The growing embryo is protected by amniotic fluid produced by the amnion.
- After birth, a young mammal is fed on milk from its mother. This provides it with exactly the correct balance of nutrients, as well as antibodies which protect it from infectious diseases.
- An egg is released from an ovary about once a month. If it is not fertilised, the thick lining of the uterus breaks down, in menstruation. The menstrual cycle is controlled by the hormones oestrogen and progesterone.
- Birth control helps a couple to avoid having unwanted children. There are natural, surgical, mechanical, barrier and hormonal methods, each of which has its own advantages and disadvantages to be weighed up when making the choice of which to use.
- In plants, the flowers are the reproductive organs. Male gametes are made inside pollen grains, produced by anthers. Female gametes are made inside ovules, produced by ovaries.
- The movement of pollen from an anther to a stigma is called pollination, and may be brought about by insects, birds or the wind.
- After landing on a suitable stigma, a pollen grain germinates and the gametes travel down the style to the ovules. Here, fertilisation takes place and a zygote is produced. The zygote develops into an embryo, and the ovule develops into a seed. The ovary develops into the fruit, containing the seeds which contain the embryos.
- Fruits are adapted to disperse seeds.

End-of-chapter questions

1 Match each of these words with its definition: zygote, mitosis, meiosis, gamete, pollination, fertilisation, pericarp, fruit, seed.

- a a sex cell, containing only half the normal number of chromosomes
- b an ovary after fertilisation
- c a diploid cell, formed by the fusion of two gametes
- d a type of cell division which produces daughter cells just like the parent cell
- e a type of cell division which produces daughter cells with only half the number of chromosomes of the parent cell
- f an ovary wall after fertilisation
- g the transfer of pollen from an anther to a stigma
- h an ovule after fertilisation
- i the fusion of two gametes

2 a Which type of cell division is involved in (i) the production of a new organism by asexual reproduction, (ii) the production of gametes, and (iii) the growth of a zygote?

- b With the aid of diagrams, describe one way in which a named plant naturally reproduces asexually.
- c What advantages are there to the plant in reproducing this way?
- d Many plants also reproduce sexually. What are the advantages to a plant in reproducing in this way?

3 The diagram shows two types of flower found in the same species. These types of flower are often found growing close together. Any one plant, however, only has one type of flower. Note: this condition is found in the West Indies in species of *Cordia* and *Pentas*.

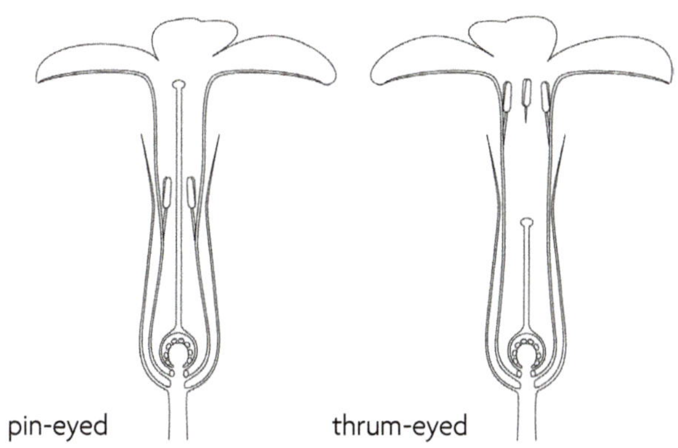

- a Describe the difference in the arrangement of the anthers and stigmas in the pin-eyed and thrum-eyed flowers.
- b This species is pollinated by insects, which reach into the bottom of the flower to get the nectar. Which part of the insect's body would pick up pollen in (i) a pin-eyed flower, and (ii) a thrum-eyed flower?
- c Which part of the insect's body would touch the stigma in (i) a pin-eyed flower, and (ii) a thrum-eyed flower?
- d Explain how this will help to ensure that cross-pollination takes place.
- e Self-pollination sometimes occurs in this species. Would you expect it to occur more often in pin-eyed or thrum-eyed flowers? Explain your answer.
- f Why is cross-pollination usually preferable to self-pollination?

4 a Where does meiosis occur in humans?

- b Describe how the egg and sperm are brought together.
- c How is the developing fetus supplied with food?
- d Suggest some advantages of breast-feeding a baby rather than using dried milk.
- e What precautions do you think should be taken when using dried milk products for babies?

5 Describe one example in each case of a plant storage organ which is:

- a also an organ of vegetative propagation
- b formed as a result of sexual reproduction.

6 Tissue culture is being increasingly used to propagate plants commercially. Find out what tissue culture is. (The University of the West Indies may be a good source of information. You could also try the internet.) How is tissue culture used in agriculture in the Caribbean?

14 Continuity

In this chapter, you will find out:

- the roles of mitosis and meiosis in reproduction
- why asexual reproduction results in genetically identical individuals, but sexual reproduction causes variation
- how our genes determine our characteristics
- the meanings of many specialist terms used when describing inheritance
- how to construct genetic diagrams to predict the genotypes and phenotypes of the offspring of two parents
- how blood group is determined and inherited
- how sex is inherited
- some of the causes and effects of mutations.

Genes and species characteristics

14.1 Each species has its own set of genes.

Each species of living organism has a specific number of **chromosomes** in its cells, and its own number and variety of **genes**. This is what makes their body chemistry, their appearance and their behaviour different from those of other species.

This ensures that the special characteristics of each species are preserved. It is the genes on the chromosomes which determine all sorts of things about you – what colour your eyes are, how tall you are, whether you have a snub nose or a straight one, whether you can roll your tongue or not.

The genes for each species are passed on from one generation to the next when they reproduce. In asexual reproduction (section **13.2**), the cells of the new organism are produced by **mitosis** of some of the cells of the parent. These new cells are all genetically identical to the parent. This is why asexual reproduction does not result in variation. Mitosis is described in Figure **12.2** (page **213**).

In sexual reproduction, special reproductive cells called **gametes** are produced by **meiosis**. Meiosis produces new cells with half the number of chromosomes of the parent cell, and with different combinations of genes. Meiosis is described in Figure **13.8** (page **231**). Two gametes – one male and one female – then fuse together in the process of fertilisation, producing even more possible combinations of genes. Sexual reproduction therefore produces genetic variation.

Humans have a large number of genes. The Human Genome Project has given us a great deal of information about our genes. The current estimate is that we have about 20 000 of them.

You have 46 chromosomes inside each of your cells, all with many genes on them. Every cell in your body has an exact copy of all your genes. But, unless you are an identical twin, there is no-one else in the world with exactly the same combination of genes that you have. Your genes make you unique.

Genes are carried on the **chromosomes** which are in the nucleus of every cell (Figure **14.1**). Chromosomes are long threads made of **DNA** (section **14.19**) and protein. Each chromosome is made up of many genes.

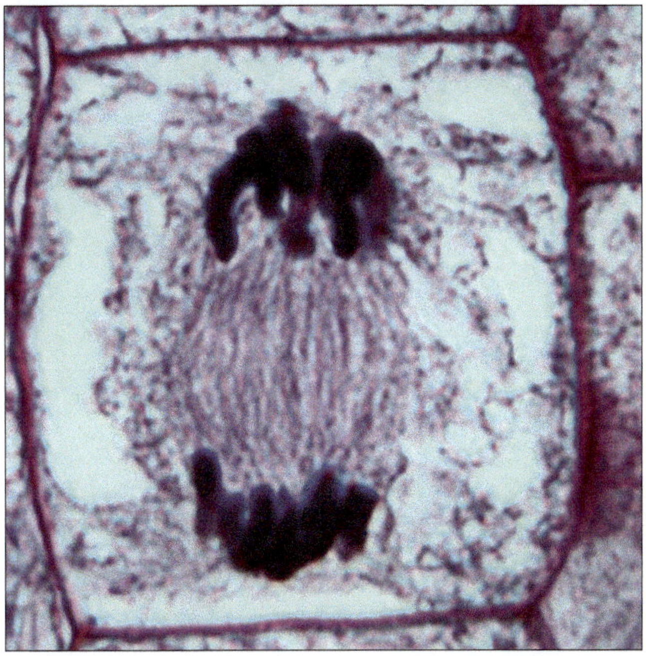

Figure 14.1 This photograph, taken with a microscope, shows a cell dividing by mitosis. The chromosomes have just arrived at each end of the cell.

14.2 Genes describe how to make particular proteins.

Genes work by providing information about making proteins.

Every chemical reaction inside a living organism is catalysed by enzymes. Enzymes are proteins. So, by providing information for making enzymes, genes affect all the chemical reactions in an organism's body.

Each of your cells contains a complete set of your genes. These genes carry the information for making many proteins. But not all of these genes are used by any one cell. Just a few genes will be 'switched on' in any one cell at any one time. If you have red hair, for example, you must have a red hair gene in all of your cells. But this gene will only have an effect in cells where hair grows, such as on your scalp. In heart cells, this gene will be switched off.

14.3 Most cells contain pairs of homologous chromosomes.

Figure **14.2** is an electron micrograph of some chromosomes from a human cell which is about to divide.

In Figure **14.3** (overleaf), the photographs of the chromosomes have been rearranged. You can see that there are, in fact, 23 *pairs* of chromosomes. The two chromosomes in a pair are the same size and shape.

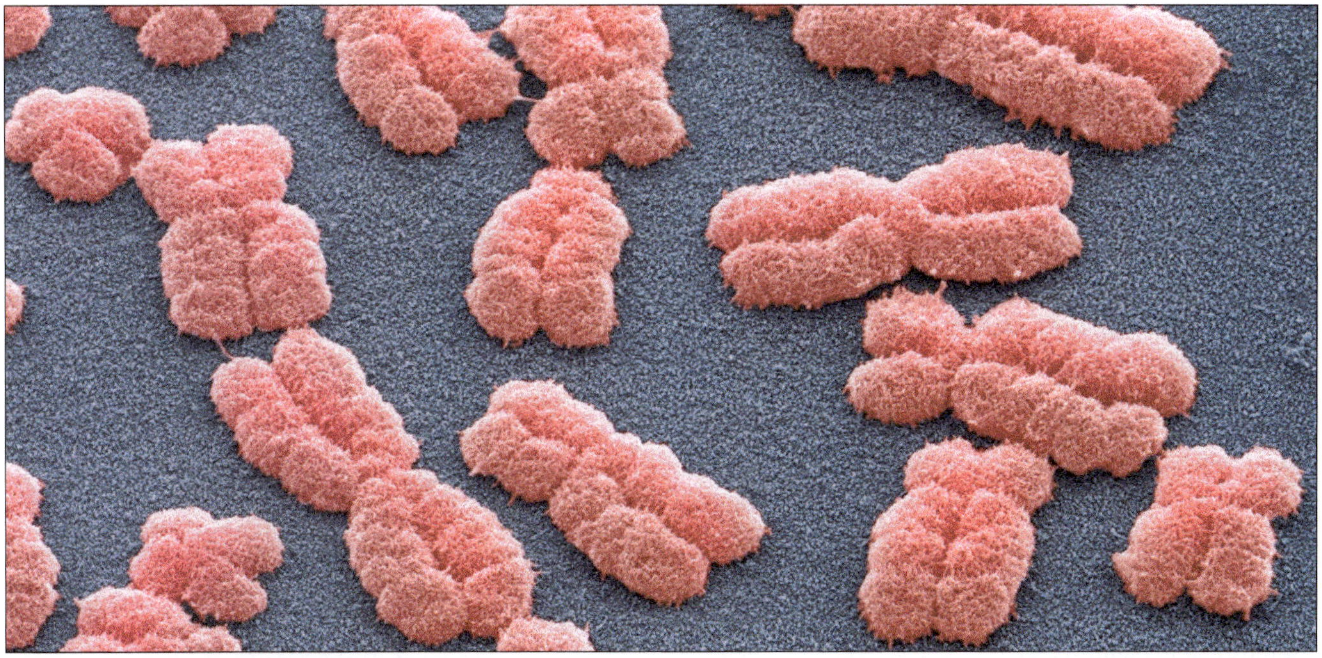

Figure 14.2 A scanning electron micrograph of human chromosomes. You can see that each one is made of two chromatids, linked at a point called the centromere.

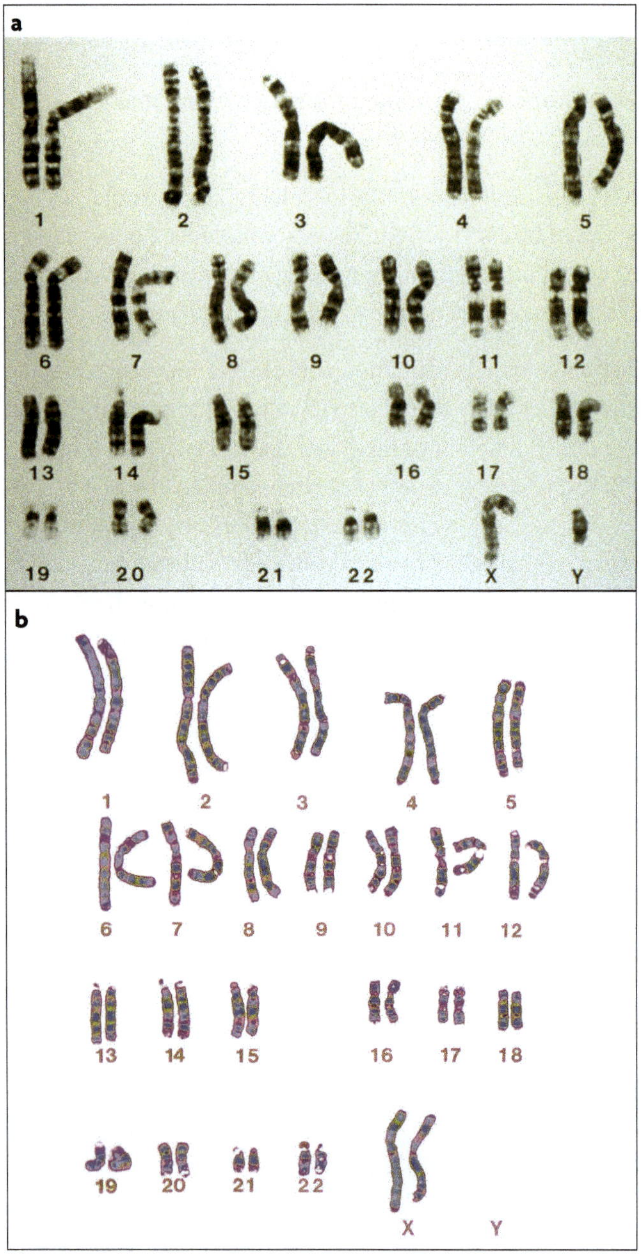

Figure 14.3 **a** Chromosomes from a man, arranged in order. **b** Chromosomes from a woman, arranged in order.

The two chromosomes of a pair are called **homologous chromosomes**. One came from the person's mother, and the other from the father.

Each chromosome of a homologous pair carries genes for the same characteristic in the same place. For example, the two chromosomes of pair number 1 might each carry a gene for tongue rolling. The tongue-rolling gene will be in exactly the same position, or locus, on each chromosome 1 (Figure **14.4**).

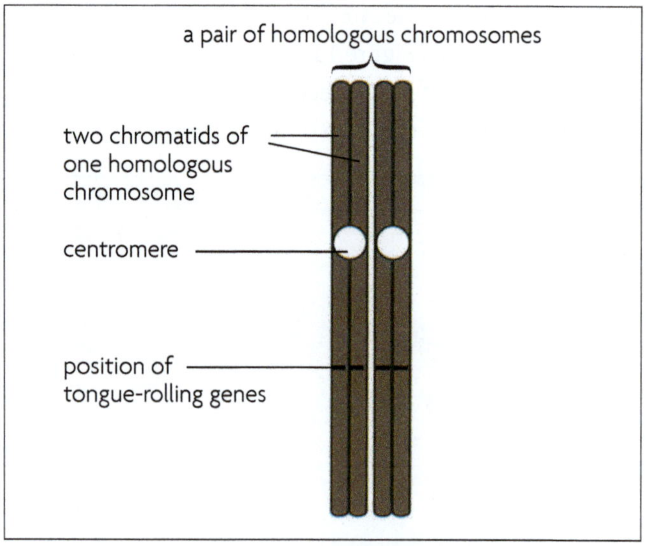

Figure 14.4 Homologous chromosomes have genes for the same characteristic in the same position.

Because there are two of each kind of chromosome, each cell contains two copies of each gene. Let us look at one gene, the tongue-rolling gene, to see how it behaves, and how it is inherited.

14.4 Each cell has two genes for any characteristic.

In each of your cells, there are two genes giving instructions about whether or not you can roll your tongue (Figure **14.5**).

In humans, there are two kinds of tongue-rolling gene. One kind, R, allows you to roll your tongue. The other kind, r, does not. These two forms of a gene, defining a characteristic in different ways, are called **alleles** (Figure **14.6**).

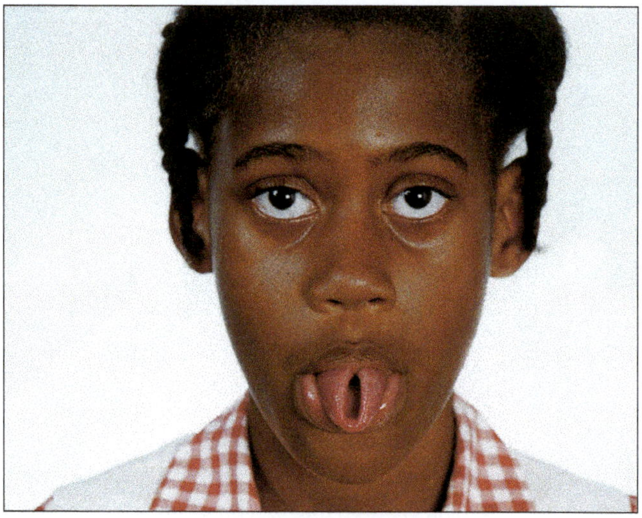

Figure 14.5 This person is a tongue roller.

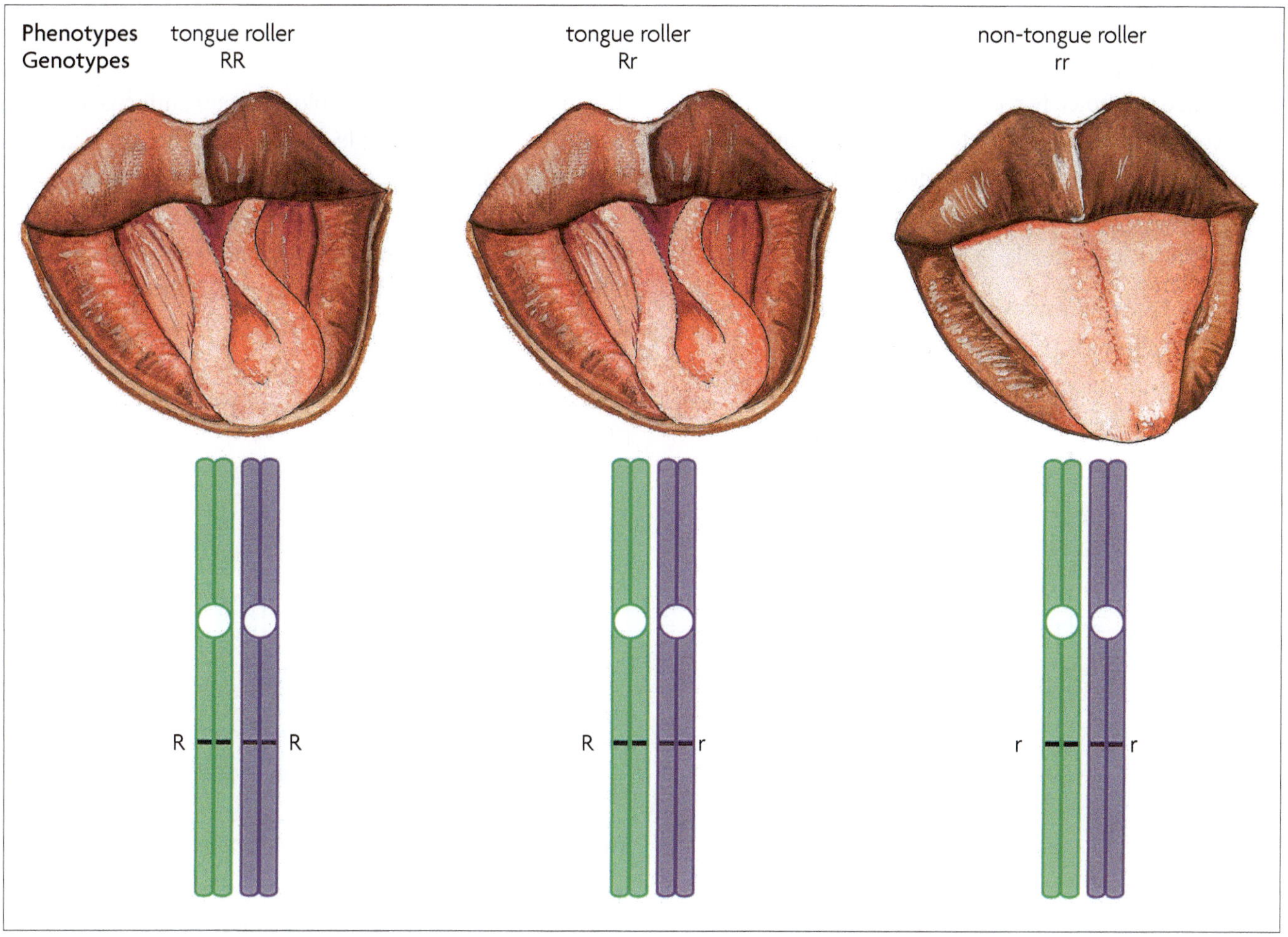

Figure 14.6 Phenotypes and genotypes for the tongue rollers and non-tongue rollers.

There are three possible combinations of alleles for tongue rolling. You might have two R alleles, RR. You might have two r alleles, rr. Or you might have one of each allele, Rr (rR is just the same).

If the two alleles for tongue rolling in your cells are the same – that is, RR or rr – then you are said to be **homozygous** for tongue rolling. If they are different – that is, Rr – then you are **heterozygous** for tongue rolling.

14.5 Genotype can determine phenotype.

The genes that you have are your **genotype**. For tongue rolling, there are three possible genotypes – RR, Rr or rr.

The genotype determines whether or not you can roll your tongue. The effect that the genotype has is called your **phenotype**. Your phenotype for tongue rolling is either being able to roll your tongue, or not being able to do it.

14.6 Alleles can be dominant or recessive.

So there are three kinds of genotype for tongue rolling, but only two kinds of phenotype. How does that happen?

It happens because the tongue-rolling allele, R, is **dominant** over the non-tongue-rolling allele, r. If you are heterozygous for tongue rolling, Rr, then it is only the R allele which actually has any effect on the phenotype. You can roll your tongue. The effect of the r allele is hidden by the R allele. The r allele is said to be a **recessive** allele.

This is summarised as follows.

genotype	phenotype
RR	tongue roller
Rr	tongue roller
rr	non-tongue roller

14.7 Some alleles show codominance.

Sometimes, neither of a pair of alleles is completely dominant or completely recessive. Instead of one of them completely hiding the effect of the other in a heterozygote, they both have an effect on the phenotype. This is called **codominance**. (You may also see the term **incomplete dominance**.)

Imagine a kind of flower which has two alleles for flower colour. The allele C^W produces white flowers, while the allele C^R produces red ones. If these alleles show codominance, then the genotypes and phenotypes are as below.

genotype	phenotype
C^WC^W	white flowers
C^WC^R	pink flowers
C^RC^R	red flowers

Snapdragons and Four o' clock are good examples of this (Figure **14.7**).

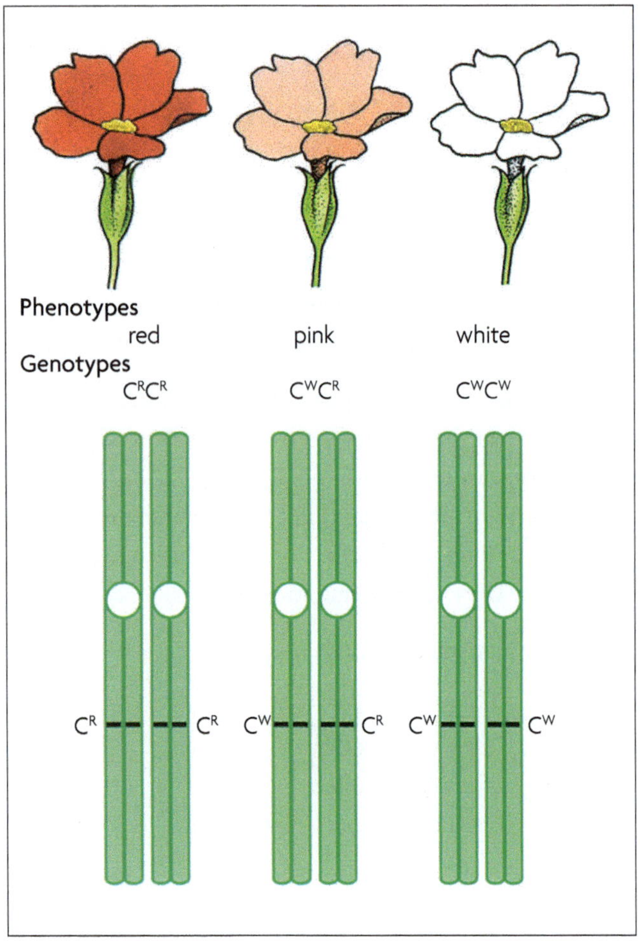

Figure 14.7 Codominance, sometimes known as incomplete dominance.

14.8 The inheritance of blood groups is another example of codominance.

The inheritance of the ABO blood group antigens in humans is another example of codominance. There are three alleles of the gene governing this instead of the usual two. Alleles I^A and I^B are codominant, but both are dominant to I^o. A person with the genotype $I^A I^B$ has the blood type AB, in which characteristics of both A and B antigens are expressed (Figure **14.8**).

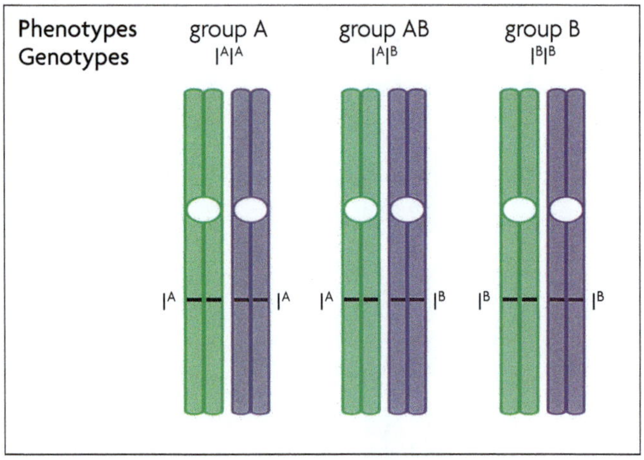

Figure 14.8 Codominance in human blood groups.

Questions

14.1 What are chromosomes made of?

14.2 Why can you see chromosomes most easily when a cell is dividing?

14.3 Explain how genes affect all the chemical reactions in an organism's body.

14.4 What are homologous chromosomes?

14.5 What are alleles?

14.6 **a** The allele for brown eyes is dominant to the allele for blue eyes. Write down suitable symbols for these alleles.

b What is the phenotype of a person who is heterozygous for this characteristic?

14.7 What is codominance?

14.8 Alleles of the gene for the ABO blood group antigens in humans show two unusual characteristics. What are these?

14.9 Figure **14.8** shows three possible genotypes for blood group. Write down all the other possible genotypes, and the phenotype that is associated with each one.

Inheritance

14.9 Gametes have only one allele of the gene for any characteristic.

Gametes (reproductive cells) are produced by meiosis, as described in section **13.8**. Each gamete has only one of each kind of chromosome instead of two as in the body cells. So, for example, human egg and sperm cells have 23 chromosomes, not 46 as in other cells. These cells, therefore, only carry *one* of each pair of alleles of all the genes.

14.10 Alleles are separated in meiosis.

Figure **14.9** shows some of the stages in meiosis, to show what happens to one pair of genes when a sperm is made.

In this example, the person is a tongue roller, genotype Rr. For simplicity, only the chromosomes carrying the tongue-rolling alleles are shown. The other 44 have been left out.

During the first division of meiosis, these chromosomes come together and then separate. Two cells are made, one carrying the R allele and the other carrying the r allele.

In the second division of meiosis, the chromosome in each cell splits into its two identical chromatids. These identical chromatids become full chromosomes during the development of the sperms. So at the end of meiosis, there are four cells, which will all grow into sperm cells. Half of them have the R allele and half have the r allele.

14.11 Genes and fertilisation.

If a man who is a heterozygous tongue roller marries a woman who is not a tongue roller (genotype rr), will their children be able to roll their tongues or not?

The eggs that are made in the woman's ovaries are also made by meiosis. If you use Figure **14.9** to work out what happens to her chromosomes during meiosis, you will see that she can only make one kind of egg. All of the eggs will carry an r allele.

During sexual intercourse, hundreds of thousands of sperm will begin a journey towards the egg. About half of them will carry an R allele, and half will carry an r allele. If there is an egg in the woman's oviduct, it will probably be fertilised. There is an equal chance of either kind of sperm getting there first.

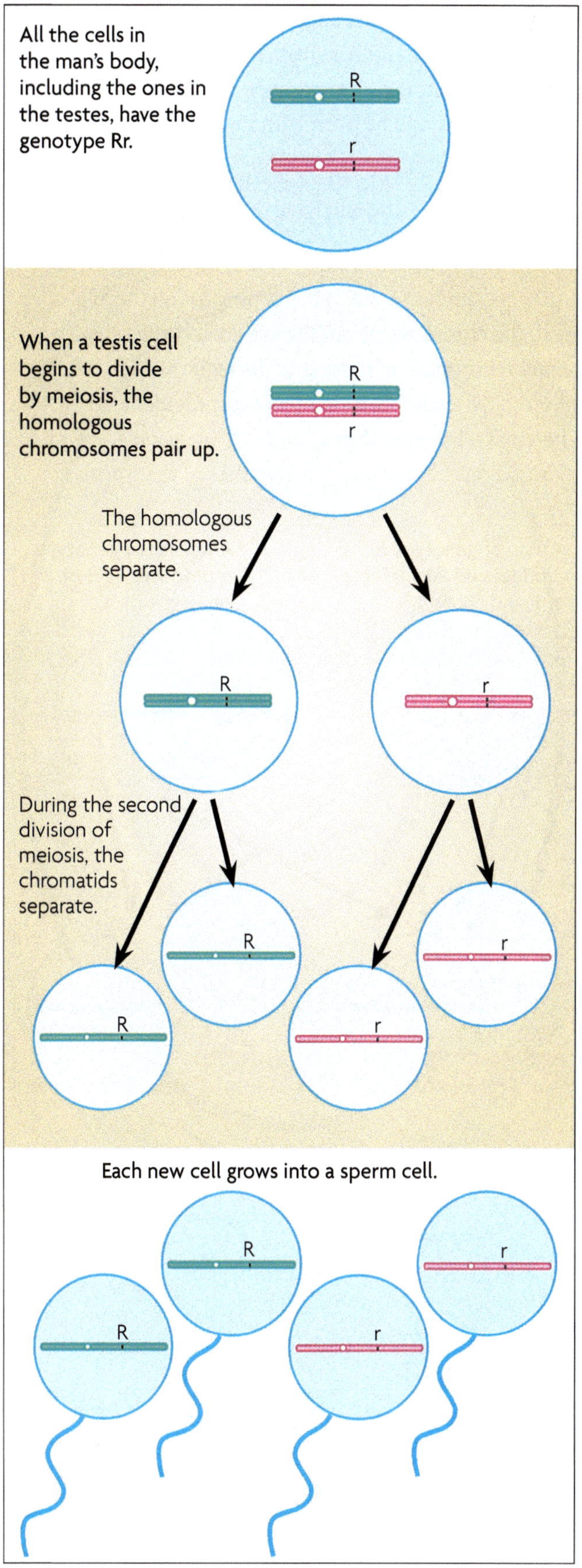

Figure 14.9 What happens to the genes of a heterozygous tongue roller during meiosis.

If a sperm carrying an R allele wins the race, then the zygote will have an R allele from its father and an r allele from its mother. Its genotype will be Rr. After nine months, a baby will be born with the genotype Rr.

But if a sperm carrying an r allele manages to fertilise the egg, then the baby will have the genotype rr, like its mother (Figure **14.10**).

A process similar to this is happening for all the alleles on all the chromosomes in the sperm and egg cells. Sexual reproduction, therefore, through this separation followed by recombination of alleles, provides a means whereby variation within a species may take place, while maintaining the special characteristics of that species.

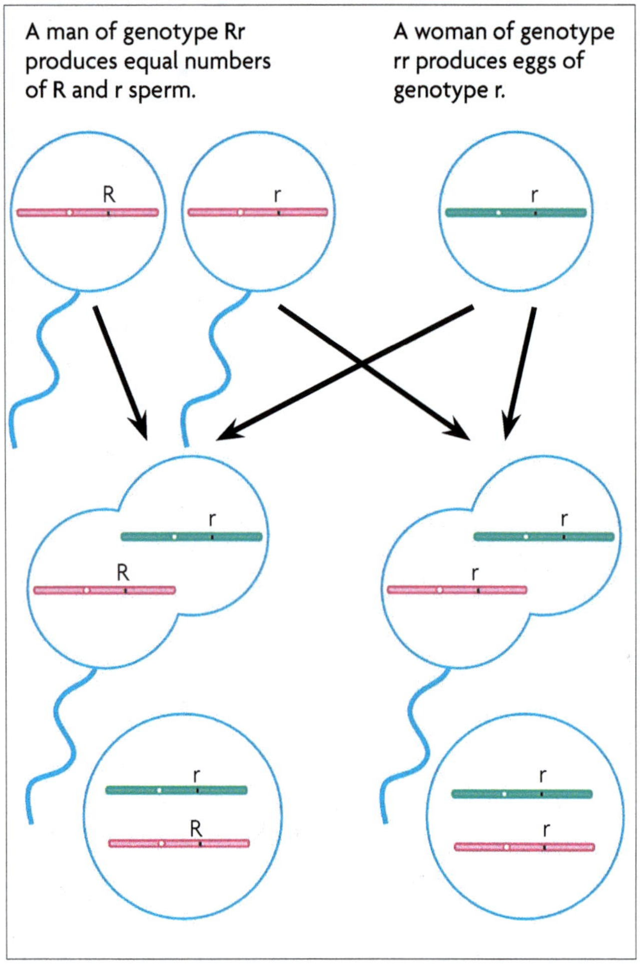

Figure 14.10 Fertilisation between a heterozygous tongue roller and a non-tongue roller.

14.12 Genetic crosses must be written clearly.

There is a standard way of writing out all this information. It is called a **genetic diagram**. First, write down the phenotypes and genotypes of the parents. Next, write down the different types of gametes they can make, like this.

Parents' phenotypes	tongue roller	non-tongue roller
Parents' genotypes	Rr	rr
Gametes	(R) or (r)	(r)

The next step is to write down what might happen during fertilisation. Either kind of sperm might fuse with an egg.

Offspring genotypes and phenotypes

		egg (r)
sperm	(R)	Rr tongue roller
	(r)	rr non-tongue roller

To finish your summary of the genetic cross, write out in words what you would expect the offspring from this cross to be.

'Approximately half of the children would be heterozygous tongue rollers, and half would be homozygous non-tongue rollers.'

14.13 If both parents are heterozygous, more offspring genotypes are possible.

What happens if both parents are heterozygous tongue rollers?

Parents' phenotypes	tongue roller	tongue roller
Parents' genotypes	Rr	Rr
Gametes	(R) or (r)	(R) or (r)

Offspring genotypes and phenotypes

		eggs: (R)	eggs: (r)
sperm	(R)	RR tongue roller	Rr tongue roller
sperm	(r)	Rr tongue roller	rr non-tongue roller

Approximately one quarter of the children would be homozygous tongue rollers, one half would be heterozygous tongue rollers, and one quarter would be homozygous non-tongue rollers.

The above example illustrates the inheritance of one pair only of contrasting characteristics (tongue rolling and non-tongue rolling). This is known as **monohybrid inheritance**.

14.14 Genetic cross diagrams give genotype probabilities.

In the last example, there were four offspring genotypes at the end of the cross. This does not mean that the man and woman will have four children. It simply means that each time they have a child, these are the possible genotypes that it might have.

When they have a child, there is a 1 in 4 chance that its genotype will be RR, and a 1 in 4 chance that its genotype will be rr. There is a 2 in 4, or rather 1 in 2 chance, that its genotype will be Rr.

However, as you know, probabilities do not always work out. If you toss a coin up four times you might expect it to turn up heads twice and tails twice. But does it always do this? Try it and see.

With small numbers like this, probabilities do not always match reality. If you had the patience to toss your coin up a few thousand times, though, you will almost certainly find that you get much more nearly equal numbers of heads and tails.

The same thing applies in genetics. The offspring genotypes which you work out are only probabilities. With small numbers, they are unlikely to work out exactly. With very large numbers of offspring from one cross, they are more likely to be accurate.

So, if the man and woman in the last example had eight children, they might expect six of them to be tongue rollers and two to be non-tongue rollers. But they should not be too surprised if they have three non-tongue rollers!

14.15 Test crosses help to determine genotype.

An organism that shows a dominant characteristic could have either of two possible genotypes. It could be homozygous for the dominant allele, or it could be heterozygous.

We can find out the genotype of an individual with the dominant phenotype for a particular gene by crossing it with one known to have the homozygous recessive genotype for the same gene. This is called a **test cross**.

For example, if we know that tallness is dominant to dwarfness in a certain species of peas, then the genotype of any tall plant could be determined by crossing it with a dwarf plant. If any of the offspring are dwarf, then this must mean that the tall parent had an allele for dwarfness. It must have been heterozygous. Try this out for yourself, using a genetic diagram.

If none of the offspring are dwarf, this almost certainly means that the tall parent was homozygous for the tallness allele. However, unless there are large numbers of offspring, this could also happen if the tall parent is heterozygous but, just by chance, none of its gametes carrying the recessive allele were successful in fertilisation.

14.16 'Pure breeding' means homozygous.

Some populations of animals or plants always have offspring just like themselves. For example, a rabbit breeder might have a strain of rabbits which all have brown coats. If he or she interbreeds them with one another, all the offspring always have brown coats as well. The breeder has a **pure-breeding** strain of brown rabbits. Pure-breeding strains are always homozygous for the pure-breeding characteristics.

The offspring of two different pure-breeding (homozygous) strains are sometimes called the first filial generation, or **F1 generation**.

Questions

14.10 If a normal human cell has 46 chromosomes, how many chromosomes are there in a human sperm cell?

14.11 Using the symbols W for normal wings, and w for vestigial wings, write down the following:

a the genotype of a fly which is heterozygous for this characteristic.

b the possible genotypes of its gametes.

14.12 Using the method shown in section **14.12**, work out what kind of offspring would be produced if the heterozygous fly in question **14.11** mated with one which was homozygous for normal wings.

14.13 In humans, the allele for red hair, b, is recessive to the allele for brown hair, B. A man and his wife both have brown hair. They have five children, three of whom have red hair, while two have brown hair. Explain how this may happen, using a genetic diagram to explain your answer.

14.14 In Dalmatian dogs, the allele for black spots is dominant to the allele for liver spots. If a breeder has a black-spotted dog, how can he or she find out whether it is homozygous or heterozygous for this characteristic? Use genetic diagrams to explain your answer.

14.15 A man of blood type A married a woman of blood type B. They had three children, of blood types O, B and AB respectively. What are the genotypes of the parents and children? Use genetic diagrams to explain your answer.

14.16 The pedigree diagram shows the known blood groups in three generations of a family. Squares represent males and circles represent females. What are the genotypes of **1** and **3**? What is the blood group of **2**?

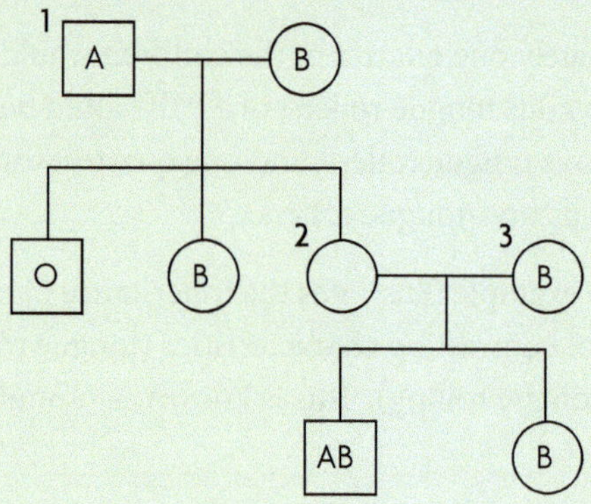

14.17 Sex is determined by X and Y chromosomes.

If you look carefully at Figures **14.3a** and **14.3b**, you will see that the last pair of chromosomes is not the same in each case. In the second photograph, of a woman's chromosomes, the last pair are alike. In the first photograph, which is of a man's chromosomes, the last pair are not alike. One is much smaller than the other.

This last pair of chromosomes is responsible for determining what sex a person will be. They are called the **sex chromosomes** (Figure 14.11). A woman's chromosomes are both alike and are called X chromosomes. She has the genotype XX.

A man, though, only has one X chromosome. The other, smaller one, is a Y chromosome. He has the genotype XY.

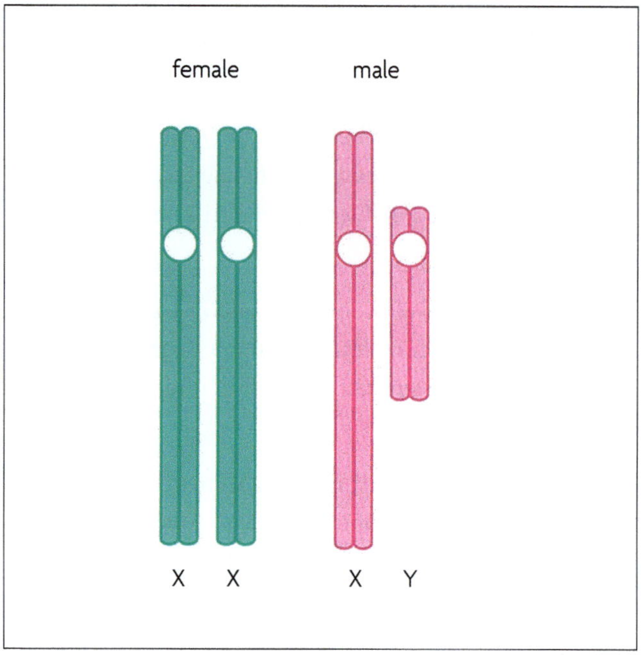

Figure 14.11 The sex chromosomes.

14.18 Sex is inherited.

You can work out sex inheritance in just the same way as for any other characteristic, but using the letter symbols to describe whole chromosomes, rather than individual alleles.

Parents' phenotypes	male	female
Parents' genotypes	XY	XX
Gametes	(X) or (Y)	(X)

Offspring genotypes and phenotypes

		egg (X)
sperm	(X)	XX female
	(Y)	XY male

So each time a child is conceived, there is a 1:1 chance of its being either sex.

Investigation 14.1
Flower colour in *Impatiens*

SBA skills
Analysis/Interpretation

Impatiens grows easily, either from stem cuttings or seed. Prepare for planting two plots on the school grounds where the soil is similar, each say 5 m square. (If the space is not available, fill four large boxes or half-drums with soil.) In one plot, randomly sow selected *Impatiens* seeds. In the other plot, plant an approximately equal number of cuttings from red- and white-flowered *Impatiens* plants. Both plots must be given the same care in terms of tilling and watering.

At the first flowering, count the numbers of plants bearing flowers of one colour and note the time taken for the plants to flower. Tabulate your observations.

Explain similarities or differences noticed in the colour distribution of the blooms from the two plots.

Investigation 14.2
'Breeding' beads

SBA skills
Analysis/Interpretation

In this investigation, you will use two containers of beads. Each container represents a parent. The beads represent the gametes they make. The colour of a bead represents the genotype of the gamete. For example, a red bead might represent a gamete with genotype R, for tongue rolling. A yellow bead might represent a gamete with the genotype r, for non-tongue rolling.

1 Put 100 red beads into the first beaker. These represent the gametes of a person who is homozygous for tongue rolling, RR.

2 Put 50 red beads and 50 yellow beads into the second beaker. These represent the gametes of a heterozygous person with the genotype Rr.

3 Close your eyes, and pick out one bead from the first beaker, and one from the second. Write down the genotype of the 'offspring' they produce. Put the two beads back.

4 Repeat step 3 100 times.

5 Now try a different cross – for example, Rr crossed with Rr.

Questions

1 In the first cross, what kinds of offspring were produced, and in what ratios?

2 Is this what you would have expected? Explain your answer.

3 Why must you close your eyes when choosing the beads?

4 Why must you put the beads back into the beakers after they have 'mated'?

Mutation

14.19 Accidental changes in DNA produce mutations.

DNA is a very important material. Almost everything that happens in a living organism is controlled by it. So all of the processes that DNA is involved in – mitosis, meiosis and protein synthesis – are very carefully controlled. The working of the cell is designed to ensure that the instructions carried on the DNA molecules are never damaged.

But occasionally things do go wrong. One time that this can happen is during meiosis. Sometimes, instead of homologous chromosomes separating perfectly, one may go the wrong way. Gametes will then be formed with the wrong number of chromosomes.

This sometimes happens when eggs are being made in a woman's ovaries. The chromosome 21s may fail to separate. Some eggs are made with two chromosome 21s instead of one. If such an egg is fertilised by a normal sperm, the child which results will have three chromosome 21s in every cell. It will have **Down's syndrome** (Figure **14.12**).

Figure 14.12 A person with Down's syndrome has an extra chromosome in each of their cells. They are usually very happy people, but are prone to problems such as heart disease, and often have learning difficulties.

Another type of change that may occur is in the DNA molecule itself. A DNA molecule is made up of a long string of smaller molecules, containing four different **bases**. (Figure **14.13**). Normally, the sequence of the bases in the DNA never changes. It is copied very carefully, and passed on unchanged from parent to offspring. But sometimes, one or more bases in the DNA may be altered, or moved out of sequence or deleted (left out). This changes the sequence of amino acids in the protein that the particular piece of DNA codes for. The result is to upset the normal functioning of the body.

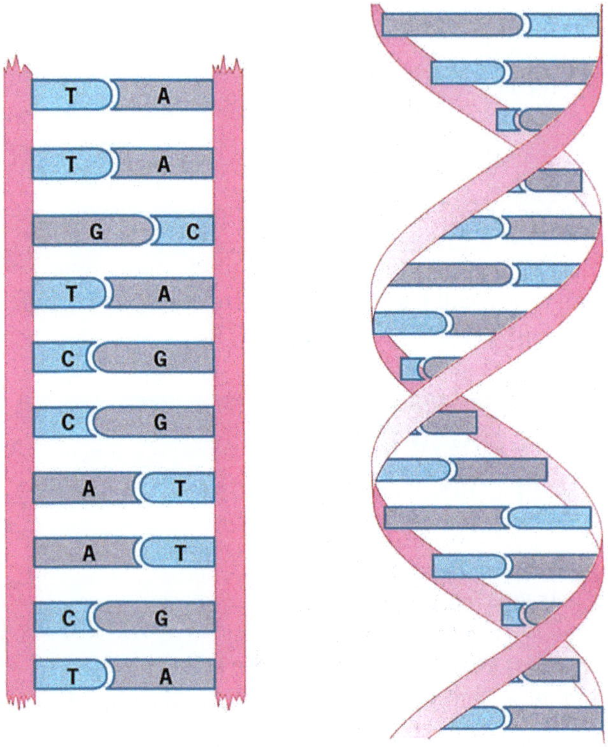
T A
T A
G C
T A
C G
C G
A T
A T
C G
T A
A DNA molecule is made of two strands, linked through the bases A, T, C and G.
The two strands twist round each other, forming a double helix.

Figure. 14.13 Part of a DNA molecule.

For example, in **albinism** such a change prevents the production of the brown pigment, melanin. Although this condition is not confined to dark-skinned people, its effect is more noticeable in these people (Figure **14.14**). The lack of skin pigment makes the skin very vulnerable to damage by the ultraviolet rays in sunlight.

Figure 14.14 A mutation in the gene that normally causes melanin to be produced has caused the loss of skin colour in this albino person.

Deletion of bases from a specific gene on chromosome 11 causes a large proportion of the cases of **cystic fibrosis**, a common and serious disease of Caucasians. The disease causes very thick mucus to clog the lungs, and the bile and pancreatic ducts leading from the liver to the gut. Cystic fibrosis significantly reduces life expectancy to about 38 years.

Most mutations are harmful, but just occasionally a mutation may turn out to produce a better characteristic than the original. An example of this is the mutation of the pale form of the peppered moth to a dark form in some parts of Great Britain. This is described in section **15.5**.

Harmful mutations are generally kept from rising in human populations because many of the fetuses die before birth, and those children who are born alive often die before they can reproduce and pass on this defect.

14.20 Sickle cell anaemia.

Sometimes, however, environmental factors encourage the persistence of a harmful mutation in a population. A good example of this is the mutation which causes sickling in human red blood cells (Figure **14.15**). This mutation seems to have arisen on at least four occasions – three times in Africa, and once in the Middle East or India.

The mutation produces a very small change in the base sequence in the DNA that codes for the production of haemoglobin. (Haemoglobin is the red protein found inside red blood cells, which transports oxygen.) The result is that the amino acid valine is inserted in the amino acid chain instead of glutamine.

This leads to the production of a form of haemoglobin called haemoglobin S or sickle cell haemoglobin instead of normal haemoglobin A in humans. The two haemoglobins differ by one amino acid only, but the change causes haemoglobin S to perform differently from haemoglobin A.

Normal haemoglobin 'loads up' with oxygen in the lungs where the oxygen level is high and 'unloads' this oxygen in the tissues where there is less oxygen. It then returns to the lungs to be 'loaded'.

Sickle cell haemoglobin, on the other hand, behaves very differently when oxygen concentrations are low – for example, if a person has been exercising hard and has used up a lot of oxygen in their muscles. In these

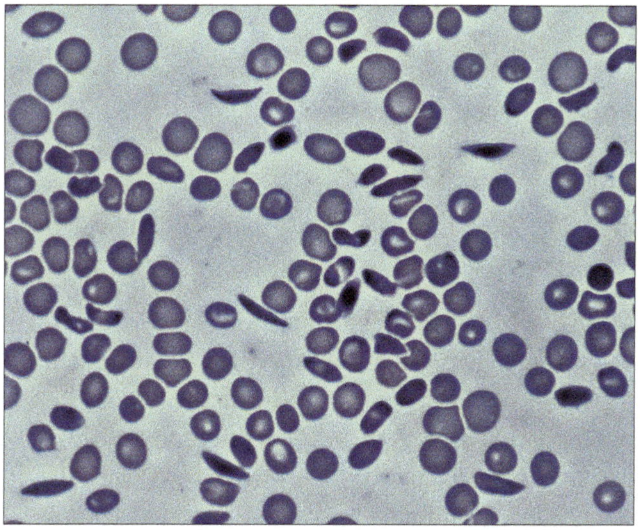

Figure 14.15 Some of these red blood cells (which have been stained blue) have become sickle shaped.

conditions, haemoglobin S forms crystals which change the shape of red blood cells from their normal round shape to a characteristic sickle shape (Figure **14.15**). The sickled red blood cells then clog or block small blood vessels, cutting off oxygen from some tissues.

The type of haemoglobin a person has is determined by two codominant alleles, Hb^A and Hb^S. If a person has the genotype Hb^AHb^A, then all of their haemoglobin is normal. If their genotype is Hb^SHb^S all of their haemoglobin is the sickle type. They have **sickle cell anaemia**. If they have the genotype Hb^AHb^S, they have a mix of both types of haemoglobin. They are said to have **sickle cell trait**.

A person with the genotype Hb^SHb^S is very likely to have sickle cell 'crises', when the red blood cells sickle and cause dangerous and painful blockages in the circulatory system. The red cells are destroyed within the circulatory system. Without treatment, most people with this genotype die before they can reproduce. However, the Sickle Cell Centre, sited at the University of the West Indies, Mona, has carried out extensive research into the disease over more than three decades. The centre operates an on-going programme of monitoring, treatment, follow-up and education for patients. Today, more than half of patients in Jamaica with sickle cell anaemia live beyond the age of 55. In Chapter **15**, we will see why this malfunctioning allele has remained in the human population.

14.21 Environmental factors can increase mutation rate.

Mutations often happen for no apparent reason. However, we do know of many factors which make mutation more likely. One of the most important of these is ionising radiation. Radiation can damage the bases in DNA molecules. If this happens in the ovaries or testes, then the altered DNA may be passed on to the offspring.

Many different chemicals are known to increase the risk of a mutation happening. The heavy metals lead and mercury and their compounds can interfere with the process in which DNA is copied. If this process goes wrong, the daughter cells will get faulty DNA when the cell divides. Chemicals which can cause mutations are called **mutagens**.

14.22 Mutations may occur in non-reproductive cells.

Mutations may occur in normal body cells. These would not be passed on in sexual reproduction, but can be spread vegetatively. For example, navel orange and several varieties of cultivated crotons (*Codiaeum variegatum*) are grown by grafts, buds and cuttings to preserve desirable phenotypes resulting from mutations that did not originate in sexual cells.

Questions

14.17 Albinism is caused by a recessive allele, a.

- **a** What is the genotype of an albino person?
- **b** If an albino woman marries a man with normal skin colouring, what are the chances of their first child being albino? Use two genetic diagrams to explain your answer.

14.18 Two people with sickle cell trait have children. Draw a genetic diagram to show the chances that their first child will have sickle cell anaemia.

14.19 Even if everyone with sickle cell anaemia in a population died, there could still be people in the next generation who have sickle cell anaemia. Suggest how this could happen. (You should be able to think of two different reasons.)

14.20 What is meant by a mutagen? Give two examples of metals that are mutagens.

Key ideas

- The nucleus of every cell contains long threads of DNA called chromosomes. Each chromosome is made up of many genes. These determine the proteins that are made by the cell, and therefore many of the characteristics of the organism.
- In asexual reproduction, cells divide by mitosis, resulting in genetically identical offspring. In sexual reproduction, cells divide by meiosis, resulting in genetically different gametes. Two gametes then fuse to form a zygote, resulting in yet more possible combinations of genes and therefore even more variation.
- In a body cell, there are two complete sets of chromosomes. The two similar chromosomes from the two sets are said to be homologous. They carry genes for the same characteristics in the same positions.
- Different forms of a gene are called alleles. There are two copies of each gene in a cell, which may be both the same allele, or two different alleles. If the alleles are the same, the cell is homozygous. If they are different, it is heterozygous.
- The genes of an organism are its genotype. The organism's characteristics are its phenotype.
- An allele that only has an effect on phenotype when there is no other kind of allele present is said to be recessive. An allele that has its full effect on phenotype even when a recessive allele is present is said to be dominant. If both alleles in a heterozygous organism affect its phenotype, these alleles are said to be codominant.
- Genetic diagrams are used to show how alleles are passsed on during sexual reproduction. They show us the chances of each different genotype and phenotype being produced.
- Test crosses can be used to find out the genotype of an organism showing the dominant feature in its phenotype.
- Sex is determined by the two sex chromosomes. A woman is XX and a man is XY.
- Normally, the DNA that makes up our genes is copied perfectly before a cell divides. Sometimes, however, this goes wrong and mistakes are made in the DNA copying. This is called mutation. Ionising radiation and chemicals such as lead and mercury increase the chances of mutation occurring.

End-of-chapter questions

1. Some breeds of cattle may have white coat, red coat or a coat made up of a mixture of red and white hairs, called roan.
   a. Write down suitable symbols for the two alleles responsible for these characteristics.
   b. List the three possible genotypes and their phenotypes.
   c. Use a genetic diagram to show the possible offspring that could be produced by a cross between a roan cow and a roan bull.

2. Two women gave birth in the same hospital on the same afternoon. Their babies were taken away, and then brought back to them one hour later.

   One of the women was worried that she had been given the wrong baby. She asked for blood tests to be carried out.

   The hospital found that she was group A and her husband was group O. The other was mother was group AB and her husband was group A.

   The woman with group A had been given the baby with group O blood. The woman with group AB was given the baby with group B blood.

   Use genetic diagrams to determine whether the women had been given the right babies.

3. The family tree shows the incidence of a genetic disease called PKU in four generations of a family.

   a. Describe one piece of evidence from the diagram that suggests PKU is caused by a recessive allele.
   b. If PKU is caused by a recessive allele, explain why it is unlikely that mutation in person 4 was responsible for their disease.
   c. Deduce the genotypes of persons 1, 2, 3 and 4. Use the symbol p for the PKU allele and the symbol P for the normal allele.
   d. Person 5 is worried that her children might have PKU. She talks to a genetic counsellor. What might she be told?

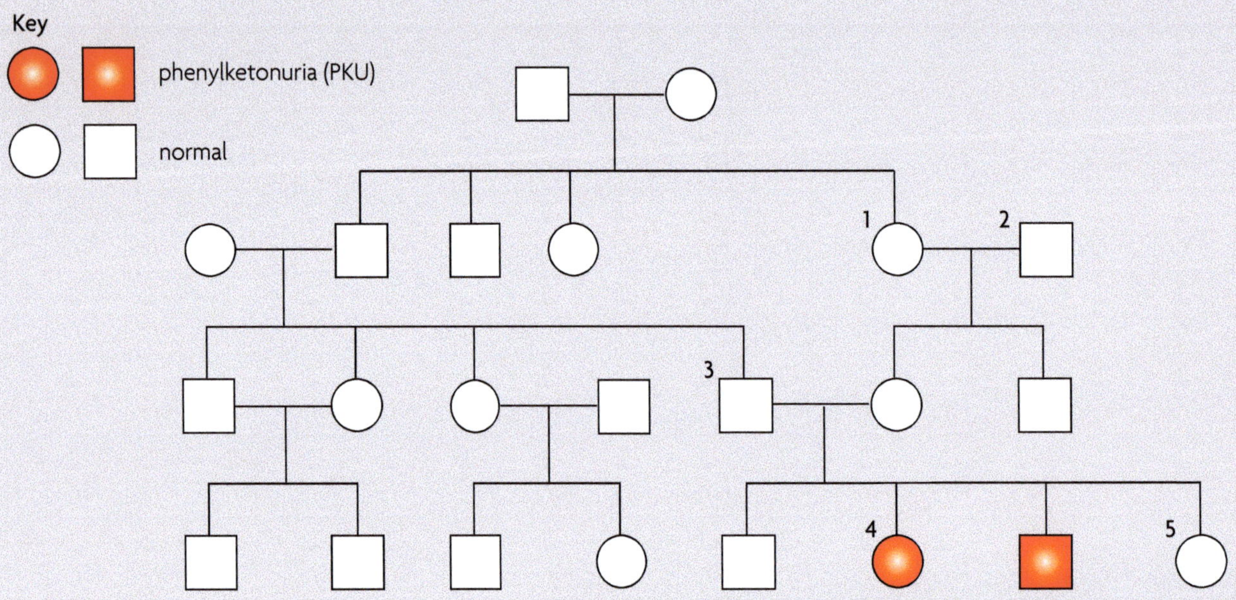

Key

● ■ phenylketonuria (PKU)

○ □ normal

15 Variation and selection

In this chapter, you will find out:

- about continuous and discontinuous variation, and what causes them
- how variation is the raw material on which natural selection acts
- how natural selection can lead to evolution
- how new species are formed
- how humans have used artifical selection to develop crop plants and animals with desired features
- how genetic engineering allows us to produce new varieties of organisms by inserting particular genes into them
- about the possible advantages and disadvantages of genetic engineering.

Variation

15.1 Individuals of the same species show differences.

You have only to look around a group of people to see that they are different from one another. Some of the more obvious differences are in height or hair type. We also vary in intelligence, blood groups, whether we can roll our tongues or not, and many other ways.

There are two basic kinds of variation. One kind is **discontinuous variation**. Tongue rolling is an example of discontinuous variation. Everyone fits into one of two definite categories – they either can or cannot roll their tongue. There is no in-between category.

The other kind is **continuous variation**. Height is an example of continuous variation. There are no definite heights that a person must be. People vary in height, between the lowest and highest extremes.

You can try measuring and recording discontinuous and continuous variation in Investigation **15.1**. Your results for continuous variation will probably look similar to Figure **15.1**. This is called a **normal distribution**. Most people come in the middle of the range, with fewer at the lower or upper ends. Human height (Figure **15.2**, overleaf) shows a normal distribution.

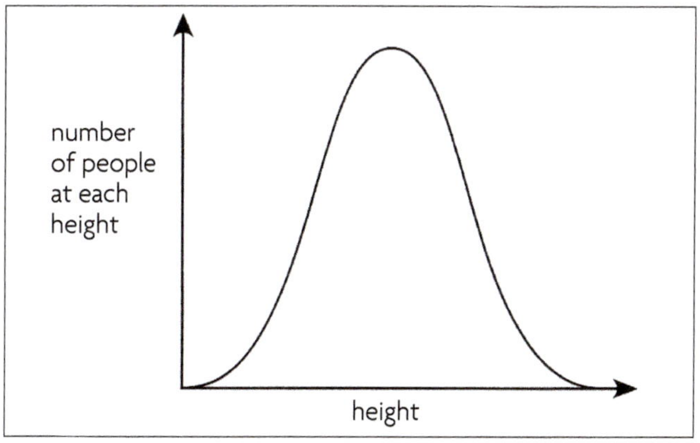

Figure 15.1 A normal distribution curve. This is a graph that shows the numbers of people of different heights.

Investigation 15.1
Measuring variation

SBA skills

Observation/Recording/Reporting
Manipulation/Measurement
Analysis/Interpretation

1 Make a survey of at least 30 people, to find out whether or not they can roll their tongue. Record your results.

2 Measure the length of the third finger of the left hand of 30 people. Take the measurement from the knuckle to the finger tip, not including the nail.

3 Divide the finger lengths into suitable categories, and record the numbers in each category, like this.

length / cm	number
8.0 – 8.4	2
8.5 – 8.9	4

and so on ...

4 Draw a histogram of your results.

Questions

1 Which characteristic shows continuous variation, and which shows discontinuous variation?

2 Your histogram may be a similar shape to the curve in Figure 15.1. This is called a normal distribution. The class which has the largest number of individuals in it is called the modal class. What is the modal class for the finger lengths of your samples?

3 The mean finger length is the total of all the finger lengths, divided by the number of people in your sample. What is the mean finger length of the sample?

15.2 What causes variation?

By describing variation as continuous or discontinuous, we can begin to explain *how* organisms vary. But the *cause* of the variation is another question altogether.

Genetic variation One reason for the differences between individuals is that their genotypes are different. Tongue rolling, for example, is controlled by genes. There are also genes for hair colour, eye colour, blood groups, height and many other characteristics (Figure **15.3**).

Figure 15.2 Human height shows continuous variation. What characteristic here shows discontinuous variation?

Environmental variation Another important reason for variation is the difference between the environments of individuals. Pine trees (*Pinus caribbea*) possess genes that enable them to grow to a height of about 30 m. But if a pine tree is grown in a very small pot, and has its roots regularly pruned, it will be permanently stunted (Figure **15.4**). The tree's genotype gives it the potential to grow tall, but it will not realise this potential unless its roots are given plenty of space and it is allowed to grow freely.

Characteristics caused by an organism's environment are sometimes called **acquired characteristics**. They are not caused by genes, and so they cannot be handed on to the next generation.

Figure 15.3 The presence of horns in cattle is controlled by a dominant allele of a gene. Polled (hornless) cattle have two copies of the recessive allele of this gene.

Variation caused by the environment is not inherited. A cutting from a bonsai pine would grow into a full size tree, if it were allowed to.
bonsai

A bonsai pine tree is dwarfed by being grown in a very small pot and so starved of mineral nutrients. Also its roots and stems are continually pruned.

Figure 15.4 Small size is an acquired characteristic for a bonsai pine tree.

Questions

15.1 Decide whether each of these features shows continuous variation or discontinuous variation.

- **a** blood group in humans
- **b** foot size in humans
- **c** leaf length in a species of tree
- **d** presence of horns in cattle

15.3 Genetic variation arises in several ways.

Meiosis During sexual reproduction, gametes are formed by **meiosis**. In meiosis, homologous chromosomes exchange genes, and separate from one another, so the gametes which are formed are not all exactly the same.

Fertilisation Any two gametes of opposite types can fuse together at **fertilisation**, so there are many possible combinations of genes which may be produced in the zygote. In an organism with a large number of genes the possibility of two offspring having identical genotypes is so small that it can be considered almost impossible.

Mutation Sometimes, a gene may suddenly change. This is called **mutation**. Mutations are the only source of brand-new characteristics in the gene pool. So they are really the final source of all genetic variation.

Most mutations are harmful, but occasionally one may happen which gives the mutant organism an advantage in the struggle for existence. It will then survive to pass its new characteristics on to the next generation. The mutant may even replace the normal form over a period of time.

15.4 Variation is the raw material for natural selection to work on.

Over the many millions of years that living things have existed, there have been gradual changes in organisms and populations. Fossils tell us that many animals and plants that once lived no longer exist. Archaeological finds are constantly revealing that early humans were different from humans today.

In the 19th century, several ideas were put forward to suggest how this might have happened. One, still widely accepted today, was suggested by Charles Darwin (Figure 15.5, overleaf). He put forward his theory in a book called *On the Origin of Species*, which was published in 1859.

Darwin's theory of how evolution could have happened may be summarised like this.

Variation Most populations of organisms contain individuals which vary slightly from one to another. Some slight variations may better adapt some organisms to their environment than others.

Over-production Most organisms produce more young than will survive to adulthood.

Struggle for existence Because populations do not generally increase rapidly in size, there must therefore be considerable competition for survival between the organisms.

Survival of the fittest Only the organisms which are really well adapted to their environment will survive (Figure **15.6**).

Advantageous characteristics passed on to offspring Only these well-adapted organisms will be able to reproduce successfully, and will pass on their advantageous characteristics to their offspring.

Gradual change In this way, over a period of time, the population will lose all the poorly adapted individuals. The population will gradually become better adapted to its environment.

The theory is often called the theory of **natural selection**, because it suggests that the best-adapted organisms are selected to pass on their characteristics to the next generation.

Darwin proposed his theory before anyone understood how characteristics were inherited. Now that we know something about genetics, his theory can be stated slightly differently. We can say that natural selection results in the genes producing advantageous phenotypes being passed on to the next generation more frequently than the genes which produce less advantageous phenotypes (Figures **15.6** and **15.7**).

Figure 15.5 A portrait of Charles Darwin at the age of 72.

Figure 15.6 When large numbers of organisms, such as these wildebeest of East African plains, live together, there is competition for food, and the weaker ones are likely to be killed by predators. Individuals best adapted to their environment survive and reproduce.

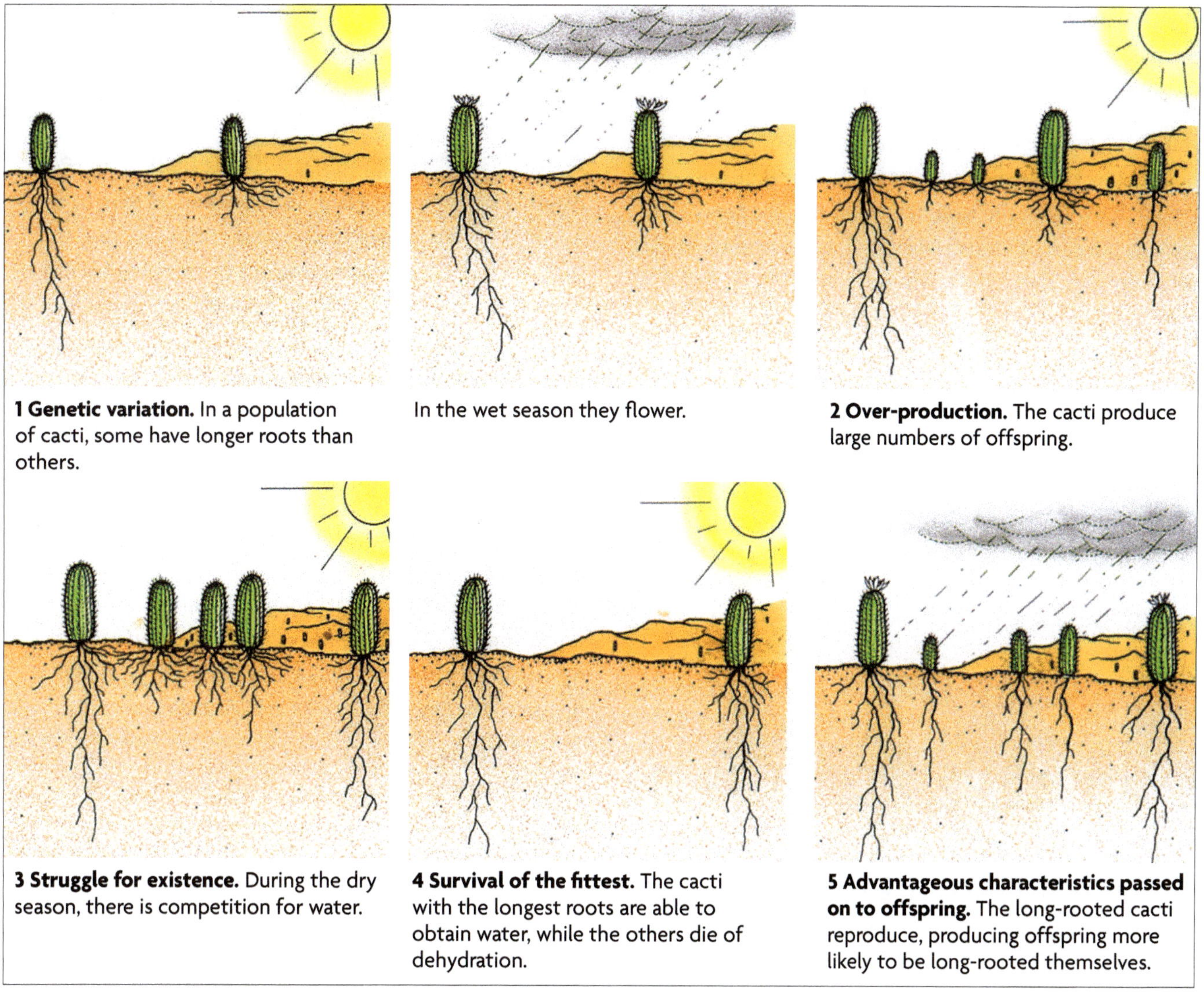

1 Genetic variation. In a population of cacti, some have longer roots than others.

In the wet season they flower.

2 Over-production. The cacti produce large numbers of offspring.

3 Struggle for existence. During the dry season, there is competition for water.

4 Survival of the fittest. The cacti with the longest roots are able to obtain water, while the others die of dehydration.

5 Advantageous characteristics passed on to offspring. The long-rooted cacti reproduce, producing offspring more likely to be long-rooted themselves.

Figure 15.7 An example of how natural selection might occur.

Evidence for natural selection

15.5 The distribution of the peppered moth in Great Britain and Eire.

Darwin's theory of natural selection provides a good explanation for our observations of the many types of animals and plants. It could explain what we see in the fossil record. But it is almost impossible to prove that these were produced by natural selection. The only way we can really be sure that natural selection works is if we can watch it happening.

The peppered moth, *Biston betularia*, lives in most parts of Great Britain and Eire. It flies by night, and spends the daytime resting on tree trunks. It has speckled wings, which camouflage it very effectively on lichen-covered tree trunks (Figure **15.8**, overleaf).

People have collected moths for many years, so we know that up until 1849 all the moths in collections were speckled. But in 1849, a black or melanic form of the moth was caught near Manchester. By 1900, 98% of the moths near Manchester were black.

The distribution of the black and speckled forms in 1958 is shown in Figure **15.9** (overleaf).

How can we explain the sudden rise in numbers of the dark moths, and their distribution today?

We know that the black colour of the moth is caused by a single dominant allele of a gene. The mutation from a normal to a black allele happens fairly often, so it is reasonable to assume that there have always been a few black moths around, as well as pale speckled ones.

Up until the beginning of the Industrial Revolution, the pale moths had the advantage, as they were better camouflaged on the lichen-covered tree trunks.

But in the middle of the 19th century, some areas became polluted by smoke. Because the prevailing winds in Britain blow from the west, the worst affected areas were to the east of industrial cities like Manchester and Birmingham. The polluted air prevented lichens from growing. Dark moths were better camouflaged than pale moths on trees with no lichens on them.

Proof that the dark moths do have an advantage in polluted areas has been supplied by several investigations. Figure **15.10** summarises one of them.

The factor which confers an advantage on the dark moths, and a disadvantage on the light moths in polluted areas, is predation by birds. This is called a **selection pressure,** because it 'selects' the dark moths for survival. In unpolluted areas, the pale moths are more likely to survive.

Figure 15.8 Peppered moths. **a** Lichen-covered bark hides a speckled moth perfectly. **b** Dark moths are better camouflaged on lichen-free trees.

15.6 Antibiotic resistance in bacteria is selected.

Another example of natural selection can be seen in the way that bacteria may become resistant to **antibiotics**, such as **penicillin**. Penicillin works by stopping bacteria from forming cell walls. When a person infected with bacteria is treated with penicillin, the bacteria are unable to grow new cell walls, and they burst open.

However, the population of bacteria in the person's body may be several million. The chances of any one of them mutating to a form which is not affected by penicillin is quite low, but because there are so many bacteria, it could well happen. If it does, the mutant bacterium will have a tremendous advantage. It will be able to go on reproducing while all the others cannot. Soon, its descendants may form a huge population of penicillin-resistant bacteria (Figure **15.11**, page **276**).

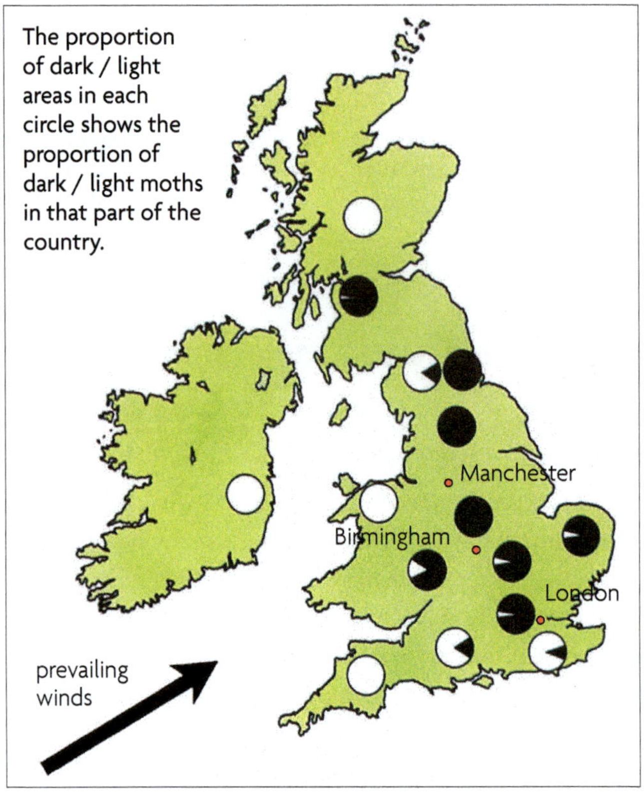

Figure 15.9 The distribution of the pale and dark forms of the peppered moth, *Biston betularia*, in 1958. Since then, the number of dark moths has dramatically decreased, because now there is much less air pollution.

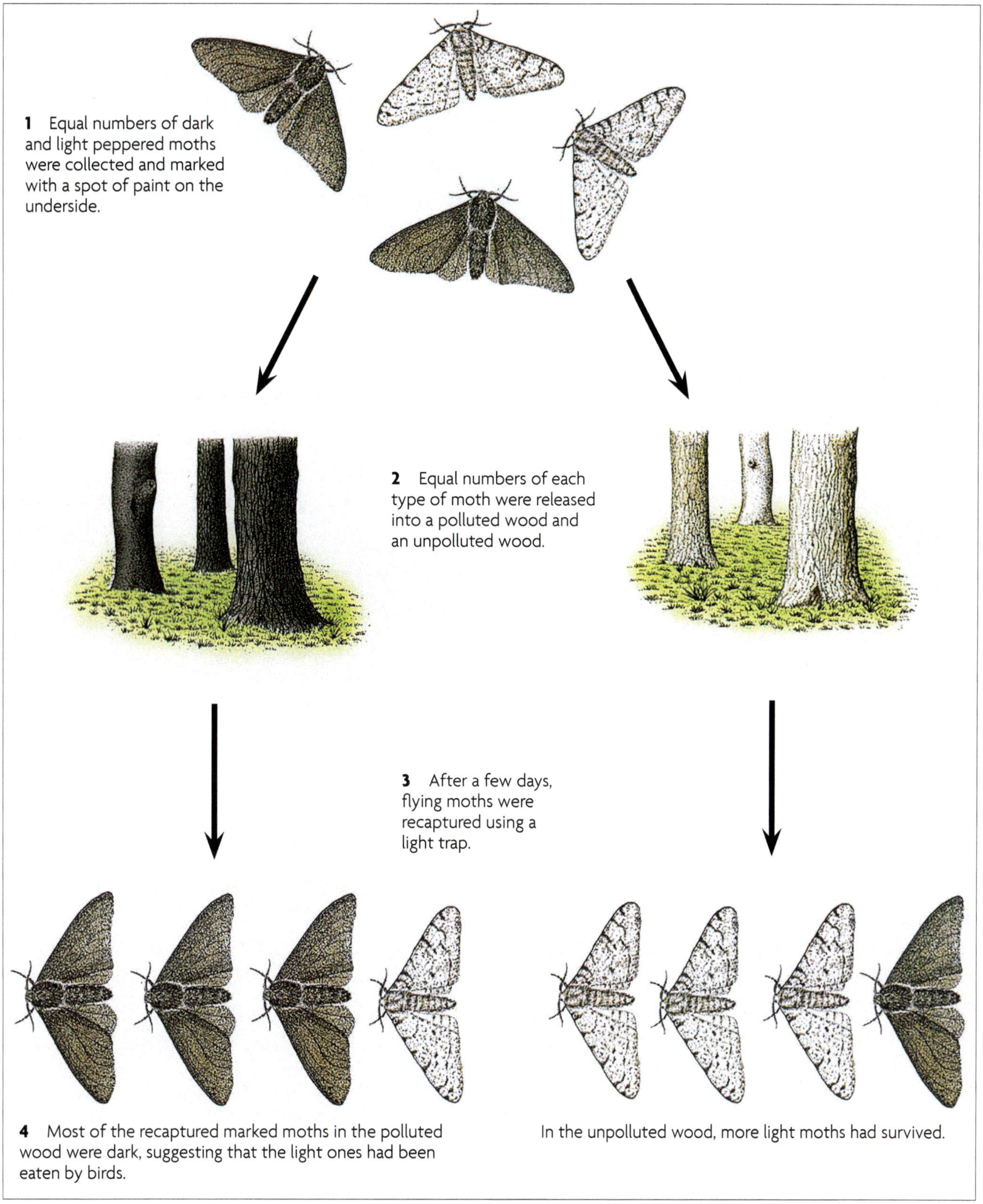

1 Equal numbers of dark and light peppered moths were collected and marked with a spot of paint on the underside.
2 Equal numbers of each type of moth were released into a polluted wood and an unpolluted wood.
3 After a few days, flying moths were recaptured using a light trap.
4 Most of the recaptured marked moths in the polluted wood were dark, suggesting that the light ones had been eaten by birds.
In the unpolluted wood, more light moths had survived.

Figure 15.10 An investigation to measure the survival of dark and light peppered moths in polluted and unpolluted environments.

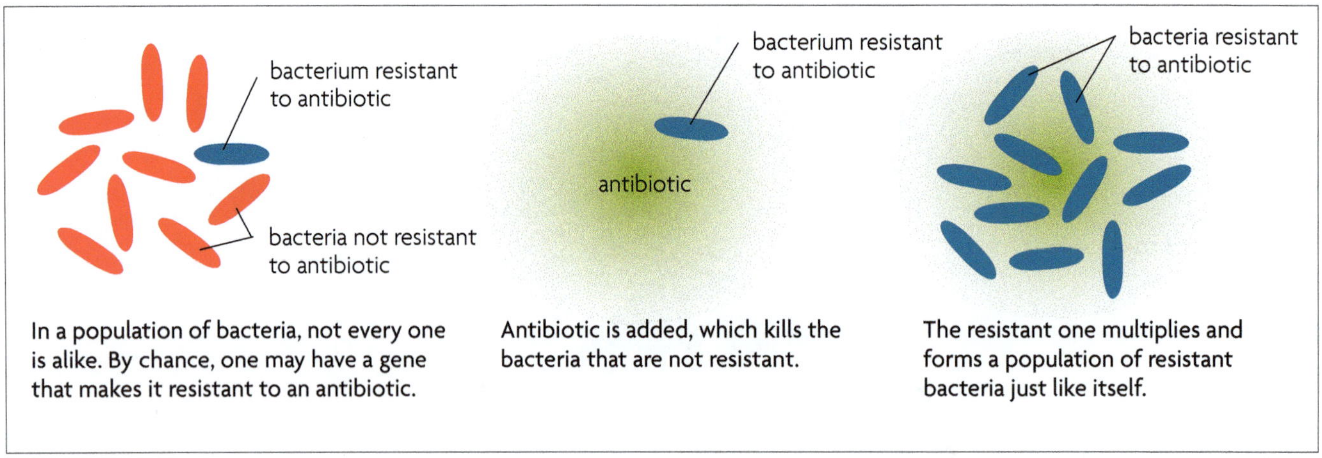
bacterium resistant to antibiotic
bacteria not resistant to antibiotic
In a population of bacteria, not every one is alike. By chance, one may have a gene that makes it resistant to an antibiotic.
bacterium resistant to antibiotic
antibiotic
Antibiotic is added, which kills the bacteria that are not resistant.
bacteria resistant to antibiotic
The resistant one multiplies and forms a population of resistant bacteria just like itself.

Figure 15.11 How resistance to antibiotics increases in a population of bacteria.

This does, in fact, happen quite frequently. This is one reason why there are so many different antibiotics available – if some bacteria become resistant to one, they may be treated with another.

The more we use an antibiotic, the more we are exerting a selection pressure which favours the resistant forms. If antibiotics are used too often, we may end up with resistant strains of bacteria that are very difficult to control.

15.7 Natural selection does not always cause change.

Natural selection does not always produce change. Natural selection ensures that the organisms which are best adapted to their environment will survive. Change will only occur if the environment changes, or if a new mutation appears which adapts the organism better to the existing environment.

For example, in the south-west of Britain, the environment of the peppered moth has never changed very much. The air has not become polluted, so lichens have continued to grow on trees. The best camouflaged moths have always been the pale ones. So selection has always favoured the pale moths in this part of Britain. Any mutant dark moths which do appear are at a disadvantage, and are unlikely to survive.

Most of the time, natural selection tends to keep populations very much the same from generation to generation. It is sometimes called **stabilising selection**. If an organism is well adapted to its environment, and if that environment stays the same, then the organism will not evolve. Coelacanths, for example, have remained virtually unchanged for 350 million years. They live deep in the Indian Ocean, which is a very stable environment (Figure **15.12**).

Figure 15.12 Coelacanths, which live deep in the Indian Ocean, have existed almost unchanged for 350 million years. Humans have existed for only about 4 million years.

15.8 Natural selection and the sickle cell allele.

In section **14.20**, we saw how people who are homozygous for a recessive allele of the gene that is responsible for making haemoglobin suffer from a serious disease called sickle cell anaemia. Without treatment, they are unlikely to survive to adulthood and have children. People who are heterozygous have sickle cell trait; they have few if any symptoms but, of course, can pass on their sickle cell allele to their children.

If sickle cell anaemia is such a dangerous disease, then why has natural selection not removed it from the human population? The answer lies with another disease – malaria.

Malaria is a serious disease caused by a single-celled parasite that is injected into the blood when an infected mosquito bites. Millions of people are killed by this disease each year, most of them children. A person who lives in a part of the world where malaria is present, and who has some resistance to the disease, will be at an advantage compared with others who are susceptible.

Malaria is common in many parts of the world where the sickle cell allele is present in the population (Figure **15.13**). In the past, people homozygous for the sickle cell allele often died early from sickle cell disease. People homozygous for the normal allele often died early from malaria. Those, however, who were heterozygous (with one Hb^S allele and one Hb^A allele) were more resistant to malaria than those with all normal haemoglobin. In parts of the world where malaria was present, people with the heterozygous genotype were most likely to survive until they were old enough to reproduce.

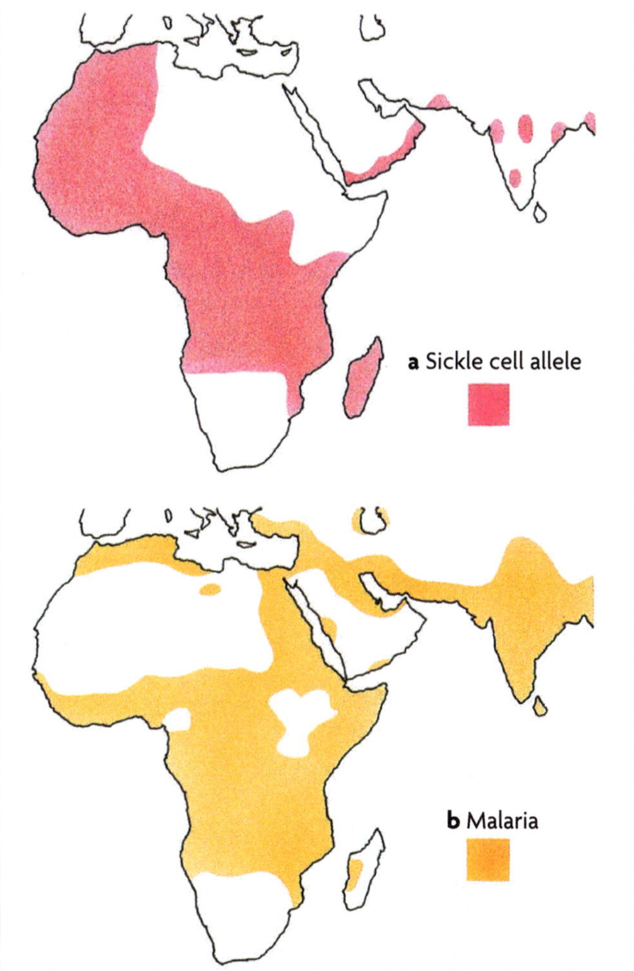

Figure 15.13 The distribution of **a** the sickle cell allele and **b** malaria.

The result was that a high proportion of the living population carried this recessive Hb^S allele.

Will this situation remain the same for the future? If malaria is ever completely controlled, then the original condition which favoured retention of Hb^S will disappear. This has happened in some parts of the world, but malaria is still claiming many lives in sub-Saharan Africa and South East Asia. As people have intermarried, the Hb^S allele has spread. Those affected are receiving better medical care. How do you think this will affect what happens to the Hb^S gene in the world population?

Sickle cell 'carriers' (genotype Hb^AHb^S; one Hb^A allele and the other Hb^S) appear to be healthy and well, and often do not know they are carriers until they have a child with a more serious form of the disease, or they have a special blood test done. For example, about 10% of all Jamaicans are carriers. Many individuals born with both mutant alleles (Hb^SHb^S) die in infancy. For those who survive, one expects decreased life expectancy, but the span varies greatly, and many live to old age.

It is very important that Caribbean people understand sickle cell disease, as it is present throughout the region (Table **15.1**, overleaf). The region is fortunate in that the Sickle Cell Centre, situated at the University of the West Indies, Mona, has carried out extensive research into the disease over more than three decades. The centre operates an on-going programme of monitoring, treatment, follow-up and education for patients.

Questions

15.2 When was the idea of natural selection first suggested?

15.3 Using the six points listed in section **15.4**, explain why the proportion of dark peppered moths near Manchester in Britain increased at the end of the 19th century.

15.4 Why is it unwise to use antibiotics unnecessarily?

15.5 What is meant by stabilising selection? Give one example.

Table 15.1 Distribution of sickle cell carriers in the Caribbean

Country	Population	Number tested	Number of sickle cell carriers	Percentage of sickle cell carriers	Reference
Haita-Tortuga	adults	965	119	12.3	Gentilin et al, 1964
Puerto Rico	adults	388	9	2.3	Pons et al, 1934
		602	29	5.5	Suarez et al, 1959
Guadeloupe	adults	3 000	240	8.0	Lanquillon, 1951
		1 000	92		Bideau et al, 1965
St. Vincent	adults	748	65	8.7	Parker and Williams, 1964
Dominica	adults	664	63	9.5	Parker and Williams, 1964
Barbados	adults	912	64	7.0	Parker and Williams, 1964
St. Lucia	adults	825	115	14.0	Parker and Williams, 1964
Jamaica	adults	1 520	167	11.0	Miall et al, 1967
	pregnant women	1 018	106	10.8	Went, 1957
	newborns	100 000	10 049	10.0	Serjeant et al 1986

The origin of species

15.9 What is a species?

All living organisms may be classified into groups. You learned about some of these in Chapter **1**. The smallest groups are called **species**.

A species is a group of living organisms that are all very similar to one another, and that can interbreed successfully with one another. Members of different species cannot interbreed to produce fertile offspring.

Sometimes, it is not possible to tell whether organisms can interbreed or not. Garlic, for example, only reproduces asexually, and never produces seeds. We can never know anything about the breeding behaviour of extinct organisms, such as dinosaurs. In cases like this, the decision about whether a group of organisms is a species or not has to be made according to how similar they are to each other, and how different they are from other groups of organisms.

15.10 New species from old.

According to the theory of evolution, the millions of different species that exist today have all evolved from other species which existed in the past. One of the big questions in evolution is, 'How can a new species be formed?'

Darwin's theory of natural selection can explain how new varieties of an organism can become more common. The appearance of the dark form of the peppered moth since 1849 can be explained very neatly in this way. But this moth is not a new species. It is still a peppered moth; it can still interbreed with the pale peppered moth.

The problem to be solved is this. How can one species split into two groups, which can no longer interbreed with one another? Although Darwin's book is called *On the Origin of Species*, he did not succeed in answering this question.

15.11 Isolation can produce new species.

Figure **15.14** shows one way in which we think new species are formed. The first stage is for the existing species to be split into two groups. They must be separated by some kind of barrier which they cannot cross.

Each group continues to live and breed in its environment. If the two environments are different, then the selection pressures on the organisms will be different. They will gradually become less and less alike.

After many years, the two populations may become so different that they will no longer be able to breed with one another. Two species now exist, where there was only one before.

Like many of the theories concerned with evolution, this one sounds very convincing, but is difficult to prove. The main difficulty is that it takes so long to happen. We can find examples where we think it has happened in the past, and other examples where it is beginning to happen now. But usually the formation of new species in this way is such a slow process that no one has yet been able to watch it happening from beginning to end.

15.12 New species often develop in island chains.

Island chains, like the West Indies, provide the kind of isolation that could help to make possible the development of new species.

Some geologists believe that the islands of the Greater Antilles were once connected to Central America. Then they separated. Some parts of the present land area of the islands may even have been beneath the sea for a time. This connection followed by separation could give the chance for new species to develop from one original species (Figure **15.15**, overleaf).

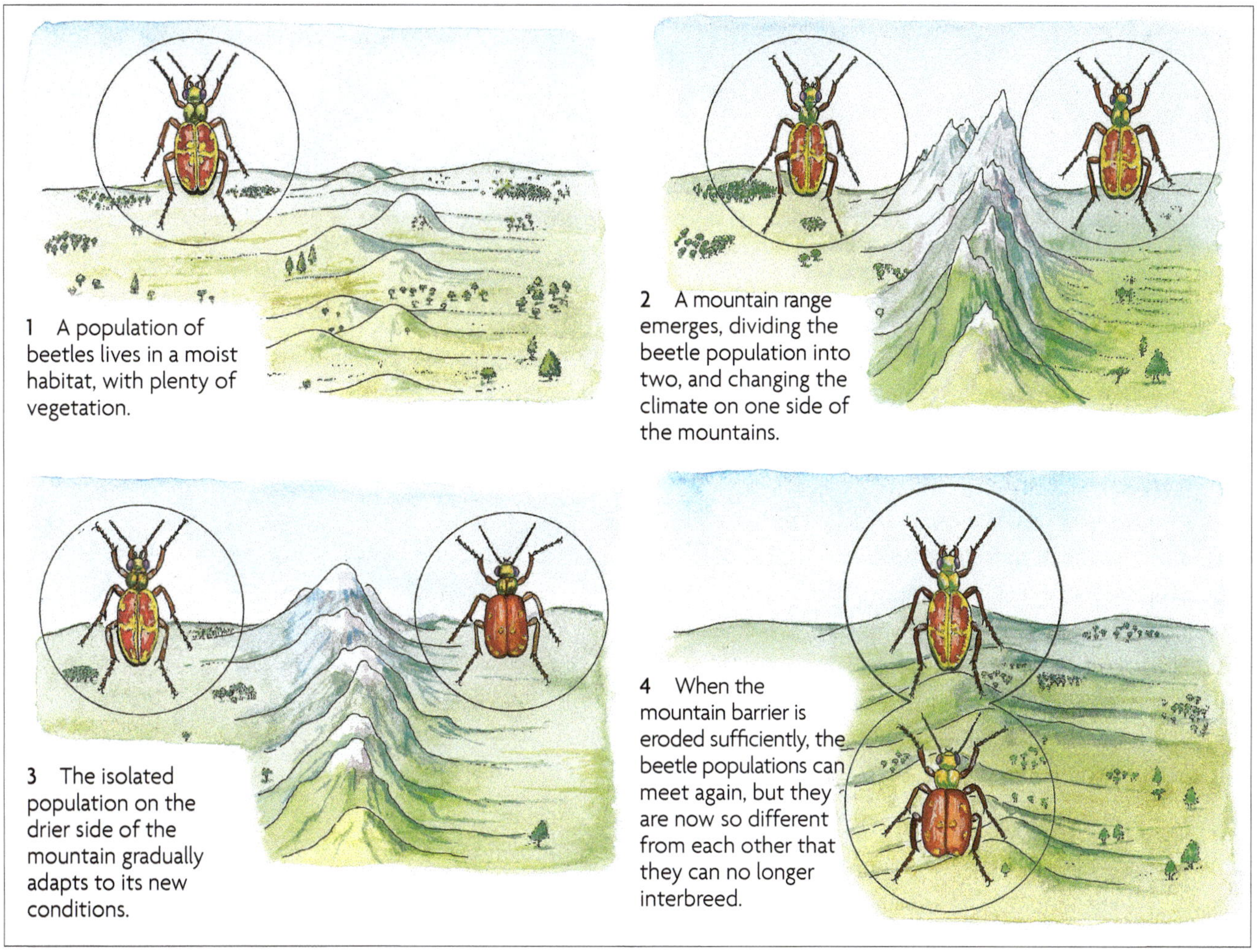

1 A population of beetles lives in a moist habitat, with plenty of vegetation.
2 A mountain range emerges, dividing the beetle population into two, and changing the climate on one side of the mountains.
3 The isolated population on the drier side of the mountain gradually adapts to its new conditions.
4 When the mountain barrier is eroded sufficiently, the beetle populations can meet again, but they are now so different from each other that they can no longer interbreed.

Figure 15.14 How a new species may evolve.

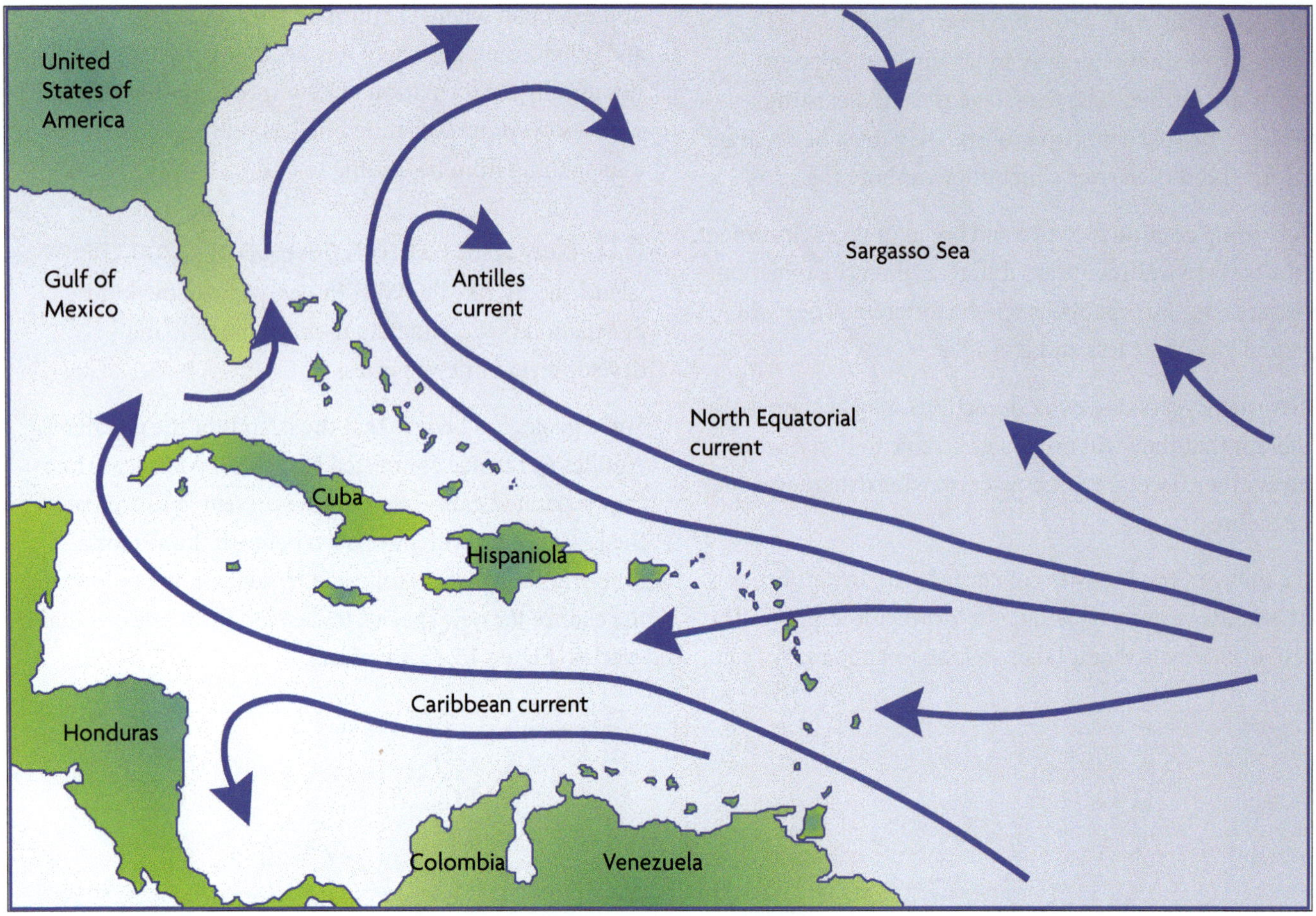

Figure 15.15 Isolated islands can sometimes be colonised by animals and plants brought to them by ocean currents. The new isolated individual colonies may eventually develop into new species.

15.13 *Calisto* butterflies are only found in the West Indies.

Calisto butterflies show no close relationship to other genera in their family (Satyridae). This is believed to be a very ancient family, perhaps over 70 million years old.

No-one knows how or when *Calisto* reached the Greater Antilles, except that it must have been very long ago. Some have suggested that it may have a common ancestor with the South American Mountain genus *Eretris*, and that it may have come to the West Indies by land. Everything that is known about the satyrids suggests that they tend to remain restricted to small niches. There is little contact with neighbours. Colonies, therefore, tend to remain discrete. This makes it easier for new species to emerge.

Calisto (Figure **15.16**) is now found only in the West Indies. There are about 20 species. Puerto Rico and Jamaica each have a single species. In Hispaniola alone there are believed to be 15 species, and in Cuba there are seven. The latter are the larger islands. Two of the species found in Cuba are also found in the Bahamas. All other species are endemic to – that is, found only in – one particular island.

Figure 15.16 *Calisto* butterflies.

15.14 Some parrot species are endemic to islands of the West Indies.

Many West Indian birds, including the parrots, came originally from Central America. The parrots are all of the genus *Amazona*. All, except one species, are endemic to particular islands (Figure **15.17**). This suggests that the different species have evolved by geographic isolation, each one evolving to suit the conditions on one island or group of islands.

Most of the species are becoming scarce. Their natural forest feeding grounds have been cleared, and they have been captured as pets sometimes. Legal measures are being taken to protect them.

Genetics and humans

15.15 Artificial selection is carried out by humans.

Humans can bring about changes in the plants and animals that they grow, using a process called **artifical selection**. For example, if a farmer wants to increase the milk yield of his herd of cattle, he will pick out only the best milk-producing cows and allow them to breed with a bull whose mother, sisters or daughters are good milk producers. The cows which do not produce as much milk will not be allowed to breed. If the farmer continues to do this over many generations, he can steadily increase the mean milk yield of his herd of cattle.

Farmers may also decide to start off with two quite different varieties of cattle and breed them together. For example, they might take one variety that is an excellent milk producer, and another variety that is able to survive in a very hot climate. With artificial selection of several generations, this could produce a new variety that is both good at producing milk and tolerant of a hot climate (Figure **15.18**, overleaf).

You will see that this is really very similar to natural selection. The only difference is that the farmer is choosing traits that *he* finds useful, rather than ones which would give the cows a better chance of surviving in the wild.

Plant and animal breeding research originally centred on the farm and the farmer. In this century, most of this research has been done in an organised way at special institutes and laboratories. Many of these are responsible for developing varieties for worldwide or regional agriculture. Examples of such institutes are the International Rice Research Institute in the Philippines and the West Indies Central Sugar Cane Breeding Station in Barbados.

Figure 15.17 Parrots of the genus *Amazona* occurring in the West Indies.

Figure 15.18 Bred for high milk production, the Jamaica Hope is productive, fertile and heat tolerant. It has a genetic make-up that is 80% Jersey, 15% Sahwah and 5% Holstein.

Developing higher yielding crop plants and animals is one of the main aims of breeders. This is very important in a world with an ever-increasing human population. Crops harvested for products other than food are also important. So there are breeders working with plants grown for timber, fibre, oil and other commodities. Plant breeding is also done with plants grown and sold for their aesthetic value, such as flowers and ornamental plants.

Increased yield may be achieved in several ways. The most obvious way is to increase the size of animals, fruits or seeds. The yield of plants can also be increased by developing plants that mature earlier. This may make it possible to grow more crops per year. For both plants and animals, increased resistance to a particular disease would enhance yields when plants are grown, or animals are raised, in environments where the disease is present.

Quality may be as important as yield. In animal breeding, reduction in body fat is a serious consideration. In part, this is due to the increased health consciousness among consumers. In the case of pigs, those who make pork products, such as bacon and ham, will reject a farmer's animal if it has too much fat.

Plants which are a staple for large numbers of people often contain little protein and can lead to nutritional problems when other food sources are scarce. Breeders working with these crops are therefore trying to increase the protein content. Rice, for instance, is a staple for almost one-third of the world's population. Although rice breeders have gradually increased its protein content, it is still low.

Farming is a business, and production costs affect both the farmer's profit and the cost to the consumer. Thus, an important aim of plant breeders is to make plants use fertilisers more efficiently. Breeding for pest and disease resistance also reduces the need for pesticides, which are not only expensive but can have negative effects on the environment. Developing breeds of animals that more effectively convert food into protein and grow faster would reduce production costs.

It is an alarming fact that about 25% of the plant products harvested each year are lost in storage. Just halving this would provide enough food for the millions of hungry people in the world. Thus, developing better storage qualities is an aim of the breeders of many crop plants.

15.16 Wild relatives of crop plants are very valuable to plant breeders.

All our crop plants were developed from plants growing wild and, in most cases, the crop plants still belong to the same species. One exception is sugar cane, *Saccharum officinarum*, which is only found in cultivation. The wild relatives of crop plants often contain genes not found in the crop. These may have been lost during domestication, or the plants used to develop the crop varieties may not have had them. Among these genes there may be ones that gave resistance to various pest and disease organisms, or other desirable traits.

Today, most plant-breeding institutes maintain collections of wild relatives for use in their breeding programmes and expeditions are mounted to collect other representatives. However, it is of major concern that the habitats of many of these wild plants are being destroyed.

The use of wild relatives in plant breeding can be seen by examining the pedigree of a recently developed sugar cane variety, B 79474 (Figure **15.19**). This variety was obtained from crosses involving varieties of *Saccharum officinarum*, *S. robustum* and *S. spontaneum*, as well as a number of previously developed commercial varieties. All of the commercial varieties used were the products of interspecific hybridisation.

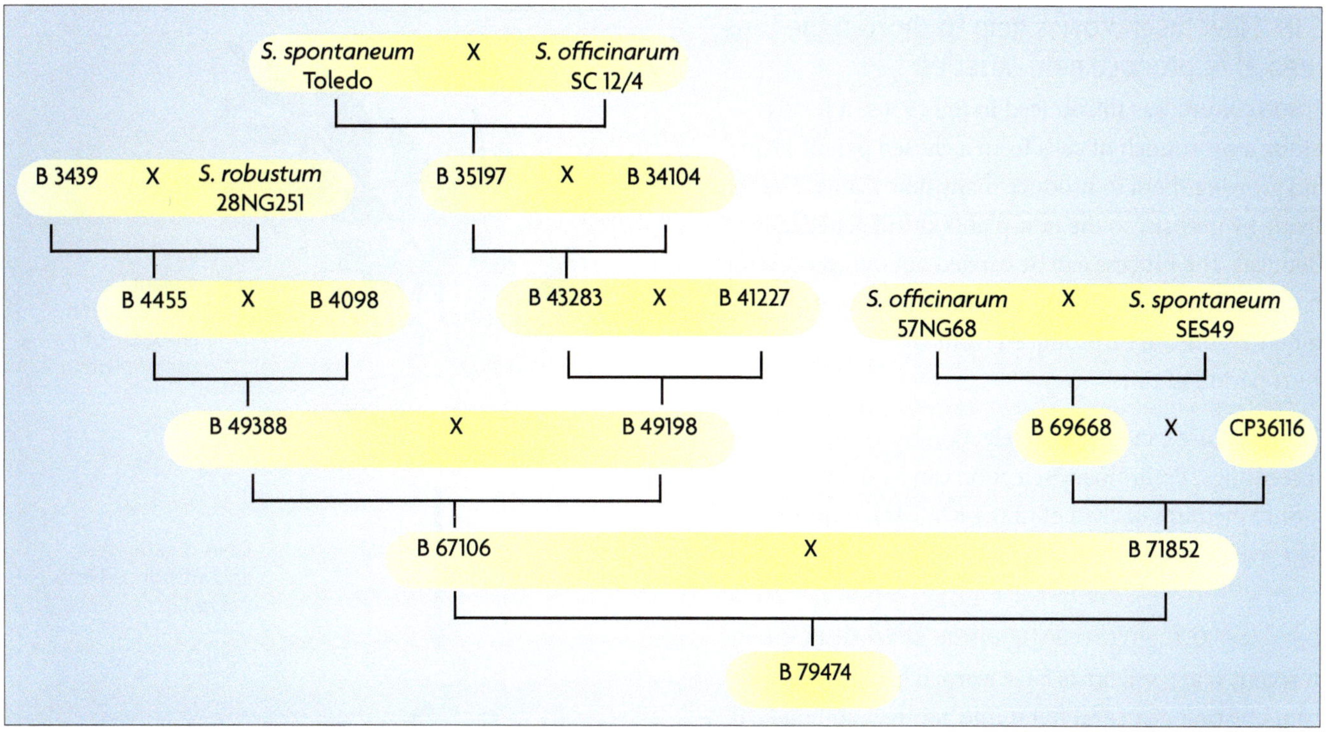

Figure 15.19 The pedigree of a recently developed sugar cane variety, B 79474.

15.17 Traditional plant and animal breeding takes a long time.

We have seen that the simplest breeding scheme involves the selection of two parents, crossing them and selecting those offspring that show the desired characteristics. For fruit trees that take several years before they bear fruit, this process could take five years or more. The two parents would have been selected because they each had desirable characteristics. One or two of the offspring may inherit some of these, but it is unlikely that any would have all of them. The best offspring would have to be back-crossed to the parent with the traits not inherited to try to get a new offspring which has the correct mix of characteristics. Often this will require back-crossing with both parents several times.

As you might realise, there are obvious problems with this, particularly with animal species. First, the parents may not live long enough for all these back-crosses to be made and other individuals with the parent's characteristics would have to be found. Second, a female offspring cannot be back-crossed with its mother, so a male with similar traits to the mother would have to be found.

Depending on generation time of the species, and the number of crosses required, this process may take a few years or very many years. Also, the process is not complete at this stage. The plants and animals have to be multiplied without losing their good characteristics. It is only after this stage that the new plant variety, or animal breed, can be given to the farmers.

Plant breeders have an advantage over animal breeders in that plants produce many more offspring. Cows normally produce a single calf, Barbados black-belly sheep normally produce twins, and pigs produce about a dozen piglets as a result of a single mating. Thus, the probability that any offspring will have all the desired characteristics is much less. Also a plant such as sugar cane, that can be cloned, will provide a number of genetically identical parents (section **13.4**). With animals, other than those which are long lived, the parents may be different at each cross.

With fewer offspring to select from in each generation and genetically different parents in each generation, it is not surprising that progress in animal breeding is normally slower than in plant breeding. Plants with long generation times are an obvious exception.

The breeding of Jamaica Hope cattle represents a success story. It is the only dairy breed that has been developed in Jamaica and has gained worldwide recognition.

15.18 New technologies help to shorten the time needed to produce new varieties.

Tissue culture was introduced in the 1930s. It involves taking a tiny bunch of cells from a chosen parent plant, and growing them to produce many new plants. The cells divide by mitosis, so the new plants are all genetically identical. The process can be carried out on a large scale in controlled conditions in a laboratory. Huge numbers of new plants can be produced from just one parent in a short period of time.

Tissue culture can speed up selection from large numbers of seedlings. Preliminary selection can be done on a culture medium instead of in the field. The technique can also give large quantities of material in a short time.

15.19 Genetic engineering alters DNA directly.

In recent years, scientists have learned how to take DNA from one organism and put it into another, and make it work there. This is called **gene technology** or **genetic engineering**.

Genetic engineering makes it possible to develop new varieties directly. A gene is found which confers a desirable trait on the organism that possesses it. The gene is then removed from this organism and inserted into the one which is to be altered. This organism then uses this gene just like the rest of its DNA, following its instructions to make a particular protein. This may confer the desired trait on the genetically engineered organism.

That may sound very simple, but the process is complex and expensive. It requires very well-equipped laboratories and highly trained personnel. Nevertheless, more and more successes have been achieved, and we now use genetically modified organisms in many different ways (Figures **15.20** and **15.21**).

Genetic engineering has been used with plants to:

- give crop plants immunity to viruses, for example, to protect tobacco from the tobacco mosaic virus (TMV)
- cause delay in ripening, and therefore in spoilage, for example, in the 'Flavr Savr' tomato marketed in the USA in 1994 and rapidly withdrawn due to its unpopularity
- give resistance to insects, for example, the natural insecticide quality of *Bacillus thuringiensis* that has been built into some crops like corn, rice and cotton.

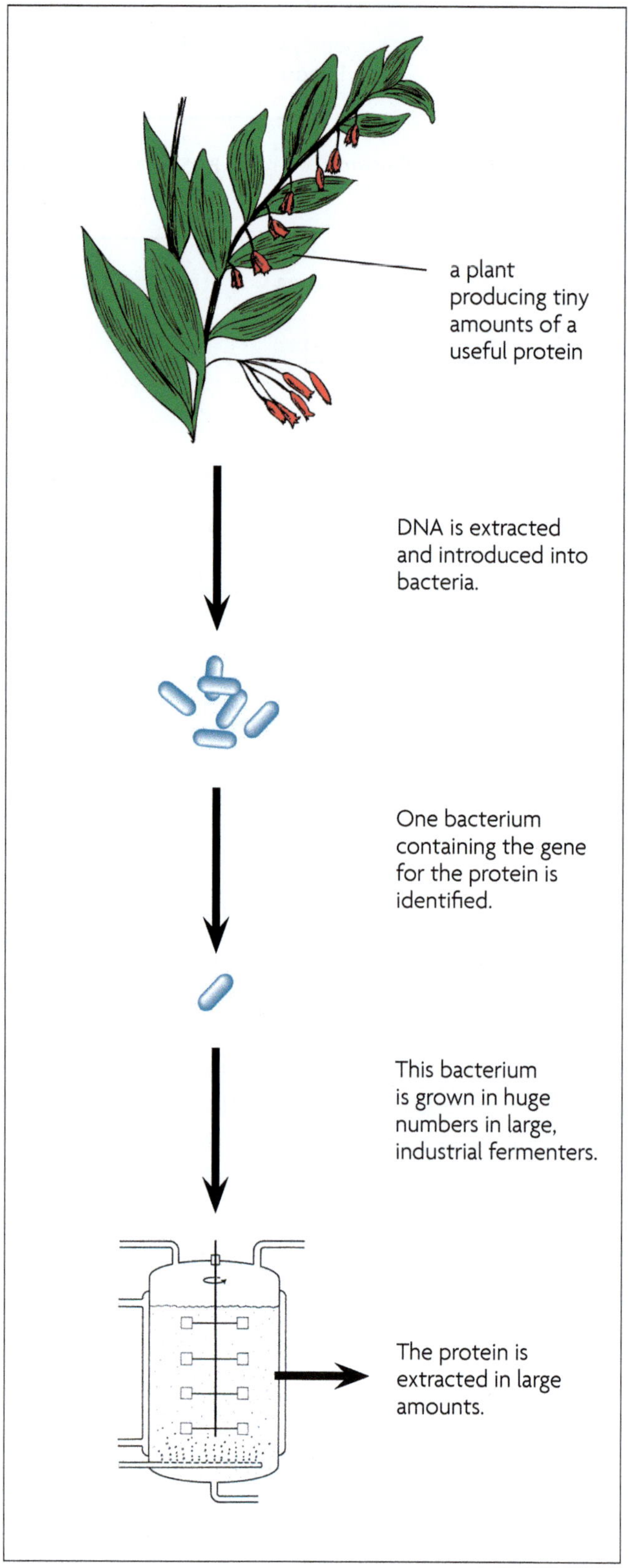

Figure 15.20 How genetic engineering can be used to produce a desired protein in large quantities.

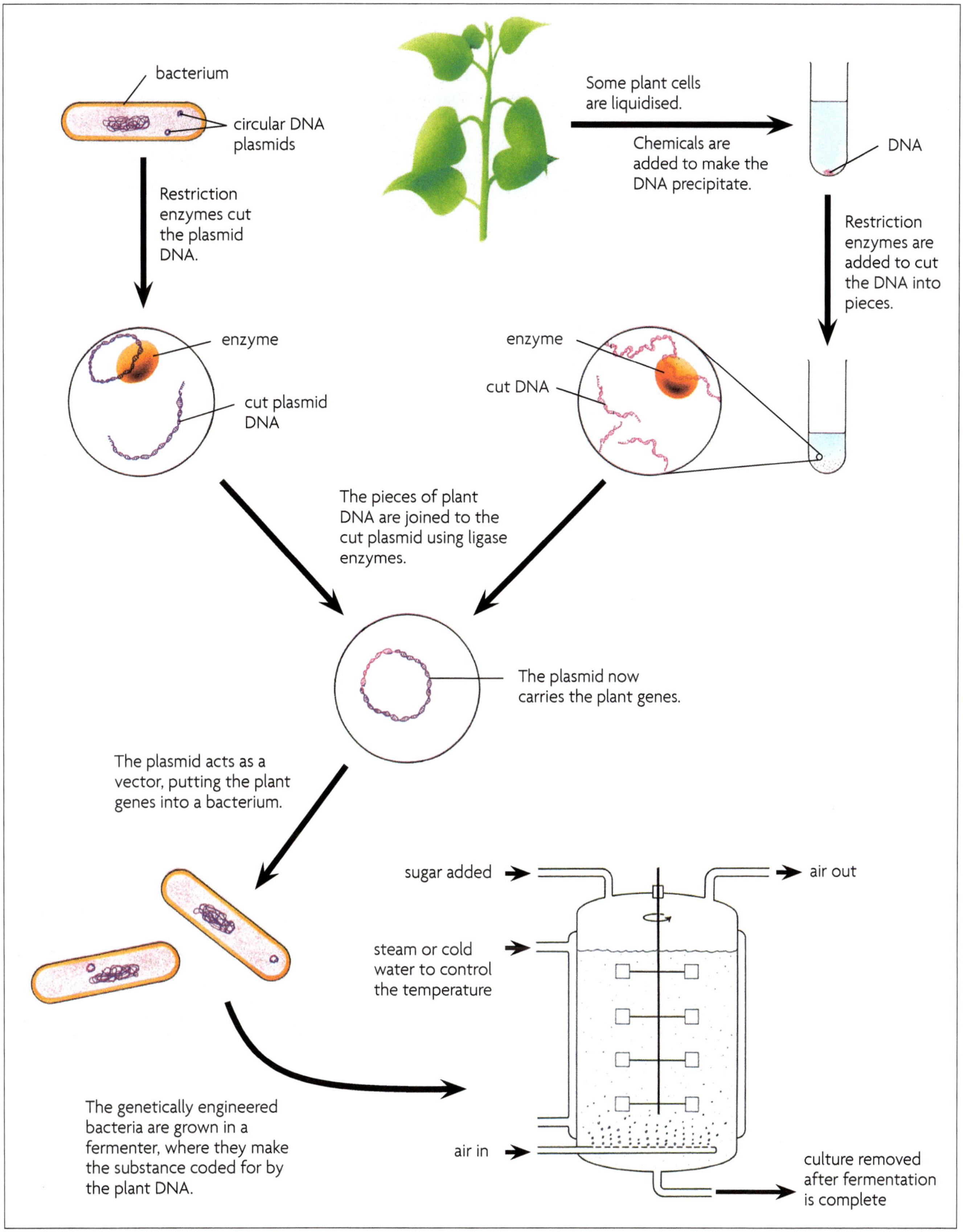

Figure 15.21 Detail of how genetic engineering can be used to produce a protein in large quantities. In this example, the required protein is one that is normally made by a plant. The gene which codes for this protein is extracted from the plant and inserted into a bacterium, using a tiny circle of DNA called a plasmid as a vector.

15.20 Human insulin is made by genetically engineered bacteria.

Genetic engineering is useful in medicine, as well as in agriculture.

Some people are not able to make the hormone insulin. Normally, insulin is secreted when blood glucose levels rise too high. Insulin causes the liver to remove glucose from the blood, bringing levels back to normal (section **11.4**). People who cannot make insulin have the disease diabetes. Those with a form of the disease called type I diabetes can be treated by giving insulin injections.

For a long time, the only source of insulin was from animals which had been killed for food, such as pigs. Now, genetic engineering has produced bacteria that make human insulin.

The insulin gene was first extracted from human cells. This may sound easy, but the length of DNA containing that gene had to be identified, and then separated from all the rest – a process requiring great expertise and expensive technology. The gene was then inserted into bacteria called *Escherichia coli*. The bacteria took the genes into their cells. Each time a bacterium divided, it copied the human insulin gene just as if it was one of its own genes, so that each new bacterium received a copy. Soon, there was a very large clone of bacteria all possessing the human insulin gene.

These bacteria are now grown in huge numbers in large containers called fermenters. They make and secrete insulin, which is identical to human insulin. This is sold and used to treat people with diabetes. It is much cheaper than insulin extracted from pigs, and also has the advantage that it is identical to human insulin (pig insulin is not quite the same).

15.21 Industry has profited from genetic engineering.

Bacteria with altered DNA have been produced for the breakdown of various forms of garbage. Research is under way to produce such a bacterium for breaking down oil slicks. Work on a bacterium called *Pseudomonas* is promising, but this bacterium would only be able to work on thin oil films, where it can get oxygen. It also does not work very well at low temperatures.

Bakers' and brewers' yeast, *Saccharomyces cerevisiae*, normally breaks down glucose, giving alcohol as one end product (section **6.7**). This fungus has been genetically changed to produce varieties that can convert lactose into alcohol. This allows manufacturers to make use of whey, a waste product from the processing of cheese. Whey contains much lactose, which now can be used to make alcohol.

15.22 There are social, ethical and moral concerns about genetic engineering.

We have seen that genetic engineering has opened up many possibilities of improving people's lives. It has also opened up many possible dangers.

For example, genetic engineering often involves producing bacteria and viruses with different genes from their usual ones. This could possibly cause **health hazards**. What if some of these normally harmless micoorganisms were changed in such a way that they became able to infect humans and cause disease? They might cause a new and highly dangerous disease, against which we have no natural body defences and no vaccines. To try to make sure that this does not happen, there are strictly enforced regulations about the kinds of microorganisms which can be used in genetic engineering, the kinds of genes which can be put into them and the conditions in which they must be kept. However, what if someone wanted *deliberately* to produce a new pathogen, and release it into the environment?

As well as health hazards, genetic engineering could produce **environmental hazards**. For example, imagine that a new variety of crop is produced, which has been genetically engineered to be resistant to a particular insect that feeds on it. This gene might be passed – in pollen, for example – to closely related, wild plants living nearby. The gene could then theoretically spread through the population of wild plants. This could upset the food web in the ecosystem, because the insect would no longer be able to eat those plants. So far, there have been no instances of this happening, but it is certainly possible. In most countries, extensive field trials of any new genetically engineered crop have to be carried out before farmers are allowed to grow it on a commercial scale. These trials can help to check if there is any possibility of the genes spreading into wild populations.

Genetic engineering also raises questions about what is morally and ethically acceptable in society. For example, in theory, it will eventually be possible to check the genes in a human zygote, to make sure that there are no major genetic faults. If a fault was found, then the 'right' allele could be inserted into the zygote, so that all the cells in the embryo which developed from it contained a correct version of the gene. Should this be allowed? Should it be allowed just for serious diseases such as cystic fibrosis or sickle cell anaemia? Or should it be allowed for things like height or intelligence? This is all a long way in the future, but perhaps we should think hard about it now, before things begin to happen that we are not prepared for.

Like all major new discoveries and technologies, genetic engineering has the potential to provide all sorts of benefits to people and perhaps also for other living things. It also has the potential to cause immense harm. Scientists and everyone else must remain well aware of this. If as many people as possible, whether they are scientists or not, try to stay well informed about the developments that are taking place, then we can do our best to ensure that the 'good' uses of genetic engineering go ahead, while the potential problems are stopped in their tracks.

Key ideas

- In discontinuous variation – for example, human blood groups – each individual fits into a definite category. In continuous variation – for example, human height – an individual can have any value between two extremes.
- Discontinuous variation occurs when one or two genes control a characteristic, and where the environment has no effect. Continuous variation generally occurs where the environment has an effect on the characteristic.
- Individuals with characteristics that give them an advantage over others are more likely to survive and reproduce. If these characteristics are caused by genes, then these characteristics will also appear in their offspring. Individuals without these features are more likely to die before they can reproduce. This is called natural selection.
- Examples of changes in the characteristics in a population caused by natural selection include peppered moths and antibiotic-resistant bacteria.
- New species are formed when a population is isolated from another, so that it develops along its own lines. Eventually, it becomes unable to interbreed with members of the original species, and has therefore become a new species.
- Humans use artificial selection and breeding programmes to produce populations of organisms with features that they find useful. Crop plants and farm animals have been bred in this way.
- More recently, genetic engineering has been used to take genes from one organism and place them into a different species. Examples include the introduction of insulin genes into bacteria and pest-resistance genes into crop plants.
- Genetic engineering has the potential to produce great benefits, but there are many ethical, moral, social and ecological issues that need to be addressed.

End-of-chapter questions

1 Match each term with its definition:
evolution, speciation, natural selection, species, artifical selection, genetic engineering.

- a a group of organisms that are very similar to each other and that can interbreed to produce fertile offspring
- b gradual changes in the characteristics of living organisms over a long period of time
- c the transfer of genes from one organism to another of a different species
- d the choice, by humans, of which animals or plants to allow to breed
- e the way in which new species are formed
- f a process in which only those organisms best adapted to their environment survive and reproduce

2 Many species, including various birds, insects, reptiles and ratbats, are found only in the Caribbean. Choose any three such species peculiar to your own territory, and investigate their history.

3 Natural selection causes living organisms to become well adapted to their environment. The best-adapted organisms are the most successful. Explain each of the following.

- a A population of organisms that can reproduce sexually often becomes adapted to a new environment more quickly than organisms that reproduce asexually.
- b Evolution does not always come to a halt once a population of organisms has become adapted to its environment.

4 Choose an organism with which you are familiar, which has been produced by artificial selection. Try to trace the history and aims of the breeding process and its present status.

16 Humans and health

In this chapter, you will find out:

- the various categories of disease
- how lifestyle can affect health
- the causes and management of diabetes
- the health implications of obesity
- the dangers of drug abuse and misuse
- how the body defends itself against pathogens
- how we can become immune to a disease
- the causes of sexually transmitted diseases, and how their spread can be limited
- the importance of mosquitoes and houseflies as vectors of disease
- some diseases of crops and livestock, and their implications.

Health and disease

16.1 Health is more than absence of disease.

What does is mean to say that we are 'healthy'? The World Health Organization, which researches into health all over the world and tries to improve health in developing countries, believes that being healthy means more than simply not having a disease. One definition of health is: feeling well, having a positive outlook and being able to carry out the physical and mental tasks needed for everyday life.

There are many different ways in which the human body can become unhealthy. The obvious causes of ill health are microorganisms, such as bacteria and viruses, but there are many other illnesses that have nothing to do with these. A person's lifestyle, including their diet, use of drugs and the amount of exercise they do, can have a very large impact on their health. We have already seen how the genes that we inherit from our parents can affect health. And, of course, our bodies become more likely to develop diseases such as arthritis as we age.

16.2 There are different types of disease.

A **disease** is something that is wrong with your body.

Nutritional deficiency diseases **Nutritional deficiency diseases** are caused by an unbalanced diet in which a nutrient is missing. Some of these are described in Tables **5.2** and **5.3** (pages 72 and 73). Figure **16.1** (overleaf) shows the foods that should be included in a balanced diet.

Physiological diseases **Physiological diseases** are caused by the body just going wrong by itself. Sometimes it simply wears out as it gets older. For example, a person's joints might get damaged so they swell and feel painful. This is called **arthritis**. **Cancer** is also a degenerative

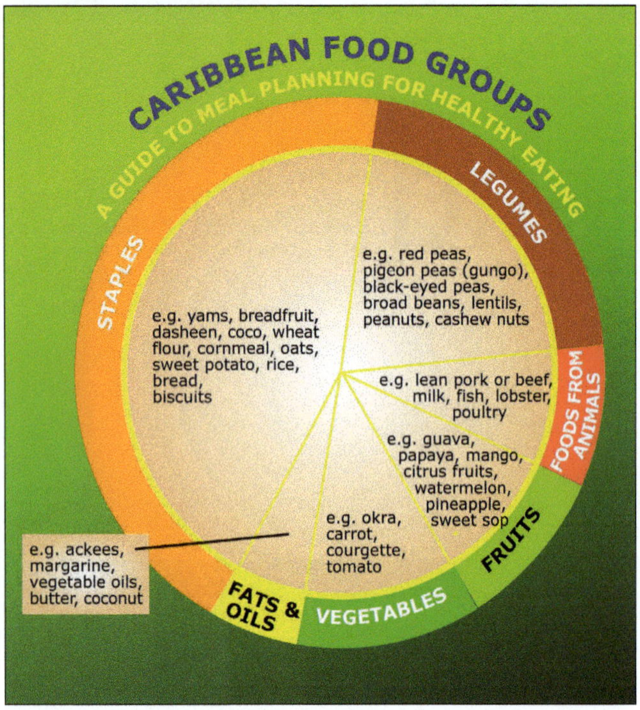

Figure 16.1 Foods to include in a balanced diet.

disease. Cancer happens when the control mechanisms for cell division go wrong. A cell divides uncontrollably, causing tumours that can spread to many parts of the body.

Hereditary diseases **Hereditary diseases** are caused by our genes. **Sickle cell anaemia** is one example.

Pathogenic diseases **Pathogenic diseases**, also called **infectious diseases**, are caused by microorganisms that get into the body and breed. **HIV/AIDS** and **tuberculosis** are infectious diseases.

Questions

16.1 Copy this table and fill it in.

Type of disease	Description	Some examples
deficiency	caused by a lack of an important nutrient in the diet	scurvy (lack of vitamin C), rickets (lack of vitamin D or calcium)
physiological		
hereditary		
pathogenic		

16.2 Which of the diseases that you have listed in the table in Question **16.1** could be caught from someone else?

Lifestyle and health

16.3 Obesity increases risk of disease.

Obesity means being very overweight. Doctors and researchers have worked out the range of body mass that appears to mean that a person is most likely to stay healthy. Figure **16.2** shows a body mass chart. You might like to use it to check if your body mass falls within the correct range.

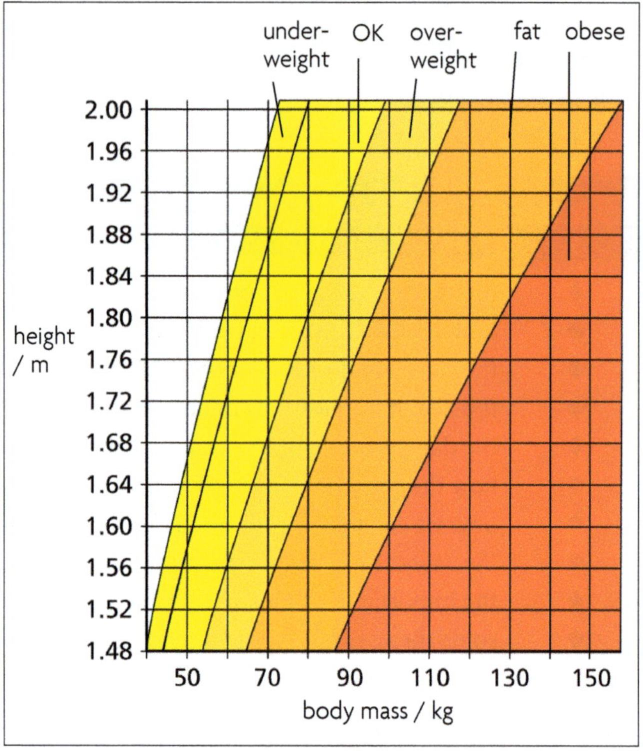

Figure 16.2 Height and body mass chart.

Obesity happens when a person takes in more kilojoules in their diet than they need, over a long period of time. The extra kilojoules are turned into fat and stored under the skin and around the body organs (Figure **16.3**).

A person's genes also have an effect on how easily they might become obese. In some people, quite a bit of the extra food that they eat gets used by the cells to produce extra heat, rather than changing into fat. In others, the body stores as much of the extra food as it can.

So, the three main causes of obesity are:

- eating too much food, especially fatty foods
- not exercising enough
- having genes that make the body likely to store 'extra' food as fat.

Figure 16.3 An obese person.

Being obese makes it much more likely that a person will get diabetes or heart disease. It is important to try to keep weight down through eating a good diet and taking regular exercise. Fad diets and diet pills are not the answer, and may be dangerous.

16.4 There are two types of diabetes.

In section **11.4**, we saw how the hormones **insulin** and **glucagon** control blood glucose levels. When this control breaks down, a person has **diabetes**.

There are two types of diabetes.

Type I diabetes This usually develops when a person is very young. The pancreas does not make enough insulin. It is not known exactly why this happens, but one theory is that the body's immune system (sections **16.23** to **16.24**) attacks the cells in the pancreas that make insulin.

Type II diabetes This develops later in life. The pancreas still makes insulin, but the liver does not respond to it.

16.5 Uncontrolled diabetes is dangerous.

You may remember that, in a normal person, insulin is secreted by the pancreas when the blood glucose levels go up. The insulin causes the liver to remove glucose from the blood and change it into **glycogen**, which is stored in the liver cells. This brings the blood glucose levels back down to normal. If, later in the day, the blood glucose level starts to fall, then the liver can break down some of its glycogen stores and release glucose back into the blood.

However, if a person with type II diabetes eats a sugary meal, the blood glucose level goes up – and stays up (Figure **16.4**). If it gets very high, the person will feel ill, with a dry mouth and blurred vision. They may be confused and could go into a coma. This happens because the high level of glucose in the blood and tissue fluid produces a highly concentrated solution. Water therefore moves out of body cells into this solution, by osmosis. The cells are left with insufficient water, and the metabolic reactions that should take place in them can no longer happen in the normal way.

If this person goes without food for more than a few hours, their blood glucose level can drop very low. This is because there are no glycogen stores in the liver to

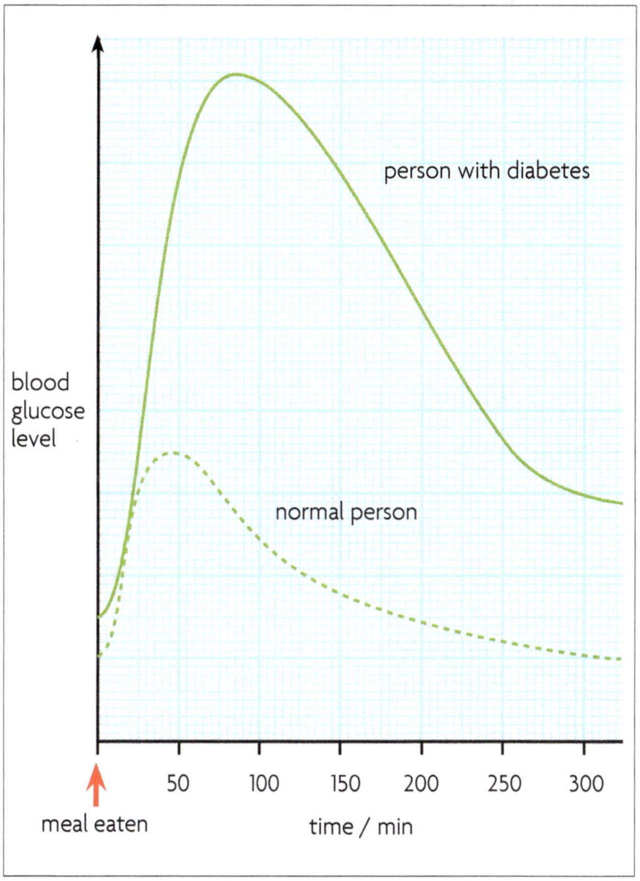

Figure 16.4 Blood glucose levels after a meal, in a normal person and a person with diabetes.

draw on. The person will feel very, very tired and become confused. They might lose consciousness and go into a coma. This happens because cells need glucose for respiration – the way in which they release energy and make ATP. Without glucose, they quickly run out of energy. Brain cells are especially susceptible to glucose shortage.

These wildly swinging blood glucose levels gradually damage many organs in the body. They especially harm blood vessels, kidneys and eyes.

16.6 Diabetes can be treated with good diet, exercise and sometimes insulin injections.

Normally, there should be no glucose at all in the urine. However, if a person has diabetes then blood glucose levels may soar so high that the kidneys do allow some of it to leave the body in urine. The presence of glucose in the urine is often used by doctors to make an initial diagnosis of diabetes.

A person with diabetes can keep track of what is happening to their blood glucose levels by testing their urine for glucose. Even better, they can test their blood, and find out what the glucose concentration is. One way of doing this is to use test strips. These are dipped into the urine or blood, and change colour according to the concentration of glucose (Figure **16.5**). Many people, however, now use electronic biosensors to do this. The biosensor gives a digital readout of the blood glucose concentration (Figure **16.6**).

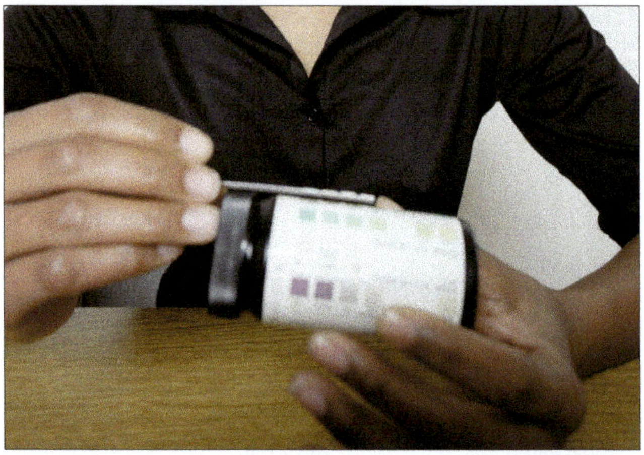

Figure 16.5 Glucose test strips contain an enzyme which acts on any glucose in urine or blood, and causes a colour change in the strip. The colour of the strip is checked against a colour chart to find the approximate concentration of glucose.

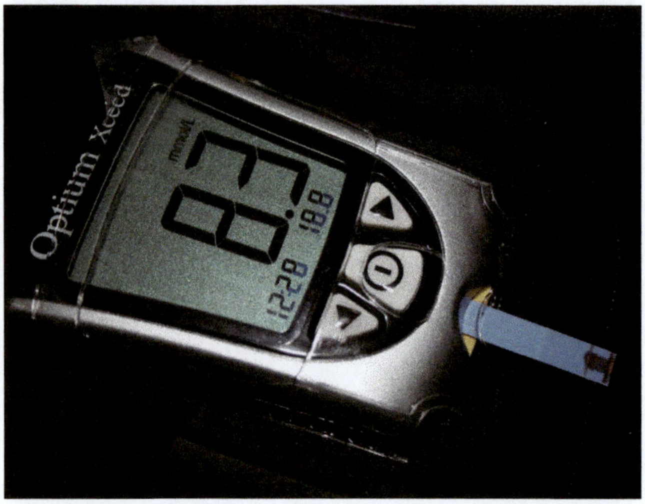

Figure 16.6 This biosensor is used by a person with diabetes to check their blood sugar level. A tiny droplet of blood is placed on the sensor, and the screen immediately shows the blood glucose reading.

If the person has type II diabetes, he or she can often control their blood glucose level by eating small meals at regular intervals. They should regularly test their blood or urine for glucose. If the person is obese, then it is very important that they try to lose weight through diet and exercise. Exercise is also helpful in reducing the concentration of glucose in the blood, as it increases the rate of use of glucose by muscle cells. Many people with type II diabetes lead very active lives – there are several world-class sportsmen and sportswomen who have type II diabetes.

If a person has type I diabetes, then diet and exercise alone are not enough to control their blood glucose levels. They may also need to inject themselves with insulin to help to keep their blood glucose levels down. Some people with type II diabetes also need to do this. If the person leads a very predictable lifestyle, so that the amount they eat and the exercise they do is very similar from day to day, then they may be able to follow a regular regime of injecting insulin, too. For most people, however, they will need to do regular blood tests to check when they need to inject insulin.

16.7 Obesity increases the risk of hypertension.

In section **7.12**, we saw how high blood pressure, known as **hypertension**, can affect a person's health. More than 20% of people in the Caribbean have hypertension. The risk of developing hypertension increases if a person is obese, smokes, does little exercise, eats a diet containing a lot of fat or salt, or lives a stressful life. It is also affected by the genes that a person inherits from their parents.

Losing weight, by eating a balanced diet and taking regular exercise, is the most important way of treating hypertension. Untreated, it often leads to heart disease or a stroke (Figure **16.7**).

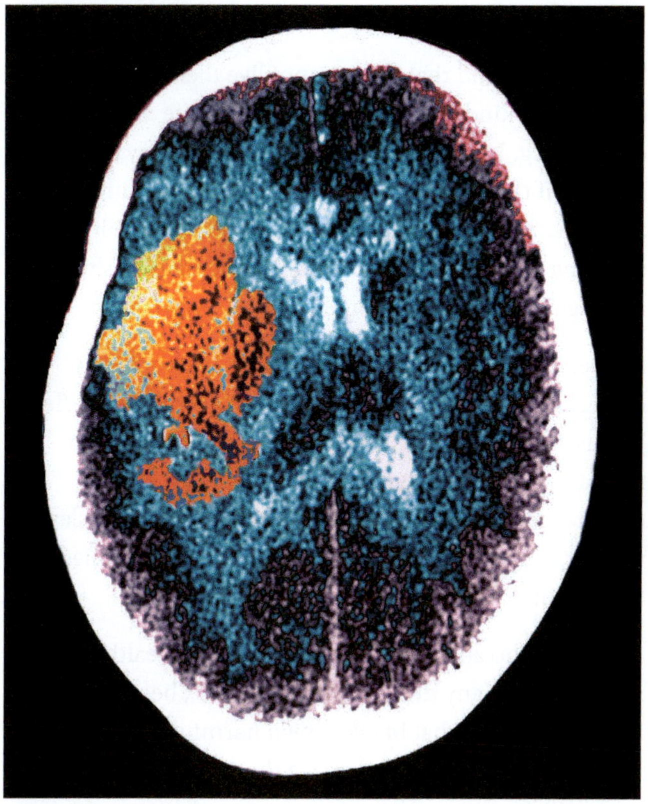

Figure 16.7 The red area in this brain scan shows where blood has damaged the brain tissue after a stroke.

16.8 Good diet avoids deficiency diseases.

A deficiency disease is caused by insufficient quantities of one or more nutrients in the diet. Deficiency diseases are most likely to occur when people do not get enough to eat, or only have a very small choice of foods. For example, people in a developing country where there is little to eat except rice may not get anough vitamin A in their diet, and may suffer from night blindness.

The best way of avoiding a deficiency disease is to eat a balanced diet containing a wide variety of different foods. It should include fresh vegetables and fruits, as these are good sources of several different vitamins, such as vitamin C. Tables **5.2** and **5.3** (pages 72 and 73) list some of the main deficiency diseases.

Some deficiency diseases are associated with childhood. For example, **rickets** is a disease that results when children do not enough vitamin D. The signs of rickets are malformed bones. Vitamin D is made in the skin when it gets enough sunshine.

Energy protein malnutrition (**EPM**) may be a problem after a baby ceases to be breast-fed. Severe forms of EPM, like kwashiorkor and marasmus, are not a great problem in the Caribbean but chronic EPM often manifests itself as stunting (Figures **16.8a** and **16.8b**).

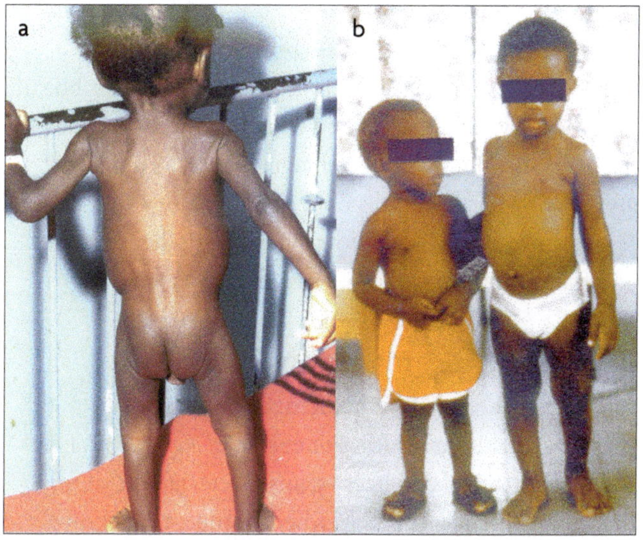

Figure 16.8 **a** This child has marasmus, one form of energy protein malnutrition (EPM). **b** The shorter of the two children is stunted. He has a chronic form of energy protein malnutrition.

Anaemia is also common in adolescents and young women of child-bearing age. Anaemia results from a lack of iron. Iron is needed for the formation of haemoglobin (Hb), the pigment in the blood which carries oxygen to body cells (section **7.20**). Rickets, EPM, and anaemia can all be treated using proper diet regimes.

The risk of developing **dental caries** may be increased by a lack of calcium in the diet, resulting in brittle teeth. However, inadequate dental hygiene is an important cause. We often eat without brushing the teeth immediately, or even sometimes before going to bed. This provides the environment for the growth of the bacteria which cause tooth decay. This condition is more frequent in the Caribbean than it should be.

Anorexia and **bulimia** appear to be more common in adolescents than in adults, though they are not restricted to this group. In anorexia, sufferers often begin to diet.

Then they continue even after they have already lost too much weight, and are hungry. There is not enough carbohydrate or fat in the diet for respiration, so the body uses protein. Much of the body protein is in the muscles. When this begins to be used, the person becomes wasted, and is really starving. The weakened body will pick up infections more easily.

In bulimia, the person eats, but readily loses a meal through induced vomiting. The end result is, as in anorexia, loss of too much weight. Both conditions seem to be associated with psychological fears. The reasons may be deep seated. This makes the conditions difficult to correct.

So far, these two diseases seem to be rare in the Caribbean. Traditionally, Caribbean people tend to appreciate the 'well rounded figure', especially in women, so anxiety about being overweight is not common. However, a few cases of anorexia are now emerging in the female adolescent population.

16.9 Drugs affect the way the body works.

Many drugs are used in medicine to help the body regain or maintain health. For example, **antibiotics** help the body's natural defences against bacterial infection. Sometimes, drugs may help where homeostatic control systems break down. For example, people who are hypertensive or diabetic may take various drugs to help them to maintain proper blood pressure or blood sugar levels. Drugs such as aspirin are used to relieve pain. Stronger drugs like morphine may be needed for those in intense pain, perhaps after surgery or in some terminally ill patients.

Many commonly used drugs may be categorised as follows.

- **Stimulants** **Stimulants** speed up the action of the central nervous system. Examples are caffeine, nicotine and cocaine.
- **Depressants** **Depressants** relax the central nervous system. They include alcohol and tranquillisers like Valium.
- **Hallucinogens** **Hallucinogens** temporarily distort reality. They include marijuana and lysergic acid (LSD).
- **Analgesics** **Analgesics** lower the perception of pain. Among these are aspirin, codeine, morphine and heroin.

16.10 Drug abuse causes damage to people and their families.

Often, however, drugs are abused. They are taken for non-medical reasons to affect our body processes, mind or nervous system, or behaviour. For example, marijuana and cocaine may be used to change one's mood, to get a 'high'. Drug abuse does serious harm to a person, and also to their friends and family.

Some people find that they cannot live their lives without a particular kind of drug. They have become **dependent** on the drug. In many instances, the person may become really ill if they do not take the drug. They may undergo severe **withdrawal symptoms** if they do not take it, suffering from continuous vomiting and nausea, shivering and feeling generally extremely unwell.

If a person takes a drug for some time, the body may change so that more drug is needed to get the same effect. This is called **drug tolerance**. The person has to keep increasing the quantity of the drug that they take, to experience the same effects. The person becomes a slave to their drug, and to the person who illegally supplies them with it.

A person who abuses drugs puts their own health at serious risk. Many drugs damage the liver, because the liver is the organ that breaks down harmful substances in the body. Some drugs damage the nervous system, especially the brain. They may affect a person's behaviour so that they put their own life at risk, or the lives of others.

When a person becomes dependent on a drug, they may be prepared to do anything to get it. They may use most of their money buying drugs. They may resort to criminal activity to get money to buy drugs. The drug abuser also harms their family, and can be a burden on society. They may become so obsessed by the drug that they neglect their friends and family and lose touch with them. They may lose their job. They cannot help to support their family. They may resort to prostitution to get money for their drugs. Some drugs can make a person aggressive and more likely to commit crimes.

16.11 Cocaine is an addictive stimulant.

Cocaine is a drug that comes from the coca plant, which grows in South America. It is an illegal drug. Cocaine is a **stimulant**. This means that it makes people feel more alert. It can also make a person feel really happy, with all their worries gone, a condition called **euphoria**.

People in South America have chewed coca leaves for thousands of years. They used it to help them to cope with hunger and tiredness, and with the problems of living or working at high altitude in the Andes mountains.

But now the drug is available in a much more pure and concentrated form. This makes it highly dangerous. Cocaine is an **addictive** drug. A person can become dependent on it very quickly.

Many people who abuse cocaine find that they become **tolerant** to it. They have to take more and more to get the same effect. They may get it into their body by injecting it, so that the drug acts more quickly. This involves an extra risk, because the needles used for injection may be dirty and transmit diseases such as HIV/AIDS (section **16.26**).

A person who keeps on taking cocaine will seriously damage their health. It especially harms the heart and circulatory system, the liver and the brain (Figure **16.9**). They may suffer from psychiatric problems such as anxiety, depression and paranoia (imagining that people are trying to harm them).

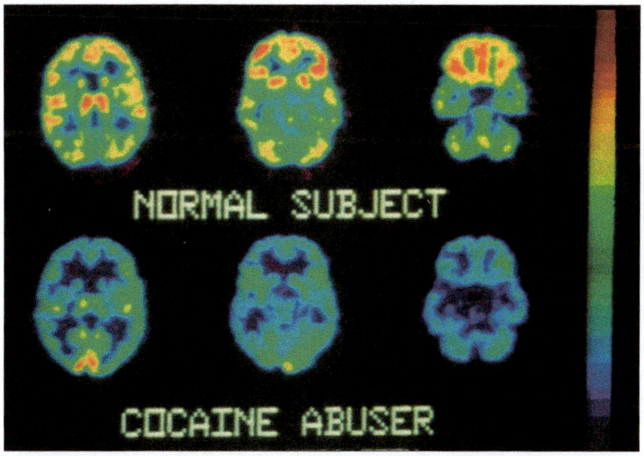

Figure 16.9 These are PET scans of the brain of a regular cocaine user, compared with the brain of someone who has never taken cocaine. The colours at the top of the scale (red) indicate activity, while the ones at the bottom (blue) indicate inactivity.

16.12 LSD is an illegal hallucinogen.

Like cocaine, LSD is an illegal drug. LSD is a **hallucinogen**. It makes the user imagine things that do not really exist. They see, hear and feel things that are not there. The hallucinations last up to 12 hours.

This can sometimes be pleasurable, but the hallucinations can be very unpleasant. A person cannot predict what the hallucinations will be like. They could be terrifying. This can have severe effects on mental health. A person who uses LSD a lot runs a serious risk of developing long-term mental problems.

LSD causes increases in blood pressure and blood glucose level. Large doses can cause convulsions, heart failure or a stroke.

People do not become dependent on LSD in the same way as they become dependent on cocaine. LSD is not an addictive drug.

16.13 Heroin is an addictive opiate.

Heroin comes from opium poppies. It is an **opiate** drug. Heroin and another similar opiate, morphine, are used in medicine to help to prevent severe pain. Used in this way, opiates are very helpful drugs.

However, they can also be abused. Heroin is very addictive and does serious damage to a person's health and social relationships.

Taking heroin gives an almost immediate feeling of euphoria. The person may feel alternately drowsy and wakeful. The activity of their brain slows down and they cannot think clearly. A person rapidly becomes tolerant to heroin, so that they need to take more and more of it. They have extremely unpleasant withdrawal symptoms if they stop taking the drug. They have pain all over their body, feel sick, have diarrhoea and cannot sleep.

A long-term user of heroin develops health problems. These include damage to the blood vessels and heart and liver disease. People who inject heroin often get serious diseases, such as HIV/AIDS.

16.14 Ecstasy is an illegal stimulant.

Ecstasy is a stimulant and a hallucinogen. It is illegal to take ecstasy.

Ecstasy affects the activity of the brain. People take it because it makes them feel more energetic and helps them to get more enjoyment out of dancing or interacting with other people (Figure **16.10**).

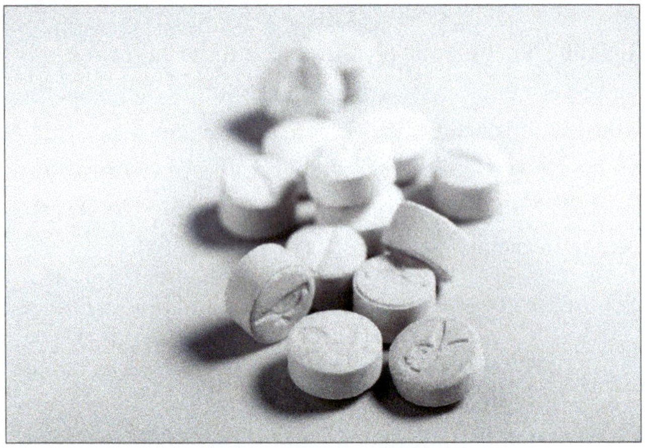

Figure 16.10 Ecstasy pills.

Unfortunately, ecstasy also has harmful affects. It can upset the body's temperature regulating mechanisms. It increases heart rate and can worsen any circulatory problems that the user has. It can cause nausea and sweating.

Most people feel tired and depressed after the effects of ecstasy have worn off. This may lead them to go on taking it, so they become dependent on it. However, ecstasy is not as addictive as cocaine or heroin.

16.15 Alcohol is a socially acceptable depressant.

Alcohol is a drug that can be taken legally. It is a **depressant**. This means that it slows down the working of the brain and nervous system.

Alcohol is generally a socially acceptable drug. At a party or other social occasion, it is almost expected that people will drink alcohol, and it may be difficult to refuse even if you do not want to drink. People drink alcohol because it helps them to relax and to be able to talk and be part of the crowd. If they drink only small amounts, they will not harm their health. Yet alcohol is responsible for many unnecessary deaths, not only of the person who drinks it but also of others who are killed by the drinker's violence or poor driving.

A person who has drunk a lot of alcohol has slow reactions. They will not be able to think clearly, and may make wrong decisions. They frequently do not recognise that they have been affected by alcohol. This is why it is very important that a person does not drive when they have drunk any alcohol. They might not judge the road conditions correctly, and they might not be able to stop quickly enough to avoid hitting a person on the road (Figure **16.11**).

Figure 16.11 A high proportion of road accidents involve drivers or pedestrians who have been drinking alcohol.

Alcohol is a poison. People can die if they drink too much of it. They become unconscious, and many alcohol-related deaths result from the person vomiting while they are unconscious and then choking on their vomit.

People who drink a lot of alcohol over several years often develop liver problems, such as cirrhosis (Figure **16.12**). The liver cells die because they get worn out trying to break down the toxic alcohol in the body. There is concern world-wide that drinking habits among young people are building up a 'time bomb' of liver disease. Liver disease is often incurable and fatal.

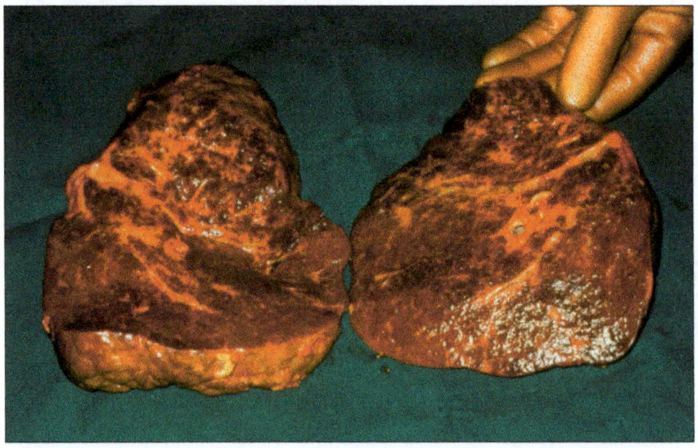

Figure 16.12 This was a person's liver. She was a heavy drinker, and you can see that there are fibres and dark areas in her liver. This is cirrhosis.

Alcohol easily crosses the placenta, so pregnant women should not drink it.

Some people become **addicted** to alcohol, but others do not. It is difficult to predict who is likely to develop addiction and who is not.

16.16 Marijuana comes from the cannabis plant.

Marijuana (ganja) is an illegal drug. It comes from the cannabis plant (Figure **16.13**). People smoke cannabis because it makes them feel more relaxed and happy. Some people with chronic painful diseases, such as multiple sclerosis, say that it makes them feel better.

Figure 16.13 These are cannabis plants, whose leaves are the source of marijuana.

For a long time, it was thought that marijuana was not a particularly harmful drug. However, it is now thought that smoking marijuana increases the risk of developing serious mental health problems, such as schizophrenia.

Like smoking tobacco, smoking cannabis can cause bronchitis and lung cancer.

Marijuana is not an addictive drug. However, people who use it may go on to use more dangerous drugs, such as cocaine or heroin.

16.17 Misuse of legal drugs can be dangerous.

Illegal drugs are made illegal because of the serious harm they are likely to do to a person's health, and the serious effects they have on their family and other members of society. However, some very harmful drugs are *not* illegal. We have seen, for example, how **alcohol** is a legal drug and yet can cause serious harm. The **nicotine** in cigarette smoke has severe effects on smokers (section **6.23**).

Many drugs that are prescribed by doctors to improve a person's health can be harmful if they are misused.

Tranquillisers are drugs that are used to treat people who have long-term problems with feeling anxious, stressed and nervous. The two types that are most frequently used as benzodiazapines and beta blockers. They may also be used in a hospital to calm a person who is having to undergo unpleasant medical treatment. Used carefully, they are valuable drugs, especially if efforts are made to tackle the underlying causes of the person's anxiety. However, if too many are taken, or if they are taken by a person who does not need them, or over too long a time period, then they can be harmful. They make a person feel drowsy and unmotivated, so they do not want to work or even to do anything very much at all. There is a risk that people will become dependent on them.

Steroids are drugs that act in a way that is similar to some of our own hormones. They are used in the treatment of many different diseases, including asthma and eczema. However, some people use steroids inappropriately. For example, some athletes have used steroids to help them to build up large amounts of muscle, increasing their strength and speed. This is not only illegal in the world of sport, but is also highly unfair and very dangerous (Figure **16.14**, overleaf). More than one athlete is thought to have died young because they had used steroids. Used incorrectly, these drugs damage the liver and circulatory system.

Antibiotics are drugs that are used to cure diseases caused by bacteria. They are very useful drugs, and save millions of lives each year. However, they should not be used unnecessarily, as this increases the risk of resistant strains of bacteria developing (section **15.6**). Many people do not understand that antibiotics are only useful against diseases caused by bacteria. They have no effect against viral diseases, and so should not be taken for them.

Figure 16.14 Marion Jones won the 100 m event at the 2000 Olympic Games, but was later disqualified and banned from further competition when it was discovered she had been taking illegal steroid drugs to improve her performance.

Caffeine is the drug in coffee and also in tea and cola drinks. It is a stimulant. There is no evidence that small amounts of caffeine do any harm, and many people use it to help them to wake up in the morning, or to stay alert as they work during the day. Very large quantities of caffeine, however, may be harmful, especially to people with hypertension because it tends to increase blood pressure. Pregnant women are also advised not to take too much caffeine, as it may affect the development of the unborn child.

Questions

16.3 Describe and explain why a person with diabetes must try to control their blood glucose levels.

16.4 Why should a person with diabetes test their blood glucose level?

16.5 Why may a person with diabetes need to inject insulin?

16.6 How can diet help a person with diabetes?

16.7 What is obesity?

16.8 Why should an obese person lose weight?

16.9 What is hypertension, and why is it dangerous?

16.10 What is energy protein malnutrition?

16.11 How can diet cure anaemia?

16.12 What is meant by **(a)** drug dependence and **(b)** drug tolerance?

16.13 Why do people who have drunk alcohol run a high risk of an accident?

16.14 How can drug addiction harm a person's family?

Defences against pathogenic diseases

16.18 Pathogenic diseases are caused by microorganisms.

Microorganisms that can cause disease are known as **pathogens**. The diseases that they cause are known as **pathogenic** diseases. Other terms that are sometimes used are **infectious** diseases, **transmissible** diseases or **communicable** diseases. There are many different ones, and we will look at several important ones later in this chapter. Table **16.1** lists some of the most important pathogenic diseases.

Figure **16.15** (page **300**) summarises the different ways in which pathogens can enter the body.

Through the skin Some bacteria and viruses can get into the body through the skin, even when it is undamaged. Wart viruses can do this. Others are more likely to cause infections when the skin is damaged. *Staphylococcus* bacteria, which can infect wounds and turn them septic, or cause boils, enter through damaged skin.

Through the respiratory system Cold and influenza viruses are carried in the air in small droplets of moisture. If you breathe these in you may become infected. This is called **droplet infection**.

In food or water Bacteria, such as *Salmonella*, that cause food poisoning are taken into the alimentary canal in food. Many pathogens, including the virus that causes polio and the bacterium that causes cholera, are transmitted in water. If you drink untreated water you run the risk of catching these diseases.

By vectors A vector is an organism that transmits a pathogen to its host. Malaria is caused by a protozoan called *Plasmodium*. It lives in the salivary glands of some types of mosquito, and is injected into a person's blood when the mosquito feeds (Figure **16.28**, page **309**). Mosquitoes are a vector for *Plasmodium*. The parasite, therefore, has two hosts, but causes disease only in one. A knowledge of the life cycle of vectors helps humans in the fight against the diseases they spread (Figures **16.29** and **16.31**, pages **310** and **311**).

Through sexual intercourse Sexually transmitted diseases are passed on by sexual intercourse (sections **16.25** to **16.30**).

16.19 Natural body defences keep pathogens out.

Many built-in mechanisms in the human body provide protection against the entry of pathogens. These are summarised in Figure **16.16** and Table **16.2** (overleaf).

Blood clotting is an important way of preventing the entry of pathogens through a break in the skin (Figure **16.17**, page **301**).

When blood platelets come into contact with a damaged tissue, they stick to the edges of the damaged area, and then to each other, forming a platelet plug. If the wound is small, this will be enough to stop bleeding.

Large wounds, however, need a larger barrier than this (Figures **16.17** and **16.18**, pages **301** and **302**). Blood plasma contains thirteen substances which are involved in blood clotting. If any one of these blood clotting factors is defective, then blood will not clot.

Table 16.1 Some important pathogenic diseases

Disease	Causative organism	Transmission	Symptoms	Prevention	Other points
AIDS	HIV (virus)	by sexual intercourse; from infected blood; from infected mother to baby	constant fatigue; weight loss; swollen lymph glands; diarrhoea and loss of appetite over a long period of time; persistent skin rash	good sexual habits; avoiding the use of non-sterile needles	the virus mutates often, so new strains keep appearing; it has proved very difficult to develop a vaccine, and there is no cure
influenza	virus	droplets in air	fever, headache, muscular pain	vaccine	new strains of the virus keep appearing, so vaccines have limited use
tuberculosis (TB)	bacterium	inhalation, or by drinking infected milk	usually no symptoms in the early stages; later, fever, loss of weight, damage to lungs	eliminating poverty and overcrowding; pasteurisation of milk; radiography to detect early infection; BCG injections to immunise young people	if untreated, may last for several years
gonorrheoa	bacterium	by sexual intercourse	in a man, a thick discharge from the urethra, and pain when passing urine; often no symptoms in a woman	antibiotics; tracing and treatment of sexual contacts	
ringworm	fungus	by contact with infected people or animals	circular, bald patch on head on circular scaly patch on body	good personal hygiene	
malaria	protozoan, *Plasmodium*	in saliva of mosquitoes	several types, with various symptoms, all including fever	drainage of wet areas where mosquitoes may breed; wearing clothing to prevent bites; sleeping under nets; anti-malarial tablets	

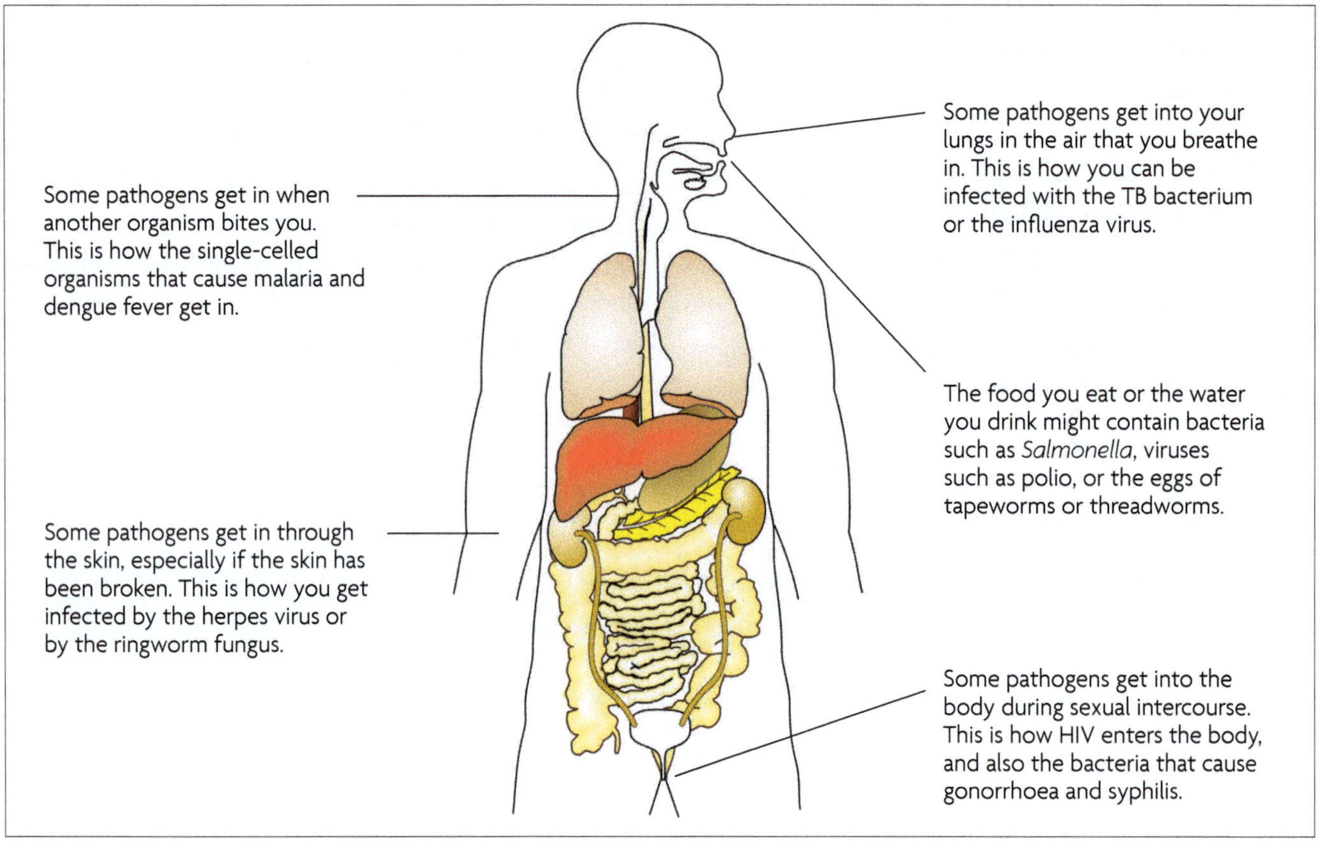

Some pathogens get into your lungs in the air that you breathe in. This is how you can be infected with the TB bacterium or the influenza virus.
Some pathogens get in when another organism bites you. This is how the single-celled organisms that cause malaria and dengue fever get in.
The food you eat or the water you drink might contain bacteria such as *Salmonella*, viruses such as polio, or the eggs of tapeworms or threadworms.
Some pathogens get in through the skin, especially if the skin has been broken. This is how you get infected by the herpes virus or by the ringworm fungus.
Some pathogens get into the body during sexual intercourse. This is how HIV enters the body, and also the bacteria that cause gonorrhoea and syphilis.

Figure 16.15 How pathogens get into the body.

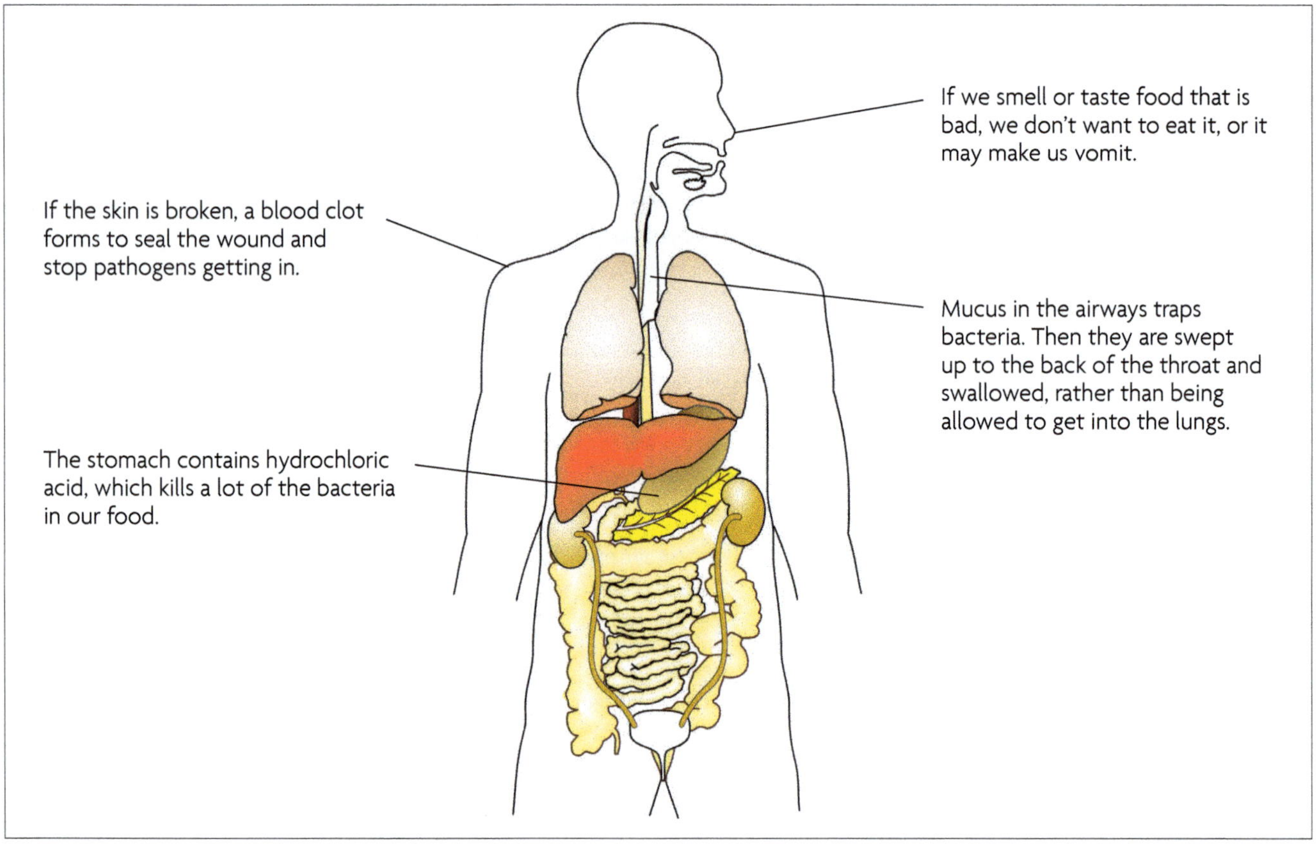

If we smell or taste food that is bad, we don't want to eat it, or it may make us vomit.
If the skin is broken, a blood clot forms to seal the wound and stop pathogens getting in.
Mucus in the airways traps bacteria. Then they are swept up to the back of the throat and swallowed, rather than being allowed to get into the lungs.
The stomach contains hydrochloric acid, which kills a lot of the bacteria in our food.

Figure 16.16 How pathogens are kept out of the body.

Table 16.2 How the body prevents infection

Method of entry	Example	Natural defences
through skin	*Staphylococcus* bacterium	1 Epidermis is a barrier between pathogens and the body 2 When skin is damaged, blood clots seal wound and prevent entry of pathogens. 3 Tears contain lysozyme, which helps to prevent eye infections.
into respiratory system	influenza virus	Cilia and mucus in respiratory passages trap dust particles which may carry pathogens, and sweep them upwards away from the lungs
in food or water	*Salmonella*	1 Distaste for food which looks or smells bad 2 Hydrochloric acid in the stomach kills many bacteria
injection into body by a vector	*Plasmodium*	None
by sexual intercourse	HIV	None

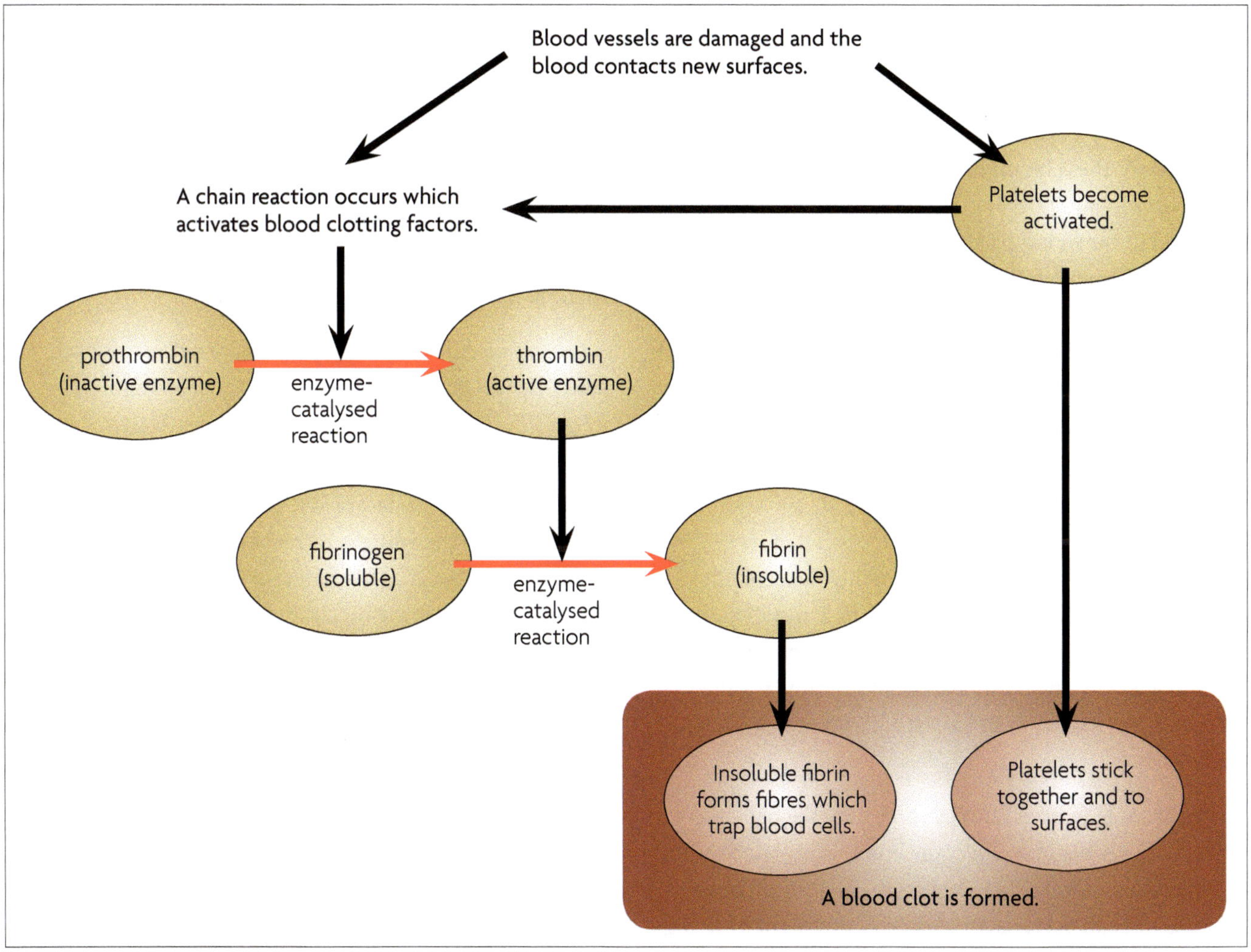

Figure 16.17 The sequence of events which occurs as blood clots.

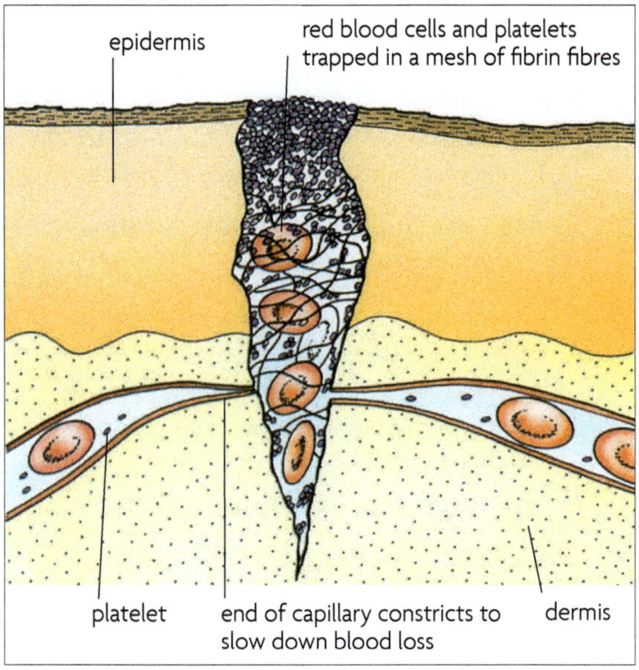

Figure 16.18 Vertical section through a blood clot.

Continued bleeding from a small wound due to a missing blood clotting factor called **factor VIII** is a disease called haemophilia. This is an inherited disease, caused by a faulty gene on the X chromosome.

Two more of these blood clotting factors are **prothrombin** and **fibrinogen**, which are soluble proteins dissolved in the blood plasma. If a tissue is damaged, it releases a chemical called **thromboplastin**. This converts prothrombin to **thrombin**. Thrombin acts on fibrinogen, converting it to the protein **fibrin**. Fibrin is insoluble, and forms fibres across the wound (Figure **16.19**). Blood cells and platelets get caught up in the fibres forming a clot.

16.20 Fever may help to kill bacteria.

The entry of a pathogen into the body is called **infection**. Once a pathogen such as a bacterium has successfully entered the body, it begins to reproduce. It usually takes some time before the colony has become large enough to have an effect on the body. This length of time is called the **incubation period**. It may be a few hours, or several days.

If they are able to breed successfully, then the bacteria will eventually begin to affect the body. The **symptoms** of the infection appear. Many symptoms are caused by the remains of dead bacteria, or substances released by living bacteria. These are called **toxins**.

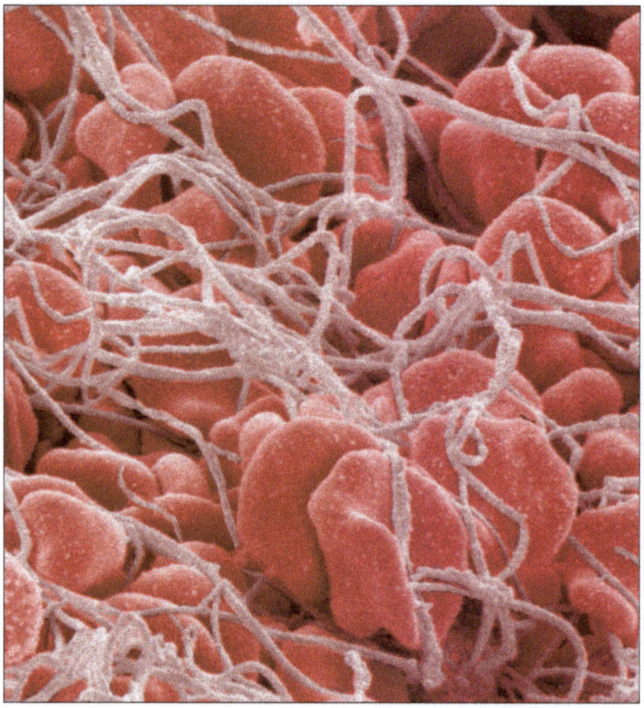

Figure 16.19 A scanning electron micrograph showing red cells tangled up in fibrin fibres.

Some of these substances may affect the hypothalamus in the brain. Because the hypothalamus is responsible for regulating body temperature, temperature may become much higher than usual. This is a fever. It is thought that this may actually help us to fight off some types of bacteria. The high temperature in the body may stop the bacteria from breeding, or even kill them.

A fever is usually only one symptom of a disease. Each kind of pathogen produces its own set of symptoms.

16.21 Phagocytes destroy invaders.

Some white blood cells are able to take up bacteria and destroy them. The white cells recognise the invading pathogen as 'foreign'. This is because the pathogen has chemicals on its cells which are not found on the cells in the body. These chemicals are called **antigens**.

These white cells are known as **phagocytes**. Phagocytes are able to crawl out of the blood, through gaps in the walls of capillaries, and move around all through the body in search of invading microorganisms. Phagocytes tend to congregate at a wound, where they rapidly destroy bacteria that may otherwise get into the body. Figure **16.20** shows a phagocyte ingesting a group of bacteria.

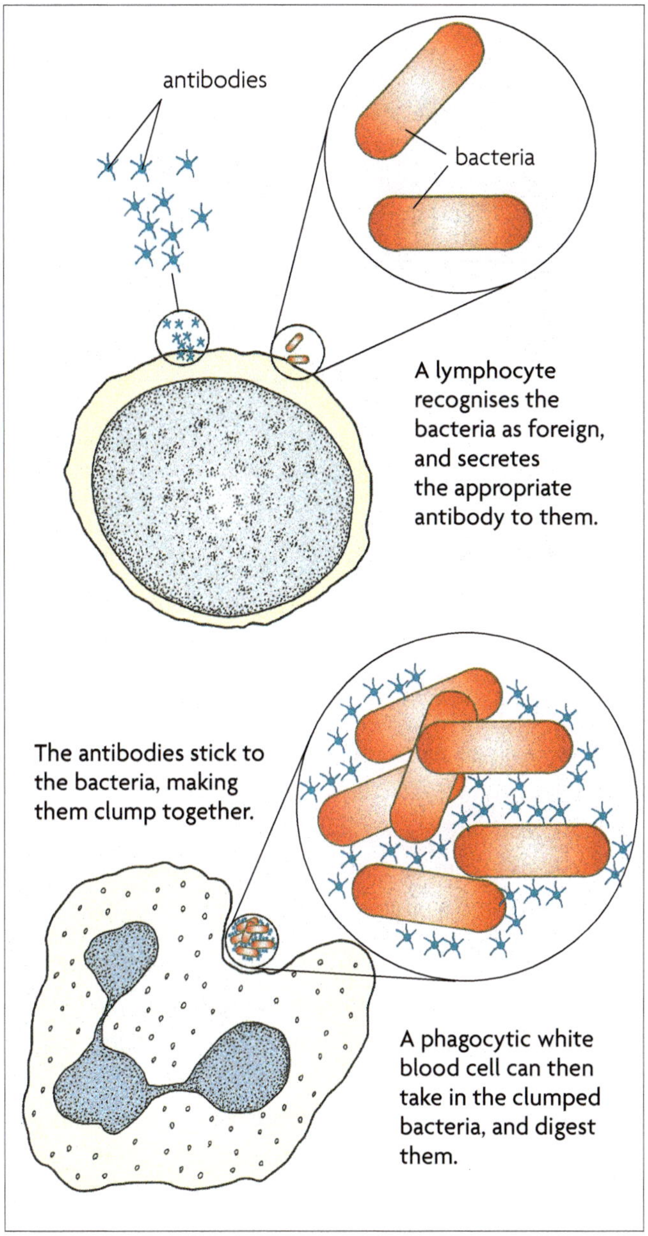

antibodies
bacteria
A lymphocyte recognises the bacteria as foreign, and secretes the appropriate antibody to them.
The antibodies stick to the bacteria, making them clump together.
A phagocytic white blood cell can then take in the clumped bacteria, and digest them.

Figure 16.20 How white cells destroy bacteria.

16.22 Lymphocytes make antibodies.

Another group of white cells, called **lymphocytes**, is able to make another set of chemicals in response to the antigens. These chemicals are called **antibodies**. The antibody molecules bind onto the antigen molecules. Each lymphocyte can make only one type of antibody, and this antibody will only fit onto one kind of antigen. We have thousands of different lymphocytes in our bodies, each capable of making one particular antibody.

The binding of the antibody to the antigen can have several different effects. One effect is that the cells carrying the antigens clump together (Figure **16.20**). The phagocytes can then destroy them, by phagocytosis.

It may take some time for the lymphocytes to make enough of the right antibody. This gives the pathogen a chance to breed, and produce the symptoms of the disease. Eventually, though, the white cells usually manage to make enough antibodies to destroy the pathogen, and you recover from the illness.

Figure **16.21** (overleaf) shows how the numbers of a pathogen (in this case a virus) and antibodies change over the time course of an illness and recovery.

16.23 Having a disease once can make you immune.

When a lymphocyte encounters its specific antigen, it divides repeatedly, forming a **clone** of lymphocytes like itself. Most of these secrete antibodies. However, some of them do not, but just remain in the blood. They are called **memory cells.**

What happens if the same kind of pathogen invades your body again some time later? This time, the memory cells are present. They recognise the antigen straight away, and quickly divide to form more lymphocytes like themselves. These secrete large amounts of the antibody that can destroy that pathogen. The pathogen is destroyed before it has a chance to breed. You have become **immune** to the disease.

Figure **16.22** (overleaf) shows how a person may become immune to a bacterium. On the first infection, the person got ill, because it took time for the appropriate lymphocytes to recognise the bacterium and divide to form a large clone, able to secrete enough antibodies to destroy the bacterium. On the second infection, her lymphocytes responded much more quickly, because she had many memory cells already present.

16.24 Vaccination can confer immunity.

Having a disease and recovering from it is one way of becoming immune to it. This sort of immunity is called **active immunity**, because your white cells make the antibodies themselves.

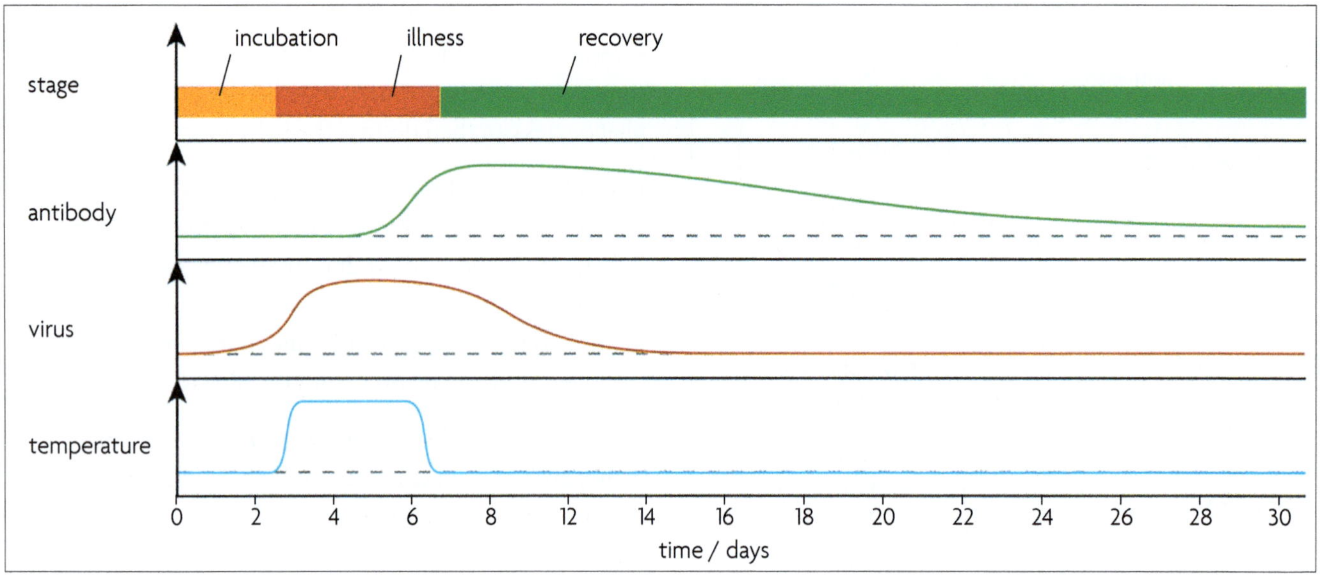

Figure 16.21 How the number of viruses and antibodies in your body and your body temperature change during a bout of influenza.

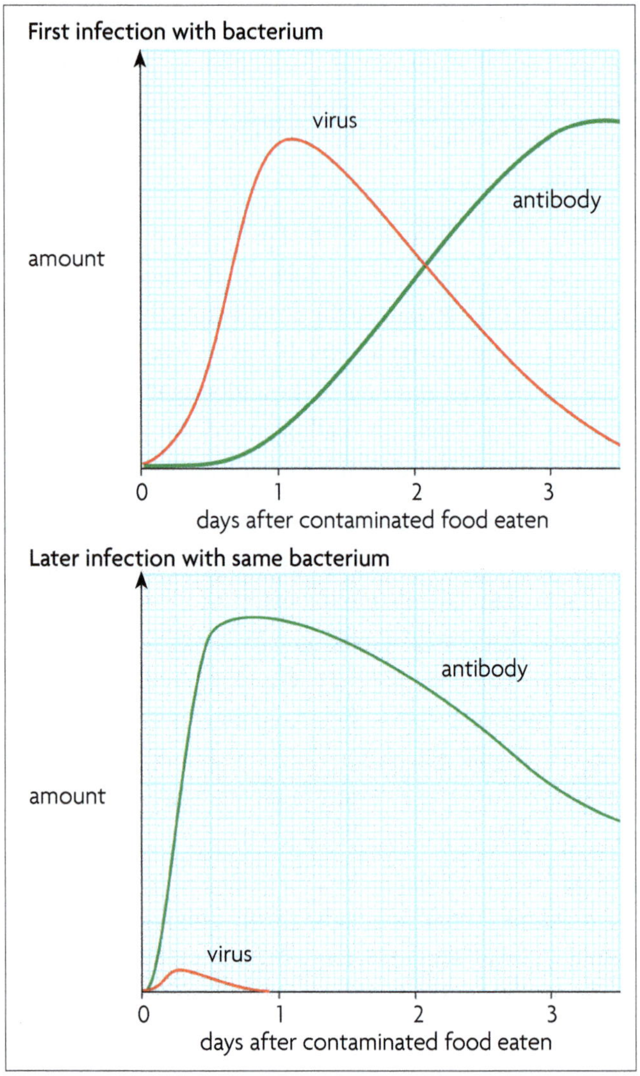

Figure 16.22 The immune response on a first and second encounter with a pathogen.

You can also acquire immunity by having a **vaccination** (Figures **16.23** and **16.24**). Some vaccines, for example the BCG vaccination for tuberculosis, contain bacteria which have been weakened. When they are injected into your body, they are too weak to reproduce. But the white cells recognise them as foreign, and 'learn' to make the antibodies to destroy them.

In the Caribbean, children are vaccinated against diphtheria, whooping cough, tetanus, tuberculosis, hepatitis B, haemophilus influenza B (hib), measles, mumps, rubella and poliomyelitis. Without vaccinations, these diseases would quickly become very common, and would cause much unnecessary ill-health and death.

Another type of immunity is called **passive immunity** (Figure **16.24**). Here your white cells do not make the antibodies. Instead, the antibody is put into your blood ready-made. Breast-fed babies get immunity to many diseases, because there are antibodies in breast milk.

Some vaccinations contain ready-made antibodies. An anti-tetanus injection given by the doctor to patients with a cut, contains anti-tetanus antibodies from a horse. They are obtained by injecting the horse with a weakened form of the bacterium, and later taking some blood plasma from it and extracting the antibodies. It is, however, also possible to be given an anti-tetanus vaccination containing weakened forms of the bacterium, which will induce a longer-lasting active immunity, but does not act as quickly as a vaccine containing ready-made antibodies.

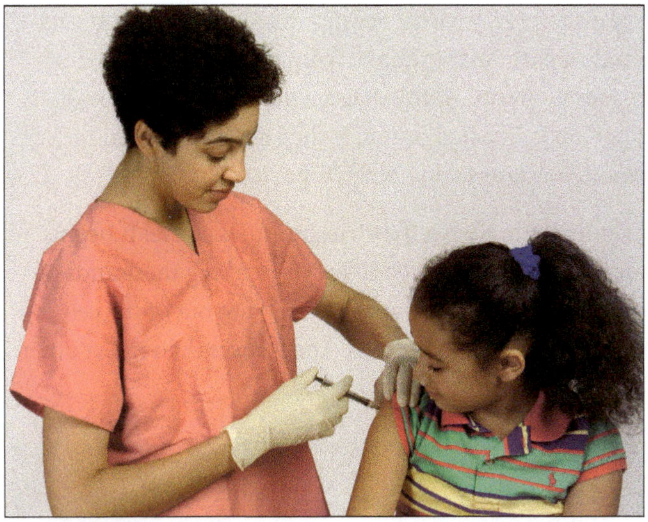

Figure 16.23 Vaccination is not much fun, but it can protect you from serious diseases.

Passive immunity does not last indefinitely, because the antibodies gradually disappear from your blood. This is why you are usually given an anti-tetanus injection whenever you go to a doctor with a cut.

Active immunity lasts much longer, because lymphocytes will have multiplied to form memory cells, which remain in the blood. One BCG injection will last you a lifetime.

Questions

16.15 How do each of these pathogens enter the body?
(a) *Staphylococcus* **(b)** *Salmonella* **(c)** *Plasmodium*

16.16 What is the role of each of these substances in blood clotting?
(a) thromboplastin **(b)** thrombin **(c)** fibrinogen

16.17 What do phagocytes do?

16.18 What do lymphocytes do?

16.19 What is the difference between an antigen and an antibody?

16.20 How do memory cells make you immune to a disease?

16.21 How can vaccination make you immune to a disease?

16.22 Why does active immunity last longer than passive immunity?

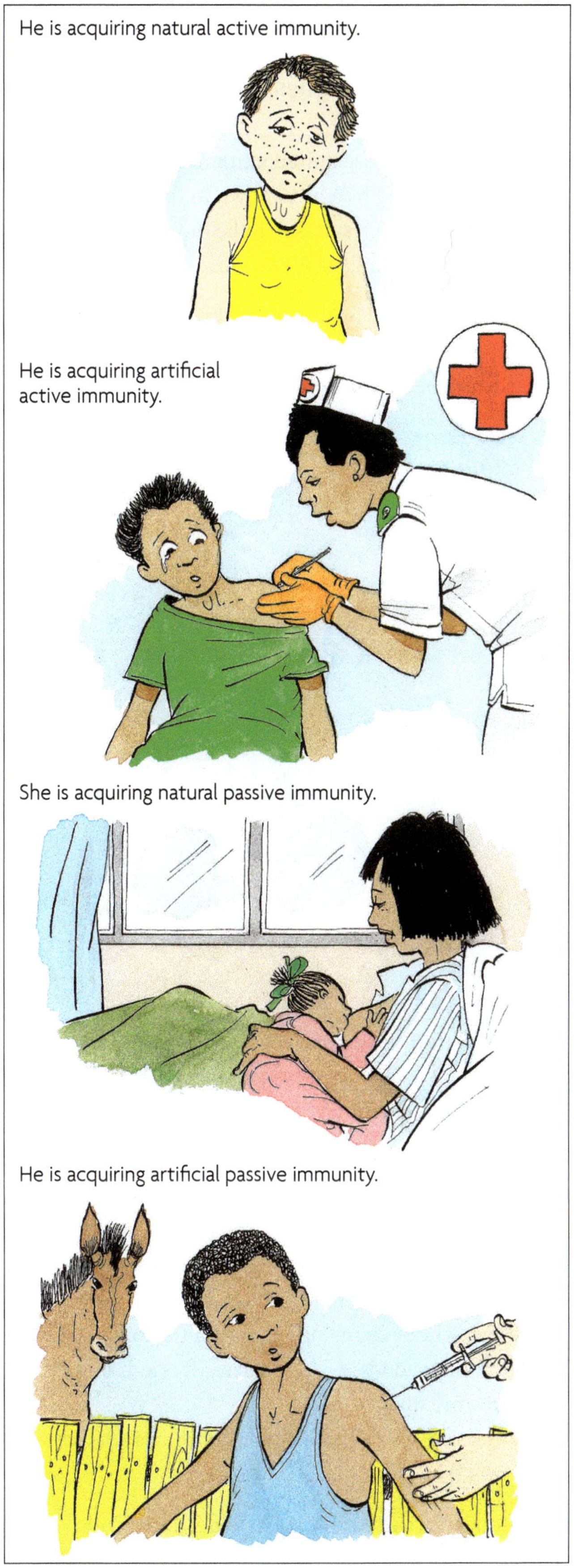

He is acquiring natural active immunity.
He is acquiring artificial active immunity.
She is acquiring natural passive immunity.
He is acquiring artificial passive immunity.

Figure 16.24 Active and passive immunity.

Sexually transmitted diseases

16.25 People can lose their ability to be immune to infections.

The disease **AIDS**, or acquired immune deficiency syndrome, is caused by a breakdown in the body's natural defence system. The result is that the individual cannot cope with even the mildest infections.

The disease is caused by infection with the human immunodeficiency virus, **HIV** (Figure **16.25**). This virus infects lymphocytes, and so damages the immune system.

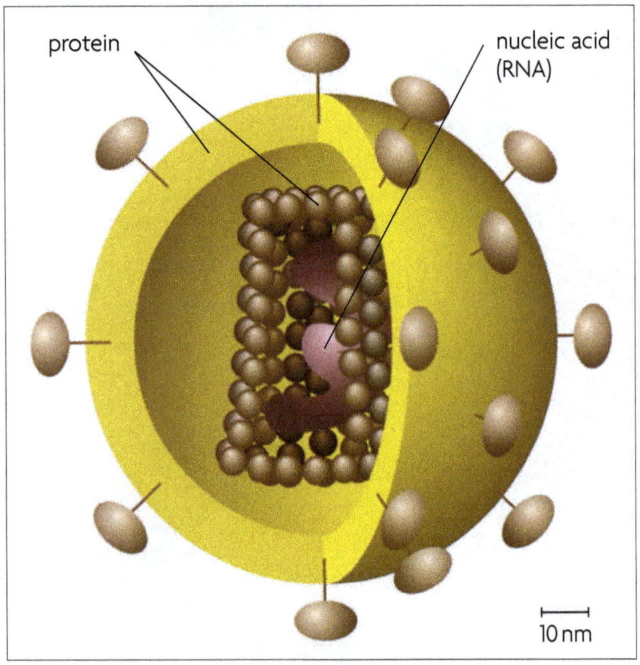

Figure 16.25 The human immunodeficiency virus, HIV.

Some of the symptoms of AIDS are:

- a fever that goes on for a long time
- sudden and severe weight loss without good reason
- constant fatigue
- swollen glands in neck, armpit and groin
- persistent skin rashes or spots
- a thick white coating or patches on the tongue
- diarrhoea and loss of appetite over periods of longer than a month
- cancers are also a feature of AIDS; cancers of the lymph tissue may develop early.

In most people, these symptoms do not appear until some time after they have been infected with HIV. In many cases, this is years after the infection took place. This is because the HIV virus 'lies low' inside their cells. It gets inside a particular group of lymphocytes, where at first it does no harm. At this stage, a blood test can show if a person is infected or not. If they do have HIV in their blood, they are said to be **HIV positive**.

Eventually, however, the virus becomes active. It begins to reproduce inside a lymphocyte, making thousands of copies of itself. These new viruses burst out of the cell, destroying it (Figure **16.26**). The viruses then infect other lymphocytes, and the cycle continues.

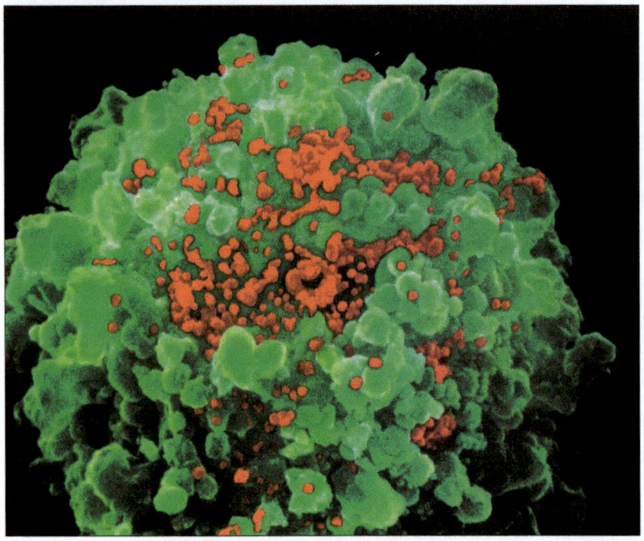

Figure 16.26 This large, green cell is a lymphocyte (the photo has been coloured by computer). The red particles are viruses escaping from it. They burst through its membrane and kill it.

16.26 HIV is transmitted in body fluid.

HIV is spread in the following ways (Figure **16.27**):

- by sexual contact with an infected person
- by getting blood from an infected person into one's bloodstream, from a blood transfusion or an infected injection needle (such as when drug abusers share needles)
- from an infected mother to her baby.

The virus is *not* spread by social contact – for example, by shaking hands, using swimming pools, sharing cutlery or working with or caring for someone with the disease.

In the Caribbean, HIV first appeared among homosexual people. However, it is now also a risk to heterosexual people. In 2008, about one in every 100 people was HIV-positive. Each year, about 37 000 new people are infected with HIV.

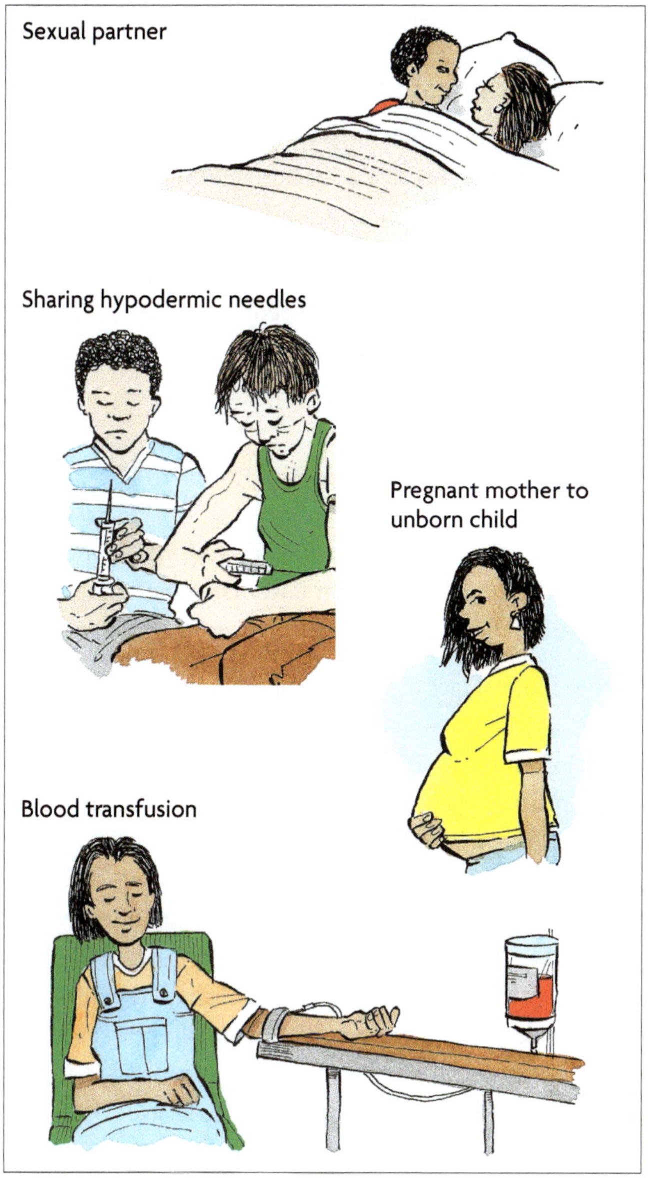

Figure 16.27 The transmission routes for HIV.

16.27 Individual action can control the spread of HIV/AIDS.

HIV/AIDS is very difficult to treat. Despite huge sums of money being spent world-wide in the search for a vaccine or drugs, none has yet been found that destroy the viruses once they are inside a person's body. However, there are now some drugs that, if taken from an early stage and taken regularly, can delay the onset of the symptoms of AIDS and enable an HIV-positive person to continue to live an active and enjoyable life. Most of these drugs, such as AZT, work by interfering with the virus's ability to reproduce, but they do not actually kill the virus. Antibiotics, of course, do not work against HIV, because antibiotics only kill bacteria.

Education about the steps one can take to protect oneself and others is an important part of the fight against the disease. The most common way in which the virus is passed from one person to another is during sexual intercourse. Individuals can protect themselves if they do the following:

- keep only one sexual partner
- refrain from sexual intercourse with those who themselves have several partners (for example, prostitutes) and those whose sexual preferences and habits of cleanliness one does not know about
- use a condom during sexual intercourse.

When a person is diagnosed as being HIV-positive, it is very important to trace all of his or her sexual contacts, in case they too have the virus. If a person knows that they are HIV-positive, it is essential that they do not indulge in any activity that might pass the virus on to someone else. Responsible sexual behaviour is our strongest weapon in the fight against AIDS.

Infection through contact with another person's blood can be avoided by:

- insisting that blood for transfusions should be tested for the virus before it is used
- using sterile needles for all injections.

Drug abusers who share needles expose themselves to infection, and the rate of infection with HIV among people who are addicted to drugs is much higher than in the rest of the population.

If a mother is HIV-positive, there is a great risk that her baby may also become infected. Beginning your life as an HIV-positive child is not good, and women who are HIV-positive should seek medical advice before they allow themselves to become pregnant. If no treatment is given, there is about a one-in-two chance that the child will be HIV-positive, as a result of some of the viruses from its mother getting into its blood. However, treatment of the mother with AZT and other measures can greatly reduce this chance, and there are now many HIV-positive women who have become mothers of healthy, uninfected children, as a result of good medical care before and during their pregnancies.

16.28 Herpes genitalis is a sexually transmitted disease caused by a virus.

Herpes genitalis is caused by the herpes simplex virus. There are two forms of the virus. The form of the virus that infects the genitals is called Type I. Type II usually infects the skin on the face. As with most viral diseases, we have no drugs that can cure herpes.

The Type I herpes virus is spread during sexual intercourse. Type II is spread by kissing or contaminated hands.

The symptoms of herpes are sores and blisters on the lips or genitals. Between two and 20 days after infection, the site begins to tingle or burn. Blisters form and burst to form ulcers. On the face, these are called cold sores. Ulcers formed as a result of herpes infection heal spontaneously but symptoms may reappear without fresh infection. In females infected with Type I herpes, urination may be painful.

Much more serious is the infection of the new-born during birth. Babies so infected may die, or have brain damage.

16.29 Gonorrhoea is another sexually transmitted disease.

Gonorrhea is caused by the bacterium *Neisseria gonorrhoeae*. In the male, the bacterium infects the urethra and two to ten days after infection he may have pus discharge from the penis. Alternatively, he may experience a burning sensation during urination. The untreated infection may spread to his prostate gland and testes. If the testes become infected, he may become sterile.

In the female, the initial infection affects the cervix. Without treatment it often spreads to the oviducts (Fallopian tubes). These may become blocked. This poses the risk of a fetus developing in the oviduct rather than in the uterus, known as tubal pregnancy. It is highly dangerous to both the mother and the fetus. The female may also become sterile.

The symptoms of gonorrhoea do not always develop, so it is possible for a person to have this bacterium in their body and not know it.

The bacterium can spread to other parts of the body in the blood. Small red pustules may develop on the skin and arthritis may result.

Early treatment with antibiotics is an effective cure. There is now some concern about the choice of antibiotic, as strains resistant to the antibiotics are developing. For example, penicillin, once the antibiotic selected for this treatment, is no longer effective, because of bacterial resistance.

Chlamydia is another bacterium which causes symptoms similar to those of gonorrhoea. The disease is milder than gonorrhoea, so again many people may have this infection without knowing it. If left untreated, the bacterium can cause infertility.

16.30 Syphilis is a serious sexually transmitted disease.

Syphilis is caused by the bacterium *Treponema pallidum*. Congenital syphilis is passed by a woman to her unborn child. Acquired syphilis is passed on by sexual intercourse.

There are four stages in the development of acquired syphilis. Primary syphilis takes about three weeks to develop and hard ulcers are formed at the site of infection. These are usually painless and last about a month. After two to four months, the symptoms of secondary syphilis may develop. These are a generalised rash of red flat lesions. The rash may reappear at intervals over two years. Then the symptoms disappear, and the person may live for many years not realising they still have the bacterium in their body. Eventually, however, serious symptoms appear in about 30% of untreated individuals. This affects the brain and the heart. There may be severe complications and death.

Untreated syphilis can cause a pregnant woman to have a miscarriage, a stillborn baby, or a baby born with syphilis who may become blind or crippled or die.

Questions

16.23 What does HIV stand for?

16.24 Which disease does HIV cause?

16.25 What is the difference between being HIV-positive and having AIDS?

16.26 How can HIV be transmitted from one person to another?

16.27 Why is it easier to treat gonorrhoea and syphilis than to treat AIDS?

Insect vectors

16.31 Malaria is caused by a protozoan.

Malaria is an infection caused by a **protozoan** called *Plasmodium*. The protozoan is transmitted by *Anopheles* **mosquitoes**. The symptoms of malaria include:

- high temperature
- headache and muscle aches
- nausea and diarrhoea.

A particularly unpleasant and dangerous form of malaria, known as malignant malaria, has even more symptoms. These include low blood pressure, severe anaemia, kidney failure, internal bleeding, coma, convulsions and paralysis. It is often fatal.

If it is not treated, a bout of malaria can last for weeks. If it is malignant malaria, it can kill. Malaria can usually be cured using anti-malarial drugs which kill the protozoan. These include chloroquine, doxycycline and mefloquine.

Malaria has been eliminated from almost all of the islands in the Caribbean. However, there is always a danger that it might be reintroduced.

16.32 Mosquitoes are vectors for malaria.

The *Plasmodium* protozoan that causes malaria is transmitted between one person and another by mosquitoes belonging to the genus *Anopheles* (Figures **16.28** and **16.29**, overleaf). Female mosquitoes need to feed on blood in order to get enough protein to make their eggs – male mosquitoes do not bite. When she bites a person, a mosquito injects fluid from her salivary gland to prevent her victim's blood from clotting. If she has previously bitten someone with malaria, then she may have *Plasmodium* in her saliva.

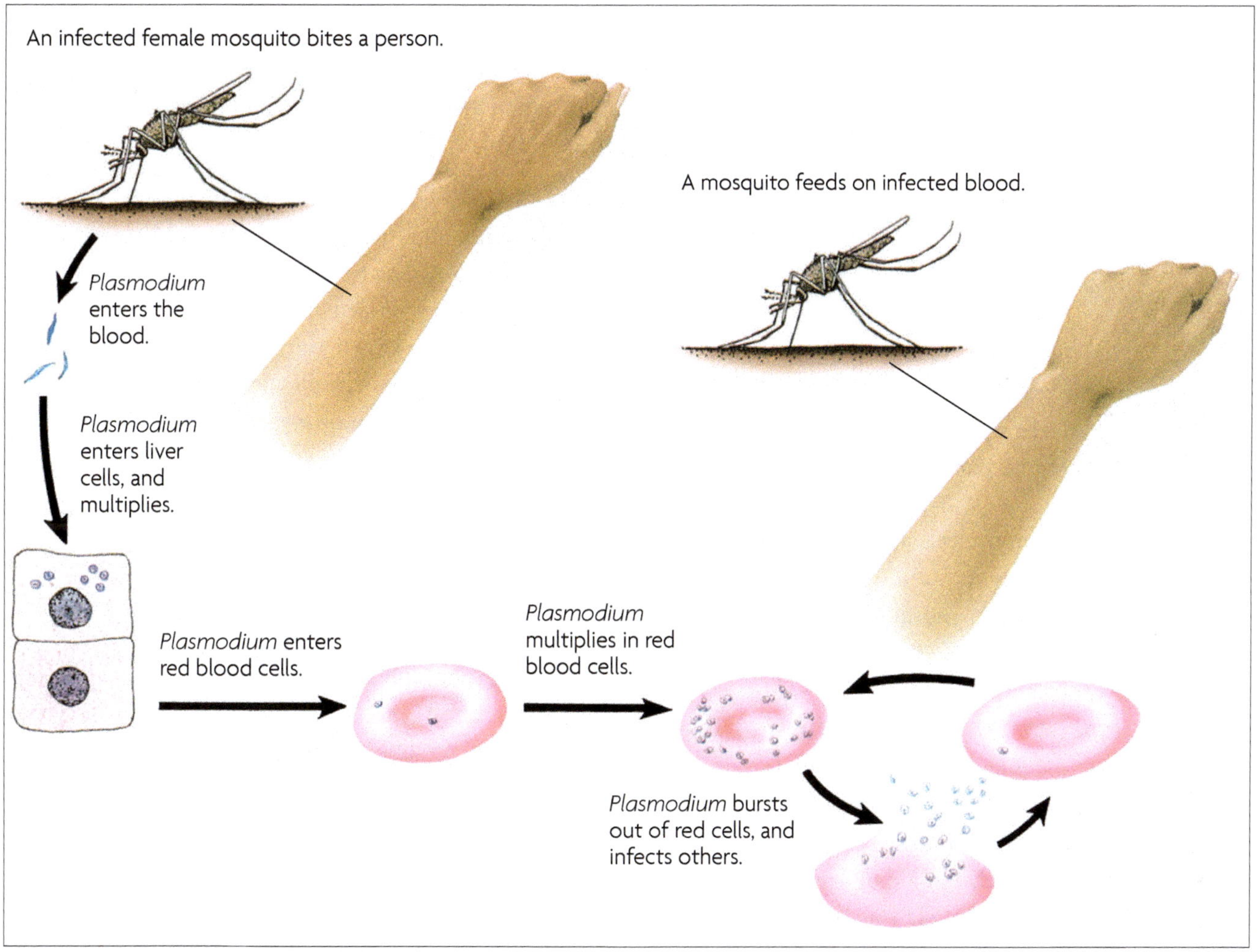

Figure 16.28 How malaria is transmitted.

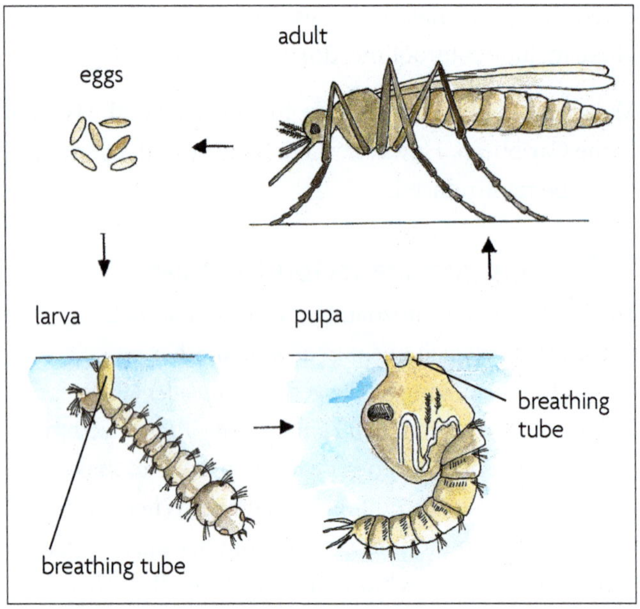

Figure 16.29 Life cycle of a mosquito.

An organism like this, which transmits a pathogen from one person to another, is called a **vector**. Other examples of vectors include the mosquito *Aedes aegypti*, which transmits the virus causing dengue fever, and blood-feeding bats, which can transmit the rabies virus.

If we can control the population of mosquitoes, then we can control the spread of malaria. Knowledge of their life cycle provides us with various possiblities for doing this. They include:

- making sure there are no pools or containers lying around near to where people live, in which mosquito larvae might develop
- introducing fish into ponds, where they will eat the larvae
- sleeping under a mosquito net, so you cannot be bitten by mosquitoes
- using insecticides to kill mosquitoes in or close to houses.

16.33 Houseflies are vectors for various diseases.

Most people get food poisoning at some time in their lives. A common form of food poisoning is **gastroenteritis**. This illness is caused by pathogenic bacteria that enter the body in food or drink. They breed in the alimentary canal and make you ill.

Houseflies are vectors for gastroenteritis. Houseflies will feed on almost any kind of food, and are often found around rubbish tips. They produce saliva which runs over the food (Figure **16.30**). The saliva contains enzymes, which digest the food to a liquid, which the fly then sucks up through its proboscis. If you eat food on which a housefly has been feeding, you are eating its half-digested meal.

FACT!

The most potentially dangerous insect in the world is the common housefly. It can transmit as many as 30 diseases to humans. These include cholera, typhoid, dysentery, meningitis and diphtheria.

Houseflies spread the bacteria that cause gastroenteritis. When they walk on food remains or on the bodies of dead animals, they pick up bacteria on their feet. They may also suck up bacteria when they feed. Then they might walk on *your* food. Their feet can leave bacteria on it. When they spit saliva onto it, they may leave more bacteria.

Figure **16.31** shows the life cycle of the housefly. Adult houseflies mate and then lay eggs in the remains of food, especially meat. After a few days, the eggs hatch into maggots. The maggots feed on the meat or other food. When they are fully grown, the maggots turn into pupae (singular: pupa). The pupae eventually hatch into adult flies.

As with mosquitoes, knowing the life history of houseflies helps us to control the spread of the diseases they carry. Measures include:

- keeping food covered at all times, so flies cannot walk on it
- keeping rubbish bins covered, so that flies cannot get to the rubbish
- disposing of rubbish well away from places where people live.

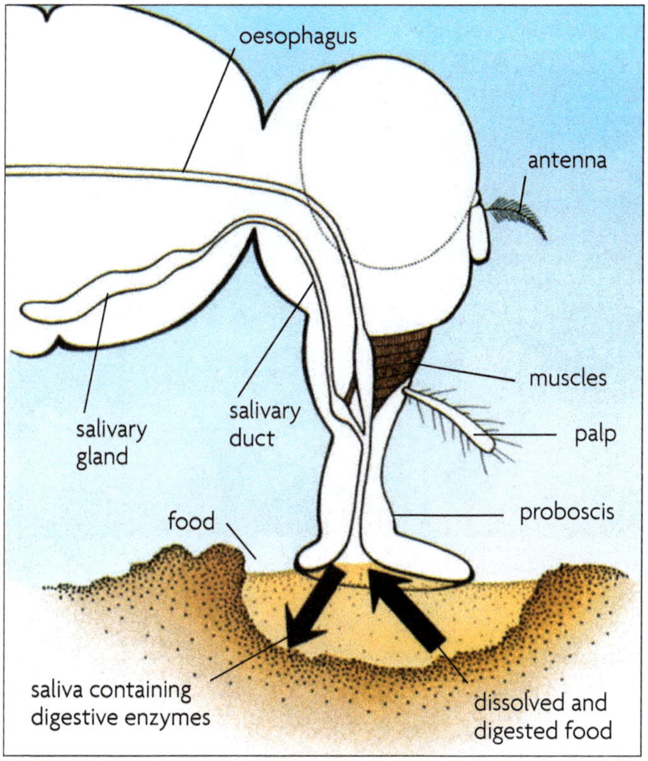

Figure 16.30 Feeding in a housefly.

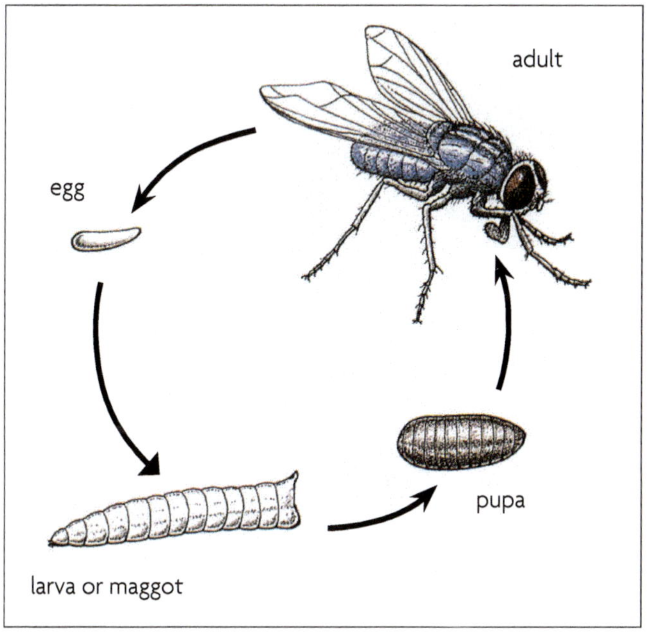

Figure 16.31 The life cycle of the housefly.

Questions

16.28 What is the difference between a vector for a disease, and the cause of a disease? Give an example to illustrate your answer.

16.29 How do houseflies spread gastroenteritis?

Some diseases of crop plants and livestock

16.34 Fungi and viruses cause disease in many important crop plants.

Several crop plant diseases are caused by fungi. **Sugar cane smut** is caused by the fungus *Ustilago scitaminea.* Pimento rust, black pod of cocoa, and leaf spot of bananas are all caused by different types of fungi.

Papaya ringspot is a virus disease probably spread by the aphids *Aphis gossypii* and *Myzus persicae.* Plant leaves become distorted in shape, but the characteristic sign is the series of circles and semicircles on the skin of the fruit (Figure **16.32**, overleaf). The taste of the fruit is unpleasant. Control is by prevention. Farmers remove affected plants immediately, and keep fields free of weeds. Current research by the University of the West Indies is investigating the use of resistant transgenic plants. Genes from the virus are introduced into papaya DNA, the aim being to produce a plant with pathogen-derived resistance.

The cause of lethal yellowing of coconut trees is believed to be a microorganism. The leaves of the plant become yellow, the nuts fall, and eventually the crown of the plant falls off, leaving the bare stem (Figure **16.33**, overleaf). There is no known cure, nor is it known how the disease is spread. Farmers plant resistant varieties, like the Malayan Dwarf.

All of these diseases greatly reduce the yield from the affected crops. In some cases, they make any crop that is obtained inedible. They therefore have considerable economic impact, reducing the income of growers and increasing the prices of foods.

16.35 Livestock yield is affected by diseases.

As with crop plants, farmers need to use constant observation, sanitation and quarantine measures to maintain healthy animals. They also have to remember that sometimes a pathogen that attacks livestock may affect humans.

The bacterium *Bacillus anthracis* causes anthrax. The disease can affect many different kinds of farm animals, although we hear about it mainly with cattle. The disease appears suddenly, often with high fever, and animals die

Figure 16.32 Appearance of fruit and leaves in papaya ringspot disease.

Figure 16.33 Lethal yellowing in coconut trees.

quickly. Affected animals that die, with their litter, should be burnt. Infected herds should be quarantined, and no milk or meat from them used. Animals may be vaccinated against the disease. The bacteria are able to form spores, which remain in the soil in a dormant state for many years. Humans can get anthrax, so great care has to be taken if an animal is found to have this disease.

Bacteria also cause mastitis in cattle. The mammary glands in the cows' udders become infected, especially if there has been irregular milking or blows to the udder. Parts of the udder may be lost, or animals may die. Udders may be treated by milking out, baths, massages and medication. Infected animals should be isolated and milkers should wash their hands thoroughly when dealing with the animals, so that they do not spread the disease.

Piglets often get scours (diarrhoea) in the Caribbean. The bacterium *Escherichia coli* is often the cause. Pregnant sows should be vaccinated against the bacterium. Some forms of this bacterium cause food poisoning in humans, and a few forms can cause death through kidney failure.

Screwworms may affect any homeothermic (endothermic) animals, including humans. The screwworm is the maggot of the New World screwworm fly *Cochliomyia hominivorax*. The larvae eat only living material. The female fly lays eggs on any wound or bruise on an animal's skin. Larvae feed on the flesh for about a week, then fall off to pupate and become adult in a few days. Untreated animals die. Those which recover often get other diseases more easily, as their immune system is weakened. Pets are often affected. Unfortunately, there are often some human cases, mostly among the very young, very old, or mentally impaired.

Screwworm is costly to farmers, through loss of animals, the cost of medicines, and the extra labour needed.

Key ideas

- A disease is anything that prevents a person from being healthy. Diseases may be physiological, hereditary, pathogenic or caused by a nutritional deficiency.
- Obesity increases the risk of developing diabetes, hypertension and heart disease.
- A person with diabetes can control their condition with a careful diet and exercise, and in some cases with injections of insulin.
- Many drugs are useful in medicine. These include antibiotics and analgesics (painkillers).
- Drug abuse causes great harm and misery. If a person becomes dependent on a drug, it takes over their life and can harm their family and friends.
- Cocaine and heroin are addictive, illegal drugs. Ectasy and marijuana are also illegal. Regular use of marijuana increases the risk of developing schizophrenia.
- Alcohol, nicotine and caffeine are legal drugs. Abuse of alcohol causes many deaths and much unhappiness. Caffeine is not thought to be harmful, but over-use should be avoided by pregnant women.
- Many prescription drugs are harmful if misused. These include tranquillisers, diet pills, and steroids. Antibiotics should not be used unnecessarily, as this can increase the risk of resistance developing in bacteria.
- The body has many natural defences against infection, including the skin, blood clotting, and hydrochloric acid in the stomach.
- White blood cells protect us against pathogenic microorganisms. Phagocytes surround, ingest and digest bacteria. Lymphocytes secrete antibodies.
- Following recovery from an infection, a person may become immune to that disease because they have memory cells ready to act if that pathogen appears again. Immunity can also be conferred through vaccination, through breast milk to a baby, and by injection with ready-made antibodies.

(*continues on page* **314**)

(*... continued*)

- HIV/AIDS, gonorrhoea and syphilis are transmitted through sexual intercourse. HIV/AIDS is also transmitted through blood contact and from mother to baby. HIV/AIDS is caused by a virus and cannot be cured, but gonorrheoa and syphilis can be cured with antibiotics.
- Mosquitoes are vectors for malaria, which is caused by a protozoan called *Plasmodium*. Control of mosquitoes is the best way of reducing infection.
- Houseflies are vectors for gastroenteritis and many other diseases. Removal of potential breeding and feeding places for flies helps to prevent infection.
- Diseases of crops and farm livestock can greatly reduce yields, causing financial hardship for farmers and making food more expensive.

End-of-chapter questions

1 This table shows the numbers of people in some parts of the Caribbean who had HIV/AIDS at the end of 2005.

Country	Number of people with HIV/AIDS	Percentage of adults with HIV/AIDS	Deaths due to AIDS in 2005
Bahamas	6800	3.3	at least 500
Barbados	2700	1.5	at least 500
Cuba	4800	0.1	at least 500
Dominican Republic	66000	1.1	6700
Haiti	190000	3.8	16000
Jamaica	25000	1.5	1300
Trinidad and Tobago	27000	2.6	1900

a Which country in the Caribbean had the highest percentage of people with HIV/AIDS?

b Which country had the greatest number of people with HIV/AIDS

c Calculate the total number of people in these parts of Caribbean who had AIDS in 2005.

(*continues on page* **315**)

(*... continued*)

2 The table below gives the number of cases of AIDS in one particular country, from the detection of the first case. Of the total of 96 cases reported by the eighth year, 47 were heterosexuals, 13 homosexuals, 6 bisexuals, 14 were children, and the sexual habits of 16 were not known. Thirty of the cases had been 'imported' or the infection acquired overseas. Up to that time 59 of the cases had died. Later figures from the second month of the tenth year of reporting showed 141 males and 67 females with AIDS, of which 133 had died.

Year	Male	Female	Number of cases	
			Annual total	Cumulative total
1	1	0	1	1
2	0	0	0	1
3	1	0	1	2
4	4	0	4	6
5	5	0	5	11
6	20	13	33	44
7	22	8	30	74
8*	17	5	22	96
totals	70	26	96	

*As at March 31

What do the figures suggest about:

a the rate at which the disease is spreading in the country

b the main route through which it is spread

c the possible impact of the movement of many people in and out, such as where there are many tourists

d the death rate due to the disease?

3 For each of the following types of disease, **(i)** name one example, **(ii)** briefly describe the cause of your example and **(iii)** briefly describe the symptoms of your example.

a a nutritional deficiency disease

b a hereditary disease

c a pathogenic disease

d a physiological disease

4 Explain each of the following.

a You can get measles only once, but you can get influenza over and over again.

b Babies fed on breast milk are less likely to get infectious diseases than those fed on milk made from powder.

c It is no use trying to treat influenza with antibiotics.

5 Discuss the ways in which lifestyle can affect a person's health.

6 Explain the difference between each of the following pairs of terms.

a pathogen, antigen

b antibody, antibiotic

c bacterium, virus

d phagocyte, lymphocyte

e vector, cause

f HIV, AIDS

7 a Explain why a person with diabetes must take great care over their diet.

b How can a person with type I diabetes maintain their health?

17 Living organisms in their environment

In this chapter, you will find out:

- the meanings of some important terms in ecology
- how quadrats and transects are used to investigate the distribution and abundance of species
- how to estimate species frequency and density
- how abiotic and biotic factors influence the population size and distribution of organisms
- about some important ecosystems in the Caribbean.

Studying ecosystems

17.1 Organisms interact with their environment.

Ecology is the study of organisms in their environment. It is a very important branch of biology. You cannot really learn about ecology without doing some practical work outside your classroom. Perhaps you have already investigated some of the plants and animals near your school, when you covered the work in Chapter **1**.

This chapter describes some of the ways you can study organisms in their natural environment, and also some of the ways in which they interact with their environment and with each other. It builds on the work you did about food chains and nutrient cycles, in Chapter **1**, so you may like to briefly look through that again before you begin this chapter.

17.2 Ecology uses many specialist terms.

There are many terms used in ecology with which you need to be familiar. It is important to learn their biological meanings, because many of them have slightly different meanings when used in everyday life. You met most of these terms in Chapter **1**, but it is worth revisiting them here as that may have been a long time ago!

The type of place where an organism lives is called its **habitat** (Figure **17.1**). The habitat of a tadpole might be a pond. There will probably be many tadpoles in the pond, forming a **population** of tadpoles. A population is a group of organisms of the same species, living in the same place at the same time, and able to interbreed with each other.

Tadpoles will not be the only organisms living in the pond. There will be many other kinds of plants and animals, making up the pond **community**. A community is all the organisms, of all the different species, living in the same place at the same time.

The living organisms in the pond, the mud and stones at the bottom, the water in it and the air above it, make up the pond **ecosystem**. An ecosystem consists of a community and its environment; they interact with one another and affect each other.

Within the ecosystem, each species of organism has its own role to play. This is called its **niche**. Tadpoles,

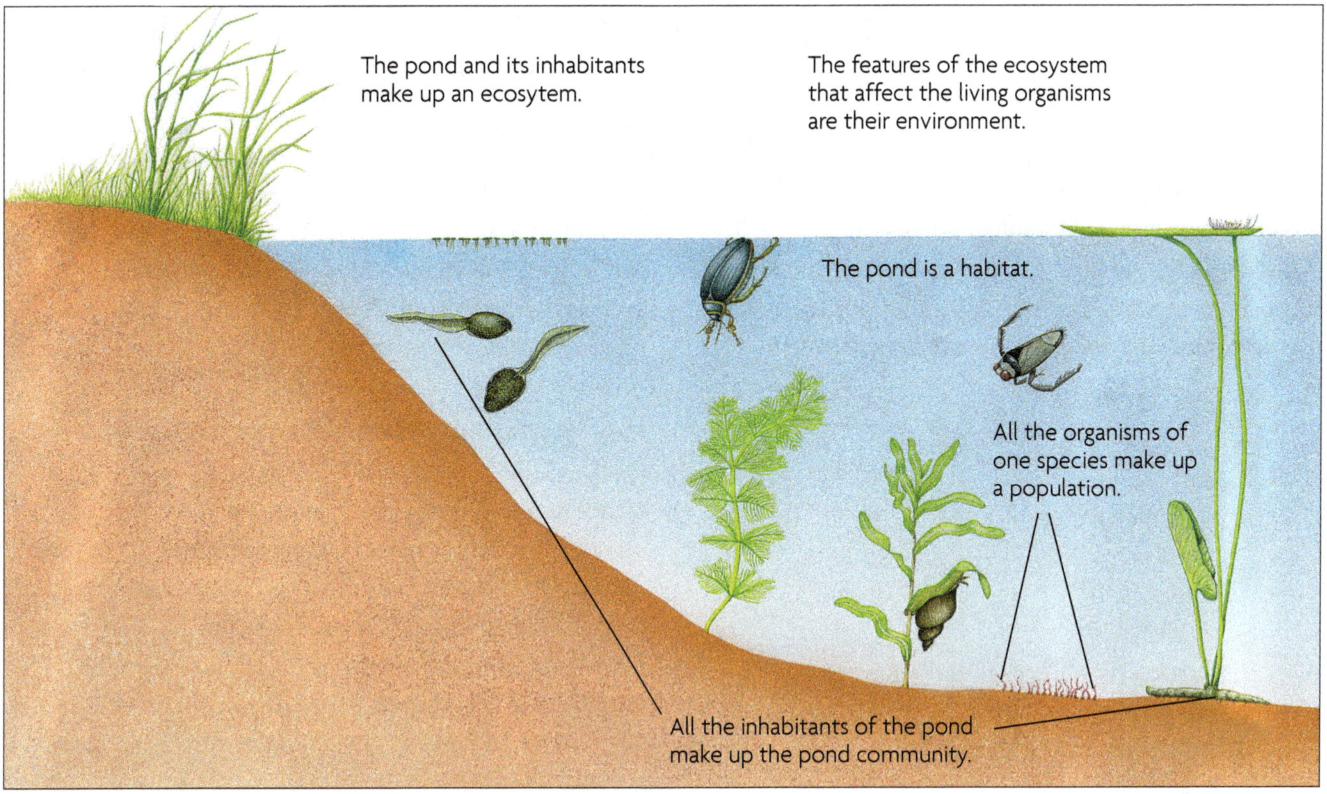

The pond and its inhabitants make up an ecosytem.
The features of the ecosystem that affect the living organisms are their environment.
The pond is a habitat.
All the organisms of one species make up a population.
All the inhabitants of the pond make up the pond community.

Figure 17.1 A pond and its inhabitants – an example of an ecosystem.

for example, feed on water weeds and are preyed on by fish. They use oxygen dissolved in the water, and they produce carbon dioxide. These activities, and all the other acitivities and needs of the tadpoles, describe the tadpole's niche in this environment. Each species has its own niche which is not identical to the niche of any other species.

The **environment** of the tadpoles is everything around that affects them. This includes other living things – for example, the fish that eat them and the plants that they eat – and the non-living things – the water in which they swim, the light falling onto the pond, the temperature and so on. We will look more closely at these environmental factors and how they affect living organisms in sections **17.10** to **17.33**.

Questions

17.1 What is ecology?

17.2 Explain the difference between each of these pairs of terms:

a population, community

b environment, habitat.

17.3 Sampling can estimate distribution and abundance.

When ecologists study an ecosystem, they usually begin by trying to find out which species live there. If you were able to do Investigation **1.1**, you may already have identified some different species of animals and plants in a particular ecosystem.

Ecologists frequently want to know which species are most common and which are most rare in the ecosystem, as well as how they are spread out. Does the species have a large population or a small one? Are they all in one place, or are they spread out over a wide area?

To find the answers to these questions, you may be able to simply count the organisms. This would be possible, for example, if you wanted to know the numbers and distribution of a particular species of tree in a small wood, or the numbers of sea anemones in a small rock pool. But often it is not quite that easy. How could you find the size of the population of daisy plants on a school playing field, or the numbers of tadpoles in a pond?

In these circumstances, it is best to take a **sample** of a small part of the field or pond. If you can answer your questions for this small area, then you can just multiply up to estimate the numbers of each kind of organism in the whole area you are studying.

One very useful way of sampling is to use a **quadrat**. This is just a square – you can make one out of pieces of wire, wood, or even string (Figure 17.2). You place the quadrat on the ground and count the organisms inside it.

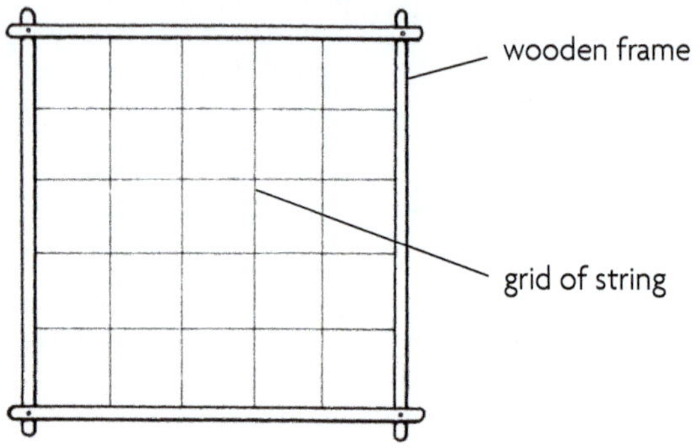

Figure 17.2 A gridded quadrat.

A quadrat can be any size you like, but a particularly useful size is with sides of 0.5 m. This is very convenient to use in a field or a rocky sea shore, for example. If you are studying small organisms – for example, growing on the surface of a wall – then you may want to use a smaller quadrat, perhaps with sides 25 cm long. If you are studying huge organisms, like trees, then you might need to use a huge quadrat, with sides perhaps 10 m long. In that case, you would just mark out the square using string or a long measuring tape. If you are planning to use quadrats in a forest, you will need more than one size. For the ground level, a square metre quadrat could be suitable. For the shrub layers, a nine square metre size might be considered. Quadrats may not be practical for the tree layer(s).

A quadrat may be gridded to allow really small areas to be studied in detail. For example, a 25 cm square quadrat may be gridded into smaller squares of sides each 5 cm.

Your quadrat sample only gives you an idea of the numbers of plants in one small area. You cannot guarantee that that area is representative of the whole field. You will need to do many quadrats, and average your results from each, to be sure of getting a representative sample (Figure 17.3).

17.4 Species frequency is the percentage of quadrats containing that species.

Quadrats allow you to estimate the **frequency** of each species. This simply means the percentage of the number of quadrats in which the particular species has been found. For example, if you put down 100 quadrats and found broomweed (*Sida* sp.) in 20 of them, then the frequency of broomweed is 20%. If you put down 10 quadrats and found it in 6 of them, then its frequency is 60%.

17.5 Species density is the number per unit area.

If you count the number of each species in every quadrat, then a figure representing the number per unit area can be obtained. This is called the **density** of the species.

For example, you could use quadrats to estimate the density of limpets on a rocky shore. You might obtain results like this:

Quadrat (0.5 m × 0.5 m)	1	2	3	4	5	6	7	8	9	10
Number of limpets	0	5	6	2	0	27	14	0	6	13

If the quadrats had sides of 0.5 m, then the area enclosed by each quadrat is 0.5 m × 0.5 m, which is 0.25 m^2. There were 10 quadrats, so the total area sampled was:

$10 \times 0.25 = 2.5\,\text{m}^2$.

Species	Quadrat number										Quadrat size =			
	1	2	3	4	5	6	7	8	9	10	Total in quadrats	Frequency in %	Density	Comments

Figure 17.3 One way of recording a species count.

The total number of limpets in this area was 73. So we can calculate the number of limpets per square metre like this:

mean number of limpets per square metre

$$= \frac{73}{2.5} = 29.2$$

This is the species density of limpets on this rocky shore.

With some species, like grasses, though, it is impossible to say where one plant stops and another begins. This makes it impossible to count the number of them inside a quadrat. In this case, you can estimate what percentage of the quadrat area is covered by grass, and by other plants (Figure 17.4). This is much easier to do if your quadrat is gridded.

If the plants in your quadrat are quite tall, there may be more than one layer of plants. In this case, the total of all your percentages may be more than 100%.

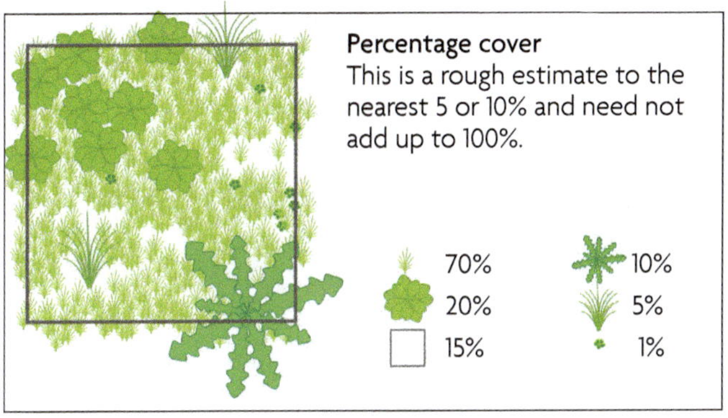

Percentage cover
This is a rough estimate to the nearest 5 or 10% and need not add up to 100%.
70%
20%
15%
10%
5%
1%

Figure 17.4 Estimating percentage cover.

17.6 Sampling should be random.

The placing of your quadrat is very important. If you just choose where to put it, the part of the field full of thorn bushes and cacti, with a bull standing behind them, will probably not get sampled very often. So you must use some way of placing your quadrats randomly in the field.

There are several ways of doing this. One way is to divide the piece of ground into squares and use pairs of random numbers as coordinates (Figure 17.5). These you can get from tables. If your numbers are (12,8) for example, you could go twelve squares forward from a corner along an edge, and then eight squares out into the field, and put your quadrat down at that point.

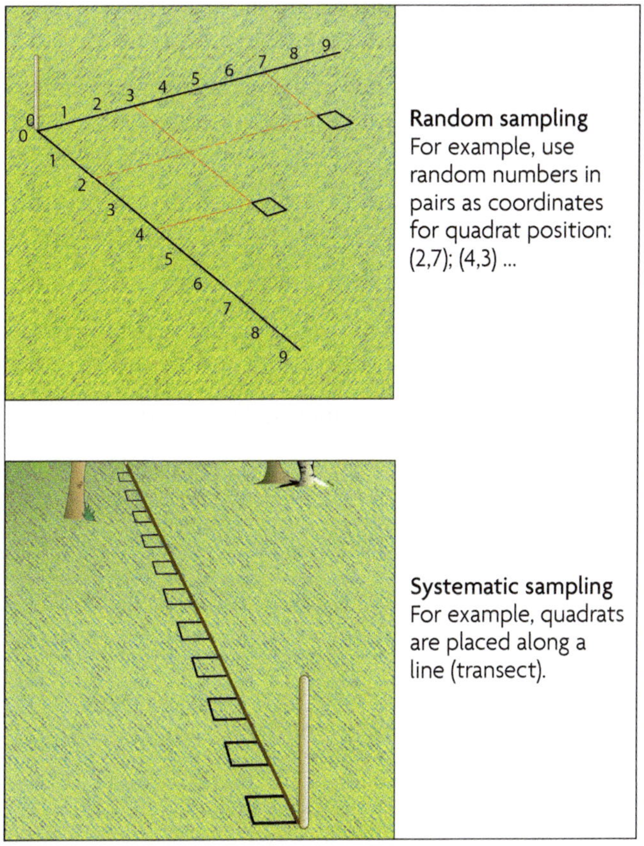

Figure 17.5 Placing quadrats for random sampling and transects.

Questions

17.3 A survey was made of *Crotalaria* plants growing on a lawn and in a cultivated vegetable patch. Ten 0.25 m^2 quadrats were placed radomly in each area, and the number of *Crotalaria* plants in each quadrat was counted. The results are shown in the table.

Quadrat	1	2	3	4	5	6	7	8	9	10
Number of *Crotalaria* on lawn	0	0	4	3	0	1	2	4	0	3
Number of *Crotalaria* on cultivated ground	0	0	0	2	5	0	0	1	0	0

Calculate the density of *Crotalaria* in each area.

17.7 Transects sample changes between habitats.

Another way of sampling the distribution of organisms in an area is to use a **transect**. A transect is a line crossing the area. You can use a long tape measure or rope to mark the transect. You then record the species of plants touching the tape.

Often, it would take far too long to record all the plants touching the tape. Instead, you might record them at intervals, say every 10 cm or every 10 m. You could place quadrats against the tape, and use them to estimate species frequency or percentage cover.

Transects are particularly useful where one kind of habitat merges into another. You could use one, for example, where the sparse vegetation on the shoreline merges into woodland. A transect will give you information about how the numbers and kinds of species change, as the environment changes (Figures **17.6** and **17.7**).

The example in Figure **17.6** shows a pattern that we often find when studying a sandy shore in the Caribbean. Different species tend to grow at different distances from the shore, so that we find different communities in each area. This is called **zonation**. Zonation happens because the environmental factors in each place are different, so certain species are better adapted to live in some areas than in others.

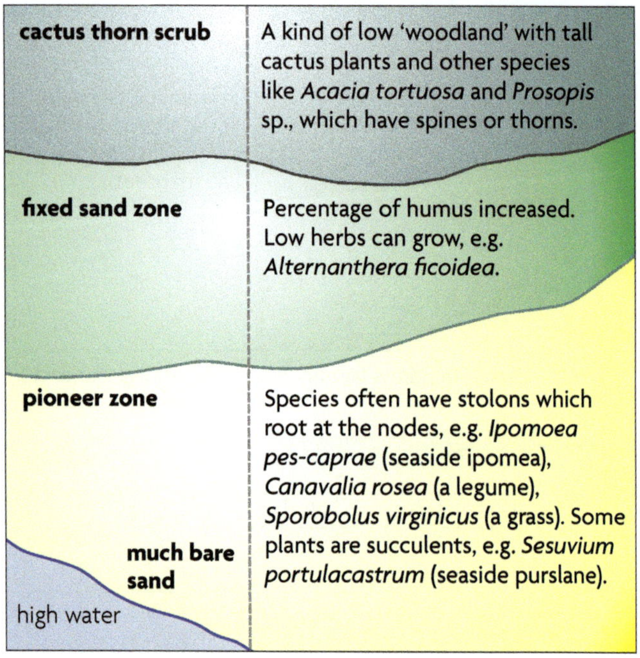

cactus thorn scrub
A kind of low 'woodland' with tall cactus plants and other species like *Acacia tortuosa* and *Prosopis* sp., which have spines or thorns.
fixed sand zone
Percentage of humus increased. Low herbs can grow, e.g. *Alternanthera ficoidea*.
pioneer zone
Species often have stolons which root at the nodes, e.g. *Ipomoea pes-caprae* (seaside ipomea), *Canavalia rosea* (a legume), *Sporobolus virginicus* (a grass). Some plants are succulents, e.g. *Sesuvium portulacastrum* (seaside purslane).
much bare sand
high water

Figure 17.6 Distribution of plants on a sandy shore in the Caribbean.

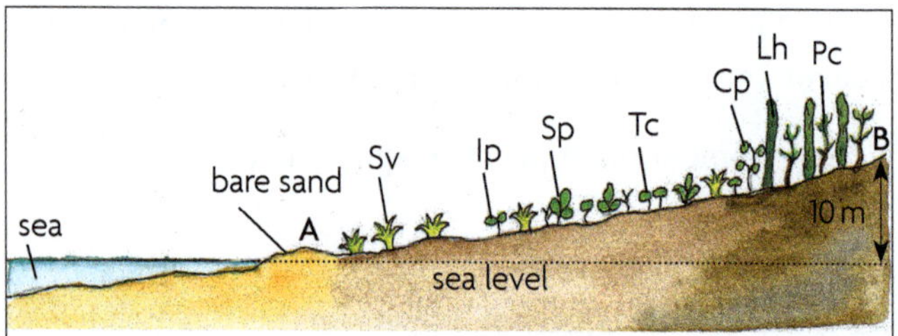

Sv	*Sporobolus virginicus*		✓	✓	✓	✓	
Ip	*Ipomoea pes-caprae*			✓			
Sp	*Sesuvium portulacastrum*			✓	✓	✓	
Tc	*Tribulus cistoides*			✓	✓	✓	
Cp	*Calotropis procera*					✓	
Lh	*Lemaireocereus hystrix*					✓	✓
Pc	*Prosopis chilensis*					✓	✓

0 point A — 10 — 20 — 30 — 40 — 50 — 60 point B (distance in metres)

Figure 17.7 Results of a transect of a sandy shore.

17.8 The point centre method is useful in a forest.

Using large quadrats for the trees in a forest may be difficult. Instead, the point-centred quarter method may be used for sampling. For this, you need to follow this procedure.

1 Select sampling points at random along a line transect.
2 Use each point as a centre, and determine the distances to the nearest individual of a particular species in each quarter (Figure **17.8**).
3 Find the mean of the distances measured.
4 Calculate the density of this species using the formula:

$$\text{density} = \frac{1}{(\text{mean distance to nearest individual})^2}$$

5 From similar measurements for different species, their relative densities can be calculated.

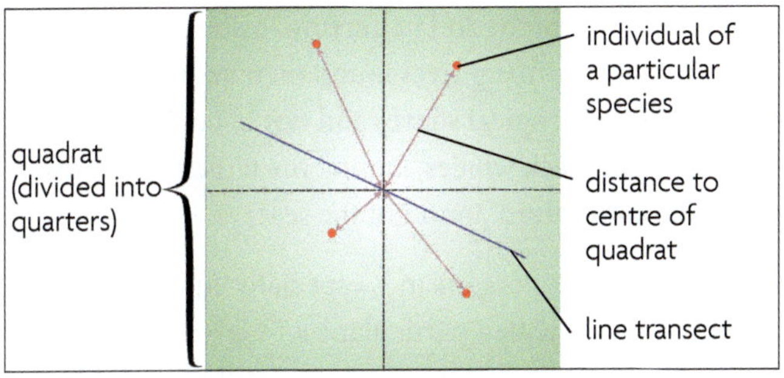

Figure 17.8 Point centre quarter method of sampling.

17.9 Mark, release, recapture estimates numbers.

Quadrats and transects are very useful ways of finding out how many organisms of different species are living in a habitat. But they can only be used with organisms which stay in one place for most of the time. This usually means plants, though on a seashore you can count limpets, barnacles, sea anemones and other animals this way.

You need a different method for estimating the numbers of animals that move around a lot. One method is the **mark, release, recapture** technique. It works so long as there are reasonable numbers of each kind of animal, and so long as they move around quite freely.

Suppose that you wanted to estimate the size of a population of woodlice. First, you need to capture a sample of perhaps 30 woodlice. You could do this just by hunting for them under stones and logs. For other animals, you might need to catch them using nets. Each woodlouse is marked with a small spot of waterproof paint, and then released.

The woodlice are then left alone for about a day, to give the marked ones a chance to become mixed up with any unmarked ones. You then capture a second sample, of as

Investigation 17.1
Estimating the size of a bead population, using the mark, release, recapture technique

SBA **skills**

Observation/Recording/Reporting

Analysis/Interpretation

1 Fill a bucket or large tray with a large number of beads, all the same colour and size.

2 Capture a sample of about 50 beads.

3 'Mark' the captured beads, by exchanging them for beads of a different colour. Return the marked beads to the population.

4 Thoroughly mix the marked beads with the rest of the population.

5 Capture a second, quite large but random, sample of beads. It may be best to use a blindfold when taking this sample to ensure that it is random.

6 Count the number of marked beads in your second sample, and the total number of beads in this sample.

7 Work out the estimated population of beads using the formula:

$$\text{population} = \frac{\text{number of beads in the first sample} \times \text{number of beads in the second sample}}{\text{number of marked beads in the second sample}}$$

8 Now count the actual number of beads.

Questions

1 How close was your estimate to the actual number of beads in the population? Do you consider it was close enough for this to be a useful technique?

2 When using the technique in the field, how could you ensure that your estimate came as close as possible to the real size of the population?

3 For which of these populations would this method be suitable?

a snails in a small garden

b nutgrass in a lawn

c killer whales in the Atlantic Ocean

d lichens on a tree trunk

Give reasons for your answers, and suggest alternative methods if you do not think that mark, release, recapture would be suitable.

many woodlice as you can. Count the total number, and the number of marked ones.

Suppose that you caught 100 woodlice in your second sample, and 10 of them had been marked. You have recaptured 10 of the 30 you originally marked, or $\frac{1}{3}$ of them. So it is probable that you have caught about $\frac{1}{3}$ of the whole woodlouse population. The size of the population will therefore be about 3 × 100 woodlice, that is 300.

Questions

17.4 When using a quadrat, how can you estimate the amount of a plant such as grass, in your sample?

17.5 Why is it important to place quadrats randomly?

17.6 When might you use a transect?

17.7 A sample of 50 water beetles were caught and marked, before being returned to their pond. The next day, another 50 water beetles were caught, 10 of which had been marked. About how many water beetles were in the pond altogether?

17.8 What other data besides that on living organisms should be collected when studying an ecosystem and why?

Environmental factors

17.10 Environmental factors partly determine organism distribution.

Why do living organisms live where they do? Why do polar bears live in the Arctic and not in Africa? Why do earthworms live in the soil in burrows instead of above ground? Why are mangroves found on marshy coastal tropical and subtropical shores and not in cold climates? Why are humpback whales, among the largest creatures which have ever lived, found in the sea?

Each kind of living organism is especially equipped, or adapted, to cope with a particular set of **environmental factors**. Polar bears, for example, are adapted to live in the intense cold of the Arctic. They have thick fur and a thick layer of fat beneath their skin to insulate their bodies. Earthworms can obtain their 'food' supply by literally eating the earth, while their bodies are being kept moist below ground. They cannot cope with the drier air above ground.

Humpback whales (Figure **17.9**) have a very ready supply of food. They take in large mouthfuls of water containing krill, then press out the water with the tongue, leaving the krill behind. Their mammalian skeleton could not support their large size on land but the water supports their bodies.

The cold of the Arctic, the moisture in the air and the presence or absence of water around the organism, are all examples of environmental factors.

Environmental factors alone, however, cannot completely explain the distribution of living organisms. Sometimes, an environment may seem just right for an organism, and yet it is not found there. This may be because it has never been able to spread to that area.

Figure 17.9 A humpback whale showing the filtering plates hanging in the mouth.

17.11 Biotic and abiotic factors.

Because there are so many different environmental factors, it is useful to try grouping them in some way. The two main groups are **biotic** factors, which are the influences of other living things, and **abiotic** factors, which are the influences of non-living parts of the environment.

Each of these main groups includes several kinds of environmental factors.

Abiotic factors These include climatic factors, such as sunlight, rainfall, humidity and temperature. Also important are chemical and physical factors, such as the amount of oxygen dissolved in a pond or stream, the amount of hydrogen sulfide gas in the air, or the pH of pond water. Factors caused by the soil are also very important. They are sometimes called **edaphic** factors.

Biotic factors These include availability of food, and how many predators there are. Parasites and pathogens (disease-causing organisms) are also important biotic factors. Another is the amount of **competition** with other organisms for food, shelter, or anything which an organism needs.

Environmental factors affect living organisms in many ways. For example, they affect their distribution, their size, their numbers, and their ability to reproduce. You will find many examples when studying any ecosystem. This chapter can describe only a few factors, and some of the effects they have on some organisms.

Questions

17.9 What is an environmental factor?

17.10 Describe at least four ways in which **(a)** an earthworm, and **(b)** a grasshopper are adapted to their way of life.

17.11 What is meant by **(a)** a biotic factor, and **(b)** an abiotic factor?

17.12 What are edaphic factors?

Abiotic factors

17.12 Climate influences natural vegetation.

On a world scale, climate has a great influence on the kinds of plants and animals that can live in different areas (Figures **17.10**). The two most important factors are temperature and rainfall.

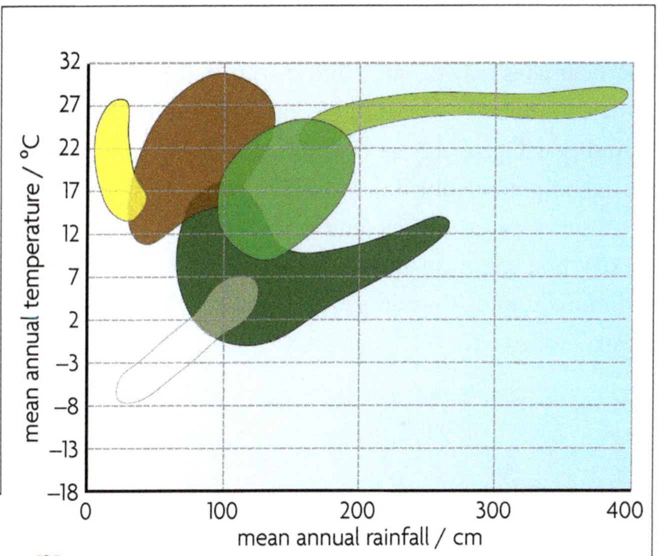

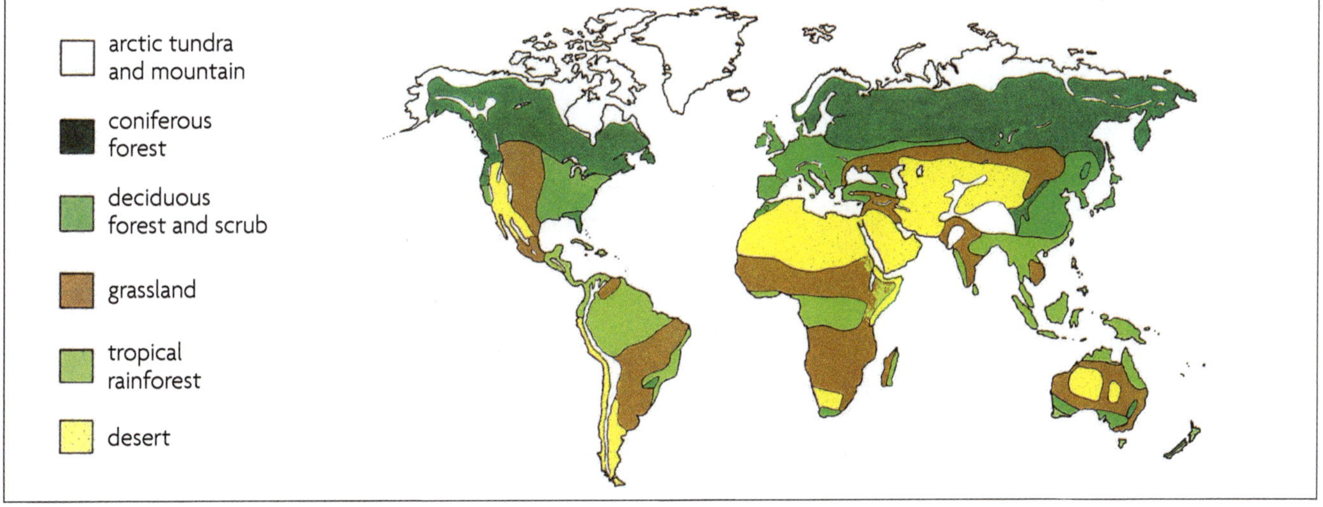

Figure 17.10 The influence of climate on world vegetation.

For example, in hot places with plenty of rainfall, a large variety of plants can thrive, and tropical rainforest is formed. This provides a very rich and varied environment for animals, and so the number and variety of animals are also large (Figure **17.11**).

Dry or desert areas, whether hot or cold, are more difficult for both plants and animals, because they lose water by evaporation and cannot easily replace it. Only a very few plants and animals are adapted to live in these conditions, so deserts are sparsely populated (Figure **17.12**).

17.13 Microclimate is important to many organisms.

Climate is also important to living organisms on a much smaller scale. To a woodlouse, for example, the climate which immediately affects it is the climate where it lives, perhaps under a rotting log. The climate in a small space like this is called a **microclimate**.

Microclimates may be quite different from the general climate in that area. Beneath the log, for example, humidity will probably be nearly 100%, whereas the air outside might be quite dry. Woodlice are not well adapted to conserve water, so they tend to stay under cover during the day, and come out at night when the air is cooler and more humid. They are cryptozoic animals ('crypto' means hidden).

17.14 Oxygen is needed for respiration.

Most living organisms need oxygen, for respiration. Usually, there is plenty of oxygen available in the air.

Aquatic organisms rely on oxygen which is dissolved in the water. Some of this will come from the air, and some from water plants, which give off oxygen during photosynthesis.

Oxygen can quite often be in short supply in water, and it does not diffuse through water very quickly. So the bottom of a deep pond or lake may have little or no oxygen, especially as it will be too dark for plants to grow there. Polluted water may have less oxygen (Figure **17.13**).

Shallow, fast-flowing streams, however, always have plenty of oxygen. Many fish that are active swimmers, such as the mountain mullet, live in unpolluted streams with plenty of oxygen (Figure **17.14**) and cannot survive in deep, poorly oxygenated water.

Pollution of the ocean, streams and rivers by sewage causes the amount of oxygen dissolved in them to decrease. This is because the sewage provides food for bacteria. A large population of bacteria builds up. This uses up the oxygen in the water so fish and other organisms cannot live there (Figure **18.11**, page **357**).

Figure 17.11 A great variety of plants grows densely where the climate is always warm and moist, as here in the tropics.

Figure 17.12 In deserts such as the Namib, plants are few and far between.

Figure 17.13 The harbour in St. George, Grenada. Water near towns and cities often becomes polluted.

Figure 17.14 **a** A shallow fast-flowing stream flowing through the rainforest in Tobago has plenty of dissolved oxygen. **b** Some fish, such as these salmon, will only breed in unpolluted streams with plenty of dissolved oxygen.

17.15 Light is needed for photosynthesis.

Light is a very important environmental factor for plants because they need it for photosynthesis. Since all plants need light, there is great competition for light. Plants have developed different ways of either reaching up to the light, or else tolerating shade (Figures **17.15**, **17.16** and **17.17**). Wild pines (Figure **17.15**) grow on the branches of tall trees, taking nothing from them but a position in the sunlight. *Philodendron* (Figure **17.16**) twines its way up the stems of trees for the same reason, while ferns and mosses can use the light that filters down through the trees above them (Figure **17.17**).

Figure 17.15 Wild pines growing in a Trinidad rainforest.

Figure 17.16 *Philodendron* growing on a tree trunk in Jamaica.

Figure 17.17 Ferns growing in the shade.

Questions

17.13 What are the two most important factors influencing the type of vegetation found in an area?

17.14 What type of vegetation would you expect to find in an area with a mean annual temperature of 20 °C and a rainfall of 80 cm?

17.15 What is a microclimate?

17.16 Why are woodlice more active at night than in the daytime?

17.17 West Indian fishermen used to be able to make a livelihood without going too far offshore for their catch. Why do you think that this is no longer true?

17.16 Soil affects plants, and therefore animals too.

Soil is a very important environmental factor, because plants rely on it for many of their requirements.

Anchorage Soil provides an anchorage for plant roots. A thin or very loosely structured soil will not support many plants, because their roots will not be able to grip it.

Nutrient minerals Soil provides nutrients for plants, particularly minerals such as nitrates and potassium salts.

Water Plants obtain water from the soil.

Air Plant roots and other soil organisms need air, to provide them with oxygen for respiration. A good soil has plenty of air spaces.

So the type of soil in a particular area has a large effect on the plants growing in it. This in turn will affect the animals that live there.

17.17 Soil is slowly formed from rock.

Soil is formed from rock. When rocks are weathered or broken down by wind, by freezing and thawing, or by water flowing over them, they are broken down into small particles, called rock waste.

These particles are colonised by pioneer plants and lichens and mosses. As the plants die and decay, their remains add organic materials to the mineral particles of the rock waste. Other plants and animals can then colonise the soil. This takes a very long time. It probably takes thousands of years to form good, deep, agricultural soils.

17.18 Soil has several components.

Figure **17.18** shows a vertical section through a good agricultural soil. The top layers are called **topsoil**.

Topsoil has six main constituents. They are mineral particles, humus, water, nutrient ions, air and living organisms.

17.19 The size of soil particles is important.

Mineral particles are formed from rocks, by weathering. The size of the mineral particles in a soil is very important. Very small particles form a soil called **clay**, while larger ones form **sand**.

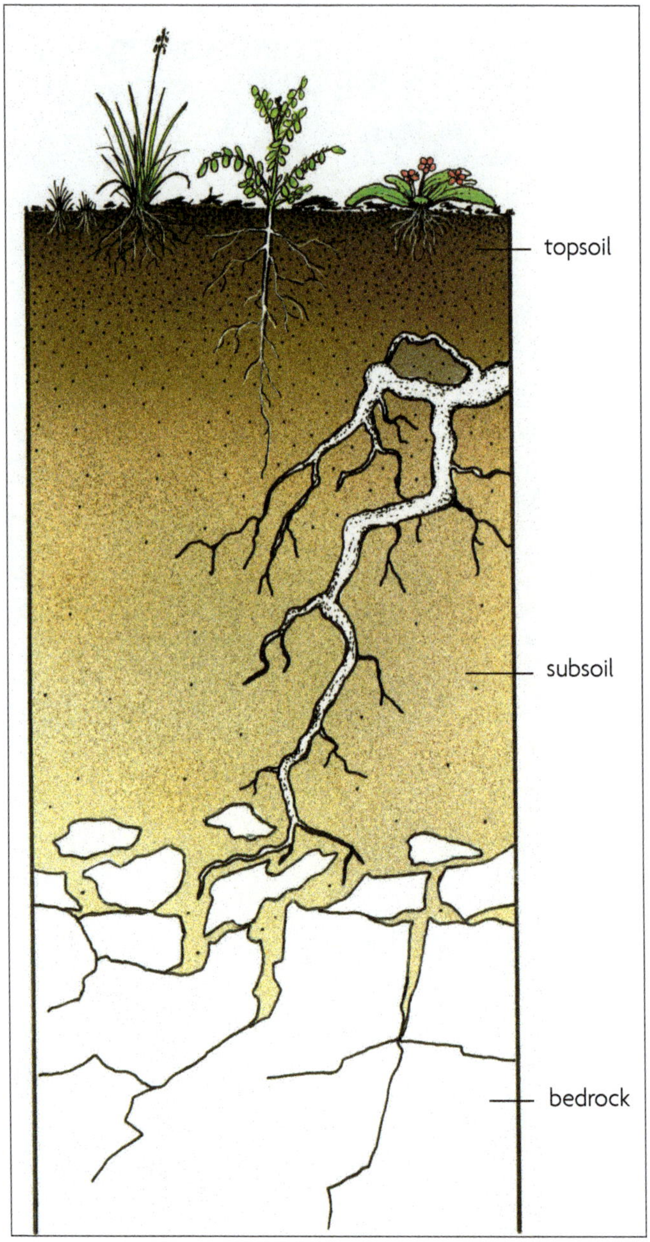

Figure 17.18 A vertical section through an agricultural soil.

Clay soils A clay soil contains very small soil particles, which can pack tightly together (Figure **17.19a**). Because they are so closely packed, they tend to hold water between them by **capillarity**. Capillarity is the tendency for water to move into very narrow spaces. Clay soils do not dry out quickly in dry weather.

However, this can be a disadvantage. In wet conditions, the small spaces between the soil particles fill up with water, so there is no room for air. The soil becomes **waterlogged** (section **17.23**).

Clay particles have a slight electrical charge, and so mineral ions like potassium (K^+) and calcium (Ca^{2+}) are attracted to them. This is useful, because the clay particles hold the ions, stopping them from being washed or leached out of the soil by rainwater.

Sand soils A sandy soil contains larger soil particles (Figure **17.19b**). The large particles cannot pack very closely together, so there are large air spaces between them. Sandy soils are usually well aerated.

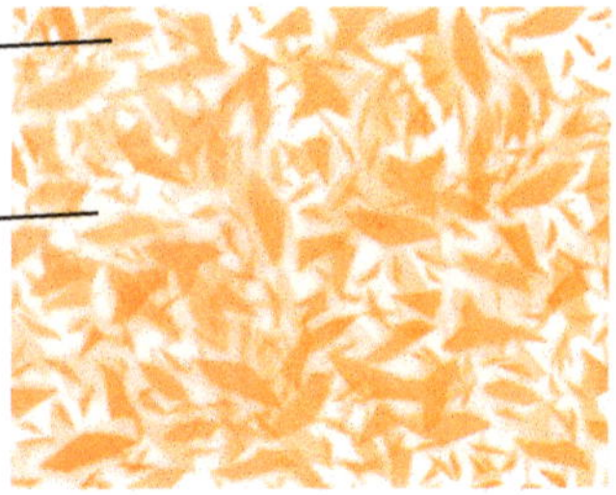

a A clay soil contains small particles which pack closely together.

b A sandy soil contains large particles, with large air spaces between them.

Figure 17.19 Soil particles.

The large spaces, however, mean that water is not held by capillarity. Sandy soils drain very quickly. Sand particles do not hold mineral ions in the same way that clay particles do. So minerals are leached out of a sandy soil more quickly.

Loam A loam is a soil that contains a good mixture of sand and clay particles. If the balance is right, it will hold water and mineral ions, but will not get waterlogged too easily.

Investigation 17.2

Making a rough estimate of the proportions of particles of different sizes in a soil sample

SBA skills

Observation/Recording/Reporting

Analysis/Interpretation

1. Put the soil sample into a gas jar.
2. Fill the gas jar to within 5 cm of the top with tap water.
3. Stir or shake the jar, to mix the soil and water completely.
4. Leave the jar undisturbed, until the particles have settled into layers.

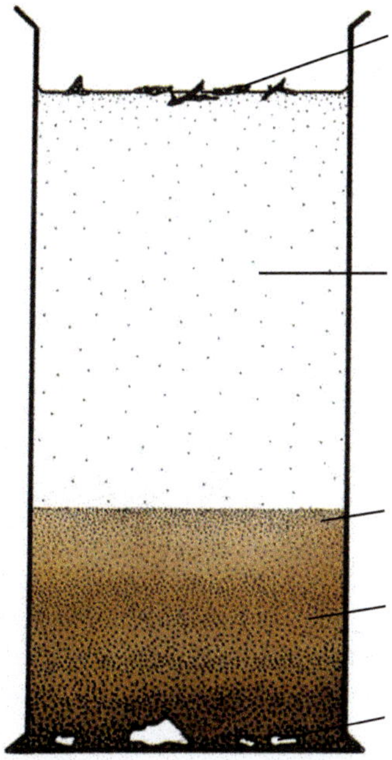

17.20 Remnants of decayed organisms form humus.

The dead bodies of animals and plants, and any other organic waste such as faeces, are decomposed by bacteria and fungi in the soil. They are slowly broken down to a dark, sticky material called **humus**.

Humus forms a coating over the mineral particles in soil. It sticks the soil particles together into small groups called crumbs. A soil with a good crumb structure tends to be well drained and aerated, and yet holds water and minerals.

It takes a long time before bacteria and fungi can break humus down completely. So humus provides a long-term store of useful substances such as nitrogen, which plants can eventually use.

Humus also provides food for other living organisms in the soil, such as earthworms.

17.21 Water coats soil particles.

Plants obtain all their water from the soil. The water is absorbed by osmosis, through root hairs.

Even in dry weather, a good loam with plenty of humus will hold water. The water forms a film around each soil particle. Too much water in soil, however, causes waterlogging.

Investigation 17.3
To estimate the percentage of water in a soil sample

SBA skills

Observation/Recording/Reporting

Manipulation/Measurement

Analysis/Interpretation

1. Find the mass of an evaporating dish.
2. Put your soil sample into the dish, and reweigh. Work out the mass of the soil sample, and record it.
3. Put the dish and soil into a warm oven (about 90 °C). The warmth will dry out the soil. The oven must not be too hot, or the organic material in the soil will break down.
4. After a day or so, find the mass of the dish and soil again. Replace in the oven, and leave for a few hours more. Find the mass. If the two masses are the same, the soil is dry. If not, replace in the oven. This is called drying to constant mass.
5. Work out the mass of water in the soil, by subtracting the mass of the dried soil plus dish from the mass of the wet soil plus dish.
6. Work out the percentage of water in the soil like this:

$$\%\text{ water in soil} = \frac{\text{mass of water in sample}}{\text{original mass of soil sample}} \times 100$$

Questions

1. Why must the oven not be hot enough to break down organic material in the soil?
2. What type of soil would you expect to contain the highest percentage of water?

Investigation 17.4
To estimate the percentage of humus in a soil sample

SBA skills

Observation/Recording/Reporting
Manipulation/Measurement
Analysis/Interpretation

1 Take the dried soil sample in its dish from Investigation **17.3**. Find its mass. If necessary, dry to constant mass again.

2 Heat the soil strongly, either in a very hot oven, or over a Bunsen burner. The high temperature will oxidise the humus.

3 Allow the sample to cool, and find its new mass.

4 Heat again, cool, and find the mass, until the mass is constant.

5 Work out the mass of humus in the soil, by subtracting the mass of heated soil plus dish, from the mass of dried soil plus dish.

6 Work out the percentage of humus in the soil like this:

$$\text{\% humus in soil sample} = \frac{\text{mass of humus in sample}}{\text{original mass of soil after drying}} \times 100$$

Questions

1 Why was dried soil used for this investigation?

2 If the dried soil has been left for a while since the last investigation, you may find that its mass has increased slightly when you check its mass at the beginning of this investigation. Explain this.

3 How could you use your results from Investigations **17.3** and **17.4** to calculate the percentage of minerals in the soil?

17.22 Mineral ions are dissolved in soil water.

Plants obtain nutrient or mineral ions from soil. They are absorbed by diffusion or active transport through root hairs. Table **4.2** (page **61**) lists the main mineral ions required by plants.

The mineral ions in soil are dissolved in the soil water. The kind and number of ions depend partly on the kind of rock from which the soil was made, and partly on the activities of bacteria in the soil. For example, a soil with plenty of nitrogen-fixing and nitrifying bacteria will contain plenty of nitrate ions.

17.23 Organisms in soil need air.

Some of the spaces between the soil particles in soil are filled with air. If all the spaces are filled with water, so that there is no room for air, then the soil is said to be waterlogged.

Soil animals need oxygen for respiration. Nitrogen-fixing bacteria need nitrogen and oxygen from the air in the soil. They cannot live in waterlogged soils, so these soils are often short of nitrates (section **1.24**).

Plant roots also need oxygen for respiration. Some plants which can tolerate these waterlogged conditions have special ways of getting oxygen into their roots. The mangroves are a good example. The red mangrove (*Rhizophora mangle*), which can grow offshore, has stilt roots which raise it above the level of the water (Figure **17.20**, overleaf). The black mangrove *Avicennia nitida* (*germinans*) has pneumatophores (sometimes called 'breathing roots') which stick up above the surface of the swampy soil (Figure **17.21**, overleaf). All these roots have many lenticels, which are special 'breaks' in the outer covering allowing air to enter (see Figure **6.25**, page **111**).

Figure 17.20 Stilt roots of red mangrove.

Figure 17.21 Pneumatophores of black mangrove.

17.24 Soil is a habitat for many organisms.

A good soil contains a large variety of living organisms. They include plant roots, earthworms, ants, termites, fungi and bacteria (Figure 17.22).

Earthworms can help to improve soil for plant growth. Their burrows help to aerate soil, and improve drainage. They also add humus to the soil by pulling in dead leaves, by excreting waste material, and from their decaying bodies after death. Earthworms feed by eating soil particles and extracting organic material from them, and the remains which they egest improve the texture of the soil.

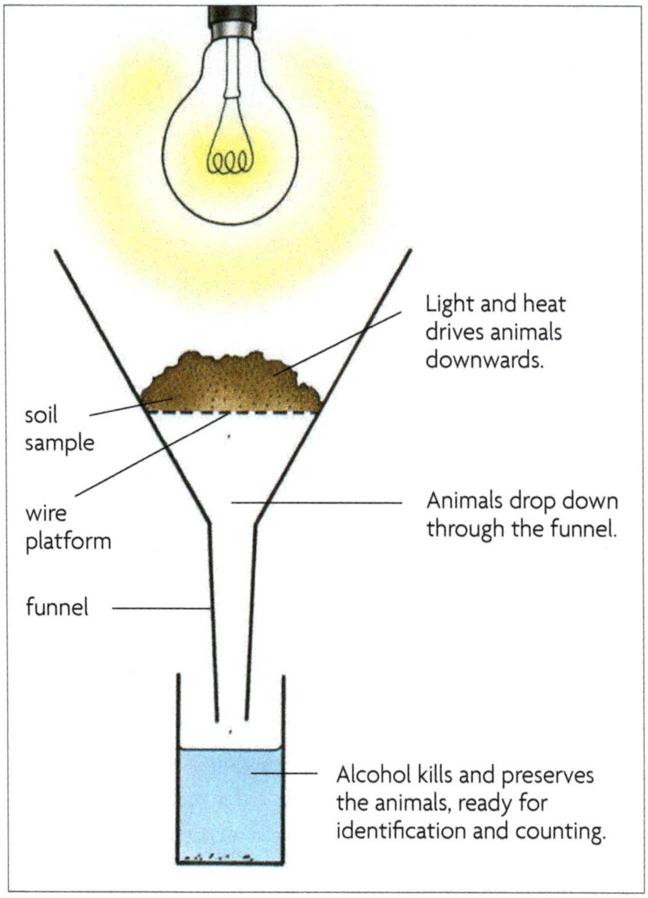

Figure 17.22 A Tullgren funnel – a method of collecting small soil animals.

Bacteria occur in soil in huge numbers. These bacteria, along with other decomposers such as fungi, feed on the dead bodies and faeces of animals and plants. They form humus. They help to release nutrients into the soil so that these can be re-used by other living organisms (section **1.19**).

In marshy areas, decay of dead plants and animals is slow because the decay bacteria need air in order to carry out their functions. So there is a build-up of partly decayed organisms. These release acids, which make the situation worse, since few bacteria can survive in these acid conditions. Release of nutrients is, therefore, very slow and only a few types of plants can live in these conditions.

17.25 Clay soils are heavy and hard to cultivate.

A clay soil has the advantage that it holds water and mineral ions well. However, drainage and aeration are poor.

A clay soil is difficult to dig or plough. When wet, it is soft and sticky, and heavy farm machinery will compact it, squeezing out air from between the soil particles (Figure **17.23**). When dry, it becomes very hard, and difficult to break up (Figure **17.24**).

Figure 17.23 A wet clay soil can be compacted by heavy machinery. You can see how water is trapped in the wheel ruts made by a tractor.

Figure 17.24 Clay soils shrink and crack when dry.

A clay soil may be made easier to work, and better for plants to grow in, by improving its crumb structure. There are two main ways that this can be done.

One way is by adding **lime** to the soil. Lime is calcium hydroxide. It reacts with the clay particles, making them clump together, or flocculate. The large crumbs improve the drainage and aeration of the soil.

Another way of improving the crumb structure is by adding humus to the soil, in the form of manure or compost. This also sticks the clay particles together to form crumbs. Other advantages of adding humus are that it adds nutrients to the soil, and encourages soil organisms.

The addition of sand may also help to improve a clay soil for cultivation, but sand adds no nutrients. If added in sufficient quantities, the larger particles will help to improve drainage and aeration.

A clay soil, if properly managed, can become an excellent agricultural soil.

The natural advantage of a sandy soil is its good drainage. This makes it easy to work because the large particles separate easily, and do not become compacted (Table **17.1**).

Sandy soils, though, lack nutrients and have poor water-retentive properties. Both of these conditions can be improved by the addition of humus.

Table 17.1 A comparison of clay and sandy soils

	Clay soil	Sandy soil
Particle size	small	large
Aeration	spaces between particles are small, so soil is often poorly aerated	spaces between particles are large, so soil is usually well aerated
Water-holding capacity	water is held in the small spaces by capillarity	water is not held by capillarity, because the spaces are too large
Drainage	water only drains slowly through the small spaces	water drains quickly through the large spaces
Mineral ions	many, because they are bound to the clay particles; slow drainage prevents them being leached out	few, because they are quickly leached out as water drains through

Investigation 17.5
To find the effect of lime on clay particles

SBA skills

Observation/Recording/Reporting
Manipulation/Measurement
Analysis/Interpretation

1 Put a small amount of powdered clay into a container and mix thoroughly with plenty of tap water. The fine clay particles will form a cloudy suspension in the water.

2 Now add a small amount of lime (calcium hydroxide or calcium oxide) to the clay suspension. Watch carefully to see what happens:
  a immediately
  b after 5 to 10 minutes.

Questions

1 What effect did the lime have on the clay particles?

2 What are the main problems that farmers have when trying to cultivate a clay soil?

3 How might the addition of lime improve such a soil?

Biotic factors

17.26 There are many relationships between living organisms.

Biotic factors are caused by other living things. Every living organism is affected by others in some way (Chapter **1**).

There are many kinds of relationships between living organisms, which may be close or casual, beneficial or harmful. They include relationships between:

1 competitors – organisms that need the same things, and so may compete with each other if these things are in short supply
2 mutualistic partners – organisms that live together for mutual benefit (section **1.17**)
3 predators and their prey
4 parasites and their hosts.

17.27 Organisms compete with one another.

Competition happens whenever two or more organisms need the same thing, which is in short supply.

Plants compete for light, root space, and sometimes for water and minerals from the soil. Animals compete for food and a place to live and reproduce.

If the competition is between individuals belonging to the same species, it is called **intraspecific competition**. If it is between individuals belonging to different species, it is called **interspecific competition**. The bark beetles *Ips calligraphus* and *Ips grandicollis* show both intra- and interspecific competition. These are small (3 to 5 mm) brown beetles which attack the Caribbean pine, *Pinus caribbea*. They tunnel through the bark of the tree to lay

Questions

17.18 List four reasons why soil is important to plants.

17.19 What is topsoil?

17.20 List the six constituents of topsoil.

17.21 Explain why a clay soil usually contains plenty of mineral ions.

17.22 Why are sandy soils better aerated than clay soils?

17.23 What is a loam?

17.24 What is humus?

17.25 List three advantages of having plenty of humus in a soil.

17.26 What is meant by a waterlogged soil?

17.27 Why do many plants die if their soil becomes waterlogged?

17.28 How does a large earthworm population benefit a soil?

17.29 What are the problems of trying to cultivate a clay soil?

17.30 How may a sandy soil be improved?

their eggs in the soft phloem tissue beneath. There the eggs develop into larvae, pupae, and then young adults which bore their way out through the bark to start the cycle in another tree.

In both species, competition for food and space among the larvae (intraspecific) results in the reduction of the average size of the adults. When competition is very high, many more larvae die than is usual.

17.28 Occupying different niches reduces competition.

Competition between living organisms only happens when their niches, or lifestyles, overlap. The more they overlap, the more likely it is that they will compete.

Both *Ips* species of bark beetles can live on the trunk or branches of the Caribbean pine. If a tree is attacked by one species only, this species will spread all over the tree. When both species are present, however, *Ips calligraphus* confines itself to the thicker portions of the main trunk, while *Ips grandicollis* attacks the branches and the thinner parts of the trunk. This spatial separation reduces competition and allows the two species to live together on the same tree.

17.29 Competition among human beings has special results.

Human beings as a species are also in competition within the species and with other species for food and shelter. In other species, competition tends to stabilise populations over time. With human beings, populations may continue to grow. Often, a shift in concentration of the species accompanies the growth. More and more of the species may crowd together in one place, in towns and cities. This has consequences for humans and for other species too. These consequences are discussed in section **18.15**.

17.30 Predators kill prey for food.

A predator is an animal which kills and then feeds on another living organism, called its prey. An example of a predator is the nymph of a dragonfly (Figure **17.25**). The nymph lives at the bottom of fresh-water ponds, and feeds on any small organisms that it can catch.

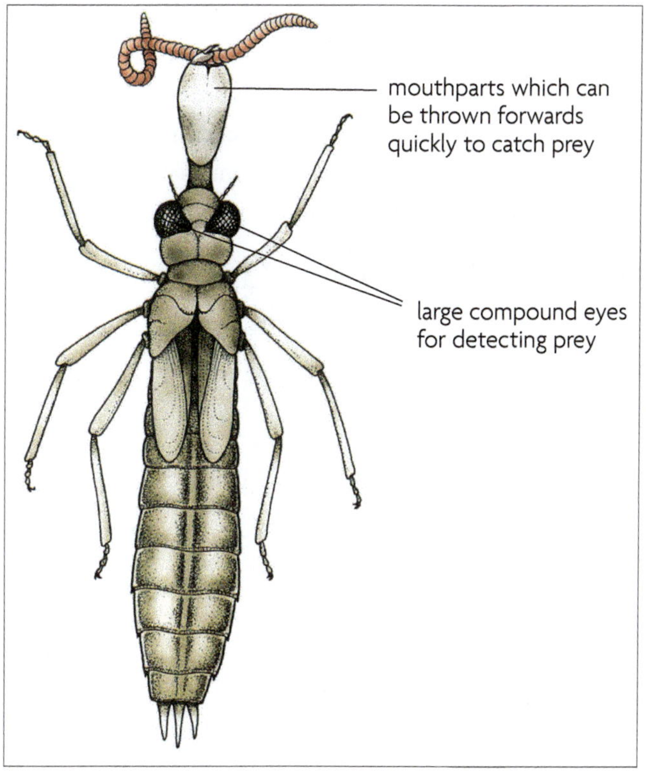

Figure 17.25 A dragonfly nymph – an example of a predator.

Predators need to be adapted to catch their prey. Some of the adaptations of the dragonfly nymph are shown in Figure **17.25**.

Animals which may be preyed on must also be adapted to protect themselves from their predators. This is often by camouflage. Stick insects, for example, look like twigs of the tree on which they are feeding (Figure **17.26**).

Other means may also be used. In some West Indian mangrove communities, the crab *Goniopsis cruentata* is

Figure 17.26 This stick insect is well camouflaged from its predators by its resemblance to the twig on which it is resting.

found (Figure 17.27). It lives at the base of the mangrove plants in the mud near the edge of the water. Part of its diet is another crab *Aratus pisonii* (Figure 17.27) which also lives in the mangrove trees. This crab lives high in the trees, however. It is only in danger from its predator when it has to go to the water's edge to wet its gills for breathing.

Figure 17.27 The crabs **a** *Goniopsis cruentata* and **b** *Aratus pisonii.*

17.31 Parasites harm their host.

A parasite is completely dependent on its host. Therefore, although it usually harms its host, a well-adapted parasite does not kill its host. If the host dies, the parasite will probably die too.

A tapeworm (Figure 17.28) is an example of a parasite. It lives inside the body of its host, so it is an endoparasite. The head louse (Figure 17.29) lives on the outside of a person's body. It is an ectoparasite.

17.32 Parasites have special adaptations.

A parasite's life is not always an easy one. Although it has plenty of food, it has many other problems.

One problem is staying in position. Tapeworms have hooks and suckers to fix them firmly to the wall of the alimentary canal (Figure 17.28). If they did not, then peristalsis would push them through the digestive system.

Head lice can grip hair firmly when it is combed, so they do not get dislodged. Their flattened shape lets them lie close against the scalp (Figure 17.29). Their eggs are cemented firmly to the hairs.

Another problem for parasites is for their offspring to find a new host. Many parasites, such as the tapeworm, have complicated life cycles which help them to do this. The tapeworm has two hosts.

Because finding a host is such a risky business, many parasites produce large numbers of eggs and young. Even though most of them will not find a host, there is then a better chance that at least some of them will. When mature proglottids of a tapeworm are passed out in human faeces, they are full of eggs.

Plant parasites often have special outgrowths which go into host tissue. Dodder or love vine (*Cuscuta* sp.) has slender orange-yellow stems which twine around herbs and shrubs. It has no chlorophyll, and leaves have become scales. There are no roots either, except in a very young seedling. These soon die as the plant attaches itself firmly to its host by suckers (Figure 17.30). Through these, it absorbs water and nutrients from the host.

Dodder bears many clusters of small whitish-pink flowers. So it produces many seeds. The plant can also reproduce vegetatively; small broken-off pieces of stem may attach themselves to new host plants.

17.33 Many parasites cause disease.

You have already seen (Chapters **1** and **16**) that many diseases of humans, of livestock and of crops are caused by parasitic microorganisms. These disease-causing organisms or pathogens include bacteria, viruses, fungi and some protozoans. Pneumonia, tetanus ('lock-jaw') and syphilis are caused by bacteria. Viruses cause the common cold, and AIDS. Pimento rust, black pod of cocoa, leaf spot of bananas and ring worm in humans, are all caused by fungi. Protozoans cause malaria and amoebic dysentery. Pathogens are discussed in more detail in Chapter **16**.

Questions

17.31 How does a parasite differ from a predator?

17.32 List three problems that a tapeworm has in trying to survive and reproduce.

17.33 Love bush is regarded as a pest in Caribbean hedges and gardens. What characteristics of this plant make it so difficult to get rid of?

17.34 What is a pathogen?

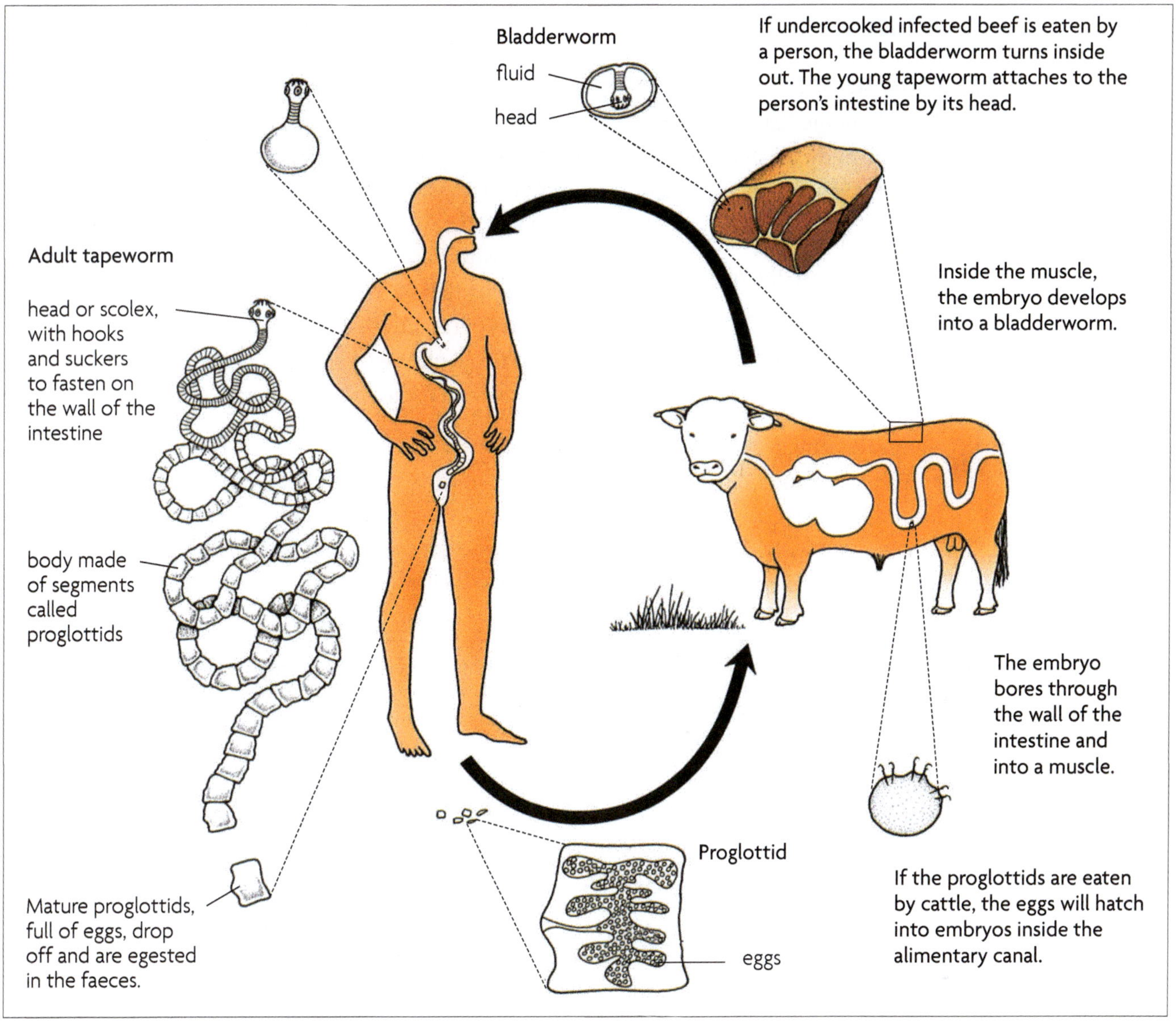

Figure 17.28 Life cycle of the beef tapeworm.

Figure 17.29 Head lice and their eggs on human hair,

Figure 17.30 Dodder (*Cuscuta* sp.) growing on another plant.

Some Caribbean ecosystems

17.34 Looking at life on the sea shore.

Sea-shore communities throughout the Caribbean show many features in common. On a sandy sea shore, one usually finds a zoned community (Figure **17.6**, page **320**).

The sandy shore is a changing environment. Over time, sand builds up behind the shore. At first, the sand is a very difficult place to live – it is constantly shifting and holds very little water or nutrients. Just a few tough species of plants are able to grow in it. Over time, they add humus to the soil, and their roots stabilise it. This allows other species to colonise. Eventually, the soil becomes fully stable and a fairly stable community, called the **climax community**, is found. These progressive changes in a habitat and its community over time are called **succession**.

We can see these changes in time by looking at the different parts of the shore at one moment in time. The part of the shore nearest to the sea is at the very earliest stage of succession, and the parts furthest away are in the later stages. Figure **17.31** shows a small part of a sandy shore in the Caribbean.

Figure 17.31 Colonisation of a sea shore in Barbados.

Species in the **pioneer zone** are early colonisers that can withstand the shifting sand and heavy salt spray on the immediate edge of the water. These are low-growing species. In the fixed sand zone, hardy herbs rise to 60 cm or so above ground. Some like *Plumbago scandens* climb over other plants. Many may be succulent or hairy. Gradually, the plants increase in height and number, and the cactus/thorn scrub represents one type of climax community that the soil and other environmental factors can support (Figure **17.32**). Another type might be a kind of woodland, often with seaside mahoe, *Cordia*, button mangrove and *Casuarina*.

Crabs, insects, lizards, and birds are likely to be found among the plants, either as 'visitors' to the area, or sometimes as 'permanent residents'. Sometimes, sea grape trees grow on the water line, and barnacles can be seen clinging to their roots.

If the water is shallow by the shore, with many coral rocks on the seabed, several species may easily be seen.

There may be clumps of turtle grass and manatee grass growing submerged. Sea fans, sea urchins, sea anemones, starfish, brittle stars, sea cucumbers, chitons, bivalves, limpets and nerites, annelids like *Hermodice*, and *Nereis*, tube worms and shrimps are some of the many animals which may be found.

Figure 17.32 Coastal cactus/thorn scrub.

Seaweeds like mermaid's wineglass and *Padina*, are common, and *Sargassum*, with its 'floats', may be washed up on to the shore (Figure **17.33**).

On a rocky sea shore there is likely to be an abundance of molluscs and hermit crabs. Often a zonation of these can be seen. *Chiton* clings to rocks where the waves break. Other species, like the nerites, winkles and limpets, distribute themselves according to their tolerance to drying out. Rock pools often contain sea urchins, starfish, sea anemones and shoals of small fish (Figure **17.34**).

Figure 17.33 *Sargassum* weed and sargassum fish. The sargassum fish is perfectly camouflaged to match the weed amongst which it lives. It even has small bladder-shaped structures on its skin and fins which resemble the bladders on the branches of the weed.

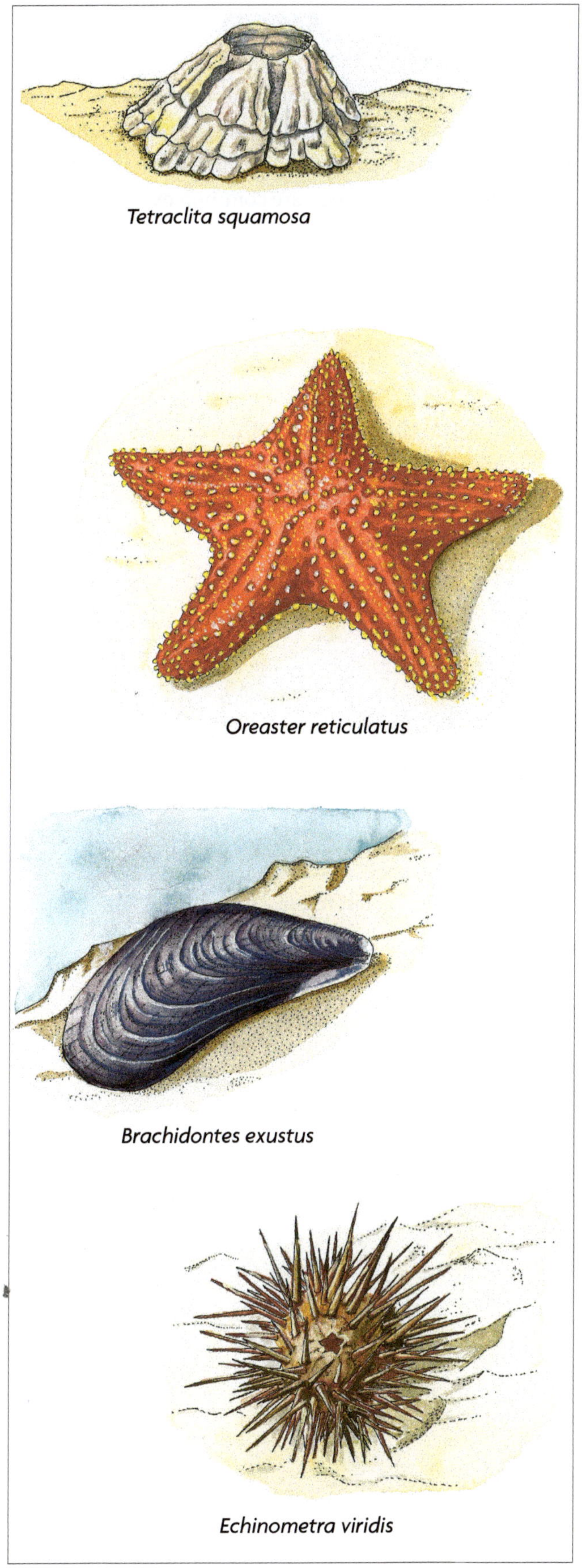

Figure 17.34 Variety of animals found on the sea-shore.

17.35 A tree may be an interesting ecosystem.

Many trees, especially those with widely spreading branches like the guango (Saman, rain tree), *Samanea saman*, and mango, *Mangifera indica*, are often found with epiphytes on them. Wild pines and cacti, like the triangular-stemmed *Cereus*, are common examples.

Tree frogs live in the wild pines which have pools of water at the bases of their leaves. Birds, lizards and ants are other animals that may all find food and shelter on the tree.

17.36 Life in a forest is layered.

On the higher mountains all over the Caribbean may be found montane mist forest (Figure **17.35**). Rainfall and atmospheric humidity are always high. Mist conditions exist for many hours each day. Such forests are damp, cool and dark. The vegetation shows definite stratification. Four main layers may be seen (Figure **17.36**).

Figure 17.35 Montane mist forest.

1 An arborescent (tree) layer: This layer forms the main canopy of the forest. It gets all the light available, but also the full force of the winds. On average, trees in this type of forest are about 9–12 metres high.
2 An upper shrub layer: Plants in this layer are about 3–6 metres high. The layer above them protects plants in this layer. But they still receive much of the available light. Here are the tree ferns, *Cyathea* spp., many species of 'jointers', *Piper* spp., and saplings of the trees.
3 A lower shrub layer: Less light reaches this layer, because it is shaded by the layers above, and there are fewer plants. Ferns are often the most common plants in this layer.
4 A ground layer: Little light reaches this layer, after it is filtered down through all the other layers. Species in this layer are shade-loving mosses, liverworts, low ferns and lichens. Some areas of soil are bare, and fallen leaves cover much of the surface.

Many epiphytes such as wild pine species (Figure **17.15**, page **325**), ferns and orchids are found at all layers. Scarcer are climbers, like the climbing bamboo, *Chusquea abietifolia*, and scramblers.

Figure 17.36 Profile of montane mist forest.

In Trinidad and Guyana, where the rainfall is very heavy, there are tropical rainforests (Figure **17.11**, page **324**). The vegetation is denser than in montane mist forest, but still layered. There may be more than one layer of trees. The lower wooded slopes of the Blue Mountains in Jamaica, and wooded valleys as in Barbados, have drier mesophytic forest.

The trees may be quite tall. They may be 30 metres tall in Turner's Hall Woods, Barbados.

Species and their abundance will differ with the type and location of these tropical forests, but their general form is similar. The trees provide a habitat for a wide variety of insects, lizards, birds and small mammals. Many organisms are also sheltered in and under the leaf litter on the forest floor.

17.37 Mangrove woodlands are coastal ecosystems.

The name 'mangrove' refers to a group of plants found in river estuaries, and in coastal swamps. These different species are all adapted to living in brackish water, and in waterlogged conditions, without much air in the soil. Once the mangroves are established, no other species seem able to survive with them. In the Caribbean , there are four species. All may be found growing together, as at the edge of a lagoon, but often there is a zonation of the species.

The red mangrove, *Rhizophora mangle*, is the species found furthest out to sea. Its prominent stilt roots identify it easily (Figure **17.20**, page **330**). These roots have many lenticels (Figure **6.25**, page **111**). These allow air into the root tissues (section **6.29**). The button mangrove, *Conocarpus erecta*, can grow furthest away from shore, and tolerate the dryer conditions. The shape of the fruit explains why it is called the button mangrove. The other two species, *Avicennia nitida*, the black mangrove, and *Laguncularia racemosa*, the white mangrove, are found in shallower water than the red mangrove, or in swampy mud. The black mangrove has short, erect roots, coming from the larger spreading roots (Figure **17.21**, page **330**). These short roots or pneumatophores also have many lenticels.

Another special feature of the mangroves is that the seeds begin to germinate while they are still on the parent plant

Figure 17.37 These seedlings are germinating on the parent mangrove tree, an example of vivipary.

(Figure **17.37**). This is termed **vivipary**. The early stages of germination which require much oxygen therefore take place before the seed falls off into water or mud, where the oxygen supply is low.

The mangroves are a habitat for a variety of animal life. They are a breeding ground for many kinds of fish and crustaceans. Rotting litter from the trees provides food for very small invertebrates. The stilt roots of the red mangrove also often develop rich communities of invertebrates and algae. These in turn are food for fish and birds.

Many birds live in the mangroves. Wetland birds feed on the crabs, molluscs and fish. Cattle egrets feed elsewhere, but roost and nest in mangrove areas. Migratory birds from temperate regions often spend the winter months in these woodlands.

Mangroves protect the shoreline from wave erosion. They also protect coral reefs by holding back sediment which might damage coral by shading or suffocation.

Questions

17.35 Why do plant and animal communities in some areas gradually change?

17.36 What is the name for this process?

17.37 What is a climax community?

17.38 Name a pioneer plant. Why did you choose that plant?

17.39 Give two factors that might affect the zonation of molluscs on a rocky sea shore.

17.40 What is an epiphyte? Give an example.

17.41 Name three functions of mangrove woodlands.

17.42 Give two adaptations of mangroves to life in a swampy habitat.

Figure 17.38 How many different species can you see in this tiny part of a coral reef?

The coral reef ecosystem

17.38 Corals are living things.

Coral reefs are a vitally important part of the marine environment in the Caribbean, for these natural underwater habitats provide shelter and feeding grounds for a varied and fascinating collection of life forms (Figure **17.38**). A reef can be huge, yet it is formed by very tiny animals – coral polyps.

Corals are often seen as white, stone-like material found washed up on beaches. They are also sold in some stores as souvenirs. This rocky material is really the skeleton of microscopic invertebrate animals called coral **polyps**. These animals belong to a large group of invertebrates which are placed in the phylum Cnidaria (Chapter **1**).

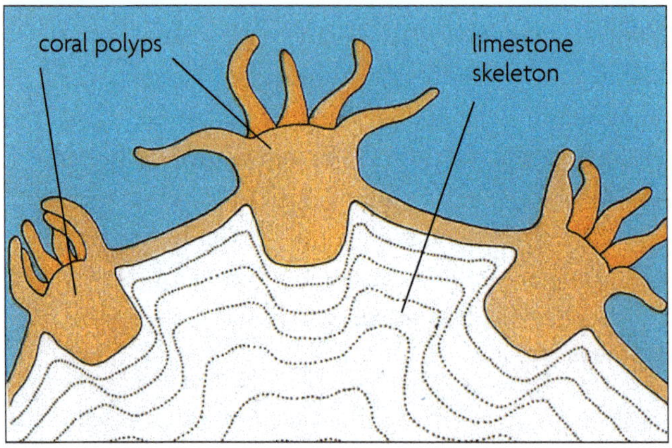

Figure 17.39 Generalised structure of a small section of coral reef.

Coral polyps are builders of a very important part of the marine environment in the Caribbean – that is, coral reefs.

A coral polyp is a soft transparent animal that builds a hard limestone skeleton (calcium carbonate) outside its body. The polyps sit in cups in this skeleton (Figure **17.39**).

The coral polyp has three identifiable parts: a base, a middle section and a mouth section (Figure **17.40**). The base is attached to the stony skeleton. The middle section has a tube-like appearance. Within this tube is a hollow gut. The mouth has tentacles surrounding it. On the tentacles are special stinging cells called nematocysts.

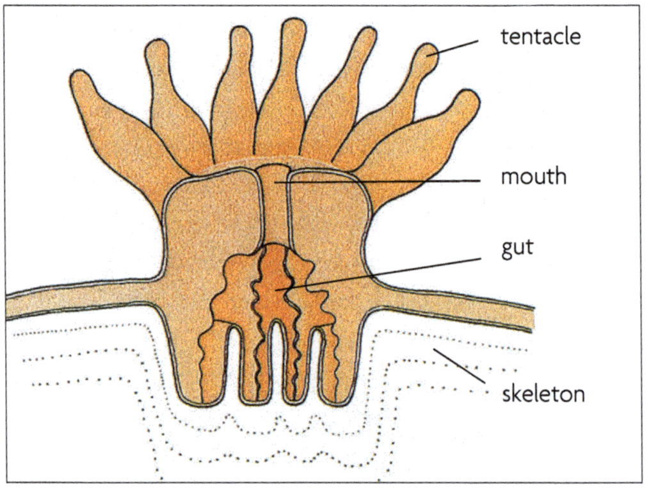

Figure 17.40 External appearance and section through a coral polyp.

17.39 Coral reefs.

A coral reef is a massive rock-like structure, many metres thick, on the surface of which are attached colonies of corals. This rocky mass is firmly anchored to the bottom of the sea, and has been laid down by the corals over many years. Its occupants are a complex community of plants and animals that live and depend on one another in harmony with their physical environment. The reef therefore offers an interesting study of many interactions that occur within a marine ecosystem.

The corals which build reefs are found in warm, shallow waters. They do not grow well where they are directly exposed to sunlight or rain for long periods, or where the water is too salty or muddy. The clear waters of the Caribbean are thus ideal for corals.

17.40 Formation of a coral reef.

A coral reef starts with tiny coral larvae, called planulae, which have developed from fertilised female gametes. The larvae are set free in the sea and float in the water until they find a hard surface such as a rock. They attach themselves onto the hard surface, thus becoming the 'parent' coral polyps.

Very soon, the polyps begin to extract minerals from the water and produce their hard skeleton of calcium carbonate. After the parent polyps have grown for a while, little polyps begin budding (asexual reproduction) out of their bodies. As the buds grow, they begin to form buds of their own. The result of this repeated budding is a large number of polyps living together in a group or 'colony'. The polyps are usually connected to each other by a layer of tissue which spreads over the hard stony skeleton. Figure **17.41** shows how buds can form in this tissue.

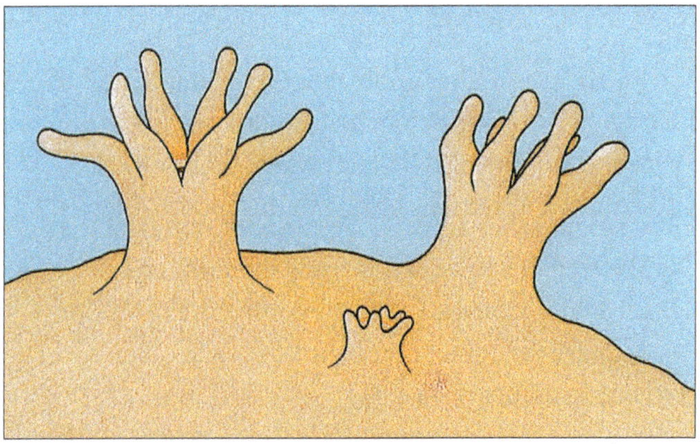

Figure 17.41 Budding of polyps to form a colony.

The corals also reproduce sexually. Adults have both male and female sex organs. These sex organs set free their gametes into the gut where fertilisation takes place. The fertilised eggs develop into planula larvae which float away in the water. Planulae form part of the microscopic zooplankton in the sea. If they are not eaten, these larvae may start a new coral reef, perhaps thousands of miles away.

When polyps die, their skeletons remain, and a new generation of polyps can grow on top of them. After many years, coral growth can form solid rocky structures of great size that are described as reefs.

Polyps always stay on the outside of the growing coralline mass, because they build their stony 'skeletons' underneath them. This pushes them upwards and outwards, and keeps them even with the surface (Figure **17.42**).

Although coral reefs can be massive, they grow very slowly. It takes about one thousand years for a reef to grow just one metre.

Figure 17.42 Star coral growing on the outside of a coralline mass.

17.41 Nutrition in corals.

Coral polyps feed by catching tiny animals brought by water currents. Feeding takes place at night. During the day, polyps withdraw into their cup-like homes in their stony skeletons. At night, they stretch out their tentacles to capture the microscopic animals and plants called plankton, brought by water currents (Figure **17.43**, overleaf). The tentacles have special cells that paralyse the prey. The trapped animal is then covered in mucus, and wafted by hair-like cilia into the mouth. Digestion of the prey takes place in the hollow gut.

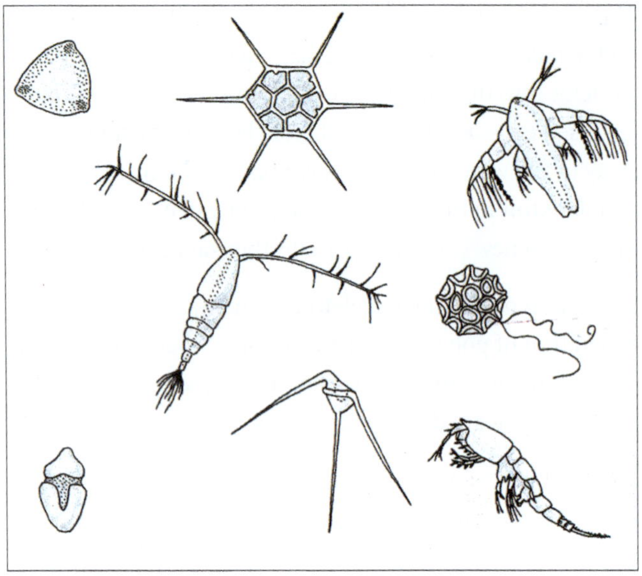

Figure 17.43 Marine plankton.

Another way in which corals get food is from tiny one-celled plants called **zooxanthellae**, that live within the polyps' tissues lining the folds of the digestive cavity (Figure **17.44**). Zooxanthellae are so named because they live within animals and are green or yellow-brown in colour. They have chloroplasts, carry out photosynthesis, and give coral polyps their attractive colours.

Zooxanthellae and coral polyps together provide an interesting example of a **mutualistic** relationship between a single-celled organism and an animal.

Carbohydrates and oxygen, products of photosynthesis, are produced by the zooxanthellae. These products are taken in and used by the polyp cells during respiration.

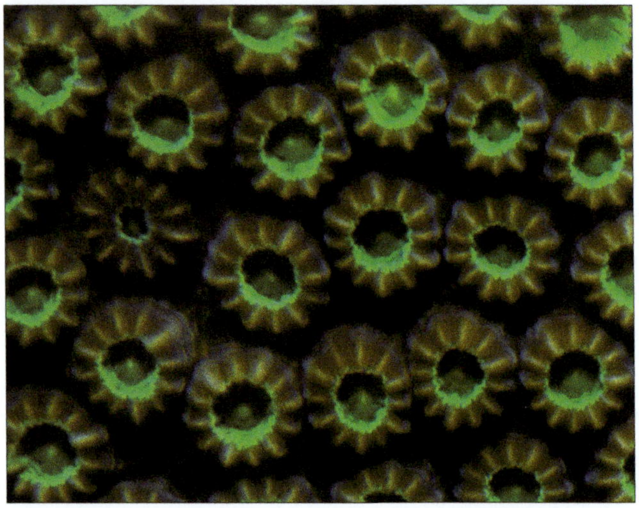

Figure 17.44 Coral and its algal partners. The chloroplasts of the zooxanthellae give the polyps their green colour.

In return, the zooxanthellae receive the raw materials of photosynthesis, carbon dioxide and water, which are the polyps' waste products of cellular respiration. The zooxanthellae also use the ammonia produced by their hosts during protein metabolism. Ammonia is the zooxanthellae's source of nitrogen, needed for protein synthesis.

The zooxanthellae's use of the polyps' waste products (carbon dioxide and water) helps to reduce the level of acidity inside the polyps' bodies. Carbon dioxide and water react to form carbonic acid which can dissolve the calcium carbonate skeleton of the polyp. The zooxanthellae also receive phosphate-containing substances which the polyps filter from the sea water. The coral polyps therefore provide the zooxanthellae with a stable, safe and self-sufficient internal environment in which there is a constant recycling of nutrients. Investigations have also shown that corals with zooxanthellae in their tissue can accelerate the process of depositing the calcium carbonate skeleton, and that neither zooxanthellae nor coral polyps can survive well without each other.

17.42 Corals may be stony or soft.

Those corals that put down stony outer skeletons belong to a group called **stony corals**. It is stony corals that build the hard structures known as coral reefs. Stony corals have different forms, shapes and sizes, and the pattern of tiny holes in the skeleton made by the polyps can be very distinctive. Corals are often given names that match their appearance – for example, brain coral (Figure **17.45**), rose coral, staghorn coral (Figure **17.46**), elkhorn coral, tube coral and lettuce-leaf coral. Of these, the elkhorn and staghorn corals are the most abundant reef-building corals in the Caribbean.

Soft corals are another group, but these do not produce a hard outer stony skeleton. Instead their skeletons are formed within their bodies. Sea whips (Figure **17.47**), sea feathers and sea fans belong to this group of corals.

The skeleton of a soft coral is really a central axis of flexible horny material called gorgonin, on the outside of which are the coral polyps joined to each other by connecting tissue.

Figure 17.45 Brain coral, a member of the stony coral group.

Figure 17.48 A sea fan.

Figure 17.46 Staghorn coral is another member of the stony coral group.

Figure 17.47 A sea whip is an example of a soft coral.

Figure 17.49 Black coral is becoming rare because it is used for making expensive jewellery.

Sea whips, sea feathers and sea fans have beautiful branching plant-like appearances (Figures **17.47** and **17.48**). Their short main trunk is usually attached to the reef, while their long colourful branches of bright reds, oranges, purples and yellows wave gracefully in the water currents.

Another type of coral with an internal skeleton is the black coral (Figure **17.49**). Black corals are slender and branching as well. They may be a few centimetres long or several metres, and are often used for making jewellery. For this reason the incidence of plunder is high and black corals are becoming rare. However, the reaping of any coral is now prohibited.

17.43 There are three types of coral reef.

Coral reefs are placed into three main groups. They are fringing reefs, barrier reefs and atolls.

Fringing reefs are found close to the shores of land masses where the water is shallow (Figure **17.50**, overleaf). This type of reef has two areas. The front area, which is on the ocean side, is called the **reef front**. Corals grow very fast in this area, because it is where conditions are most favourable. There are many reasons why conditions on the **reef flat** are not as good as those on the reef front. Water is often trapped here at low tide. When the sun is very hot, water evaporates and the water that is left becomes very salty and hot. Then when it rains, fresh water collects here, causing the water to be not salty enough. Whereas on the reef flat the conditions change, on the reef front the conditions are always about the same.

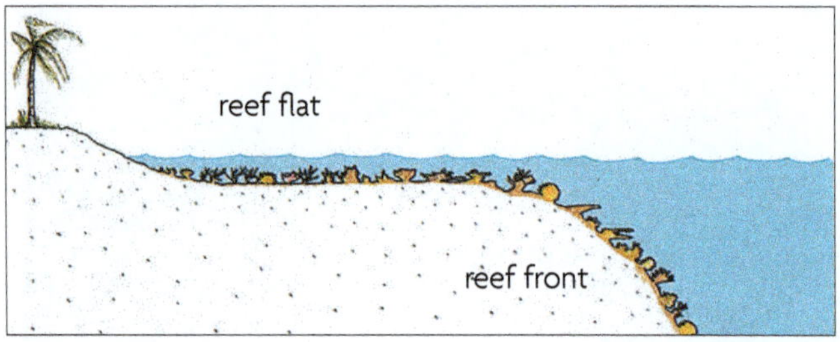

Figure 17.50 A fringing reef.

Like the fringing reef, the **barrier reef** has a reef front and a reef flat (Figure **17.51**). However, the barrier reef is formed much farther from the shore. Usually a very wide and deep lagoon is found between the reef and the shore. Corals grow well in the lagoon, forming an 'inner reef'. Ships often use the quiet, protected waters of the lagoon, but they have to be careful not to run into the section of reef which is near the surface. The biggest barrier reef in the world is the Great Barrier Reef of Australia.

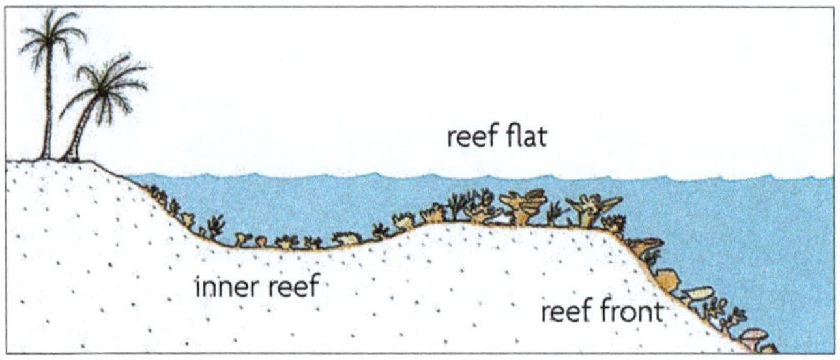

Figure 17.51 A barrier reef.

Atolls are located in the middle of the ocean, far from any shore (Figure **17.52**). They are really small islands of coral. The coral reef forms a circle, and in the middle of the circle is a deep lagoon. Atolls can have palm trees growing on them from nuts deposited by the tide, and beautiful sandy beaches.

Figure 17.52 An atoll.

17.44 The coral reef ecosystem.

Coral reefs are made up of much more than corals and their skeletal remains. Many other organisms live in the reef, and some of these also deposit limestone material. Certain molluscs, crustaceans and even tiny plants (called 'coralline algae') leave behind hard deposits which help build up the reef. But it is the stony coral that creates the foundation and most of the structure of the reef.

Coral reefs provide a home, food and shelter for a variety of plants and animals (Figures **17.53**, **17.54** and **17.55**). The spaces, sinks and cracks in the hard coral mass make suitable shelter and feeding grounds for marine worms, sea urchins, sponges, molluscs, crabs, shrimps, sea anemones and fish. Some of the animals use the dead coral skeletons as a solid place to attach themselves.

Figure 17.53 Feather worms.

The energy which flows between the organisms in the reef keeps all these animals and plants alive. The source of this energy is sunlight. Figure **17.56** shows the path of energy from sunlight to green plants (producers), then to animals which eat the plants (primary consumers) and to animals which eat the animals (secondary and tertiary consumers).

Sunlight provides the energy for the ecosystem, but water currents also bring animals, plants and nutrients to the reef. The reef plants use the sunlight and the nutrients during photosynthesis.

Figure 17.54 A lettuce sea slug.

Figure 17.55 A hermit crab in a mollusc shell.

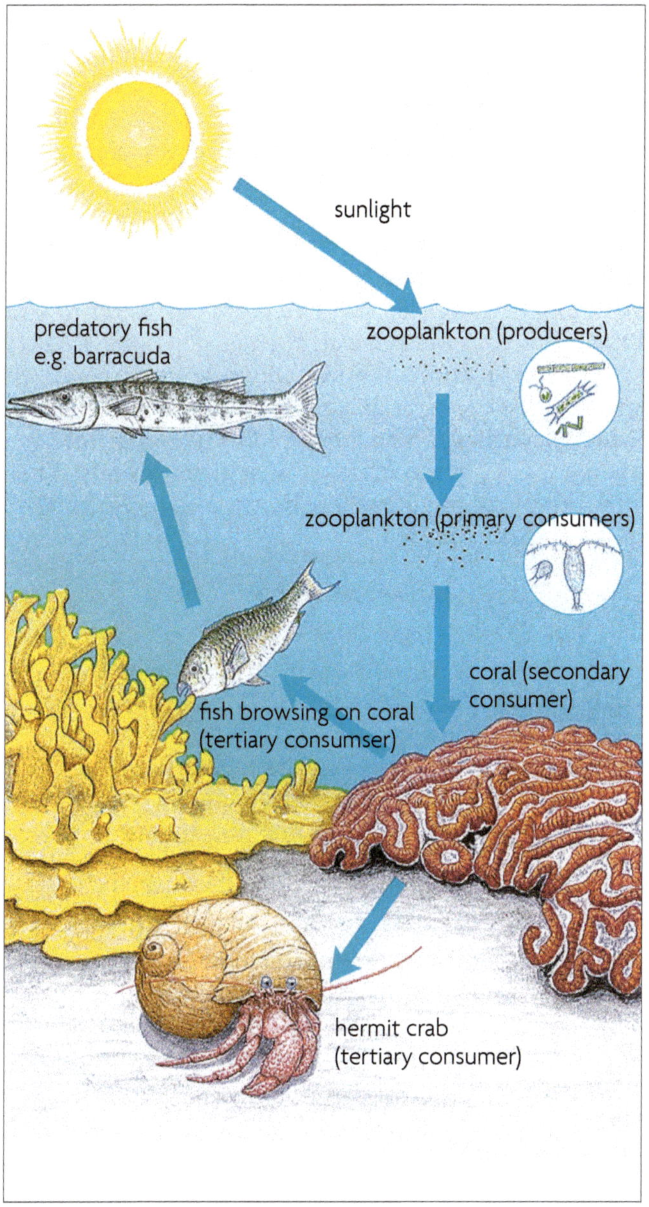

Figure 17.56 Energy flow in a coral reef.

Photosynthetic organisms are everywhere on the reef. Some float in the water. They are microscopic green organisms called phytoplankton. Some algae live in the coral polyps and their skeletons and add colour to the living reef, while algae of varying colours – red, brown and green – grow over the surface of dead coral. The algae help cement loose pieces of coral limestone together and they provide food and shelter for small animals. As well, anchored by roots in the sandy bottom of the reef, are sea grasses, food of sea urchins and other herbivores.

These organisms are, therefore, the producers in the system, providing the basic food supply for the entire ecosystem. Many reef animals feed on these organisms, and they in turn are eaten by other animals. The energy is passed along a food chain which leads from small photosynthetic organisms to the large meat-eaters, such as sharks and barracuda. When organisms in the chain die, they fall to the reef floor. **Decomposers** feed on them, and release calcium and phosphates to the environment.

On a coral reef, therefore, the many levels of the trophic pyramid can be identified; **producers**, such as phytoplankton and sea grasses, **primary consumers**, such as zooplankton and sea urchins; **secondary** and **tertiary consumers**, as well as decomposers.

But energy from food is not the only thing that is exchanged on the reef. Gas exchange takes place between animals and photosynthesisers. The photosynthetic organisms give out oxygen during photosynthesis, and the animals use this oxygen for respiration. Carbon dioxide and water, the waste products of respiration, are the raw materials of photosynthesis. The photosynthetic organisms also use nitrogenous animal waste to make protein compounds. A constant recycling of substances is taking place on the reef, creating a stable and balanced environment.

17.45 There are symbiotic relationships among reef dwellers.

Since a coral reef serves as a habitat for a wide range of living organisms, interesting patterns of survival have been developed by some organisms. For example, there are various types of **symbiotic** relationships found on a coral reef. One such relationship in which both organisms benefit is seen in coral polyps and their algae partners, zooxanthellae (section **17.41**).

The small man-o-war fish and the jellyfish, Portuguese man-o-war, also live together in a mutualistic relationship. The small fish find safe swimming grounds among the deadly tentacles of the jellyfish, and at the same time lure larger fish within the reach of the jellyfish's stinging cells (Figure **17.57**). This living arrangement between the Portuguese man-o-war and the small fish is not an obligate one, like that of the coral polyp and the zooxanthellae.

Hermit crabs and sea anemones offer another interesting example of two different species living together. Anemones are usually seen attached to the shells which the crabs occupy. The anemones benefit by being transported to wider feeding grounds, while the crabs are protected by the anemones' stinging cells. The anemones offer added protection by acting as a camouflage: they give the shells an appearance similar to that of the reef floor.

Parasitic relationships are also found on the reef. Small ectoparasites are often seen attached to the skin, fins, gills and buccal cavity of snappers, grunts or butterfly fishes. These ectoparasites are small crustaceans called isopods (Figure **17.58**). Isopods are related to shrimps and lobsters. The isopods feed on the blood and tissue fluids of their hosts, and are equipped with special

Figure 17.57 A symbiotic relationship between an anemone and a clownfish.

Figure 17.58 A soldier fish with an isopod ectoparasite.

mouthparts that can pierce the host's tissues and thus extract their liquid food. But some shrimps and small fish feed on ectoparasites or damaged tissues of large fish. These cleaners help rid fish of troublesome parasites while getting a meal for themselves. This cleaning arrangement provides yet another example of mutualism.

The blue streak wrasse is a small cleaner fish. It feeds on the parasites and waste particles found on the skin of larger fish such as the platax batfish. Blue streak wrasse is often seen hovering near to its host.

17.46 Reef dwellers and their physical environment.

Other interesting patterns of survival, protection and feeding are shown by reef dwellers. Parrot fish eat chunks of coral, egesting particles of fine coral sand through the anus. The reef also offers protection to parrot fish. These fish are easily detected by their predators during the night. So when night approaches, the parrotfish enter small holes in the reef and seal themselves in with a protective coat of mucus.

On the other hand, long-spined black urchins are night-time feeders and they hide in holes in the coral during the day. So necessary is this reef protection to the urchins that they do not venture too far from their safe shelters in the reef. In fact, it is very easy to identify areas of urchin habitation. These areas are almost bare of marine vegetation due to overgrazing by the herbivorous urchins.

Minnows, such as hardhead silverside, use other means of survival. They produce large numbers of offspring and can adapt quite easily to a wide range of environmental conditions. They do, however, face the disadvantage of a high death rate and brief lifespan.

When changes in the reef environment cause the death of some species of reef dwellers, rapidly reproducing organisms, such as minnows, will quickly establish themselves, occupying all available space left by the dead inhabitants.

Gall crabs' survival technique is quite unusual. They make their homes on the branches of the elkhorn coral. After the crabs' eggs hatch, the young developing females settle on the branches of the elkhorn corals. The corals' skeleton grows around the crabs producing a gall-like growth. Once the crabs are enclosed in their stony homes they cannot leave the cavities. They feed on plankton swept towards them by the water currents. The male crabs do not make galls. They are smaller in size than females, so they can freely enter their mate's coral homes and fertilise eggs.

Some organisms, such as corals, do not reproduce in large numbers but show a high degree of specialisation for their size. This offers them the advantage of being able to occupy many types of niche. Some corals, for example, are found living very close to the surface and are resistant to moderate wave action, while some live in deep waters where light is minimal. Corals, however, are very sensitive to changes in environmental conditions and often die when such changes take place.

17.47 Coral reefs are of great importance to the Caribbean.

Coral reefs are rich sources of seafoods such as fish, shrimp, lobsters, sea urchins and seaweeds. The reefs protect the coastline from erosion by acting as natural breakers of the force of powerful waves and are the suppliers of the lovely white sand of Caribbean beaches.

Reefs also provide shallow areas for safe swimming and are of very high recreational value for those interested in scuba diving and snorkelling. In fact, Caribbean states advertise their coral reefs as a tourist attraction, and some governments, as a deliberate policy for environmental enhancement, sink large old ships and dump car bodies in the sea to encourage reef formation.

Most important of all, coral reefs provide humans with living examples of recycling of materials within the environment, and of organisms surviving and existing successfully in symbiotic relationships. Indeed, this environment provides us with many lessons, such as the importance of maintaining a harmonious relationship with our environment, the need for reduction of all kinds of pollution and for making the widest use of natural resources.

The reef is indeed one of Earth's many wonders, which has taken millions of years to develop. We must try our best to preserve and conserve this vital marine ecosystem.

Key ideas

- The terms habitat, population, environment, community and ecosystem have their own precise meanings in ecology.
- Quadrats can be used to sample an area. They enable species frequency and density to be estimated.
- Transects are useful to investigate the changes in the distribution and density of species as one habitat merges into another.
- The numbers and distribution of populations are influenced by abiotic and biotic factors.
- Abiotic factors are those resulting from non-living parts of the environment. They include light intensity, availability of water, temperature and edaphic (soil) factors.
- Biotic factors are those resulting from other living organisms. They include predator–prey relationships, parasites and hosts, and competition within a species (intraspecific) and between species (interspecific) for resources that are in short supply.
- The Caribbean region has many special ecosystems, including sea shores, forests and coral reefs.

End-of-chapter questions

1 a List the components of topsoil.

b What problems are associated with the cultivation of (i) clay soil, (ii) sandy soil, and (iii) acid soil?

c Explain how each of the following can improve the properties of a clay soil.
(i) earthworms (ii) addition of humus
(iii) addition of lime

2 a What is a parasite?

b List four problems faced by most parasites.

c For one named parasite, describe how it overcomes these difficulties.

3 Explain the difference between each of the following pairs, giving examples where you can:

a habitat, niche

b community, population

c quadrat, transect

4 In Caribbean montane mist forest, there is a difference in the appearance of the leaves of the plants. Some are broad, thin, and have a thin cuticle. Others are thicker, have heavy cuticles, and tend to be stiff. What factor(s) might account for this difference? Explain your answer.

5 a If you were a farmer, and could choose the type of soil to cultivate, which would you choose and why?

b Design an investigation you could do to help to convince another farmer that your choice was a good one. You will need to state the aim of the investigation and the hypothesis on which it is built; identify the variables; sequence the steps in the procedure you will use; select the apparatus and materials; indicate the data you will collect; say how the data will be used to test your hypothesis; discuss the limitations of the procedure you have used.

18 Human population and the environment

In this chapter, you will find out:

- what affects the size of a population
- what is happening to the human population
- that we need the greenhouse effect, but enhancing it may cause global warming
- why we clear forests, and what harm this can do
- how CFCs damage the ozone layer
- about the causes and effects of acid rain
- how we are damaging coral reef ecosystems
- how care of forests and good farming practices can help the environment
- how careful disposal of rubbish and recycling can reduce our demands on the environment.

Populations

18.1 Most populations stay about the same size.

We have seen that a population is all the individuals of a particular species that live together in a habitat. In this chapter, we will look at how and why population sizes change, and begin to consider the implication of Earth's rapidly increasing human population (Figure **18.1**).

Figure 18.1 Streets are much more crowded today than in the past.

Most populations tend to stay roughly the same size over a period of time. They may go up and down – fluctuate – but the average population will probably stay the same over a number of years. The population of greenfly in a garden, for example, might be much greater one year than the next. But their numbers will almost certainly be back to normal in a year or so. Over many years, the sizes of most populations tend to remain at around the same level.

Yet if all the offspring of one female greenfly survived and reproduced, she could be the ancestor of 600 000 000 000 greenfly in just one year! Why doesn't the greenfly population shoot upwards like this? Why isn't the world overrun with greenfly?

The answers to those questions are of great importance to human beings, because our own population is doing just that; it is shooting upwards at an alarming rate. Every hour, there are 9000 extra people in the world. We need to understand why this is happening, and what is likely to happen next. Can we slow down the increase? What happens if we don't?

18.2 Birth rate and death rate determine population size.

The size of a population depends on how many individuals leave the population, and how many enter it.

Individuals leave a population when they die, or when they migrate to another population. Individuals enter a population when they are born, or when they migrate into the population from elsewhere. Usually, births and deaths are more important in determining population sizes than immigration and emigration.

A population increases if new individuals are born faster than the old ones die – that is, when the birth rate is greater than the death rate. If birth rate is less than death rate, then the population will decrease. If birth rate and death rate are equal, the population will stay the same size.

This explains why we are not knee-deep in greenfly. Although the greenfly population's birth rate is enormous, the death rate is also enormous. Greenfly are eaten by ladybirds and birds, and sprayed with insecticides by gardeners. Over a period of time, the greenfly's birth and death rates stay about the same, so the population doesn't change very much.

18.3 Yeast experiments give some clues about population growth.

By looking at changes in population sizes in other organisms, we can learn quite a lot about our own. Many experiments on population sizes have been done on organisms like bacteria and yeast, because they reproduce quickly and are easy to grow. Figure **18.2** shows the results of an experiment in which a few yeast cells are put into a container of nutrient broth. The cells feed on the broth, grow and reproduce. The numbers of yeast cells are counted every few hours.

At the beginning of the experiment, the population grows quite slowly, because there are not many cells there to reproduce. But once they get going, growth is very rapid. Each cell divides to form 2, then 4, then 8, then 16. There is nothing to hold them back except the time it takes to grow and divide.

But as the population gets larger, the individual cells can no longer reproduce as fast, and begin to die off more rapidly. This may be because there is not enough food left for them all, or it might be that they have made so much alcohol that they are poisoning themselves. The cells are now dying off as fast as new ones are being produced, so the population stops growing and levels off.

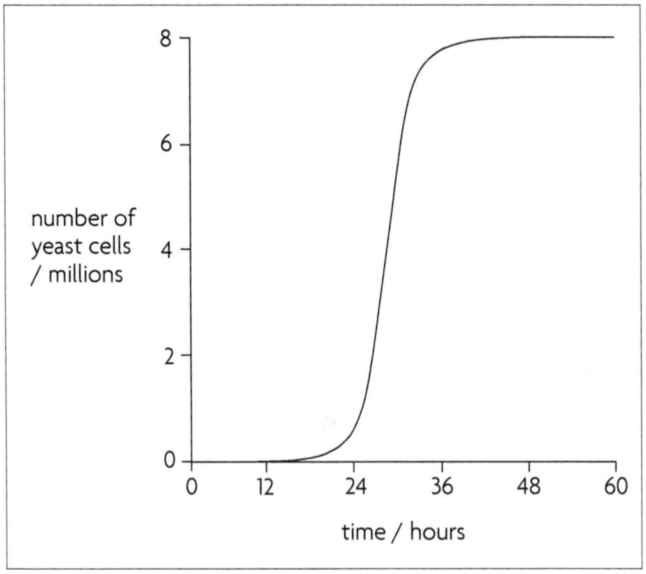

Figure 18.2 The growth of a population of yeast in a flask of broth.

18.4 Environmental factors control population size.

Although the experiment with the yeast is done in artificial conditions, a similar pattern is found in the growth of populations of many species in the wild. If a few individuals get into a new environment, then their population curve may be very like the one for yeast cells in broth. The population increases quickly at first, and then levels off.

The levelling off is always caused by some kind of environmental factor. In the case of the yeast, the factor may be food supply. Other populations may be limited by disease, or the number of nest sites, or the number of predators, for example. The factor that stops the population from getting any larger is called a limiting factor.

18.5 Population sizes often oscillate.

It is usually very difficult to find out which environmental factors are controlling the size of a population. Almost always, many different factors will interact. A population of kingbirds, for example, might be affected by the number of hawks and the amount of food and tree cover available.

Figure **18.3** shows an example of how the size of population of a predator may be affected by its prey. This information comes from the number of skins which were sold by fur traders in Northern Canada to the Hudson Bay Company, between 1845 and 1935. Snowshoe hares and northern lynxes were both trapped for their fur, and the numbers caught probably give a very good idea of their population sizes.

Snowshoe hare populations tend to vary from year to year. No-one is quite sure why this happens, but it may be related to their food supply. Whenever the snowshoe hare population rises, the lynx population also rises shortly afterwards, as the lynxes now have more food. A drop in the snowshoe hare population is rapidly followed by a drop in the lynx population.

The numbers tend to go up and down, or oscillate, but the average population sizes stay roughly the same over many years.

18.6 Age pyramids show whether a population is increasing or decreasing.

When scientists begin to study a population, they want to know whether the population is growing or shrinking. This can be done by counting the population over many years, or by measuring its birth rate and death rate. But often it is much easier just to count the numbers of individuals in various age groups, and to draw an age pyramid.

Figure **18.4** (overleaf) shows two examples of age pyramids. The size of each box represents the numbers of individuals of that age.

Figure **18.4a** is a bottom-heavy pyramid, because there are far more young individuals than old ones. This indicates that birth rate is greater than death rate, so this population is increasing.

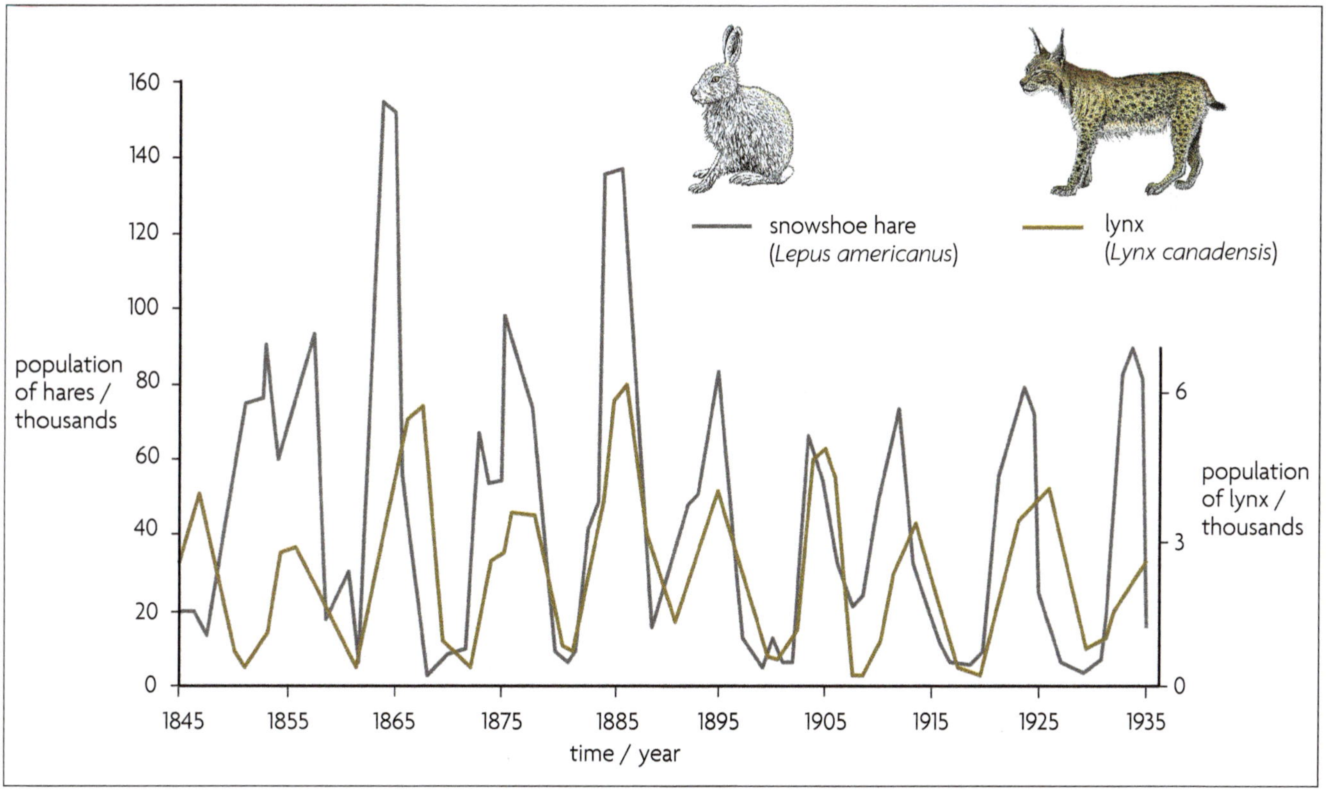

Figure 18.3 Variations in snowshoe hare and lynx populations in northern Canada.

a An increasing population. If all the organisms in the younger age groups grow up and reproduce, the population will increase.

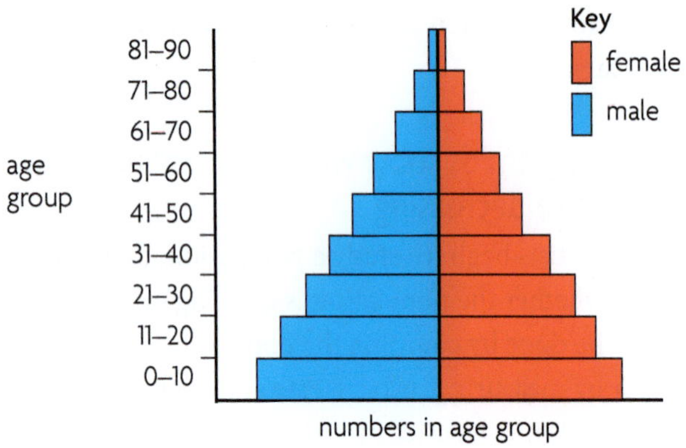

b A stable population. The sizes of the younger age groups are only a little larger than the older ones, so this population should not change much in size.

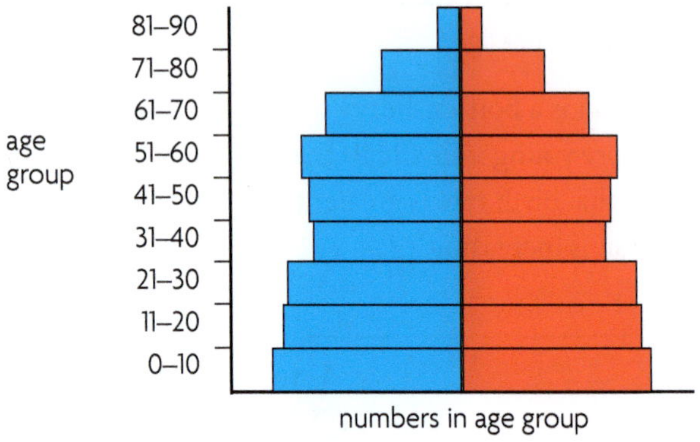

Figure 18.4 Age pyramids.

Figure **18.4b** shows a much more even spread of ages. Birth rate and death rate are probably about the same. This population will remain about the same size.

If an age pyramid is drawn for the human population on Earth, it is bottom-heavy, like Figure **18.4a**. Age pyramids for most of the world's developing countries are also this shape, showing that their populations are increasing. But an age pyramid for a European country such as France looks more like Figure **18.4b**. The human population in France is staying about the same.

18.7 The human death rate has decreased dramatically.

Figure **18.5** shows how the human population of the world has changed since about 3000 BC. For most of that time, human populations have been kept in check by a combination of disease, famine and war. Nevertheless, there has still been a steady increase.

Twice there have been definite 'spurts' in this growth. The first was around 8000 BC, not shown on the graph, when people in the Middle East began to farm, instead of just hunting and finding food. The second began around 300 years ago, and is still happening now.

There are two main reasons for this recent growth spurt. The first is the reduction of disease. Improvements in water supply, sewage treatment, hygienic food handling and general standards of cleanliness have virtually wiped out many diseases in developed countries – for example, typhoid and dysentery. Immunisation against diseases such as polio has made these very rare indeed. Smallpox has been totally eradicated. And the discovery of antibiotics has now made it possible to treat most diseases caused by bacteria.

Secondly, there has been an increase in food supply. More and more land has been brought under cultivation. Moreover, agriculture has become more efficient, so that in many parts of the world each hectare of land is now producing more than ever before.

18.8 Birth rate now exceeds death rate.

The human population has increased dramatically because the death rate has been brought down. More and more people are now living long enough to reproduce. If the birth rate doesn't drop by the same amount as the death rate, then the world population will continue to increase.

In developed countries, the dramatic fall in the death rate began in about 1700. To begin with, the birth rate stayed high, so the population grew rapidly. But since 1800, there has been a marked drop in birth rate. In 1870, for example, the 'average' British family was 6.6 children, but by 1977 it was only 1.8. In Britain, birth rate and death rate are now about equal, so the population is staying the same.

However, in many developing countries, the fall in the death rate only began about 50 years ago. As yet, the birth rates have not dropped, and so the populations are rising rapidly.

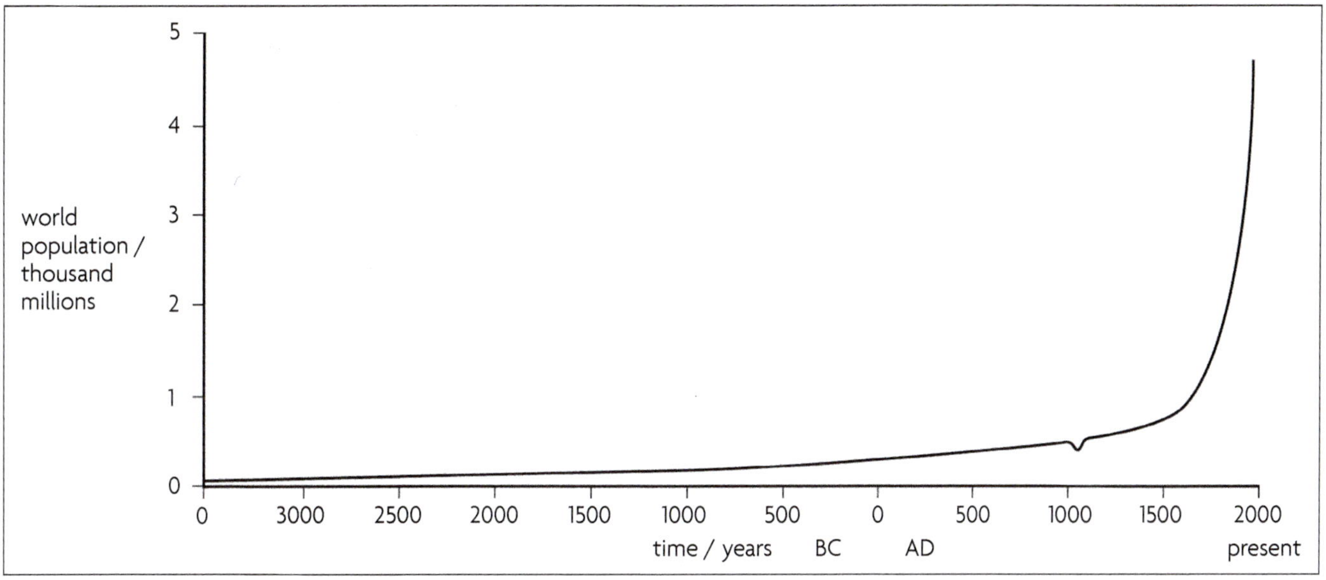

Figure 18.5 The growth of the human population on Earth.

18.9 Birth rate must be reduced to slow population growth.

The human population could be brought back under control in two ways – increasing the death rate or decreasing the birth rate. There is no question as to which of these is the best.

In the developed countries, the single largest factor which brought down the birth rate was the introduction of contraceptive techniques. But many people are suspicious of contraceptive methods, or barred from using them by their religion, or simply want to have large families.

If we do not control the overall human birth rate, then it may happen that famine, war or disease will increase the death rate. The more of us there are on Earth, then the more likely it is that many people will go hungry, or that there will not be enough clean water for everyone, or that serious disease will spread rapidly. This cannot be the best thing for the human race. We must do our best to stabilise the world population at a level at which everyone has a fair chance of a long, healthy life.

Human impact on the environment

18.10 Human activity often affects ecosystem equilibrium.

In Chapter 17 we looked at some of the environmental factors that influence the distribution of living organisms throughout the world. We recognised that interconnecting and orderly relationships exist among organisms. We saw how equilibrium is maintained in ecosystems. Recycling of materials is important for this.

In this chapter we consider the interactions of the dominant species, *Homo sapiens*, with other species and with the non-living world. We look at some of the effects of these interactions.

In the search for food, clothing and shelter, humans use the raw materials and organisms in the physical and biological environment as resources. However, humans are subject to the same constraints as other organisms. If these resources are used in such a way that the ecosystem, of which humans are a part, cannot continue

Questions

18.1 If a population remains about the same size, what can you say about its birth rate and death rate?

18.2 A population of mice is increasing rapidly. How could competition bring about a reduction in the population size?

18.3 If humans have to live in very crowded conditions, the prevalence of infectious diseases increases. Suggest why this happens. (You should be able to think of several reasons.)

to support itself, there will be an imbalance. That is to say, many resources have limits and can be used up.

For thousands of years, humans were able to live in ways that allowed most resources to regenerate naturally. This situation has changed, and more noticeably so in the last 50 or 60 years.

One very important reason for this change is the rapid growth of the human population. What is of concern is not just that total numbers are increasing. The rate of that increase is also growing. It has been estimated that it took more than two million years for the world population to reach one billion (1000 million). Between 1960 and 1975 the fourth billion was added. In October 1999, the United Nations registered the birth of the six billionth human being.

As we have seen, much of this growth is taking place in the developing countries of the world. Although on a global scale resources may be enough, no country has everything it needs. All have to buy what they need but many do not have the money to import goods from elsewhere. With many people to serve, it is difficult for developing countries to provide for all their people.

18.11 Many forests have been destroyed.

The removal of forest cover is one of the most noticeable effects of human demand on natural resources. Unfortunately, many territories in the Caribbean have high levels of deforestation. Rates of 5.3% for Jamaica, 3.9% for Haiti, compare with 2.6% for Costa Rica and 2.5% for the Dominican Republic (FAO assessment 1994/95). The rate for Mozambique, the highest in Africa, is one quarter of that for Jamaica.

Forests are cleared for housing, for fuel and for agriculture. This deforestation causes many problems. Plants and animals are destroyed, along with their habitats. Sometimes these organisms are found in few other places, so eventually species may become totally extinct. Once lost, they can never be retrieved. The St. Lucia muskrat, once common along the island's riverbanks, seems to have disappeared.

Other species have become scarce, and have to be protected by law. These include the Pawi, an indigenous bird of Trinidad, the parrots of St. Lucia and of Jamaica, and the Giant Citrus Swallowtail, the largest butterfly in the Americas, also found in Jamaica. Iguanas throughout the Caribbean are threatened with extinction.

Transpiration from the aerial part of plants is very important in maintaining the water cycle (section **1.25**). Wide-scale removal of trees considerably reduces the amount of water vapour put back into the air. The air becomes drier, fewer clouds form and there is less rain. Less rain means less water to go into rivers. Eventually, some will cease flowing. In Jamaica, it has been estimated that, in the last 60 years, more than 100 rivers and streams have stopped flowing. Left undisturbed, forests are a reservoir of water, which they release slowly. They form healthy watersheds.

The root systems of trees hold the soil together. The forest cover also breaks the force of raindrops before they reach the earth. When the earth is bare of vegetation, the soil loosens easily. Much of the soil is then washed away or eroded (Figure **18.6**). The water from the rain is no longer absorbed by the soil, but rushes down in torrents taking the soil with it. It has been estimated that, in the Caribbean, removal of forest cover from a hill slope can increase loss from 6 tonnes per hectare per year, when a forest is well managed, to 580 tonnes after clearance.

The soil fills up stream and river beds, so there is less space for water to flow. When there is heavy rain this can cause flooding. Eventually, some of the soil reaches the sea, where it can endanger the coral reefs around the islands (section **18.22**).

18.12 Forests are important in recycling elements in nature.

The large tropical forests of the world are its most productive natural systems. This means that it is in these forests that the greatest amount of photosynthetic activity takes place. So they are storehouses for carbon compounds, both in the plants and their products and in the soils.

High rates of photosynthesis also mean that these forests absorb large quantities of carbon dioxide and give out a lot of oxygen. They represent large oxygen pools as well. So they play a very important role in recycling carbon dioxide and oxygen in the atmosphere, and in keeping

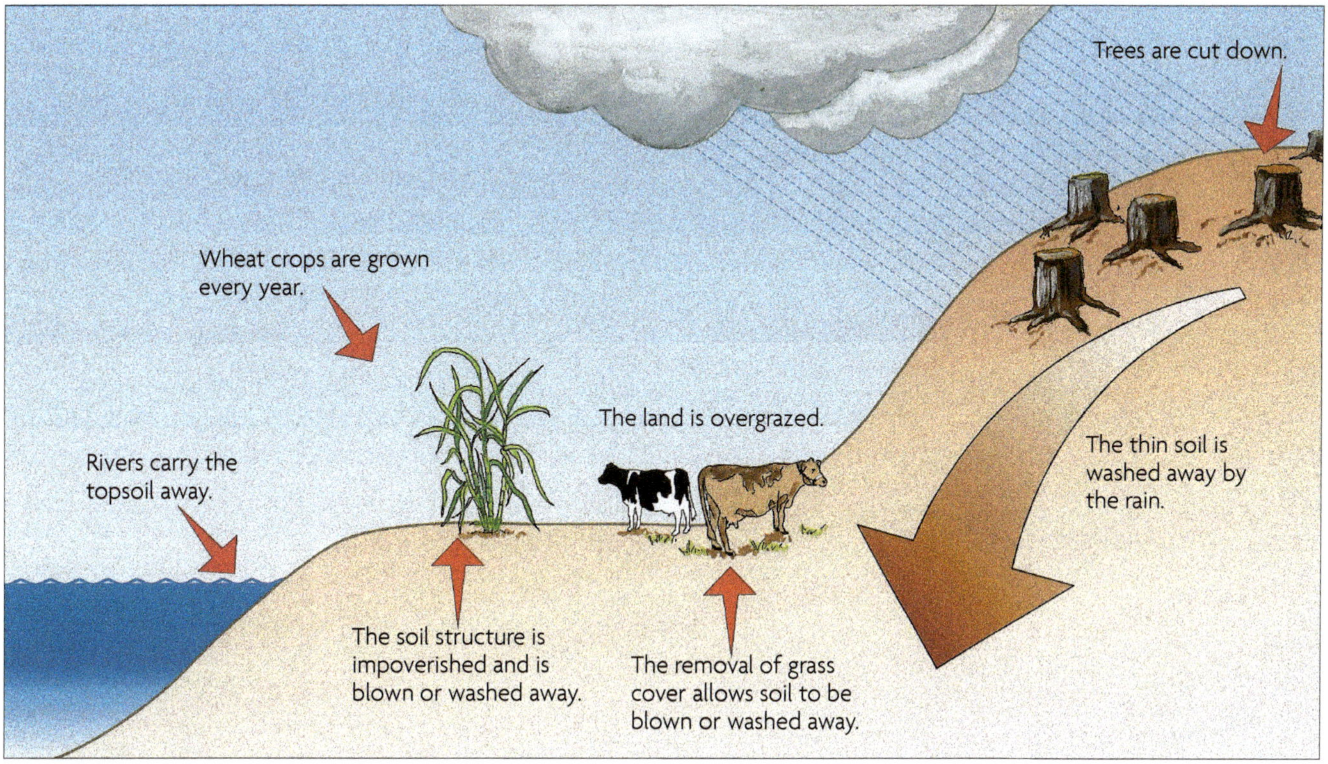

Figure 18.6 How human activities can increase soil erosion.

the level of these gases fairly constant (Figure **1.22**). The destruction of these forests is, therefore, cause for concern (Figure **18.7**).

Increasingly large amounts of carbon dioxide are being released into the atmosphere by several human activities. More fuel is being burnt for domestic use, transport, industries, space exploration and war, by an ever-increasing human population. Fewer trees remain to use carbon dioxide for photosynthesis. If carbon dioxide is not absorbed, either by green plants or by the oceans, then carbon dioxide levels in the atmosphere could rise (Figure **18.8**, overleaf). This is not desirable.

18.13 Greenhouse gases keep the Earth warm.

Carbon dioxide in the atmosphere, along with some other gases such as methane (Table **18.1**, page **359**), helps to absorb some of the heat that is reradiated from the Earth's surface. This is termed the **greenhouse effect** (Figure **18.9**, overleaf). Without this, the Earth would be about 30 °C colder than it is now. The planet could not support life as we know it. The greenhouse effect is, therefore, a normal part of the patterns of nature. But the effect is increased as the quantity of the gases which cause it increases.

Figure 18.7 When rainforest is cut down and burnt, as here in Brazil, large amounts of carbon dioxide are released to the atmosphere.

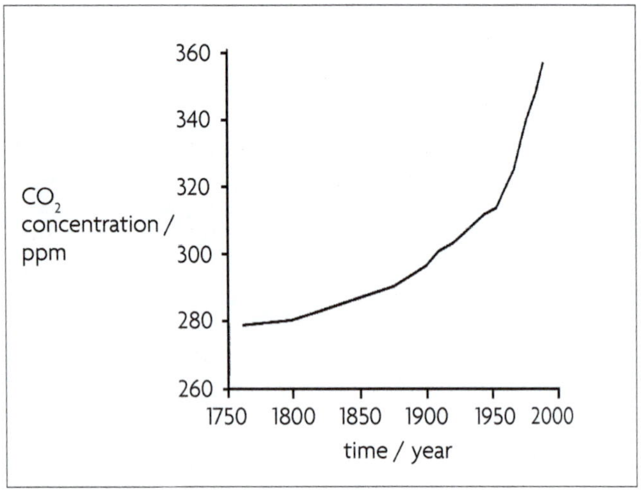

Figure 18.8 How carbon dioxide concentrations in the atmosphere have changed since 1750.

Temperatures around the world are rising, as the quantity of carbon dioxide in our atmosphere increases because less radiation is escaping from the Earth into space. We are already seeing early signs that the upper layers of the ocean are expanding with the added warmth, and ice caps are melting. This is beginning to cause a rise in sea levels which could put some low coastal areas under water. The Caribbean region has many such areas.

These temperature increases also mean that there is more energy in the atmosphere. Tropical storms seem to be developing more often, and are more violent. All over the world, the climate seems to be changing. At least some of this change is due to the increase of carbon dioxide in the atmosphere that we are causing.

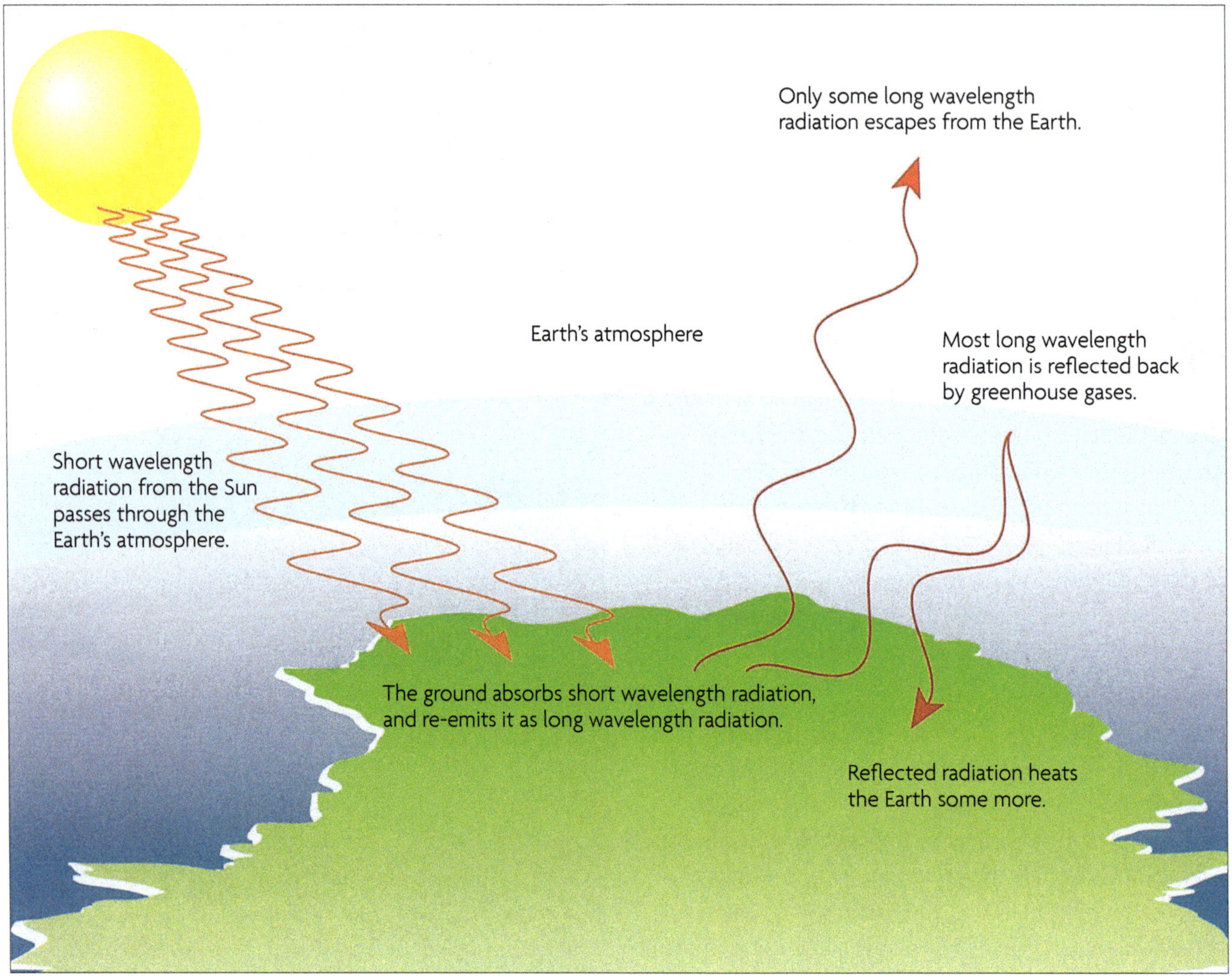

Figure 18.9 The greenhouse effect.

18.14 Forests are cleared for planting crops.

There are two types of agricultural patterns in the Caribbean. There are small mixed farms, intended mostly to feed the farmers and their families, and support cash crops like vegetables. These farms are often on marginal and hilly lands where some farmers still practise 'slash and burn' methods. Land is cleared by cutting larger trees by hand, then burning the vegetative cover. As pointed out in section **18.11**, removal of the vegetation causes loss of the flora and fauna and encourages soil erosion.

Secondly, there are the larger estates. These usually concentrate on one or two crops only – for example, sugar cane, bananas (Figure **18.10**) or coconuts. Cattle or sheep might be reared. Here, environmental damage may be even greater. Land is often cleared by bulldozers. Trees are overturned and topsoil removed, so the loss of plants and animals is greater.

Monoculture, or the cultivation of a single crop, also causes some alleles of genes to be lost from the population of crop plants. High-yielding strains of crops, produced through research, are chosen for planting, instead of wild strains. So these wild strains are often lost and, with them, their genes. If disease strikes, all of a particular crop plant may die, since the genes in all the plants are the same. There is no variation to allow some plants to survive (section **15.4**).

In both types of agricultural patterns, artificial fertilizers may be used to make up for loss in soil fertility. Also chemicals may be used to kill the pests and weeds. These substances can pollute the air, soil, underground water and streams (Figures **18.11** and **18.12**).

Figure 18.10 A banana plantation has replaced natural forest.

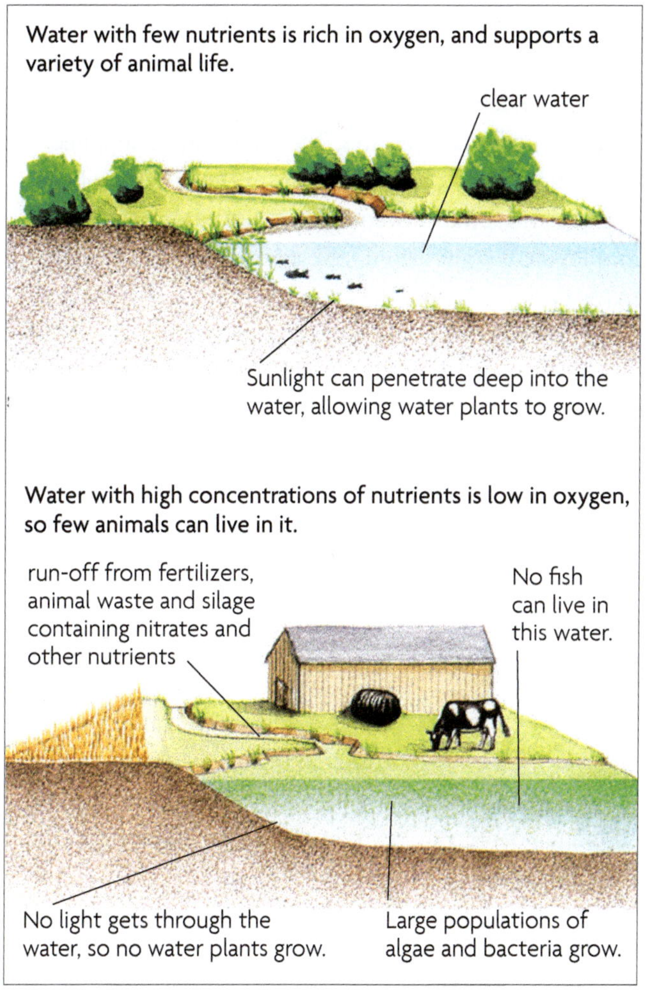

Figure 18.11 Plant nutrients from fertilizers flowing into the water increase plant and bacterial growth. This reduces oxygen levels, killing fish. This process is known as eutrophication.

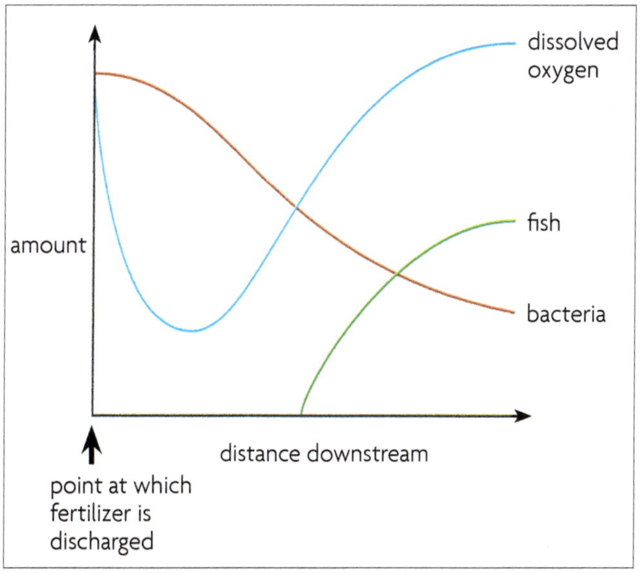

Figure 18.12 The effect of fertilizer pollution on a stream.

18.15 Urban centres often replace forests.

As we have seen, world population is increasing rapidly, and people need housing. Forests are sometimes cleared for building housing estates. These need to be supplied with water, electricity, and means for the disposal of garbage and sewage. Eventually, urban centres develop. Employment comes from industries, not from farming. In 1960, about 20% of the population of the world lived in cities. In 2000, the figure was estimated to be around 60%.

These large centres of human population have a great impact on the natural environment. Ecosystem relationships will change, as forests are cleared, and buildings and roads put in. Many species will lose their normal habitats. So, for example, fewer birds and soil animals are likely to be found. But houseflies, mosquitoes and rodents will increase, as conditions favourable for their growth abound.

Urban centres are extreme examples of the built environment created by human beings. Large quantities of food, water, energy and oxygen are needed to support so many people. But towns and cities give back little to help to maintain nature's balance. They continually have to 'import' supplies to meet their human needs. They concentrate waste, increasing problems of disposal. More people are quickly exposed to hazards like contagious diseases, floods, fires and earthquakes. There have been many recent examples which demonstrate this. The smoke from the 1997 widespread land fires in Indonesia covered Asian skies for months, until the rains came in November. Many millions are said to have experienced respiratory problems. Earthquakes in Japan and Turkey in 1999 caused thousands of deaths as high-rise city buildings crumbled. The destruction was made worse through faulty construction and failure to obey building codes.

Urban centres also generate high levels of noise, which becomes an irritant and health hazard for humans and other animals. They also make it easier for habits of substance abuse to spread.

While forest removal helps to provide city dwellers with shelter, it robs forest-dwelling indigenous peoples of their homes and livelihoods. Indians of the rainforests of Guyana are losing their forest homes as logging and goldmining activities increase in the territory. Forest dwellers of Brazil are at risk as the Amazon rainforest is cleared for roads and agriculture.

18.16 Industries pollute the environment.

Industries provide employment and create wealth. They provide material for human needs and comfort. These include building materials, clothing, means of transportation, communication, recreation and intellectual stimulation.

For all this, we pay an environmental price. The burning of fossil fuels, in vehicles, power plants (Figure **18.13**), and industry generally, sends large quantities of carbon dioxide into the air. In section **18.13**, we saw how this could contribute to an increase in the global temperature. Though carbon dioxide is an important greenhouse gas, it is not the only pollutant sent into the air by human activity (Table **18.1**). Methane is also an important greenhouse gas. So are CFCs.

18.17 CFCs damage the ozone layer.

Chlorofluorocarbons (**CFCs**) were used in the past in spray cans, refrigerators and air conditioning. They not only contribute to the greenhouse effect, but also damage the ozone layer. CFCs do not readily break down. So they can go very high up into the upper levels of the atmosphere. Here they may be broken down by ultraviolet (UV) radiation from the Sun. Some of the products so formed can destroy ozone molecules (O_3) at a fast rate. So more ozone molecules are destroyed than are produced.

Figure 18.13 A power generating station in Jamaica releases polluting gases.

Table 18.1 Gases contributing to the greenhouse effect

Gas	% estimated contribution	Main sources
carbon dioxide	55	burning fossil fuels
methane	15	decay of organic matter, e.g. in waste tips and paddy fields; waste gases from digestive processes in cattle and insects; natural gas leaks
CFCs	24	fridges and air conditioning units; plastic foams
nitrous oxides	6	fertilizers; car engines

Ozone that is high up in the atmosphere absorbs much of the UV radiation from the Sun before it reaches the Earth. So it protects living things on Earth from tissue damage by UV radiation. When the high ozone layer is damaged (Figure **18.14**), more UV radiation reaches the Earth. Living things are at a greater risk of being harmed by UV radiation (Figure **18.15**).

As with the greenhouse effect, it is difficult to predict the true impact of damage to the ozone layer. Both involve extremely complex interactions. What is certain is that both phenomena upset nature's equilibrium. So we should be careful not to make them any worse. New compounds are now replacing CFCs and legal measures are enforcing their use. However, because it takes so long for CFCs to break down, even though we have stopped using them it will be many years before they disappear from the atmosphere.

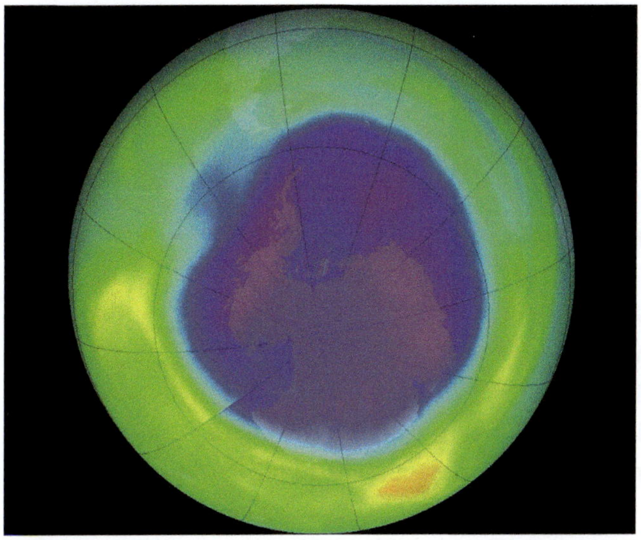

Figure 18.14 A satellite map showing the hole in the ozone layer in Antarctica in 2007. Purple and blue show the lowest amount of ozone, and orange shows the most.

18.18 Sulfur dioxide and nitrogen oxides produce acid rain.

Compounds of sulfur and nitrogen also reach the air from industry. These dissolve in water in the air forming weak acids, which come down in falling rain. This acid reduces the pH of the soil and water, killing plants and animals. Acid rain also destroys buildings, since it corrodes metals and minerals, and dissolves limestone. Since air currents mix, acid rain may affect countries that are far away from those in which the gases are produced (Figure **18.16**, overleaf).

So far, the Caribbean region has suffered little from acid rain. The trade-winds carry away the gases, produced in the region, that cause acid rain.

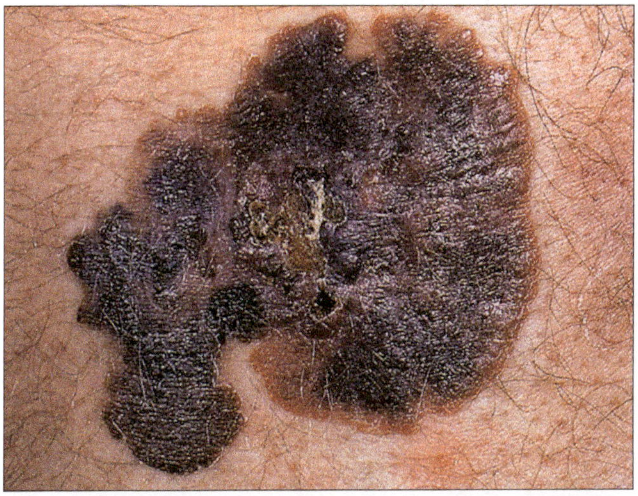

Figure 18.15 This type of skin cancer, called melanoma, can be caused by ultraviolet radiation from the Sun damaging the DNA in skin cells. It can affect people of any skin colour.

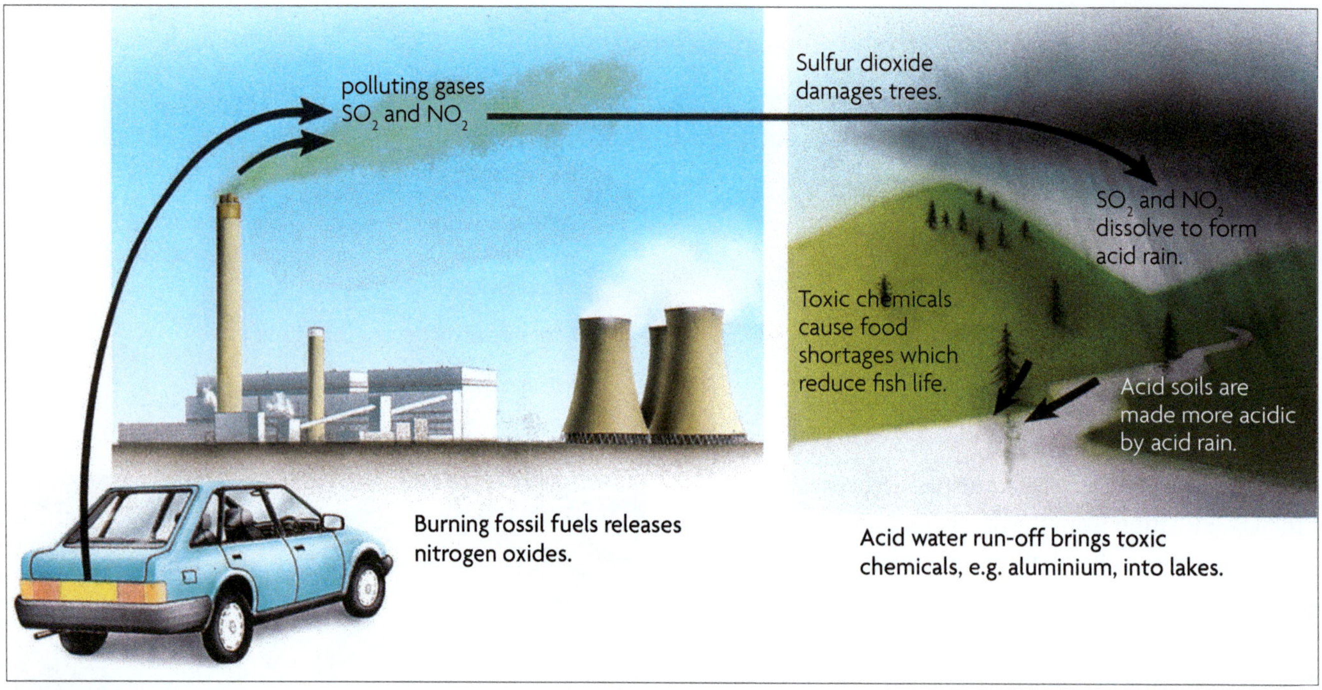

Figure 18.16 Acid rain.

18.19 Many other pollutants affect air, land and water.

Dust and smoke are other end-products of industry in the region. Bauxite mining (Figure **18.17**) and the manufacture of alumina (Figure **18.18**) in Jamaica and Guyana, gypsum mining in Jamaica, oil refining, especially in Trinidad (Figure **18.19**), limestone quarrying, the manufacture of cement and the burning of sugar canes before harvesting, all cause this type of problem. Factories for making chemicals and car batteries release toxic chemicals like lead which pollute air and water.

Figure 18.18 Manufacture of alumina in Guyana.

Figure 18.17 Bauxite mining in Jamaica.

Figure 18.19 Oil refinery at Pointe-a-Pierre, Trinidad.

The region is also exposed to the effects of possible accidents at nuclear plants which might cause leakage of radioactive substances. The small nuclear reactor at the Mona campus of the University of the West Indies, used for research (Figure **18.20**), is not thought to be a threat. However, nuclear plants exist in Cuba and in nearby Florida in the United States of America.

Investigation 18.1
To determine the environmental impact of an industry

SBA skills
Observation/Recording/Reporting

It is probably best to carry out this investigation as a group, rather than on your own.

1 Visit a factory site near your school.

2 Observe, and make notes on the following:
- the main product manufactured
- the processes involved in the manufacture
- the raw materials used
- the source of energy for the factory
- the by-products and waste materials from the manufacturing processes
- the arrangements for disposal of these by-products and waste (consider waste gases, dust and smoke, liquid waste, solid waste).

3 Note the approximate number of employees, and the working conditions (for example, number of working hours, provisions for safety and for meals, sanitation).

4 Note the suitability of the siting of the factory from a geographical point of view, and from the viewpoint of people who may be living nearby.

5 Prepare a report on the basis of your observations.

6 Discuss, from the standpoint of its impact on the environment, the advantages and disadvantages of having the factory. Include a consideration of the employment opportunities provided by the industry.

There are other 'imported' problems. Much of the oil going to the United States crosses the Caribbean Sea, posing the constant risk of oil spills at sea. Some Caribbean countries, for economic reasons, have even considered accepting waste from industrialised countries. In one island, some dumping has actually occurred.

18.20 People's lifestyles influence how they use resources.

The industrialised countries support about 30% of the world's population. They use, however, most of the world's resources. Their wealth is linked to technological advance. The lifestyle is mostly urban and service demands are high. People use more water, more electricity, more refined foods, more artificial materials like plastics, than are used in the poorer countries. Farmers use more mechanical tools for their tasks.

Developing countries use less of the world's resources, but poverty itself causes ecological damage. The damage is made worse because it is often in these countries that the population is increasing very rapidly. Traditional beliefs which encourage large families often still exist. Many women in the Caribbean still believe they should have their 'quiverful' of children.

In order to feed themselves, people clear more and more forest. The soil becomes poorer, crops yield less, so poverty increases. The whole process becomes a cycle, difficult to break. In the Caribbean, Haiti is a stark example of this situation. In Africa, famine is increasing, as land becomes desert as a result of this process.

Figure 18.20 The Slowpoke nuclear reactor at the Mona campus, University of the West Indies.

People seeking employment flock to cities and towns. Often they have to live in makeshift houses on the margins of the cities. 'Shanty towns' develop. Sometimes, because of where these are sited, there can be no proper provisions for water, electricity, garbage and sewage disposal.

For example, it is estimated that in south-east and central Asia about two-thirds of those who live in cities have no supply of clean water. Therefore, they use untreated water, exposing themselves to waterborne diseases like cholera, typhoid and dysentery. In the Caribbean, people usually have a source of potable (drinking) water, but the other problems remain.

The fast communication systems of today also have a great impact on how people use resources. Television is especially powerful. People in poorer tropical and subtropical countries copy the lifestyle of the wealthier temperate countries. In the Caribbean, this is very true of the influence of North America. For example, people copy building designs which are not suitable for the climate, especially the hurricanes and storms we often experience. The end result is that the lifestyles of most of the world's population, rich or poor, are not sustainable.

18.21 The Caribbean is prone to naturally occurring environmental problems.

We are not to blame for all of our environmental problems. Hurricanes and storms, floods, earthquakes and, less frequently, volcanic eruptions are naturally occurring environmental problems experienced in the Caribbean. However, many scientists believe that the addition of more and more greenhouse gases to the atmosphere will increase the violence and intensity of the weather events that we experience.

Hurricanes develop over tropical oceans. They result from disturbances in the atmosphere when air masses move to areas of low pressure. They are characterised by high winds, and often there is torrential rain. Huge waves or storm surges often follow them and are a further source of danger. The people of Central America faced another kind of danger after powerful hurricane Mitch in 1998. Prolonged heavy rainfall caused gigantic mudslides which covered residents, leaving many thousands dead and millions homeless.

Earthquakes are sudden movements in the Earth's crust. Buildings may be destroyed; landslides and fires are possible. Coastal regions may be raised or lowered, as in the destruction of Port Royal in Jamaica in 1692. The West Indian islands are in both the earthquake and hurricane belts of the globe (Figure **18.21**).

When volcanoes erupt, molten lava and hot gases destroy anything in their path. Fine dust from broken bits of lava is also carried long distances. St Vincent lost its entire banana crop in 1979 when La Soufrière erupted. Ash from the volcano was carried to other islands like Barbados. In Guadeloupe, La Grande Soufrière, which had been dormant for over 100 years, erupted in 1976. People had to be evacuated from most of the Basse-Terre region. In July 1995, the Soufrière Hills volcano in Montserrat, which had been dormant for about 300 years, erupted. A second eruption took place in September 1996. The entire south of the island has been evacuated. Some 4000 people, about one-third of the island's population, have emigrated to Britain and other Caribbean islands. The rest are crowded together in the 'safe' region to the north of the island. The volcano is still being monitored, as there is uncertainty as to future eruptions.

Natural disasters cause loss of plant and animal life, and destruction of human property. A safe water supply, electricity and means of communication with the outside world may not be available for some time after a disaster. Health services often break down, increasing the possibility of outbreak and spread of disease.

All countries, and especially those in disaster-prone areas like the Caribbean, should have permanent plans for dealing with natural disasters. The public should know what these plans are. Through modern technology, warnings of approaching hurricanes or possible volcanic activity can be given. Arrangements should exist to transfer people away from danger zones, and to look after the ill and injured.

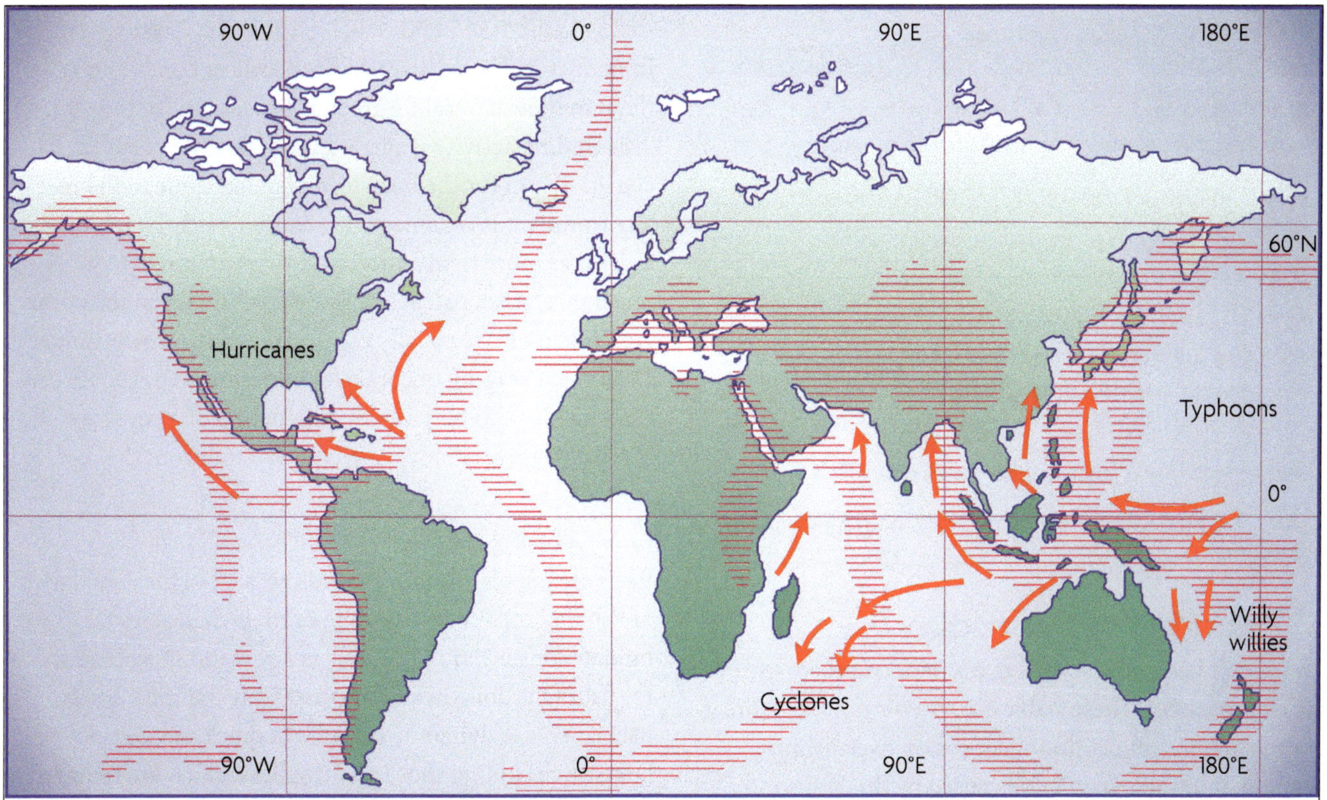

Hurricanes are tropical cyclones. As indicated in the diagram, cyclones are called different names in different parts of the world.

Key
earthquake zones
paths taken by tropical cyclones

Figure 18.21 The hurricane and earthquake belts of the globe.

Investigation 18.2

To find out the effect of hurricanes on local building practices

SBA skills

Observation/Recording/Reporting

Analysis/Interpretation

1 From personal observation, library and museum records, and interviews with older people, get information on the types of houses that have best withstood hurricanes over the last 100 years.

2 Find out the materials used in these buildings, the style of the houses and shape of the roofs.

3 Compare your findings from part **2** with data relating to recently built houses.

4 On the basis of what you have found out, suggest precautions for hurricane resistance for future buildings. Take into account new building materials which have been developed.

5 Prepare a written, illustrated report of what you have found out.

Questions

18.4 'Resources have limits'. Explain what this means, using at least two examples to illustrate your answer.

18.5 What are the main effects of deforestation on the environment?

18.6 What is the 'greenhouse effect'?

18.7 How may the practice of cultivating single crops like sugar cane on a large scale affect **(a)** the crop species itself, **(b)** other plants and animals, and **(c)** soil fertility?

18.8 What is acid rain and what are its effects?

18.9 Why is the ozone layer important for living things?

18.22 Coral reefs face destruction.

Coral reefs have not escaped man's indiscriminate use of the environment. These stable ecosystems now face threat of destruction from collectors of corals, over-fishing, siltation and water stagnation caused by dredging and filling, oil spills, thermal pollution, sewage and fertilisers (Figure **18.22**).

18.23 Collectors cause long-term damage.

In many Caribbean islands, divers collect corals and sell them in their natural form, or as ornaments, to tourists. This trading activity is carried out with little or no consideration for the long-term damage done to the reef environment. It is damage that cannot easily be repaired, as it takes more than a thousand years for a reef to grow one metre. Also, patches of stone left bare when the corals are broken off are usually colonised by fast-growing algae. Continued reaping of corals for commercial purposes can therefore lead to permanent destruction of a coral reef. It is now illegal to remove any type of coral from the reef.

18.24 Fishing harms many different species.

Reefs are popular fishing grounds because of the abundance of fish and other sea life, some of them delicacies for human consumption. But this is not without problems, for fishing is done in an indiscriminate manner. Some fishermen use dynamite on reefs (a quick way to get a large catch) killing those reef dwellers which are required for their market and also those which are not. Mature and young organisms are killed, and parts of the reef destroyed.

Figure 18.22 Destructive influences affecting coral reefs.

Fishermen also use fish traps of heavy steel or iron mesh to catch those large reef fish and lobsters that live in the deep waters of the reef. The openings of the metal mesh of these traps are usually very small; once fish enter, they cannot escape. Thus large and small are caught. The small ones, which are unwanted, are often dumped on the shore and left to die.

Sometimes the traps, which are lowered by rope, separate from the rope detachments and become lost. These traps then continue to 'fish' for years, with their trapped inhabitants imprisoned until they die. Their decomposing remains attract more fish and lobsters and they too join their unfortunate mates. Anchors dropped from fishing boats also damage reefs.

This problem of over-fishing has had serious effects on fish populations in the Caribbean. In fact, the results of over-fishing on reefs are now becoming evident in some Caribbean countries. Indigenous fish populations are decreasing and harvests from the sea are declining (Figure **18.23**). One mollusc, the conch, has been declared commercially endangered. Catches of 'sea eggs' (sea urchins), a delicacy of Barbadian households, have decreased so considerably that the government has passed a law to regulate harvesting. Fishing for 'sea eggs' is now permitted only during the 'in-season' period.

18.25 Industrial activity causes pollution.

Construction work, such as dredging of lagoons and blowing apart of reefs to make deep-water harbours for sea-going ships, filling shallow parts of the sea to reclaim land, building of coastal roads, beach-side hotels and groynes, all release clouds of dust and debris into the sea; dust from cement plants, almost always 'conveniently' located right on the shoreline, and the red mud waste from bauxite plants, also contribute to the silting which settles on reefs. This shuts out light and air from the coral polyps. Polyps are very sensitive to changes in light intensity, temperature and salinity of their marine environment. They react to these changes by expelling their resident zooxanthellae; an act injurious to the polyps themselves, for it has been shown that the polyps cannot live very long without their plant associates.

Figure 18.23 Conch shells for sale in St George's Harbour. Heavy harvesting of these molluscs has severely reduced their numbers.

In Barbados, the construction of groynes along the west and south coasts by hoteliers to protect their beach front areas has had far-reaching effects. The groynes break the natural flow of inshore tidal currents, contributing to severe beach erosion in some areas along the coasts. In addition, the break in the natural flow of inshore tidal currents also prevents the deposition of nutrients that are needed by marine life such as seaweeds, sea grasses and by coral polyps for formation of their limestone skeleton.

Sea grasses grow on the reef floor; they are true flowering plants with roots, stems, flowers and seeds. Sea urchins inhabit coral reefs and feed mainly on algae and sea grasses. Building of groynes has thus been given as one of the most likely reasons for the marked decline in this country's sea urchin catch in the past ten years.

18.26 Thermal pollution harms marine organisms.

When hot water from electricity-generating stations and desalination plants is discharged into the sea, the temperature of the coastal water can rise to as high at 32 °C. Corals and marine organisms cannot tolerate these high temperatures. The result is the death of coral polyps and obvious destruction of coral reefs. Another effect of the high water temperature is the decrease in oxygen content of the water. More oxygen dissolves in cold water than in warm water.

18.27 Sewage causes eutrophication.

An international study carried out in 1981 of 27 Caribbean countries found that nine-tenths of the sewage from 30 million people was discharged untreated into the sea. Fertilisers and chemical insecticides are also washed into the sea during heavy rainfall. These pollutants all contribute to coral reef destruction.

Large amounts of sewage and fertilisers provide marine algae with an excessive supply of nutrients. The algae grow rapidly, almost beyond control. The spreading mass of algae cuts off light from the coral reef, depriving the coralline inhabitants, zooxanthellae, of the light needed for photosynthesis, and thus upsetting the natural cycle of substances between zooxanthellae and coral polyps.

Further decomposition of large masses of dead algae by aerobic bacteria leads to a decrease of the oxygen content of the water. The oxygen depletion may result in the death of many fish and other marine animals.

Figure 18.24 The queen angel fish bites off chunks of coral with its sharp teeth.

18.28 Natural enemies eat coral.

Corals also have sea-dwelling enemies. Butterfly fish, angelfish and parrotfish, all of which have strong jaws and several rows of sharp teeth, bite off chunks of coral, swallowing the coral polyps, their limestone skeletons and their algal inhabitants (Figures **18.24** and **18.25**). The fish digests the living parts of the meal and expels the fine bits of sand through its anus. Marine biologists estimate that every year about 2.5 tonnes of solid coral skeleton is converted into fine sand for every hectare of coral reef. The crown of thorns starfish also feeds on corals.

Figure 18.25 The puffer fish eats coral.

Other species of worms, sponges, mussels and sea urchins actually live in the coral reef, using the hard skeleton as shelter. They bore their way into the coral, causing a weakening of the structure. When strong waves from hurricanes and tropical storms hit the reef, those parts weakened by burrowing animals break away (Figure **18.26**). Corals are killed, and fast-reproducing groups such as algae, sponges and anemones quickly take over the bare areas of hard rock. It takes between 20 and 50 years for renewed polyp growth to occur following such destruction by hurricanes.

Figure 18.26 Hurricane damage to a coral reef.

18.29 Oil spills harm coral.

Offshore oil exploration and the refining of crude oil take place in a number of Caribbean islands. The Caribbean Sea also serves as an important shipping lane for oil tankers, linking North and South America and the east and south coasts of the United States of America with the Pacific Ocean via the Panama Canal. The Caribbean Sea is therefore constantly exposed to accidental oil spillage from tankers and offshore wells. Not to be overlooked are the slicks from tankers flushing out their holds into the sea.

Marine biologists have found that black slimy patches appearing on the reefs are caused by oil slicks. When the tide is low, the crude oil sticks onto those corals which are near the surface of the water. The polyps react to this coat of oil by secreting large amounts of mucus. The mucus attracts colonies of bacteria that decompose both the mucus and the entrapped polyps into a black slimy mass. The damage which oil slicks cause to coral reefs is widespread and permanent, and conservation programmes recognise this as an area for urgent action.

Solutions to environmental problems

18.30 Environmental problems can be solved.

Having a sustainable lifestyle means living in such a way that a good quality of life can go on indefinitely. So we need to make sure that we leave for future inhabitants the level of resources we enjoy. We can only do this if we conserve resources, and protect and improve the environment.

But, as we seek to satisfy the need for shelter, food, clothing and social relationships, our activities alter the natural environment constantly. So the total Earth environment interacting with living things includes not just the natural environment, but a built or manufactured component. Therefore, when we think of the environment, we need to be conscious of many aspects. There is the physical, biological and physiological base which supports all life. But there are also social, economic, political, cultural, technological, aesthetic and ethical aspects to consider. All aspects affect not only humans, but all other living organisms as well.

Achieving sustainability means that humans need to find solutions to the problems they have created. They must also correct, as far as is possible, the environmental damage already done. Harmony between the natural environment and all the other facets of the total environment must be sought and maintained. Resources which cannot be renewed must be used very sparingly. Resources which can be renewed must be managed, so that they can yield without being destroyed. Nature's cyclical patterns in managing resources must be copied, so as to avoid waste and maintain equilibrium.

Left undisturbed, interactions in ecosystems maintain a balance which allows species to exist with each other indefinitely. These interactions include the recycling of nutrients, water and essential gases. Whenever the balance is upset, problems result. Sometimes, this happens in nature. For example, flooding of a river delta restores the supply of nutrients for the organisms living there. Hurricanes and earthquakes in the Caribbean and elsewhere cause considerable environmental distress, but over time, equilibrium is restored.

Human beings often make the results of these natural disasters worse. They crowd into towns and cities, exposing more people quickly to disaster effects. Sometimes people live on marginal lands – on dumped coastal wetlands, on steep slopes, at the base of volcanoes, along the banks of rivers. They dump solid waste in gullies and other drainage ways, causing unnecessary flooding.

In the Caribbean, there are many things we can do to reverse damage, conserve resources and improve the environment.

18.31 Forests can be preserved or replaced.

Forests (Figure **18.27**) are an immense resource pool. We have noted that they protect water and soil, and provide a habitat for wildlife. They provide energy, as wood for fuel, for about half the world's population. They yield food, fodder, rubber, gums and medicinal products. They are a rich source of genetic variety, serving to preserve the biodiversity of an area or region. This variety of

Figure 18.27 Tropical forests must be preserved.

organisms is necessary as nature's safeguard against environmental change. So it is important that we both preserve the forests left, and plant new trees to replace those removed.

We must manage the remaining forest cover so that it can yield, without destroying the areas from which our rivers draw their water. We must select areas to be kept as national parks and protected areas so that these are kept in their natural state for the future. Establishing national parks may also be a way of preserving the traditional ways of life of forest dwellers. For example, the Guyana Iwokrama Rain Forest Programme proposes to use nearly one million acres of Guyana's rainforests as a huge national park. Part of this is to be kept in its natural state to preserve biodiversity. But there will also be experiments in sustainable forestry. The people who have always lived in the forest, the indigenous Amerindians, are an integral part of the project. They will contribute their knowledge of, and experience and skill in managing the forest.

Where we have to replant forest, choices must be made scientifically. Trees used must be suited to local conditions. But in some cases, it might be wiser to allow the natural forest to regenerate itself without interference. We have to resolve to replace any trees used in the future as they are removed.

Plans for urban centres should include the preservation of large green areas. These would provide not only habitats for wildlife and places of recreation for humans, but also reduce extremes of temperature. Topsoil from construction sites should be saved for later use in creating gardens. Similarly, mined-out areas, such as those left after bauxite mining, should be filled and planted out. In Jamaica, several of these areas have been used successfully for cattle rearing.

18.32 Better farming practices can preserve soil fertility.

Farming practices should copy nature's diversity. Mixed farming should be emphasised. Different crops require different proportions of soil minerals. So each crop is more likely to obtain what it needs. The same is true if crops are rotated. Different crops are also likely to have different pests. Whether crops are mixed in the same field or planted one after the other in rotation, it would be more difficult for pests to find their host plants. Fewer pests mean easier control. Also, this is an alternative to control by chemicals. These pollute air, soil and water and sometimes directly affect organisms other than those for which they were intended.

The use of predators to control pests is closest to what occurs in nature. For example, fish may be introduced into ponds to feed on mosquito larvae. This type of control is called biological control. The introduction of predators, however, needs to be very carefully studied beforehand, as these could in time become pests themselves.

Where it is necessary to cultivate large areas of one crop to provide food, wild strains should also be grown to preserve genetic variety.

Terracing, contouring and strip-cropping help to prevent soil erosion on slopes (Figure **18.28**).

Figure 18.28 Terracing on a hill slope.

Fire should not be used, either in preparing land for farming or for burning sugar cane before reaping. Using organic manure – for example, pen manure – is often preferable to using artificial fertilisers. Organic manure decomposes and replaces nutrients through natural cycles (sections **1.19** to **1.23**). It also improves the crumb structure of the soil (section **17.20**) and is less likely to cause pollution.

18.33 Energy resources can be conserved.

Energy is necessary for our social, cultural and economic activities. Most of the energy used in the Caribbean comes from oil, a fossil fuel and non-renewable resource. Trinidad has its own oil supply (Figure **18.19**, page **360**), and Barbados has some natural gas. In other territories, oil has to be imported at tremendous cost. So there is good reason to use other sources of energy whenever possible. Some electricity is generated by hydropower. Damming the water before use may cause habitat changes which some organisms cannot tolerate. The temperature of the water leaving the turbines is also higher than the original. This may kill some organisms. However, the water itself is not used up and no pollutants are released into the air. In electricity plants powered by diesel fuel, the gases produced in combustion are discharged into the air. Wind energy was once used extensively in the region in sugar factories. Windmills could be reintroduced where conditions are favourable for their use.

Throughout the year, there is abundant sunshine in the Caribbean. Other territories could copy Barbados, where the norm for households is a solar water heater. Solar driers could also be used for some crops, like ginger, and solar cookers for foods which need a long cooking time.

Wood is still a popular cooking fuel, especially in rural areas. The use of charcoal is also increasing because of the high cost of electricity and cooking gas. Charcoal is made by slowly burning wood in the absence of air. The use of these fuel sources increases the problems caused by the removal of forest cover. One possible way of controlling this would be to plant fast-growing tree species in selected areas, which would be maintained as sources of fuel. Such a programme would need rigid monitoring by the agricultural authorities. More efficient kilns for producing charcoal also need to be put into use.

Another source of energy is 'farm waste', which may be converted into biogas. Biogas contains 60–70% methane, which can be used for cooking, heating and refrigeration. Organic waste is allowed to break down in an oxygen-free environment. The residue after the gas is produced is good organic manure. Making biogas therefore provides a way of supplying fuel and nutrients for crops, as well as a way to dispose of waste properly.

Investigation 18.3
To find out the sources of energy most used in a community

SBA skills

Observation/Recording/Reporting

Analysis/Interpretation

1 Find out the sources of energy used in your own and four other families in your community, for laundry, cooking, house-cleaning, transportation and the three commonest recreational activities. Use personal observations and interviews to get the information desired.

2 Record your findings in a results table like the one below.

3 Rank the tasks according to the possible effects of their energy requirements on the environment.

4 Compare your results with those obtained by other members of your class.

5 From both sets of data, how well is your community managing to conserve energy resources? How can the situation be improved?

Tasks	Energy source					
	Direct sunshine	Human muscle power	Wood	Charcoal	Petroleum products	Electricity
Laundry						
Cooking						
House-cleaning						

18.34 Our fragile island ecosystem must be handled carefully.

Many Caribbean nations look to the development or maintenance of a vibrant tourist industry as a means of support for their people. Our beaches and coral reefs are the basic attractions. These must be preserved for ourselves and for our visitors. However, marine and coastal ecosystems are very fragile. As the number of visitors grows, we must be increasingly careful how we treat these ecosystems.

Mangrove swamps (Figure **18.29**) along island coasts provide food and shelter for crustaceans, molluscs, fish and water-fowl. Organisms found in the swamps are important links in marine food chains. Sea grass beds in shallow water are 'nurseries' for fish. Coral reefs are a habitat for a variety of organisms. They also help to build our beaches. Mangrove swamps and coral reefs also protect the shoreline against storms, which are frequent in the region.

Unfortunately, some mangrove swamps have been cleared, filled in and used as building sites. This practice has worsened with increasing urbanisation. Others have been used as illegal dump sites for solid waste. Mangrove trees have also been cut for burning charcoal. Our coral reefs also face destruction from human activities. When we remember that coral reefs have been called the tropical forests of the ocean, we see how serious this destruction is. In some cases, the damage already done is extensive. For example, studies of Jamaican coral reefs have revealed that only about 5% of these reefs are still alive. The natural ecology of shorelines has been further disturbed by the building of artificial beaches and by pollution (Figure **18.30**).

Figure 18.29 Mangrove swamps protect the coastline.

Caribbean interests are now promoting community-based eco-tourism. Inland trails are being established for nature lovers and hikers. In doing so, we need to remember constantly that these inland ecosystems interact with and influence coastal and marine ecosystems. Protecting and preserving the hills and forests, the watersheds, also protects coastal ecosystems.

We must stop the destructive activities so that, in time, trends may be reversed. There need to be strict, well-enforced laws to prevent the destruction of, and to protect, all of these habitats. Establishing marine parks, as has already been done in some islands, would help to protect coral reef systems.

In addition, environmental impact assessments should be required for all proposals for new 'developments.' Criteria for these assessments should be set by governments which, in turn, have taken technical advice. Such assessments should include the expected social consequences and should be examined thoroughly by government authorities. A satisfactory assessment should be an important criterion for approval of any proposal.

Figure 18.30 Beach pollution in the Dominican Republic.

18.35 Waste can be carefully disposed of.

We produce a huge amount of rubbish each year. Cardboard and paper packaging, bottles and cans, newspapers and magazines, old tyres, waste food and many other things get thrown away each day.

Some of these things are **biodegradable**, meaning that they will break down naturally in the environment. These include waste food and paper. Others are **non-biodegrable**, meaning that they stay in the environment for a very long time without breaking down. These include metals and most plastics.

A lot of our rubbish goes into landfill sites. The rubbish is piled up and compacted. When the site is full, it is covered with soil. Eventually, the site can be used to grow plants again, or it can be developed for recreational use. In some countries, such as Guyana, landfill sites have been used to reclaim 'extra' land from the sea.

Landfill sites can cause problems. If they are close to places where people live, the smells and pests (such as rats and flies) that they attract can cause health risks. Fires from spontaneous combustion may occur, causing heavy smoke which causes respiratory distress. If the landfill sites are placed too close to the sea, run-off can carry pollutants into the water. However, with careful planning and construction, many of these problems can be avoided (Figure **18.31**).

As biodegradable materials in the landfill are broken down by bacteria, methane is produced. We have seen that, if this goes into the air, it can contribute to global warming. Far better is to collect the methane gas and use it as a fuel.

There are various alternatives to dumping waste in landfill sites. One is to burn – incinerate – the waste. This uses up much less land than landfill. However, the temperature at which the waste is burnt must be carefully controlled. If the temperature is too low, then chemical reactions can produce harmful chemicals which are released into the air. These include dioxins. Incinerators need to be carefully designed and controlled to avoid these problems. When the only landfill site in Bermuda was reaching its capacity, an incinerator was built, and this now treats a large proportion of Bermuda's waste. The incinerator reduces the volume of waste by 90%.

However, the best solution to reducing pollution from our waste materials is to produce less of them. Recycling can also help.

18.36 Recycling reduces waste.

Recycling means getting back the materials that were used to make a product, and using them again. They might be used for the same purpose, or for something completely different.

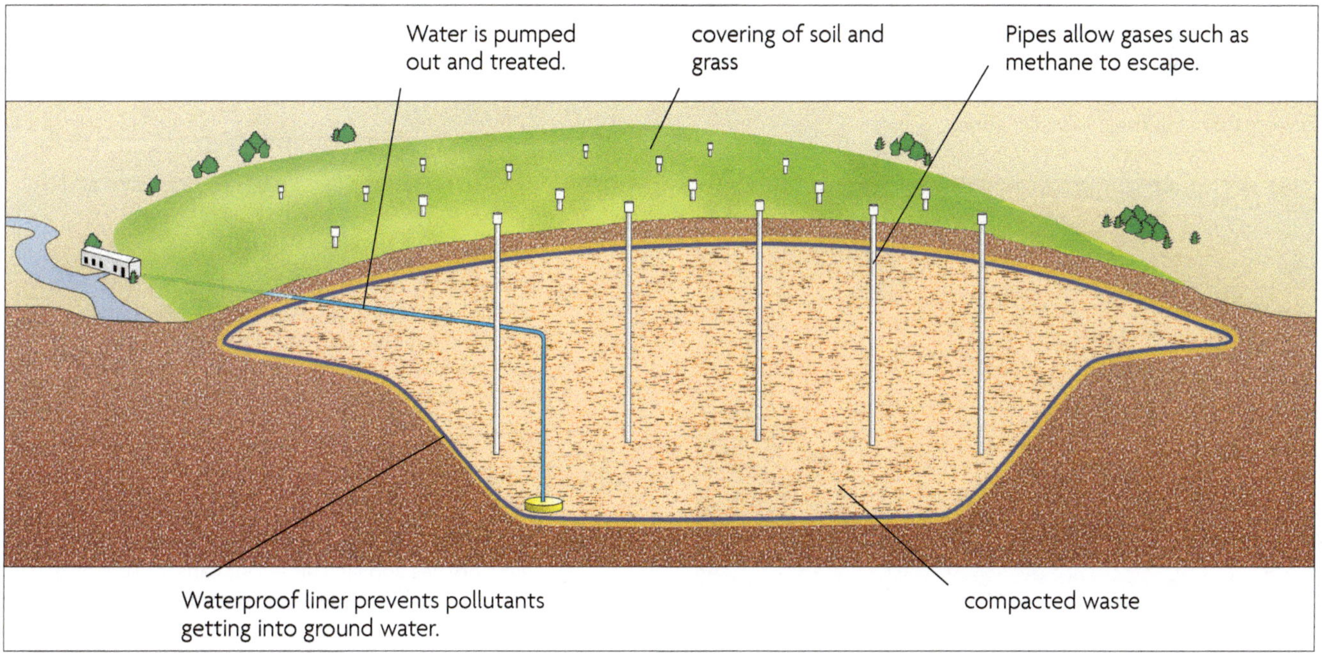

Figure 18.31 A well-constructed landfill site.

Various materials can be recycled. They include paper and cardboard (used for making more paper or cardboard), glass, metals and some kinds of plastics (Figures **18.32** and **18.33**). Recycling these materials reduces our demand on the original sources. For example, if we recycle metals, then we do not need to mine so much from the ground. Plastics are made from fossil fuels, so if we can recycle plastics, then we can reduce our use of this non-renewable resource. Things that can be recycled often have the globally recognised recycling logo on them (Figure **18.34**).

Figure 18.32 Scrap metal bales being stored in Trinidad before being sold on to companies who can melt the bales and convert them into new metallic goods.

Figure 18.33 Glass recycling on Saint Kitts

Figure 18.34 The recycling logo.

Recycling obviously reduces the amount of waste we dump in landfill sites or incinerate. However, it is not always straightforward to do, and it can be costly. Someone has to collect the waste materials and sort them. They have to be transported to the recycling plant, which means using fossil fuels in a vehicle engine.

Many countries in the Caribbean ask people to sort their waste. The waste for recycling is picked up at different times from the other household waste. Figure **18.35** shows the waste management schedule that was used in Bermuda in April 2005, and the guidelines that were given to people about how to manage their household waste.

APRIL

s	m	t	w	t	f	s
					1	2
3	4	5	6	7	8	9
10	11	12	13	14	15	16
17	18	19	20	21	22	23
24	25 WEST	26 EAST	27	28 WEST	29 EAST	30

GARBAGE: Please put garbage in lidded bins and do not put liquids in your garbage.

ANIMAL & HUMAN FAECES: Must not be put in the garbage. Animal waste must be flushed down the toilet or dried out, wrapped in newspaper, placed in a plastic bag and disposed of in the bin at Tynes Bay Drop-Off. All human waste must be flushed down the toilet.

CHRISTMAS TREES: Remove tinsel, nails and ornaments and place out on your scheduled day. Do not use a tree bag.

RECYCLING: Aluminium and steel (tin) cans and glass bottles and jars. Rinse out cans, bottles and jars. Place in blue recycling bag and place out for collection.

Figure 18.35 A waste-collection schedule in Bermuda.

18.37 The success of environmental measures depends on our attitude.

If we are to be successful in correcting environmental problems and trying to prevent new ones, human attitudes to the environment must be different. We can no longer see the natural environment just as 'resources' for our use. We need to move from a culture of power over, and control of, the environment. Instead, we need to see ourselves as being part of this environment. We are part of the world ecosystem, and, therefore, subject to many of the same checks as other species.

We need to show this belief in our personal, community and regional decisions and actions. For example, in Jamaica, deforestation is a known problem. The recent upsurge in the production of yams for export has made the situation worse. But the sale brings in good earnings in foreign exchange in the short term. So it is encouraged at the national level. The traditional way of cultivating yams requires the use of wooden stakes to support the twining stem and its leaves. To get these 'yam sticks', many saplings are removed from the forest. It will be interesting to see whether farmers can be persuaded to change traditional habits, and use the new 'yam sett' technique. This new method, a result of biotechnology research, produces smaller yams, but the plant stems do not require the support of 'sticks'. Thus the forest would no longer be at risk from reaping these sticks.

We need to make unceasing efforts to promote an understanding of, and respect for, the environment. The educative process is necessary to bring about the attitude change which will make solutions possible and lasting, and help to ensure continuing good quality of life for all.

Questions

18.10 What are the advantages of mixed farming?

18.11 How can you prevent soil erosion on slopes if these have to be used for farming?

18.12 Organic manure is preferable to artificial fertilisers. Why?

18.13 Why is it especially important to conserve oil? What sources of energy, other than oil, could be used in your territory, and for what purposes?

18.14 Why should mangrove swamps and coral reefs be protected?

Key ideas

- If birth rate and death rate are equal, population remains the same. If one is greater than the other, the population either increases or decreases.
- The human population is growing, because in many developing countries birth rate is greater than death rate. A population pyramid with a very wide base indicates an increasing population.
- Destruction of forests causes habitat loss for many species. With fewer trees to photosynthesise, more carbon dioxide can build up in the atmosphere. If the trees are burnt, carbon dioxide is released from them. Increased carbon dioxide increases the greenhouse effect, causing global warming.
- Methane, CFCs and nitrous oxides are also greenhouse gases.
- The ozone layer, high in the atmosphere, protects us from harmful ultraviolet radiation from the Sun. CFCs damage the ozone layer.
- Burning fossil fuels produces sulfur dioxide and nitrogen dioxides, which cause acid rain.
- Coral reefs are easily damaged by pollution and over-fishing.
- With care, we can live comfortable lifestyles and still preserve the natural environment. Good farming practices, careful siting and management of industry and forest preservation maintain soil fertility, reduce the emission of greenhouse gases and CFCs and reduce the production of acid rain.
- Careful disposal of waste in properly managed facilities, and recycling, can help to improve our environment and reduce demands on natural resources.

End-of-chapter questions

1 The 'hurricane watch' is a yearly event in the Caribbean. Describe the precautions you would take before a hurricane, and the steps you would take to deal with its after-effects.

2 Explain how the continuing destruction of forests, and especially of large tropical rainforests, may affect:

a the composition and temperature of the air
b coral reef habitats
c life in a Caribbean coastal resort town.

3 Accepting waste from industrialised countries for disposal in the Caribbean has been aired as a possible way for some Caribbean countries to earn foreign exchange. Discuss the implications of such a step for the environmental health of the region.

4 Throughout the Caribbean and other parts of the tropics, mangrove wetlands have been dumped up, and the land used for housing. Discuss some of the possible consequences of this practice for:

a the coral reefs
b the people who live on the dumped-up land
c biodiversity in the coastal ecosystems.

5 State any three ways you can help to promote environmental health in your community or territory. Explain in detail how you would set about any one of the tasks you set yourself.

6 The larger towns in the West Indies have developed by the sea, and attract many tourists, besides supporting their own populations. The coral reefs which fringe the islands are dying. What possible links can you suggest which might exist between these two facts?

7 The graph shows the amount of dissolved oxygen in the water of a river in a city.

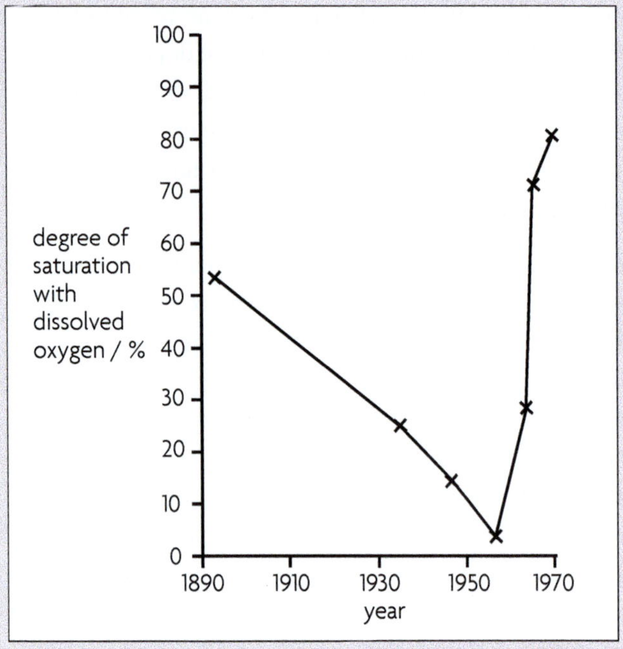

In the 19th century, sewage from the city drained directly into the river. At the begining of the 20th century sewage treatment plants were installed, which removed some of the organic material from the sewage before it entered the river. These plants have gradually become more efficient.

a Give two ways in which water obtains dissolved oxygen.
b Explain how pollution by sewage causes dissolved oxygen levels to decrease.
c Suggest why dissolved oxygen levels in the river
i decreased until 1948, and
ii have increased since the 1950s.
d What effect would you expect a decrease in dissolved oxygen to have on the fish population in the river?
e Apart from affecting the levels of dissolved oxygen, what other harmful effects can the discharge of untreated sewage into rivers have?

Appendix 1 Apparatus required for investigations

Safety note

Although great care has been taken in checking the accuracy of the information provided, Cambridge University Press shall not be responsible for any errors, omissions or inaccuracies. Teachers should always follow their school and departmental safety policies. Teachers must ensure that they consult their employer's safety documentation and modify the information provided as appropriate to meet local circumstances before starting any practical work. Risk assessments will depend on your own skills and experience, and the facilities available to you.

Everyone is responsible for his or her own safety and for the safety of others. The practicals should be carried out by teachers themselves before they are presented to students.

The apparatus listed is that required for each group performing the experiment.

1.1 Studying an ecosystem

digital camera (to share between class)
polythene bags
jars with tops
marker pens to label bags and jars or pencil and pieces of scrap paper
insect net
pooter
hand lens
sorting tray

1.2 Do animals prefer particular types of plants to eat?

12 small herbivores, e.g. slugs or caterpillars
3 leaves from each of four different types of plant
6 jars or plastic containers with perforated tops

2.1 Looking at animal cells

section lifter
very small amount of methylene blue (diluted)
slide
coverslip
filter paper or blotting paper
pipette
microscope
trachea of sheep or pig (obtainable from butcher or abbatoir)

2.2 Looking at plant cells

sections of onion bulb; these can be cut beforehand, and kept in a beaker of water
slide
coverslip
pipette
filter paper or blotting paper
iodine in potassium iodide solution with dropper
microscope
seeker or mounted needle

2.3 Demonstrating diffusion in a solution

gas jar or tall glass jar
crystals of potassium permanganate CARE!
forceps to handle crystals

2.4 Diffusion of substances through a membrane

10 cm length of Visking tubing (diameter unimportant)
pipette
strong thread
starch solution (use soluble starch and follow instructions on the container to make a starch suspension), concentration not critical
iodine in potassium iodide solution
beaker or other transparent container

2.5 Measuring the rate of osmosis

10 cm length of Visking tubing (diameter unimportant)
pipette
concentrated sugar solution (concentration not critical)
piece of glass tubing at least 250 cm long; diameter not critical but between 3 mm and 5 mm is ideal
strong thread
marker to write on glass, or sticky label with straight edge
ruler or graph paper (to be placed behind the glass tube to measure distance travelled by meniscus)
stopwatch or other timer
retort stand, clamp and boss (to support glass tube)
beaker or other transparent container

2.6 Experiment to investigate the effect of different solutions on plant cells

solution A – distilled water
solution B – 0.3 $mol\,dm^{-3}$ sucrose solution
solution C – 1.0 $mol\,dm^{-3}$ sucrose solution
Rhoeo leaves
forceps
scalpel CARE!
3 microscope slides
3 coverslips
labels for slides
filter paper or blotting paper
microscope

2.7 Osmosis and potato strips

Irish potato or other tuber
knife for peeling and cutting potato CARE!
ruler to measure in mm
containers deep enough to hold liquid to cover the strips (e.g. Petri dishes, margarine containers, beakers)
liquids A to E as follows, sufficient to completely cover the potato strips in the container
A – distilled water
B to E – range of sucrose solutions from 0.1 $mol\,dm^{-3}$ to 2.0 $mol\,dm^{-3}$ (students should be told the concentration of each solution)
filter paper or blotting paper
forceps for removing strips from liquid in container

3.1 Testing foods for sugars

variety of foods, to include some containing reducing sugars and some not
glucose solution (to demonstrate a positive result)
test-tube rack
Bunsen burner or water bath at about 80 °C CARE!
boiling tubes
test-tube holder
pipette
white tile
scalpel CARE!
Benedict's solution
dilute hydrochloric acid CARE!
dilute sodium hydrogencarbonate solution

3.2 Testing foods for starch

variety of foods, to include some containing starch and some not

iodine in potassium iodide solution
pipette
white tile
scalpel CARE!

3.3 Testing for lipids

variety of foods, to include some containing lipids and some not
white tile
scalpel CARE!
filter paper
very clean test tubes
test-tube rack
access to absolute alcohol CARE!
distilled water

3.4 Testing for protein

variety of foods, to include some containing proteins and some not
white tile
scalpel CARE!
biuret solution or 20% potassium hydroxide solution CARE! and 1% copper sulfate solution
pipettes
test tubes
test-tube rack

3.5 Investigating the effect of pH on the activity of catalase

leaves of pawpaw (or young leaves of bean)
pestle and mortar
6 50 cm^3 beakers
3% hydrogen peroxide solution
buffer solutions at pH 5.6, 6.2, 6.8, 7.4, 8.0
small measuring cylinder or syringes 5 cm^3 and 10 cm^3
distilled water
forceps
filter paper
scalpel (or scissors) CARE! or hole punch
ruler
test tube and holder
Bunsen burner CARE!
tripod
large beaker as water bath
stopwatch or other timer

3.6 Investigating the effect of temperature on the activity of catalase

Students are to plan their own investigation, so will ask for their own apparatus. However, they are likely to need the following.
access to a thermostatically controlled water bath, or Bunsen, tripod and gauze plus a beaker
thermometer
access to boiling water CARE!
access to a refrigerator and/or ice
means of crushing ice (e.g. a tea towel and mallet)
several test tubes or boiling tubes
test-tube rack
means of labelling tubes
ruler
glass rods

3.7 The effect of temperature on the activity of amylase

5 water baths
ice
thermometer
boiling water
0.1% solution of amylase
10 test tubes
1% starch solution
small measuring cylinder or syringes
5 glass rods
spotting tile
iodine in potassium iodide solution
Benedict's reagent
Bunsen burner CARE!
test-tube holder
tripod
beaker

3.8 The effect of substrate concentration on the rate of activity of catalase

2 boiling tubes
rubber bung with hole, to fit in tube
glass tubing (see diagram on page 52)
large cork borer
ruler
scalpel or sharp knife CARE!
distilled water
hydrogen peroxide solutions, 0.5 mol dm^{-3}, 1.0 mol dm^{-3}, 1.5 mol dm^{-3} and 2.0 mol dm^{-3} CARE!
stopwatch or other timer
Irish potato

4.1 Looking at the epidermis of a leaf

variety of leaves – *Rhoeo* (lady in the boat, Moses in the basket) or onion are good
forceps
slides
coverslips
pipette
clear nail varnish
microscope

4.2 Which kind of fertilizer helps plants grow best?

small plant pots or other containers, with drainage holes
dry sand, vermiculite or other growing medium containing no soil or plant nutrients
five small seedlings – for example, maize seedlings; they should have good root systems
distilled water
small measuring cylinder
four different fertilizer solutions, made to the dilution recommended by the manufacturer (following instructions on the packet)

4.3 Testing a leaf for starch

bean or *Hibiscus* plant which has been photosynthesising
boiling water bath, or beaker on tripod with Bunsen burner CARE!
boiling tube
alcohol CARE!
glass rod
iodine in potassium iodide solution
forceps
white tile
pipette
Note: have a damp cloth ready to place over any tubes of alcohol that accidentally catch fire. CARE!

4.4 To see if light is needed for photosynthesis

Session 1:
bean or *Hibiscus* plant
Session 2:
destarched plant
apparatus as for Investigation 4.3
black paper or aluminium foil
scissors CARE!
paper clips
Session 3:
apparatus as for Investigation 4.3

4.5 To see if chlorophyll is needed for photosynthesis

Session 1:
plant with variegated leaves
Session 2:
destarched plant with variegated leaves
apparatus as for Investigation 4.3
Session 3:
apparatus as for Investigation 4.3

4.6 To see if carbon dioxide is needed for photosynthesis

Session 1:
bean or *Hibiscus* plant
Session 2:
destarched plant
apparatus as for Investigation 4.3
two bell jars or two conical flasks with stoppers (see diagram on page 65)
potassium hydroxide solution CARE!
distilled water
Vaseline®
Session 3:
apparatus as for Investigation 4.3

4.7 To show that oxygen is produced in photosynthesis

Session 1:
large beaker
funnel which fits entirely inside the beaker
test tube
Canadian pondweed (*Elodea*), *Hydrilla*

or other aquatic plant
Session 2:
Bunsen burner CARE!
splint

4.8 Investigating the effect of light intensity on photosynthesis

Students are to plan their own investigation, so will ask for their own apparatus. However, they are likely to need the following.
large beaker or test tubes
aquatic plant, e.g. *Elodea* or *Hydrilla*
funnel
possibly a means of collecting gas and measuring volume, e.g. delivery tube and measuring cylinder over water, or a gas syringe (but most students are likely to opt for counting bubbles)
timer
metre ruler
lamp
means of keeping out light from other sources from around the plant, e.g. black paper screens or a few boxes that can be placed around it
piece of perspex or other transparent material that could be used to prevent too much heat from the lamp reaching the plant

5.1 To find out which of three sets of food would provide the most balanced meal

Three groups of food:
1 carrots, Irish potatos, saltfish (yellow vegetable, carbohydrates, protein)
2 gungo (pigeon) peas, rice with coconut milk (protein, carbohydrates, fat)
3 cornmeal, green plantain, pumpkin (yellow vegetable, carbohydrate, possible traces of protein)
Reagents for food tests:
Benedict's solution
dilute hydrochloric acid CARE!
iodine in potassium iodide solution
sodium hydrogencarbonate solution
potassium hydroxide solution CARE! and copper sulfate solution, or biuret reagent
absolute alcohol CARE!
distilled water
filter paper
test tubes and holders
test-tube racks
Bunsen burner CARE!
mortar and pestle
white tile
scalpel CARE!
pipette

5.2 Observing the digestive system of a mammal

For demonstration:
small mammal, either freshly killed or preserved
dissecting board or dish
dissecting instruments (scissors, forceps, scalpel CARE!)
access to warm, soapy water and paper towels

6.1 To show that carbon dioxide is producd by a respiring mammal

apparatus as shown on page 88
NB take care that the long and short tubes are in the positions shown, or limewater will be drawn back towards the mouse's container
small mammal, e.g. a mouse
hydrogencarbonate indicator solution or limewater
potassium hydroxide solution CARE!

6.2 To measure the rate of oxygen uptake during respiration in a small invertebrate

apparatus as shown on page 89
woodlice or other small, active invertebrates
soda lime
stopwatch or other timer

6.3 Comparing the energy content of two kinds of food

Students are to plan their own investigation, so will ask for their own apparatus. However, they are likely to need the following.
two foods that are likely to have different energy contents, e.g. a peanut and a cashew nut, plain popcorn and popcorn soaked in oil, plain bread and bread soaked in oil
means of setting light to the food
mounted needle (to hold the food)
boiling tube held in a clamp on a retort stand
small measuring cylinder or syringe
thermometer

6.4 Investigating heat production by germinating peas

Session 1:
pea or bean seeds
beaker
Session 2:
boiled peas or beans
soaked peas or beans from Session 1
mild disinfectant solution
two vacuum flasks
two cotton wool plugs for flasks
two thermometers
clamp stands to support flasks

6.5 Investigating the production of carbon dioxide by anaerobic respiration

4 boiling tubes, fitted with bungs and glass tubing, as shown on page 93
boiled, cooled water
sucrose or glucose
fresh or dried yeast
boiled yeast suspension
glass rod
pipette
limewater or hydrogencarbonate indicator solution
2 beakers to support boiling tubes
wax pencil or other way of marking tubes
liquid paraffin

6.6 Examining lungs

For demonstration:
set of ox's lungs
large board and dissecting instruments
long glass tube
access to hot, soapy water and paper towels

6.7 Using a syringe to show how the diaphragm works

apparatus as shown on page 102

6.8 Comparing the carbon dioxide content of inspired and expired air

apparatus as shown on page 102
NB: if more than one student is to use the same apparatus, wash the tubing in disinfectant between uses CARE!

6.9 Investigating how breathing rate changes with exercise

stopwatch or other timer

6.10 Investigating how recovery time varies with fitness

Students are to plan their own investigation, so will ask for their own apparatus. However, they are likely to need the following.
stopwatch or other timer

6.11 Investigating the structure of gills

small fish, e.g. sprat
seeker
scissors CARE!
Petri dish
tile
forceps

6.12 The effect of animals and plants on the carbon dioxide concentration in water

4 boiling or specimen tubes, fitted with bungs
Elodea, *Hydrilla* or other pond weed
snails or other pond animals
hydrogencarbonate indicator solution
(This experiment can also be performed with terrestrial animals such as woodlice, or leaves of a terrestrial plant, held above the indicator solution on a gauze platform.)

7.1 To find the effect of exercise on the rate of heart beat

stopwatch or other timer

7.2 To see which part of a stem transports water and solutes

Session 1:
freshly pulled *Impatiens* (balsam) plant with root system intact
eosin solution
beaker
Session 2:
plant from Session 1
slide
coverslip
safety razor blade or very sharp knife CARE!
tile
paint brush or section lifter
pipette
microscope

7.3 To see which surface of a leaf loses most water

potted plant with smooth leaves
forceps
cobalt chloride paper in desiccator
self-adhesive book-covering film or sticky tape
scissors CARE!

7.4 To measure the rate of transpiration of a potted plant

2 plants of similar size, in pots of the same size
2 large polythene bags
rubber bands
Vaseline®
top-pan balance

7.5 Using a potometer to compare rates of transpiration under different conditions

a potometer (not necessarily of the type shown on page 135)
plant with firm stems that will fit tightly into the apparatus
wire
pliers
Vaseline®
stopwatch
electric fan

9.1 Using a model arm to investigate the action of the biceps muscle

apparatus as shown on page 168
range of masses (weights)
spring balance to measure in newtons

10.1 Do woodlice prefer light or dark?

2 plastic Petri dishes
metal rod, heated, to make tunnel in dishes
piece of perforated zinc or mesh, as used for insect protection at windows (see diagram on page 174)
10–12 woodlice or millipedes
dark cloth or paper
glue or sticky tape

10.2 The response of an invertebrate to humidity

Students are to plan their own investigation, so will ask for their own apparatus. However, they are likely to need the following.
choice chambers as constructed for Investigation 10.1
anhydrous calcium chloride or silica gel CARE! (to create dry conditions)
cotton wool or filter paper (to be soaked in water to create humid conditions)
10–12 woodlice or millipedes
dark cloth or paper

10.3 To measure reaction time

stopwatch
ruler or tape measure

10.4 To find out which part of the skin contains the most touch receptors

two pins
plasticine or piece of polystyrene, through which pins may be pushed to support them in position
ruler

10.5 To find out which parts of the tongue can taste which flavours

labelled solutions of salt, sugar, quinine, lemon juice and soy sauce
5 straws or cotton wool sticks

10.6 Can you always see the image?

no apparatus except text book required

10.7 Observing the effect of light on the pupil

torch

10.8 Examining the form and structure of the mammalian eye

eye of a mammal (obtainable from butcher or abbatoir)
sharp blade or scalpel CARE!
forceps
seeker
cork mats
access to hot, soapy water and paper towels

10.9 To find out how shoots respond to light

3 Petri dishes
wax pencil or other means of marking
cotton wool or filter paper
pea or bean seeds
2 light-proof boxes, one with a slit in one end
clinostat
large pins (e.g. dissecting pins)

10.10 To find out how roots respond to gravity

Students are to plan their own investigation, so will ask for their own apparatus. However, they are likely to need the following.
clinostat
large pins (e.g. dissecting pins)
young bean or pea seedlings with short radicles
blotting paper or filter paper
gas jars

10.11 To find out which part of a shoot is sensitive to light

Session 1:
pots containing seed compost
maize grains
Session 2:
germinated coleoptiles
razor CARE!
foil
ruler
3 light-proof boxes with a slit in one end
Session 3:
coleoptiles from session 2
ruler

10.12 To find how auxin affects shoots

3 pots of germinated maize grains
lanolin, warmed slightly
IAA solution. Make this by dissolving 0.1 g of IAA in 1 litre of distilled water to make a solution of 100 parts per million. This can then be diluted to 1 ppm for use in the experiment. The solution should be used within a few hours of being made up.
labels
3 clinostats

11.1 Experiment to investigate the effect of size on rate of cooling

2 containers of same shape, one significantly larger than the other, e.g. beakers
2 thermometers
stopwatch or other timer
access to hot water CARE!

11.2 Investigating the effect of evaporation on the rate of cooling

Students are to plan their own investigation, so will ask for their own apparatus. However, they are likely to need the following.
2 or 3 test tubes or boiling tubes
2 or 3 thermometers
stopwatch or other timer
access to hot water CARE!

12.1 To find the conditions necessary for the germination of tomato seeds

5 test tubes, fitted with gauze or perforated zinc platforms
pyrogallol in NaOH solution CARE! (this is very caustic and should be handled only by the teacher, not students)
cotton wool
1 rubber bung to fit test tube
tomato seeds
wax pencil or other method of marking tubes

12.2 To find the effect of storage time on the germination rate of seeds

Students are to plan their own investigation, so will ask for their own apparatus. However, they are likely to need the following.
seeds of the same variety, of at least two different ages (e.g. from packets bought in previous years and in the current year)
dishes, e.g. Petri dishes
cotton wool or filter paper
access to dark environment, e.g. cupboard

12.3 To find out which part of a root is the growing region

Session 1:
soaked bean seeds
gas jar
blotting paper
Session 2:
blotting paper
Indian ink
pen or fine paintbrush
ruler

12.4 Measuring the rate of growth of a plant

Students are to plan their own investigation, so will ask for their own apparatus. However, they are likely to need the following.
at least 20 young seedlings of the same type of fast-growing plant, or soaked seeds to sow themselves
ruler
top-pan balance
thermometer
access to refrigerator

13.1 Cloning of sugar cane

3 sugar cane stems with buds
3 containers filled with soil

13.2 Investigating the structure of a flower

flower stalk of *Crotalaria* or other simple insect-pollinated flower, with flowers in various stages of development
hand lens
safety razor blade CARE!
tile
microscope slide
microscope
seeker

13.3 Pollination

Students are to plan their own investigation, so will ask for their own apparatus. However, they are likely to need the following.
coloured plastic or other material to make artificial flowers
little pots that can be filled with sugar solution
access to outdoor area on a sunny day, when bees are likely to be flying

13.4 Growing pollen tubes

4 cavity slides
Vaseline®
4 coverslips
labels for slides
variety of solutions. e.g. distilled water, 5% sucrose, 10% sucrose, 15% sucrose, each with a tiny amount of boric acid added
4 types of flowers with ripe pollen
seeker
microscope
access to incubator at 20 °C (slides must be left inside for at least 1 hour)

14.1 Flower colour in *Impatiens*

large spade or fork
Impatiens seeds
cuttings from red- and white-flowered *Impatiens* plants
2 plots in school grounds (each 5 m square), or 4 large boxes or half-drums filled with soil

14.2 Breeding beads

2 containers
150 beads of one colour
100 beads of a second colour

15.1 Measuring variation

ruler

17.1 Estimating the size of a bead population, using the mark, release, recapture technique

large tray or bucket
about 1000 beads of one colour and size
about 50 more beads of the same size, but a different colour

17.2 Making a rough estimate of the proportions of particles of different sizes in a soil sample

sample of soil, enough to quarter-fill a gas jar
gas jar
large stirring rod
access to water

17.3 To estimate the percentage of water in a soil sample

Session 1:
evaporating dish
spatula
top-pan balance
freshly collected soil sample
oven set at about 90 °C CARE!
Session 2:
soil sample from Session 1
top-pan balance

17.4 To estimate the percentage of humus in a soil sample

Session 1:
dried soil sample from Investigation 17.3
top-pan balance
Bunsen etc. and crucible, or oven at a very high temperature CARE!
Session 2:
cooled soil sample from Session 1
top-pan balance

17.5 To find the effect of lime on clay particles

small sample of powdered clay
small amount of calcium hydroxide CARE!
boiling tube
glass rod
spatula

18.1 To determine the environmental impact of an industry

No apparatus required.

18.2 To find out the effect of hurricanes on local building practices

No apparatus required.

18.3 To find out the sources of energy most used in a community

No apparatus required.

Appendix 2 To the teacher: School-based assessment (SBA) in Biology for CSEC

Three levels of understanding are necessary to enable teachers to carry out school-based assessment (SBA) competently and with fairness to both students and teachers.

A The overall philosophy behind SBA must be appreciated. In other words, why have SBA?

B The goals of SBA as they apply to a particular subject/discipline – that is, the parameters of achievement for SBA in the subject – must be understood.

C The necessity to plan carefully for, and to organise, the practical procedures for implementing assessment in the classroom should be recognised.

We shall consider each of these levels of understanding in turn.

A Why have SBA?

As teachers are aware, there are, from a time perspective, basically two ways of approaching the evaluation of students' learning. Assessment often takes place after specified blocks of time – for example, at the end of a term, semester or year. Public examinations, external to the school, are generally of this type.

Within the classroom, however, teachers must constantly monitor students' learning, and use the 'feedback' to inform their efforts to promote learning. This feedback may be obtained in a variety of ways: by oral questioning, written exercises, practical tasks, or student peer 'teaching assignments'.

This on-going assessment provides student and teacher with information as to where each student 'is'. Carefully done, this on-going evaluation gives a good picture of students' achievements, of their strengths and weaknesses, of their aptitudes and talents, and of the areas where they need greater challenges or additional help.

In SBA, CXC makes use of teachers' on-going evaluations. Thus, contributions from both 'on-going' and 'end-of-course' assessments are captured by the examining body. This allows for fairer evaluation of student performances.

B Goals for SBA in Biology

Of necessity, the inclusion of school-based assessment has meant that teachers must 'spell out', for the scrutiny of the Council's examiners, the criteria on which they base their judgements of students' work.

On the part of the Council, there has also been the necessity to delineate in its subject syllabuses the parameters for reporting SBA where it applies.

Teachers assess and guide students constantly, and often they respond to the student's needs without conscious thought. The Council requires that, in reporting on this on-going assessment, conscious and careful attention be given to particular aspects considered essential, not only for the students' understanding of the particular subject, but in order to give students skills which will be useful in their lives.

In Biology, requirements for the school-based assessments have been confined to skills associated with practical work. They are outlined as below in the syllabus (2002 edition, pages 5–7 with additional clarifications on pages 38–40). The specific expectations are listed as objectives.

Observation/Recording/Reporting

The ability to: select observations relevant to the particular activity; make accurate observations and minimise experimental errors; report and recheck unexpected results; select and use appropriate models of recording data or observations (for example, graphs, tables, diagrams); record observations, measurements, methods and techniques with due regard for precision, accuracy and units; present data in an appropriate manner, using the accepted convention of recording errors and uncertainties; organise and present information, ideas, descriptions and arguments clearly and logically in a complete report, using spelling, punctuation and grammar with an acceptable degree of accuracy; report accurately and concisely using scientific terminology and conventions as necessary.

Drawing

The ability to: make large, clear, accurate line representations of specimens, with appropriate labelling and annotations.

Manipulation/Measurement

The ability to: follow a detailed set or sequence of instructions; use techniques, apparatus and materials safely and effectively; make observations and measurements with due regard for precision and accuracy.

Planning/Design

The ability to: make predictions, develop hypotheses and devise means of carrying out investigations to test them; plan and execute experimental procedures in an appropriate sequence; modify an original plan or sequence of operations as a result of difficulties encountered in carrying out an experiment or obtaining unexpected results; take into account possible sources of error and danger in the design of an experiment; select and use appropriate equipment and techniques.

Analysis/Interpretation

The ability to: identify and recognise the component parts of a whole and interpret the relationships between those parts; identify causal factors and show how they interact with each other; infer, predict and draw conclusions; make necessary and accurate calculations and recognise the limitations and assumptions of data.

The groupings of skills given are one formulation of what are widely recognised as investigative and problem-solving skills. Acquisition of these skills is necessary for each individual to 'respond to the challenges of a rapidly changing world' (2002 edition of the Biology syllabus, page 2).

C Organising for SBA

The realities of responsible reporting demand that teachers plan carefully for SBA. They need to think through in detail the material they wish students to understand; to clarify in their own minds the concepts involved, and how best they might present them; to determine if, and when, they should use a practical approach in the particular situation, and what form this might take. Teachers also need to have a manageable and reliable strategy for recording their observations and assessment of student performance. This brings us to some variation of the familiar 'mark book'.

Preparing the records

Class reports The scores sent in to CXC originate from class records kept in the teacher's mark book. Two levels of records need to be kept.

1 The scores given for each exercise assessed, and the criteria used to obtain them (see page 43 Appendix 1, 2002 edition of the Biology syllabus and Table A2.1 on page 382 of this book).

2 The average score for each skill at each point at which CXC requires a record (see page 45, Appendix 1, 2002 edition of the Biology syllabus and Table A2.2 on page 382 of this book).

It is this average score that is transferred, for each student, to the CXC report form (see page 47, 2002 edition of the Biology syllabus).

CXC reports CXC requires school reports on SBA in Biology to be submitted on a form designed for the purpose (see page 47, Appendix 1, 2002 edition of the Biology syllabus). Average scores, obtained from several assessments on a particular skill, are recorded at selected points over the last two years of work prior to the examinations. The terminology 'last two years' is deliberate. It is expected that the syllabus outlined be covered over a two-year period, but it is made quite clear that this is on the assumption that students have already been introduced to basic physical and biological principles. It is particularly important that this introduction should have included exposure to the problem-solving skills. Each student should keep an indexed notebook, with numbered pages, which contains a record of *all practical exercises* done over the period prior to the examinations. For each practical assessed for CXC, the teacher should submit the mark scheme which guided its assessment. There should be a minimum of 18 practical exercises. Essential – but not exclusive – topic areas to be covered are photosynthesis, respiration, diffusion/osmosis, food tests, enzyme action, transpiration, response, locomotion, growth, reproduction, dispersal, genetics and field work.

Organising the class for assessment

It should always be remembered that school-based assessment is meant to help the student. It should not ever be seen as presenting an opportunity for subjecting students to continuous examination pressure all year round. The practical exercises on which the scores are based are expected to be those which teachers would normally use to support their teaching.

Although CXC has given the entire year as the assessment period for year 1, students should not be formally assessed early in the year. They should be allowed enough time to practise a skill before being assessed for CXC purposes. Additionally, no student should be denied needed assistance even while formal assessments are being made. Scores can easily be adapted to reflect the different levels of performance of students needing help as distinct from those who manage on their own.

A teacher may reasonably expect to assess about ten students in a class period on a skill. In reality, in most Caribbean schools, class sizes are 30 or more. In this situation, there are different strategies teachers may adopt to 'get around' the class within a time frame which does not allow some students the advantage of additional practice. These include the following:

1 *Team work* In schools with several class groups, teachers might arrange their work in order to assist each other for a formal recording. In this way, an entire class may be processed at the same time.

2 *Using varied exercises* A single teacher may use different exercises to assess portions of the class on the same skill at different sittings. Though the actual investigations may be different, the same skill task may be given in more than one investigation, and the same criteria used for its assessment.

3 *Using records* Several skills may be judged from written records handed in by students – for example, the ability to construct a graph from data collected, and explain relationships and patterns. Carefully chosen and taken oral reports may also be used where appropriate.

Carrying out the assessment

Although practical work should not be 'created' for the sake of recording scores for CXC, teachers should be aware of the potential of each practical as a vehicle for allowing students to display a particular skill. The skills to be tested at each stage of the course should also be taken into account. During the first year of the course, scores are required for observation/recording/reporting, drawing and manipulation/measurement. The cognitively more difficult skill of planning and designing is left for later, when students would be more mature, and have had more exposure.

Forward planning is, therefore, mandatory.

1 For each term (year if possible), decide ahead on the practical exercises which must be covered. This does not preclude spontaneous additions or changes which might be suggested by circumstances.

2 For each exercise, outline the work to be done (a) by the teacher beforehand, and possibly during the exercise and (b) by the student as he or she carries out the task.

3 Indicate all the skills which might be assessed during each exercise. These might usefully be put in order of their suitability for judging the particular skill, as seen by the teacher.

The later steps are, perhaps, more easily done for shorter spans, for example a week, especially for the inexperienced teacher. These involve:

4 Selecting from the lists prepared in step 3 the particular skill(s) to be assessed in the exercise to be carried out. The authors would advise a *maximum* of two skills from any one exercise, and preferably only one. Attempting to judge several skills from the same exercise results in unreliable scores. Teachers are also reminded that students should be corrected on, but not penalised for, one skill when another is being assessed.

5 Deciding on specific criteria to guide the teacher's judgement, and on how these criteria will be weighted to achieve scores on the 11-point scale given by CXC. Use the information to devise a check list/mark scheme for the assessment. (See Table A2.1 below.) Transfer the results to the teacher's mark book. (See Table A2.2 below.)

Several examples from exercises from the text are given below to illustrate steps 2–5. For Investigation 3.8, a possible check list/mark scheme for assessing Observation/reporting/recording (ORR) and the transferral of results to the teacher's mark book is illustrated.

The score in the last column is transferred to the teacher's mark book. CXC requires that there be at least four assessments over the two year period in observation/recording/reporting (ORR), drawing (Dr), manipulation/measurement (M/M) and analysis/interpretation (AI), and at least two in planning/design (PD) in the second year. Marks on each skill are averaged for each student. The total of these averages gives the student's mark for the year.

A similar record will be kept for Year 2, but with the addition of planning/design. For each student, the average mark for each skill and the total figures only will be transferred to the CXC report form for school based assessment in biology (see page 47, 2002 edition of the Biology syllabus). These records, for each group of students, must be presented to CXC by June 30 of Year 1, and for both years by April 30 of Year 2.

Table A2.1 Check list for assessing Investigation 3.8 Date:......................

Drawing graph Skill: ORR

Name	Criteria					Teacher's score	Score CXC scale
	Appropriate scale (1)	Axes choice, label (1)	Appropriate title (1)	Plotting – Accuracy/ Agreement with table (2)	Consistency, counts each concentration (2)	out of (7)	out of (10)
Boyd, D.	1	1	1	2	1	6	9
Chin, A.	1	1	1	1	2	6	9
King, S.	1	1	1	2	2	5	7
Smith, J.	1	1	1	2	2	7	10

Table A2.2 Teacher's Mark Book (Year 1) (Grade 10)

Skills	Observation/Recording/Reporting				Drawing			Manipulation/Measurement			Analysis/Interpretation			Total Yr. 1
Names/ Dates	Inv. 1 2/10	Inv. 2	Inv. 3	Avg. (10)	Inv. 1	Inv. 2	Avg. (10)	Inv.1	Inv.2	Avg. (10)	Inv.1	Inv.2	Avg. (10)	(40)
Boyd, D.	9													
Chin, A.	9													
King, S.	7													
Smith, J.	10													

Investigation 1.1 Studying an ecosystem

Teacher's preparation

1 Select a suitable area for study beforehand.
2 Carry out a preliminary investigation and find out the identities and habits of as many organisms as possible.
3 Construct a possible food web.

Students' task

1 Identify a range of plants and animals.
2 Collect decaying leaves and label.
3 Find disturbed soil and suggest what has caused the disturbance.
4 Make notes about large animals in the area.
5 Complete identifications in the laboratory.
6 Summarise class results in a table.
7 Make drawings of at least two animals.
8 Construct a food web using data collected.

Skills which could be assessed

Observation/Recording/Reporting
Drawing
Analysis/Interpretation

Skill selected for assessment

Analysis/Interpretation

Possible criteria for assessment

1 Identifies at least five previously unknown organisms, using keys and/or books and/or the internet. 2 points
2 Draws a correct food web, using his or her own results, those of others and information researched from elsewhere, including at least 10 different organisms, with arrows pointing in the correct direction. 3 points
3 Recognises and comments on the partial nature of the food web, and on the tentative nature of the conclusions drawn. 2 points

Scoring: Total = 7 points

Rating scale

Convert score out of 7 to a score out of 10
e.g. if the teacher's mark is 5/7,

$$\text{score on CXC scale} = \frac{(5 \times 10)}{7}$$

$$= 7 \text{ (to the nearest whole number)}$$

Investigation 3.8 The effect of substrate concentration on the rate of activity of catalase

Teacher's preparation

1 Obtain for each pair of students to set up apparatus:
two boiling tubes
rubber bung with tube
glass tubing as shown on page 52
clamps or other means of holding tubes firm
Irish or English potato
2 Have available enough for all pairs:
large cork borers
beakers or glass jars
distilled water
0.5 mol dm^{-3}, 1.0 mol dm^{-3}, 1.5 mol dm^{-3} and 2.0 mol dm^{-3} hydrogen peroxide
graph paper
timing device to measure seconds
means of measuring 10 cm^3 quantities

Students' task

1 Cut cylinders of potato and immerse in water.
2 Prepare apparatus as shown in diagram on page 52.
3 Prepare results table.
4 Add 10 cm^3 of 0.5 mol dm^{-3} hydrogen peroxide to tube 1, add water to tube 2 as shown.
5 Cut 10 thin slices of potato from cylinder. Place in tube 1, replace bung, shake slightly to separate.
6 Wait 45 seconds, then count and record in the table the number of bubbles seen in one minute.
7 Discard all contents of tube 1.
8 Repeat and record the bubble count twice, using fresh hydrogen peroxide and new slices of potato.
9 Repeat using solutions of 1.0, 1.5 and 2.0 mol dm^{-3} hydrogen peroxide.
10 Calculate mean (average) counts for each concentration of hydrogen peroxide and record in results table.
11 Draw graph with concentration of substrate on x-axis and mean number of bubbles on y-axis. Join points with a ruler, or draw smooth best fit line.

Skills which could be assessed

Observation/Recording/Reporting
Manipulation/Measurement
Analysis/Interpretation

Skills selected for assessment

Observation/Recording/Reporting
Manipulation/Measurement

Possible criteria for assessment – *Observation/Recording/Reporting*

Drawing graph

1 Correct values on x and y-axis, and both axes correctly labelled with units. 1 point
2 Appropriate choice of scales. 1 point
3 Appropriate title. 1 point
4 Accuracy of plotting – agreement with table. 2 points
5 Clear line drawn, either ruled point to point or smooth best fit. 1 point
6 Reasonable consistency in counts at each concentration of substrate. 2 points

Scoring: Total = 8 points

Rating scale

Convert score out of 8 to a score out of 10
e.g. if the teacher's mark is 5/8,

$$\text{score on CXC scale} = \frac{(5 \times 10)}{8}$$

$$= 6 \text{ (to the nearest whole number)}$$

Possible criteria for assessment – *Manipulation/Measurement*

1 Setting up apparatus. 2 points
2 Preparation of potato cylinders. 1 point
3 Cutting of potato slices (within 1–2 mm). 2 points
4 Using timing device. 1 point
5 Measurement of 10 cm^3 quantities (reading meniscus properly). 1 point

6 Measurement of 10 cm^3 quantities using correct concentration of hydrogen peroxide for each repetition of the exercise. 3 points

Rating scale

Teacher's score: mark/10. Score on CXC scale: mark/10.

Investigation 7.2 To see which part of a stem transports water and solutes

Teacher's preparation

1 Obtain *Impatiens* (balsam) or other easily 'seen through' plants, with root systems intact, microscopes and razor blades.
2 Prepare eosin solution.

Students' task

1 Wash roots of plant.
2 Place in eosin and leave overnight.
3 Set up microscope (use hand lens if not available).
4 Remove plant from eosin; wash roots carefully.
5 Cut stem sections from about half-way up.
6 Select and mount a section in water on a microscope slide. Cover with a coverslip.
7 Observe under the microscope and draw.
8 Answer questions in text on the investigation.

Skills which could be assessed

Observation/Recording/Reporting
Drawing
Manipulation/Measurement
Planning/Design (answer to question 3)
Analysis/Interpretation

Skill selected for assessment

Planning/Design (to be done after students have performed the experiment, to give reasonable basis for hypothesis)
Problem: how does a chosen environmental factor affect the rate at which dye is transported up the stem of an uprooted plant?

Possible criteria for assessment

1 States a hypothesis linking a relevant environmental factor (e.g. temperature, wind speed) to an effect on the rate of movement of dye up the plant. 2 points
2 Chooses suitable apparatus and materials, including choice of a suitable plant. 1 point
3 Describes how the variable being investigated would be changed, and suggests a range (e.g. if temperature, test at several values between 4 °C and 40 °C, or whatever can be achieved in laboratory conditions). 2 points
4 Lists at least two other variables to be kept constant (temperature, wind speed, humidity, concentration of dye, type of plant etc.) and states how they will be controlled. 2 points
5 Suggests what will be measured, how and when. 1 point
6 Repeats or replicates included in plan. 1 point
7 Makes reasonable suggestion of expected results. 1 point

Rating scale

Teacher's score: mark/10. Score on CXC scale: mark/10.

Investigation 9.1 Using a model arm to investigate the action of the biceps muscle

Teacher's preparation

1 Obtain model arm, spring balance, variety of masses. Set up demonstration bench.
2 Design results table.
NB It is assumed teachers may have only one model available sturdy enough to take weights. The exercise would then need to be carried out as a demonstration, but with students carrying out the tasks below.

Students' task

1 Hang masses and take readings on the spring balance.
2 Record readings in a table.
3 Answer questions in the text.

Skills which could be assessed

Observation/Recording/Reporting
Manipulation/Measurement
Analysis/Interpretation

Skill selected for assessment

Analysis/Interpretation

Possible criteria for assessment

Answers to questions – main points.
1 Correct answer. 1 point
2 Correct reading from table. 1 point
3 Correct position. 1 point
4 Reasonable answer linking force exerted with the position of attachment of the muscle. 2 points
5 Correct answer. 1 point
6 Correct answer. 1 point

Rating scale

Convert score out of 7 to a score out of 10
e.g. if the teacher's mark is 5/7,

$$\text{score on CXC scale} = \frac{(5 \times 10)}{7}$$

$$= 7 \text{ (to the nearest whole number)}$$

Investigation 10.4 To find out which part of the skin contains the most touch receptors

Teacher's preparation

1 Obtain enough pins for the class to work in pairs.
2 Design results table.

Students' task

1 Prepare results table.
2 Measure and maintain specific distances (2.0 cm and so on) between pins while performing experiment.
3 Record results.
4 Draw histogram.
5 Answer questions 1–3.

Skills which could be assessed

Observation/Recording/Reporting
Analysis/Interpretation

Skill selected for assessment

Observation/Recording/Reporting

Possible criteria for assessment

1	Results table complete.	1 point
2	Correct axes for histogram.	1 point
3	Title for histogram.	1 point
4	Readings in table correctly plotted in histogram.	2 points
5	Neat presentation.	1 point

Rating scale

Teacher's score: mark/6. Score on CXC scale: Teacher's mark ×10/6

Investigation 10.8 Examining the form and structure of the mammalian eye

Teacher's preparation

1 Obtain enough mammalian eyes for class use – no fewer than one between two students. (These can be collected over time and preserved.)
2 Provide blunt seekers, sharp blades/scalpels or warn students ahead to bring their own.
3 Provide cork mats or other suitable material for anchoring eyes for cutting.
4 Ensure plentiful supply of soap, warm water and towels for washing hands.

Students' task

1 Locate structures apparent on the outside of the eye: muscles, sclerotic, cornea, iris, pupil.
2 Draw and label the eye as it looks from the outside.
3 Cut through eye vertically.
4 Identify the internal structures, using the diagram on page 184 as a guide.

Skills which could be assessed

Observation/Recording/Reporting
Drawing

Skill selected for assessment

Drawing

Possible criteria for assessment

1	Accurate representation.	2 points
2	Clean lines.	1 point
3	Title.	1 point
4	Labelling.	2 poins
5	Magnification of drawing calculated.	1 point

Rating scale

Teacher's score: mark/7. Score on CXC scale: Teacher's mark ×10/7

Investigation 14.2 'Breeding' beads

Teacher's preparation

1 Provide beads of two colours. Have students assist by bringing their own sets.
2 Provide suitable unbreakable containers.

Students' task

1 Prepare a table for results.
2 Follow instructions 1 to 5.
3 Answer questions 1 to 4.

Skills which could be assessed

Analysis/Interpretation

Skill selected for assessment

Analysis/Interpretation

Possible criteria for assessment

(based on answers to questions)

1	Correct kind of offspring reported in first cross.	1 point
2	Ratios correct.	1 point
3	Reasonable explanation of comparison with expected ratios.	2 points
4	Reason for closing eyes when choosing beads.	1 point
5	Reason for replacing beads in container after 'mating'.	1 point

Rating scale

Teacher's score: mark/6. Score on CXC scale: Teacher's mark ×10/6

Investigation 18.2 To find out the effect of hurricanes on local building practice

Teacher's preparation

1 Be prepared to give guidance to students on sources of information, and provide stimulus material in the classroom.
2 Work out with students a very brief interview schedule they can use when they speak to residents.

Students' task

1 Put together a brief history of hurricanes in the country over the past 100 years.
2 Find out from libraries, museums, interviews with various residents and visits to particular sites the types of building which have best withsood hurricanes over the period.
3 Prepare a table to record the building materials used, the style and the shape of the roofs of the buildings.
4 Collect the same information for houses built in the last 20 years.
5 Work out suggestions for building for hurricane resistance.
6 Prepare written report.

Skills which could be assessed

Observation/Recording/Reporting
Analysis/Interpretation

Skill selected for assessment

Observation/Recording/Reporting

Possible criteria for assessment

The exercise will be marked initially out of 40.

1	Accuracy of information.	10 points
2	Adequacy of coverage.	10 points
3	Suitability of model for hurricane resistance based on information gathered.	10 points
4	Originality,	5 points
5	Neatness and arrangement of overall presentation.	5 points

Rating scale

Teacher's score: mark/40. Score on CXC scale: Teacher's score ×10/40

Appendix 3 Skills which may be assessed using the investigations in the text

Investigations		ORR	D	MM	PD	AI
1.1	Studying an ecosystem	✓	✓			✓
1.2	Do animals prefer particular types of plants to eat?	✓				✓
2.1	Looking at animal cells	✓	✓			
2.2	Looking at plant cells	✓	✓			
2.3	Demonstrating diffusion in a solution	✓				✓
2.4	Diffusion of substances through a membrane	✓		✓		✓
2.5	Measuring the rate of osmosis	✓		✓	✓	✓
2.6	Experiment to investigate the effect of different solutions on plant cells	✓	✓	✓		✓
2.7	Osmosis and potato strips	✓		✓	✓	✓
3.1	Testing foods for sugars	✓				
3.2	Testing foods for starch	✓				
3.3	Testing for lipids	✓				
3.4	Testing for protein	✓				
3.5	Investigating the effect of pH on the activity of catalase	✓		✓		✓
3.6	Investigating the effect of temperature on the activity of catalase	✓		✓	✓	✓
3.7	The effect of temperature on the activity of amylase	✓		✓		✓
3.8	The effect of substrate concentration on the rate of activity of catalase	✓		✓		✓
4.1	Looking at the epidermis of a leaf	✓	✓			
4.2	Which kind of fertilizer helps plants grow best?	✓	✓			✓
4.3	Testing a leaf for starch	✓				
4.4	To see if light is needed for photosynthesis	✓	✓	✓		✓
4.5	To see if chlorophyll is needed for photosynthesis	✓		✓		✓
4.6	To see if carbon dioxide is needed for photosynthesis	✓		✓		✓
4.7	To show that oxygen is produced in photosynthesis	✓		✓		✓
4.8	Investigating the effect of light intensity on photosynthesis	✓		✓	✓	✓
5.1	To find out which of three sets of food would provide the most balanced meal	✓			✓	✓
5.2	Observing the digestive system of a mammal	✓	✓			
6.1	To show that carbon dioxide is produced by a respiring mammal	✓				✓
6.2	To measure the rate of uptake of oxygen during respiration in a small invertebrate	✓		✓		✓
6.3	Comparing the energy content of two kinds of food	✓		✓	✓	✓
6.4	Investigating heat production by germinating peas	✓				✓
6.5	Investigating the production of carbon dioxide by anaerobic respiration	✓			✓	✓
6.6	Examining lungs	✓				
6.7	Using a syringe to show how the diaphragm works	✓				✓
6.8	Comparing the carbon dioxide content of inspired air and expired air	✓				✓
6.9	Investigating how breathing rate changes with exercise	✓				✓
6.10	Investigating how recovery time varies with fitness	✓			✓	✓
6.11	Investigating the structure of gills	✓	✓			✓
6.12	The effect of animals and plants on the carbon dioxide concentration in water	✓		✓		✓
7.1	To find the effect of exercise on the rate of heart beat	✓				✓
7.2	To see which part of a stem transports water and solutes	✓	✓	✓	✓	✓
7.3	To see which surface of a leaf loses most water	✓				✓
7.4	To measure the rate of transpiration of a potted plant	✓				✓
7.5	Using a potometer to compare rates of transpiration under different conditions	✓		✓		✓
9.1	Using a model arm to investigate the action of the biceps muscle	✓		✓		✓
10.1	Do woodlice prefer light or dark?	✓				✓
10.2	The response of an invertebrate to humidity	✓			✓	✓
10.3	To measure reaction time	✓				✓
10.4	To find out which part of the skin contains the most touch receptors	✓		✓		✓
10.5	To find out which parts of the tongue can taste which flavours	✓				✓
10.6	Can you always see the image?					
10.7	Observing the effect of light on the pupil	✓				✓
10.8	Examining the form and structure of a mammalian eye	✓	✓			
10.9	To find out how shoots respond to light	✓	✓			✓
10.10	To find out how roots respond to gravity	✓			✓	✓
10.11	To find out which part of a shoot is sensitive to light	✓		✓		✓
10.12	To find out how auxin affects shoots	✓		✓		✓

Investigations		ORR	D	MM	PD	AI
11.1	Experiment to investigate the effect of size on rate of cooling	✓		✓		✓
11.2	Investigating the effect of evaporation on the rate of cooling	✓		✓	✓	✓
12.1	To find the conditions necessary for the germination of tomato seeds	✓				✓
12.2	To find the effect of storage time on the germination rate of seeds	✓			✓	✓
12.3	To find out which part of a root is the growing region	✓	✓	✓		✓
12.4	Measuring the rate of growth of a plant	✓	✓	✓	✓	✓
13.1	Cloning of sugar cane	✓				✓
13.2	Investigating the structure of a flower	✓	✓			
13.3	Pollination	✓		✓	✓	✓
13.4	Growing pollen tubes	✓		✓		✓
14.1	Flower colour in *Impatiens*					✓
14.2	'Breeding' beads					✓
15.1	Measuring variation	✓		✓		✓
17.1	Estimating the size of a bead population, using the mark, release, recapture technique	✓				✓
17.2	Making a rough estimate of the proportions of particles of different sizes in a soil sample	✓				✓
17.3	To estimate the percentage of water in a soil sample	✓		✓		✓
17.4	To estimate the percentage of humus in a soil sample	✓		✓		✓
17.5	To find the effect of lime on clay particles	✓		✓		✓
18.1	To determine the environmental impart of an industry	✓				
18.2	To find out the effect of hurricanes on local building practices	✓				✓
18.3	To find out the sources of energy most used in a community					✓

Key

ORR Observation/Recording/Reporting
D Drawing
MM Manipulation/Measurement
PD Planning/Design
AI Analysis/Interpretation

Glossary

abiotic factor an environmental factor caused by non-living components – for example, light intensity, temperature

absorption the uptake of nutrients from the alimentary canal into the bloodstream

accommodation the change of shape of the lens, in order to focus on objects at different distances

acquired characteristics characteristics that develop during an organism's lifetime, as a result of its environment; they cannot be inherited

active immunity being immune as a result of having made your own antibodies against a pathogen

active site the part of an enzyme molecule into which its substrate fits

active transport the movement of a substance across a cell membrane against its concentration gradient, using energy provided by the cell

addictive a drug is said to be addictive when a person is unable to stop craving it

ADH antidiuretic hormone; a hormone secreted by the pituitary gland, which causes the kidneys to reabsorb water from urine

adipose tissue a layer of cells which store fat, found beneath the skin of mammals

adolescence the time at which a person approaches sexual maturity

ADP adenosine diphosphate; it can be made into ATP with the addition of a phosphate group and energy

adrenaline a hormone secreted by the adrenal glands, which prepares the body for flight or fight

adventitious roots roots that grow out of a stem

aerobic respiration the breakdown of glucose by combining it with oxygen, releasing energy that a cell can use

afterbirth the placenta, as it leaves the body after the baby has been born

AIDS acquired immune deficiency syndrome; the disease caused by HIV

air spaces gaps between cells in the spongy mesophyll of a leaf, through which gases can easily diffuse

albinism a condition caused by a recessive allele of the gene that codes for the brown pigment melanin, in which no melanin is produced

alcohol another term for ethanol; a chemical made by yeast during anaerobic respiration

alimentary canal the long tube through which food passes between ingestion and egestion

alkaloids waste products of plants; some alkaloids are toxic to animals

allele one of two or more different forms of a gene

alveolus (plural: alveoli) an air sac in the lungs, where gas exchange occurs

amino acids molecules that can link together in long chains to form proteins; they contain carbon, hydrogen, oxygen and nitrogen, and sometimes sulfur

ammonia NH_3; ammonia is a nitrogenous excretory product of animals

amnion a protective membrane surrounding a developing fetus

amniotic fluid viscous fluid secreted by the amnion, which supports and protects a developing fetus

Amphibia amphibians – vertebrates with smooth skins; frogs, toads, newts and salamanders

amylase a carbohydrase found in saliva and pancreatic juice, which breaks down starch to maltose

anaemia an illness caused by a lack of haemoglobin in the blood; there are many causes, such as not having enough iron in the diet

anaerobic respiration the breakdown of glucose without using oxygen, releasing a small amount of energy that a cell can use

analgesic a drug that relieves pain

androgens hormones which cause male characteristics

annual a plant that completes its life cycle in one year

anorexia a dieting illness in which a person perceives themselves as being fatter than they really are, and eats so little food that illness and even death can result

antagonistic muscles muscles that work as a pair, one causing extension and the other flexing of a joint

anther the part of a stamen in which pollen is produced

antibiotic a drug that kills bacteria in the human body, without damaging human cells

antibodies chemicals secreted by lymphocytes, which attach to antigens and help to destroy them

antigens chemicals on the surfaces of pathogens, which are recognised as foreign by the body

anti-malarial drug a drug that attacks the protozoan that causes malaria

anus the exit from the alimentary canal, controlled by a sphincter muscle

aorta the largest artery in the body; it carries oxygenated blood from the heart to the body organs

appendages in a mammalian skeleton, the limb bones, connected to the axis by girdles

Arachnida arthropods with four pairs of legs; the spiders and scorpions

artery a vessel that transports blood away from the heart

arthritis a disease in which the surfaces of the joints become rough, making movement difficult and painful

Arthropoda the invertebrates with an exoskeleton and jointed legs

artificial selection the choice by a farmer or grower of only the 'best' parents to breed, generation after generation

asexual reproduction the production of new organisms that are genetically identical to the parent

atherosclerosis the hardening of the walls of arteries, caused by the build-up of plaque containing cholesterol

atoll a coral reef formed on the top of an undersea volcano, far from land

ATP adenosine triphosphate; it can be broken down to ADP with the release of a phosphate group and energy

atrioventricular valves the valves between the atria and ventricles in the heart, which prevent the blood flowing back up into the atria

atrium (plural: atria) one of the two upper chambers of the heart, which receive blood from the veins

autonomic nervous system the part of the nervous system that controls heart rate, breathing and other functions of the internal organs

autotrophic nutrition making organic nutrients using only inorganic substances – for example, by photosynthesis

auxin a plant hormone which causes cells to elongate

Aves birds – vertebrates with feathers and a beak

axis in a mammalian skeleton, the skull, vertebral column, pelvic girdle and pectoral girdle

axon a nerve fibre that conducts impulses away from the cell body

balanced diet a diet containing some of each of the different types of nutrients, in a suitable quantity and proportions

barrier reef a coral reef formed well away from the shore, but often running roughly parallel with the shoreline; there is usually a very wide and deep lagoon between the barrier reef and the land

bases one of four components of a DNA molecule, which produce the genetic code

biceps muscle a muscle in the upper arm which causes the elbow to bend when it contracts

bicuspid valve the valve between the left atrium and ventricle

bile a greenish liquid made in the liver, stored in the gall bladder and emptied into the small intestine, where it helps to emulsify fats

bile duct a tube that carries bile from the gall bladder to the duodenum

bile pigments coloured substances found in bile; they are the breakdown products of haemoglobin

bile salts substances in bile that help to emulsify fats

biodegradable able to be broken down (digested) by microorganisms

biotic factor an environmental factor caused by other living organisms– for example, predation, competition

bladder an organ in which urine is stored

blind spot the part of the retina where the optic nerve leaves; there are no receptor cells here

blood clotting the formation of a blood clot, involving the production of fibrin fibres in which blood cells are trapped

blood vessels tubes that carry blood around the body

bolus a ball of food mixed with saliva, formed in the mouth before swallowing

bone a strong, hard tissue containing living cells surrounded by a matrix of calcium phosphate

bone marrow the tissue in the centre of a bone, in which red and white blood cells are produced

Bowman's capsule the cup-shaped structure at the start of a nephron, where filtration occurs

brain the part of the central nervous system in the head; it coordinates actions in all parts of the body

breathing muscular movements which cause air to move into and out of the lungs

brewing using yeast to convert sugars from barley seeds to alcohol, to make beer

bronchioles the small tubes into which the bronchi branch

bronchus (plural: bronchi) one of the two tubes into which the trachea branches, carrying air into each lung

bulimia a dieting illness in which a person gorges on food and then makes themselves vomit

caffeine a drug found in coffee and cola drinks; it is a mild stimulant

calcium oxalate an excretory substance of plants

calcium phosphate a hard substance that makes up a large proportion of bone tissue

cambium a thin layer of dividing cells in a plant

cancer a disease in which cells divide uncontrollably, producing lumps (tumours)

canines the teeth next to the incisors; they are long and pointed in carnivores

cannabis the plant from which marijuana (ganja) is obtained

capillarity the movement of water up a narrow tube

capillary a tiny blood vessel that delivers blood to the body tissues

carbohydrase an enzyme that catalyses the breakdown of carbohydrates

carbohydrates starches and sugars; substances whose molecules contain carbon, hydrogen and oxygen

carbon monoxide a gas produced by incomplete combustion; it is toxic to animals because it combines irreversibly with haemoglobin, preventing the transport of oxygen round the body

carcinogen a substance which increases the risk of a person's body developing cancer

cardiac arrest sometimes called a heart attack; the heart stops beating

cardiac muscle the muscle of which the heart is made

carnivore an animal that eats other animals

carpel the female part of a flower

cartilage a strong, flexible smooth tissue which covers the ends of bones and joints

catalase an enzyme found in almost all living tissues, which catalyses the breakdown of hydrogen peroxide to water and oxygen

catalyst a substance that speeds up a chemical reaction without itself being changed

cataract a condition in which the lens of the eye becomes cloudy

cell the basic unit of life; cells contain DNA and are bounded by a cell membrane

cell sap a solution of sugars and other substances inside the vacuole of a plant cell

cell surface membrane a very thin layer of lipid and protein that surrounds every living cell; often called the plasma membrane, or simply the cell membrane

cellulose a polysaccharide carbohydrate which forms fibres and is found in the cell walls of plant cells

cement a substance that holds the root of a tooth in the jaw

central nervous system the brain and spinal cord

cerebellum the part of the brain which controls muscle coordination

cerebral hemisphere one of the two sides of the cerebrum

cerebrum the part of the brain in which conscious thought occurs

cervix the entrance to the uterus from the vagina

chemical digestion the breakdown of large molecules of food into smaller ones, done by enzymes

Chilopoda carnivorous arthropods with many pairs of legs; centipedes

chlorofluorocarbons CFCs; chemicals that were used widely in the past for refrigeration and that damage the ozone layer

chlorophyll a green, light-absorbing pigment found inside chloroplasts in plant cells

chloroplast an organelle found in some plant cells, which contains chlorophyll and where photosynthesis takes place

Chordata the vertebrates

choroid a black layer inside the eye, which absorbs light

chromosomes long DNA molecules, which each contain many genes; they are found in the nucleus of a cell

chyme the mixture of enzymes, hydrochloric acid and food in the stomach

cilia tiny extensions on the surface of a cell, which can wave in unison and cause fluids next to the cell to move

ciliary muscle a ring of muscle around the lens, which can change its shape

circulatory system the network of blood vessels and the heart

cirrhosis a disease of the liver in which the cells are permanently damaged

class a group of families of organisms with similar characteristics, e.g. insects

clay small soil particles; they tend to form a soil that holds water and does not drain well

climax community the final community of organisms at the end of a succession

clone a group of genetically identical organisms

Cnidaria the jellyfish and sea anemones

codominance incomplete dominance; a situation in which both alleles in a heterozygote have an effect on the phenotype

coil an IUD; a device which is inserted into the uterus and prevents pregnancy

collagen a tough, stretchy protein found in bones and skin

colon the first part of the large intestine, in which water is absorbed

commensalism a type of symbiosis in which one partner benefits and the other does not, although it does not suffer either

communicable disease transmissable disease; a disease that can be caught from someone else; communicable diseases are caused by pathogens

community all the organisms, of all the different species, living in an area at the same time

compact bone the type of bone tissue found near the outside of the bone, with few spaces

competition an interaction between organisms that occurs when both need the same resource which is in short supply

complex sugar a disaccharide; a carbohydrate whose molecules are made of two sugar units

condensation changing from a gas to a liquid

condensation reaction linking together small molecules to form long chains

condom a sheath which can be pulled over the penis to prevent sperm or pathogens passing from one partner to the other during sexual intercourse

cones receptor cells in the retina which are only responsive to bright light, and see in colour; they are mostly found in the fovea

conjunctiva a thin, transparent tissue that covers the front of the eye

continuous variation differences in the features of a group of organisms in which there are no definite categories; each individual's features can lie anywhere between two extremes

contraceptive pill a pill containing oestrogen and progesterone, which prevents the production of eggs and therefore fertilisation

contraction the shortening of a muscle

control a part of an experimental set-up which can be used as a base for comparison with other parts, when investigating the effect of one particular factor

coordination communication between different parts of the body, enabling them to work together

cork cambium a thin layer of dividing cells in the bark of a tree, which can produce new bark cells

corm a short, swollen underground stem

cornified layer a layer of dead cells containing keratin, forming a protective layer in skin

coronary arteries blood vessels that carry oxygenated blood to the cardiac muscle in the wall of the heart

corpus luteum the structure that forms in an ovary after an egg has been released; it secretes progesterone

cortex in a kidney, the outer layer; in a plant stem or root, a tissue made of typical plant cells (usually, however, without chloroplasts)

cotyledons food storage structures in a seed, which sometimes come above ground during germination and begin to photosynthesise

cranial reflex a reflex action in which the nerve impulse passes through the brain

cross-pollination the transfer of pollen from the anther of one plant to the stigma of another plant of the same species

crown the part of a tooth that is visible above the gum

Crustacea arthropods with more than four pairs of jointed legs and which breathe through gills; they include crabs and woodlice

cuticle a layer of wax on the surface of a leaf

cuttings pieces taken from a plant, such as part of a root, stem or leaf, that can grow into complete new plants

cystic fibrosis a condition caused by a recessive allele of a gene that affects the production of mucus in the lungs and digestive system

deamination a metabolic reaction that takes place in the liver, in which the nitrogen-containing part of amino acids is removed

deciduous a plant that drops most of its leaves at a particular time of year (e.g. in winter, in a dry season)

deciduous teeth the first set of teeth, which fall out and are replaced by permanent teeth; also called milk teeth

decomposer an organism that feeds on waste material or dead organisms; many bacteria and fungi are decomposers

deficiency disease sometimes called nutritional deficiency disease; an illness caused by a lack of a nutrient in the diet

denatured an enzyme is said to be denatured when its molecule has changed shape so much that the substrate can no longer fit into it

dendrite a very short nerve fibre that conducts impulses towards the cell body of a neurone

dendron a nerve fibre that conducts impulses towards the cell body of a neurone

denitrifying bacteria bacteria that obtain their energy by converting nitrate ions into nitrogen gas

density the number of individuals of a species in a particular area

dental caries tooth decay, caused by bacteria feeding on food remains left on the teeth

dentine a living layer found beneath the enamel in a tooth

deoxygenated blood blood containing only a little oxygen

depressant a drug that inhibits the nervous system and slows it down

diabetes mellitus (often called simply diabetes) a condition in which insulin fails to control blood glucose levels correctly

dialysis exchange of substances between two solutions through a partially permeable membrane; dialysis machines are used in the treatment of people with kidney failure

diaphragm a domed sheet of tissue which separates the abdomen from the thorax; when it contracts it flattens, drawing air into the lungs

diaphragm (cap) a flexible ring, often made of rubber, that can cover the cervix and prevent the entry of sperm to the uterus

diastole the stage of a heart beat in which the muscles in the heart relax

dichotomous key a set of paired descriptions which can be used to identify an unknown organism

diet the food eaten in one day

diffusion the net movement of particles from a place where they are in a high concentration, to where they are in a lower concentration, as a result of their random motion

digestion the breakdown of large nutrient molecules into smaller ones, so that they are able to be absorbed through the walls of the alimentary canal and into the blood

digestive enzymes enzymes which break down large nutrient molecules in the alimentary canal

digestive system all the organs that work together to carry out digestion, consisting of the alimentary canal, liver and pancreas

diploid cell a cell containing two complete sets of chromosomes

Diplopoda herbivorous arthropods with many pairs of legs; millipedes

disaccharide a complex sugar; a carbohydrate whose molecules are made of two sugar units

discontinuous variation differences in the features of a group of organisms where each fits into one of a few clearly defined categories

disease a condition in which the body does not work normally; some diseases are caused by microorganisms but others – for example, arthritis – are not

dispersal spreading out over a wide area

DNA the chemical from which genes and chromosomes are made

dominant a dominant allele has an effect even if a recessive allele is present

dormant a condition in which an organism shuts its metabolism down, so that it can survive in adverse conditions

double circulatory system a system in which blood passes twice through the heart on one complete circuit of the body

Down's syndrome a genetic condition in which a person has three copies of chromosome 21

droplet infection the entry of a pathogen to the body in tiny droplets of moisture floating in the air

drug dependency unable to manage without a drug

drug tolerance a condition in which the body requires more and more of a drug in order to achieve the same effect as in the past

dry mass the mass of an organism after all water has been removed

ductless glands glands of the endocrine system, which secrete hormones directly into the blood

duodenum the first part of the small intestine, into which the pancreatic duct and bile duct open

Echinodermata the sea urchins and sea cucumbers

ecology the study of living organisms in their environment

ecosystem the living organisms and the non-living things in an area; they interact with one another

ectothermic poikilothermic; unable to regulate body temperature physiologically; the organism's temperature varies with that of its environment

edaphic to do with the soil

effector a part of the body that responds to a stimulus, e.g. a muscle or a gland

egestion the removal of undigested food, in the form of faeces, through the anus

egg a female gamete

ejaculation the forcing of semen out of the penis, a result of muscular contractions

element a substance made of one kind of atom

embryo a young organism before birth, and before all the body organs have formed

emphysema a disease in which the walls of the alveoli in the lungs break down, reducing the surface area for gas exchange

emulsification breaking large globules of fat into tiny droplets, so that they mix easily with water

emulsion a mixture of two liquids that cannot dissolve in one another – for example, oil and water – in which one liquid forms tiny droplets which float in the other

enamel the outer layer of a tooth; the hardest substance made by animals

endocrine system the endocrine glands, which secrete hormones

endoskeleton a supporting structure inside an organism's body; humans have endoskeletons

endosperm a storage tissue present in some seeds, e.g. cereal grains

endothermic homeothermic; able to regulate body temperature; the body temperature is independent of the temperature of the environment

energy protein malnutrition EPM; a condition in a child resulting from not having enough to eat over a long period of time

environment all the living (biotic) and non-living (abiotic) factors an organism encounters during its life

environmental factor a feature of the environment that affects a living organism

environmental hazard a feature of the environment that could cause harm to living organisms

enzymes proteins which catalyse metabolic reactions

ephemeral a plant that completes its life cycle in weeks or months

epidermis a tissue made up of a single layer of cells which covers the top and bottom of a leaf, and the outside of the stem and root

epiglottis a flap of cartilage which covers the entrance to the trachea when food is swallowed

epiphyte a plant that grows on another, but does not take nutrients from it

epithelium a layer of cells covering a surface in an animal, e.g. the cells lining the trachea

EPM energy protein malnutrition; a condition in a child resulting from not having enough to eat over a long period of time

euphoria a condition in which a person forgets all their worries and feels completely happy

evaporation changing from a liquid to a gas, at temperatures below boiling point

evergreen a plant that keeps its leaves all the year round

excretion the removal of metabolic waste products from the body

excretory product a waste substance produced by a metabolic reaction, which must be removed from the body

exoskeleton a supporting structure on the outside of an organism's body; insects have exoskeletons

extensor muscle a muscle that causes a limb to straighten when it contracts

eyelid a flap of skin that can cover the eye to protect it

F1 generation the offspring from a parent homozygous for a dominant allele and a parent homozygous for the recessive allele

factor VIII one of several different substances in the blood that help it to clot

faeces the remains of undigested food and old cells from the lining of the alimentary canal, which are egested through the anus

Fallopian tube the tube leading from an ovary to the uterus

fatty acids molecules containing carbon, hydrogen and a very small amount of oxygen, which can form part of a lipid molecule

feed to take in and use chemicals that provide energy or material for building cells

fermentation the breakdown of glucose by yeast, using anaerobic respiration; it produces carbon dioxide and alcohol

fertilisation the fusion of the nuclei of two gametes

fetus a young organism before birth, once all the body organs have formed

fibres structures that help to hold a tooth in the jaw, allowing some movement

fibrin a fibrous protein, formed from fibrinogen during blood clotting

fibrinogen a soluble protein found in blood plasma, which changes to the fibrous protein fibrin when a blood vessel is damaged, helping to form a blood clot

fibrous joint a joint in which two bones are connected by fibres and cannot move

fibrous root system the type of root system found in grasses, where many fine roots branch out from the base of the stem

filament the stalk of a stamen

first trophic level the first stage in a food chain, always occupied by a producer, which is generally a plant

flaccid a term used to describe a cell that has lost a lot of water, becoming soft and floppy

flexor muscle a muscle that causes a limb to bend when it contracts

follicle a space inside an ovary in which an egg develops

food chain the sequence of organisms through which energy passes after entering an ecosystem

food web several interlinking food chains

fossil fuel a substance that can be combusted to release energy, formed millions of years ago from the partially-decomposed and compressed bodies of organisms

fovea the part of the retina in which cones are most tightly packed

frequency the percentage of quadrats in which a species is found

fringing reef a coral reef that runs roughly parallel to the shoreline, not far from the shore

fruit an ovary of a plant after fertilisation; it contains seeds

FSH follicle stimulating hormone; a hormone secreted by the pituitary gland which causes the development of eggs in the ovaries

fully permeable able to let most substances pass through

gall bladder a small organ within the liver, where bile is stored

gametes sex cells, e.g. eggs and sperm

gas exchange the entry of oxygen into an organism's body, and the loss of carbon dioxide

gastroenteritis an infection of the stomach, causing vomiting

gene a part of a chromosome (a length of DNA) that codes for the production of one protein, or for one characteristic

gene technology the manipulation of the genes of an organism

generic name the first word in a binomial; the name of the genus to which an organism belongs

genetic diagram the conventional way to set out a genetic cross

genetic engineering placing a gene from one organism into another, often of a different species

genotype the genes an organism possesses

gestation period the time between fertilisation and birth

gibberellin a plant hormone which causes stems to grow taller

gill an organ in which gas exchange takes place in a fish or other aquatic organism

gill bar a piece of bone that supports a fish's gills

gill pouches the spaces between the gills of a fish, through which water flows

gill rakers stiff structures attached to a fish's gills, which filter out particles from the water as it flows over the gills

glaucoma a condition in which the pressure of fluid in the eye becomes too great

glomerulus a tangle of blood capillaries in a Bowman's capsule in the kidney

glucagon a hormone secreted by the pancreas, which increases blood glucose level

glucose a monosaccharide (simple sugar); the form in which carbohydrate is transported in the blood of animals; its molecular formula is $C_6H_{12}O_6$

glycerol a molecule containing carbon, hydrogen and oxygen, and which can form part of a lipid molecule

glycogen the polysaccharide that is used as an energy store in animal cells and fungi

goblet cells cells which secrete mucus

gonads organs in which gametes are made; ovaries and testes

Graafian follicle a space inside an ovary containing a mature egg

grafting producing a new plant by joining a piece of the desired plant to the roots of another

greenhouse effect the warming effect of carbon dioxide, methane and other greenhouse gases, on the Earth

growth an irreversible increase in mass or complexity of an organism

growth hormone a hormone secreted by the pituitary gland which causes growth

guard cell one of two sausage-shaped cells between which there is a hole called a stoma; the guard cells can change shape to open and close the stoma

guide-lines markings on petals which lead insects towards the centre of the flower

habitat the place where an organism lives

haemoglobin a red pigment that transports oxygen; it is a protein and is found inside red blood cells

hair follicle an indentation in the skin from which a hair grows

hallucinogen a drug that causes a person's brain to distort reality

haploid cell a cell containing only a single set of chromosomes

health hazard something that poses a risk to health

heart a muscular organ which contracts and relaxes regularly to pump blood through the circulatory system

heart attack sometimes called cardiac arrest; the heart stops beating

heart disease a condition in which the heart muscle is unable to work normally – for example, because of the development of plaques in the coronary arteries

hepatic artery the artery that carries oxygenated blood to the liver

hepatic portal vein the blood vessel that carries blood from the alimentary canal to the liver

hepatic vein the vein that carries deoxygenated blood away from the liver

herbaceous plant a plant that does not have a woody stem

herbivore an animal that eats plants

hereditary disease a disease caused by faulty genes, which can be passed from parent to offspring

hermaphrodite an organism that can produce both male and female gametes

heterotrophic nutrition feeding on organic substances; this is the way that animals feed

heterozygous having two different alleles of a gene

hilum the scar where a seed was attached to a fruit

HIV positive having antibodies in the blood which have been produced as a result of exposure to HIV

HIV/AIDS HIV is the human immunodeficiency virus, which causes AIDS

homeostasis the maintenance of a constant internal environment

homeothermic endothermic; able to regulate body temperature; the body temperature is independent of the temperature of the environment

homologous chromosomes the two chromosomes of a pair in a diploid cell; they have genes for the same features at the same positions

homozygous having two copies of the same allele

hormone a chemical secreted by an endocrine gland, which affects target organs in a different part of the body

host an organism on which a parasite lives and feeds

humus the partly decayed remains of living organisms or their waste products, found in soil

hydrochloric acid a strong acid; it is produced in the stomach where it helps to destroy bacteria

hydrolysis breaking down large molecules into small ones, by the addition of water; this is done, for example, by digestive enzymes in the alimentary canal

hypertension high blood pressure

hypha (plural: hyphae) one of the long, thin threads of which the body of a fungus is made; each hypha is just one cell thick

hypothalamus a part of the brain which is involved in temperature regulation and osmoregulation

ileum the longest part of the small intestine, in which most digested nutrients are absorbed

immune able to fight off a particular type of pathogen before it causes any symptoms in the body

implantation the movement of a young embryo into the lining of the uterus, and its attachment there

incisors chisel-shaped teeth at the front of the mouth

incomplete dominance codominance; a situation in which both alleles in a heterozygote have an effect on the phenotype

incubation period the time between infection and the development of disease symptoms

infection the entry of a pathogen to the body

infectious disease a disease caused by a pathogen, which can be passed from one person to another

ingestion taking food into the mouth

inorganic a term used to describe substances that are not made by living organisms

Insecta arthropods with three pairs of legs and, usually, two pairs of wings

insulin a hormone secreted by the pancreas, which reduces blood glucose level

integuments the protective coverings around an ovule

intercostal muscles muscles between the ribs, which help to produce breathing movements

interspecific competition competition between members of different species

intervertebral discs discs of cartilage between the vertebrae

intraspecific competition competition between members of the same species

iris the coloured part of the eye, which controls the amount of light allowed through to the lens

irritability sensitivity; the ability to sense and respond to stimuli

islets of Langerhans groups of cells in the pancreas which secrete insulin and glucagon

IUD intrauterine device; a device which is inserted into the uterus and prevents pregnancy

jejunum the middle section of the small intestine

joint a place where two bones meet

keratin a tough, waterproof protein found in skin

key a set of paired descriptions which can be followed through to identify an unknown organism

kingdom the largest grouping in the classification system

labour muscular contractions that bring about the birth of a baby

lactase an enzyme that breaks down the disaccharide lactose into glucose and galactose

lactation production of milk by mammary glands

lamellae the many tiny flaps of tissue in a fish's gills; they increase the surface area for gas exchange

lamina the flat part of a leaf; the leaf blade

large intestine the colon and rectum

larynx the voice box; it contains cords which vibrate when air passes over them, making sounds

lenticel a break in the bark of a woody plant, allowing gases to enter and leave the tissues inside the stem

LH luteinising hormone; a hormone secreted by the pituitary gland which causes an egg to be released from an ovary

ligament a strong, stretchy cord that joins two bones together at a synovial joint

light microscope a microscope that produces a magnified image by sending light rays through the specimen and lenses

lignin a tough, waterproof material that makes up the walls of xylem vessels; wood is mostly lignin

lime calcium hydroxide; it helps to improve the structure of clay soils

limiting factor an environmental factor which prevents a reaction happening any faster, or a population growing any more

lipase an enzyme that digests fats (lipids) to fatty acids and glycerol

lipids fats, oils and waxes

liver a large organ in the abdomen, with many different roles including the control of blood glucose concentration and the breakdown of toxins

locomotion movement of the whole body from one place to another

lumen the space in the centre of a tube

lungs soft, dark pink organs in the chest cavity, well-supplied with blood and with millions of tiny air sacs (alveoli), where gas exchange occurs

lymph the fluid found inside lymph vessels, formed from tissue fluid

lymph nodes organs in which large numbers of white blood cells (which can destroy bacteria or toxins) collect

lymphocytes white blood cells that secrete antibodies

lysozyme a bacteria-killing enzyme found in tears

malignant a type of tumour in which cells can break away and begin to produce new tumours in other parts of the body; a cancerous tumour

Malpighian layer the part of the skin in which new cells are produced

maltase a carbohydrase found in the small intestine, which breaks down maltose to glucose

maltose a disaccharide produced by the digestion of starch

Mammalia the mammals – vertebrates with hair, who feed their young on milk from mammary glands

mark, release, recapture a method used for estimating the population of mobile animals

marrow the central part of a bone, in which red and white blood cells are produced

mechanical digestion the breakdown of large pieces of food to smaller ones, increasing their surface area; it is done by teeth in the mouth and by the contraction of muscles in the stomach wall

medulla the middle layer of a kidney

medulla oblongata the part of the brain which controls breathing and heart rate

meiosis a type of cell division used to produce gametes; it produces four haploid, genetically different cells from one diploid parent cell

melanin a brown pigment which protects the skin from ultraviolet light

memory cells white blood cells that have been exposed to a particular antigen and remain in the blood after infection; they are able to respond rapidly if the same antigen enters the body on another occasion

meninges the membranes that surround the brain

menstruation the loss of the uterus lining through the vagina

meristem a part of a plant where cell division takes place

mesophyll the tissues in the centre of a leaf, where photosynthesis takes place

metabolic reactions the chemical reactions that take place inside a living organism

metabolism all the metabolic reactions occurring in the body

microclimate the climate in a small part of a habitat

micropyle a tiny hole in the testa of a seed

milk teeth the first set of teeth, which fall out and are replaced by permanent teeth; also called deciduous teeth

mitochondrion an organelle in which aerobic respiration takes place, producing ATP

mitosis a type of cell division in which one cell produces two genetically identical daughter cells; used in growth and repair

mitral valve the bicuspid valve; the valve between the left atrium and left ventricle of the heart

molars teeth with broad ridges and grooves

monohybrid inheritance the inheritance of a single gene (one pair of characteristics)

monosaccharide a simple sugar; a carbohydrate whose molecules are made of one sugar unit

mosquitoes insects found almost all over the world, some of which act as vectors for diseases including malaria and denque fever

movement the change of shape or position of the whole or part of the body

mucus a viscous, sticky substance which is secreted in many parts of the body for lubrication or the removal of dust or bacteria

mutagen a substance that causes mutations

mutation a change in the structure of a gene or a chromosome

mutualism a type of symbiosis in which both partners gain

mycelium the mass or network of hyphae that makes up the body of a fungus

mycorrhizae fungal hyphae closely associated with plant roots; they help the plant to absorb water and minerals from the soil

myelin a fatty substance that surrounds the axons of many neurones, insulating them and enabling the nerve impulse to travel faster

myoglobin a dark red pigment found in muscles, which can store small amounts of oxygen

natural selection the increased chance of survival and reproduction of those organisms best adapted to their environment

nectary a gland producing a sugary fluid, found in many insect- or bird-pollinated flowers

negative feedback a mechanism used in homeostasis, in which a change in a parameter brings about actions that push it back towards normal

nephron one of the thousands of tiny tubules in a kidney, in which urine is produced

nerve a bundle of axons or dendrons belonging to many different neurones (nerve cells)

nerve cell a neurone; a cell specialised for the rapid transfer of electrical impulses

nerve fibre a long strand of cytoplasm leading out from the cell body of a neurone

nerve net a network of neurones, found – for example – in cnidarians

nervous system the brain, spinal cord, nerves and receptors

neurone a nerve cell; a cell specialised for the rapid transfer of electrical impulses

niche the role of an organism in an ecosystem

nicotine the addictive drug in tobacco

nitrifying bacteria bacteria that obtain their energy by converting ammonia or nitrite ions to nitrate ions

nitrogen-fixing able to change unreactive nitrogen gas into a more reactive nitrogen compound such as nitrates or ammonia

nitrogenous waste excretory products containing nitrogen – for example, ammonia, urea, uric acid

non-biodegradable not able to be broken down by microorganisms

normal distribution a curve in which the largest number occurs near the midpoint, with approximately equal quantities on either side of this point and a gradual decrease towards the extremes

nucleus a part of a cell surrounded by a nuclear membrane, in which DNA is found

nutrition taking in substances from the environment which can be used to build cells or provide energy

nutritional deficiency disease an illness caused by a lack of a nutrient in the diet

obese being more than 20% heavier than the average for your height

obligate essential and unavoidable – for example, an obligate parasite is an organism that can *only* live as a parasite

oesophagus the tube that carries food from the mouth to the stomach

oestrogen a hormone secreted by the ovaries that helps to control the menstrual cycle

omnivore an animal that eats food of both animal and plant origin

operculum a bony covering over the exit from the gills in a fish

opiate a drug obtained from opium poppies, such as heroin

optimum temperature the temperature at which something happens most rapidly

orbit the bony socket that protects the eye

organ a group of tissues which work together to carry out a particular function

organ system a group of organs which work together to carry out a particular function

organelle a structure within a cell

organic a term used to describe substances that have been made by living organisms, or whose molecules contain carbon, hydrogen and oxygen

organism a living thing

osmoregulation the control of the quantity of water in the body tissues

osmosis the diffusion of water molecules from a place where they are in a higher concentration to a place where they are in a lower concentration, through a partially permeable membrane

ovary an organ in which female gametes are made

oviduct the tube leading from an ovary to the uterus

ovulation the release of an egg from an ovary

ovule a structure in the ovary of a flower which contains a female gamete

oxygen debt the extra oxygen that must be taken in by the body following strenuous exercise, when anaerobic respiration took place; the oxygen is needed to break down the lactic acid that accumulated as a result of anaerobic respiration

oxygenated blood blood containing a lot of oxygen; in humans, blood becomes oxygenated in the lungs

oxyhaemoglobin the compound formed when oxygen combines temporarily with haemoglobin

pacemaker also known as the sinoatrial node or SAN; a patch of muscle in the heart that determines the rate at which the heart beats

palate a structure made of bone and cartilage, which separates the nasal cavity from the mouth

palisade layer the upper mesophyll layer in a leaf, made up of rectangular cells containing many chloroplasts

pancreas an organ lying close to the stomach, which is both an endocrine gland (producing insulin and glucagon) and an exocrine gland (producing pancreatic juice)

pancreatic duct a tube that carries pancreatic juice from the pancreas into the duodenum

pancreatic juice the liquid secreted into the pancreatic duct by the pancreas; it flows into the duodenum where its enzymes help with digestion of fats, proteins and carbohydrates

parasite an organism that lives in a close relationship with an organism of another species, called the host; the parasite feeds on the host and does it harm

parthenogenesis the production of young from unfertilised eggs

partially permeable selectively permeable; able to let some substances, but not others, pass through

particulates tiny pieces of carbon and other substances found in smoke, which can irritate the lungs

passive immunity being immune as a result of being given antibodies against a pathogen

pathogen a microorganism that causes disease

pathogenic disease a disease caused by a pathogen – bacteria, virus, protozoan or fungus

pelvis the inner part of a kidney, which leads into the ureter

penicillin an antibiotic which destroys bacteria by damaging their cell walls

penis an organ that can be inserted into a female's vagina, through which sperm pass

pepsin a protease enzyme found in the stomach

perennial a plant that lives for many years

pericarp the outer tissues of a fruit

peristalsis rhythmic contractions of muscles that ripple along a tube – for example, peristalsis pushes food through the alimentary canal

permanent teeth the second set of teeth, which replace the deciduous (milk) teeth

petals often brightly coloured structures, which attract insects or birds to flowers

petiole a leaf stalk

phagocytes white blood cells that surround, engulf and digest pathogens

phenotype the characteristics of an organism, affected by its genes and its environment

phloem tubes long tubes made up of living cells with perforated end walls, which transport sucrose and other substances in plants

photosynthesis the production of carbohydrates and oxygen from water and carbon dioxide, using light energy

phylum (plural: phyla) one of the major groups of organisms into which each of the five kingdoms is split

physiological disease an illness caused by something going wrong in the body, often linked with ageing

pigment a coloured substance, for example chlorophyll, haemoglobin

pioneer zone an area where pioneer species are found – a difficult place to live, in which only well-adapted organisms can survive

Pisces fish – vertebrates with scales and fins

pistil the female part of a flower

pituitary gland a gland in the centre of the head, which secretes several hormones including ADH

placenta an organ made up of tissues of both the mother and embryo, through which the mother's and embryo's bodies exchange nutrients and waste materials

plant growth substance a hormone found in plants, e.g. auxin, gibberellin

plant hormone a hormone found in plants, e.g. auxin, gibberellin

plantlets new young plants

plasma the liquid part of blood, in which the cells float

plasma membrane the membrane surrounding a cell; often called the cell surface membrane

plasmolysed the condition of a plant cell that has lost so much water that its cytoplasm shrinks and pulls the cell membrane away from the cell wall

platelets tiny fragments of cells found in blood, which help with clotting

pleural fluid a viscous fluid which fills the space between the two pleural membranes, providing lubrication

pleural membranes two strong, slippery membranes which surround the lungs

plumule the young shoot in an embryo plant

poikilothermic ectothermic; unable to regulate body temperature physiologically; the organism's temperature varies with that of its environment

pollen grains tough, resistant structures containing the male gametes of a flower

pollination the transfer of pollen from anther to stigma

pollinator an organism that carries pollen from one flower to another, e.g. some types of insects and birds

polyps the individual animals that make up a coral colony

polysaccharide a carbohydrate whose molecules are made of hundreds of sugar units linked in long chains; for example starch, glycogen and cellulose

population all the organisms of one species living in one area, and able to interbreed with one another

potometer a piece of apparatus that can be used to measure the rate of uptake of water by a shoot

precipitation water falling from the sky to earth, as rain, hail or snow

predator an animal that kills and eats other animals

premolars teeth with broad ridges and grooves

primary consumers herbivores

primary growth in plants, upward growth

primary producer the organism at the start of a food chain, which uses energy from an external source to make energy-containing organic substances

producers organisms at the first level in a food chain, which use sunlight (or another form of energy) to produce organic substances from inorganic ones; sometimes known as primary producers

product the substance produced by an enzyme-controlled reaction

progesterone the pregnancy hormone; a hormone secreted by the ovaries and placenta which maintains the lining of the uterus

prostate gland a gland close to a male's bladder, that secretes fluid in which sperm can swim

protease an enzyme that catalyses the breakdown of proteins

protein a substance whose molecules are made of long chains of amino acids; proteins contain carbon, hydrogen, oxygen and nitrogen, and sometimes sulfur

prothrombin an inactive enzyme found in blood plasma; it can be changed to thrombin when a blood vessel is damaged, helping a clot to form

protoplasm the material of which a cell is composed

protozoan an organism made of a single animal-like cell

psychiatric problems difficulties resulting from the brain not working quite correctly, such as depression and chronic anxiety

puberty the stage of development during which sexual maturity is reached

pulmonary artery the artery that carries deoxygenated blood from the heart to the lungs

pulmonary embolism the blockage of a blood vessel in the lungs caused by a blood clot

pulmonary veins veins that carry oxygenated blood from the lungs to the heart

pulp cavity the central part of a tooth, containing nerves and blood vessels

pupil the gap in the middle of the iris, through which light can pass

pure-breeding homozygous

pyramid of biomass a sideways-on graph, in which the size of the boxes represents the dry mass of organisms in each trophic level of a food chain

pyramid of numbers a sideways-on graph, in which the size of the boxes represents the number of organisms in each trophic level of a food chain

quadrat a square frame inside which a sample of an area is studied

radicle the young root in an embryo plant

receptor a cell that is able to detect changes in the environment; often part of a sense organ

recessive a recessive allele only has an effect if a dominant allele is not present

rectum the final part of the alimentary canal, in which faeces are formed and stored before egestion

red blood cells also known as erythrocytes; they contain haemoglobin and transport oxygen

reduction a type of chemical reaction in which oxygen is lost or electrons are gained

reef flat the part of a fringing reef between the reef front and the land

reef front the part of a fringing reef that faces the open sea

reflex action a fast, automatic response to a stimulus

reflex arc the arrangement of neurones along which an impulse passes during a reflex action

region of cell division a part of a plant where cells are able to divide – for example, the area just behind the tip of a root

region of cell elongation a part of a plant where cells grow and get longer

relay neurone a neurone in the central nervous system which passes an impulse between a sensory neurone and a motor neurone

renal relating to the kidneys

rennin a protease enzyme found in the stomach, which helps to digest milk

reproduction producing new organisms from one or two parents

Reptilia reptiles – vertebrates with scales

respiration the release of energy from carbohydrates; it happens in every cell

respond to carry out an action as the result of stimulus

retina the part of the eye that contains receptor cells

rhizome an underground stem

rickets a disease caused by a lack of vitamin D or calcium, in which bones are not as hard as they should be and can grow in a bent shape

rods receptor cells in the retina which are responsive to dim light, but see only in black and white

root the part of a tooth embedded in the jaw

root cap a tough, protective covering over the tip of a root

root meristem the part of a root where cells are able to divide; it is found just behind the tip

runners young plants growing out a parent by means of stems creeping above the soil surface

sample a small part of a whole – for example, a small part of a field that is investigated to represent the entire field

sand large soil particles; they tend to form a fast-draining soil

saprophytism feeding by secreting digestive enzymes outside the body, and then absorbing the products of digestion

schizophrenia a psychiatric condition; it can cause serious problems for a person and their family, but can be treated by drugs

sclera a tough, white tissue surrounding the eyeball

scrotum the part of the body that contains the testes

sebaceous gland an oil-producing gland in the skin

second trophic level the second stage in a food chain, occupied by a primary consumer

secondary consumers carnivores that eat herbivores

secondary growth in plants, widthways growth of a stem or root

secondary sexual characteristics features of the body that develop at puberty, as a result of the increased secretion of sex hormones

seed an ovule after fertilisation; it contains an embryo plant

selection pressure an environmental factor that causes organisms with certain characteristics to have a better chance of survival than others

selectively permeable partially permeable; able to let some substances, but not others, pass through

self-pollination the transfer of pollen from the anther to the stigma on the same plant (but not necessarily the same flower)

semen a mixture of sperm and fluids from the prostate gland and seminal vesicles

seminal vesicles glands that secrete fluid in which sperm can swim

sense organ a group of tissues, including receptor cells, that detects changes in the environment

sensitivity the ability to detect changes in the environment

sepals structures that cover a flower bud and protect it

septum the tissue that separates the right and left sides of the heart

sex chromosomes the X and Y chromosomes, which determine sex

sexual intercourse mating; the introduction of sperm into a woman's vagina

sexual reproduction the production of new organisms involving gametes and fertilisation; the offspring are genetically different from their parent or parents

sickle cell anaemia a condition caused by a codominant allele of the gene that codes for haemoglobin, in which a person has two copies of the gene and suffers serious health problems

sickle cell trait a condition caused by a codominant allele of the gene that codes for haemoglobin, in which a person has one copy of each of the two different alleles of the gene and does not usually suffer health problems

sieve plates the perforated end walls of phloem sieve tube elements

simple sugar a monosaccharide; a carbohydrate whose molecules are made of one sugar unit

sinoatrial node also known as the SAN or pacemaker; a patch of muscle in the heart that determines the rate at which the heart beats

skeleton a structure which supports the body of a living organism

small intestine the longest part of the alimentary canal, in which digestion is completed and absorption takes place

smooth muscle the type of muscle found in the walls of the alimentary canal, which can contract smoothly, slowly and strongly

sodium hydrogencarbonate an alkaline substance; it is found in pancreatic juice and helps to neutralise the acidic mixture entering the small intestine from the stomach

soft corals corals that do not form hard outer skeletons

species a group of organisms with similar characteristics, which can interbreed with each other to produce fertile offspring

specific name the second word in a binomial; the name of the species to which an organism belongs

sperm a male gamete

sperm duct the tube that leads from the testis to the penis

sphincter muscle a muscle surrounding a tube, which can contract to close the tube

sphygmomanometer an instrument for measuring blood pressure

spinal cord part of the central nervous system; it is connected to the brain and lies within the vertebral column

spinal reflex a reflex action in which the impulse passes through the spinal cord

spongy bone the type of bone tissue found towards the centre of a bone, with many air spaces

spongy layer the tissue beneath the palisade layer in a leaf; it is made up of cells that contain chloroplasts and can photosynthesise, with many air spaces between them

stabilising selection natural selection that tends to keep things the same from generation to generation

stamen the male parts of a flower

starch the polysaccharide that is used as an energy store in plant cells

stem tuber a swollen part of a stem, which stores food

sterilisation a method of birth control in which the oviducts or sperm ducts are cut

steroids drugs that have molecules similar to, or identical with, some types of hormones, such as sex hormones

stigma the part of a flower that receives pollen

stimulant a drug that makes the nervous system work faster

stimulus a change in an organism's surroundings that can be detected by its sense organs

stoma (plural: stomata) a gap between two guard cells, usually on the lower surface of a leaf

stomach a muscular organ in which protein digestion is carried out

stony corals corals with hard outer skeletons

striated muscle the type of muscle attached to the bones, sometimes called voluntary muscle because it is under conscious control

stroke damage caused to the brain by an interruption in blood supply, caused either by a blood vessel bursting or a blood vessel becoming blocked by a blood clot

style the connection between the stigma and ovary of a flower

subclavian veins veins lying close to the collarbone, into which lymph drains

suberin a waxy, waterproof substance that is found in bark

substrate the substance on which an enzyme acts

succession gradual and progressive changes in a community over time

succulent a plant with swollen stems or leaves, in which water is stored

sucrase a carbohydrase found in the small intestine, which breaks down sucrose to glucose and fructose

sucrose a disaccharide, non-reducing sugar, made of a glucose molecule and a fructose molecule linked together; the form in which carbohydrates are transported in the phloem of plants

sugar cane smut a fungal disease of sugar cane

suspensory ligaments a ring of ligaments that holds the lens in position in the eye

suture a fibrous joint between the bones of the cranium

sweat gland a gland in the skin which secretes sweat, helping to cool the body

symbiosis the relationship between two organisms of different species that live closely together

symptoms the effects of a pathogen on the body, e.g. fever or a rash

synovial joint a joint at which the two bones can move freely

systole the stage of a heart beat in which the muscles in the walls of the heart chambers contract

tap root a root system comprising one main root from which others branch; the tap root is sometimes swollen and stores food

tapeworm a parasite that lives in the alimentary canal

tar a mixture of substances in tobacco smoke which increases the risk of cancer

target organ an organ that is affected by a hormone

tear gland a gland at the side of the eye that secretes tears to lubricate the eye surface

tendons strong, inelastic cords of tissue, which attach muscles to bones; they are also found in the heart, where they attach the atrioventricular valves to the wall of the ventricle

tertiary consumers organisms that feed at the fourth stage in a food chain; they eat carnivores

test cross breeding an offspring with the dominant phenotype with an organism with the recessive phenotype; the offspring of the cross can help to determine the genotype of the parent with the dominant phenotype

testa the tough waterproof covering of a seed

testis (plural: testes) an organ in which sperm are made

testosterone a hormone secreted by the testes, which causes male characteristics

third trophic level the third stage in a food chain, occupied by a secondary consumer

thrombin a clotting agent produced in the blood from prothrombin when a blood vessel is damaged

thromboplastin a substance released by tissues when they are damaged, which helps to stimulate blood to clot

thrombosis a clot that forms inside a blood vessel

thyroid stimulating hormone a hormone secreted by the pituitary gland, which stimulates the production of thyroxine by the thyroid gland

thyroxine a hormone secreted by the thyroid gland, which speeds up metabolic rate

tissue a group of similar cells which work together to carry out a particular function

tissue culture growing small groups of cells in culture solutions; this is one way of producing many new plants from a few parents

tissue fluid the fluid that surrounds all the cells in the body, formed from blood plasma that leaks out of capillaries

topsoil the top layers of soil, which generally contain humus and are well-aerated

toxins poisons

trachea the tube that carries air from the nose and mouth down to the lungs; it is surrounded by C-shaped rings of cartilage for support

tranquillisers drugs that make a person feel calm

transect a line along which a habitat is studied

translocation the transport of sugars and other organic substances through the phloem tubes of a plant

transmissible disease communicable disease; a disease that can be caught from someone else; transmissible diseases are caused by pathogens

transpiration the loss of water vapour from a leaf; the vapour diffuses out through the stomata

transpiration stream the pathway of water from the root hairs of a plant, up the root and stem and out of the leaves into the atmosphere

triceps muscle a muscle in the upper arm which causes the arm to straighten when it contracts

tricuspid valve the valve between the right atrium and ventricle

trophic level the position in a food chain at which an organism feeds

tropism a growth response to a stimulus, in which the direction of growth is related to the direction of the stimulus

trypsin a protease enzyme found in pancreatic juice

tuberculosis an infectious disease caused by a bacterium, which usually infects the lungs

tumour a lump caused by cells dividing uncontrollably

turgid cell a plant cell that has absorbed water and has cytoplasm that is pressing outwards on the cell wall

umbilical cord an organ linking an embryo to the placenta, containing blood vessels

urea the main nitrogenous excretory product of mammals, produced in the liver from excess amino acids

ureter a tube that leads from a kidney to the bladder

urethra a tube that leads from the bladder to the outside

uric acid the main nitrogenous excretory product of birds, insects and reptiles

urine a solution of urea and other excretory products in water, produced by the kidneys

uterus the organ in a mammal in which the embryo develops

vaccination the introduction to the body of dead or weakened pathogens, to make a person immune to an infectious disease

vagina the tube that leads from the uterus to the outside

vas deferens (plural: vasa deferentia) the tube that leads from the testis to the penis

vascular bundle a vein in a plant, containing xylem vessels and phloem tubes

vascular system the blood system of an animal or the transport system of a plant

vasoconstriction narrowing of blood vessels

vasodilation widening of blood vessels

vector an organism that transmits a pathogen from one host to another – for example, mosquitoes are vectors for the malarial parasite

vegetative propagation asexual reproduction in a plant

vein in an animal, a vessel that transports blood towards the heart; in a plant leaf, a collection of xylem vessels and phloem tubes

vena cava (plural: vena cavae) a large vein that carries deoxygenated blood back to the heart

ventricles the two lower chambers of the heart, which pump blood into the arteries when they contract

villus (plural: villi) a tiny, finger-like process on the inner wall of the small intestine; villi increase the surface area for digestion and absorption

vivipary giving birth to live young – for example, the germination of mangrove seeds while still on the parent plant

vocal cords tissues in the larynx which vibrate when air passes over them, making sounds

waterlogged full of water, so that there are no air spaces

white blood cells cells which help to defend the body against invading pathogens

wilting the drooping of a plant as a result of excessive water loss

withdrawal symptoms the very unpleasant effects of ceasing to take a drug to which one is addicted

wood a dead, strong tissue made largely of xylem vessels

xerophyte a plant adapted to live in dry conditions

xylem vessels long hollow tubes made up of dead, empty cells with lignified walls, which transport water in plants and help to support them

yeast a single-celled fungus, used in brewing and baking

zonation distribution of organisms in which different species live at different places, in an area where there is a steady change in a factor from one place to another – for example, on a rocky seashore

zooxanthellae unicellular algae (plant-like organisms) that live inside the tissues of coral polyps

zygote the diploid cell produced when two gametes fuse

Index